The British Palaeolithic

The British Palaeolithic provides the first academic synthesis of the entire British Palaeolithic, from the earliest occupation (currently understood to be around 980,000 years ago) to the end of the Ice Age. Landscape and ecology form the canvas for an explicitly interpretative approach aimed at understanding how different hominin societies addressed the issues of life at the edge of the Pleistocene world.

Commencing with a consideration of the earliest hominin settlement of Europe, the book goes on to examine the behavioural, cultural and adaptive repertoires of the first human occupants of Britain from an ecological perspective. These themes flow throughout the book as it explores subsequent occupational pulses across more than half a million years of Pleistocene prehistory, which saw *Homo heidelbergensis*, the Neanderthals and ultimately *Homo sapiens* walk these shores.

The British Palaeolithic fills a major gap in teaching resources as well as in research by providing a current synthesis of the latest research on the period. This book represents the culmination of 40 years combined research in this area by two well-known experts in the field, and is an important new text for students of British archaeology as well as for students and researchers of the continental Palaeolithic period.

Dr Paul Pettitt is Reader in Palaeolithic Archaeology at Sheffield University and specialises in the Middle and Upper Palaeolithic of Britain. He is the author of *The Palaeolithic Origins of Human Burial* (Routledge 2010).

Dr Mark White is Reader in Archaeology at Durham University and specialises in the Lower and Middle Palaeolithic of Britain.

Routledge Archaeology of Northern Europe

Forthcoming

Formative Britain: An Archaeology of Britain AD 400–1100
Martin Carver

The British Palaeolithic

Hominin societies at the edge of the Pleistocene world

Paul Pettitt and Mark White

Routledge
Taylor & Francis Group

LONDON AND NEW YORK

First published 2012
by Routledge
2 Park Square, Milton Park, Abingdon, Oxon OX14 4RN

Simultaneously published in the USA and Canada
by Routledge
711 Third Avenue, New York, NY 10017

Routledge is an imprint of the Taylor & Francis Group, an informa business

British Library Cataloguing in Publication Data
A catalogue record for this book is available from the British Library

Library of Congress Cataloging in Publication Data
A catalog record for this book has been requested

ISBN: 978–0–415–67454–6 (hbk)
ISBN: 978–0–415–67455–3 (pbk)
ISBN: 978–0–203–14144–1 (ebk)

Typeset in Helvetica Neue
by Swales & Willis Ltd, Exeter, Devon

Printed and bound in Great Britain by
CPI Antony Rowe, Chippenham, Wiltshire

Contents

List of figures		vi
Text boxes and figures within text boxes		xii
List of tables		xviii
Acknowledgements		xx

1 One million years of the British Pleistocene   1

2 Pioneers at the edge of the Pleistocene world: the earliest hominin visitors to Britain, ~1 ma–700 ka BP   10

3 Landscapes of habit: the hominin occupation of Britain, ~550–300 ka BP   55

4 Behaviour and society in Lower Palaeolithic Britain, ~550 ka–300 ka BP   143

5 Neanderthals of the forest steppe: the Early Middle Palaeolithic, ~325–180 ka BP   209

6 The Neanderthal steppe: landscapes and human environments of the Late Middle Palaeolithic, ~60–35 ka BP   293

7 Liminal worlds: the British Early Upper Palaeolithic and the earliest populations of *Homo sapiens*   373

8 Settling the north-west frontier: the Late Upper Palaeolithic, ~14.6–11.6 ka BP   423

Notes   502
Bibliography   506
Index   586

List of figures

2.1   Major British sites pertinent to the earliest hominin occupation of Britain   13
2.2   Schematic representation of the prevailing habitat character of western
        Eurasia during the Early Pleistocene and early Middle Pleistocene
        (~2.0–0.4 ma BP)   18
2.3   Schematic representation of vegetation cycles in Early Pleistocene Europe   19
2.4   Maxilla and frontal bone of *Homo antecessor*   21
2.5   The Marine Isotope Curve from MIS1 back to MIS21   23
2.6   Tentative correlation of the English Cromerian temperate stages with
        the Rhine River System, deep sea Marine Isotope Stages and
        magnetostratigraphy   24
2.7   Palaeogeography of southern Britain at ~1.4 ma BP, ~1.15 ma BP
        and ~0.6 ma BP   26
2.8   Composite sketch maps showing the principal river systems of Britain
        during the Early Pleistocene and early Middle Pleistocene, excluding
        the Solent system   28
2.9   (a) Schematic section through the Cromer Forest Bed Formation at
        Pakefield, showing main environmental contexts and location of the
        flint artefacts. (b) Photograph of Pakefield Sections exposed during
        the Quaternary Research Associations' Easter 2000 Field Excursion   30
2.10   Selected artefacts from Pakefield   31
2.11   *Mimomys* teeth from Pakefield   33
2.12   Carnivores and Herbivores from Pakefield   34
2.13   Overhead view of the Happisburgh 3 site and detail of excavations in
        progress   36
2.14   The implementiferous fluvial (lag) gravels and laminated estuarine sands
        and silts from Happisburgh 3   40

2.15 Stratigraphical context of the Happisburgh 3 artefacts and biological
remains 41
2.16 Artefacts from Happisburgh 3 42
2.17 Selected fauna from Happisburgh 3 43
2.18 The dating evidence for Happisburgh, particularly palaeomagnetism
and mammalian biostratigraphy 44
3.1 Main British sites discussed in Chapters 3 and 4 59
3.2 The Marine Isotope Curve from MIS1 to MIS21 with the period covered
in this chapter highlighted 60
3.3 Pollen diagram from the Noordbergum Interglacial IV in the Dutch
Cromerian Sequence 61
3.4 (a) Taxonomic habitat index for the Boxgrove sequence (b) Top:
Excavations in Q1B at Boxgrove. Bottom: Section through the
Boxgrove sequence at GTP13, sowing three cycles of marine
deposition, overlain by the Slindon Silts of Unit 4 and the Pleistocene
landsurface of Unit 4c 64
3.5 Composite pollen diagram of the Hoxnian (MIS11) Interglacial at Marks
Tey 68
3.6 Tentative correlation of recently excavated critical Hoxnian (MIS11)
sites, showing pollen zonation, the presence of characteristic
'Rhenish' molluscan fauna and archaeological industries 74
3.7 Palaeodrainage maps of eastern Essex during MIS 11 (a) and MIS 9 (b) 86
3.8 Section through the channel deposits at Cudmore Grove, showing
location of boreholes and channel margins 86
3.9 MIS9 pollen record from Cudmore Grove 87
3.10 Section through the deposits at Greenland's Pit, Purfleet from the 1996
excavations 96
3.11 Reconstructions of the Palaeogeography of Eastern England during
MIS11 and MIS13 100
3.12 Map of the English Channel (a) with distribution of palaeochannels
(b), and sonar bathymetry of the north-central Channel Shelf (c) 101
3.13 Sea level estimates from the benthic isotope record and other sea-level
indicators, with periods during which Britain was an island during MIS11
and MIS9 indicated 104
3.14 Map showing (a) the immediately pre-Anglian route of the Thames and
(b) the diversion of the Thames during the Anglian Glaciation 109
3.15 Derek Roe's distribution map of Lower and Middle Palaeolithic sites
and findspots 112
3.16 Schematic diagram showing tentative phases of colonisation, isolation
and abandonment during marine isotope sub-stages 113
4.1 The complete corpus of Lower Palaeolithic human fossils from Britain 144
4.2 Two historically important handaxes from Britain 145
4.3 Diagrammatic illustration of the two main classification systems for
handaxes used in Britain since the 1960s 148

4.4	Graphs showing the relationship between dominant handaxe shape and raw material sources	153
4.5	McPherron's model showing how handaxes may change in shape, elongation and refinement throughout a prolonged use-life	156
4.6	Handaxe from Boxgrove with refitting tranchet removal	157
4.7	Selection of British 'cleavers' illustrating the effects of tranchet removals and the use of flake blanks in accidentally creating this rare form in a British context	158
4.8	Paired handaxes from Foxhall Road, possibly representing the idiosyncratic styles of two Palaeolithic individuals	162
4.9	Artefacts from Hoxne and Clacton with functions inferred from microwear analysis	164
4.10	Clactonian Chopper Cores	165
4.11	Handaxe from South Woodford, showing area of incipient percussion cones resulting from repeated localised battering (inset = magnified image of percussion area)	167
4.12	Clactonian flake tools	175
4.13	Handaxes in the Clactonian	180
4.14	The Furze Platt Giant and the Wansunt Pit Miniatures, the largest and some of the smallest handaxes in the British Palaeolithic	201
4.15	Soft-hammers from Boxgrove	202
4.16	Horse scapula from Boxgrove GTP17	204
4.17	Rhino butchery area from Boxgrove Q1, showing rhinoceros pelvis and handaxes	205
4.18	Viewsheds from three upland sites in the Chiltern Hills: Round Green, Caddington and Gaddesden Row	206
4.19	Handaxe retaining fossils that hominins appear to have deliberately preserved during manufacture	208
5.1	Major British sites discussed in Chapter 5	210
5.2	The Marine Isotope Curve from MIS1 to MIS21, with the period covered in Chapter 5 highlighted	211
5.3	Key features of Marine Isotope Stage 7	212
5.4	Sea level estimates from the benthic isotope record and other sea-level indicators, with periods during which Britain was an island during MIS7 and MIS5 indicated	213
5.5	The palaeogeography of eastern England during MIS7	215
5.6	Raised beaches and sea caves in the Torbay area	216
5.7	Pollen profile from the Lower Channel Deposits at Marsworth	222
5.8	Number of known British Levallois sites and findspots by modern county	243
5.9	Number of known British Levallois sites and findspots by river valley	243
5.10	Pseudo-Levallois cores	251
5.11	Two proto-Levallois cores from Botany Pit, Purfleet alongside a classic linear Levallois core from the same pit	252

5.12 A retouched Levallois flakes from Baker's Hole, essentially a unifacial handaxe 259

5.13 Diagrammatic representation of the variety evident in Levallois surface preparation, based on the location of flake scars 262

5.14 Diagrammatic representation of the variation evident in Levallois exploitation methods 262

5.15 Levallois points and an exhausted core from Creffield Road, Acton 263

5.16 Cores from Baker's Hole 267

5.17 Levallois artefacts from the Lion Tramway Cutting, West Thurrock 268

5.18 Refitting laminar flakes from Crayford found by Spurrell 271

5.19 The gradually declining numbers of artefacts over time in the terraces of the Middle Thames 276

5.20 Geological sequences at Crayford, Ebbsfleet and West Thurrock, illustrating how hominin activity persisted only as long as a source of raw materials was available at each site 281

5.21 Major size differences of astragali between MIS6 caballine horse (left) and MIS7 caballine horse (right) 288

6.1 Chronology of the British Middle Palaeolithic, shown relative to the Marine Ice Oxygen Isotope records, mammalian assemblage zones, and Greenland interstadials 294

6.2 Major British Late Middle Palaeolithic sites and *bout coupé* findspots 329

6.3 Middle Palaeolithic artefacts from Uphill Quarry 338

6.4 Handaxes and scrapers from Lynford 339

6.5 The organic sediments of Facies Association B at Lynford Quarry, Mundford, Norfolk 339

6.6 Extreme recycling at Lynford 343

6.7 *Bout coupé* handaxes 350

6.8 *Bout coupé* handaxe from Castle Lane, Bournemouth 350

6.9 Aerial view of Creswell Crags (Nottinghamshire/Derbyshire), looking west 354

6.10 The Creswell Heritage Area, showing caves with Late Middle Palaeolithic materials 355

6.11 Church Hole Cave 357

6.12 Quartzite flakes from discoidal technology 358

6.13 Quartzite flakes from discoidal technology from Church Hole, Creswell. (Photo Paul Pettitt.) 358

6.14 Section through the archaeological deposits in Pin Hole cave, Creswell, reconstructed by Roger Jacobi, showing Pin Hole MAZ dated fauna. (Courtesy Museums Sheffield.) 359

6.15 Map of the Axe Valley and adjacent countryside, showing location of sites mentioned in the text 363

6.16 The Hyaena Den, Wookey 366

6.17 Handaxes from the Hyaena Den 366

6.18 Late Middle Palaeolithic artefacts from Rhinoceros Hole, Wookey 368

6.19 View of the Axe Valley from the plateau above the Hyaena Den, Rhinoceros Hole and Badger Hole, Wookey 370

7.1	CT scan of the KC4 human maxilla	383
7.2	Bladepoints from Robin Hood Cave, Creswell Crags	384
7.3	Distribution of Early Upper Palaeolithic bifacially worked leafpoints in Britain	388
7.4	Distribution of Early Upper Palaeolithic bladepoints in Britain	389
7.5	Bifacially worked 'bladepoints' (leafpoints) from Badger Hole, Wookey, Somerset	390
7.6	Bifacially worked leafpoint from Kent's Cavern, Devon	391
7.7	Welsh Early Upper Palaeolithic bladepoints	393
7.8	Bifacially worked bladepoint (leafpoint) from Beedings, Sussex	397
7.9	Distribution of British sites/findspots classified as Aurignacian	403
7.10	Aurignacian shouldered endscrapers from Paviland	405
7.11	*Burins busqué* from the Welsh Aurignacian	406
7.12	Organic points from Aurignacian contexts in Somerset	407
7.13	Representation of raw material types among the Aurignacian lithics from Paviland	410
7.14	Tanged points of Font Robert type	418
7.15	Distribution of British sites/findspots classified as Gravettian	420
7.16	Conical bone pin from Kent's Cavern, Devon	422
8.1	Late Magdalenian ('Creswellian') lithics from Robin Hood Cave, Creswell Crags	437
8.2	Cheddar Points from the Hoyle's Mouth, Dyfed, Wales	437
8.3	Proximity of British, Belgian and Dutch Late Magdalenian/Creswellian sites	439
8.4	Distribution of Late Magdalenian sites and findspots in Britain	444
8.5	Cheddar Gorge from above Gough's Cave	451
8.6	Reindeer antler javelin foreshafts from Fox Hole, Peak District	454
8.7	British Late Magdalenian *bâtons percé*	455
8.8	Mammoth ivory *sagaie* from Pin Hole, Creswell, bearing engraved 'fish/line' decoration	456
8.9	Engraved 'vulva' of three converging lines on the east wall of the main chamber of Robin Hood Cave, Creswell Crags	464
8.10	Engraved cervid (probably red deer) on the east wall of Church Hole, Creswell Crags	464
8.11	Engraved bovid on the east wall of Church Hole, Creswell Crags	465
8.12	Engraved 'vulva' on the west wall of Church Hole, Creswell Crags	465
8.13	Possible Havelte Point from Cat Hole, Wales	470
8.14	Shouldered points of Hamburgian affiliation	471
8.15	Distribution of sites and findspots with Hamburgian shouldered points	474
8.16	View from just above Fox Hole Cave, Peak District	476
8.17	Distribution of sites with curved backed points/*federmesser*	481
8.18	*Federmessergruppen* lithics from Mother Grundy's Parlour, Creswell Crags	482
8.19	Backed bladelet and curved backed points from Kilmelfort Cave, Argyll	483

8.20   Antler harpoon from Victoria Cave, near Settle, North Yorkshire   486
8.21   Bruised blade from Avington VI   496
8.22   Tanged points of Ahrensburgian type, from Avington VI, Berkshire   497
8.23   Reindeer antler points from Victoria Cave, near Settle, North Yorkshire 498
8.24   Reindeer antler 'Lyngby' axe from Earl's Barton, Northamptonshire   499
8.25   Knapping scatters at Seamer Site C   501

Text boxes and figures within text boxes

2.1	A short chronology for Europe, or there and back again	11
2.2	Beetle faunas and environmental reconstructions	34
2.3	The age of the Happisburgh Till	37
2.4	A resurrected short chronology for northern Europe?	44
Figure 1	Westaway's interpretation of the palaeomagnetic (a) and amino-acid data (b) from Pakefield and Happisburgh	46
3.1	Barnfield Pit, Swanscombe, Kent	56
Figure 1	Section through the Swanscombe sequence, showing stratigraphical units and phases, climatic interpretation, archaeology and correlation with the Hoxnian pollen zones	56
3.2	Hoxne, Suffolk	69
Figure 1	Schematic section through the Hoxne Lake basin, with a detailed cross-section through the deposits re-exposed during the 2000–2003 excavations	69
Figure 2	Artefacts from the University of Chicago excavations at Hoxne	71
3.3	Clacton-on-sea, Essex	76
Figure 1	(a) Map showing distribution of Pleistocene deposits at Clacton, and the location of the various excavations (b) Section through the Clacton area showing the various Clacton Channel occurrences (c) Section through the main fill of the Clacton Channel as exposed at the West Cliff	77
3.4	Barnham and Elveden, Suffolk	79

Figure 1	Schematic sections through the Barnham and Elveden sequences, showing stratigraphy, archaeology and possible correlation with the Hoxnian pollen zones	79
Figure 2	Artefacts from Barnham and Elveden	80
3.5	Beeches Pit, West Stow, Suffolk	81
Figure 1	Schematic section through the Beeches Pit sequence, showing sedimentology, climatic interpretation, archaeology and correlation with the Hoxnian pollen zones	82
Figure 2	The series of handaxes from Beeches Pit showing the variety of form and size found in the Acheulean	83
3.6	Bridgland's model of terrace formation	88
Figure 1	Schematic representation of the 6-Phase Terrace Formation Model	89
Figure 2	Schematic representation of the Thames Terrace Staircase	91
3.7	Stoke Newington, London Borough of Hackney	93
Figure 1	(a) Map showing location of nineteenth- and twentieth-century investigations at Stoke Newington. (b) Possible correlation of the MIS9 Stoke Newington Sands and Highbury Sands and Silts	94
3.8	Greenlands and Bluelands Pit, Purfleet, Essex	105
Figure 1	Map showing location of the main pits in the Purfleet area	106
Figure 2	Greenlands Pit, 1996	106
3.9	Foxhall Road, Ipswich	110
Figure 1	Nina Layard's section through the Foxhall Road sequence, showing location of two main archaeological horizons within the Grey Clay and Red Gravel	110
3.10	Waverley Wood, Bubbenhall, Warwickshire	115
Figure 1	Section through the Waverley Wood sequence, showing location of implementiferous channel fills	115
Figure 2	Andesite and lava handaxes from Waverley Wood	116
3.11	Boxgrove, West Sussex	117
Figure 1	Map showing Amy's Eartham Quarry, Boxgrove with main areas of archaeological excavation	118
Figure 2	Section through the Boxgrove sequence	119
Figure 3	Excavations in progress	119
Figure 4	*In situ* knapping scatter from Q1/A, and refitted reduction sequence 492 from Boxgrove	120
3.12	High Lodge, Mildenhall, Suffolk	121
Figure 1	Schematic section through the High Lodge sequence, showing stratigraphical units, interpretation and archaeology	121
Figure 2	A selection of scrapers from the classic High Lodge Industry	122
3.13	Wolvercote Channel, Oxfordshire	125
Figure 1	Section through the Wolvercote sequence	126

Figure 2   The classic Wolvercote-style handaxe   127

3.14   Cuxton, Kent   128
Figure 1   (a) Sections through the Cuxton deposits as recorded by Tester (1961),
            Cruse (1987) and the MVPP (Wenban-Smith 2004) (b) Location map
            showing position of various excavations (c) Longitudinal Section
            showing the positions of Tester's and Cruse's sections   129
Figure 2   A very large and elegant ficron handaxe from Cuxton, discovered
            during the MVPP 2005 excavation   130

3.15   Globe Pit, Little Thurrock, Essex   130
Figure 1   Section through the Globe Pit sequence, showing the relationship
            between the different beds and their contained archaeology   131

3.16   The Chiltern Hills   135
Figure 1   Map showing location of Worthington Smith's main sites on the
            Chiltern Hills (closed circles) and major modern towns (open circles)   135
Figure 2   Broken handaxe and refitting flake sequence from Caddington   136
Figure 3   Handaxes from Worthington Smith's sites at Caddington; Round
            Green and Gaddesden Row   136

4.1   The Clacton spear   160
Figure 1   The Clacton spear, discovered by Samuel Hazzledine Warren at
            Clacton in 1911   160

4.2   Growing up in the Middle Pleistocene   171

4.3   Were handaxes sexy?   191

4.4   Fire use at Beeches Pit   194
Figure 1   Evidence of highly localised burning at Beeches Pit, Suffolk   194

5.1   Lion Pit Tramway Cutting, West Thurrock, Essex   217
Figure 1   Excavation Plan and geological section through the archaeological
            levels exposed in the recent excavations at the Lion Tramway Cutting,
            West Thurrock   217
Figure 2   Levallois cores from the Lion Tramway Cutting, showing two
            different operational schema   218
Figure 3   Photograph of the 1984 excavations at the Lion Tramway Cutting,
            showing the depth of sands and silts overlying the Levallois
            knapping floor   218

5.2   Sandy Lane Quarry and Purfleet Road, Aveley, Essex   223
Figure 1   Schematic Section through the Mucking formation deposits at
            Sandy Lane, Aveley   224
Figure 2   Photo of 1997–8 investigations at Aveley   224
Figure 3   Levallois core from Aveley   224

5.3   MIS7 biostratigraphy   230

5.4   Pontnewydd Cave, Clwyd, North Wales   232

Figure 1   View of the entrance to Pontnewydd Cave   233
Figure 2   Hard stone bifaces from the Early Middle Palaeolithic of
            Pontnewydd Cave   233

5.5   The Crayford Brickearths   235
Figure 1   (a) Composite section through the Crayford and Erith brickpits
            (b) Spurrell's original section showing position of main archaeological
            horizon and band of flint at Stoneham's Pit   235

5.6   The Stanton Harcourt Channel (Dix's Pit), Oxfordshire   237
Figure 1   Photograph of the site under excavation   237
Figure 2   Artefacts from Stanton Harcourt   238

5.7   Rich tapestry of MIS7 environments   240

5.8   Levallois technology   247
Figure 1   Boëda's technological criteria that is now accepted as identifying and
            conceptually underwriting Levallois reduction   247

5.9   West London   255
Figure 1   John Allen Brown's section from Eastwood's Pit, Yiewsley   255
Figure 2   John Allen Brown's Section from Pit 2 at Creffield Road   255
Figure 3   Artefacts from the Hillingdon Pit   256

5.10   Botany Pit, Purfleet   257
Figure 1   Proposed correlation of the botany sediments with the sequence
            recorded at Bluelands/Greenlands Pits   258
Figure 2   A Proto-Levallois or simple prepared core from Botany Pit   258

5.11   Ebbsfleet   264
Figure 1   Location map of sites located in the Ebbsfleet Valley   264
Figure 2   Section through the Ebbsfleet Channel deposits excavated by the
            British Museum   265

5.12   The Suffolk Rivers   268
Figure 1   Levallois core from the Stoke Bone Bed   269
Figure 2   Section through the deposits of the River Stour at Brundon   269

6.1   Temperate floras   309

6.2   Cold floras   310

6.3   Why was MIS3 treeless?   311

6.4   Cold interval at Sandy, Bedfordshire   315

6.5   The Late Middle Palaeolithic open-air site of Little Paxton,
            Cambridgeshire   334
Figure 1   Late Middle Palaeolithic lithics from Little Paxton   335

6.6   Coygan Cave, South Wales   336
Figure 1   Classic *bout coupé* handaxe from Coygan Cave   337

6.7   Lynford environments   340

6.8	Neanderthals among the Mammoths	345
Figure 1	Montage of Lynford during excavation	345
6.9	Late Middle Palaeolithic findspots in the Thames Valley	352
Figure 1	*Bout coupé* handaxe from Marlow	352
6.10	Ash Tree Cave, Derbyshire	355
6.11	Uphill Quarry, Somerset	363
6.12	Picken's Hole, Somerset	364
6.13	Kent's Cavern	371
Figure 1	Artefacts from Kent's Cavern. Scale in cm. (After Evans 1897.)	371
Figure 2	View of excavations by the authors in the Wolf's Cave area of Kent's Cavern, Devon, 2009, looking west	372
7.1	Last Glacial Maximum	374
Figure 1	Approximate limits of the Last Glacial Maximum ice over Britain	375
7.2	The arrival of the Gravettians	377
Figure 1	Calibrated age ranges of direct AMS radiocarbon measurements on fauna from Pontnewydd Cave, plotted against NGRIP climate curve	378
7.3	Glaston, Leicestershire	395
Figure 1	The location of Glaston	395
Figure 2	Leafpoint and fragmentary leafpoint from Glaston	396
Figure 3	Horse limb bones from Glaston	396
7.4	Paviland Cave and the 'Red Lady'	412
Figure 1	The bones of the 'Red Lady' of Paviland in frontal view	412
Figure 2	Paviland. The Goat's Hole is the triangular opening to the right	413
Figure 3	Section drawing of excavations in the Goat's Hole, Paviland Cave, from Buckland 1823	413
Figure 4	Fragments of mammoth ivory rods polished with ochre and apparently associated with the Red Lady burial	414
Figure 5	The 'Sollas Egg', a pathological fragment of mammoth tusk pierced for suspension	414
Figure 6	Two basal fragments of Chopped-base points	415
Figure 7	Horse bone 'spatulae' from the Goat's Hole, Paviland	415
Figure 8	Fragmentary Font Robert Point from Paviland	416
Figure 9	Recent excavations in the Goat's Hole, Paviland, directed by Stephen Aldhouse-Green	416
7.5	Pin Hole, Creswell Crags	421
Figure 1	Complete Font Robert point from Pin Hole	421
8.1	The Condover mammoths	431
Figure 1	The mandible of the adult mammoth from Condover	432
Figure 2	Russell Coope holding bone from the Condover site	432

8.2	Late Magdalenian archaeology of Creswell Crags	445
Figure 1	The Creswell Crags gorge, looking east	445
Figure 2	Creswell Crags in the winter, looking west	446
8.3	Gough's Cave skull cups	448
Figure 1	Distribution of percussion marks on cranial bones from Gough's Cave	448
Figure 2	Cut-marks and percussion marks on human facial bones from Gough's Cave	449
8.4	Late Magdalenian clothing	449
Figure 1	Church Hole sewing (1) eyed bone needle (2) thread-winder made on vertebral process of horse (3) Arctic hare tibia awl (4) reindeer antler javelin foreshaft	450
8.5	Gough's Cave, Cheddar Gorge	452
8.6	Kent's Cavern	457
Figure 1	View of the Vestibule from the Passage of Urns, with approximate location of the original position of the Black Band	457
Figure 2	Antler uniserial and biserial harpoons from Kent's Cavern	458
8.7	The Poulton Elk	458
Figure 1	The Poulton Elk	459
Figure 2	Uniserially barbed bone harpoons associated with the Poulton Elk	459
8.8	Art Mobilier from Creswell Crags	462
Figure 1	The engraved humanoid from Pin Hole	462
Figure 2	Engraved horses head from Robin Hood Cave	463
8.9	Church Hole rear engravings	466
Figure 1	Engraved birds or stylised human females from the west wall of the rear chamber in Church Hole, Creswell Crags	466
8.10	Hengistbury Head, Dorset	471
Figure 1	Location map of Hengistbury Head	472
Figure 2	Core H refitting group	473
Figure 3	Hengistbury knapping scatter	473
8.11	Rookery Farm, Cambridgeshire	483
Figure 1	Distibution of lithics at Rookery Farm	484
Figure 2	Conjoined sequence of laminar removals from Rookery Farm	484
8.12	Kendrick's Cave, Conwy	488
Figure 1	Engraved and ochred roe deer metapodia from Kendrick's Cave	488
Figure 2	Horse maxilla with engraved chevron designs	489
8.13	Three Ways Wharf, Uxbridge	492
Figure 1	Location of the Three Ways Wharf site	493
Figure 2	Distribution of used lithics, retouched tools and reindeer upper limb bones in Scatter C East	494
Figure 3	Refitting group 10	494

List of tables

3.1   List of mammalian fauna for the MIS13, 11 and 9 interglacials, and the
MIS12, 10 and 8 glacials   65

3.2   List of Lower and Middle Palaeolithic findspots by county, including the
historical counties of Huntingdonshire, Rutland and Middlesex   141

4.1   British handaxe traditions according to Derek Roe   150

4.2   Selected technological and morphological attributes on handaxes from
20 British assemblages   152

4.3   Frequency of various uses (counting edges) of stone tools from Clacton
and Hoxne Lower Industry   164

4.4   British handaxe traditions according to Derek Roe with inferred ages   170

4.5   Key Clactonian occurrences   173

4.6   Key moments in the history of the Clactonian industry   174

4.7   Selected typologies for the Clactonian   176

4.8   Handaxes in the Clactonian   178

4.9   The chronological occurrence of Clactonian sites   183

5.1   Summary of the pollen evidence from Selsey LBS   221

5.2   Pollen zones from Aveley   226

5.3   Mammalian fauna of MIS7 Britain   227

5.4   The characteristic faunas of the Ponds Farm and Sandy Lane MAZs   229

5.5   Summary of main archaeological sites from MIS8–7   245

5.6   Population estimates for Pleistocene Britain based on different
ethnographically observed densities   282

5.7   Claimed human presence during MIS6 to MIS4 with reasons for their
rejection   286

5.8   Upper Pleistocene mammalian assemblage zones   289

6.1   Suggested ages (ka cal BP) of Heinrich events, Greenland stadials and
      Greenland interstadials   295
6.2   Multi-proxy climatic conditions at select British Devensian sites   296
6.3   Published temperature estimates for Devensian beetle assemblages   297
6.4   Key British Late Middle Palaeolithic sites   301
6.5   The Pin Hole mammalian assemblage zone   318
6.6   Dietary preferences of the mammoth steppe fauna   320
6.7   Direct and indirect AMS radiocarbon dates for MIS3 hyaenas in Britain   321
6.8   A list of claimed *bout coupé* handaxe findspots, by county   327
6.9   List of *bout coupé* handaxes that can be attributed to MIS3 or a broader
      Devensian context   329
6.10 Population estimates for Middle Palaeolithic hominins in Britain based
      on ethnographically observed densities   330
6.11 Artefacts originally reported by Dawkins vs. Coulson's assessment of
      the extant assemblage from Robin Hood Cave   360
7.1   Major British Late Middle Palaeolithic sites   385
7.2   British sites with Aurignacian material   401
7.3   Diagnostic Aurignacian endscraper and burin forms (bladelet cores)
      represented in Britain and on the continent   404
7.4   British sites and findspots with material attributable to the early Gravettian   419
8.1   Chronology of the main climatic oscillations of the Late Glacial in
      calendar (ice core, varve and INTCAL calibrated) years   427
8.2   The Dimlington Stadial mammalian assemblage zone   430
8.3   Selected British Late Magdalenian (Creswellian) sites   441
8.4   Quantities of worked lithics from selected European Late Magdalenian
      sites   446

Acknowledgements

We have benefited considerably from the help of numerous colleagues who have been kind enough to read sections of the manuscript and provide information and illustrations. We thank most kindly (and alphabetically) Juan-Luis Arsuaga, Nick Ashton, Colin Ballantyne, Nick Barton, Mark Bateman, Martin Bates, David Bridgland, Barry Chandler, Chantal Conneller, Jill Cook, Lynden Cooper, Andy Currant, Andrew David, Rob Dinnis, Helen Drinkall, Julie Gardiner, John Gowlett, Chris Green, Sonja Grimm, Sanjeev Gupta, Emma Heslewood, Jon Humble, Roger Jacobi, Paul Jeffery, David Keen, Nigel Larkin, John Lewis, Adrian Lister, Shannon McPherron, Keith Moore, Julian Murton, Simon Parfitt, Matt Pope, Richard Preece, Chris Proctor, Mark Roberts, Penny Robinson, Helen Roe, Danielle Schreve, Beccy Scott, Kate Scott, Chris Stringer, Hartmutt Thieme, Erik Trinkaus, Beth Upex, Jeff Veitch, Ian Wall, Elizabeth Walker, Francis Wenban-Smith, Rob Westaway and John Wymer. We are also grateful to the following institutions for permission to reproduce figures: Bolton Museum, The Trustees of the British Museum, Creswell Heritage Trust, Harris Museum and Art Gallery Preston, University of Hull, Museum of London, National Museums and Galleries Wales, the Natural History Museum, Oxford University Museum of Natural History, Portsmouth City Museum, the Prehistoric Society, the Royal Society, Torquay Museum.

One million years of the British Pleistocene

GREATER LONDON, NEARLY 12,000 YEARS AGO

At this point the waters of the Colne River ran through a wide floodplain, cutting a gravelly route due south towards its confluence with the mighty Thames barely 15 km downstream. The lower slopes leading to the river allowed access to the waters, to the flint and chert nodules glinting in its shallows that sufficed for knapping, and to fording points that could be used to trap fish and disadvantage prey in the hunt. The patchy stands of pine trees provided wood for fuel and for replenishing the hafts and shafts of tools and weapons. After several months of snow the region was greening up; although it was still cold, reindeer were passing through in number on the way to their spring calving grounds and, here and there, small herds of wild horse grazed on the grassy tundra. From the high ground above this place their numbers could be seen for a great distance across the floodplain and their movements studied. The familiar path of the Thames and Colne – preserved as folk knowledge despite infrequent visits to this edge of the world – had guided these people here.

They were present in small numbers – a task group you could count on one hand – charged with monitoring the reindeers' movements and beginning the hunt that would provide meat and fat, antler for tools and calfskin and sinew for clothing. A few days in the area should provide enough to take back to the remainder of the small band left behind where the two rivers meet. The day's hunt had been a success; an adult reindeer had been killed at the ford just downstream; its legs had been removed and carried to this place, a low slope overlooking the river. Fish traps set at this place had produced a freshwater fish and fallen pine wood had been gathered to set a hearth against the growing afternoon chill. While there was still enough light each person set to their tasks, huddling as close as they could to the hearth to benefit from its heat. Sometimes they sat, sometimes they stood, each preoccupied with swiftly and efficiently executing the tasks on which they were dependent. When the hearth had been lit, two wiped dry the nodules of flint they had selected from the chilly waters and knapped them. After removing the chalky cortex they skilfully produced a small series of long, regular blades, using time-honoured techniques to shape the cores and control the flakes and blades knapped from them. Some of these were passed on to the two members busy with completing the dissection of the reindeer legs. In addition to the sinew, meat and marrow the foot-pads of the animal would be saved to make boot soles. A fifth individual – the last – set to descaling the fish for immediate consumption. After eating, as night fell, the group would set to repairing their javelins and nets before retiring under lightweight bivouacs tethered to the pines. Tomorrow they would rejoin their band, paddling downriver in the skin boats drawn up out of the water and now packed with reindeer antler and meat carefully wrapped in skins. They would leave offerings to placate the waters and the spirits of this place, ensuring a successful return next year, set their paddles in the water, and take one last look back before setting their minds on the brief journey south.

They would never return. They could not know it but their world was coming to an end. Soon, the reindeer and horse would be gone from here, and the grasslands would give way to woodland and forest. First, the boreal woodlands would thicken; later a thick mat of warmth-loving forest would cover the land. Although their hunter-fisher-gatherer way of life would continue for several thousand years more, the vast open lands that had been home to the large herds and their Palaeolithic predators would be no more. The world of gravelly rivers, hills and plains would disappear.

They could not know, but this little group – one of only several scattered about in this vast and untamed world at the northern edge of humanity's reach – had inherited the legacy of nearly one million years of intermittent visits into this land. Soon, with the reindeer, it would be completely gone.

Hominins stretched to their limits: living on the edge of the Palaeolithic world

The fanciful reconstruction above is based on interpretation of Scatter A at the Terminal Pleistocene/Early Holocene Long Blade Industry site of Three Ways Wharf in Uxbridge, Greater London (see Chapter 8). It has a little of our imagination mixed in for sure but is otherwise based on analyses and interpretations of the site's excavators (Lewis and Rackham 2011). Here, at the Pleistocene/Holocene transition, a small group of terminal Palaeolithic hunter-gatherers camped, leaving several lithic scatters and bones of reindeer and horse. Long Blade Industry sites – which almost certainly are linked to the continental Ahrensburgian culture – are not common in Britain. It seems that there were few people of this cultural attribution in the country – probably for a very brief time – a small and barely perceptible dispersal into a vast landscape during a brief window of opportunity when climate and environment allowed. If we were to go back in time from this point to that of the earliest known hominin dispersal into Britain – currently ~750-980,000 years ago – we would find essentially the same thing; remarkably small groups of humans, in this case a different species, engaged in similar social and economic tasks registered mainly through their involvement with stones and bones.

Our central aim in this book is a synthesis and interpretation of the entire British Palaeolithic record in terms of the occupation, behaviour and societies of the ancient hominins who once roamed these shores. Several of the elements touched upon in the opening vignette are constant themes in this book. Rivers are critical to Palaeolithic archaeology and their 'fluvial archive' contains by far the richest record of hominin presence. Equally, rivers were central to the lives of Palaeolithic hominins, forming a focus of critical resources (water, plants, animals and stone), as well as conduits for movement through the landscape. Since at least MIS12 the Thames has formed a main route of dispersal into Britain, being connected at times of low sea level to the Rhine–Meuse systems of Europe, while its many tributaries formed a network for incursions into large parts of the country. Prior to MIS12, the erstwhile Bytham River served a similar function.

The landscapes and environments of the Pleistocene are both alien and familiar. As we shall see in later chapters, during the warm interglacials the vegetation of Britain had a remarkably British feel, a mosaic of woodland and grassland in which most of the component species still occur today. The animals that walked this land, though, were often rather exotic, with mammoth, bison, reindeer, and rhinoceros forming key prey species for humans and non-human carnivores such as lion and hyaena. During colder periods, however, Britain was a truly alien place, its geography unrecognisable as low sea levels connected it to Europe across the vast plains of 'Doggerland' (Coles 1998). Ice sheets at times extended as far as the Thames Valley, beyond which existed polar deserts with frozen ground, biting winds and minimal tundra vegetation. During the 'non-analogue' environments of MIS3, though, Britain, like much of northern Europe, formed part of the so-called 'Mammoth-Steppe' (Guthrie 1982), a rich grassland populated by vast herds of megafauna, in which trees were a rare commodity.

Located at the north-western corner of North-western Europe, Britain formed the edge of the hominin range throughout most of the Palaeolithic. 'Here, at the very edge of their range, biological and cultural adaptations were stretched to their limits' (Roebroeks et al. 2011, 113). When combined with the frequency and amplitude of climatic and environmental change, this made Britain a very hard place to live. It is therefore not surprising that for much of the Pleistocene Britain appears to have been unoccupied, or occupied only very briefly by small groups of humans. To paraphrase a geological axiom: the Palaeolithic record of Britain is essentially a long series of hiatuses, interrupted by a few handaxes. While the same may be said of neighbouring regions of Europe, the occupational gaps in Britain are longer and more frequent (Roebroeks et al. 2011). As such, Britain may be considered a population sink, where regular abandonment and/or extirpation necessitated the constant influx of people originating from elsewhere; even during periods of occupation populations may have been reproducing below replacement levels and thus required 'topping-up' from outside. This has had a profound impact on the record we find here.

A VERY BRIEF HISTORY OF TIME: THREE CENTURIES OF PALAEOLITHIC ARCHAEOLOGY IN BRITAIN

This is not a book about the history of Palaeolithic archaeology in Britain. In order that we may present a coherent interpretation of the British Palaeolithic record we do not even seek to integrate discussion of the history of investigation of British Pleistocene deposits into the main text. Where we discuss key sites – usually in boxes – we note the major excavators and phases of investigation but this is not intended to constitute a comprehensive account of the history of the discipline. There are colleagues better suited to undertaking this and, indeed, excellent accounts of the British contribution to the development of Palaeolithic archaeology and of the historical investigation of British sites already exist. The reader is directed in particular to Grayson (1983) and O'Connor (2007) for general accounts contextualised in the wider scientific world; various papers in *Great Prehistorians: 150 Years of Palaeolithic Research, 1859–2009* (Volume 30 of *Lithics: the Journal of the Lithic Studies Society* for 2009) for accounts of specific individuals; Pettitt and White (2011), White and Pettitt (2009), Weston (2008) and particularly Sommer (2007) for discussion of the work of Buckland, MacEnery and their contemporaries in the first half of the nineteenth century; Gamble and Kruszynski 2009 for discussion of the British involvement in the shattering of the 'time barrier' at Amiens and acceptance of deep time in that *annus mirabilis* of 1859; McNabb (1996b, 2007) for the history of Lower Palaeolithic archaeology with particular reference to the Clactonian and Swanscombe; Scott (2010) for the investigation of what came to be defined as the Early Middle Palaeolithic and Campbell (1977) for the Upper Palaeolithic. A very brief survey, is nonetheless warranted.

Britain was central to the development of Palaeolithic archaeology, along with its closest continental neighbours. The absence of an understanding of deep time until the mid-nineteenth century meant, however, that the earliest discoveries of what we now know to be Palaeolithic materials – the handaxes discovered at Gray's Inn Lane, London (1679) and Hoxne, Suffolk (1797) – passed largely unnoticed. Similarly, John MacEnery's discoveries of Middle and Upper Palaeolithic tools stratified under stalagmite floors in association with extinct animals at Kent's Cavern during the early 1820s remained unpublished during his lifetime, largely due to his deference to the 'antediluvian' theories of the Reverend William Buckland, his friend and mentor (White and Pettitt 2009; Pettitt and White 2011). Even Buckland's involvement with the discovery of an Upper Palaeolithic burial, fauna, stone and bone tools at Goat's Hole, Paviland, in 1823 and his excavation of a Pleistocene hyaena den at Kirkdale Cave in 1822, did little to shake his conviction. Although MacEnery's findings were adequately vindicated by the publication of his notes by Edward Vivian in 1845, this came after his and Buckland's death because Buckland's validation – which MacEnery was waiting for – never came (White and Pettitt 2009). The world, it seems, was not ready for such an epochal shift.

This would not occur for another 35 years, and then, sadly, not in Britain. At Amiens, in April 1859, Joseph Prestwich and John Evans gave their seal of approval to Jacques Boucher de Perthes' claims to having found early evidence of humans in association with the bones of extinct animals. A frenzy of discovery occurred over the decades that followed, during which time several of the 'flagship' British sites were investigated, including the caves of Creswell Crags, Swanscombe on the North Kent terraces of the Thames, the Hyaena Den at Wookey, Gough's Cave in Cheddar, Clacton-on-Sea in Essex, and High Lodge in Suffolk, and more systematic investigations in Kent's Cavern. By the beginning of the twentieth century thousands of new sites and findspots had been identified, most of which still remained undated and poorly understood chrono-logically. As the number of sites grew, in Britain and especially in France, attempts were made to place some sense of order on the record. The most influential of the resulting chrono-cultural systems was that of Gabriel de Mortillet, who introduced terms such as Acheulean, Mousterian and Magdalenian; still in use today, for better or for worse. Culture history had begun, and from this time dominated British Palaeolithic archaeology until well into the 1960s. Developments during the early decades of the twentieth century also saw the birth of the Clactonian (Chapter 4), the infamous Piltdown hoax and the re-emergence of the pointless eolith debate, with Ray Lancaster and James Reid Moir picking up the reins from Benjamin Harrison and Joseph Prestwich in the quest to prove the existence of 'Tertiary Man' (O'Connor 2007). These latter controversies can be seen in the wider context of the 'scramble' for evidence of the development of humanity. At this time everything was up for grabs; it had not yet been recognised that Africa was the cradle of humanity and, therefore, it seemed plausible that humans may have originated in Europe. The embarrassing forgery of the Piltdown remains – a recent human cranium matched with the mandible of an orang-utan, both chemically stained to appear fossil and teeth filed clumsily to occlude together (Spencer 1991) – fooled scientists of the time but its authenticity had begun to be questioned by the 1950s.

Emphasis on fieldwork has been constant throughout the history of the British Palaeo-lithic. The large-scale excavation of caves was largely restricted to the nineteenth and early twentieth centuries. Sadly, this too often took the form of wholesale clearing of vast sedimentary deposits, archaeology and palaeontology from which were selectively retained, lost, distributed across the world and rarely published comprehensively. Cave and rockshelter excavations of the latter half of the twentieth century were typically smaller in scale and usually comprised very small trenches, in many cases thankfully, as they remain unpublished: certain British scholars put trenches through critically impor-tant deposits in a number of caves and failed to undertake even the most basic analysis and publication. In worst case scenarios we know they excavated in flagship caves such as Kent's Cavern but don't even know the location of their trenches.

By contrast, the monitoring and excavation of productive pits and quarries has profit-ably continued for the best part of one 150 years. The rate of discovery of archaeological sites in these contexts has diminished over time, as extraction procedures have become increasingly mechanised and urban expansion has made many Pleistocene deposits inac-cessible, although these sites continue to provide world-class information. During the sec-ond half of the twentieth century, the excavations of John Wymer, Mark Roberts, Francis Wenban-Smith, David Bridgland, Nick Barton, John Gowlett, Danielle Schreve, and the British Museum/AHOB (led by Nick Ashton, Simon Parfitt and Simon Lewis) have been particularly important in drawing together the understanding of the British Quaternary discussed in Chapters 2, 3 and 4. With a few key exceptions, for example Pakefield and Happisburgh (Chapter 2), Lynford (Chapter 6), Glaston (Chapter 7), Three Ways Wharf at Uxbridge (Chapter 8), and to an extent Boxgrove (Chapter 4), most excavations of the past 50 years have concentrated on re-investigating old sites to answer specific chronological, environmental or cultural issues. Sadly, many of the very early discoveries at such sites were, with the best of contemporary intentions, poorly and sometimes completely excavated, meaning that they are now effectively lost to us (Roe 1981). Britain may have taken an early lead in the race to study the Palaeolithic but unfortunately quickly ran out of steam: now is an exciting time to be working in the British Palaeolithic, but we sorely need more new sites, something that only renewed and extensive survey will achieve.

Alongside fieldwork, more sophisticated methods of artefact analysis have been developed in Britain since the 1960s, resulting in classificatory schemes still in use today such as the handaxe classifications of Roe (1968a); and in considerable advances in our understanding of assemblage variation in the Lower Palaeolithic (e.g. McNabb 1992) and Early Middle Palaeolithic (White et al. 2006; Scott 2010) and the establishment of a chronology for the Late Middle and Upper Palaeolithic (e.g. Campbell 1977; Barton and Roberts 1996; Barton et al. 2003 and the numerous publications of Roger Jacobi). In recent years popular (but nevertheless weighty) accounts of the British Palaeolithic have been published (Barton 1997; Stringer 2006), although it is perhaps no surprise that the relatively brief coverage of the Palaeolithic in general accounts of British prehistory (e.g. Pryor 2004; Darvill 2010), however useful, fail to do justice to a period which represents 98.5–99% of British Prehistory.

THE SOMEWHAT LONGER (PRE)HISTORY OF TIME: SOME CONVENTIONS IN QUATERNARY SCIENCE

In the same way that this is not a book about the history of the British Palaeolithic, it is also not a book about Palaeolithic chronology, although we are, of course, entirely reliant upon the ability to hang sites as precisely in time as we can in order to make sense of the record. The host of relative and absolute dating techniques on which Quaternary specialists rely have been developed since the mid-twentieth century (Walker 2005), and it may be said that we have entered a period of maturity in which we can now place our confidence in the reliability of several techniques. We simply make some points here about our use of Quaternary time.

Rhythms of the planet: climate, environment and Pleistocene timescales

It is not a straightforward task to marshal the variety of complex relative and chronometric dating techniques and seriation schemes into one consistent whole for the purposes of clarity, but that is what we have attempted here. Overall we refer to the Marine Isotope Stage (MIS, alternatively Oxygen Isotope Stage, OIS) system, which has become the global standard among Quaternary scientists (e.g. Shackleton 1987). If the recent dating of Happisburgh is upheld (see Chapter 2) then hominins have visited Britain intermittently over a period spanning at least 25 of such stages.

Marine Isotope Stages reflect relatively long periods of time – typically ~15,000 years (MIS2) to ~60,000 (MIS11). They are subsumed in or define the old units of 'glacials' and 'interglacials'. As such they form the largest definable units of the highly complex climatic and environmental instability of the Pleistocene. Within these, however, several nested scales of change are also observed, and it has become necessary to subdivide each Marine Isotope Stage further. The ice cores, deep sea cores, and terrestrial records preserve evidence of these climatic and environmental fluctuations on the millennial and sub-millennial scale. At the level of hominin dispersals and behavioural change it is probably these scales that provided the adaptive pressures that determined whether Palaeolithic societies survived and ultimately propagated the changes that are visible in the archaeological record.

Two conventions have been established for the naming of these isotopic substages. MIS 11, for example, has been divided into substages based on an alphanumeric system, that is, 11c, 11b and 11a (e.g. Tzedakis et al. 2001). In other records, however, (e.g. MD900963, Bassinot et al. 1994) a more complex pattern can be seen with additional warm–cold oscillations (Figure 2.5). Therefore, an alternative system identifies negative and positive isotopic events, which are numbered using a decimal system (Imbrie et al. 1984; Bassinot et al. 1994; Desprat et al. 2005). This has the advantage of allowing additional isotopic events to be incorporated as they are discovered. The two conventions differ because the first denotes *periods of time*, whereas the second identifies specific *isotopic events*, and therefore the terminology is not directly interchangable. We discuss issues where they appear in the text.

From an environmental point of view, the Hoxnian Interglacial (MIS11) and the Ipswichian Interglacial (MIS5e) have been divided into pollen subzones, the identification of which has proved critical to our understanding of exactly when hominins were present in Britain. Alongside these, micro- and macro-faunal, coleopteran and molluscan biostratigraphy are critical to the division of time and correlation of sites. In chronometric terms, palaeomagnetism and amino-acid racemisation techniques have proven invaluable in the seriation of sites, but do not produce dates. Correlating such seriated sites with Marine Isotope Stages is nowadays possible with high degrees of confidence, but it is not without its problems, as will be seen, for example, in Chapter 2. Non-radiocarbon dating methods such as thermoluminescence (TL), optically-stimulated-luminescence (OSL) and Uranium-series underpin our chronology and, for the Middle Pleistocene and earlier stages of the Upper Pleistocene, are associated with measurement imprecision consistent with that of the other techniques. The powerful combination of all these methods has resulted in the impressive chronological control of British Middle Pleistocene sites we rely on in Chapters 2, 3, 4 and 5.

How old is a *Homotherium*? Radiocarbon chronology and the British Late Middle and Upper Palaeolithic

Non-radiocarbon dating techniques noted above, particularly Uranium-series, TL and OSL, while of critical use from MIS3 backwards, are associated with relatively large measurement errors (imprecision) which render them of limited use for structuring late MIS3 and MIS2 archaeology in time, at least where radiocarbon measurements are available. As a result we rely in Chapters 6, 7 and 8 almost entirely on radiocarbon for our chronological framework. We will not rehearse in detail here the usual issues relating to radiocarbon accuracy and precision, but make some simple points which, we hope, justify why we use calendrical (calibrated) radiocarbon dates in the way we do. Correction for radiocarbon inaccuracy has been available back to ~50 ka (^{14}C) BP for the last decade, notably in the form of the CALPAL curve (see below). INTCAL09 now calibrates back to a little beyond ~44.5–45 ka ^{14}C BP, that is ~48 ka BP in calendrical terms (Reimer et al. 2009). The result of calibrating measurements using these curves has revealed how considerably radiocarbon measurements underestimate real time in this period; the cause being the complex factors relating to the influx and production of ^{14}C in the Earth's atmosphere, itself, it seems, governed to a large extent by changes in the Earth's magnetic field. Here is one example of such age underestimation which we revisit in Chapter 7: a tooth of the scimitar-toothed cat *Homotherium latidens* dredged from the North Sea close to the Brown Bank that has been directly dated to 28100 ± 220 (^{14}C) BP (UtC-11000, tooth) and 27650 ± 280 (^{14}C) BP (UtC-11065, mandibular bone). These calibrate to ~31–32 ka BP, revealing that the uncalibrated radiocarbon measurements on the dentary underestimate its real age by four to five thousand years.

The ability of specialists to remove contaminating sources of carbon from dating samples and thus isolate only the carbon relevant to the actual age of the sample has also had a significant effect on chronometric accuracy. Recent improvements in pretreatment methods, notably ultrafiltration, seem to be far more efficient at removing contaminating sources of carbon and thus of producing more reliable (i.e. accurate) age estimations. Although the technique was not invented at Oxford – and was indeed practised in other laboratories before it was adopted there – it has perhaps become particularly associated with this laboratory's work on the chronology of the Late Middle and Upper Palaeolithic (e.g. Higham 2011). The redating of ultrafiltrated carbon from samples originally pretreated using non-ultrafiltration methods has often resulted in new (and one assumes more reliable) measurements that are either younger or older than the original results. It would be fair to say, however, that new results typically produce *older* ages. There is, therefore, a *strong tendency* for more recently produced measurements to be older, and thus shift back in time our chronologies for the Late Middle and Upper Palaeolithic, while at the same time eliminating chronometric noise.

All dates we use in the book may be considered to be 'calendrical', that is we present calibrated radiocarbon dates. In order to correct the uncalibrated radiocarbon measurements pertinent to Chapters 6, 7 and 8 we have used the CALPAL curve, a splined, multi-component curve based on high-precision U/Th and radiocarbon data from Hulu Cave synchronised with palaeoclimatic data from the Greenland ice cores (Weninger and Jöris 2004, 2008). The reason we use this rather than the INTCAL09 curve is familiarity and loyalty: the effort expended into developing CALPAL over the last 15 years or more made this available long before INTCAL was extended back beyond ~25 ka BP although the two datasets are very similar. Reimer et al. (2009, 1112) suggest that where calibrated dates are used original radiocarbon measurements on which they are based should also be cited. We do this where we think it is necessary, but in the interests of space do not make a habit of it. We cite references to the publications in which the original radiocarbon measurements were presented and thus, where we do not present original measurements in tables or text, readers, should they wish, may follow a trail back to original sources and check the accuracy of our calibration. In any case we do not attempt any correlations of dated material (between sites, or with climate, for example) that require high degrees of precision, and even towards the end of the Pleistocene there is still a large degree of imprecision; *single* radiocarbon measurements around 12,000 BP produced in recent years using ultrafiltration pretreatment methods – which may be considered to be the most precise currently available – typically have errors in the order of 50 (^{14}C) years (see for example the results on samples from Gough's Cave – Jacobi and Higham 2009); *sets* of such measurements from contexts that one might assume to be chronometrically contemporary (e.g. assemblages such as Gough's) typically produce age ranges of three to four centuries, and even Bayesian analyses – which perhaps specialists put a little too much faith in – result in modelled ranges of around two centuries *for samples that are assumed to be contemporary or which reflect single events.* This is some achievement for which the radiocarbon community should be justifiably proud, but also a degree of imprecision with which we are probably stuck and thus that, in our opinion, merits our use of calibrated dates. When we quote a date '~14.5 ka BP' it should be assumed that there is a spread of uncertainty of around a century either side at 2σ. Where a set of dates have been produced for a given assemblage we state the range over which measurements overlap at 2σ; it will be seen in the text that, for the Late Glacial, this typically results in ranges of two, three, four or more centuries (Chapter 8). Needless to say, the further one goes back the greater the imprecision; measurements at around five half lives of radiocarbon, for example ~30 ka (^{14}C) BP – pertinent to the arrival in Britain of the first *Homo sapiens* groups – typically possess age ranges of some seven centuries (Chapter 7), and at around seven half lives/~42 ka (^{14}C) BP – pertinent to late Neanderthals – around two millennia.

CHAPTER 2

Pioneers at the edge of the Pleistocene world

The earliest hominin visitors to Britain, ~1ma–700 ka BP

INTRODUCTION

Little more than a decade ago, most European Pleistocene specialists would have denied the presence of humans in Europe prior to ~600–500 ka BP (e.g. Roebroeks and van Kolfschoten 1994; papers in Roebroeks and Van Kolfschoten 1995; cf. Roebroeks 2001; Roebroeks 2006: see Text Box 2.1). Today, however, there is incontrovertible and ever-increasing evidence – in the form of both hominin fossils and genuine humanly modified lithics – that humans arrived in some areas of Europe by at least ~1.2 ma BP, and probably earlier. Until very recently these earliest incursions were also understood to be restricted to familiar semi-arid (savannah-like) grassland habitats and to warmer southern latitudes below 40° N (Dennell and Roebroeks 1996, 2005; Dennell 2003). This proposition must now be called into question, at least on the basis of the earliest evidence on hominin presence in Britain. In this chapter we review this earliest evidence of human settlement during the Early and early Middle Pleistocene, relating to the first demonstrable dispersal of humans into Europe.

The record of human occupation between ~1.6 ma–700 ka BP is very different from that found ~600–500 ka BP onwards, in terms of both technological character and quantity of evidence (Roebroeks 2006). The earliest occupation appears to be one of patchy, short-lived and modest settlement (Dennell 2003), whereas from ~600 ka BP onwards far more substantial and continuous occupation is evident (Roebroeks 2001; 2006). Some have seen this as suggestive of a two-phased sequence of colonisation – the first before ~1.2 ma BP and the second ~700–600 ka BP – although in reality these phases are more likely to have been a stochastic series of multiple dispersals and local extinction events at a continental scale, rather than linear and directed waves of migration (Carbonell et al. 1999a, 2010; Moncel 2010; Dennell et al. 2011).

A SHORT CHRONOLOGY FOR EUROPE, OR THERE AND BACK AGAIN

The quest to identify the earliest Europeans is a perennial and often divided pursuit. By the beginning of the 1990s, many workers were ready to accept an age of ~1 ma BP for hominin dispersals into the continent (e.g. Rolland 1992; cf. Roebroeks and van Kolfschoten 1994) with some specialists accepting sites of up to ~2 ma BP in age (Bonifay and Vandermeersch 1991). In a reversal of the normal trend in origins research, however, where things simply get pushed back earlier in time the more they are researched, the outcome of the 1993 European Science Foundation Workshop at Tautavel, France (Roebroeks and van Kolfschoten 1995) promoted a much shorter chronology for Europe, arguing that no convincing evidence of hominin presence existed prior to ~0.5 ma BP.

In a critical review of a number of claimed early sites, Roebroeks and van Kolfschoten (ibid.) concluded that most contained only pseudo-artefacts, were poorly dated and/or contained fossils thought to be hominin that on critical inspection belonged to other species. Qualitative and quantitative differences between sites before and after ~0.5 ma BP, provided a number of falsifiable propositions: (Table 1).

Table 1 **Qualitative and quantitative differences between sites before and after 500 ka BP. (After Roebroeks and Van Kolfschoten 1994.)**

Before 0.5 ma BP	After 0.5 ma BP
Small series of isolated pieces selected from a natural pebble background	Large collections of obvious artefacts from excavated knapping floors with conjoinable material
Secondarily (disturbed) context (coarse matrix)	Primary context sites (fine-grained matrix)
Contested primitive assemblages	Uncontested Acheulean and non-Acheulean industries
No hominin remains	Hominin remains 'common'

This original 'Short Chronology' was itself shortlived. New discoveries at Orce, Spain, the redating of TD6 at Atapuerca to below the Brunhes-Matuyama palaeomagnetic boundary (Carbonell et al. 1995; it had originally been dated to ~MIS13 on the basis of palaeomagnetism and biostratigraphy, cf. Carbonell and Rodriguez 1994) and the announcement of the discovery of *Homo antecessor* (Bermudez de Castro et al. 1997), falsified almost all of its original tenets. Dennell and Roebroeks subsequently forwarded a 'modified Short Chronology', which accepted that hominins had occasionally and temporarily dispersed into southern Europe prior to ~0.5 ma BP, as and when conditions allowed, but were

Text Box 2.1

still confined by winter foraging requirements and minimum daylight tolerance to areas south of latitude 35° N. Thus, while southern Europe occasionally threw up surprises (due to a closer environmental match and its much shorter and less intensive research history) Dennell and Roebroeks maintained that a 'quantum leap' in adaptive abilities was required to take humans into northern and central Europe, where their absence prior to ~0.5 ma BP was 'beyond reasonable doubt' (Dennell and Roebroeks 1996, 535). Dispersals into the north, and more permanent occupation of southern latitudes, therefore occurred only after ~0.5 ma BP.

This modified position was upheld in the face of growing evidence for more continuous and widespread occupation of southern Europe as early as perhaps ~1.6 ma BP (see main text), and discovery of ~0.75 ma BP occupation at Pakefield, Suffolk (Roebroeks 2005; 2006). In this case, it was suggested that the warm Mediterranean climate underlined the ecological signal of the Short Chronology, with pioneer hominin groups dispersing as integral parts of their familiar habitats. In this way, Pakefield did not contradict the assertion that humans only spread into colder latitudes from about ~0.5 ma BP because at this time Britain was not part of the cold north but apparently an extension of the Mediterranean zone (although we dispute this – see main text). The discovery of Happisburgh, if accepted (see Text Box 2.4) must be seen as finally falsifying and signalling the last death throes of the Short Chronology.

Situated at the northwest tip of Eurasia – a cul-de-sac at the edge of the Pleistocene world – Britain is sometimes considered a 'good laboratory' for studying the ebb and flow of human colonisation and adaptation (Roebroeks 2006; Figure 2.1). This is only partly true. While Europe may be largely a political construct (ibid.), several countries – including Britain – are geographically defined. When not isolated from Europe as an island, Britain formed an upland peninsula surrounded by two deep basins (the Channel and the North Sea) through which flowed wide, deep and possibly impassable rivers (White and Schreve 2000; papers in Preece 1995; Pettitt 2008). The British 'laboratory' was thus only periodically open for experiments and we should therefore expect it to show different settlement patterns from the European mainland. These issues are taken up further in the following chapters.

FAMILIAR SETTINGS IN UNFAMILIAR LANDSCAPES: THE EARLIEST OCCUPATION OF EURASIA

The earliest artefactual and/or fossil evidence for human presence outside the 'cradle of Africa' dates to the Early Pleistocene. The oldest artefactual claims come from the ~2.4–1.9 ma BP deposits at Riwat, Pakistan (Dennell et al. 1988) and the Pabbi Hills,

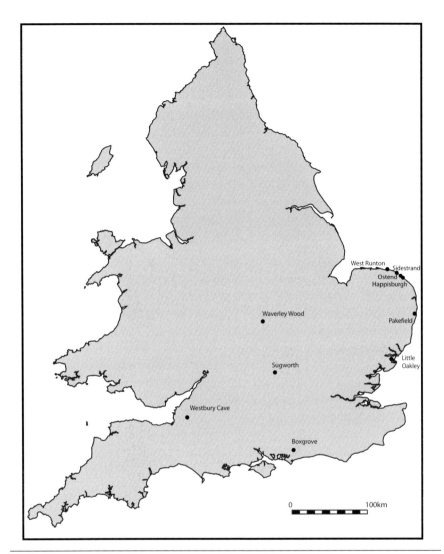

FIGURE 2.1
Major British sites pertinent to the earliest hominin occupation of Britain.

Pakistan, where a series of poorly contextualised artefacts have been argued to originate from deposits ~2.2ma BP in age (Dennell 2004). The earliest uncontested human remains are slightly younger: the ~1.77 ma BP fossils and associated artefacts from Dmanisi, Georgia (Gabunia et al. 2000; Rightmire et al. 2006; Mgeladze et al. 2010) and ~1.8 ma BP material from Mojokerto and Sangiran, Java (Swisher et al. 1994; Antón and Swisher 2004).

The earliest European sites are all situated within the Mediterranean belt. The two oldest claimed sites are currently Lézignan-le-Cébe, Hérault, France, which has been dated by Ar-Ar on overlying basalts to at least ~1.57 ma BP (Crochet et al. 2009), and Pirro-Nord, Italy, dated to ~1.6–1.3 ma BP on biostratigraphical grounds (Arzarello et al. 2007, 2009).[1] Other sites dated to >1 ma BP include Fuente Nueva 3 and Barranco León 5 at Orce, Spain (~1.4–1.2 ma BP; Oms et al. 2000); Sima de Elefante TE9, Atapuerca, Spain (~1.2 ma BP; Carbonell et al. 2008) and Pont-de-Lavaud in the Creuse Valley (~1.1 ma BP; Despriée et al. 2006). Continued, if not necessarily continuous, occupation of these Mediterranean and southern European landscapes is further attested by a series of sites dating to between ~1 ma BP and ~800 ka BP, including the Trinchera Dolina Levels 6 and 4 at Atapuerca, Spain (~960 ka BP; Berger et al. 2008); Vallparadis, Barcelona, Spain (a newly excavated site dated to ~830 ka BP; Martinez et al. 2010); Ca' Belvedere di Monte Poggiolo, Italy (~1 ma BP; Gagnepain et al. 1992, 1998; Peretto et al. 1998); Lunery-Rosières, Cher Valley and Pont-de-la-Hulauderie, Loire Valley, France (~930 ka BP and ~980 ka BP respectively; Despriée et al. 2010)[2].

The last of these, as well as the British sites that form the principal subject of this chapter, show that the common assumption that evidence for Early Pleistocene human occupation is limited to sites below 40° N latitude with little or no evidence north of the Alps (e.g., Doronichev and Golovanova 2010) is no longer sustainable (although see note 1). The notion that the very earliest occupation – between ~1.6 and 1.2 ma BP – was restricted to these low latitudes still holds true, however, with incursions beyond 45°N taking a further ~300,000 years to achieve. Even then, any human presence seems to have been so sparse as to remain archaeologically undetected or undetectable in most regions of Europe – if any is actually out there to be found. There is presently absolutely no evidence of human settlement in Central Europe until ~600 ka BP (Marine Isotope Stage [MIS] 15) (Haidle and Pawlik 2010), Eastern Europe saw only insignificant incursions before this date (Doronichev and Golovanova 2010) and the same may be true of much of southwest France (Turq et al. 2010 – see note 1). After ~600 ka BP, this situation was very different, as we shall see in Chapter 3.

Technical systems

While human occupation by at least ~1.6–1.2 ma BP is now well attested in Europe, the lithic assemblages from sites of this age are generally poor in quality and quantity. They are without exception core and flake industries lacking handaxes (Clark's [1969] Mode 1). Débitage was based around a number of simple flaking systems, described in European terms as orthogonal (i.e. with flaking angles close to 90°), unipolar and multidirectional (Arzarello and Peretto 2010; Carbonell et al. 1999b). In Britain most lithic technologists would probably subsume these under the heading of migrating platform cores (Ashton 1992; Ashton and McNabb 1996; Ashton 1998a), involving a number of simple flaking episodes (single, alternate or parallel sequences, the latter sometimes forming part of an alternate episode) that proceeded from a number of different (migrating) platforms. While this is neither random nor unskilled, knapping operated in a varied and organic fashion that was minimally planned or controlled. The raw materials used at the earliest sites were, regardless of rock type, usually cobbles and pebbles (Arzarello and

Peretto 2010). Sequences were initially dictated by the size and shape of these blanks, and subsequently by the evolving morphology of the core, each removal influencing the location and character of the next. The resulting cores are morphologically diverse and show varying degrees of working (White and Ashton 2003; White and Plunkett 2004). Selection of such materials may reflect the exploitation of familiar settings (i.e. fluvial corridors) in otherwise unfamiliar landscapes. On a number of early European sites the use of an anvil has also been noted, resulting in a 'pseudo' bipolar technique with flakes showing two opposing bulbs (Martinez et al. 2010; Peretto et al. 1998; Carbonell et al. 1999b; Despriée et al. 2010); these have also been claimed for Britain, particularly in the Clactonian (Wymer 1968) although their presence has been questioned (McNabb 1992).

Façonnage ('shaped' tools) in these assemblages is limited to simple 'choppers', a typological category plagued by controversy and variously interpreted as either tools or cores and of course in reality probably functioning as both (Warren 1922; Breuil 1932; Leakey 1971; Toth, 1985; Ashton et al. 1992a). At Monte Poggiolo, Italy, use-wear analyses showed no evidence of utilisation, suggesting that here, at least, they were simply by-products of flake production, although given a million years and the whole of Europe it is unwise to generalise these conclusions too widely. Retouched tools are also extremely rare in these assemblages, the only reported examples >1 ma BP presently coming from Pont-de-Lavaud (Despriée et al. 2006) and perhaps Barranco León 5 and Fuente Nueva 3 (Palmqvist et al. 2005), although the irregular retouch seen on many small flakes in the latter two assemblages may not be intentional but rather edge damage and crushing (Barsky et al. 2010). Retouch may be more common among sites within the ~1 ma–700 ka BP time range, although this appears to be regionally or functionally specific: retouched tools are abundant at Vallparadis, Barcelona (Martinez et al. 2010) and Atapeurca TD6 (Carbonell et al. 1999b) but are very rare from Lunery-Rosières (n = 2; Despriée et al. 2010) and absent from Monte Poggiolo (Arzarello and Peretto 2010).

This association of a Mode 1 technological repertoire and the earliest incursions into new territories appears to hold true almost everywhere (White 2000; Doronichev and Golovanova 2010). In the Levant, the Early Pleistocene site at 'Ubeidiya, Israel contains several levels with handaxes dating to ~1.4–1.2 ma BP although the basal levels have yielded only Mode 1 assemblages (Bar-Yosef 1998). Mode 1 is also found in Dursunlu, Turkey (Kuhn 2002) and Bizat Ruhama, Israel (Ronen et al. 1998) both dated to ~1–0.8 ma BP.

The emergence of the Acheulean (Mode 2) in Europe (see Chapter 3) probably relates to a separate, later phase of colonisation. In the Levant, where the Acheulean appears ~1.4–1.2 ma BP at 'Ubeidiya, evidence for continued handaxe production is limited until ~780 ka BP, as seen at Gesher Benot Ya'aqov (Goren-Inbar 1992, 2000; Bar-Yosef 1998). The earliest Acheulean in Europe also appears to belong to this period, the oldest securely dated examples occurring in the ~700–600 ka BP Level 'P' at Caune de l'Arago, France, its 'sudden' appearance suggesting that it was not an *in situ* development but an introduction from elsewhere (Barsky and de Lumley 2010). Following MIS15 (~600 ka BP), Acheulean industries are found throughout Europe (e.g. papers in Roebroeks and Van Kolfschoten 1995; Piperno et al. 1998; Tuffreau and Lamotte 2010; Despriée et al. 2010), with the notable exception of Central Europe, where a Mode 1 technology persisted until the advent of the Middle Palaeolithic (McBurney 1950; White 2000; Moncel 2010; Doronichev and Golovanova 2010; Haidle and Pawlik 2010). Only in Spain have claims for an older Acheulean been made – with a date of ~900 ka BP proposed for handaxes from Estrecho del Quípar and ~760 ka BP for Solana del Zamborino (Scott and Gibert 2009) – although some doubt has been expressed over the provenance of these handaxes and their relationship to the dated levels (Robin Dennell pers. comm.).

The palaeoclimatic and palaeoecological background to Early Pleistocene dispersals

Hominin dispersals out of Africa have often been correlated with the development of more arid conditions in Africa beginning ~2.5 ma BP (which required terrestrial hominins to widen their range to match the spread of animal resources of the African savannah and/or their analogous Eurasian grasslands) or with the dispersal of other animals (Vrba 1995; Turner 1992; Rolland 1992; Martínez-Navarro and Palmqvist 1995; deMenocal 2004; Dennell and Roebroeks 2005; Martínez-Navarro et al. 2007; Muttoni et al. 2010). The dates of these major climatic shifts in Africa, however, (~2.8, 1.7 and 1 ma BP; deMenocel 2004) do not fit neatly with the currently understood pattern of Early Pleistocene hominin dispersals, as Carbonell et al. (2010) point out, and the notion of multi-species dispersal events from Africa has also been questioned (O'Regan et al. 2009). By contrast, recent work by Trauth et al. (2009) detected a previously overlooked dust-flux in the marine sediments off West Africa indicating a period of aridity beginning ~1.5 ma BP and ending ~1 ma BP, which fits far better with documented dispersal events, in Europe at least. Lake sediments from ten Ethiopian, Kenyan, and Tanzanian rift basin localities furthermore suggest that three humid periods of ~200,000 years duration existed ~2.7–2.5 ma, ~1.9–1.7 ma and ~1.1–0.9 ma BP, which overlap and are largely superimposed on the longer-term process of aridification (Trauth et al. 2005). Trauth et al. (2009) suggest that the mismatch between evidence from dust fluxes and lake levels is best explained by regional responses to global climate change combined with local variations in insolation.

A key problem with most environmental hypotheses for hominin dispersals is that they generally rely on wiggle-matching environmental processes operating at scales of tens or hundreds of millennia with patterns of human dispersal and contraction operating at generational scales, and make uncritical assumptions of causal links between the two. Against the scale of geological time dispersals into Europe were effectively instantaneous. Based on an average rate of advance of one kilometre per year, hominins could move from the tip of the Levant into Georgia, and from there reach southern Spain – or indeed southern Britain – in only 6,000 years (Lewin and Foley 2004). Thus, given the errors involved in accurately dating deposits of the relevant age, the incompatibility of different dating methods, and the often regional or local responses to global climate change (e.g. Trauth et al. 2005), such wiggle-matching must be considered at best terribly inaccurate and at worst grossly misleading. In fact, one might suggest that rather than emphasising environmental push factors within Africa that *forced* hominins to disperse out of the continent, one would be better served examining the ecological pull factors in Europe that *encouraged* or permitted hominins to disperse in. This might also bring us closer to the complex interplay of demographic, social, adaptive, behavioural, technological and cognitive factors involved and also eliminates the almost universal assumption that all 'outs' were from Africa.

The tempo and scale of global climatic fluctuations during the two main phases of hominin colonisation were also markedly different. The Early Pleistocene was a period of muted climatic cycles of low amplitude and high frequency, operating on an average duration of ~41 ka (controlled by orbital precession). The Middle Pleistocene, by contrast, saw low frequency but high amplitude climatic cycles of ~100 ka average duration (controlled by orbital eccentricity), triggering the familiar pattern of prolonged glacials and interglacials in Europe. The earliest severe glacial across Northern Europe occurred during MIS16 (~650–620 ka BP), although a series of discrete cold events can be seen in the marine record as early as MIS36 (~1.2 ma BP; Head and Gibbard 2005). Neither of these two significant dates coincides with an archaeologically visible major human dispersal. Moreover, as Dennell et al. (2011) emphasise, these ~100 ka cycles often conceal millennial scale variability similar to that seen during MIS3 (see Chapter 6), which may be of far greater consequence to patterns of human dispersal than the longer cycles, although matching these elusive wiggles is even more fraught with difficulty.

The archaeological significance of these global climatic cycles lies in their impact on regional climates and ecosystems. A number of recent studies of mammalian faunas have suggested that the first human dispersals into Europe were conditioned by the availability of familiar open grassland landscapes, which extended from North Africa, the Levant and Central Asia (Van der Made and Mateos 2010; Palombo 2010; see also Dennell and Roebroeks 2005). Palombo (2010) detected a faunal turnover ~1.4 ma BP, signalling the spread of more open environments and the presence of more scattered habitats across Europe, followed by a modest extinction of forest ungulates of all sizes ~1 ma BP. This opening up and fragmentation of the landscape was accompanied by a decline in highly gregarious small–medium herbivore species and a rise in herbivores living in small herds. As Palombo implies, this removed the element of 'safety in numbers' from these groups, providing humans with greater opportunities to hunt by pursuit, ambush or pack.

In an extensive study of large mammalian communities accompanying the earliest human dispersals, Kahlke et al. (2011) found evidence for a high diversity of habitats and a high diversity of resources, facilitating human expansion by offering the widest resource base possible for a colonising species. Similarly, the mild climates, low seasonality and lack of strong environmental fluctuations indicated by their data suggested that humans moved into stable, low-risk environments requiring little in the way of major new behavioural adaptations (Figure 2.2). These conclusions are largely in agreement with studies of palaeoherpetological remains (reptiles and amphibians), which have shown that the first occupation of Iberia, ~1.4–1.2 ma BP, was associated with a sharp rise in temperature and increasing precipitation (Agustí et al. 2009, 2010). No human activity has yet been reported during the cold, arid phase that followed the earliest incursions (probably MIS22) but there is abundant evidence for human occupation during the renewed warm conditions of the late Early and early Middle Pleistocene. These authors therefore suggest that human dispersals were strongly influenced by climate (mediated by physiology and culture) with hominins preferring relatively warm, wet phases and shunning cold, dry phases.

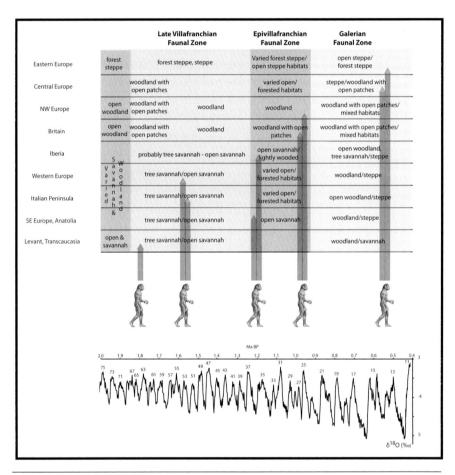

FIGURE 2.2
Schematic representation of the prevailing habitat character of western Eurasia during the Early Pleistocene and early Middle Pleistocene (~2.0–0.4 ma BP) inferred from the large mammal fossil records, in relation to global temperatures and the earliest records of human occurrence. A forward slash indicates the temporal alternation of habitats. (Redrawn and modified after Kalkhe et al. 2001; Elsevier, used with permission.)

Reconstructions of vegetation reveal a similar picture. In a study of pollen and large mammals from 12 Early Pleistocene sites, Leroy et al. (2011) found that the vegetation of the Early Pleistocene was characterised by closed forests for most of the time, even in the southern peninsulas (Figure 2.3). Although only half the sites studied provided a reliable pollen record, the combined floral and faunal record revealed that during the periods of human dispersal open 'Mediterranean-type' environments prevailed, with diverse ecosystems ranging from forested steppe to completely open grasslands. Climatic modelling further suggested that the areas occupied by humans had a minimum temperature range of 0–6° C, and summer precipitation of 30–60 mm a month: in short, during these early dispersals humans appear to have been moving into open woodland

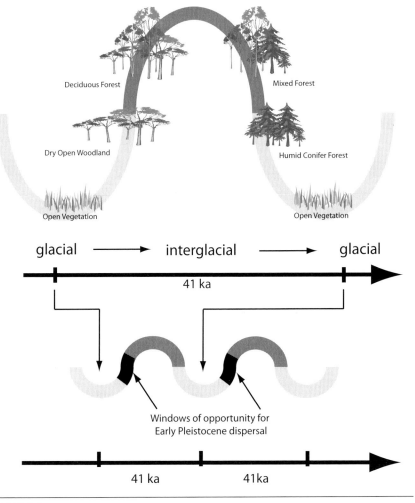

FIGURE 2.3
Schematic representation of vegetation cycles in Early Pleistocene Europe, showing periods of optimum opportunity for hominin dispersal during periods of warm, open environmental conditions. (Redrawn and modified after Leroy et al. 2011; Elsevier, used with permission.)

environments during periods when the climate was relatively warm and dry, but not arid (Leroy et al. 2011). The only exception to this pattern was found at Pont-de-Lavaud, where human occupation took place in deciduous forests during warm, wet conditions (Leroy et al. 2011; Messager et al. 2011).

Muttoni et al. (2010), somewhat at odds with the conclusions of most recent studies, suggested that all of the oldest European sites can be fitted into a temporal window between ~0.99 and 0.78 ma BP, the period which witnessed the establishment of ~100 ka climatic cycles and the inception of Northern Hemisphere glacial oscillations. According to these authors this led to aridity in the Sahara from ~950 ka BP and the development of steppic grasslands across the Eastern European Plain, with a number of large herbivore species (including both the steppe mammoth *Mammuthus trogontherii* and straight-tusked elephant *Palaeoloxodon antiquus*) seeking refuge in southern Europe. Humans probably followed these herds.

Whether this interpretation of the dating evidence stands up or not, from ~0.8 ma BP the 100 ka climatic periodicity became dominant, leading to much longer glacial–interglacial episodes, with net decreases in both moisture and temperature, and longer lasting switches between steppic and forested conditions (Van der Made and Mateos 2010; Palombo 2010). In fact, optimum forested conditions made up only a very small percentage of Pleistocene time (~8%; Gamble in Roebroeks et al. 1992), most of the period hosting a rich mosaic of grassland and open woodland, presaging the final expansion of the Mammoth Steppe across Northern Europe during the Upper Pleistocene. These environments were enriched by herbivore species with diverse feeding strategies and also saw a decrease in carnivore diversity (Turner 1992; Palombo 2010). It is under these conditions that the more 'permanent' occupations discussed in the next chapter took place.

Founder populations

The only human fossil remains associated with the earliest occupation of Europe currently come from Trinchera Dolina Level 6 and Sima de Elefante Level TE9 at Atapuerca, Spain. These have been classified as *Homo antecessor,* the probable ancestor of the European Middle Pleistocene hominin lineage that includes *Homo heidelbergensis* and *Homo neanderthalensis* (Bermúdez de Castro et al. 1997, 2010; Carbonell et al. 2008; see Figure 2.4). Bermúdez de Castro et al. (2010) argue that *Homo antecessor* colonised Early Pleistocene Europe from the east, and may have evolved from the Dmanisi humans, *Homo georgicus*, as yet the earliest known hominin taxon from Eurasia. A full consideration of the small-brained and highly dimorphic Dmanisi fossils lies outside our scope, but it is worth noting that their taxonomic status is unclear and they may represent more than one palaeodeme (Rightmire et al. 2006; Martinón-Torres et al. 2008). Rightmire et al. (2006) suggested that despite some habiline characteristics they were best placed within *Homo erectus,* suggesting the sub-species designation *Homo erectus georgicus*. De Lumley et al. (2006), on the other hand, considered them to be closest to *Homo rudolfensis*.

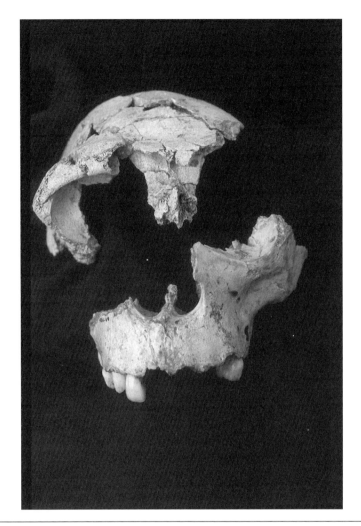

FIGURE 2.4
Maxilla and frontal bone of *Homo antecessor*. (Courtesy of Javier Troeba: Madrid Scientific Films.)

Based on the most recent fossil discoveries, however, it has been suggested that *Homo erectus* was not in fact an African species but evolved in Western Eurasia from the early human populations represented at Dmanisi, from there spreading east across Asia and south into East Africa (Lordkipanidze et al. 2006; Martinón-Torres et al. 2008; cf. T.D. White 1995; Dennell and Roebroeks 2005; Dennell et al. 2011). In a study of human teeth across the Old World, Martinón-Torres et al. (2007) similarly concluded that Asia had played a more important role in populating Europe than Africa. The dental record showed evidence of continuity in European populations from the Early Pleistocene until the Neanderthals, suggesting that Eurasia and Africa had independent evolutionary trajectories for much of the Pleistocene. Human prehistory was thus not a series of high-impact dispersals from Africa but a complex interplay of populations on both continents.

This 'Out of Asia' model represents a significant paradigm shift away from an Afro-centric view of human evolution. Robin Dennell – one of its principal architects – and colleagues have recently formulated this model into a series of formal testable hypotheses (Dennell et al. 2010, 439):

1   Humans (including early *Homo*) left Africa ~1.8 ma BP

2   *Homo erectus* originated in Southwest Asia, which was a central area for the dispersal of hominins in Eurasia

3   Hominin dispersals (and extinctions) in Eurasia during the Early Pleistocene were primarily driven by climate change that was both long-term (glacial–interglacial cycles) and short-term (millennial-scale oscillations)

4   Dispersals into southern Europe were possible by the early part of the Early Pleistocene (~1.75 ma BP)

5   At least one hominin dispersal event into Europe led to a speciation event by ~1.2 ma BP leading to *Homo antecessor*

6   Sub-Saharan Africa was isolated from Eurasia after ~0.8 ma BP because of the desert barrier between the Sahara and Arabia

7   *Homo heidelbergensis* is primarily a West Eurasian taxon that is absent from Africa and East Asia

8   The Acheulean in Europe (and possibly India) was introduced from Southwest Asia, not sub-Saharan Africa

9   After *H. heidelbergensis* dispersed into Europe, it replaced or may have interbred with some remnant populations of its own ancestor *Homo antecessor*.

This has a major bearing on how we interpret the evidence presented both here and in the following chapter.

EMPTY LANDSCAPES: BRITAIN ON THE EVE OF OCCUPATION

Environmental and climatic sequences of the Early and early Middle Pleistocene

The pioneering and largely ephemeral phases of human colonisation of Britain occurred in the Early Pleistocene and early Middle Pleistocene, during an extended, climatically variable period, referred to as the 'Cromerian Complex' (~MIS13–21) and late Beestonian (MIS22–25). This long period, extending from ~0.98 ma to 0.47 ma BP, includes at least eight interglacial and six glacial stages, as well as numerous interstadial and stadial sub-stages within these (Bassinot et al. 1994; see Figure 2.5). Traditionally, archaeological sites belonging to the Cromerian Complex have been treated together, mostly for geological convenience (e.g. Hosfield 2011). As this is a book about the human settlement of Britain, not its geological succession, we deliberately break with this practice and draw our dividing line ~0.6 ma BP. This marks the period during which human settlement became more intensive and probably more continuous on a European scale, and also probably saw the emergence or arrival of the Acheulean (Roebroeks 2006; contra Scott and Gibert 2009). We therefore discuss Lower Palaeolithic archaeological sites belonging to MIS15 and thereafter in Chapters 3 and 4, although for ease of reference the entire Cromerian Complex is summarised diagrammatically here.[3]

Other than the key river terraces outlined below, the Early Pleistocene and early Middle Pleistocene in Britain is principally represented by the richly fossiliferous Cromer Forest-bed Formation (CF-bF) of Norfolk and Suffolk, a complex and spatially varied sequence of sediments that are exposed discontinuously for 80 miles along the North Sea coast. These sediments primarily comprise organic detrital muds and sands laid down in the channels and floodplains of rivers draining central and eastern England. West (1980) interpreted the CF-bF as representing a single interglacial stage, subdivided into four pollen zones (Cr I–Cr IV). It is now known, however, on the basis of mammalian and molluscan biostratigraphy, that as many as five discrete temperate episodes are represented (Preece and Parfitt 2000, 2008; Preece et al. 2009; Stuart and Lister 2001). These are unlikely all to be sub-stages of the same interglacial, but are equally unlikely to equate one-to-one with major, odd numbered interglacials in the isotope record, so some sub-stage divisions are almost certainly represented (Preece and Parfitt 2008). In the Netherlands, a series of four distinct interglacials (Interglacials I–IV) separated by periods of cold climate has similarly been recognised on the basis of palynology, lithology and heavy mineral analysis from borehole data (Zagwijn 1985, 1996). Correlation of the British and Dutch sequences remains extremely problematic. The earliest Dutch

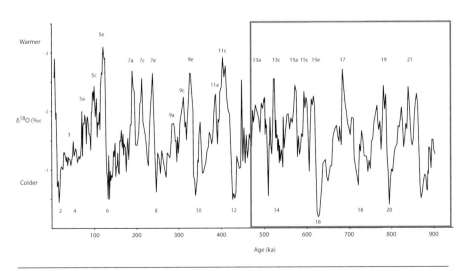

FIGURE 2.5
The Marine Isotope Curve from MIS1 back to MIS21. The Early Pleistocene and early Middle Pleistocene highlighted. (Data from Bassinot et al. 1994.)

Interglacial – Interglacial I – is magnetically reversed and has a highly diagnostic pollen zone characterised by *Carpinus* (hornbeam) and *Eucommia* (Chinese rubber tree) that is unknown from any subsequent interglacial event. Apart from those at Happisburgh 3, all interglacial sediments within the CF-bF are normally polarised and must therefore post-date the Dutch Interglacial I.

Recent stratigraphical and palaeontological investigations in East Anglia have shed some light on the complex nature of this period and identified a succession of temperate-climate episodes with diagnostic floral and faunal assemblages, within which periods of early human occupation may be identified (Turner 1996; Preece and Parfitt 2000, 2008; Stuart and Lister 2001; Parfitt et al. 2005, 2010). One of the key divisions between these early Middle Pleistocene assemblages is based on the evolution of the water vole from the extinct form *Mimomys savini* (in which the molars are rooted in older individuals) to the extant *Arvicola terrestris cantiana* (in which the molars are always unrooted). This transition is thought to have occurred during MIS15 (Preece and Parfitt 2008), an estimate supported by last appearance dates of *Mimomys savini* in a number of key European localities (e.g., 602 ± 52 ka at Gran Dolina, Atapuerca, Spain (Berger et al. 2008), Ar/Ar dates correlated with MIS15 from Isernia, Italy (Coltorti et al. 2005) and the presence of *Mimomys* in deposits above MIS16 Don Till in Russia (Preece and Parfitt 2008)). Other important markers among the microtine voles include *Mimomys pusillus*, which apparently became extinct ~0.7 ma BP, and the evolutionary transition from *Microtus gregaloides* to *M. gregalis* (see Figure 2.6).

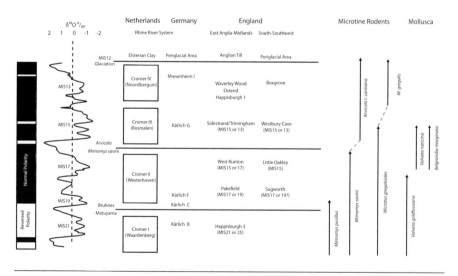

FIGURE 2.6
Tentative correlation of the English Cromerian temperate stages with the Rhine River System, deep sea Marine Isotope Stages and magnetostratigraphy. Direct correlation with the Dutch and British interglacials is not implied. (Revised and Modified after Preece and Parfitt 2000, incorporating data and ideas from Preece and Parfitt 2008; Ashton et al. 2008b; Preece et al. 2009; Parfitt et al. 2010.)

In Britain, the 'vole-clock' provides a ready method for dividing a series of early 'Cromerian' sites with *M. savini* (including the CF-bF sites at Pakefield, Happisburgh and West Runton and the Kesgrave sites of Little Oakley, Essex and Sugworth, Oxfordshire) and later 'Cromerian' sites with *A. terrestris cantiana* (e.g. Sidestrand and Ostend in Norfolk; Westbury-sub-Mendip, Somerset; Waverley Wood, Warwickshire; and Boxgrove, West Sussex). Entirely coincidentally, this evolutionary juncture in microtine voles also marks the division between the 'pioneer' and 'settler' phases of human occupation. Recent investigations of molluscan faunas have similarly identified three biostratigraphically significant assemblage groups (Meijer and Preece 1996; Preece and Parfitt 2000):

1   *Valvata goldfussiana – Tanousia runtoniana – Bithynia troschelli – Viviparus viviparous gibbus* – associated with *Mimomys savini* and found at West Runton, Pakefield and Sugworth

2   *Valvata naticina – Bithynia troschelli – Tanousia* cf. *stenotoma – Belgrandia marginata* – associated with *Mimomys savini* and found at Little Oakley

3   *Valvata naticina – Bithynia tentaculata – Belgrandia marginata* – associated with *Arvicola terrestris cantiana* and found at Sidestrand and Trimingham

A tentative correlation of key sites with the oxygen isotope record is presented in Figure 2.6.

The long temporal duration and associated climatic complexity of the period under consideration renders a full discussion of the environmental sequence impractical, even if the relevant information actually existed in sufficient detail. Furthermore, the fact that hominins are currently understood to have been present on only two brief occasions prior to ~0.6 ma BP renders it unnecessary for present purposes. Suffice it to say that, based on our current understanding of the Early Pleistocene and early Middle Pleistocene in general, and the periods of hominin occupation in particular, there appear to be no simple climatic or environmental factors that allowed or prevented human dispersal into Britain.

Palaeogeography of Earlier Pleistocene Britain

The palaeogeography of Britain for the periods before and during the earliest human incursions has been summarised by Funnell (e.g. 1995, 1996; Figure 2.7). Sedimentological and biological evidence suggests that during the late Pliocene (>2.6 ma BP) Britain took the form of an island surrounded by warm seas, with free circulation of water around or across southern Britain (Funnell 1995, 1996); the depth of the Coralline Crag, which formed during this period, suggests relative sea levels ~70m above those of today. The first terrestrial connection with mainland Europe occurred during the earliest Pleistocene (~2.5 ma BP) and is associated with a global fall in sea-level corresponding to climate change beginning ~MIS100. These climatic changes also triggered modifications in the behaviour of major European rivers, which began to extend their headwaters and increase bedload transport, leading to progressive deltaic progradation in the southern

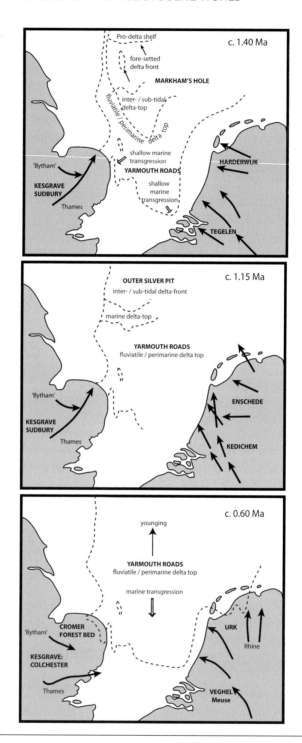

FIGURE 2.7
Palaeogeography of Southern Britain at ~1.4 ma BP, ~1.15 ma BP and ~0.6 ma BP. (Redrawn after Funnell 1996, Elsevier, used with permission.)

North Sea basin. This combination of lower sea-level and progressive sedimentation temporarily converted Britain into a peninsula of the European mainland ~2.3 ma BP; the ensuing 600 ka saw a number of marine transgressions and regressions.

By ~1.7 ma BP, however, progressive deltaic progradation saw the continued growth of the 'Great European (Ur-Frisia) Delta Top' which reinforced the terrestrial link, excluding all marine influence from the southern North Sea basin between ~1.7 and 0.5 ma BP. During this period, Britain was permanently a northwestern peninsula of Europe, even during periods of high sea level. Consequently, flora, fauna and early humans were able to disperse across the top of the Great European Delta Top and the Weald-Artois chalk ridge that closed the Dover Strait to the south (Figure 2.7). By the end of the Cromerian Complex (whatever that may mean), degradation and subsidence of the delta top allowed interglacial seas to encroach southwards across it, although circulation was still bounded in the south by the Weald-Artois chalk ridge, the breaching of which is discussed in Chapter 3.

During the Early Pleistocene and early Middle Pleistocene, therefore, southeast England lay at the western edge of a broad isthmus, while East Anglia was located at the margin of a large coastal embayment around the North Sea basin. The shallow marine deposits that formed in this basin are widespread in the eastern part of East Anglia, and often underlie the key archaeological and palaeontological deposits of the CF-bF. From oldest to youngest these comprise the Red Crag, Norwich Crag and Wroxham Crag. Recent summaries of the distribution, sedimentology and stratigraphy of these deposits can be found in Hamblin et al. (1997) and Rose et al. (2001, 2002). The terrestrial landscapes of eastern England during this period (i.e. the Wash Basin and the Fens) were characterised by greater elevations than the present day, with a higher-relief chalk escarpment (lying to the west of the modern East Anglian escarpment) linking the Chilterns and the Yorkshire Wolds (Lewis 1998; Clayton 2000; Hosfield 2011). The Wash and the present-day flat relief of this region is a product of later (MIS12) lowland glacial erosion.

The fluvial landscape of Britain during the Early and early Middle Pleistocene was dominated by four principal river systems (Bridgland 2010; Hosfield 2011; Rose 2009; Figure 2.8):

1   The extinct Bytham River, which flowed eastwards from the West Midlands, through East Anglia and into the North Sea, until its destruction during the Anglian Glaciation/MIS12 (Rose 1987, 2009). Six distinct terrace formations have been identified, from oldest to youngest: Seven Hills, Ingham, Knettishall, Timworth (MIS16), Warren Hill[*4] (MIS14) and Castle Bytham* (MIS12) (Lee et al. 2004). Using the 'simplified version' of Bridgland's terrace formation model advocated by Rose, Lee and colleagues, which assumes one terrace formation for every 100 ka climatic cycle, we presume the three oldest terraces would date from MIS22, 20 and 18 respectively. A very different interpretation was proposed by Westaway (2009, in press), who recognises only three terraces – the Timworth terrace (MIS12–13), Knettishall terrace (MIS14–15) and Seven Hills terrace (MIS16–15) – although Rose (2009) has refuted this sug-

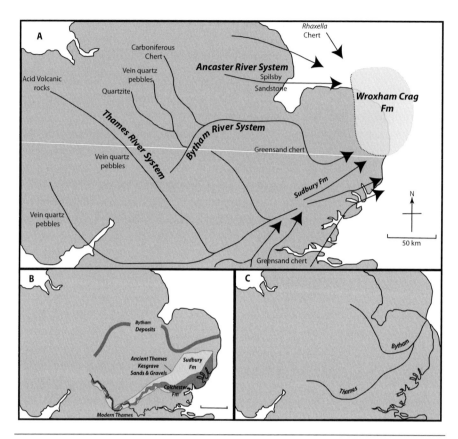

FIGURE 2.8

Composite sketch maps showing the principal river systems of Britain during the Early Pleistocene and early Middle Pleistocene, excluding the Solent system. (a) The Thames, Bytham and Ancaster Rivers, with principal sources of diagnostic rock lithologies. (Redrawn after Rose 2009, used with permission Elsevier.) (b) Extent of Thames and Bytham sediments of the Early Pleistocene and early Middle Pleistocene. (Redrawn and simplified from Whiteman and Rose 1992, used with permission Elsevier.) Note that, to date, no convincing archaeology older than MIS13 has been found in the Kesgraves, or inland within the Bytham system. (c) Proposed (alternate) palaeogeography during the occupation of Happisburgh. Note that the Bytham and Thames are confluent in this reconstruction. (Redrawn after Parfitt et al. 2010, and courtesy Simon Parfitt.)

gestion, arguing that Westaway conflated Bytham terraces with glaciofluvial and post-glacial deposits of the Waverney and for ignoring the implications of palaeosols within the various deposits.

2   The ancestral form of the River Thames, which rose in the Cotswolds and followed its present valley until Reading, from which it flowed north-eastwards through the Vale of St Albans, into eastern Essex and out into the North Sea (Rose and Allen 1977; Whiteman and Rose 1992; Bridgland 1994; Rose et al. 1999). Large spreads of sand and gravel of the Kesgrave Formation of the ancestral Thames ranging from MIS65 to MIS12 have been mapped across

East Anglia (Rose et al. 1999; Rose 2009; Bridgland and Westaway 2008; Bridgland 2010 – see Figure 2.8). The Early Pleistocene and early Middle Pleistocene terraces comprise (from oldest to youngest): Beaconsfield Terrace (~MIS22), Gerrards Cross Terrace (~MIS18), Walringfield Terrace, Ardleigh Terrace* (~MIS17–15), Wivenhoe Terrace* (~MIS14–13) and the Lower St Osyth Terrace* (MIS12).

3   The extinct Solent River which drained most of the Hampshire basin, flowing eastwards past the Isle of Wight before turning southwards into the area of the English Channel (Allen and Gibbard 1993; Westaway et al. 2006). At least six terraces of Early Pleistocene and early Middle Pleistocene age have been mapped in the Solent system: Whitefield Hill Terrace (MIS22), Holmsley Ridge Terrace (MIS18), Wootton Terrace (MIS16), Sway Terrace* (MIS15b), Tiptoe Terrace* (MIS14) and Setley Plain Terrace* (MIS13).

4   The Ancaster-Trent, which possibly flowed northwards from the southern Pennines, across the carboniferous uplands, before veering eastwards through a series of gaps in the Jurassic escarpment at Lincoln and Ancaster and on into the North Sea. This reconstruction remains speculative; no deposits exist within the Trent of this age, high-level terraces of the Ancaster River have not been identified and its possible course is largely based on rockhead relief (Clayton 2000; Rose et al. 2001; Rose 2009; Howard et al. 2007; Bridgland et al. in press).

Despite recent evidence for hominin occupation in Britain during MIS17 and MIS21–25, not a single convincing artefact has been recovered from contemporanous sediments of any of these major river systems, outside the two find spots detailed below. One might infer from this that hominin presence was exceptionally sparse, possibly confined only to the east of England.

PIONEERS AT THE EDGE OF THE WORLD: THE EARLIEST OCCUPATION OF BRITAIN

At the end of the last century, there was a widespread consensus amongst British and European workers that the earliest occupation of Britain occurred during MIS13 (e.g. Roberts et al. 1995; Roebroeks and Van Kolfschoten 1995; Wymer 1999). This was consistent with emerging hypotheses concerning the occupation of the north discussed above, the oldest age most 'serious' scholars were even willing to entertain being MIS15 (~565 ka BP) at Westbury-sub-Mendip (Andrews et al. 1999) and Waverley Wood (Shotton et al. 1993; Bowen et al. 1989; Bowen 1999). Despite many early claims to the contrary (e.g. Moir 1917, 1921a and b; 1939), it was also universally agreed that there was no evidence of human activity within the CF-bF (Preece and Parfitt 2000; Stuart 1996; Wymer 1999). Discoveries at Pakefield, Suffolk during the Quaternary Research Association field trip in 2000, and subsequent excavations under the auspices of the Ancient Human Occupation of Britain Project (AHOB), changed all this[5].

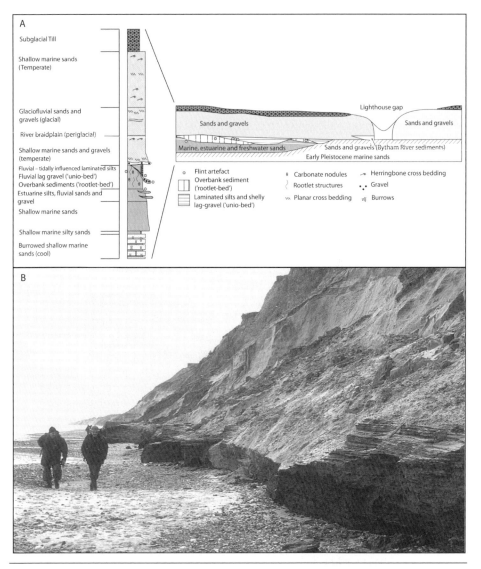

FIGURE 2.9
(a) Schematic section through the Cromer Forest Bed Formation at Pakefield, showing main environmental contexts and location of the flint artefacts (Redrawn after Parfitt et al. 2005, courtesy Simon Parfitt.) (b) Photograph of Pakefield Sections exposed during the Quaternary Research Associations' Easter 2000 Field Excursion. (Courtesy Simon Parfitt.)

Pakefield, Suffolk

Pakefield is situated on the Suffolk coast of East Anglia, at latitude 52° N. Some 34 flint artefacts were recovered from the interglacial fill of a channel (part of the CF-bF), incised into Early Pleistocene marine sediments, and overlain by a series of marine sands, glaciofluvial sediments and Lowestoft (MIS12) Till (Parfitt et al. 2005; Parfitt 2008) (Figure 2.9). The mineral composition of the fluvial sediments suggests deposition by the Bytham River, which at this time drained the English Midlands (ibid; Rose et al. 2001; Lee et al. 2006).

The artefacts (Figure 2.10) include two cores, a crudely retouched flake and débit-age; a small sample but nevertheless conforming to the general Mode 1 technology seen across Europe at this time (Parfitt et al. 2005; Parfitt 2008). They are all in a fresh preservational state and all on good quality black flint with water-worn cortex, suggesting that the raw material was gathered from local river gravels. The artefacts were recovered from four different contexts within the Pakefield sequence. The old-est evidence of hominin activity was recovered from the upper levels of an estuarine silt bed, which also yielded marine and brackish-water ostracods, foraminifera and marine mammals such as dolphin and walrus. The remainder were found in sediments

FIGURE 2.10
Artefacts from Pakefield. (Photographs by Harry Taylor and © Natural History Museum.)

attributed to the CF-bF (from top to bottom): the 'Rootlet bed' (overbank sediments with well-developed soil features including numerous fossil root-casts and pedogenic carbonate nodules (n = 2), the 'Unio-bed' (a lag gravel cutting into the overbank sediments (n = 30) and laminated silts at the edge of the channel (n = 1). The presence of micro-débitage indicates that knapping occurred on-site, while the occurrence of artefacts in several contexts has been argued to show that hominins were present for more than one phase of occupation (Parfitt et al. 2005; Parfitt 2008) although vertical and horizontal displacement cannot be ruled out.

The CF-bF sediments at Pakefield are normally magnetised, meaning that they post-date the Bruhnes-Matayama magnetic boundary and cannot therefore be older than 0.78 ma BP (ibid.). The sequence is capped by Lowestoft Till of Anglian (MIS12) age, meaning they cannot be younger than ~0.5 ma BP. The sediments between the CF-bF and the till were originally interpreted as Anglian glaciofluvial deposits (West 1980) which, parsimoniously, would make the Pakefield sediments late Cromerian, probably MIS13 or 15. Lee and colleagues, however, have proposed a longer chronology, in which the CF-bF was separated from the MIS12 Till by two high sea-level stands and two cold episodes. Counting back on the oxygen isotope record, this would suggest that the interglacial deposits at Pakefield date to MIS17 (~0.68 ma BP) at the youngest, and could possibly be as early as MIS19 (~0.75 ma BP) (Parfitt et al. 2005)[6].

An age within an early Middle Pleistocene interglacial is supported by evidence from mammalian biostratigraphy and amino acid geochronology. Although Pakefield was previously correlated with the deposits at West Runton on the basis of pollen and molluscs (West 1980; Preece 2001) the recent work of Parfitt and colleagues has suggested that this is not the case. West Runton lacks the southern thermophilous plants (e.g. water chestnut (*Trapa natans*), floating water fern (*Salvinia natans*) and Portuguese crowberry (*Corema album*)) and exotic beetles (*Cybister lateralimarginalis*, *Oxytelus opacus* and *Valgus hemipterus*) found at Pakefield. The mammalian fauna also shows a number of key differences that cannot be explained by different facies composition or collection history. In the large mammal assemblage several species from Pakefield – including *Hippopotamus* sp., *Megaloceros dawkinsii* (giant deer) and *Palaeoloxodon antiquus* (straight-tusked elephant) – have never been found at West Runton. Pakefield also has two species of the water vole genus *Mimomys*: *M. savini* and *M. aff. pusillus* (Figure 2.11). The latter is unknown from West Runton. In Eurasia, the last appearance of *M. pusillus* is in the Ilynian Complex of Russia, which underlies the MIS16 Don Till (Parfitt et al. 2005 and references therein). This suggests an age of at least MIS17 for the Pakefield *Unio* Bed. However, the oxygen isotope record reveals numerous short-lived sub-Milankovitch warm episodes to which any or all these sites might convincingly be related (cf. Westaway 2009a and b, and in press).

Palynological evidence suggests that the channel at Pakefield was infilled during a warm interglacial dominated by broad-leaf woodland (Parfitt et al. 2005). The combined palaeoenvironmental evidence suggests that locally the environment centred on a meandering river surrounded by marshy ground with reedy vegetation and alder-carr, with nearby areas of

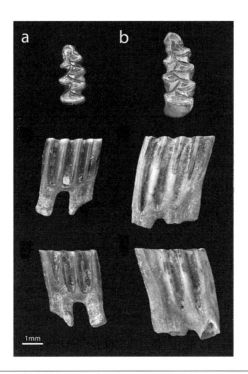

FIGURE 2.11
Mimomys teeth from Pakefield. (Photograph Phil Crabb and © Natural History Museum.)

oak woodland and open grassland (ibid.). These rich and varied habitats were exploited by a number of large herbivores including open-grassland species such as steppe mammoth (*Mammuthus trogontherii*), rhinoceros (*Stephanorhinus hundsheimensis*), bison (*Bison cf. schoetensacki*) and giant deer (*Megaloceros dawkinsii and Megaloceros savini*); forest species such as straight-tusked elephant (*Palaeoloxodon antiquus*), wild boar (*Sus scrofa*) and fallow deer (*Dama dama*); the river-dwellers hippopotamus (*Hippopotamus* sp.) and beaver (*Castor fiber*); as well as their predators/scavengers including scimitar-toothed cat (*Homotherium sp.*), lion (*Panthera leo*), spotted hyaena (*Crocuta crocuta*) and wolf (*Canis lupus*) (Figure 2.12). The floodplain would therefore have presented diverse plant and animal resources for early humans, in addition to raw material from the flint-rich river gravels, which was otherwise scarce in the immediate vicinity.

The warmth-loving and frost sensitive plants and insects alongside hippopotamus indicate warm summers and mild winters. MCR on beetles (see Text Box 2.2) has suggested mean July temperatures of 18–23° C and mean January/February temperatures between –6 and +4° C. Stable isotope analysis on pedogenic carbonate nodules from the 'Rootlet Bed' revealed intense moisture evaporation during their formation, suggesting highly seasonal precipitation regime (Candy et al. 2006; Parfitt et al. 2005). Together with the palaeotemperature reconstructions, this is argued to show that warm, seasonally dry 'Mediterranean' climates prevailed in Britain during the Pakefield interglacial.

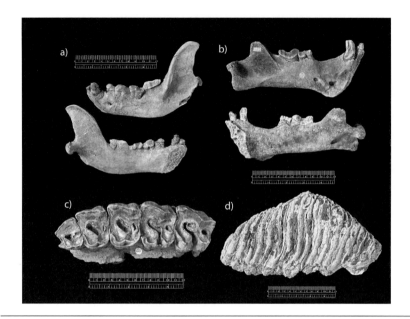

FIGURE 2.12
Carnivores and Herbivores from Pakefield. (a) Spotted hyaena (*Crocuta crocuta*); (b) scimitar-toothed cat (*Homotherium* sp.) (c) Rhinoceros (*Stephanorhinus hundsheimensis*); (d) Steppe mammoth (*Mammuthus trongontherii*). (Photographs Harry Taylor and © Natural History Museum.)

BEETLE FAUNAS AND ENVIRONMENTAL RECONSTRUCTIONS

Text Box 2.2

Insect remains, particularly those of coleoptera (beetles), provide a valuable tool for reconstructing Quaternary environments, and are often found in anoxic (oxygen depleted) waterlain sediments that both preserve and concentrate a range of organic detritus (Elias 1994). Beetles occupy a very wide range of terrestrial and freshwater habitats, and many species are stenotopic (precisely adapted to particular habitats and temperature ranges), meaning they can provide a high-resolution picture of a wide range of localised palaeoenvironments and palaeoclimates (Coope 2006). As many taxa have very specific feeding habits, they are also useful in augmenting our understanding of local (rather than regional) vegetation, herbivore and avian communities, and the type of carcasses that littered the landscape, even if these are not themselves recovered from palaeofaunas (Elias 1994). Critically, the similarities between suites of associated beetles found in fossil and modern contexts, as well as a range of independent proxies, suggest that beetles have not greatly altered their ecological preferences during the course of the Pleistocene (ibid.), and are thus a reliable proxy.

As with pollen, however, there is an ever present danger that at a local level allochthonous 'background faunas' may have strayed into deposits or been carried there by animals; a particular problem when dealing with small numbers of individuals, and perhaps most significant when dealing with later human settlements or closed environments (Kenward et al. 1985). For Palaeolithic studies, however, seeking to understand both the local and regional environmental structure, the issue of scale becomes important. Precisely because beetles are highly sensitive to factors such as vegetation, temperature, soil type, chemical variation and hydrology, they emphasise the micro-habitats of the preservational basins being sampled rather than providing a picture of a wider landscape. Some are totally dependant on their particular hosts and do not stray far from them at all (Coope 2006). Thus, the very specificity that makes them such sensitive environmental and ecological indicators, may also limit their scope when trying to reconstruct Palaeolithic landscapes (depending of course on the scale of preservation and the sample strategy).

At regional scales, coleopteran data are very useful for reconstruction palaeoclimates. As climate changes, beetles respond not by evolving in terms of Darwinian natural selection, but by altering their geographic ranges, which they can do much more rapidly than many other terrestrial biota (Coope 2002). In some cases, this may lead to the beetle faunas being out of phase with other proxies (ibid.). Several methods of inferring past climates from beetle assemblages have been devised. One depends on mapping the modern geographical distribution of individual species and taking the conditions in the region of maximum overlap as the most likely palaeoenvironment for the fossil assemblage (e.g. Coope 1959). Coope (2002) highlights several problems with the method: it assumes complete knowledge of modern distributions; it fails to consider the possibility that modern distributions may not fully cover the potential range of a species; and the patchy distribution of many species makes simple overlapping in geographical space difficult. The method most often applied today is the 'mutual climatic range' (MCR) (Atkinson et al. 1987; Coope 2000, 2002), which plots species distribution not in geographical space but climatic space. This creates a series of 'climatic envelopes', the inferred palaeoclimate being derived from the coordinates of the area of maximum overlap of these envelopes. To keep temperature estimates independent from other complicating factors, such as the distribution of host plants, only carnivorous species are used. The results are usually presented as T_{max} (mean temperature of the warmest month) and T_{min} (mean temperature of the coldest month). A range of values is usually provided, the figures indicating that the actual T_{max} and T_{min} lay somewhere between these limits and not that it ranged between them (Murton et al. 2001). Individual daily figures would obviously fluctuate enormously around the mean. Sensitivity tests on the MCR procedure, using modern coleopteran faunas living near to meteorological stations, show that there is often a disparity in the MCR estimates and the actual mean monthly temperatures measured at those stations – winter temperature estimates are usually too warm.

Text Box 2.2

Happisburgh Site 3, Norfolk

Happisburgh Site 3 was discovered in 2005, during an excavation programme designed to examine the Pleistocene sequence between Happisburgh and Ostend, Norfolk (N. Ashton pers. comm. November 2010). One objective of the project was to recover artefacts and fauna from interglacial sediments beneath the Happisburgh Till, in order to establish a probable age for material recovered from the beach (including a handaxe found *within* the interglacial sediments), which had become embroiled in a wider debate concerning the glacial sequence in Norfolk (e.g. Rose et al. 2001; Lee et al. 2004, 2006; Preece and Parfitt 2000; Preece et al. 2009; see Text Box 2.3). The results of this project suggested that the Happisburgh Till was deposited during MIS12, and that the immediately underlying implementiferous and fossiliferous deposits at Happisburgh I belonged to MIS13 (Ashton et al. 2008b; Preece et al. 2009). Those from Happisburgh 3 (Figure 2.13), however, are possibly much older (Parfitt et al. 2010).

FIGURE 2.13
Overhead view of the Happisburgh 3 site, and detail of excavations in progress. (Courtesy Nick Ashton.)

THE AGE OF THE HAPPISBURGH TILL: GLACIAL STRATIGRAPHY VERSUS BIOSTRATIGRAPHY

For the past 30 years, the glacial tills of East Anglia have been widely understood as deposits laid down by an oscillating British and Scandinavian ice sheet during a single glacial event – the Anglian (MIS12) glaciation (e.g. Perrin et al. 1979; Rose 1987; Table 1). Over the past decade, however, a research team from Royal Holloway and the British Geological Survey has made a strong and vocal challenge to this, provoking an equally robust response from supporters of the traditional model. The age(s) of the glacial deposits of East Anglia has major ramifications for the dating of the Early Pleistocene and early Middle Pleistocene occupation of Britain. Of key concern here is the age of the Lowestoft and Happisburgh Formations.

Table 1 The glacial stratigraphy model compared to the biostratigraphical model for the ages of the East Anglian tills (data combined after Preece and Parfitt 2008; Preece et al. 2009)

Glacial stratigraphy model				Biostratigraphical age model
Proposed MIS age	Formation	Member	Key fossil sites (MIS)	MIS: water voles
			Sidestrand Cliff Formation (Trimingham Lake Bed)	11 or 9
6	Briton's Lane Fm	Britons Lane Sand and Gravel Mb		12
10	Sheringham Cliffs Fm	Weybourne Town Till Mb		12
		Runton Till Mb		12
		Bacton Green Till Mb (3rd Cromer Till)		12
12	Lowestoft Fm	Walcott Till Mb (=2nd Cromer Till)		12
				12
		Lowestoft Till Mb		
16	Happisburgh Fm	Corton Till member Mb		12
		Happisburgh Till Mb		12

≥17	Cromer Forest Bed Fm	Sidestrand Hall Mb (≥17)	13 or 15: *Arvicola*
		Happisburgh 1 (≥17)	13 or 15: *Arvicola*
			15 or 17: *Mimomys*
		West Runton (17/19)	17: *Mimomys*
		Pakefield (17/19)	

The glacial stratigraphy model (e.g., Hamblin et al. 2000, 2005; Lee et al. 2004, 2006; Rose 2009; Lee 2009)

Advocates of the glacial stratigraphy model argue that the sedimentary character, lithology and ice-flow direction of the East Anglia tills demonstrate that they represent a series of glacial episodes dating to MIS6, MIS10, MIS12 and MIS16, rather than belonging to a single MIS12 glaciation (Lee et al. 2004; Hamblin et al. 2005; Rose 2009). Only the deposits of the Lowestoft Formation are considered to be MIS12, with the glacial deposits of the Happisburgh Formation suggested to belong to MIS16. This conclusion is founded on a simplified version of Bridgland's terrace formation model (Bridgland 1994; Bridgland and Allen 1996), whereby terraces are assumed to form at regular 100 ka cycles. In this reconstruction, the three lowest terrace aggradations of the Bytham River are assigned to MIS16 (3rd or Timworth Terrace), MIS14 (2nd or Warren Hill Terrace) and MIS12 (1st or Castle Bytham Terrace); the latter age being supported by evidence for continuous sedimentation from fluvial to ice-dammed lake conditions during MIS12. Concomitantly, the presence of till-balls, erratics and heavy minerals characteristic of the Happisburgh Till in deposits of the 'MIS16' Timworth Terrace at Leet Hill (Lee et al. 2004; Hamblin et al. 2005) demands that the Happisburgh Till is older than the terrace formation, a date earlier within the MIS16 glaciation being favoured (Rose et al. 1999; Lee et al. 2004; Rose, 2009). Unconformable contacts and differential weathering between the Lowestoft and Happisburgh Formations (Hamblin et al. 2005), combined with evidence that a shallow (non-glacial) marine phase separates the Happisburgh Formation (Corton Till) from the Lowestoft Till at Chapel Hill (Read et al. 2007), also demand their attribution to different climatic cycles.

The conclusions of this model contradict several long-held biostratigraphical frameworks, particularly the dating of the *Mimomys–Arvicola* transition. Lee et al. (2004) therefore suggested that the first and last appearances of these biostratigraphical markers is uncertain, and may not relate to full MIS stages but substages, and the assumption that evolution and replacement was synchronous across Eurasia is unproven – the two species could have co-occurred in some regions.

Text Box 2.3

The biostratigraphical model (Preece 2001; Stuart and Lister 2001; Preece and Parfitt 2008; Preece et al. 2009)

In contrast, the biostratigraphical model reinforces the traditional viewpoint that the East Anglian tills all belong to MIS12. The foundation of this model has undoubtedly been the evolution of the water vole from *Mimomys savini* (with rooted molars in older individuals) to *Arvicola terrestris cantiana* (with molars that are always unrooted), a transition thought to have occurred during MIS15 (Preece and Parfitt 2008), as on the continent. For Preece and Parfitt it is difficult to reconcile this pattern with the glacial stratigraphy model, which would require all sites with *Mimomys savini* to fall between the end of MIS19 and MIS17, before being replaced by *Arvicola* just before the Happisburgh Glaciation (*Arvicola* occurring in deposits directly beneath Happisburgh Till at Sidestrand, Happisburgh 1 and Ostend). There is also no evidence for the interdigitation of *Mimomys* and *Arvicola* that would support claims for progressive and diachronic evolution with significant ebb and flow of populations over time. Other important markers among the microtine voles include *Mimomys pusillus*, which apparently became extinct in MIS17.

This model is supported by multiple and independent lines of evidence, including molluscs, ostracods and beetles (Preece and Parfitt 2008; Preece et al. 2009). A recent OSL dating programme also supported an MIS12 age for all the sampled East Anglian tills (Pawley et al. 2008), while AAR estimates on molluscs from Sidestrand indicated an MIS11 or MIS9 age for temperate sediments capping the Happisburgh Till, but an MIS13 or 15 age for the interglacial sediments underlying it (Preece et al. 2009; Penkman et al. 2010). The inescapable conclusion is that the intervening till is of MIS12 age. Re-mapping and uplift modelling of the Bytham Terraces by Westaway (2009a), furthermore, resulted in the incorporation of the first three terraces of Lee *et al.* (2004) into a single aggradation belonging to MIS13 and MIS12. While Rose (2009) offered a critical rebuttal to Westaway, Preece and Parfitt (2008) also suggested that the lowest three Bytham Terraces belonged to MIS12, stressing the effects of crustal movement and glacial displacement on terrace formation, which cannot be expected to operate in a regular 100 ka cycle in all river systems. Indeed, this fact has long been recognised by David Bridgland, the architect of the prevailing model of climatically driven terrace formation, and is exemplified in the two MIS12 terraces of the Thames (Winter Hill and Black Park) (Bridgland 1994; Maddy et al. 2000; Bridgland and Westaway 2008) and the paired terraces of the Solent (Bridgland 2001; Westaway et al. 2006).

We follow the biostratigraphical model, with the caveat that if this ultimately proves to be wrong, our preferred dates for some sites may require adjustment.

Text Box 2.3

Artefacts at Happisburgh 3 were recovered from fluvial (lag) gravels and laminated estuarine sands and silts filling a series of stacked, overlapping channels (Figure 2.14). These
were incised into sands and silts of the Norwich Crag Formation and overlain by Happisburgh Till (Parfitt et al. 2010; see Figure 2.15). The implementiferous deposits have
been assigned to the newly defined Hill House Formation. Their sedimentology suggests
deposition in the upper part of the estuary of a large river. Non-local and exotic clasts
included vein quartz and quartzite from the Midlands, Carboniferous chert, Hertfordshire
Puddingstone and Greensand chert from southeast England and acid volcanic rocks
probably derived from Ordovician strata in North Wales. Together this suite is consistent
with deposition by the ancestral Thames – flowing some 150 km north of its present
estuary – with some contribution by the Bytham River (ibid.).

A total of 78 artefacts were recovered from six horizons in Layers C, D, E and F. Many
were in a fresh preservational state (Figure 2.16). The assemblage is characterised by
large flakes (>145 mm) with sharp cutting edges and cortical backs. The unusual size
range and proportion of naturally backed knives was argued to show that the artefacts
had been transported to the site from knapping areas elsewhere (ibid.).

The human environment of Happisburgh 3 has been reconstructed through a number
of terrestrial and marine proxies, including pollen, plant macrofossils, beetles, molluscs,

FIGURE 2.14
The implementiferous fluvial (lag) gravels and laminated estuarine sands and silts from Happisburgh 3. (Courtesy Nick Ashton.)

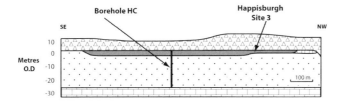

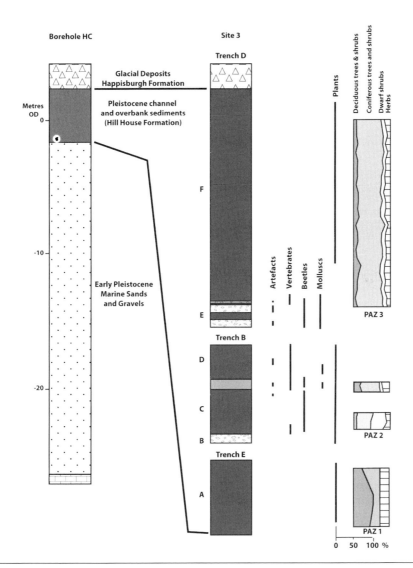

FIGURE 2.15
Stratigraphical context of the Happisburgh 3 artefacts and biological remains. Top: Coastal section showing location of R.G. West's Borehole HC. Below: Lithostratigraphy of Borehole HC, alongside composite lithostratigraphy for Site 3. (Redrawn and simplified after Parfitt et al. 2010, and courtesy Simon Parfitt and Nick Ashton.)

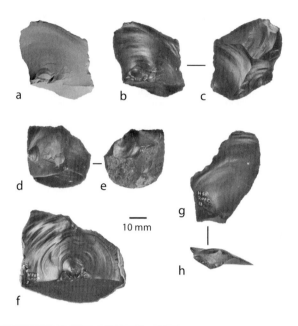

FIGURE 2.16
Artefacts from Happisburgh 3. (After Parfitt et al. 2010 and courtesy Nick Ashton.)

foraminifera, barnacles, fish and mammals (Parfitt et al. 2010). The pollen revealed a vegetation succession through three major zones. The earliest archaeology (two arte-facts) is associated with pollen assemblage zone 2, which was dominated by heathland taxa, together with pine and spruce. The majority of the artefacts, though (76), were associated with pollen assemblage zone 3, characterised by an abundance of pine and spruce with deciduous elements, suggesting regional conifer-dominated forests (ibid.). The presence of local grassland is indicated by a number of large grazers such as horse and bison, as well as pollen from a hyaena coprolite. The beetle remains, plant macrofossils and fish showed the presence of a large, slow-moving river surrounded by reed swamp, alder carr, marshes, pools, and coniferous woodland; while the marine molluscs, barnacles and foraminifera testify to the proximity to the estuary.

Temperature estimates based on the mutual climatic range of the beetles indicated mean July temperatures of 16–18° C and mean January temperatures of 0 to –3° C, sug-gesting warm summers slightly hotter than present, and mild but slightly colder winters. On the basis of these temperatures and the dominance of coniferous forest, Parfitt et al. (2010) draw an analogy with modern southern Scandinavia, close to the transition between the temperate and boreal zones. In general, the environment at Happisburgh 3 can be seen to conform to the general pattern highlighted above – whereby humans moved into areas of rich diverse resources that cushioned them from failure. Although coniferous forests are nutritionally poor with low edible biomass, Happisburgh appears to have been in an ecotonal situation with a large tidal river, freshwater pools, and marshes providing a range of aquatic resources, vegetation such as tubers and rhizomes and both open and closed environment herbivores (Parfitt et al. 2010).

The age of the Happisburgh deposits has been constrained by reversed palaeomagnetism, (suggesting an age >0.78 ma BP) and biostratigraphy. The deposits have yielded pollen of *Tsuga* (hemlock) and *Ostrya* (hop-hornbeam type), which are unknown in northern Europe after the Early Pleistocene, alongside a mammalian suite (Figure 2.17) comprising southern mammoth (*Mammuthus* cf. *meridionalis*), extinct equid (*Equus suessenbornensis*), extinct elk (*Cervalces latifrons*), red deer (*Cervus elaphus*), 'advanced' forms of *Microtus*, and the two species of *Mimomys* found at Pakefield, *M. savini* and *M. pusillus*. The overlapping ranges of the plant and mammalian taxa indicate a date towards the end of the Early Pleistocene which, together with the palaeomagnetic evidence, suggests human occupation towards the end of the Matuyama Chron, between 0.99 and 0.78 ma BP. The vegetation succession from Happisburgh 3 can be correlated with the upper part of West's (1980) much longer log from Borehole HC (Parfitt et al. 2010). This suggest that hominins occupied the cooling limb of an interglacial, which would further constrain the age of Happisburgh 3 to either MIS21 (0.86–0.81 ma BP) or MIS25 (0.97–0.93 ma BP) (Figure 2.18). Others have disputed this reading of the record (see Text Box 2.4)

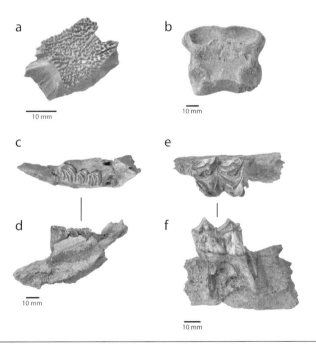

FIGURE 2.17
Selected fauna from Happisburgh 3: a, Skull bone of *Acipenser* cf. *sturio* (sturgeon) (Bed E). (b), Phalanx II of *Equus* sp. (Horse) (Bed D). (c)–(d), Mandible with P4–M2 of *Trogontherium cuvieri* (Giant Beaver) in (c) occlusal view and (d) lingual view (Bed D). (e)–(f), Mandible fragment with M2 of *Cervalces latifrons* (Extinct Elk) in (e) occlusal and (f) labial views (Bed E). (After Parfitt et al. 2010 and courtesy Nick Ashton.)

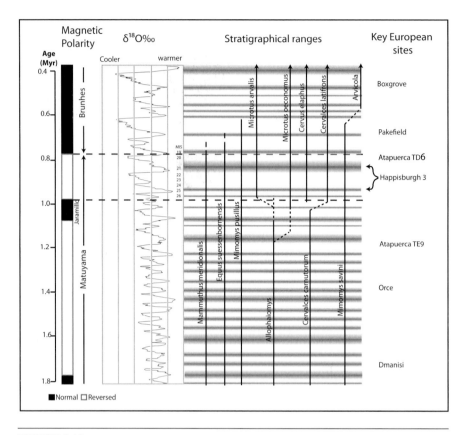

FIGURE 2.18
The dating evidence for Happisburgh, particularly palaeomagnetism and mammalian bios-tratigraphy. (Modified after Parfitt et al 2010 and courtesy Simon Parfitt.)

Text Box 2.4

A RESURRECTED SHORT CHRONOLOGY FOR NORTHERN EUROPE?

Recent claims for human occupation at Pakefield during MIS17 or 19 and at Happisburgh 3 during MIS21 or 25 have transformed our understanding of the hominin settlement history of Britain and have brought into focus their adaptative capabilities (see main text). These claims have been well received in the archaeological world (Roebroeks 2005; Roberts and Grün 2010). There is, however, a compelling voice of dissent: the geophysicist Rob Westaway (Westaway 2009a; 2009b; in press and personal communication to MJW; for full argument see cited papers and references therein). Westaway's views deserve to be taken seriously and are summarised below.

The age of Pakefield

The key lines of evidence employed by Parfitt et al. (2005) to support the MIS17 or MIS19 age for Pakefield were:

1   The sediments are normally magnetised and overlain by Anglian Till, providing an age range between MIS19 and MIS12. The correlation of Pakefield with the 3rd (Timworth) Terrace of the Bytham River at Leet Hill, argued to be of MIS16 age by Lee et al. (2004), suggests that the interglacial deposits are MIS17 or older.

2   The presence of *Mimomys pusillus* alongside *Mimomys savini*, the former unknown in sites in southwest Russia after MIS17 (Pevzner et al. 2001).

3   Amino-acid dating evidence showing that Pakefield is older than Waverley Wood.

Westaway (2009a, b) unpicks each of these principles in turn. Remapping and redating the Bytham terraces using uplift modelling, Westaway (2009a) subsumed the first three terraces of the Bytham into a complex sequence of incision and aggradation during MIS12 and MIS13 (similar to that seen in the Thames), thus refuting the MIS16 age of the critical Leet Hill deposits. He rejected the value of *Mimomys pusillus* as a biostratigraphic indicator, given its rarity and poorly understood chrono-geographical distribution. The amino-acid dating was considered equally uninformative.

Westaway instead constructs an argument for a much younger age. That Pakefield is older than MIS13 is undisputed, as by this time *Mimomys savini* had been replaced across Europe by *Arvicola cantiana*. But, taking MIS14 and not MIS16 (Preece and Parfitt 2000, 2008) as the age of that transition and following the biostratigraphical scheme of Tyráček et al. (2004), Westaway suggested that Pakefield belonged to MIS15 (along with other CF-bF sites at Corton and Kessingland). This date was refined to MIS15e based on differences in molluscan faunas found at these CF-bF sites and the Kesgrave site at Little Oakley – the latter being attributed to a later part of the same cycle, MIS15c or MIS15a – and using calibrated amino-acid dating, which supports an MIS15e date for both Pakefield and West Runton (Westaway 2009b; see Figure 1). The type-site of West Runton, which has a notably cooler climatic signature than Pakefield, is thus argued to represent the warming transition at the start of the MIS15e sub-stage, with Pakefield representing the climatic optimum. Penkman et al. (2010) later supported the suggestion that Pakefield and West Runton are very similar in age, although refrained from attributing either to a specific isotope stage.

The age of Happisburgh 3

Parfitt et al. (2010) proposed an Early Pleistocene (MIS25 or 21) age for Happisburgh 3 on the basis of magnetostratigraphy, pollen mammalian biostratigraphy

Text Box 2.4

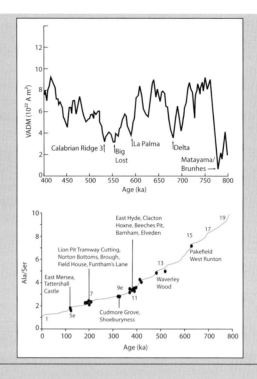

FIGURE 1

Westaway's interpretation of the palaeomagnetic (a) and amino-acid data (b) from Pakefield and Happisburgh. (Redrawn and simplified after Westaway 2009 and in press. Courtesy Rob Westaway.)

and clast lithology, arguing that their combination provided a robust argument for an Early Pleistocene age. For Westaway each is open to question.

Magnetostratigraphy

The reversed magnetisation of Happisburgh beds C, D and F forms the cornerstone for the Early Pleistocene, pre-MIS19 age of these deposits. However, according to Westaway (in press, and the original commentators in *Nature* (Roberts and Grün 2010) the palaeomagnetic data shows significant variability in magnetisation directions and are more consistent with the complexity expected during a geomagnetic excursion rather than a full reversal. One such event, the Calabrian Ridge 3 excursion, is dated to ~0.59 ma BP, within the end-MIS15e cooling-transition, a suggestion consistent with the environmental evidence at Happisburgh of progressive cooling throughout the sequence.

Pollen

Parfitt et al. (2010) reported the presence of *Tsuga* (hemlock) and *Ostrya* (hop-hornbeam) pollen in the Happisburgh sequence, both of which they considered to be unknown in northern Europe after the Early Pleistocene. *Ostrya*-type pollen is abundant (up to ~15%) in Happisburgh 3 Bed A, occurred as a trace (<~1%) in Bed C, and was absent from other beds (Westaway in press). Similarly, trace amounts (<1%) of *Tsuga* pollen were found in only one sample from Bed F. Westaway therefore argues that the abundance of *Ostrya*-type pollen in Bed A provides a strong indication that this bed is Early Pleistocene, but the trace amounts in Bed C could parsimoniously result from reworking; the same is true of the single occurrence of *Tsuga* pollen in bed F.

Mammalian biostratigraphy

Four mammalian taxa are critical to the Early Pleistocene age attribution of the Happisburgh succession: the water voles *Mimomys savini* and *M. pusillus*, the horse *Equus suessenbornensis*, and the elephant *Mammuthus meridionalis*. Westaway rejects all of these. *Mimomys savini* is known from many CF-bF and fluvial sites, including Pakefield, West Runton, Little Oakley and Sugworth, its extinction during MIS14 (Westaway 2009a) or MIS16 (Preece and Parfitt 2008) rendering it irrelevant to the Early Pleistocene. *E. suessenbornensis* is similarly found at many CF-bF sites, including West Runton and Sidestrand (assigned respectively, to MIS15 and 13). *Mimomys pusillus* is recorded at Pakefield and although this species is suggested to have become extinct by MIS17 in eastern Europe, and even earlier in western and central Europe (Maul and Markova 2007). Westaway's reading of the age of Pakefield questions this last appearance datum in Britain of a rare species. *Mammuthus meridionalis* is known from European early Middle Pleistocene deposits, including Kärlich F (dated to MIS15 on the basis of counting loess–palaeosol couplets, relative to beds that provide age control). Here, *M. meridionalis* post-dates the earlier occurrence (in Kärlich B) of its nominal evolutionary descendant, the steppe mammoth *Mammuthus trogontherii*, suggesting the co-occurrence of distinct elephant forms in the early Middle Pleistocene (van Kolfschoten and Turner 1996). A late form of *Mammuthus meridionalis* is also known from the *Lehmschicht* deposits at Voigtstedt (e.g., Kahlke 2002), which can also be assigned to part of MIS15. These occurrences suggest that both *Mammuthus trogontherii* and a late form of *Mammuthus meridionalis* coexisted in western/central Europe in early MIS15, the latter becoming extinct later in the same interglacial.

Clast lithology

'Exotic', fluvially transported clasts at Happisburgh (from beds B and E) do not support the Thames-Bytham palaeo-drainage model of Parfitt et al. (2010) but could easily have been derived from older deposits which are widespread locally. That the land surface was uplifting during the early Middle Pleistocene provides a mechanism for incision.

In summary, Westaway suggests that nothing precludes West Runton belonging to the early MIS15e warming transition (~0.62 ma BP), Pakefield to the (~0.61 ma BP) climatic optimum and Happisburgh beds B-F to the subsequent cooling transition (~0.59 ma BP). This redating highlights the fact that the CF-bF exposures may typically mark brief time spans – in the region of a few thousand years at most – and represent fragments of temperate MIS sub-stages rather than different sub-stages or full stages.

Text Box 2.4

THROUGH SMALL WINDOWS: THE EARLIEST HUMANS IN BRITAIN

The discoveries of the past ten years, made largely under the auspices of the AHOB, have completely transformed our understanding of the chronology and settlement history of Lower Palaeolithic Britain. Finding sites of such vintage is also an exciting spectacle capable of generating intense interest in academia, the media and the public eye. But this initial feeling of satisfaction is quickly replaced by a hunger for more. Simply knowing that a site is older than all others that have gone before it, that humans made stone tools and that the British climate and ecology was – well, pretty much British – leaves a lot of questions unanswered. The real importance of these discoveries is that they challenge our perceptions of past human adaptation at a very early date. While the discoveries of occupation during a 'Mediterranean excursion' at Pakefield could perhaps be accommodated into prevailing paradigms (e.g. Roebroeks 2005, but see below), the colonisation of the boreal zone at Happisburgh is ostensibly at odds with everything previously known and demands of hominins a range of novel adaptive skills (Parfitt et al. 2010). To go further, we need to untether our archaeological imaginations. This is not a call to stray from 'science to séance' (Binford 1989b), but to step beyond the empirically proven and into the logically inferred (Roebroeks 2001; White 2006). If correctly framed, such 'thought exercises' can provide useful testable hypotheses for future work. So, what do we want to know?

Who were the earliest visitors?

While one cannot eliminate the possibility that groups of Asian *Homo erectus*, African *Homo* cf. *ergaster* or even an unrecognised Eurasian species occasionally ventured westwards, only one species of human – *Homo antecessor* – is presently known from Early Pleistocene Europe. As long as fossil remains are restricted to the Atapuerca region of Spain, the geographical distribution of this species remains open to conjecture. However, given that by ~1.2 ma BP, a speciation event is argued to have given rise to a new European lineage (Martinón-Torres et al. 2008, Bermúdez de Castro et al. 2010; Dennell et al. 2010), we predict that should fossil remains ever be found in British Early Pleistocene deposits, they will probably be ascribable to this taxon.

Where did they come from?

The proximal and therefore most parsimonious source populations for the earliest incursions into Britain undoubtedly lie in neighbouring regions of France, particularly the sites in the Loire Basin dated to ~0. 93–0.98 ma BP, and more distally Spain and Italy. Stone tool technology is a very poor indicator of origin, as Mode 1 core and flake reduction is the lowest common denominator with few means of making cultural links, and idiosyncratic practices have not yet been identified. The test of such an assertion must therefore come from continued research in these potential source areas, linked to explicit research agendas aimed at understanding what ecological or demographic factors made humans spread *from* rather than *to* southern Europe.

How continuous was human presence?

Two sites, temporally separated by up to 200 ka, forms a poor basis on which to construct the MIS25–17 settlement history of Britain, but one may predict that human presence was ephemeral and possibly restricted to eastern England, populations extremely sparse and local extinction frequent (cf. Hublin and Roebroeks 2009). Human presence is thus unlikely to have been continuous, and we would expect humans to forego Britain during each glacial period when temperatures certainly dropped below those seen at Pakefield and Happisburgh, and probably below those faced by Neanderthals during MIS3 (Davies and Gallop 2003). However, given that the British record is still liable – after over 150 years of investigation – to throw up fabulous surprises on the scale of Pakefield and Happisburgh, it would be premature to look for reasons why humans were not present during the apparently unpopulated interglacials after ~1.2 ma BP. Such lacunae may be entirely illusory because, as Rose (2009) reminds us, our sequences are in fact largely composed of hiatuses. Taking the example of the Cromerian stratotype at West Runton, Rose suggested that the vegetation succession represented a typical seral development on a floodplain, whereby a new surface was colonised by temperate woodland. Such an event could realistically occur within a period of 100 years, an estimate that is in agreement with isotopic analysis on molluscs that provided no evidence for climate change throughout the sequence, and the coarse-grained sedimentation (organic sands) indicative of rapid deposition over timescales of tens or hundreds of years, not thousands. Our windows on the past may therefore be very small, the chances of preservation and visibility remarkably slight, and the chances of recovery even slighter. We predict that, now the veil of incredulity has been lifted, these gaps will ultimately be filled.

What adaptations were necessary?

The 'Out of Asia' model implies that, rather than spreading directly from tropical Africa in a geological 'blink of an eye', humans had in fact already spent some 300,000 years evolving within western Eurasia.[7] When this new 'Europe-ready' lineage eventually moved westwards, it spread first along familiar habitats with familiar genial climates, taking ~600,000 years to finally occupy the far northwest fringe (cf. Parfitt et al. 2005, 2010). This suggests that while several hundred millennia in western Eurasia may have equipped humans with all the resources to disperse successfully throughout the Mediterranean zone, the northern boreal zone of Britain was quite a different proposition (Roebroeks 2001, 2006; Rolland 2010). This region clearly placed significant environmental constraints on human colonisation, although even these had been successfully overcome by at least one million years ago. In short, there probably never was a tropical ape in the English country garden, rather a well adapted Eurasian one.

In two thought-provoking essays, Roebroeks (2001, 2006) urged us to go beyond the limits of preservation and, by drawing on advances in cognate disciplines, infer a number of social, physiological and behavioural prerequisites that must logically have pertained by the time humans first settled the north. At the time, Roebroeks considered the earliest occupation of the north to have occurred ~0.6 ma BP, and to have been undertaken by *Homo heidelbergensis*. It would now appear that this occupation took place some 400 ka earlier and by a different species. Regardless of this fact, those same prerequisites must surely still apply.

The climate and ecology of Europe vary along two well-known axes – longitudinally from west to east (the 'continentality' variable) and latitudinally from south to north (the 'boreal variable') (Roebroeks 2006; Rolland 2010) – presenting a range of different affordances and challenges to Pleistocene humans colonising along these gradients. At a most basic level, northern Europe is simply colder with far greater extremes in winter temperatures, the coldest months in the more continental northeast today reaching between −40° and −60° C (Rolland 2010). Britain, however, benefits from a more oceanic climate (although a more continental regime may have prevailed for parts of the Pleistocene), is relatively warm compared to inland continental Europe, and has a much narrower annual temperature range with (in mean terms) moderately cool summers and comparatively warm winters. Nevertheless, the extremes in southern England alone can vary from 32° C in the height of summer to −11° C in the depths of winter.[8]

Indeed, the reconstruction of Pleistocene winter temperatures in Britain is highly problematic (Parfitt et al. 2010). The mutual climatic range of beetles is probably the best method available (e.g. Parfitt et al. 2005; 2010; Coope 2001, 2002, 2006; Text Box 2.2) but often underestimates the severity of winter temperatures (Coope 2001; Murton et al. 2001) and perhaps should not be taken at face value. MCR estimates are usually presented as a temperature range, but this does not imply that temperatures fluctuated between these limits, rather that the actual mean lay somewhere within them (Murton et al. 2001; Coope 2001). The absence of robust statistical methods through which the actual temperature might be determined is a weakness of the method (Bray et al. 2006). However, even given perfect precision, mean monthly values homogenise the world into an artificial ideal, totally obscuring the fact that temperatures in Britain fluctuate on a daily basis, sometimes wildly, and that it is the (humanly experienced) extremes that posed threats of freezing, hypothermia and death, not the middling values.

Interpreting the values provided by the MCR procedure is therefore difficult, but one reading of the average winter temperature at 'boreal' Happisburgh and 'Mediterranean' Pakefield – estimated to fall between 0 to −3° C and 4 to −6° C respectively – could suggest that they were actually identical. In fact, given the range limits provided we might even suppose that winter temperatures at Pakefield were colder than those at Happisburgh; although frost *sensitive* plants and the presence of hippopotamus possibly suggests otherwise, assuming that an unidentified Pleistocene European hippopotamus (*Hippopotamus* sp. according to Parfitt et al. 2005, supplementary information) had the same tolerances as modern African examples (cf. Stuart and Lister 2001; Candy et al. 2006). Critically interrogating the MCR, rather than simply opting for the temperature that makes the best story, thus casts something of a shadow over the 'Costa del Cromer' (Roebroeks 2005).

In his commentary on Pakefield, Roebroeks (2005, 2006) posited only fleeting occupation during an uncharacteristically warm period, which served to underline the environmental signals highlighted by the 'Short Chronology'. It did not, for him, testify to the colonisation of the colder temperate environments of northern Europe, but to a short-lived range expansion in rhythm with climatic oscillations; humans simply expanded into familiar ecological settings using existing adaptations. This may be true of the summers, but compatible climatic signatures and pre-adapted humans only hold if winter temperature in the Early Pleistocene Spanish sites fell at the lower end of the MCR for herpetofauna (–0.5 to 12.5° C) generated by Agustí et al. (2009, 2010). In this case the conditions facing these pioneering Europeans may not have been entirely genial, and could potentially have demanded that humans coped with temperatures that hovered a few degrees above freezing from at least ~1.2 ma BP, which fits the minimum temperature tolerances of 0–6° C proposed by Leroy et al. (2011) and suggests that any interglacial with mild winters would have been suitable for humans to move north. Indeed, we strongly advocate that it is winter temperatures that are critical to discussions of dispersal and adaptation, and that mean summer temperatures during interglacials are of little consequence, unless they become so hot they begin to present dangers of dehydration and heat stroke, which we assume were probably not major problems in Pleistocene Britain. Concomitantly, it seems unlikely that humans were 'pulled' into Britain simply because summers were 2–4° C warmer than today, suggesting that any range expansion relates to demographic factors operating over long time periods on the source populations and not the climate of East Anglia. Precisely determining the age of Pakefield, to facilitate comparison with southern European environments during the period of human presence, is critical to an understanding of why humans expanded northwards at this time.

Regardless of how warm interglacial summers may have been, the over-wintering problem in Britain and elsewhere remains. Humans are poorly equipped physiologically to cope with low temperatures. In modern humans the lower critical temperature[9] is 28.2° C, while the minimal sustainable ambient temperature[10] is 10.5° C (Aiello and Wheeler 2003). For Pleistocene humans these values may require major adjustment to reflect the possibility of elevated basal metabolic rates (due to factors such as high protein diets and the effects of temperature and day length on thyroid function), the insulating effects of increased muscle mass, and a suite of other physiological and genetic adaptations (e.g. thermogenic brown adipose tissue; subcutaneous fat; enhanced vasoconstriction and localised vasodilation; aerobic fitness and ontogenetic acclimatisation) but these do not provide a total solution[11] and carry additional energetic costs (Aiello and Wheeler 2003; Steegmann et al. 2002). Life in Britain would therefore have posed the threat of hypothermia and freezing without adequate cultural solutions (White 2006; Rolland 2010) and would also have required greater energy expenditure merely to maintain homeostatis and reproduce (Roebroeks 2001; Aiello and Wheeler 2003; White 2006). This might suggest that by at least 1 ma BP, humans had developed rudimentary clothing (cf. Roberts 1996a; White 2006), fire (Gowlett 2006, although see Roebroeks and Villa 2011) and shelter (Chu 2009), all of which offer very significant thermal advantages.

Little evidence for any of these technologies in Europe exists at this date, the earliest evidence for fire use outside Africa coming from Gesher Benot Ya'aqov, dated to ~0.79 ma BP (Goren-Inbar et al. 2004). Gowlett (2006) and Roebroeks and Villa (2011) suggest that northern Europe was first colonised by humans who did not possess fire technology, but to us it seems unlikely that a purely physiological adaptation would have allowed *Homo antecessor* to survive the cold winters without it (cf. Aiello and Wheeler 2003; White 2006; Sørensen 2009). We suspect that the apparent absence of fire evidence prior to MIS11 will, like most of the absences noted over the past 20 years, ultimately prove to be an issue of taphonomy and recovery rather than a real absence. Evidence of the use of hides, for either clothing or structures is equally lacking. Simple clothing or wraps would have been very easy to produce, but may not have provided good thermal buffering (White 2006). Tools to produce tailored clothing to trap body heat are not in evidence until the Upper Palaeolithic (Kuhn and Stiner 2006), although experiments have shown that perfectly good clothes can be manufactured using a much simpler lithic tool kit (MJW pers. obs.). Claims for structures in the Lower Palaeolithic, those at Terra Amata, France and Bilzinsleben, Germany being amongst the most famous (De Lumley 1969; Mania and Mania 1995, 2005) have been dismissed on the basis of taphonomic problems (Villa 1982; Beck et al. 2007). Still, that Lower Palaeolithic humans were skinning animals for their hides might be shown at Schöningen 13II–4, Germany, where cut-mark patterns made during horse butchery and the lack of cordal vertebrae point to the careful removal of hides with their tails still attached (Voormolen, 2008). If humans were taking hides, then clothing and shelter are obvious uses. Seasonal migration is of course always an option, but how far and in which direction would humans have had to travel to reach warmer conditions, and what reception would they get from the local residents?

The previously mentioned temperature gradients also mean that resources become more spatially segregated as one move from south–north and west–east. Beyond 56° N, photo-periods became short, reducing growing seasons for vegetation and diminishing primary biomass production. The availability of edible plant foods in Britain is markedly seasonal, with short periods of plenty and a complete winter shut down. This problem is also greatly exacerbated in the coniferous forests which have few edible plants and dispersed game (Kelly 1995). Access to other resources – running water, lithic raw materials, animals – and the maintenance of the high mobility necessary to access them, may also have been restricted by thick snow, dense fog and prolonged frost (Rolland 2010). Shorter days – daylight only lasts for ~6–7 hours during some winter months – would have further impacted on daily foraging (Dennell and Roebroeks 1996; Roebroeks 2006; Rolland 2010) and any night-time activity would have been restricted by the presence of crepuscular carnivores, and the apparent lack of fire. Acute food shortages would therefore have been a frequent risk during cold seasons, requiring a year-round dependence on animal fats and proteins (Roebroeks 2001, 2006; Rolland 2010).

The 'boom and bust' character of vegetal resources demanded that, in order to survive, humans must have practised high levels of carnivory with routine and unhindered access to meat resources. One might suppose that humans achieved this by scavenging, especially the meaty leftovers of the machairodont cats *Megantereon whitei and Homotherium latidens* (Turner 1992; Palombo 2010; cf. Turner 2009), the latter possibly a pack hunter (Antón et al. 2005). Europe between ~1.5 ma and 0.9 ma BP was also home to three species of hyaenid (a form of brown hyena *Pliocrocuta perrieri*, giant hunting hyaena *Pachycrocuta brevirostris*, spotted hyaena *Crocuta crocuta*)*;* three felids (giant European cheetah *Acinonyx pardinensis,* European jaguar *Panthera gombaszoegensis,* and leopard *Panthera pardus*); and three canids (*Canis arnensis*, *Canis mosbachensis, Canis falconeri*) (Hemmer 2000; O'Regan et al. 2002). With so many members in the guild, one might predict rich opportunities for any scavenger, but given the energy requirements needed simply to maintain health, survive the cold and reproduce (cf. Sorenson and Leonard 2001), failure to procure sufficient meat would have carried severely high costs. Humans could not therefore afford to be passive recipients of ravaged carcasses, but must surely have depended at the very least on aggressive confrontational scavenging at carnivore kills. Moreover, in northern latitudes, lean meat alone would not have been enough, and a fat-rich diet would have been needed to avoid the types of metabolic problems highlighted by Speth (1987, 1989). This would have required time to process carcass parts, and could not have operated on a hit and run basis. Given all these issues, it seems maladaptive to attempt to steal a horse from a hyaena or lion (perhaps at night), when one could hunt it during the day. Sadly, at present, only the juvenile dominated assemblage from Atapuerca TD6 has provided any evidence of possible hunting at this time (Villa and Lenoir 2009); and at the same site evidence of nutritional cannibalism has been found (Fernández-Jalvo et al. 1999), although whether this indicates dietary stress is unclear.

Prey–predator density relationships and resource sustainability also indicate that hunting would have demanded large home ranges (Guthrie 1990). In northern latitudes these ranges would have been even larger because the boreal gradient means that resources become more spatially segregated and the need for residential moves is greater; the same is also true as one moves from the west to the east along the continentality gradient (Roebroeks 2001; Kelly 1995). This would have major implications for social networks, information exchange and fission–fusion dynamics amongst small band societies attempting to make a living while maintaining social cohesion and reproductive viability. Just how large these territories might have been during the early Pleistocene is completely unknown, and we await raw material movement studies once the corpus of sites and assemblages reaches a sufficient size. However, even later studies of lithic transfers (e.g. Gamble and Steele 1999) are really only giving us an indication of tool husbandry and resource distribution in the landscape, not a measure of human home ranges (cf. Roebroeks 2001). We can assume, though, that for most of the Pleistocene humans existed in very low numbers in the landscape. In this regard, Gamble's conclusion that the major wave of expansion ~0.6–0.5 ma BP involved encephalisation *and* larger community size – engendering cooperation in subsistence and defense against predators, as well as extended fission–fusion dynamics – seems rather overstated, especially given the clear overlap in predicted group sizes for *Homo erectus* (~70–120 at 1σ) and *Homo heidelbergensis* (~100–140 at 1σ) (Gamble 2009, 153 and Figure 2).

For Roebroeks (2001, 2006), hunting *must* have become increasingly important during the Pleistocene, humans being an established part of the carnivore guild by 0.6–0.5 ma BP, as shown by the evidence from Boxgrove, Sussex and Schöningen, Germany (Roberts and Parfitt 1999; Thieme 2005). Large quantities of meat were required not only to feed and heat the body, but also to fuel the brain (Aiello and Wheeler 1995). Human brains are energetically costly, using ~20% of energetic resources in adults and 60% in neonates; in pregnant females an astonishing 70% of energy in the final phase of pregnancy goes to feed the foetus' brain. Roebroeks uses these figures to good effect, reasoning that a regular supply of meat for nursing females suggests cooperation between the sexes and a greater reliance on males (or perhaps 'grandmothers' (cf. O' Connell et al. 1999)) to provide food, a situation exaggerated by the seasonal lack of anything to independently forage. Such a hypothesis carries a well-known cascade of social implications such as food sharing, social gatherings in central places and pair-bonding, although these views (cf. Isaac 1978; Lovejoy 1981) have been strongly criticised in the past (e.g. Binford 1985). Nonetheless, some support may now be found in the 'modern' levels of sexual dimorphism seen in the Sima de los Huesos fossil assemblage (dated to 0.4–0.5 ma BP or earlier; Bischoff et al. 2007), which may indicate that a modern type of male–female relationship was in place by the Middle Pleistocene. Furthermore, the ethnographic record shows that large game hunting also requires cooperation among males, who use knowledge of animals and the landscape to outsmart their faster, stronger prey (Roebroeks 2001). This may well have required language (Roberts 1996b). Indeed, Roebroeks concludes that such a high quality diet released the constraints on encephalisation and facilitated the expansion in brain size seen after 0.5 ma BP (cf. Gowlett 2006), with the permanent settlement of Europe demonstrating that humans had totally cracked the super-carnivore niche. But if such a meat rich diet and all its corollaries was required to fuel the large brains of *Homo heidelbergensis* (~1200cc; Rightmire 2004), would a similar set of conditions not also apply to the large brains of *Homo antecessor* (~1000cc; Bermúdez de Castro et al. 1997)?

WHERE DO WE GO FROM HERE?

As we have argued elsewhere (White and Pettitt 2011), the key to further understanding can only be new excavations. British scholars have for too long picked over the scraps left behind by Victorian pioneers and their pre-1950 successors, the result being that large swathes of the British Palaeolithic is in danger of becoming a footnote in prehistory. The successes of AHOB show what can be achieved, but to go beyond dates and environments and begin to tackle the behavioural issues highlighted here the scale of investigations needs to be expanded by several orders of magnitude. This is easier said than done. The logistical issues of excavating within the tidal zone beneath 20 m high cliffs of glacial till, sand and gravel should not be underestimated. The finances needed to conduct excavations that could ultimately provide the kinds of evidence being uncovered at Atapuerca are also prohibitive, and any proposal to remove a sizable portion of a Norfolk and Suffolk coastline already being obliterated by erosion might raise more than a few objections in the local community. But, this is a rapidly disappearing resource and the very processes that are exposing the sediments are destroying them forever. If ever there was an opportunity to discover the missing organic element of early human cultural adaptation in Britain then it is now and within the superb organic preservation of Cromer Forest Bed Formation.

CHAPTER 3

Landscapes of habit

The hominin occupation of Britain 550–300 ka BP

INTRODUCTION

The next two chapters deal with the principal Middle Pleistocene, Lower Palaeolithic occupation of Britain, which we define as spanning the period from the Cromerian (MIS13) interglacial to the advent of the persistent use of Levallois technology ~300 ka BP. As noted in the previous chapter, in many books and papers this period is divided into two, the first part dealing with early Middle Pleistocene occupation (MIS15 and 13), the second part with late Middle Pleistocene (MIS11 and 9) occupation, with the disjuncture of the Anglian glaciation or belief that MIS13 was the earliest (and therefore somehow special) occupation and thus apparently the rationale behind the separation. This makes little sense from an archaeological, technological or behavioural perspective, and we accordingly combine them here into a unified 'classic' Lower Palaeolithic record. The beginning of this period also corresponds to that in which Roebroeks (2006) detects a major transformation in the occupation of Europe, with the arrival of larger and more continuously present populations armed with bifacial handaxe technology. Across Europe, this period is associated with fossils assigned to *Homo heidelbergensis*, a species to which the only two British fossils of the period – the Swanscombe cranial remains (Text Box 3.1) and the Boxgrove tibia and incisors – have been referred (Roberts et al. 1994; Stringer and Hublin 1999; Hillson et al. 2010). Although hominin fossils are extremely rare, in archaeological terms the British Lower Palaeolithic record is remarkably rich relative to later periods, and contains a number of exceptionally well-preserved *in situ* sites and some very long sequences of multiple assemblages.

This chapter and the next therefore subsume some 250,000–300,000 years, spanning three major warm periods (MIS13, 11 and 9), two major cold periods (MIS12 and 10) and

Text Box 3.1

BARNFIELD PIT, SWANSCOMBE, KENT

Barnfield Pit, Swanscombe lies on the southern edge of the Lower Thames Basin, 5 km east of Dartford. It is justifiably one of the most famous archaeological sites in Britain, preserving an exceptional sequence of fluvial deposits and Palaeolithic industries, as well as three conjoining fragments of a human cranium assigned to *Homo heidelbergensis* (Marston 1937; Wymer 1964; Stringer and Hublin 1999). The site was first noted by Spurrell (1883), although the first systematic excavations, by Smith and Dewey, did not take place until 1912 (Smith and Dewey 1913, 1914). The discovery of conjoining skull fragments by Marston in 1935 and 1936 has been followed by a long string of investigations, including excavations by Cotton (Swanscombe Committee 1938), Montagu (1949), Wymer (1955, 1964), Waechter (1970, 1971, 1973; Conway et al. 1996), the Geological Conservation Review (Bridgland et al. 1985; Bridgland 1994), and the Quaternary Research Association (Ashton et al. 1995). As a result well over 100 primary articles, three monographs and innumerable citations exist. Only the briefest of summaries and key references can be provided here.

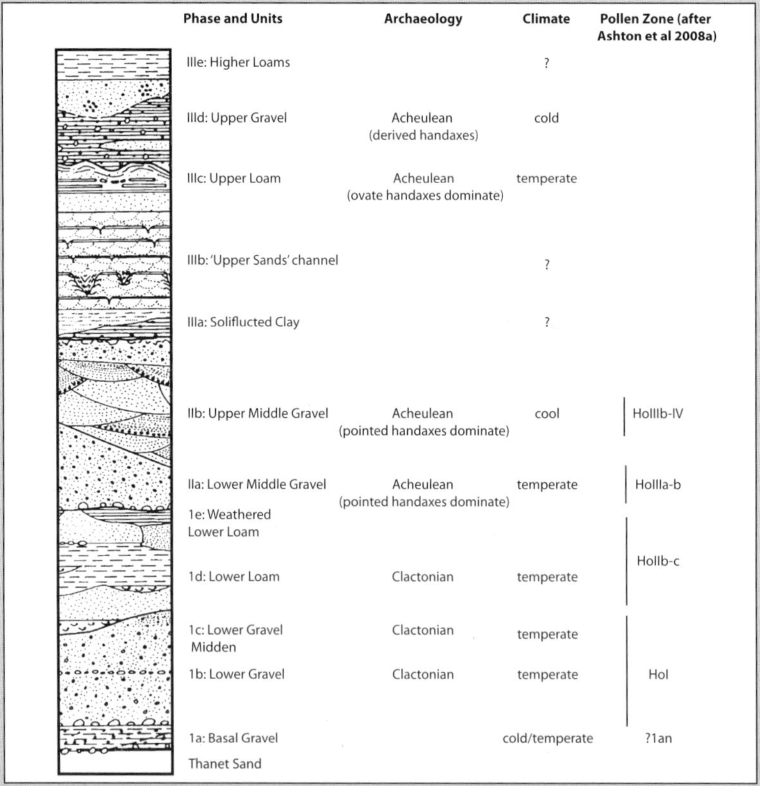

Phase and Units	Archaeology	Climate	Pollen Zone (after Ashton et al 2008a)
IIIe: Higher Loams		?	
IIId: Upper Gravel	Acheulean (derived handaxes)	cold	
IIIc: Upper Loam	Acheulean (ovate handaxes dominate)	temperate	
IIIb: 'Upper Sands' channel		?	
IIIa: Soliflucted Clay		?	
IIb: Upper Middle Gravel	Acheulean (pointed handaxes dominate)	cool	HoIIIb-IV
IIa: Lower Middle Gravel	Acheulean (pointed handaxes dominate)	temperate	HoIIIa-b
1e: Weathered Lower Loam			
1d: Lower Loam	Clactonian	temperate	HoIIb-c
1c: Lower Gravel Midden	Clactonian	temperate	
1b: Lower Gravel	Clactonian	temperate	HoI
1a: Basal Gravel		cold/temperate	?1an
Thanet Sand			

FIGURE 1
Section through the Swanscombe sequence, showing stratigraphical units and phases, climatic interpretation, archaeology and correlation with the Hoxnian pollen zones. (Redrawn after Conway et al. 1996, with additional data from Ashton et al. 2008a. © Trustees of the British Museum.)

The Swanscombe deposits form part of the Boyn Hill/Orsett Heath Formation, the highest post-Anglian terrace formation of the Thames. They comprise a remarkably full and rich archaeological and palaeontological sequence, with evidence for human occupation stretching through 14 m of sediment from the terminal part of the Anglian, through the MIS11 interglacial and into the ensuing cold phase. The sequence is summarised in Figure 1.

The key Phase I deposits are the Lower Gravel and Lower Loam, which contain organic remains characteristic of fully temperate climatic conditions. Molluscs and ostracods indicate a swift-flowing river with a stony bed in the Lower Gravel, succeeded by slowly moving water with reed swamps and marshes surrounded by grasslands and calcareous woodland in the Lower Loam. The mammalian fauna is dominated by inhabitants of deciduous woodland, such as the 'Clacton' subspecies of fallow deer (*Dama dama clactoniana*) and straight-tusked elephant (*Palaeoloxodon antiquus*), alongside large grazers of open grassland, including horse (*Equus ferus*), narrow-nosed rhinoceros (*Stephanorhinus hemitoechus*) and aurochs (*Bos primigenius*). Water vole (*Arvicola terrestris cantiana*) and European beaver (*Castor fiber*) indicate aquatic habitats. The faunal assemblages from the Phase I deposits have been equated with those from the Clacton Freshwater Beds (Kerney 1971; Turner and Kerney 1971; Schreve 1997); while a contentious pollen profile assigned the Lower Loam to pollen sub-zone HoIIb (Hubbard 1996). The Phase I deposits contain only Clactonian material – mostly in secondary context in the Lower Gravel, but mostly *in situ* with refitting sequences in the Lower Loam (Smith and Dewey 1913; Wymer 1964; Waechter 1970, 1971; Ashton and McNabb 1996). A soil at the top of the Lower Loam represents an old land surface (Kemp 1985), on top of which were observed white-patinated flint flakes and mammalian footprints, including those of wild cattle and horses (Waechter 1970; Davies and Walker 1996).

The Phase II deposits comprise the Lower Middle Gravel (LMG) and Upper Middle Gravel (UMG). The LMG is extremely poor in vertebrate remains but the presence of southern species in the molluscan assemblage indicates the persistence of warm conditions. The Phase II deposit also marks the full appearance of the characteristic 'Rhenish' molluscan fauna, some members of which appear at the top of the Lower Loam. The UMG reflects a change in climatic and environmental conditions, with a sharp decline in woodland-adapted species and a rise in taxa indicative of open grassland, such as field vole (*Microtus agrestis*), northern vole (*Microtus oeconomus*) and horse. The occurrence of the Norway lemming (*Lemmus lemmus*), currently a boreal and arctic species, presumably reflects slightly cooler conditions as well as more open vegetation. The beginning of Phase II also marks a major archaeological transition, with the appearance of Acheulean handaxe assemblages. Both the LMG and UMG are dominated by pointed handaxes alongside a range of débitage, scrapers and choppers. Only the material from the Wymer (1964) excavation in the UMG has any real contextual control, the rest of the Middle Gravel material mostly deriving from earlier collections. The distribution of artefacts from the UMG appeared to thin out, wedge-like, to a point, suggesting small-scale derivation from an adjacent river beach. Above the basal 20–30 cm, the UMG is virtually sterile.

Text Box 3.1

By contrast, the palaeoecology and archaeology of the Phase III deposits is rather poorly understood. No mammalian remains have been recorded from the Upper Loam although pollen of frost-sensitive species such as ivy (*Hedera*) and holly (*Ilex*) suggests that temperate conditions prevailed (Hubbard 1996). The Upper Gravel has also yielded musk ox (*Ovibos moschatus*), implying a return to cold climatic conditions at the top of the sequence. The archaeology from the Upper Loams, although often mentioned (Dewey 1919, 1930; Marston 1937; Roe 1981; *inter alia*), is actually rather elusive. Records suggest the assemblage was dominated by white-patinated ovate handaxes, with possible *in situ* knapping scatters. Derived ovates have also been reported from the Upper Gravels (Roe 1981).

The sequences at Rickson's Pit and Dierden's Pit (Ingress Vale) at Swanscombe are lateral continuations of the Barnfield Pit sequence and show a broadly similar archaeological succession (Smith and Dewey 1914; Dewey 1932; Wymer 1968; Roe 1981; Bridgland, 1994).

myriad smaller climatic fluctuations. The present chapter provides the environmental, landscape and settlement background to the Lower Palaeolithic, providing the backdrop against which the interpretation of human societies and behaviours presented in the next chapter can be situated. The reader is referred to the relevant text boxes on each of the sites discussed below for a brief summary and illustration of the geological sequence at each site; a map showing the distribution of the main sites mentioned in this chapter is provided in Figure 3.1.

THE MIS13, 11 AND 9 INTERGLACIALS – DIFFERENT BUT THE SAME

The isotopic record

From the isotopic record (Figure 3.2), the MIS13 (Cromerian) interglacial spans the period ~524–474 ka BP (Bassinot et al. 1994) and comprised two pronounced warm peaks, MIS13c and MIS13a, separated by a short cold interval, MIS13b. According to some records, MIS13a was relatively unstable, with a marked cooling (MIS13.12) separating two warm intervals (MIS13.13 and 13.11; Bassinot et al. 1994[1]). The cooling limb of MIS13–MIS12 appears to have been rather protracted, with an initial sharp decline followed by a long period of fluctuating climate, interrupted by a marked warming ~454 ka BP (MIS12.3). The glacial maximum (MIS12.2) occurred ~434 ka BP. In Britain MIS12 was the most severe glaciation of the past 500,000 years, with ice advancing as far south as London, and lobes of ice extending to Watford, Finchley and Hornchurch in greater London and adjacent areas of Essex (Bridgland 1994).

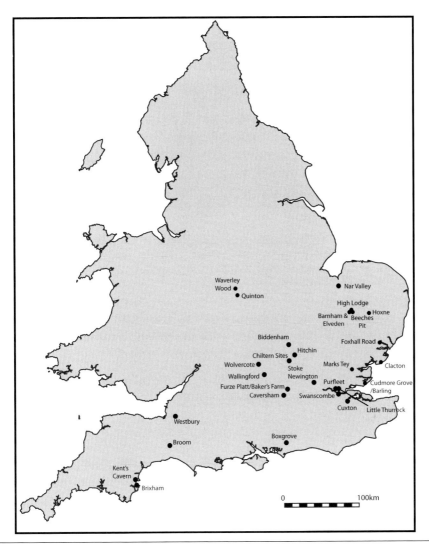

FIGURE 3.1
Major British Lower Palaeolithic sites referred to in Chapters 3 and 4.

As with most interglacials, the onset of renewed warm conditions during MIS11 was isotopically rapid[2]. MIS11 was also remarkably long, persisting, from warming to cooling limb, for ~62,000 years from ~427 to 364 ka BP (Bassinot et al.'s dates for MIS12.0 and MIS11.0). It comprised two pronounced warm peaks, MIS11c and MIS11a, separated by a short return to cooler conditions during MIS11b. Some records (e.g. Prokopenko et al. 2001) reveal a short-lived initial warm peak, MIS11e, but this is not prominent in the stacked sequences of either SPECMAP or Bassinott and colleagues (Ashton et al. 2008a). Cooling into MIS10 again appears to have been a slow, staggered process, with a series of cold–warm oscillations before the onset of more extreme cold conditions during MIS10 (~357 ka BP). A notably 'warm' isotopic event (MIS10.3) occurred ~349 ka

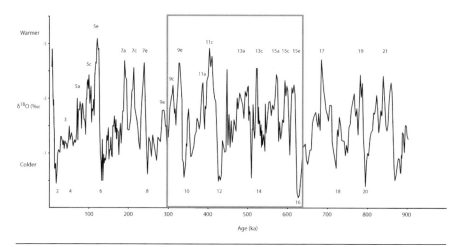

FIGURE 3.2
The Marine Isotope Curve from MIS1 to MIS21 with the period covered in this chapter high-lighted. (Data from Bassinot et al. 1994.)

BP, immediately prior to the glacial maximum (MIS10.2) ~334 ka v. At present there is no widely accepted evidence of an MIS10 ice advance onto the British mainland (D.R. Bridgland pers. comm. to MJW 2011).

The onset of MIS9 was, once again, isotopically rapid. It consisted of three pronounced warm peaks, MIS9e, MIS9c and MIS9a, separated by two cold troughs MIS9d and MIS9b, but overall was significantly shorter than either MIS13 or MIS11, lasting just 27,000 years (~328–301 ka BP). Each successive MIS9 warm event was isotopically more depleted in $\delta\ ^{18}O$ than the last. This pattern is similar to the three progressively weaker peaks of MIS5; there is some palynological and faunal evidence that during the latter period the less enriched isotopic stages were relatively cool (Hopkinson 2007a; Currant and Jacobi 2011). MIS9 may similarly have become progressively cooler.

The human environment of MIS13

The environmental record for MIS13 in Britain is extremely patchy and no complete sequence exists, even in composite form. Reconstructions of MIS13 environments are further complicated by the difficulty of confidently assigning many of the 'Cromerian Complex' sites to a specific isotopic stage, as discussed in Chapter 2. More complete sequences have been documented on the continent, particularly the Netherlands (Zag-wijn 1985, 1996; de Jong 1988) but British and Dutch workers often disagree on how sites from the two countries should be correlated (cf. papers in Turner 1996; Preece and Parfitt 2000, 2008).

If the sequence from the Noordbergum (Cromerian IV) interglacial in the northern Nether-lands can be correlated with MIS13, it is possible to reconstruct a basic vegetation his-tory (Figure 3.3). The Dutch pollen record shows that the early interglacial was dominated by pine, birch and spruce, with the rapid development of mixed-oak temperate forest in which alder, oak, hornbeam and hazel formed the principal deciduous taxa (de Jong 1988). *Abies* (fir) also formed an important species during the beginning and middle of Interglacial VI but is totally absent from Interglacial III. The end of Interglacial IV was dominated by alder, pine, birch and spruce, with a reduction in mixed-oak forests and the complete disappearance of hornbeam and hazel.

Environmental reconstruction based on multiple proxies is possible for only a small number of British archaeological sites dating to MIS13. At High Lodge, Suffolk, pollen evidence showed an environment dominated by pine and spruce forest with juniper and heathland plants (Hunt 1992) and a suggestion that the environment became more open over time. Pollen from wetland plants was also present, suggesting marshy conditions immediately adjacent to the river; a picture enhanced by the beetle assemblage from the site, which showed an array of wetland habitats, from reed swamp to meadow-like areas, but little evidence of trees in the immediate vicinity (Coope 2006). Temperature estimates based on the MCR method (see Chapter 2) showed mean summer temperatures between 15 and 16° C and winter between −4 and 1°C (Coope 2006). The coleoptera also suggested that the water in the marsh may have, in part, dried up in the summer, probably due to relatively low rainfall. Mammalian remains were poorly preserved and only five taxa were recovered, the straight-tusked elephant [*Palaeoloxodon antiquus*], extinct rhinoceros [*Dicerorhinus etruscus*], horse, deer and a large bovid (Stuart 1992), but together the beetles and pollen indicate a cool temperate climate with boreal forest, similar to southern Scandinavia today.

Pollen and macrofossils from Channel 2 at Waverley Wood, Warwickshire, were similarly characterised by boreal forest and shrub, dominated by pine, spruce and small quantities of birch (Shotton et al. 1993: the presence of temperate species such as oak, elm and lime was attributed to derivation from older deposits). The composition

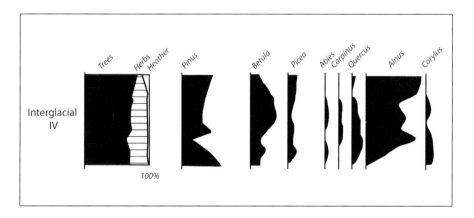

FIGURE 3.3
Pollen diagram from the Noordbergum Interglacial IV in the Dutch Cromerian Sequence. (Redrawn after de Jong 1988, Figure 6 and © The Royal Society.)

of the forest flora and sedimentogical evidence suggested that this belonged to the post-temperate phase at the end of an interglacial, rather than the pre-temperate phase at the beginning. Grasses and sedges dominated the non-tree pollen, revealing the presence of an open grassy floodplain. The macrofossils, which included the sedge *Carex palacea*, were characteristic of a plant community today associated with central Scandinavia. The insects from Channel 2 (Shotton et al. 1993; Coope 2006) also indicated marshy reed vegetation and meadow-like habitats close to the channel, with scattered stands of conifer forest further afield. Dung beetles were rare, suggesting that large animals (i.e. dung-producers) were uncommon in the landscape; a suggestion not contradicted by the sparse mammalian fauna of straight-tusked elephant, horse, bison and cervid. Most of the beetles still live in Britain today and provided a temperature estimate of ~15° C, but northern and continental species from near the top of Channel 2 testified to a brief arctic phase when summer temperatures deteriorated to ~10° C. This was followed by a return to cool temperate conditions, with temperatures similar to those seen at the start of the infilling of the channel (Coope 2006). The taxonomic diversity of the molluscan fauna, which generally suggested a cool climate, reduced through the sequence, indicating the gradual onset of cold conditions (Shotton et al. 1993).

Similar conditions may be inferred from the palaeobotanical remains, beetles and mammals from Happisburgh 1, Norfolk (Ashton et al. 2008b), although the site has yet to be fully published and currently only the insects and vertebrate remains from the organic muds have been properly analysed (Nick Ashton pers. comm.). The coleoptera are dominated by wetland species characteristic of marsh, shallow ponds and occasional running water, with more distant heathland and coniferous woodland beyond (Coope 2006). MCR estimates suggest summer temperatures lay between 12 and 15° C and winter temperatures between −11 and −3° C. These estimates indicate a climate much cooler than that of southern England today, although the vertebrate remains still suggest an interglacial environment with the presence of roe deer (*Capreolus capreolus*), red deer (*Cervus elaphus*), giant beaver (*Trogontherium cuvieri*) and tench (*Tinca tinca*). It is worth remarking that the winter temperatures for Happisburgh 1 are far lower than those reconstructed for the earlier site at Happisburgh 3, possibly testifying to new hominin solutions to the overwintering problem. Overall the evidence points to humans inhabiting a river valley with still ponds and marshes with areas of heathland and coniferous forest in a cool interglacial climate.

By far the best palaeoenvironmental evidence for MIS13 comes from the remarkable site at Boxgrove, West Sussex. The best evidence is associated with the main period of human occupation in Units 4 and 5, when the site was, first, part of an intertidal (lagoonal) mudflat and, following a marine regression, a grassy plain in a small coastal embayment flanked by a high chalk cliff. The lagoonal silts of Unit 4a and 4b contain a mammalian fauna dominated by grassland species, including the heavyweight grazers *Stephanorhinus hundsheimensis* (extinct rhinoceros) and horse, although the presence of mouse (*Apodemus sylvaticus*), roe deer (*Capreolus capreolus*) and wild cat (*Felis sylvestris*) indicate woodland or dense scrub nearby, probably on the chalk downland above the cliff (Parfitt 1999). Poorly developed soil horizons within the lagoonal silts, often associated with scatters of flint and bone, suggest periodic drying out accompanied by an expansion of grassland.

The terrestrial phase marked by the palaeosol of Unit 4c, shows an increase in vegetation diversity, with a rich mosaic of grassland, woodland and shrub (Parfitt 1999). The small mammal fauna is dominated by pine vole (*Microtus subterraneus*), which inhabits open grassland and forest, with the field vole (*M. agrestis*) and common vole (*M. arvalis*) also showing open habitats (Parfitt 1999). Open scrub and woodland species are also common, and include squirrel (*Scurius* sp.), birch mouse (*Sicista* cf. *betulina*), badger (*Meles* sp.) and roe deer – these animals probably venturing from woodland on the chalk downland above and inland of the site to feed. Soil micromorphology (MacPhail 1999) shows that the area in front of the cliff was open grassland and that trees and shrubs did not colonise it. A moist, well-shaded land surface is also indicated by some mollusc taxa (Preece and Bates 1999). Similar conditions may be inferred for the spring deposits of Unit 4d. Although pollen preservation at Boxgrove was poor, the vegetation record from Units 4c and 5a were consistent with the picture of a wooded downland block and grassy foreshore. Boreal arboreal taxa predominated, especially pine, spruce and fir, but small quantities of oak and beech were present; greater frequencies of thermophilous taxa and high levels of herbs and grasses were also recorded from samples taken from just above the marine sands (Scaife in Roberts 1986).

The mammals from Unit 4 were analysed using the Taxonomic Habitat Index (Figure 3.4) which showed that the majority of species can be found in the deciduous and mixed-forest zones of Western Europe today, although the number of boreal and tundra elements was higher, suggesting that cooler and more continental conditions prevailed. This picture is supported by temperature estimates based on the Mutual Ostracod Temperature Range, which indicate summer values between 16 and 20° C and winter values between −4 and 4° C (Holmes et al. 2010), as well as MCR estimates on herpetofauna, which suggested mean summer temperatures between 15 and 24° C and winters falling to between −12 and 4° C (Sinka 1993, cited in Holmes et al. 2010). These figures indicate that summers were similar or slightly warmer than those in southern England today, but that winters were potentially much colder.

Following the deposition of Unit 4, conditions began to deteriorate, with a thin brickearth at the top of Unit 5a showing a brief, very cold interlude, followed by a return to warmer conditions, similar to that seen at Waverley Wood. The main body of the brickearths of Unit 6 are dominated by a cold-climate, boreal forest fauna, including the northern vole (*Microtus oeconomus*). As a whole the sequence marks climatic deterioration during a late temperate phase, with a brief warm interval before the onset of periglacial conditions. There is possible evidence that humans were also present at Boxgrove into the earlier part of the succeeding MIS12 glaciation, possibly during temporary warmer interstadials (see below).

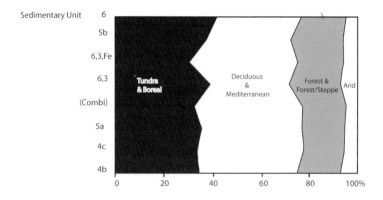

FIGURE 3.4

(a) Taxonomic habitat index for the Boxgrove sequence. Redrawn after Parfitt 1999 and courtesy Simon Parfitt. (b) Top: Excavations in Q1B at Boxgrove. Bottom: section through the Boxgrove sequence at GTP13, showing three cycles of marine deposition, overlain by the Slindon Silts of Unit 4 and the Pleistocene landsurface of Unit 4c (top). (Courtesy Mark Roberts.)

The fauna from Boxgrove, by far the largest and most representative assemblage of MIS13 fauna available for Britain, contains ~99 species of vertebrate, including fish, birds, mammals reptiles and amphibians. The large mammal fauna contained a mixture of familiar (red deer, fallow deer, horse) and exotic animals (rhinoceros), modifications on the bones of which reveal that they were apparently all preyed upon by hominins, and contemporary carnivores including wolf, spotted hyaena and lion (Table 3.1). Overall, the evidence from MIS13 sites in Britain indicates that humans were present only at the end of the interglacial, when a cool continental climate and a boreal forest environment pertained.

Table 3.1 List of mammalian fauna for the MIS13, 11 and 9 interglacials, and the MIS12, 10 and 8 glacials. (Data derived from Schreve 1997 and Parfitt 1998a, 1999.)

Taxon		MIS13	MIS11c	Hoxne (MIS11a?)	MIS9
Insectivora					
Erinaceus sp.	Hedgehog	*			
Crocodura cf. *leucodon*	Bicoloured shrew				*
Crocodura sp.	White-toothed shrew		*		
Sorex araneus	Eurasian shrew		*		*
Sorex minutus	Pygmy shrew	*	*	cf.	*
Sorex runtonensis	Extinct shrew	*			
Sorex savini	Extinct shrew	*			
Sorex sp.1				*	
Neomys browni	Water shrew				
Neomys sp.	Water shrew	*	*	*	
Desmana moschata	Russian desman		*	*	
Talpa europaea	Common mole	*	*		
Talpa minor	Extinct small mole	*	*	*	
Primates					
Macaca sylvanus	Macaque		*	*	*
Homo sp.	Human	*	*	*	*
Lagomorpha					
Lepus timidus	Mountain hare	*			
Oryctolagus cuniculus	Rabbit	*	*		
Chiroptera					
Plecotus auritus	Long-eared bat	*			
Plectorus sp.	Long-eared bat		*		
Myotis mystacinus	Whiskered bat	*			
Myotis bechsteini	Bechstein's Bat	*			
Eptesicus serotinus	Serotine bat				*

Table 3.1 *Continued*

Rodentia					
Scuirus	Squirrel	*			*
Castor fiber	European beaver		*		*
Trogontherium cuvieri	Giant beaver		*	*	
Lemmus lemmus	Norway lemming		*	*	
Clethrionomys glareolus	Bank vole		*	*	*
Arvicola t. cantiana	Water Vole		*	*	*
Microtus agrestis	Field vole		*	*	
Microtus arvalis	Common vole		*	cf.	*
Microtus oeconomus	Northern vole		*		
Microtus subterraneus	European pine vole		*	cf.	
Apodemus sylvaticus	Wood mouse		*	*	*
Apodemus maastrichtiensis	Extinct mouse		*		
Eliomys quercinus	Garden dormouse		*		
Cetacea					
Tursiops truncatus	Bottle-nosed dolphin		*		*
Carnivora					
Canis lupus	Wolf	*	*		*
Vulpes vulpes	Fox				*
Ursus deningeri	Extinct bear	*			
Ursus spelaeus	Cave bear		*		
Ursus arctos	Brown bear				*
Ursus sp.	Bear			*	
Mustela cf. *putorius*	Pole Cat				*
Mustela erminea	Stoat	cf.	*		
Mustela martes	Marten		*		
Mustela lutreola	Mink	*			
Mustela nivalis	Weasel	cf.			
Meles meles	Badger	sp.			*
Lutra lutra	Otter		*	*	*
Felis lynx	Lynx		*		
Felis sylvestris	Wild cat	*	*		
Panthera leo	Lion	*	*	*	
Crocuta crocuta	Spotted hyaena	*			*
Proboscidea					
Palaeoloxodon antiquus		*	*	*	*
Perissodactyla					
Equus ferus	Horse	*	*		*
Equus hydruntinus	European ass		*		
Stephanorhinus hemitoechus	Extinct steppe (narrow-nosed) rhinoceros		*		*

Stephanorhinus kirchbergensis	Extinct forest (Merck's) rhinoceros		*		*
Stephanorhinus hundsheimensis	Extinct rhinoceros	*			
Artiodactyla					
Sus scrofa	Pig		*		*
Megaloceros giganteus	Extinct giant deer		*	*	*
Megaloceros dawkinsi	Extinct giant deer				
Megaloceros verticornis	Extinct giant deer				
Dama dama clactoniana	Clacton fallow deer		*		
Dama dama	Fallow deer	*	*	*	*
Cervus elaphus	Red deer	*	*	*	*
Capreolus capreolus	Roe deer	*	*	*	*
Alces alces	Elk/Moose				
Bos primigenius	Aurochs		*		*
Bos priscus	Bison	*	*		*
Bos/Bison	A bovine			*	

Taxon		**MIS12**	**MIS10**	**MIS8**
Primates				
Homo sp.	Human	*	*	*
Rodentia				
Microtus arvalis	Common vole	*		
Microtus oeconomus	Northern Vole			
Carnivora				
Canis lupus	Wolf			
Vulpes vulpes	Fox			
Ursus arctos	Brown bear			
Panthera leo	Lion	*		*
Proboscidea				
Palaeoloxodon antiquus	Straight-tusked elephant	*		*
Mammuthus primigenius	Woolly mammoth	*		*
Perissodactyla				
Equus ferus	Horse	*		*
Stephanorhinus hemitoechus	Narrow-nosed rhino			
Coelodonta antiquatis	Woolly rhino	*		*
Artiodactyla				
Cervus elephas	Red deer	*		*
Rangifer tarandus	Reindeer	*		
Bos primigenius	Aurochs			*
Bos priscus	Bison			*
Ovibos moschatus	Musk-ox		*	

The human environment of MIS11

The environments of (parts of) MIS11 are remarkably well understood. Long pollen records from sites such as Marks Tey, Essex, (Turner 1970, see Figure 3.5) and Quinton, Birmingham, (Thomas 2001) have provided a virtually complete vegetation history at least for the first warm sub-stage (cf. Ashton et al. 2008a). A range of vertebrate and invertebrate fossils provide additional means of environmental reconstruction, as well as a biostratigraphical tool for correlating the various records and seriating them into a acceptable order. In this section we will again concentrate on the records from a series of key archaeological sites that provide evidence for the types of environments and climates that humans were exploiting during MIS11, augmented by palaeoenvironmental data from key sites and sequences, notably the long pollen record from the Hoxnian parastratotype at Marks Tey, Essex. Here, ~35m of interglacial lacustrine sediments have been preserved in a deep, sub-glacial trough, overlying MIS12 till. These provided the first complete pollen sequence through the Hoxnian interglacial (Turner 1970). As the pollen zones form the basis of much correlation it is worth describing them in some detail.

Pollen Zone 1An marks the end of the Anglian glaciation and witnessed the rise of open grassland and birch copse with the decline of *Hippophaë* (sea buckthorn, which dominates Zone 1An at Hoxne). Evidence from Hoxne (Turner 1968; Text Box 3.2) suggested

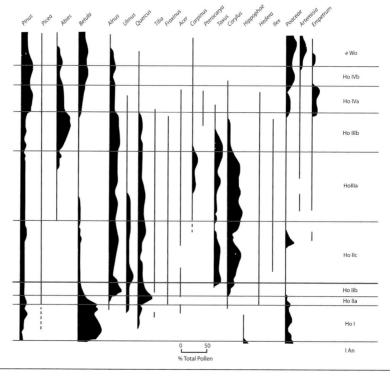

FIGURE 3.5
Composite pollen diagram of the Hoxnian (MIS11) Interglacial at Marks Tey. (Redrawn after Turner 1970, Fig. 15, and © The Royal Society.)

HOXNE, SUFFOLK

Hoxne lies on the interfluve of the Rivers Dove and Goldbrook, some 26 miles north of Ipswich. The deposits, which form the stratotype for the Hoxnian inter-glacial (Mitchell et al. 1973), are situated in two clay and gravel pits to the east and west of the Hoxne–Eye Road: the Old Brick Pit and the Oakley Park Pit. Hoxne has a long history of investigation, beginning in 1797 with Frere (1800). Excavations were conducted by Reid in 1895 (Evans et al. 1896); Moir between 1924 and 1934 (Moir 1926, 1935); McBurney and West from 1952–3 (West and McBurney 1954; West 1956); the University of Chicago led by Wymer and Singer from 1974–8 (Wymer 1983; Singer et al. 1993); and by the Ancient Human Occupation of Britain Project between 2000 and 2003 (Ashton et al. 2008a). The site thus has a long history of interpretation and reinterpretation. The following account is based on the conclusions of the most recent excavations which rec-onciled the various interpretations offered over the past 100 years.

The solid geology at Hoxne consists of Chalk at –17 m OD, overlain by a Lower Pleistocene Crag Series, Anglian Corton Beds, and about 16 m of Lowestoft (Anglian, MIS12) Till (Gladfelter 1993) (see Figure 1 and Table 1). A hollow in the till, about 570 m wide and 14 m deep, has been infilled with a series of Middle Pleis-tocene lacustrine and fluvial deposits. The most recent investigations suggest the following sequence.

Text Box 3.2

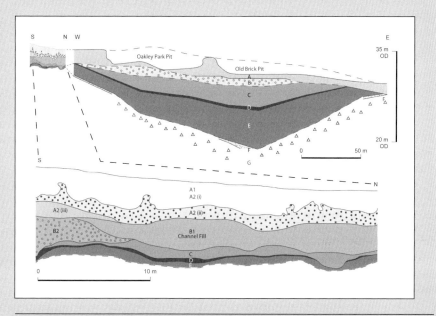

FIGURE 1
Schematic section through the Hoxne Lake basin, with a detailed cross-section through the deposits re-exposed during the 2000–2003 excavations. (After Ashton et al. 2008a, used with permission from Elsevier.)

Table 1 Summary of stratigraphy, palynology, climate and archaeology at Hoxne (after Ashton et al. 2008a).

Bed	Description	Pollen Zone	Climate	Archaeology
Stratum A1	Coversand		Cold	
Stratum A2(i)	Cryoturbated sand and gravel		Cold	
Stratum A2(ii)	Solifluction gravel		Cold	Derived Upper Industry
Stratum A2(iii)	Alluvial sandy clay		Warm	Upper Industry
Stratum B1	Fluvial sand, silt and clay		Warm	Lower Industry
Stratum B2	Fluvial chalky gravel		Warm	
Stratum C ('arctic bed')	Lacustrine sands and silts		Cold	
Hiatus				
Stratum D	Peat (representing a drop in lake levels)	HoIIIa	Warm	
Stratum E	Lacustrine clay	Hol–IIc	Warm	
Stratum F	Lactustrine clay	1An	Cool	
Stratum G	Till		Cold	

The base of the sequence (F–D) represents a kettle hole lake that gradually infilled with clayey-muds throughout much of the Hoxnian interglacial (Pollen Zones Hol–HoIIIa: West 1956; Turner 1970; Wymer 1983; Mullenders 1993). Following deglaciation, Stratum F began accumulating under cool conditions, followed by rapid climatic amelioration to full interglacial conditions. The environment of the thickest lake bed, Stratum E, was characterised by fully temperate deciduous woodland, with a prominent non-arboreal pollen zone at the top representing a brief period of deforestation. This non-arboreal phase has been recognised on a regional scale; its cause is unclear it but does not appear to have been due to climatic cooling (Turner 1970; Ashton et al. 2008a). Bed D represents a drop in the water table and the onset of marshy conditions locally, characterised by the development of alder carr during HoIIIa. The rest of the interglacial – HoIIIb–HoVI – is apparently missing from the sequence due to a depositional hiatus. Renewed lacustrine sedimentation began in Bed C (the famous arctic beds of Clement Reid, in Evans et al. 1896) under very cold climatic conditions.

Stratum B marks a major transformation in the hydrology of the site with the establishment of a fluvial system. The fauna from Stratum B includes macaque, (*Macaca sylvanus*), beaver (*Castor fiber*) and fallow deer (*Dama dama*) indicative of temperate woodland, with field vole (*Microtus agrestis*), horse (*Equus ferus*), lion (*Panthera leo*) and giant deer (*Megaloceros giganteus*) suggesting more open, grassy conditions. Fish and aquatic mammals (otter, beaver) confirm the presence of water (Stuart et al. 1993). Warm conditions persisted during the deposition of Stratum A2(iii) followed by deteriorating climatic conditions in the remainder of Stratum A2 and Stratum A1.

Text Box 3.2

This new interpretation makes it clear that hominins were not present at Hoxne during the long lake phase (contra Wymer 1983; Singer et al. 1993). They are first represented by the Lower Industry, associated with renewed temperate conditions at the base of Stratum B1. This assemblage is in mint condition and includes ovate and cordiform handaxes in association with manufacturing débitage, flakes, cores and hammerstones. An interesting element of the Lower Industry is a series of 12 stone clusters which may represent transported raw material accumulations. The Upper Industry was recovered from the upper part of Stratum A2(iii). Comprising ~450 artefacts, it is in mint condition and may be *in situ*, lying where it was discarded on a floodplain. It differs from the Lower Industry by virtue of a dominance of pointed bifaces and the presence of 12 scrapers (see Figure 2).

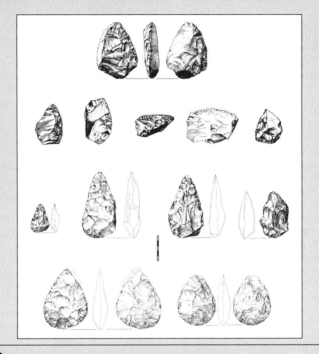

FIGURE 2
Artefacts from the University of Chicago excavations at Hoxne. Top two rows: scrapers from the Upper Industry. Third Row: Handaxes from the Upper Industry. Bottom Row: Handaxes from the lower Industry. (After Wymer 1985, used with permission.)

Establishing the age of Hoxne has been marked by controversy. Correlation with MIS9 was suggested by AAR on *Valvata* shells from Bed E (Bowen et al. 1989). TL dates on burnt flints from the Lower Industry yielded a mean age of 210 ± 20 ka BP – suggesting a date within MIS7 – although problems with dosimeter readings indicate that this is unreliable and should be discarded (Bowman 1993). ESR dates on enamel from horse teeth associated with the Lower Industry originally provided a mean age of 319 ± 38 ka BP, again suggestive of an MIS9 age (Schwarcz and Grün 1993); these were later remodelled, yielding an age of 404 ± 33/42 and 437 ± 38 ka BP, indicating an MIS11 age (Grün and Schwarcz 2000). The latter is in accord with

Text Box 3.2

Text Box 3.2

the biostratigraphical evidence from the Lower Industry, which has been correlated with that of the Swanscombe MAZ (Schreve 2001a and b). It was not possible to distinguish between late MIS11 and early MIS9 on the basis of amino-acid determinations on *Bythinia* opercula from Stratum B2 (Ashton et al. 2008a).

Ashton et al. (2008a) concluded that the lacustrine beds belonged to the first prolonged sub-stage of MIS11c, and Strata C and B to the cold and warm events within the same isotope stage, probably MIS11b and MIS11a. This would suggest that the archaeology from Hoxne was deposited during the second warm sub-stage, and therefore that it is of a younger age than most of the other known British Hoxnian assemblages; assuming of course that they have all been assigned to the correct isotopic sub-stage . Based on continental scale correlations of pollen records, Ashton et al. (ibid.) further suggest that the environments would have been characterised by boreal forests, with warm summer temperatures and colder winters, which of course raises a number of survivorship issues and cultural adaptations discussed in the main text and Chapter 2.

that this period was much warmer than suspected, with mild summers that permitted the spread of tree birch and growth of *Typha* (bulrushes) which require summer temperatures above 14° C.

An expansion of birch forest, an increase in pine and a decrease in grassland characterised Pollen Zone HoI (pre-temperate), marking the beginning of the interglacial. Oak and spruce also appeared in small quantities and, towards the end of HoI, oak and elm increased dramatically at the expense of pine and birch, alongside small quantities of hazel, alder, lime and ivy. This expansion of temperate deciduous trees was short-lived, however, possibly due to a sudden drop in winter temperatures.

Pollen Zone HoII (full temperate) saw the full development of mixed-oak woodland and an abundance of plants of the forest floor, such as *Geranium*, *Urtica* (nettle), rosaceous shrubs, *Caryophyllacaea* (chickweeds) and ferns. An initial persistence of grassland shrub communities including juniper, *Artemesia* and grasses was quickly eliminated as the forests took hold. Three sub-zones are recognised on the basis of changes in the composition of the forest: HoIIa in which oak was the most important species; HoIIb in which alder and hazel assumed importance; and HoIIc in which elm, yew and hazel were abundant. A dramatic return to grassland conditions – the so-called non-arboreal pollen phase, also seen at Hoxne (West 1956) – occurred during the final sub-zone, HoIIc, and Turner thought this may have been caused by a forest fire; annual laminations in the lacustrine sediments suggested that the forests became re-established after ~350 years.

The late temperate phase of Pollen Zone HoIII saw the expansion of late immigrating trees, notably hornbeam and spruce, and the gradual decline in the mixed-oak forests. This pattern is a well-established feature of many interglacials and, based on the presence of thermophilous exotics such as grapevine (*Vitas*), is probably associated with degradation and acidification of forest soils rather than severe climatic deterioration (Turner 1970). At the beginning of HoIII winters were still mild, as shown by frost-sensitive plants such as *Hedera* (ivy), *Ilex* (holly) and *Buxus* (box), but their later decline suggests the onset of colder winters. Grapevine is important because, while it can survive cold winters, it needs warm summers, suggesting the beginning of more continental conditions.

The post-temperate phase of the interglacial, Pollen Zone HoIV, saw a complete shift to boreal forest, with pine and birch once again assuming dominance. Open grassland and *Empetrum* (crowberry) heath environments also spread. In sub-zone HoIVa fir was still important, but in HoIVb birch predominates, and grassland communities become more widespread at the expense of oceanic heathland plants. Warm winter indicators such as ivy, which had survived into HoIVa, vanish entirely and the climate at this point became drier and colder.

In summary, the Hoxnian shows a classic interglacial vegetation succession related to climatic and pedological factors; beginning and ending with an open grassland phase, the middle seeing the rise, first of pine-birch coniferous forest, then by fully temperate deciduous oak woodland, that in turn gives way to boreal forest as soils degrade and climate deteriorates.

These forests were home to a wide range of mammalian taxa (see Table 3.1) although a number of regional extinctions had taken place during MIS12, including the shrews *Sorex* (*Drepanosorex*) *savini* and *S. runtonensis*, the vole *Pliomys episcopalis*, two species of giant deer *Megaloceros verticornis* and *Megaloceros dawkinsi*, Hundsheim's rhinoceros *Stephanorhinus hundsheimensis*, and the archaic cave bear *Ursus deningeri* (Schreve 1997; Parfitt 1998a). The MIS11 interglacial also marks the first appearance of a number of species, including field vole (*Microtus agrestis*), European/Steppe ass (*Equus hydruntinus*), the forest (Merck's) rhinoceros (*Stephanorhinus kirchbergensis*), the steppe (narrow-nosed) rhinoceros (*Stephanorhinus hemitoechus*), giant deer (*Megaloceros giganteus)* and aurochs (*Bos primigenius*). Important absences from the MIS11 interglacial notably include hyaena (*Crocuta crocuta*) and hippopotamus (*Hippopotamus amphibious)* (Schreve 1997; 2001a and b; Parfitt 1998a).

A number of key Palaeolithic sites allow us to place hominins within this landscape. Here, we examine hominin habitats at both the regional and the local scale, as evinced at five key MIS11 Palaeolithic sites. At Swanscombe, primary context or minimally derived archaeology occurs in at least five separate stratigraphical contexts, spanning a range of climatic and environmental conditions through much of the MIS11 interglacial (see Text Box 3.1). The Swanscombe deposits contain a rich molluscan and mammalian assemblage, although pollen preservation is limited and the subject of some controversy (Hubbard 1982, 1996; Turner 1985). However, by comparing the molluscan fauna from Swanscombe with those at Clacton, Kerney (1971) was able to correlate fossiliferous parts of the Swanscombe sequence with the pollen biozones found at both Clacton and Hoxne (Turner and Kerney 1971; West 1956).

Fossil remains from the Phase I deposits (the Basal Gravel, Lower Gravel and Lower Loam) indicate fully temperate climatic conditions. The molluscs and ostracods are characteristic of a swift-flowing river with a stony bed in the Lower Gravel, which Ashton et al. (2008a; see Figure 3.6) tentatively correlated with HoI and HoIIa, which would suggest

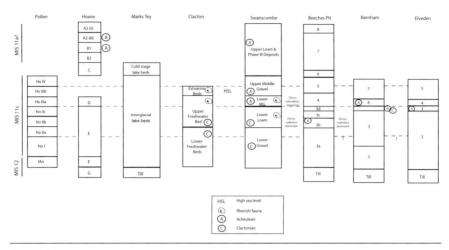

FIGURE 3.6
Tentative correlation of recently excavated critical Hoxnian (MIS11) sites, showing pollen zonation, the presence of characteristic 'Rhenish' molluscan fauna and archaeological industries. (Based on data in Ashton et al. 2005 and 2008a; former courtesy of The Prehistoric Society, latter Elsevier, with permission.)

that hominins were active here when the Thames was regionally enclosed by a boreal pine–birch forest with decreasing grassland, developing into a fully temperate mixed-oak forest, as described above. It was suggested that the base of the Lower Gravel belonged to the terminal part of the Anglian Glaciation which, at Marks Tey, was a relatively warm period characterised by grassland and birch copse (Turner 1970, see above).

The Lower Loam, a floodplain deposit, has yielded refitting flakes on the 'knapping floor' and an abundance of palaeoenvironmental data (not necessarily in direct association). The pollen spectrum reveals a mixed-oak forest with hazel and occasional peaks of alder (probably caused by periodic flooding) which has been attributed to HoIIb (Hubbard 1996). An increase in grasses and herbaceous taxa towards the top of the Lower Loam was interpreted as a change in pollen catchment, although this could equally correspond to the non-arboreal pollen phase of HoIIc, as seen at Hoxne and Marks Tey (Ashton et al. in press; West 1956; Turner 1970). The molluscs from the Lower Loam suggested sluggish water surrounded by reed swamp and marshes and some dry ground (Kerney 1971). The ostracods further indicate shallow pools of still water, possibly abandoned meander channels on the floodplain (Robinson 1996). The mammalian fauna is dominated by animals characteristic of temperate deciduous or mixed woodland, such as the 'Clacton' sub-species of fallow deer and straight-tusked elephant, with nearby open grassland indicated by the presence of horse, narrow-nosed rhinoceros and aurochs.

The overlying Phase II deposits (Lower Middle Gravel (LMG) and Upper Middle Gravel (UMG)) documents a cultural change from a non-handaxe to handaxe industry and gradual change in environment. The LMG is poor in vertebrate remains but the presence of southern species in the molluscan assemblage indicates the persistence of warm conditions. The LMG also contains the 'Rhenish molluscan' fauna, a diagnostic suite of aquatic species including *Theodoxus serratiliformis*, *Pisidium clessini*, *Viviparus diluvianus* and *Corbicula fluminalis*. Members of this suite today have central European distributions and were thought to indicate that the Thames was confluent with the River Rhine at this time (Kennard 1942a and b). Some 'Rhenish' taxa appear at the top of the Lower Loam but its main full occurrence at Clacton (Kerney 1971) and Tillingham (Roe 2001) appears to correlate with HoIIIa (cf. Ashton et al. 2008a). Based on this correlation, the climate during the deposition of the LMG would have been mild, and dominated by mixed-oak forest, with the appearance of late colonisers such as horn-beam and spruce. The UMG reflects a change in climatic and environmental conditions, with a steep decline in woodland-adapted species and a rise in taxa indicative of open grassland, such as field vole, northern vole (*Microtus oeconomus*) and horse. The unu-sual occurrence of the Norway lemming (*Lemmus lemmus*), a boreal and arctic species today, may reflect slightly cooler conditions as well as more open vegetation. Ashton et al. (2008a) correlate the UMG with Pollen Zones HoIIIa–IVa which, at Marks Tey and Hoxne, show the onset of colder winters, a shift to boreal forests, and the rise of open grassland and heathland communities.

The Phase III deposits at Swanscombe are largely sterile and their environmental context (or indeed correlation with other MIS11 deposits) is unclear. The basal Phase III depos-its, though, reflect cold conditions, as revealed by ice-wedge casts, micro-faulting and cryoturbation structures. While no mammalian or molluscan remains have been found in the Upper Loam, the presence of frost-sensitive plants such as ivy and holly suggest that temperate conditions prevailed. This would make a correlation with HoIVb at Hoxne and Marks Tey difficult as these species had disappeared entirely at the latter localities by this time. Correlation with part of MIS11a may therefore be more appropriate. Musk Ox (*Ovibos moschatus*) in the Upper Gravel implies very cold conditions at the top of the sequence, perhaps during MIS10. Swanscombe therefore preserves a long and complex succession of environmental fluctuations that appear to span most of the MIS 11 interglacial, and may have evidence of two sub-stages of MIS11.

A long sequence of MIS11 palaeoenvironments can also be reconstructed in the chan-nel deposits (of channels i, ii, v and vi) at Clacton-on-Sea, which essentially comprise the Lower Freshwater Beds, Upper Freshwater Beds and Estuarine Beds (Wymer 1985; Bridgland 1994; Bridgland et al. 1999; see Text Box 3.3). Boreholes excavated in 1950 provided a pollen sequence through the Estuarine Beds and top of the Upper Freshwa-ter Beds, which were assigned to HoIIIb and HoIIb–HoIIIa respectively. Hominins were active at Clacton only during the deposition of the freshwater sediments, the intertidal Thames estuary apparently not a favoured environment, although the arrival of 'Rhenish molluscan' species in the top of the Upper Freshwater Bed and a fully developed Rhen-ish suite in the Estuarine Beds suggests correlation with the top of the Lower Loams and the Middle Gravels at Swanscombe, showing that hominins were present during this phase further upstream. Pollen and plant macrofossils from the Freshwater Beds reveal that hominins were present during fully temperate conditions, during which time the river was surrounded by an array of wetland, marshy and dry grassland environments and flanked by dense, mixed-oak forests on its valley sides. The molluscs from the Freshwater Beds also testified to flowing water, pools and swampy areas (Turner and Kerney 1971), while the mammals showed a mixture of open and woodland taxa including fallow deer, boar and beaver *(Castor fiber)* alongside horse, rabbit *(Oryctolagus cuniculus)* and steppe rhinoceros.

The presence of ice-wedge casts, cryoturbation structures and 'frozen' clay balls in the basal gravels of the Lower Freshwater Beds at the Golf Course and Jaywick sites, which also yielded abraded artefacts, possibly show that (as at Swanscombe) hominins were active at

CLACTON-ON-SEA, ESSEX (LION POINT, JAYWICK SANDS, WEST CLIFF, GOLF COURSE AND BUTLINS HOLIDAY CAMP)

Clacton-on-Sea lies in the south-eastern corner of the Tendring Plateau in eastern Essex. The foreshore, cliffs and hinterland at Clacton preserve a series of Middle Pleistocene channels of the Thames–Medway, which occur in an arc that extends for over 2 km from Lion Point in the west to south of the pier (West Cliff) in the east. These are considered to be part of the Boyn Hill/ Orsett Heath Formation (and its downstream equivalents) and are correlated with MIS11 (Bridgland 1994). Warren (e.g. 1955) mapped six channels at Clacton, all containing temperate deposits. More recent investigations have recognised only two channels. Warren's Channels i and v are two ends of the same feature, which incorporate channels ii and vi (Bridgland 1994). Channels iii and iv are similarly two ends of a single channel, separated from the main channel complex by a ridge of London Clay; they are probably unrelated to the MIS11 river and instead represent a later channel of the Colne (Bridgland et al. 1999).

The first artefacts from Clacton were reported by Kenworthy (1898), but the site is most widely associated with Samuel Hazzledine Warren – the father of the eponymous Clactonian industry – who was active here between 1911 and the 1950s (Warren 1911, 1912, 1922, 1923b, 1924, 1933, 1951, 1955, 1958). Warren collected extensively from numerous locations, most notably at West Cliff and Lion Point, but conducted no excavations. Given its fame and vintage it is remarkable that only four excavations have ever been conducted (largely due to poor accessibility; see Figure 1): at Jaywick Sands in 1934 (Oakley and Leakey 1937), the Golf Course Site in 1969–1970 (Singer et al. 1973), the Holiday Camp in 1984 (Bridgland et al. 1999), and in a temporary exposure at the West Cliff in 1987, which otherwise had not been seen since the early years of the century (Bridgland et al. 1988).

The main channel, over 400 m wide and attaining a maximum depth of 15 m, is incised into London Clay and Holland Gravel. Although laterally variable along the various exposures, a simplified composite sequence through the Clacton deposits comprises the clayey gravels and sands of the Lower and Upper Freshwater Beds overlain by the Estuarine Beds (laminated clays followed by sands, passing into calcareous marl). Evidence of periglacial processes at the base of the sequence at the Golf Course Site suggests that sedimentation began during the

Text Box 3.3

Text Box 3.3

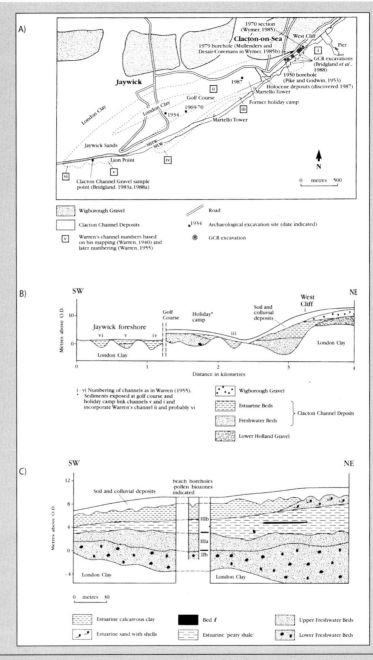

FIGURE 1

A) Map showing distribution of Pleistocene deposits at Clacton, and the location of the various excavations; B) section through the Clacton area showing the various Clacton Channel occurrences; C) section through the main fill of the Clacton Channel as exposed at the West Cliff. (After Bridgland et al. 1999, reproduced with permission from Elsevier.)

Text Box 3.3

late Anglian (Singer et al. 1973). Pioneering pollen analyses demonstrated aggradation throughout most of the ensuing interglacial, the Upper Freshwater Beds being assigned to biozone HoIIb–IIIa, the Estuarine Beds to HoIIIa onwards (Pike and Godwin 1953; West 1956; Turner and Kerney 1971). A diverse molluscan fauna also shows the arrival of the Rhenish suite beginning in the Upper Freshwater Beds, with a developed Rhenish suite and marine molluscs along with brackish/marine fish occurring during HoIIb (unequivocal evidence of sea-level rise) in the Estuarine Beds (Turner and Kerney 1971; Meijer and Preece 1995; Bridgland et al. 1999). On the basis of pollen and molluscs, the site has been correlated with the Hoxnian sites at Hoxne and Swanscombe. A rich mammalian fauna has also been recovered from the Freshwater Beds – including the type specimens (lectotypes) of the large-bodied fallow deer (*Dama dama clactoniana*) and narrow-nosed rhinoceros (*Stephanorhinus hemitoechus*) – which is considered to represent an early Hoxnian suite (Schreve 1997, 2001a and b; Parfitt 1998a).

Thousands of artefacts in both primary and secondary contexts, including flakes, flake tools and cores but definitively no handaxes, have been recovered from the Freshwater Beds at most Clacton localities. Wymer's (1985) preferred interpretation saw hominins active at the site from the Late Anglian or early Hoxnian (HoI), with the richest concentrations occurring in the upper part of the Lower Freshwater Beds (Wymer 1985). This is associated with a warm temperate climate and an oak-dominated woodland environment with areas of open grassland. Artefacts (and fauna) are very rare from the Estuarine Beds, the wide Thames estuary probably not an ideal habitat for hominins. The climate at this time was deteriorating, and the environment was dominated by boreal coniferous woodland. Clacton is also famous for having produced the only unequivocal wooden artefact of Palaeolithic age from Britain – the point of a broken wooded spear of yew, found *in situ* in interglacial deposits by Warren (1911; Text Box 4.1).

Clacton from the end of the MIS12 glaciation (Gladfelter 1972; Singer et al. 1973; Wymer 1985), by which time the climate was rapidly ameliorating and grassland and birch copse were developing. Continued hominin presence during HoI has been suggested on the basis of the pollen from the overlying marl at the Golf Course site (Mullenders and Desair-Coremans, cited in Wymer 1985). Wymer (1985) dismissed this due to the absence of sea buckthorn (*Hippophaë*), which characterises the 1An and HoI pollen profiles at Marks Tey and Hoxne, and the dominance of pine. However, sea buckthorn cannot tolerate competition and at Marks Tey it was declining during An1 and completely eliminated before the end of HoI (Turner 1970, 419) which, contrary to Wymer's contention, did contain an abundance of pine. HoI at Marks Tey further contains some evidence for a brief return to cold conditions.

Shorter sequences through MIS11 are found at Barnham (see Text Box 3.4) and Beeches Pit (see Text Box 3.5). At Barnham, the key primary context archaeological industries (both handaxe and non-handaxe) were excavated from a lag gravel and overlying silts at the edge of a deep basin, interpreted as an over-deepened fluvial channel. A non-handaxe industry in secondary context was also recovered from within and beneath the lag gravel. Palaeoenvironmental data have not survived in the marginal deposits, although organic remains were recovered from the silts and clays in the centre of the channel, associated with a small lithic assemblage (n = 16), presumably tossed by hominins into the middle of the channel. On the basis of sedimentology, Ashton et al. (1998) claim that the archaeology at the margins is contemporaneous, although the connecting deposits are missing and this cannot be proven. Nevertheless, on a regional scale the palynology suggests a mix of open grassland with deciduous, oak woodland characteristic of HoII, a correlation supported by the molluscan fauna, which includes the zone fossil *Discus ruderatus* (Preece and Penkman 2005). The herpetofauna indicate a mosaic of wetland and

BARNHAM AND ELVEDEN, SUFFOLK

Barnham and Elveden are situated in the Breckland region of East Anglia, 3.5 km south and 5 km south-west of Thetford respectively. Both sites were originally brickpits in operation around the turn of the twentieth century, when they attracted attention from local collectors. Both were excavated by T. T. Paterson in the 1930s (Paterson 1937; Paterson and Fagg 1940), and more recently by the British Museum, between 1989 and 1999 (Ashton et al. 1998; Ashton et al. 2005). Similarities between the geological sequence at the two sites led Ashton et al. (2005) to suggest that they might have formed part of the same fluvial drainage network, although it is impossible to demonstrate whether humans – who left two different archaeological signatures – truly occupied them at the same time.

Elveden comprises a depression within the Chalk, mantled by Lowestoft (MIS12) till and infilled by a sequence of lacustrine silty-clays, gravel and colluvium (brickearth) (Ashton et al. 2005; Figure 1). Pollen from the base of the lacustrine

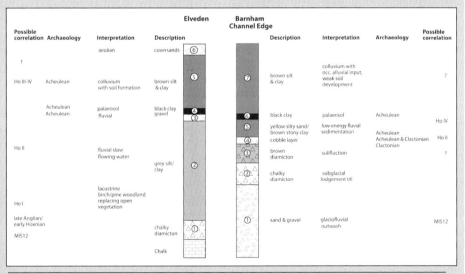

Text Box 3.4

FIGURE 1
Schematic sections through the Barnham and Elveden sequences, showing stratigraphy, archaeology and possible correlation with the Hoxnian pollen zones. (Data after Ashton et al. 1998; Ashton et al. 2005, with permission from Elsevier and The Prehistoric Society.) NB no direct correlation is implied between the two sequences as presented.

sequence, which includes sea buckthorn (*Hippophaë*), indicates cool conditions with open vegetation growing in damp, poorly drained habitats, giving way to coniferous forested conditions dominated by birch and pine higher up the sequence. A molluscan fauna from the upper part of the lake sequence signals the development of fully temperate conditions, with woodland around the edges of the basin; vertebrates were sparse although fish (rudd and tench) suggesting MJT of ~15° C were recovered. This lacustrine succession was tentatively correlated with Hol–HolI; amino acid racemisation produced ratios consistent with this attribution. The gravel, preserved above the lake sequence only at the margins of the basin, is a 'lag' deposit that formed a localised cobble band at the margins of the basin, indicating that a river capable of winnowing the finer elements of the gravel had become established through the site. A black clay overlying the gravel was interpreted as a palaeosol, indicating a period of soil formation.

Paterson (Paterson and Fagg 1940) recovered a substantial assemblage from Elveden, which he believed represented a hybrid of Acheulean and Clactonian industries (Figure 2). The recent excavations found Acheulean archaeology in a

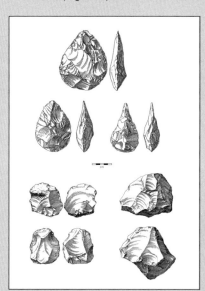

number of contexts. The most important occurred within and atop the cobble band in Area I, within the black clay and brickearth in Area III. Different activities took place in each area: Area I was predominant used for the procurement, testing and roughing out of cores and handaxes; Area II for handaxe manufacture. The activities on these two areas may be contemporaneous.

FIGURE 2

Artefacts from Barnham and Elveden. Top: handaxes from Elveden (after Smith 1931, © Trustees of the British Museum): bottom: a core and flake tools from Paterson's Series C at Barnham. (After Paterson 1937, courtesy of The Prehistoric Society.)

The Barnham sequence essentially consists of a deep glaciogenic channel filled with MIS12 till and glacial outwash. Emplaced above this lies a late MIS12–early MIS11 lacustrine and fluvial sequence, comprising 7 m of fossiliferous interglacial clays and silts, passing laterally at the channel margins into yellow-gray siltysands overlying a coarse cobble band. The sequence is capped by a colluvial brickearth. A diverse temperate vertebrate fauna of early Hoxnian character was recovered from the silts within the channel (Parfitt 1998a). The fauna suggests a variety of habitats from dense woodland to more open scrub grassland, in close proximity to still or slow-moving water. The climate appears to have been warmer than today with MJT in the order of ~17–18°C.

Text Box 3.4

Text Box 3.4

The archaeology at Barnham is also associated with a coarse cobble band (Area I and VI, laterally occurring silty-clays (Area II) and the overlying brickearth. The cobble band formed the main source of raw materials throughout the human occupation of the site, although it was probably periodically inundated by water. Paterson (1937) described five Clactonian assemblages (A–E) from below, within and atop the cobble band, with an Acheulean assemblage in the overlying brick-earths. Wymer (1979, 1985) also found an *in situ* Clactonian assemblage from near the surface of the cobble band. Recent excavations by the British Museum (Ashton et al. 1994a, 1994b, 1998), however, recovered fresh-conditioned *in situ* handaxes and manufacturing débitage in this geological context, 50 m away from the original finds but sealed by the same black horizon. The cultural affinities of Paterson's and Wymer's fresh-conditioned Clactonian industry may thus need revising, although we are of course dealing with geological and not strict occupational contemporaneity, and the two areas could have been exposed at very different times (Wenban-Smith 1996). But, even accepting that the two areas are contemporaneous and that the fresh assemblage is Acheulean, no trace of handaxe manufacture has been found within the cobble band and the presence of a rolled Clactonian assemblage is still valid.

The sediments at the margins of the basin – where the majority of the archaeology occurred – were decalcified. The sediments between the main faunal and archaeological areas were all removed by quarrying. It is thus difficult to relate the fauna with any of the archaeological horizons, other than the small undiagnostic collection of mint flakes and cores from the channel sites themselves (n = 16).

Text Box 3.5

BEECHES PIT, WEST STOW, SUFFOLK: 400,000 YEAR-OLD FIRE

Beeches Pit lies in a disused brick pit at the edge of Thetford Forest, 2.5 km from Icklingham in Suffolk. The geology was first recorded and described by Skertchly in the 1870s (Whitaker et al. 1891), and latterly investigated by a team of Quaternary specialists led by Richard Preece (Preece et al. 1991, 2000, 2006). Archaeological excavations were conducted during the 1990s by John Gowlett (Gowlett et al. 1998, 2005).

The Pleistocene sequence at Beeches Pit fills a sub-glacial channel incised into Middle Chalk, ~100m wide and >15m deep (Preece et al. 2006). The basal sediments are glacial in origin, overlain by interglacial sediments occupying a depression at their top. The interglacial deposits are highly fossiliferous, yielding molluscs, ostracods and vertebrates (but no pollen). The site is dated to MIS11 on the basis of biostratigraphy, a correlation supported by amino acid racemisation (Penkman 2005) and a thermoluminescence date of 414 ± 30 ka BP on burnt flint (see Figure 1).

Archaeological excavations concentrated on two areas on the north-western edge of the pit, labelled AF and AH. Flint artefacts were recovered from both

Bed	Description	Interpretation	Climate	Archaeology	Tentative Correlation	MIS
8	clayey gravel	slope activity	periglacial			
7	sandy clay	slow moving water	cold	Acheulean	?	?
6	black organic clay			Acheulean		
5	grey brown silts & clays	slope activity		Acheulean	Ho IV or later	
4	tufaceous silts & clays	opening of canopy / springs within closed deciduous forest	fully temperate	Acheulean	Ho III	
3d	grey brown silts and clays diamicton (remobilised)	slope activity				
3c	grey silt	shallow pool				11
3b	brown silty clay	stagnant pool on foot of grassland slope with scrub	warm	Acheulean	Ho IIb-c	
3a	grey silt	shallow pool			Ho I	
2	laminated silts and clays / chalky silty diamicton / sands and gravels	glaciolacustrine / TILL / glaciofluvial	glacial			12
1	brecciated chalk					
	Chalk					

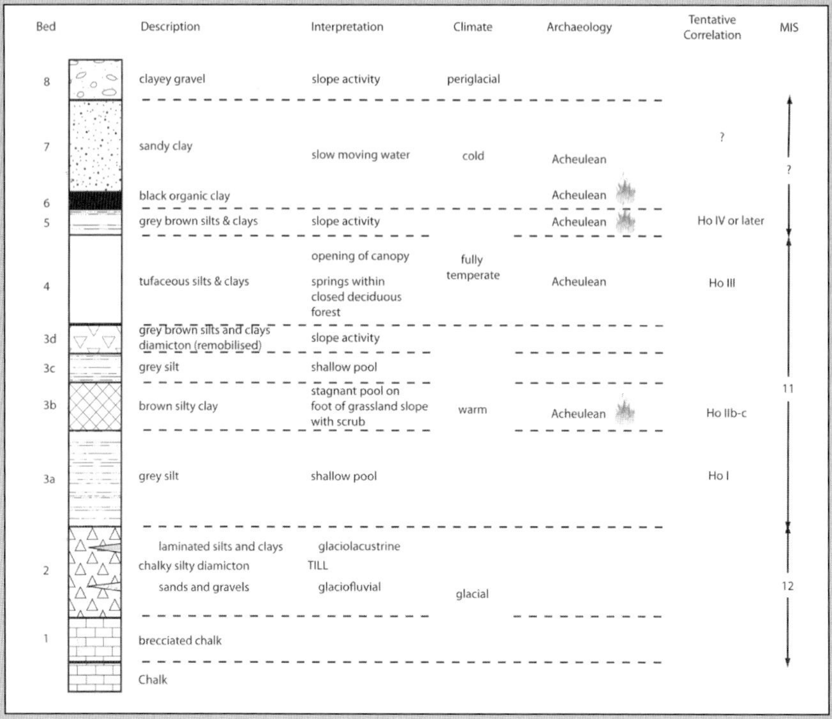

FIGURE 1

Schematic section through the Beeches Pit sequence, showing sedimentology, climatic interpretation, archaeology and correlation with the Hoxnian pollen zones. (Modified after Preece et al. 2006; reproduced with permission from Wiley.)

the interglacial beds (3b, 4 and 5) and the ensuing cold period deposits (6 and 7). Most pieces (several thousand) were recovered from the sloping horizon of Bed 3b, including four handaxes, flake tools, cores and both soft and hard-hammer débitage (95% of the assemblage), manufactured on flint available from the Chalk and till around the site (Gowlett et al. 2005; see Figure 2). Environmental data suggests that hominins were active around the margins of a pool, surrounded by marsh, with nearby areas of calcareous grassland and open woodland.

Some 100 lithics refits suggest that the archaeology is largely *in situ*, although a small degree of downslope movement may have occurred, particularly in Area AF (Gowlett et al. 2005). Knapping sequences are incomplete, suggesting spatial and temporal separation of different phases of the *chaîne opératoire*. In particular, the absence of conjoinable thinning flakes belonging to the handaxes in Area AH suggests that they were introduced from a manufacturing site elsewhere; similarly, the flake tools were not found in association with their parent cores (Gowlett et al 2005; Hallos 2005). A refitting roughout, abandoned due to a flaw in the flint, shows that handaxe manufacture did take place at Beeches Pit. The

Text Box 3.5

FIGURE 2
The series of handaxes from Beeches Pit showing the variety of form and size found in the Acheulean. All belong within MIS11, but the two small examples on the left come from a slightly higher level. (Photo John Gowlett, courtesy John Gowlett.)

Text Box 3.5

hard-hammer flake population is also consistent with full reduction sequences on site, although many of the cores used to produce them seem to have been exported. Both areas also produced evidence of fire use (see Text Box 3.2 on fire at Beeches Pit) with related clusters of artefacts.

The presence of handaxes in Bed 3b, which has been correlated on the basis of its molluscan fauna with HoIIb–c (Preece et al. 2006), indicates that the Acheulean was present in East Anglia earlier than in the Thames Valley, and possibly occurred in the same sub-stage as the Clactonian, although proving that they were contemporaneous is impossible. Hominins were also present during the height of the interglacial (Beds 4 and 5) in an environment dominated by closed woodland. During this phase the site was also located close to tufa-forming springs that would have provided clean, fresh water. John Gowlett (e.g. 2006; Gowlett et al. 2005) has interpreted Beeches Pit as a home base to which hominins repeatedly returned. This would have functioned as a social hub, where they gathered together, built fires, ate and made tools, and where objects were transported in and out as they carried out their day-to-day activities in the surrounding environs.

dry-ground habitats around the channel. The fish and molluscs from the organic sediments within the channel show still or slow-moving water but the presence of a palae-osol above the fluvial sediments, both at the margins and centre of the basin, suggests that the channel eventually dried up, perhaps in response to reduced precipitation or climatic warming. Thermophilous species such as European pond terrapin (*Emys orbicularis*) and common tree frog (*Hyla arborea*) indicate summer temperatures warmer than today, with mean July temperatures of at least 17° C (Holman 1998).

A different ecological setting under the same climatic conditions is evident for the main period of hominin occupation at Beeches Pit, in Beds 3b and 4 (Preece et al. 2006). The molluscan fauna demonstrated that Bed 3b was laid down in stagnant pools, flanked by calcareous grassland and open woodland, in concord with the mammalian assemblage which comprised a mixture of open grassland dwelling taxa such as rabbit, alongside scrub/woodland species such as fallow deer (*Dama dama*), bank vole (*Clethrionomys glareolus*) and wood mouse (*Apodemus sylvaticus*). Shrews and water voles are also well represented, indicating moist and richly vegetated waterside habitats. The tufa deposits of Bed 4 formed in shallow, spring-fed pools. The molluscs from this level allow us to infer that human occupation occurred during fully temperate conditions (with higher summer temperatures and higher rainfall than today) and *within* a closed, deciduous woodland environment. Pollen was not preserved but a change in the molluscan fauna from a dominance of *Discus ruderatus* in Bed 3b to *Discus rotundatus* in Bed 4, also seen at Barnham and Swanscombe, suggests a correlation with HoIIb–c and HoIII respectively (Preece et al. 2006). Later hominin activity in Beds 6 and 7 is associated with much colder conditions, although reworking complicates the reconstruction of the ecological conditions at the site during their deposition. Nevertheless the mammals from Beds 5 and 6 record a major shift from woodland to open-grassland species, probably due to cooling, and include a number of large grazers such as horse, red deer, steppe/narrow-nosed rhinoceros and aurochs (*Bos primigenius*). Molluscs and ostracods from the youngest deposits containing archaeology (Bed 7) indicate fluvial deposition under cold conditions, a conclusion supported by the presence of lemming, although where this lies within MIS11 is as yet unknown

The sequence at the Hoxnian stratotype at Hoxne, like Marks Tey, records a long sequence from the end of the MIS12 glaciation through much of the succeeding interglacial (Pollen Zones 1An through HoIIIa), although a hiatus at the top of Stratum D means that HoIIIb and VI are missing. The most recent fieldwork at the site suggested that hominins first appeared in Stratum B1, which marks a return to warm conditions after the cold episode registered in the 'Arctic Bed' of Stratum C (Ashton et al. 2008a). On the basis of Uranium-series dates (Grün and Schwarcz 2000), AAR and biostratigraphy (Ashton et al. 2008a), it is suggested that the 'Arctic Bed' was deposited during a post-Hoxnian cold phase within MIS11 and that the Lower and Upper Industries date to a warmer phase towards the end of MIS11.

This means that hominins were absent from Hoxne for the entirety of the Hoxnian, *sensu stricto* (probably MIS11c), when most other sites show humans to be present in the country; at Hoxne they were only present during a later warm sub-stage (probably MIS11a) for which we thus far have very little evidence. Palaeoenvironmental data were recovered from the archaeological horizons excavated during the 1970s (Singer et al. 1993). The mammalian fauna is dominated by horse, suggesting open conditions, with local woodland attested by fallow deer, beaver and macaque. Warm summers are indicated by Rudd (*Scardinius erythrophthalmus*) although Norway lemming may suggest more continental conditions. Pollen from Stratum B was dominated by birch and pine although one must remember that pollen from fluvial contexts is problematic and often reworked and may not reflect vegetation in the immediate vicinity.

Ashton et al. (2008a) suggest that the hominin occupation of Britain during MIS11a took place within cool temperate conditions dominated by boreal forest. Such conditions also prevailed at a number of European sites that probably correlated with Hoxne, for example the Polish MIS11 site at Ossowka, where the later part of the interglacial sequence is characterised by a series of climatic oscillations of open vegetation alternating with boreal forest dominated by pine. Similarly, the palynological data from the Reinsdorf interglacial in the Channel II (level 4b) deposits at Schöningen show that hominin occupation occurred within a boreal forest environment dominated by pine with some birch and larch (Urban 2007). Intriguingly, spruce (from which Schöningen's famous spears were made) seems to have been unimportant at the site (Urban 2007). Ashton et al. (ibid.) suggest that Hoxne and Schöningen date to the same sub-stage, MIS 11a, going on to suggest that this period had a relatively cool climate and was dominated by boreal forest; although it should be noted that these conditions reflect only one part of the Reinsdorf Interglacial, near to its close, and earlier parts of the interglacial show the presence of mixed-oak forest (Urban 2007). This raises the intriguing possibility that some Lower Palaeolithic sites previously attributed to the Hoxnian, *sensu lato*, on the basis of a temperate pollen assemblage may also belong to MIS11a and that many of our mammalian, molluscan and sea-level tie points may need revisiting.

THE HUMAN ENVIRONMENT OF MIS9

A series of buried channel fills at Cudmore Grove, situated on Mersea Island on the eastern coastal fringe of Essex, provides the most complete and most important sequence through MIS9. The deposits are believed to have been laid down by the River Blackwater (and not the Thames as previously suggested, e.g. Bridgland 1994; see Figure 3.7). They comprise basal sand and gravel (Bed 1) overlain by a series of organic clays (Beds 2–4) capped by an upper sand and gravel deposit (Bed 6) (see Figure 3.8). The sequence spans a considerable part of the MIS9 interglacial and provides high-resolution data facilitating reconstructions of the climate, environments and sea levels of the period (Roe et al. 2009). In terms of archaeology, Cudmore Grove has produced only three unstratified flakes and a scraper from the beach, although the potential for finding lithic scatters and associated faunal remains in the channel margin remains high.

The long pollen sequence from Cudmore Grove (Figure 3.9) provides the first detailed vegetation history of the MIS9 interglacial which has only recently been recognised in terrestrial sediments on the basis of lithostratigraphy (Text Box 3.6) and mammalian biostratigraphy (e.g. Bridgland 1994; Schreve 2001a and b; Schreve et al. 2002). In terms of vegetation the pollen sequences from MIS11 and MIS9 are practically identical which has historically precluded their separation on palynological grounds. Both even have 'Type X' pollen, which was once thought to be a Hoxnian/MIS11 zone fossil, and subtle differences in species composition are probably taphonomic (Roe et al. 2009). The following account is based entirely on the recent work of Helen Roe and colleagues (Roe et al. 2009).

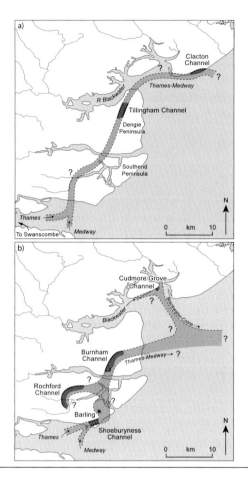

FIGURE 3.7

Palaeodrainage maps of eastern Essex during MIS 11 (a) and MIS 9 (b). Map (a) shows the tidally-influenced Thames–Medway flowing between Tillingham (East Hyde) and Clacton during the late-temperate sub-stage of the inferred MIS 11 interglacial. The sequence at Swanscombe is considered to be the upstream equivalent of this channel system. Map (b) depicts a larger, more complex palaeo-estuary inferred for the end of the early-temperate sub-stage of the MIS9 interglacial, when lower estuarine conditions prevailed at Cudmore Grove. The Cudmore Grove palaeo-channel is placed in the more northerly part of this estuarine system and is assumed to have formed a tributary of the main Thames–Medway estuary. (After Roe et al. 2009 and Elsevier, used with permission.)

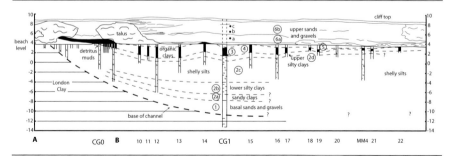

FIGURE 3.8

Section through the channel deposits at Cudmore Grove, showing location of boreholes and channel margins. (After Roe et al. 2009, and Elsevier, used with permission.)

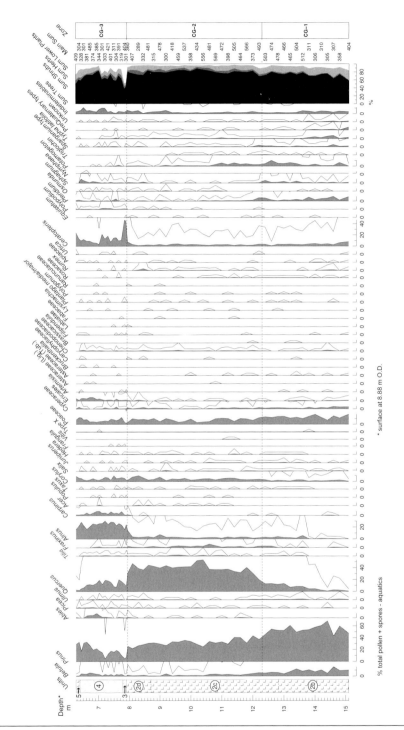

FIGURE 3.9
MIS9 Pollen Record from Cudmore Grove. (After Roe 2001, and Elsevier, used with permission.)

BRIDGLAND'S MODEL OF TERRACE FORMATION

Much of the evidence for the Palaeolithic occupation of Britain is preserved in primary and secondary contexts within the fluvial archive; the silts, sands and gravels laid down by Pleistocene rivers. Understanding the way in which artefacts become buried in fluvial deposits is a vital prerequisite to interpreting the social and behavioural meaning of artefact accumulations, and sites are routinely assessed in terms of artefact context and condition in order to establish their integrity and degree of derivation (Wymer 1968, 1999). How the terraces themselves formed is equally important to understanding settlement history and the cultural and behaviour patterning within the archaeological record.

The currently favoured interpretation of the formation of river terraces and their deposits (followed throughout this book) is that of David Bridgland (e.g., Bridgland 1994, 2006, 2010; Bridgland and Allen 1996; Maddy et al. 2000; Bridgland and Westaway 2008). Bridgland's model suggests that terrace formation is controlled by climate and tectonic uplift. In its current form, the model is divided into six main stages (see Figure 1).

Phase 1: late glacial incision

Vast releases of water previously stored in ice sheets and permafrost, together with heavy rainfall events, create powerful rivers carrying very little transportable sediment. This leads to erosion and the downcutting of the river channel into the valley floor. The processes of erosion and incision are also driven by the gradual uplift of the earth's crust during the long, succeeding interglacial period.

Phase 2: late glacial–early interglacial aggradation

This is a short-lived period in which material eroded in Phase 1 is transported downstream, leading to substantial amounts of sand and gravel being deposited in newly created riverbeds.

Phase 3: interglacial stability

During full interglacial conditions smaller, single-thread, meandering rivers form with vastly reduced discharge rates. The gravel aggradations deposited in Phase 2 are overlain by fine-grained floodplain deposits and localised channel sediments, including cut-off meanders and abandoned channels. Some of these deposits may be buried and preserved by subsequent aggradation events, although most are eroded during the preceding phase.

Text Box 3.6

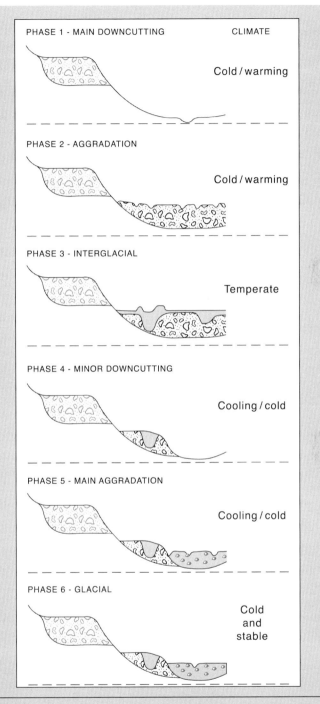

FIGURE 1
Schematic representation of the 6-Phase Terrace Formation Model. (Courtesy of David Bridgland.)

Text Box 3.6

Phase 4: late interglacial erosion

As the climatic cycle enters a cooling period, the return of spring melt flooding leads initially to erosional events similar to those in Phase 1, but as interglacials are too short for significant uplift, this usually occurs without deep downcutting and new terraces do not form.

Phase 5: late interglacial–early glacial aggradation

As the climate cools further, decreasing levels of vegetation combined with active physical weathering processes cause the mass movement of abundant coarse sediments into river bottoms. This brings about a change from single-channel river to a braided system, with large quantities of stored sediment. Sand and gravel deposits are laid down across the braid-plain, covering the interglacial surface and preserving some channel deposits.

Phase 6: full glacial stability

At glacial maxima the progressively frozen landscape reduces the activity of the river, which becomes stabilised under an arctic regime. Floods redistribute sediments deposited in Phase 5. This condition persists until the next cycle, and finally a return to Phase 1.

The key insight in Bridgland's model is that terrace formation is coupled with Milankovitch cycles, and can therefore be correlated with the marine isotope framework. For many rivers, it is possible to use the model to 'count' terrace ages, which increase up the staircase, but the model is not inviolable (see Figure 2). Flights of separate terraces tend to form only in areas where uplift has occurred (Bridgland and Westaway 2008), and major river valleys that have experienced net subsidence are underlain by stacked sequences of fluvial deposits, with all but the most recent sediments only accessible by boreholes. There are no British examples of such systems, but even here there are exceptions to the model, driven by local differences in uplift history and responses to sub-stage climatic variation. The Solent River, for example, appears to have sometimes formed two terraces per climatic cycle as a result of differential uplift and rejuvenation (Westaway et al. 2006). Nevertheless, the widespread use of the Bridgland model has, for the first time, made some sense of the British Palaeolithic record and allowed us to detect some order in an otherwise bewildering variety of materials (cf. Roe 1981).

Text Box 3.6

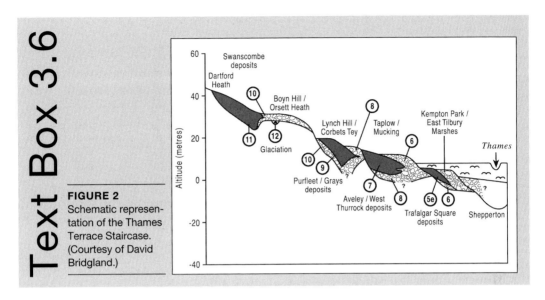

Text Box 3.6

FIGURE 2
Schematic representation of the Thames Terrace Staircase. (Courtesy of David Bridgland.)

The pollen spectrum was divided into three biozones (CG1-3).

CG1 is characterised by boreal forest in which both pine and birch were widespread. Oak, elm, ash and hazel were present in limited numbers at the start of the phase, but as the interglacial progressed the composition of the forest changed, with oak expanding and out-competing birch in places. At the same time ivy began to colonise the forest understory. Herb communities were fairly diverse throughout this period and point to the existence of lightly shaded forest-floor habitats and open areas of grassland. Mosses and bracken reveal damp, slightly acidic soils with waterside and marshland plants including sedges, ferns and marshland herbs also forming an important part of the flora, probably close to the river.

CG2 saw the development of mixed-oak forest dominated by oak, with lime, hazel and ash also being important. Pine and birch decreased and some open areas persisted. Water-side and aquatic plants declined, as a result of rising sea levels and increased salinity, the river now forming part of an estuarine regime with the development of local salt-marshes.

Unit 3, which sits between the sediments that yielded Biozones CG2 and CG3, has also produced a wealth of vertebrate and invertebrate fossils. The coleoptera indicate a sluggish river surrounded by marsh. The occurrence of alder leaf beetle (*Agelastica alni*) shows the presence of alder along the riverside, while the elm bark beetle (*Scolytus scolytus*) and *Rhyncolus elongates*, which feed on a variety of deciduous trees and on the rotting stumps of conifers respectively, show the presence of mature mixed-oak forests nearby. Dung and carrion beetles indicate the presence of large herbivores. Temperature reconstructions based on the MCR method provided summer values between 16 and 22° C and winter temperatures between –7 and 4° C.

The herpetofauna included six species not present in Britain today, including moor frog (*Rana arvalis*), tree frog (*Hyla* sp.), viperine or dice snake (*Natrix tessellata* or *Natrix maura*), aesculapian snake (*Zamenis longissimus*) and European pond terrapin (*Emys orbicularis*). Some debate surrounds the climatic significance of these exotic taxa. Holman et al. (1990) favoured an oceanic climate similar to central or southern France, with mean July temperatures above 17–18° C and warm winters. Gleed-Owen (1999), though, noted that *Z. longissimus* and *N. tessellata* are distributed throughout most of eastern Europe, where they experience cold winters, and therefore proposed more continental conditions similar to those experienced today around the southeast German border with Austria and the Czech Republic.

The mammalian and bird remains from Unit 3 also showed a range of environments, with woodland and aquatic species particularly well represented. The presence of deciduous or mixed woodland with thick ground cover is suggested by the abundance of wood mouse (*Apodemus sylvaticus*) and presence of red squirrel (*Sciurus vulgaris*), macaque, beaver and roe deer, alongside song thrush (*Turdus philomelos*), great tit (*Parus major*) and chiffchaff or willow warbler (*Phylloscopus collybita* or *P. trochilus*). Locally open vegetation is indicated by field vole (*Microtus agrestis*) and horse (*Equus ferus*), while aquatic habitats are indicated by water vole (*Arvicola terrestris cantiana*). The sandwich turn (*Sterna sandvicensis*) shows the proximity of the coast. The occurrence of bicoloured, white-toothed shrew (*Crocidura* cf. *leucodon*), which today has a southern European distribution, supports the inference that the climate may have been slightly warmer than at present.

CG3 coincided with a dramatic change in the depositional environment, the previous estuarine conditions being replaced by a lagoonal backwater. The input of regionally derived estuarine pollen (mostly oak and pine) ceased and was replaced by a strong local pollen signal. Alder carr developed, in which alder dominated the nearby woodland and indicating that the local soils were fairly wet. Some drier areas continued to support mixed-oak woodland during the early part of the zone but this declined as hornbeam and subsequently boreal forest expanded. The ground vegetation also changed, becoming dominated by ericaceous (acid-soil) plants, and waterside and aquatic plants spread. At the end of the zone thermophilous trees diminished, with a progressive shift to boreal woodland.

Cudmore Grove thus preserves evidence of regional and local vegetation development over long time scales, with a characteristic sequence of forest development complicated by local hydrographical and pedological conditions. Biostratigraphically, Biozones CG1 and CG2 span the early (Pollen Zone II) to late-temperate zones (Pollen Zone III), in which boreal forest was replaced by mixed-oak woodland under temperate conditions with soil ripening; while Biozone CG3 records the development of alder carr woodland with the expansion of hornbeam and fir during a post- temperate (Pollen Zone IV) phase during which soils deteriorated and forest cover declined. Despite a hiatus between zones 2 and 3, it is believed that the same interglacial is represented.

The pre-temperate phase of MIS9 is absent from Cudmore Grove, but may be present at the nearby site of Barling (see Figure 3.7), in deposits of the Thames-Medway system (Bridgland et al. 2001). Two pollen zones were recognised. The lower, BAR1, was dominated by boreal forest of pine and birch with a few (probably reworked) thermophilous species including chestnut, hazel, lime and ash (the latter also present as woody fragments). BAR2 saw the rise of oak and elm, at the expense of birch; grasses and sedges were present throughout the sequence, although there are indications that the canopy became more closed over time. Bridgland et al. (2001) interpreted the Barling pollen sequence as representing the transition between the pre-temperate and early temperate zones (pollen biozones I–II) of the MIS9 interglacial. Vertebrates and invertebrates associated with the early temperate zone also showed a climate somewhat warmer than today. MCR estimates from the beetle fauna provided summer temperature values between 17 and 26° C, and winter temperatures of −11 to 13. These can be refined using other taxa, notably cyprinid fish (members of the carp family) that require mean summer water temperatures of at least 18° C and the presence of ivy and bracken, which are susceptible to frost, and would suggest the extreme winter temperature estimates were simply too cold. Another tie point to the Cudmore Grove sequence is the occurrence of a nodded form of *C. torosa* at the top of the Barling sequence showing a marine influence and high sea levels during Zone II of the interglacial.

Recent investigations at the Nightingale Estate in Hackney (London) revealed organic deposits of the River Lea (the Highbury Silts and Sands) representing a short time interval, perhaps no more than a few years, within the MIS9 interglacial (Green et al. 2006). Although no artefacts were recovered, these deposits probably represent only a slightly later part of the same interglacial represented at the rich archaeological site at Stoke Newington (see Text Box 3.7) and correlate with the late temperate phase at Cudmore Grove (Green et al. 2006; Roe et al. 2009). Plants, insects and vertebrate remains from the interglacial deposits all indicated mean summer temperatures between ~18 and 19° C and mean winter values between −4° and 1° C, again indicating a more continental regime. The regional environment was similarly characterised by mixed-oak woodland, dominated by oak with smaller frequencies of beech, ash, elm and lime, with hazel forming an important shrub layer. The authors also list a number of woodland flowers – including violets, potentilla and anemone – adding a rather romantic blush to this Pleistocene canvas. The plant macrofossils, however, revealed a local environment dominated by grasses, open ground herbaceous species, aquatics and semi-aquatics; a picture enhanced by the beetles and mollusc assemblages which indicated marsh and wet grassland with scarcer patches of woodland and dry ground.

Text Box 3.7

STOKE NEWINGTON, LONDON BOROUGH OF HACKNEY

Stoke Newington lies immediately west of the River Lea in northeast London, at 27 m OD. Artefacts were first discovered on an extensive Palaeolithic horizon ('floor') by Worthington Smith in 1878, when building work north of Stoke Newington Common opened large sections in former fields and market-gardens (Smith 1878, 1884, 1894; Greenhill 1884). The 'floor' was later rediscovered by Warren in Geldeston Road (Roe 1981) but all subsequent attempts to locate it have failed. The geological assessments of Gibbard (Harding and Gibbard 1984; Gibbard 1994) and Green et al. (2004) have greatly added to our understanding of the geology of the area (see Figure 1).

The richest archaeological discoveries were made between Kyverdale Road and Alkham Road (Smith 1894). The geology here consisted of London Clay overlain by ochreous gravel containing abraded artefacts and bones. Above this lay 2–3 m of fine, buff-coloured sands containing terrestrial and freshwater molluscs. Smith's

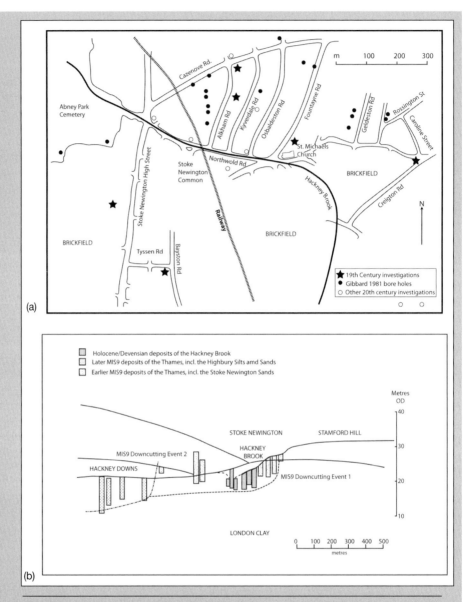

FIGURE 1
(a) Map showing location of nineteenth- and twentieth-century investigations at Stoke Newington. (b) Possible correlation of the MIS9 Stoke Newington Sands and Highbury Sands and Silts. (Redrawn after Creen et al. 2004, used with permission of Elsevier.)

Palaeolithic floor occurred within and above the sand, as a band of sub-angular, ochreous gravel up to 15 cm thick, or as a mere colour contrast. As Green et al. (2004) have noted, the heights at which Smith recorded the 'floor' vary by up to 6 m, suggesting that it either had considerable local relief or that more than one artefact horizon was present. The sequence was capped by a colluvial brickearth, although this was locally absent, allowing the floor to outcrop at the surface.

Text Box 3.7

Organic remains were recovered from both the floor and the lower gravel, Smith (1884) recording some 45 species of mollusc and 24 species of mammal.

A series of boreholes drilled by Gibbard (1994) provided a similar sequence, and he interpreted the implementiferous sands as the infill of a substantial west–east flowing meander. Green et al. (2004) assigned these to the Stoke Newington Sands (Gibbard and Harding 1994), rejecting Gibbard's attribution to the Highbury Silts and Sands. The latter include the organic deposits reported at the Nightingale Estate, Hackney Downs (Green et al. 2006), which are overlain by the Hackney Downs Gravel and form part of a discrete mappable unit with a different terrace surface height (21 m OD) and different bench level (13 m OD) to the Stoke Newington Sands. Recent investigations suggested that the organic deposits at the Nightingale Estate are MIS9 in age (Green et al. 2004, 2006). As the height of the Stoke Newington Sands is too low to be correlated with the MIS11 deposits at Swanscombe, but too high to be part of Hackney Downs Gravel, it is argued that they represent an earlier aggradation during MIS9. The molluscan fauna from the sites, which includes the stratigraphically significant taxa *Corbicula fluminalis* and *Belgrandia marginata*, supports this. The age difference may be relatively minor, with the accumulation at Stoke Newington reflecting conditions near the confluence of the Lea and the Thames (Green et al. 2004).

The artefacts from the floor include pointed and ovate handaxes (many of diminutive size), roughouts, thinning flakes, scrapers, hammers, anvils, cores and flakes. Several conjoining groups were present (Smith 1894). One handaxe is made of quartzite, and some stained artefacts (presumably from older deposits) have been resharpened and reused by the occupants of the 'floor'. Green et al. (2004) suggest that Smith found very few pieces *in situ*, collecting most from workmen or from freshly gravelled roads; if correct this would question the veracity of the Stoke Newington archaeology. Smith's original correspondence makes it clear that this was not the case, however; a letter to W.A. Sturge dated 21 February 1906 states (original emphases):

> During the first years of my N.E. London work I found *every implement* & *every flake every tool* & *every flake* myself either *in situ* or in the newly thrown out brick-earth, gravel or sand. Even the heights and levels are my own.

At some point between Cazenove Road and Northworld Road, the Stoke Newington Sands are cut by a later channel infilled with Devensian–Holocene deposits of the proto Hackney Brook (Harding and Gibbard 1984; Green et al. 2004). The Middle Pleistocene deposits in this area must therefore have been largely obliterated, although Harding and Gibbard (1984) did find derived artefacts. As the deposits are superficially similar to the sequence found immediately to the north, Smith almost certainly assumed the floor extended southwards across Stoke Newington Common, when in fact it only existed along a small corridor between Northwold Road and Cazenove Road, and possibly again on the south of the common. Sadly, this means that two artificially pointed birch stakes, found by Smith in 'Baystock' (Bayston?) Road, cannot unequivocally be regarded as Palaeolithic wooden tools, as they could derive from the later deposits of the Hackney Brook. This possibility is supported by the fact that the artefacts from the area around the common recovered by Smith are in a different preservational state to those found on the true floor.

Text Box 3.7

A much longer record, possibly through the entirety of MIS9, comes from the key site of Purfleet, Essex, where a 'sandwich' of Thames terrace deposits representing successive cold–warm–cold climatic episodes have been described (Bridgland 1994; Schreve et al. 2002; see Figure 3.10). Sedimentological evidence at the base of the sequence suggests deposition under cold climatic conditions during the end of MIS10, possibly shortly after down cutting to this terrace level. A small, non-handaxe assemblage recovered from these basal levels reveals the presence of hominins at this time. The onset of temperate conditions is first signalled by the molluscs from Bed 3, with strong temperate signatures coming from Beds 4 (silty clay) and 5 (Greenlands shell bed). Pollen from Bed 4 probably reflects the early temperate phase of the MIS9 interglacial, dominated by mixed temperate woodland rich in alder, spruce and oak, with lime, ash and elm also present. Large open areas also existed nearby, which periodically became dominant. Remains of green frog (*Rana ridibunda/lessonae/esculenta*) from Bed 4 indicate mean July temperatures of at least 15–17° C (as warm as southern Britain today). The local environment was reconstructed as a mature, vegetated water body, with a marshy floodplain surrounded by woodland and open grassland. Herbaceous pollen was poorly represented, probably due to taphonomic factors. Sedimentologically, Bed 4 consists of laminated silty-clays, which may reflect tidal sedimentation during a period of high sea level, although evidence of salinity is weak: only the noded form of the ostracod *C. torosa* and intertidal foraminifera such as *Ammonia beccarii* and *Haplophragmoides* spp. were recorded amongst an otherwise freshwater assemblage (Schreve et al. 2002).

The deposition of the Greenlands Shell Bed (Bed 5) reflects an increase in flow energy and the development of a sand flat. Pollen was not preserved, but a limited terrestrial

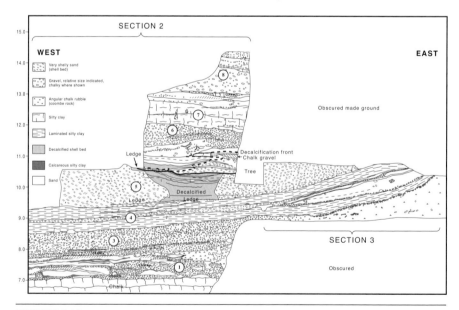

FIGURE 3.10
Schematic section through the deposits at Greenland's Pit, from the 1996 excavations. (After Schreve et al. 2002; Elsevier, used with permission.)

molluscan fauna indicates a mosaic of marsh or swamp close to the river channel, with grassland, scrub and woodland beyond (Schreve et al. 2002). The presence of the extinct hydrobid mollusc '*Paladilhia radigueli*' indicates brackish habitats and high sea levels, but as this species is very rare Schreve et al. (ibid.) suggest that Purfleet lay at some distance from the contemporary estuary. Bed 5 also yielded abundant fish remains that are indicative of slow-flowing water with some cyprinids requiring high summer temperatures (at least 18° C) for spawning. This is again in keeping with the evidence from Cudmore Grove and Hackney. The mammalian assemblage from the shell bed also reflects fully interglacial conditions. The small mammals indicate a range of habitats, including woodland, grassland, riparian and aquatic environments, whereas the larger mammals, in particular macaque monkey, beaver, roe deer (*Capreolus capreolus*) and straight-tusked elephant, suggest the proximity of deciduous or mixed woodland (Schreve et al. 2002).

The Bluelands Gravel (Bed 6) and the Botany Gravel (Bed 8) were probably deposited under cooling climatic conditions at the end of MIS9 and into MIS8, and contain an Acheulean and Levalloisian archaeological signature respectively. The mammalian assemblage from these beds (although very limited) is at least consistent with more open conditions, in particular the presence of horse.

One other MIS9 archaeological locality has yielded environmental data: the elusive Wolvercote Channel in Oxfordshire. The mammalian assemblage reflects cool but temperate conditions, with both woodland and open grassland species (straight-tusked elephant, aurochs and horse). Furthermore, 17 species of temperate mollusc, plant macrofossils representing 30 species of flowering plant and 37 mosses (Bell 1894, 1904; Reid 1899; Duigan 1956) and five coleopteran taxa (Blair 1923) were recovered from Bed 4, immediately overlying the main archaeological layers. These included the arctic-alpine Hoary whitlowgrass (*Draba incana*), several mosses characteristic of highland and sub-alpine habitats, and the northern weevil *Notaris aethiops*, indicating cool but probably temperate conditions (Briggs et al. 1985). Cooling climatic conditions were also reflected in sparse pollen assemblages obtained (probably) from Bed 5 (Briggs et al. 1985), which show a transition from pine-dominated forest to open habitats.

It is important to note here that the long sequences from Barling/Cudmore Grove and Purfleet appear to reflect only one period of warming–cooling, and that sub-stage variation is apparently absent. Whether this means that we only have evidence for one isotopic sub-stage, two different sub-stages, or that the climatic fluctuations of MIS9 are not strongly registered in the terrestrial record is unclear. MIS9 is a 'fledgling' interglacial that has only recently been properly recognised in the Quaternary record. Taking lessons from the MIS11/Hoxnian interglacial, it would seem very probable that as more sites and sequences are discovered greater complexity will become evident. Where the two short sequences from Wolvercote and Hackney might fit within this is therefore mostly guesswork based on pollen, which history has again shown us can be extremely misleading.

ENVIRONMENTAL RECONSTRUCTIONS AND HUMAN SCALAR RELATIONSHIPS

The sections above provide the standard environmental reconstructions. They show a very familiar range of habitats, mostly around river valleys or coastlines, most of which can easily be recognised in Britain today, and provide a basic canvas against which to situate Palaeolithic humans as they moved through their landscape. In some cases these reconstructions are remarkably detailed and provide evidence of habitat preferences and climatic tolerances at the micro-level. And yet, there is always a feeling that there is something not quite 'right' about them from an archaeological perspective. That is, they operate at the wrong scales, in both time and space. Temporally they represent huge, time-averaged units extending over decades, centuries or millennia or unconstrained 15-minute snapshots floating in chronological hyperspace. Geographically they exist at either regional scales – huge swathes of landscape covered in grassland or forest and dependant on the fall-out catchment of lakes, ponds and rivers – or at the micro-scales most relevant to beetles, molluscs or ostracods. Human scalar relationships, from both the individual and group perspective, are hard to attain. What, for example, did it matter to a handaxe-making hominin whether the ground they sat on was bare, sandy or bore sweetgrass? Furthermore, how did the structure of the grassland–woodland mosaic actually influence mobility and the distribution of resources? These are all important questions for Palaeolithic archaeologists seeking to use these reconstructions not for their own intrinsic value but in order to understand hominins in their specific landscapes. Only the extensive excavations of the landscapes at Boxgrove appear to have sufficient human-scale relationships – what people saw as they scanned the horizon, where animals were, what resources lay within what distance, which plants were edible without extensive processing, the smell in the air – to allow us to understand what they did there and why (Pope 2002; Pope and Roberts 2005). As Quaternary environmental reconstructions become ever more sophisticated, we run the risk of losing the humans in a matrix of data as they move through a world that resembles a computer-generated landscape – only those pixels closest to the action ever being rendered, the rest being a wireframe of uncertainty. Resolving this issue is a pressing task for the future if we wish to understand humans at the human scale; otherwise, as discussed by White and Plunkett (2004) and below, everywhere simply becomes the same place, just with different trees. True, one will probably always need to rely on time-averaged snapshots of specific vegetational regimes, but we still need to develop better ways of transforming these into an understanding of the specific locales frequented by hominins and how these impacted on human decisions.

PALAEOGEOGRAPHY

Becoming an island: Britain inside and outside of Palaeolithic Europe

The opening of the Dover Strait is of paramount importance to our understanding of the settlement history of Pleistocene Britain. While the general mechanism of opening is generally agreed – catastrophic overflow of a proglacial lake – the timing of this event is still the subject of some debate (Smith 1985, 1989; Gibbard 1988, 1995; Meijer and Preece 1995; White and Schreve 2000; Ashton and Lewis 2002; Gupta et al. 2007; Busschers et al. 2008; Toucanne et al. 2009).

As discussed in Chapter 2, during the Early Pleistocene and early Middle Pleistocene, Britain was connected to continental Europe by the Weald–Artois Ridge, part of a huge chalk anticline that once spanned the modern Straits of Dover. By the Middle Pleistocene, a reduction in sea level had also left the coast lying much further north of its Early Pleistocene position, with the massive sediment body formed by the Great European (Ur-Frisia) Delta Top emergent in the southern North Sea basin (Morigi et al. 2011). The present south coast of England thus lay on the northern edge of a large embayment, while southeast England and East Anglia was similarly located at the margin of a large coastal embayment around the North Sea basin, the two being separated by a large chalk isthmus (Figure 3.11). Therefore, at the start of the period covered in this chapter, Britain was permanently a peninsula of Europe, permitting relatively easy movement of flora, fauna and hominins in and out of the country. By the end of the Cromerian Complex, degradation and subsidence of the delta top once again allowed interglacial sea levels to encroach southwards across it and into the southern North Sea basin (Funnell 1995), although circulation was still bounded in the south by the Weald–Artois chalk ridge. The onset of the Anglian (MIS12) glaciation saw an ice sheet fill much of the North Sea, with a large proglacial lake occupying the southern North Sea basin, fed by the Rhine–Mass, Schedlt and Thames systems.

According to several authors (Gibbard 1995; White and Schreve 2000; Gupta et al. 2007), it was the overflowing of this ice-dammed lake – bounded by coalescent Fennoscandian and British ice sheets to the north and the Weald–Artois ridge to the south – that incised a channel through the land bridge at the Dover Straits, and by doing so facilitated the formation of the Channel River (Fleuve Manche) and left open the potential for Britain to become isolated from Europe during periods of high sea level. Work by Gupta and colleagues cast significant new light on this hypothesis, and suggested a more complex and multiphase sequence of events (Gupta et al. 2007; Gibbard 2007). Gupta et al. (2007) recorded a number of landforms in the English Channel, including streamlined bedrock islands and longitudinal erosional grooves that indicated rapid sub-aerial erosion by very high magnitude water discharge. A sub-horizontal bench on the northern flank of the channel, south of the Isle of Wight, suggested not one, but two such events, however, one that initially breached the land-bridge and cut the platform, and another that incised the channel further (Figure 3.12). The preservation of small, truncated and beheaded channels on one of the bedrock islands further showed a period of normal fluvial processes following the initial breach but before the final downcutting. Gibbard (2007) suggested that the initial breach occurred during the Anglian Glaciation, leaving a valley ~45 km wide (Gupta et al. 2007). The Thames and Schedlt rivers were re-routed south, flowing into the Atlantic via the Channel River, while the Rhine and Meuse continued to flow north. The second event greatly enlarged the Dover Strait and had a greater impact on the palaeodrainage of Europe, producing a combined Thames–Rhine system

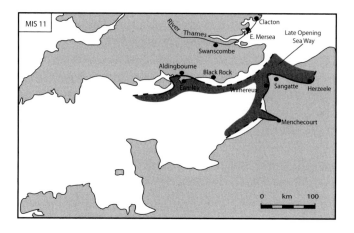

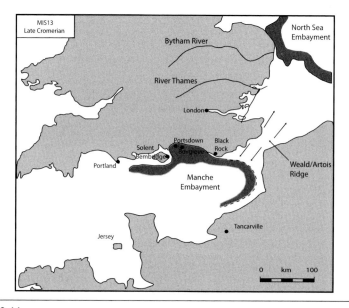

FIGURE 3.11
Reconstructions of the Palaeogeography of Eastern England during MIS11 and MIS13. (After Bates et al. 2003 and courtesy Martin Bates.)

flowing southwards, effectively carrying half the drainage of western Europe out into the Atlantic via the Channel River (Gibbard 2007). This event is suggested to have occurred during the Saalian (MIS8 or MIS6), when a second ice-dammed lake formed behind a weaker bedrock or moraine barrier further north, which also broke with immediate and catastrophic effect.

Based on their correlation of differential artefact density in different Thames terrace deposits with hominin population density, Ashton and Lewis (2002; see also Chapter 4) suggest that the breach was later than commonly supposed (possibly just prior to the Ipswichian interglacial, MIS5e) or that the initial breach was insufficient to exclude

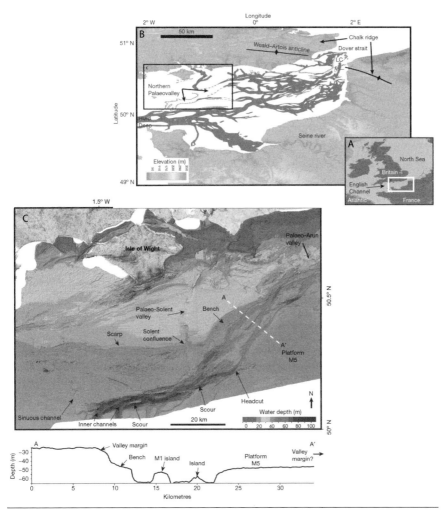

FIGURE 3.12
Map of the English Channel (A) with distribution of palaeochannels (B), and sonar bathymetry of the north-central Channel Shelf (C). (After Gupta 2007 and courtesy Sanjeev Gupta.)

hominins from Europe during periods of high sea level. The formation of the Dover Straits seems to have been polycyclic with episodes of catastrophic overspill from proglacial lakes, marine erosion during marine transgressions and fluvial dissection during periods of low sea level, but evidence suggests that the strait was a significant feature from MIS12 onwards. Difference in the ostracods and foraminifera between the MIS7 Norton–Brighton Raised beach and the MIS13 Westbourne–Arundel Raised Beach (formally the Goodwood–Slindon Raised Beach; Roberts and Pope in press) have been suggested to represent different oceanic conditions (Whitaker, cited in Bates et al. 1998, 163), while the appearance of non-flint pebbles in the intermediate Aldingbourne Raised Beach may similarly indicate a different source area to the earlier deposits. Both provide some evidence that the Dover Strait became open after MIS12 and that by MIS7 a fairly open seaway existed around Britain (Bates et al. 2003). Further evidence derives from raised beach deposits at Herzeele and Sangatte on the French side of the strait. Lying at 8 m and 10 m NGF directly within the Pas de Calais, these sites clearly provide evidence for an open Dover Strait. Unfortunately, dating these localities has proven difficult, with various estimates of MIS7 (Balescu et al. 1992; Bates 1993), MIS9 (Sommé et al. 1999) and MIS11 (Sommé et al. 1978), although this uncertainty does not detract from the fact that marine conditions existed in the strait during the Middle Pleistocene.

Studies of Channel River/Fleuve Manche activity over the last four glacial periods using mass accumulation rates and x-ray fluorescence of marine sediments also suggest that the Dover Strait was open from MIS12 (Toucanne et al. 2009). Toucanne et al. (ibid.) concluded that terrigenous inputs into the Armorican margin off the Bay of Biscay dating to MIS10, 8 and 6 provided clear evidence that the Channel River connected the southern North Sea basin with the Atlantic. Channel River activity was significantly reduced during MIS10 and 8 than during MIS6 and 2, which might be seen as evidence for a gradual increase in the size of the Dover Strait, although these authors imply that ice sheet and fluvial dynamics in the North Sea had a greater effect on discharge. Critically, the seasonal imprint of fluvial discharges, indicated by laminated facies, precluded any large sediment input ~160–150 ka BP as required by Gupta et al.'s (2007) Saalian megaflood scenario. Instead Toucanne et al. suggest that a succession of numerous Channel River discharges from ~350 ka onwards produced the valley systems and erosional features documented in the English Channel by Gupta et al., suggesting a significant breach from MIS12 onwards.

Sea levels and marine transgressions: keeping hominins inside and outside of Britain

While early Middle Pleistocene hominins could potentially have entered Britain at any time, during the late Middle Pleistocene interglacials ingress may have been precluded by a significant water barrier. The current depths of the Channel and North Sea basins are –50 m OD and –40 m OD respectively (Keen 1995), meaning that sea levels above these depths isolate Britain from Europe – keeping residents in and potential colonists out. While these may serve as a general guide to prerequisite sea level rises in the past, reconstructing the bathymetry of the Channel and North Sea basins during the Middle Pleistocene is complicated by a number of long and short-term tectonic and depositional factors, including the cyclical accumulation and (catastrophic) erosion of deltaic and lacustrine sediments, progressive downwarping of the North Sea basin, general uplift in response to erosion, glacio-isostacy and hydro-isostacy, as well as uplift of ~30–40m in the Channel (Lagarde et al. 2003).

Ashton et al. (2011) offered a model that incorporated gradual subsidence of the North Sea basin (Busschers et al. 2008) from a high stand of 0 m OD during MIS11 to a low stand of –40 m OD today. Net downwarping has certainly taken place, but such an assumption of a constant and gradual mechanism takes no account of cyclical variation in response to ice sheets, water bodies or sedimentation/erosion. Their projections, therefore, seem rather wishful, reliant upon *a priori* conclusions regarding settlement history and access times rather than empirical figures. Indeed, extrapolating the subsidence rates used (0.25

m/ka for the past 100 ka in the Netherlands, cf. Busschers et al. 2008 and Kooi et al. 1998), which one must do in order to assume a net gradual rate, it becomes clear that the North Sea basin ~450 ka BP would not have been at 0 m OD, but at 72.5 m above modern sea level, and ~350 ka BP it would have been at 47.5 m amsl. These figures are clearly negated by the direct terrestrial evidence for high sea level stands around the North Sea basin during MIS11 and MIS9, and show that assumptions of gradual downwarping over ~500 ka of glacial activity cannot be sustained.

We model here the effects of sea level based on direct terrestrial evidence for high sea level stands in the North Sea, which reveal that it was inundated during these periods and that the North Sea basin was sufficiently deep (see below). We do not claim to know what this depth was, but all five reconstructions presented in Figure 3.13 clearly show that global sea levels greatly exceeded the modern limiting depths during each interglacial and approached a few metres of modern levels several times in each cycle. Assuming a limiting depth of just −10 m throughout MIS11 and MIS9, or indeed gradual subsidence, makes very little difference to the projections offered below, and at the human scale a depth of just a metre or so would surely have prevented humans from wading several kilometres across the North Sea. But we are aware that our model remains just that – a model – and is offered as an heuristic in understanding the settlement history of Britain.

The reconstructions of Waelbroeck et al. (2002), Siddall et al. (2003) and Cutler et al. (2003) show a rapid peak in sea levels and probable isolation during early MIS11, with reconnection to Europe during later sub-stages and the cooling limb. Reconstructions based on Shackleton's (2000) data, however, show two high sea level stands in MIS11, an initial peak (possible MIS11c) and a later peak (possibly MIS11a), separated by a prolonged episode of low sea levels when Britain would have been connected to Europe. It was possibly during such a period that the terrestrial link between the Thames and the Rhine, which allowed the dispersal of the freshwater 'Rhenish' mollusc suite into Britain during Hoxnian Pollen Zone HoIIc (cf. Kerney 1971; Meijer and Preece 1995), also provided a window of opportunity for dispersing hominins, although this suggestion is hampered by a lack of fine-grained correlation between these marine sediment stacks and the pollen and molluscan evidence from terrestrial sites.

Meijer and Preece (1995) suggested that the absence of southern elements in MIS11 marine molluscan faunas around the North Sea might indicate that the strait was still closed at this time, although this pattern is closely mirrored by modern distributions. Furthermore, if Britain was still connected to continental Europe it is unclear why the Rhenish fauna did not make its first appearance much earlier. Meijer and Preece (1995) suggested that this might reflect a time lag in immigration from distant refugia, although an inundated North Sea basin provides another explanation. As discussed by White and Schreve (2000), glacio-isostatic depression of the crust of northwest Europe after the very extensive OIS12 glaciation, could have led to a highly penetrative Hoxnian transgression, the sea flooding in before the crust could recover (Kukla and Cïlek 1996). If sufficient to disconnect Britain from continental Europe, later crustal uplift combined with a global reduction in sea levels, would then have reconnected Britain to continental Europe around the end of HoII, thereby allowing the incursion of the Rhenish suite.

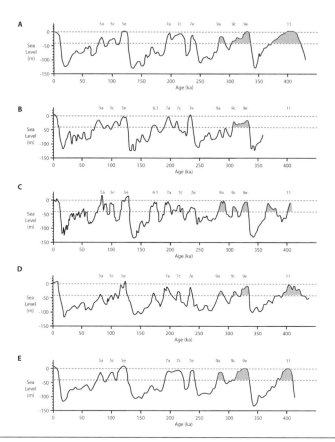

FIGURE 3.13

Sea level estimates from the benthic isotope record and other sea-level indicators, with periods during which Britain was an island during MIS11 and MIS9 indicated. Top dashed line: modern sea-level. Lower dashed line: –40 m below modern sea-level, above which Britain is assumed to become an island. Shaded area: periods of high sea level and island status as described in this chapter. (Reconstructions based on data from A: Waelbroeck et al. 2002, based on North Atlantic and equatorial Pacific benthonic isotopic record; B: Lea et al. 2002, based on foraminif-eral Mg/Ca and planktonic oxygen isotopes; C: Shackleton 2000, based oxygen isotope data from equatorial Pacific (V19-30) and Vostock air oxygen isotope ratio; D: Siddall et al. (2003), based on Red Sea salinity and oxygen isotope record; E: Cutler et al. 2003, based on scaled data from benthic isotope record of core V19–30.)

White and Schreve (2000) have discussed in detail the evidence for marine conditions around the coast of Britain during the Middle Pleistocene. Evidence for early MIS11 comes from reports of marine stenohaline fish in the Lower Loam at Swanscombe (Irv-ing 1996) and a smelt tooth and saline tolerant ostracods from the lower part of the sequence at the Clacton Holiday Camp site (Bridgland et al. 1999). A later transgression is attested at East Hyde, Essex, where marine molluscs and ostracods occur in the same deposits as the Rhenish suite during Pollen Zone HoIII (Roe and Preece 1995; Roe 1999). Similarly, brackish water ostracods have been recovered at 25 m OD at Marks Tey, towards the top of the long Hoxnian sequence at this parastratotype (Turner 1970; Turner, cited in Ventris 1996). Evidence of a marine influence have also been recorded at Swanscombe, notably brackish molluscs and the vertebra of a bottle-nosed dolphin (*Tursiops truncatus*) reported from Dierden's Pit, Ingress Vale, in deposits equivalent to the Middle Gravels at Barnfield Pit (Sutcliffe 1964; Kerney 1971). The dolphin probably became beached after swimming up the Thames estuary (White and Schreve 2000).

The sea level evidence for MIS9 is more complex. As shown in Figure 3.13 there is no general consensus but most research teams reconstructed high sea level stands during MIS9e, 9c and 9a, with reduced sea levels during MIS9b and possibly also MIS9d. Terrestrial corroboration of these estimates is extremely hard to find, mostly because of the small number of sites firmly attributed to this stage. Meagre evidence exists at only a handful of localities. At Cudmore Grove, Essex, molluscs, diatoms and ostracods from a MIS9 channel fill record a transition from freshwater to marine conditions during an early oak-dominated (Pollen Zone II) sub-stage (Roe 1994; Roe et al. 2009). At Greenlands Pit, Purfleet, (Figure 3.10) high sea-levels were inferred from a laminated silty-clay towards the base of the sequence (at 14 m OD), believed to have been deposited in an intertidal environment (Hollin 1977); similar laminated deposits at Globe Pit, Little Thurrock, were also attributed to estuarine conditions (ibid. and see Text Box 3.8). More recent work at Purfleet (Schreve et al. 2002) failed to recover any evidence that might confirm a strong marine influence in the laminated clays, although an extremely noded morphotype of the brackish water ostracod *Cyprideis torosa* was found in the overlying shelly sand (alongside a freshwater molluscan fauna) suggesting that Purfleet lay right at the limit of tidal influence some distance from the contemporary coastline (Schreve et al. 2002). The same morphotype of *C. torosa* is also found at the top of the early interglacial (Pollen Sub-stage II) sequence at Barling in Essex (Bridgland et al. 2001). Evidence for high sea levels and the onset of marine conditions during sub-zone IIc of an interglacial has also been reported from the Nar valley (Ventris 1996; West 1987). An MIS9 date for this site was favoured by White and Schreve (2000) on a number of stratigraphical grounds, and is supported by a uranium-Series measurement of 317±14 ka BP (Rowe et al. 1997).

Text Box 3.8

GREENLANDS AND BLUELANDS PITS, PURFLEET, ESSEX

Purfleet, Essex, is located in the Lower Thames valley, 20 km east of central London. Since the 1960s, a complex sequence of Pleistocene deposits has been exposed in a series of commercial pits, from east to west: Bluelands Pit, Greenlands Pit, Esso Pit and Botany Pit (see Figures 1 and 2). Investigations at Bluelands and Greenlands were first conducted by Palmer (1975) and latterly by Danielle Schreve and colleagues (Schreve et al. 2002).

The Purfleet deposits are now widely interpreted as representing an abandoned meander loop of the main River Thames (Bridgland 1994; Schreve et al. 2002), contradicting earlier suggestions that they were laid down by the tributary Mar Dyke, which joins the Thames at Purfleet (Wymer 1968, 1985; Palmer 1975; Gibbard 1994). On lithological and biostratigraphical grounds, they have been correlated with the Corbets Tey/Lynch Hill Formation, spanning MIS10–9–8

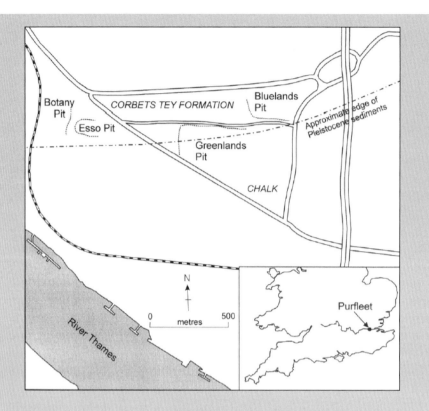

FIGURE 1
Map showing location of the main pits in the Purfleet area. (After White and Ashton 2003.)

FIGURE 2
Section through the deposits at Greenland's Pit, Purfleet from the 1996 excavations. The photograph shows the middle of the sequence. (Photo courtesy Danielle Schreve.)

Text Box 3.8

(Bridgland 1994). The MIS9 interglacial is now often informally termed the Purfleet interglacial and the distinctive mammalian suite has been designated the type for the Purfleet MAZ (Schreve 2001a and b; Schreve et al. 2002). The sequence at Greenlands and Bluelands Pits reveals the edge of a substantial river channel, up to 1 km wide and 5 m deep, flowing adjacent to a steeply sloping river cliff cut in Chalk. The deposits are tripartite, with three broadly upwardly-fining sequences, and the archaeology they contain is amongst the most interesting and complex within the British Lower Palaeolithic. Each of the main members contains a different archaeological industry, with the top of the sequence heralding the emergence of a new form of core working – the Levallois method (see Chapter 5).

The geological and archaeological sequence at Purfleet can be summarised as follows (after Schreve et al. 2002, see main text for a more detailed discussion of the environments and landscapes of Purfleet).

Table 1 Summary of the sequence at Greenlands and Bluelands Pits, Purfleet, showing geology, archaeology and inferred environment. (After Schreve et al. 2002.)

Member/Beds	Thickness	Archaeology	Environment
Botany Member			
8. Botany gravel	2 m	Levallois	Cold
Purfleet or Botany Member			
7. Grey-brown silty clay	<0.75 m		Temperate
6. Bluelands gravel	Up to 6 m	Acheulean	Cold
Purfleet Member			
5. Greenlands shell bed	Up to 2 m		Temperate. Contains an abundance of temperate shells, most articulated in life-position, as well as thermophilous fish and an interglacial mammalian fauna. A range of local marshland, woodland and grassland, and slow to fast moving aquatic habitats are indicated, including a weak, brackish influence
4. Laminated silty clay	<0.25 m		Temperate. Possibly tidal sedimentation during high sea levels. Temperate ostracods, some with brackish tolerances. Mosaic open woodland with 70% temperate arboreal pollen including oak, ash, lime, elm and spruce. Remains of green frog suggest mean July temperatures ~15–17°C
Little Thurrock Member			
3. Shelly gravel	<0.75 m	Non-handaxe (cf. Clactonian)	Temperate
2. Little Thurrock gravel	<0.4 m	Non-handaxe (cf. Clactonian)	Cold
1. Angular chalk rubble (Coombe Rock)	1 m	Non-handaxe (cf. Clactonian)	Cold
Brecciated chalk bedrock			

Purfleet is unique in the Thames Valley in having all three putative archaeological industries (Clactonian, Acheulean and Levallois) in stratigraphical

Text Box 3.8

Text Box 3.8

superposition. The non-handaxe assemblage, which derives from Beds 1–3 inclusive, is numerically small,~100 artefacts (cores, hard-hammer flakes and a few scrapers) from several different excavations. Those from the 'coombe rock' are generally in mint condition, while those from the overlying gravels of Beds 2 and 3 tend to show a mixture of preservational states. Their stratigraphic position arguably suggests that these non-handaxe occurrences represent the initial reoccupation of Britain following its abandonment during the height of the MIS10 cold episode. The small sample size led McNabb (2007) to reject the materials from the Little Thurrock Member as representative of a distinct non-handaxe assemblage, although materials have been sampled from a very extensive area and the gravels containing them equate with Bed 1 at the Globe pit, Little Thurrock (see Text Box 3.15) where thousands of similar artefacts were recovered. The Bluelands Gravel (Bed 6) has produced an Acheulean industry comprising handaxes, cores, flakes and flake tools, mostly in fresh to slightly rolled condition, the recent investigations also having produced one handaxe *in situ*, and one out of its original context.

Drainage networks and the fluvial archive

The vast majority of Lower (and Middle) Palaeolithic artefacts from Britain have been recovered from deposits of minor and major rivers – the invaluable 'fluvial archive' (Bridgland 2010). As a result, Palaeolithic archaeology has, quite rightly, been inextricably linked with research into Pleistocene river systems as noted in Chapter 1, a close relationship that has facilitated major advances in our understanding of the chronology, environments and landscapes of hominin occupation, and resulted in some seminal works (Wymer 1968, 1985, 1999, and outputs of *The English Rivers Palaeolithic Survey*; Bridgland 1994; Gibbard 1985, 1994). We here acknowledge this debt, but deliberately keep discussions concerning the nuances and uncertainties of Pleistocene fluvial stratigraphy to a minimum; these can be found in all of the above mentioned references and in major Quaternary journals. As archaeologists first and foremost, we explicitly wish to avoid the common pitfall of turning this book into a scull up and down the Pleistocene history of British waterways, and focus firmly on our main concern – Pleistocene humans: who they were, when they were present and what they did.

The major drainage systems of the early Middle Pleistocene have been described in Chapter 2. Several of these systems were dramatically remodelled or obliterated during the Anglian Glaciation. The Bytham River, which had previously flowed from the Midlands across East Anglia was completely destroyed, and the Thames was diverted from its earlier course around the Vale of St Albans into its modern valley, usurping the route of the River Medway in the process to form the 'Thames–Medway' which flowed through Essex to join the earlier course of the Thames at Clacton (see Bridgland 1994 and Morigi et al. 2011 for summaries of these fluvial histories and Figure 3.14). Keen (Keen et al. 2006; Lang and Keen 2005) suggested that the relative paucity of hominin occupation in the English Midlands following the Anglian resulted from the severing of

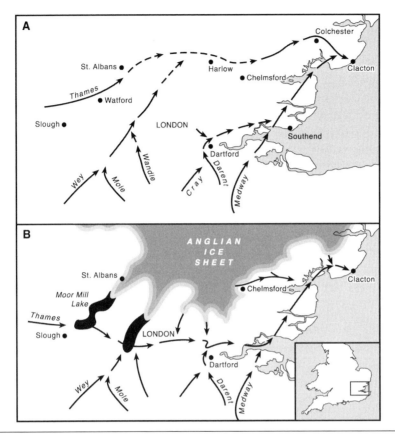

FIGURE 3.14
Map showing (A) the immediately pre-Anglian route of the Thames and (B) the diversion of the Thames during the Anglian Glaciation. (After Bridgland 1994 and courtesy David Bridgland.)

the Bytham 'artery' which had previously facilitated incursions from the east, the focus now shifting instead to the Thames, which remained thereafter a ready dispersal route.

The Anglian glaciation obliterated much of the British drainage patterns of MIS13 and earlier (Wymer 1999). The immediate post-Anglian landscape in those regions north of the maximum ice limits would have been dominated by till plains, peppered with newly exposed glacial landforms such as kettle holes and over-deepened glacial valleys, the latter often forming the basis for new drainage systems (Wymer 1999; Keen et al. 2006). Major Lower Palaeolithic sites, such as Barnham, Elveden, Hoxne and Foxhall Road (Text Box 3.9), were situated around such features (Ashton et al. 1998, 2006; 2008a; White and Plunkett 2004). As this landscape gradually matured, a very familiar drainage network evolved that included Pleistocene versions of all the major extant British rivers, albeit with some major transformations in actual courses and channels over time. A cursory glance at the distribution of Lower Palaeolithic finds shows activity concentrated around these river basins (Figure 3.15) which, for Pleistocene humans, provided concentrations of vital resources and conduits for moving through landscapes; for us this is their key importance.

FOXHALL ROAD, IPSWICH

Foxhall Road is located in eastern Ipswich, on a plateau of Kesgrave gravels at an elevation of ~40 m OD (Figure 1). Artefacts were first discovered by Nina Layard in 1902, and a series of excavations was directed by her from 1902–1905 (Layard 1903, 1904, 1906a, b). The site was re-excavated by Layard and Smith in 1914 (Smith 1921) and by Boswell and Moir in 1921 (Boswell and Moir 1923). Wymer twice attempted to work the site in the 1970s but recovered no artefacts. For many years the site lay under an engineering works, but these were demolished in 2005 in preparation for housing development, facilitating a rescue investigation (Allen et al. 2007). The rediscovery of original records left by Layard and Smith allowed White and Plunkett (2004) to reconstruct the original excavations in fine detail. This box summarises their conclusions.

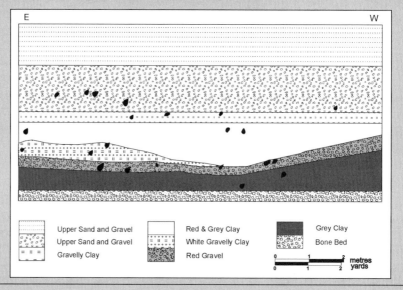

FIGURE 1

Nina Layard's section through the Foxhall Road sequence, showing location of two main archaeological horizons within the Grey Clay and Red Gravel. (After White and Plunkett 2004.)

The Foxhall Road deposits lie within a shallow dry valley, part of the erstwhile course of the Mill River, which can be traced for about 2.5 km (Allen and White 2004). The valley is filled with at least three deep but discontinuous patches of brickearth, separated by shallower sections in which only sands and gravels occur. This originated as a sub-glacial drainage line, with sections significantly over-deepened by sub-glacial scouring that later formed a series of small lakes connected by a small stream.

The site excavated by Layard, Smith and Moir represents one of these overdeepened sections. The area of the brickpit shown on an Ordnance Survey map dated 1904, which provides a rough guide to the shape of the lake, shows a narrow

Text Box 3.9

extension to the north-west (towards the archaeologically rich area) probably along the feeder stream. Coring demonstrated that its base is filled with Anglian till (MIS12), overlain by a series of sands, gravels and silts, some of which may be glacial outwash. The excavated sequence comprised two main series.

The lowers series comprise fossiliferous sands and gravel (the Bone Bed) overlain by up to 4 m of clay, the latter interrupted by a number of gravel seams and smaller pebble partings, notably the Red Gravel. These deposits slope into the depression and probably represent colluvial material from the valley sides that has undergone some aqueous rearrangement. Allen (in Allen and White 2004) suggested that part of the sloping deposits formed a minor delta feature building out from the feeder stream into the deep 'brickearth lake'. The gravel partings testify to higher energy pulses during floods, when material may have been swept off the sides and transported along the channel system.

The upper series of deposits are horizontally bedded and unconformably overlie the sloping beds, which they disturb and truncate at the contact. These consist of up to 0.5 m of Gravelly Clay capped by 2 m of Upper Sand and Gravel, in places heavily cryoturbated. These are interpreted as being deposited by a substantial river system, possibly during cool-cold climatic conditions.

White and Plunkett reconstructed eight separate assemblages, the most important being the near primary context assemblages from the Grey Clay and Red Gravel. The assemblage from the Red Gravel is dominated by small, minimally worked pointed handaxes made on small pebbles and flakes. Roughouts and soft-hammer flakes suggest that handaxe manufacture was taking place on the spot, while the cores and hard-hammer flakes similarly testify to local core reduction. A fairly complete *chaîne opératoire* is represented, although spatially rearranged by hydraulic and slope processes (White and Plunkett 2004).

The Grey Clay assemblage is dominated by well-worked ovate handaxes, several with a twisted profile, and is marked by a lack of débitage. The artefacts occurred in several discrete clusters, one of which might represent *in situ* occupation around a small hearth. The handaxes in this cluster also fall into three groups of technologically and typologically identical handaxes, possibly made by three individuals. White and Plunkett suggested that the Grey Clay assemblage represented imported artefacts used by a small group sitting round a campfire (or other group focus) out of the wind in the lee of the slope.

A small faunal assemblage comprising indeterminate species of elephant, rhinoceros, deer and bovid was recovered from the bone bed (Schreve in White and Plunkett 2004). Environmental samples taken during the 2005 investigations also produced 2 species of cold-climate ostracods from the upper series but 32 samples submitted for palaeobotanical analysis failed to produce any pollen. However, two OSL dates indicate an age range of 416 ka–434 ka BP, suggesting that the archaeology was deposited during the Hoxnian interglacial, as previously suggested from stratigraphical and heavy mineral data (Wymer 1985; Allen and White 2004).

Text Box 3.9

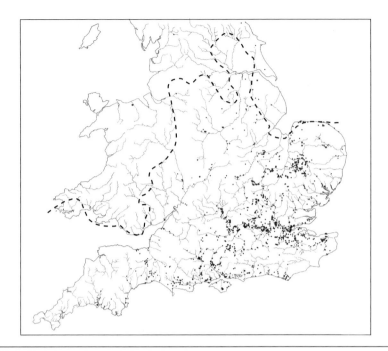

FIGURE 3.15
Derek Roe's distribution map of Lower and Middle Palaeolithic sites and findspots, showing how closely the location of sites mirrors the modern drainage systems and the maximum extent of the last glacial ice advance (dashed line shows extent of the Last Glacial Maximum ice advance: see Chapters 7 and 8). (After Roe 1981.)

HOMININ SETTLEMENT HISTORY DURING THE MIDDLE PLEISTOCENE

A revised model for hominin colonisation, abandonment and residency

Hominins appear to have been present in Britain during MIS13, 11 and 9, and at least the beginning and end of MIS12 and 10, although this settlement was certainly not continuous but rather stochastic and broken. White and Schreve (2000) proposed a three-phase framework for understanding the human settlement of Britain during the late Middle Pleistocene, based on human tolerances and major palaeogeographical and climatic fluctuations. A modified version including isotopic sub-stage variation is offered here (Figure 3.16).

Phase 1: cooling limb peninsula – residency and colonisation

Following the breach of the Dover Strait, increasing global ice volume and concomitant sea level reductions during cooling transitions connected Britain to Europe across the

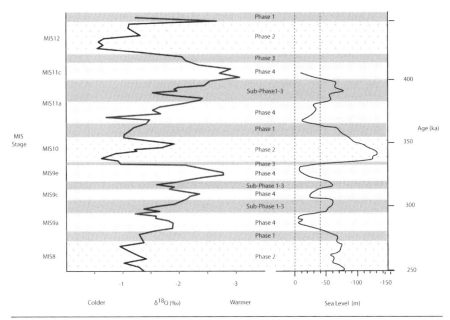

FIGURE 3.16
Schematic diagram showing tentative phases of colonisation, isolation and abandonment during marine isotope sub-stages. (Marine isotope curve data after Bassinot et al. 2004; illustrative sea level curve data derived from Shackleton et al. 2000.)

plains of Doggerland, allowing movement and occupation across the Channel and North Sea basins, barring local barriers. Cool but 'intermediate' conditions (Gamble 1986, 1987; Roebroeks et al. 1992) provided ideal mosaic habitats for human settlement, with rich floral and faunal resources. During such periods one may expect to find incursions of new animals and technologies from Europe.

Phase 2: glacial peninsula – human wasteland

As conditions worsened towards glacial maxima, ice sheets on the British mainland and North Sea basin – and polar desert for hundreds of kilometres beyond – would have rendered Doggerland and Britain totally inhospitable to hominins and most animal and plant life. This climatic threshold would have caused abandonment and local extinction of Britain during each glacial period.

Phase 3: warming transition peninsula – recolonisation

During the warming limbs of each major cycle, deglaciation, climatic amelioration and the re-establishment of animal and plant communities provided renewed opportunities for hominin occupation. Continued low sea levels maintained terrestrial conditions for several millennia (Shackleton et al. 1987 estimate that isolation occurred within ~3000 years), allowing time for humans to recolonise from their cold stage refugia (cf. Dennell et al. 2011 and see discussion below).

Phase 4: interglacial island – residency and isolation

As rising interglacial (and sub-stage) sea levels exceed the depths of the surrounding basins, Britain was cut off from Europe, locking existing hominins in and keeping continental populations out. Local extinction and perturbations in ecology, societies and technology would have profound effects on archaeological signatures during this phase.

Sub-phase 1–3: stadial peninsula

A number of sea level reconstructions (Figure 3.13) reveal that during cold sub-stages global sea levels were sufficiently reduced for Britain to be temporarily reconnected to Europe. Although conditions were far from optimum, it remains to be seen if hominins abandoned Britain during stadials. They may have remained resident, although the possibility remains for new incursions of animals, peoples and technologies, until increased sea levels into warm sub-stages isolated Britain from the continent once more. If Britain was abandoned during stadials, the archaeological record suggests that re-colonisation took place before each subsequent warm sub-stage.

Settlement history: journeys through time

Britain was connected to continental Europe for the entirety of MIS15 and MIS13, with few major obstacles to hominin colonisation. Given the attention it receives, one would be forgiven for believing that the early Middle Pleistocene record in Britain was the richest and most important (e.g. Ashton and Lewis 2002). In reality, this is another case of 'old(er) = (more) interesting', and despite the existence of this continuous connection to the continent the number of British sites known for this period is actually very small. While the corpus has increased dramatically since the first acceptance of pre-Hoxnian (that is, before MIS11) occupation during the 1980s (e.g, Wymer 1988) a recent synthesis by Hosfield (2011) identified just 26 sites and findspots, most of these bearing caveats concerning their age. Early Middle Pleistocene Lower Palaeolithic occupation is not in doubt, but is limited to a handful of informative sites such as Waverley Wood, Boxgrove and High Lodge (see Text Boxes 3.10, 3.11 and 3.12). The evidence for occupation during MIS15 is remarkably poor and based largely on two sites: Waverley Wood, Warwickshire and Westbury Cave, Somerset. The former is now widely regarded as belonging to MIS13 (Keen et al. 2006) and, while the latter may genuinely be of MIS15 age (Andrews et al. 1999; Preece and Parfitt 2000), the evidence it has apparently furnished for hominin presence – namely knapped lithics and modified bones – remains, in our opinion, totally unconvincing (White 2000). It is not considered further in this book and, at present, we find no convincing evidence for a human presence in MIS15, unless one accepts the conclusions of Westaway concerning the age of Pakefield and Happisburgh III, discussed in Chapter 2.

The four main sites discussed above in relation to the human environments of MIS13 all suggest occupation towards the end of each interglacial, when cool continental conditions

WAVERLEY WOOD, BUBBENHALL, WARWICKSHIRE

During the 1980s nine artefacts made of andesite and quartzite were recovered from the base of the Baginton–Lillington Formation at Waverley Wood Farm Quarry, Bubbenhall (situated about 25 km south of Coventry) although only a few were actually recovered *in situ* (Shotton and Wymer 1989; Shotton et al. 1993; Keen et al. 2006; see Figure 1). More recent investigations in a lateral continuation of these deposits at Wood Farm Pit (Keen et al. 2006) yielded a larger collection of 50 quartzite and andesite artefacts and a flint handaxe.

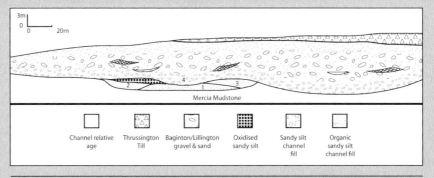

FIGURE 1

Section through the Waverley Wood sequence, showing location of implementiferous channel fills. (Redrawn after Shotton et al. 2003, used with permission from Wiley.)

The sediments at Waverley Wood represent deposition in the upper part of the Bytham River (Keen et al. 2006). The sequence comprises a series of four shallow channels incised into Mercia Mudstone bedrock, representing a single river that meandered over its floodplain depositing sediments in a range of regimes. These channels were infilled with organic interglacial clayey-sand and gravel, assigned to the Waverley Wood Member (Keen et al. 2006), and are overlain by a succession of cooling-cold climate Bytham deposits (assigned to the Thurmaston Member and Brandon Member respectively), capped by the Thrussington Till of MIS12 age (Keen et al. 2006). At Waverley Wood Farm Pit, the organic channel sediments yielded a boreal woodland pollen and fluvial molluscs including *Unio crassus,* which is today restricted to central and south-east Europe (Shotten et al. 1993; Keen et al. 2006). A limited faunal assemblage including northern vole (*Microtus oeconomus),* European pine vole (*Microtus subterraneus*) and water vole (*Arvicola terrestris cantiana*) (Shotton et al. 1993) also suggests cool temperate conditions. Fluvial and terrestrial molluscs showed changing conditions in each channel: the Channel 2 deposits being formed in a slow moving water body, such as a meander cut-off or floodplain pond, Channel 1 being a large,

Text Box 3.10

oxygenated river. A mixture of marshy conditions and drier grassland areas were indicated around Channel 3. Large mammals are rare, the most numerous species being straight-tusked elephant (*Palaeoloxodon antiquus*), and a few horse (*Equus ferus*), bison (*Bison priscus*) and cervids. Keen et al (2006) also recorded *Unio crassus* and *P. antiquus* at Wood Farm Pit, supporting a correlation with the channel deposits at Waverley Wood Farm Pit. Lithostratigraphical and biostratigraphical correlations suggest that the site dates to late MIS13 (Preece and Parfitt 2000), although MIS15 has also been suggested on the basis of aminostratigraphy (Bowen et al. 1989).

The artefacts from Waverley Wood are dominated by non-flint raw materials. The assemblage consists mostly of cores and to a lesser extent handaxes, but flakes are rare. All but four of the 60 known objects are fluvially abraded, suggesting that the assemblage has been transported from its original location, although the relative abrasion rates of non-flint objects has yet to be quantified in Britain, making it difficult to compare with abrasion on flint objects, which has been more fully studied (e.g. Hosfield 1999). The assemblage is dominated by the heavier elements, suggesting that the lighter débitage has been winnowed out, unless collection potential and opportunity is at least in part responsible. The raw materials have also had an impact on typology and technology, quartzite being particularly intractable and some of the objects 'barely recognisable' (Keen et al. 2006). At the other extreme, the andesites have facilitated fine workmanship and John Wymer even described one of the original discoveries as 'beautiful' (Shotton and Wymer 1989; Keen et al. 2006; see Figure 2). Shotton et al. (1993) note the presence of sand polish on the original finds, suggesting that they had lain exposed on the surface for a long period prior to burial.

Text Box 3.10

FIGURE 2
Andesite and lava handaxes from Waverley Wood. (After Keen et al. 2006, used with permission from Wiley.)

Petrological analysis by Shotton on the handaxes found in the 1980s indicated that the andesite originated from the Borrowdale Volcanics of the Lake District, a distance of some 320 km. If hominins were procuring this directly,

Text Box 3.10

then not only is this evidence of extensive transport beyond that general seen in the Lower Palaeolithic, but also that hominins dispersed much further north-west in Britain than presently known (Keen et al. 2006). The possibility that the andesite was obtained from erratics brought into the Midlands by earlier ice advances must also be considered however. Blocks suitable for the manufacture of handaxes – and of Lake District origin – were found at the base of the Thurmaston Member during the most recent investigations. Given that flint could be obtained within much shorter distances simply by following the route of the Bytham River, the possibility that hominins grubbed suitable erratics from the cobble lag at the edge of the channels seems very plausible. There is, however, very limited evidence for flint being introduced into the area prior to the Anglian glaciation (Keen et al. 2006). The nearest source of flint is ~100 km away in the West Midlands, which is at the extreme end of long distance transport and curation as currently understood for the Lower Palaeolithic.

Text Box 3.11

BOXGROVE, WEST SUSSEX

Boxgrove is one of Europe's most important Lower Palaeolithic sites. The several excavated areas that comprise it are located in Amey's Eartham Pit, a large quarry about 5 km northeast of Chichester and 12 km north of the current shoreline of the English Channel. It is situated on the northern edge of the Upper Coastal Plain, where the plain abuts the truncated South Downs. The area is well known for Palaeolithic archaeology, especially along the line of the Westbourne–Arundel (formerly 'Goodwood–Slindon') raised beach (e.g. Curwen 1925; Fowler 1929; Calkin 1934). Exploratory work in the 1970s (Shephard-Thorn and Kellaway 1977; Woodcock 1981) was followed by full-scale excavation from 1983–1996, under the direction of Mark Roberts (e.g. Roberts 1986; Roberts et al. 1997; Roberts and Parfitt 1999; see Figures 1 and 2).

The excavations at Boxgrove have sampled fragments of a Palaeolithic landscape, representing an erstwhile coastal embayment in the South Downs (Figure 3). The Pleistocene sediments (Roberts 1999) rest on a marine platform bounded to the north by a chalk cliff, created by a Middle Pleistocene high sea-level event that encroached northwards over the Lower Coastal Plain. Associated with this event are near-shore marine deposits, forming a localised storm beach accumulation (2) and the more widespread Slindon Sands (3). These are overlain by the lagoonal/intertidal deposits of the Slindon Silts (4a–b), marking a marine regression. Towards the cliff in Quarry 1/B, a carbonate-rich sediment (4d) accumulated in a spring-fed pool in the top of the silts, with which they are probably contemporaneous. At the end of the lagoonal phase, a soil developed on the surface of the silts (4c), marking the beginning of fully terrestrial conditions (ibid.). Subsequent sedimentation came from the downland block to the north. Freshwater flooding heralded the onset of alder carr (5), followed by the erosion of soils from the

Text Box 3.11

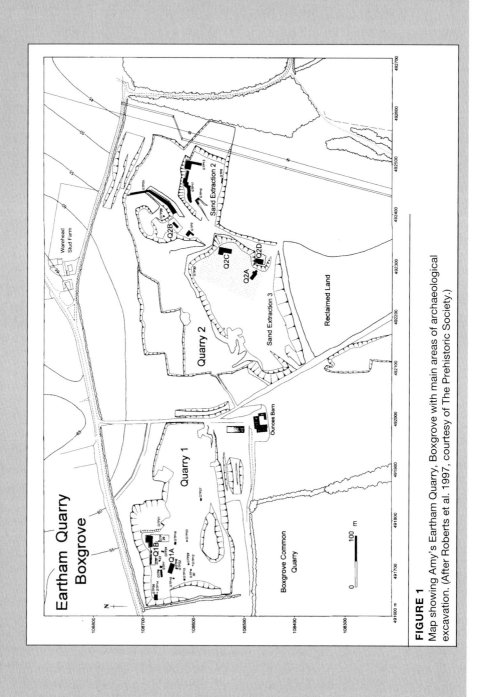

FIGURE 1
Map showing Amy's Eartham Quarry, Boxgrove with main areas of archaeological excavation. (After Roberts et al. 1997, courtesy of The Prehistoric Society.)

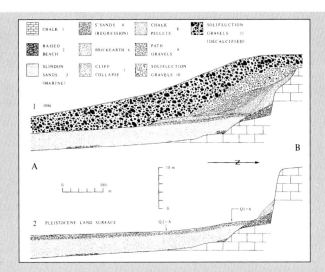

FIGURE 2
Section through the Boxgrove sequence. (After Roberts 1986, courtesy of The Prehistoric Society.)

downland and cliff to form a brickearth (6). Chalk rubble associated with a cliff collapse (7) occurs towards the northern margin, near the storm beach. At the top of the sequence lies a series of gravels (9–11), mass-movement deposits derived from the adjacent South Downs and emplaced under cold climate conditions.

A sparse pollen assemblage (possibly residual) from Bed 5 indicates the presence of boreal coniferous forest close to the site, predominately of pine, spruce and fir (Roberts 1986; Roberts and Parfitt 1999). These conditions are likely to have prevailed on the downland, but on the coastal plain foraminifera, molluscs and soil micromorphology suggest more open, marshy conditions (Whittaker 1999; Preece and Bates 1999; MacPhail 1999). The faunal assemblage from units 4–5 also indicates temperate conditions and includes horse (*Equus ferus*), water vole (*Arvicola terrestris cantiana*), rabbit (*Oryctolagus cuniculus*), roe deer (*Capreolus capreolus*), wild boar (*Sus scrofa*) fallow deer (*Dama dama*), two species of giant deer (*M. dawkinsi* and *Megaloceros* cf. *verticornis*) and two species of extinct rhinoceros, *S. hundsheimensis* and one currently undescribed (Parfitt 1999). Together, these mammals indicate a mosaic of vegetational conditions in the area, including grassland, scrub and mixed woodland. Large carnivores were also present, including wolf (*Canis lupis*), hyaena (*Crocuta crocuta*), as well as the extinct (and largely vegetarian) cave bear *Ursus deningeri*. Fish, amphibians, wildfowl and reptiles, also indicate open grassland with damp areas and small ponds. Mammals from the top of the sequence show a shift towards cold-adapted species, including Norway lemming (*Lemmus lemmus*).

In situ artefacts have been recovered throughout the sequence. Evidence of occupation during the marine phase is limited to a few flakes, handaxes and butchered red deer bones from GTP 13 (Roberts 1999). Unit 4a–4d by

Text Box 3.11

FIGURE 3
Excavations in progress.

contrast has produced tens of thousands of artefacts. Possible *in situ* remains also occur in the cliff collapse (7). Particularly rich concentrations of artefacts were recovered from the silty sediments associated with the water hole. Material has also been found in units 7–10, most of it derived, although refitting material was recovered in Bed 11, perhaps suggesting continued occupation into the early Anglian glaciations, although the possibility that this has moved *en mass* from earlier scatters above the cliff must be considered (Roberts 1999, 383).

The archaeology generally consists of extensive scatters of handaxes (dominated by ovate and limande forms, usually with tranchet tips) and handaxe manufacturing débitage (Austin et al. 1999; Roberts 1999; see Figure 4). Much of the lithic material appears to be *in situ* and extensive refitting groups have been reconstructed (Bergman et al. 1987; Bergman and Roberts 1988; Austin et al. 1999; Roberts 1999). In some cases there is a spatial (and presumably temporal) separation between different phases of production (e.g. Q1/B), in others almost whole sequences occur together (e.g. Q1/A). In Q1/A handaxes appear to have been made outside the excavated areas and imported to the site, whereas at GTP 17 handaxes were made on the spot from whole nodules and then removed. Flake tools and cores are rare, the latter often being reused, end-shocked bifaces (Roberts 1990). The archaeology in the cliff collapse of Unit 7 is mostly large, hard-hammer cortical flakes and biface roughouts (Roberts 1986) suggesting that material was tested and roughed out at the cliff, with selected flints and roughouts being transported up to 400m away from the cliff for finishing. The artefact inventory includes several stone- and bone-hammers and the 1995 excavations also yielded a well-used *antler* soft-hammer. The most celebrated finds from Boxgrove are the tibia and two lower front incisors of *Homo* cf. *heidelbergensis* (Roberts et al. 1994; Hillson et al. 2010).

In several cases *in situ* lithics are associated with butchered animal remains, including those of horse and rhinoceros. Roberts (1996a and b) interprets Boxgrove as a hunting ground on a coastal grassland plain, to which hominins repeatedly went to exploit the rich combination of herd animals, freshwater and raw materials.

Boxgrove contains a Cromerian interglacial fauna which includes the zone fossil *Megaloceros dawkinsi,* and a number of other species (including *Sorex savini, S. runtonensis, Ursus deningeri* and *Pliomys episcopalis)* which do not survive the Anglian and are absent from sites such as Swanscombe and Barnham (Roberts et al. 1994; Parfitt 1998a). A date towards the end of MIS13 is now widely accepted, despite the huge range (MIS 6–13) suggested by various scientific dating techniques (Roberts and Parfitt 1999).

FIGURE 4
In situ knapping scatter from Q1/A, and refitted reduction sequence 492 from Boxgrove. (Courtesy of Matt Pope.)

HIGH LODGE, MILDENHALL, SUFFOLK

High Lodge is located 3 km from Mildenhall, Suffolk, on the western side of a degraded chalk escarpment. It has been a focus of Palaeolithic research since the 1860s and has a long history of controversy regarding its geology and archaeology (Evans 1872; Whitaker et al. 1891; Sturge 1911; Harrison 1938; Paterson 1942). Excavations were conducted by J.E. Marr and R.A. Smith in the 1920s (Marr et al. 1921; Smith 1926) and by the British Museum from 1962–8 and in 1988 (Ashton et al. 1992b).

The Quaternary geology of the site is extremely complex (see Figure 1). The British Museum excavations divided the sequence into two main series:

1   The High Lodge Series – pre-Anglian floodplain clayey-silts and sands deposited by the extinct Bytham River.
2   Mildenhall Series – tills, sands and gravels from Anglian glaciofluvial activity.

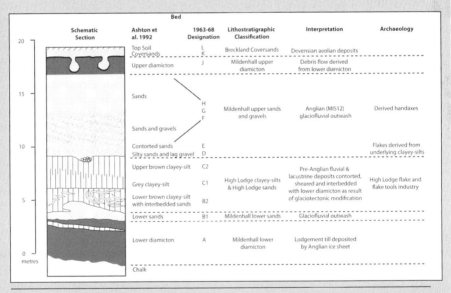

FIGURE 1
Schematic section through the High Lodge sequence, showing stratigraphical units, interpretation and archaeology. (After Ashton et al. 1992 © Trustees of the British Museum.)

These two series are sandwiched between two tills (the Mildenhall Upper and Lower diamictons) both equated lithologically with the Anglian Lowestoft Till (MIS12). To explain this, Lewis (1992) suggested that Anglian ice entrained frozen blocks of the pre-Anglian implementiferous silts and redeposited them on top of the Lower Diamicton, thus inverting the sequence and deforming the

Text Box 3.12

fluvial sediments. Following this, the retreat of the ice resulted in the deposition of the Mildenhall glaciofluvial sands and gravels over the clayey-silts. Periglacial debris flow then caused upslope exposures of the Lower diamicton to flow downhill and cover the glaciofluvial deposits. The two tills are therefore the product of a single glaciation.

The Mildenhall series were therefore laid down in an active proglacial environment. The clayey-silts of the High Lodge series, though, were deposited under interglacial conditions. Pollen and algal microfossil analysis suggested a marshy/aquatic regime with slow flowing freshwater, surrounded by boreal spruce and pine forest (Hunt 1992), and insect remains indicated a mean July temperature of 13–15° C, slightly colder than at present (Coope 2006). The sparse mammalian fauna added little to this picture, comprising only five taxa: straight-tusked elephant (*Palaeoloxodon antiquus*), rhino (*Dicerorhinus etruscus*), horse (*Equus ferus*), deer and large bovids (Stuart 1992).

Two series of artefacts are present at High Lodge:

1 Scrapers, denticulates, flakes and cores recovered from the High Lodge clayey-silts, some of which refit, suggest these occur *in situ* within the clays, even if the clays themselves have been relocated.
2 Slightly derived handaxes from the Mildenhall glaciofluvial sands, generally in fresh condition and dominated by ovates and cordates.

The classic High Lodge scraper industry is an enigmatic group that has never conformed to any traditional framework (see Figure 2). This is reflected in a long history of interpretation and reinterpretation, at times seen as Mousterian (Collins 1969; Coulson 1990), Clactonian (Breuil 1932; King and Oakley 1936), Acheulean (Bordes 1984), the missing link between the Mousterian and Clactonian (Oakley and Leakey 1937) or between the Clactonian and Acheulean (Oakley 1949; Paterson and Fagg 1940). While no handaxes are

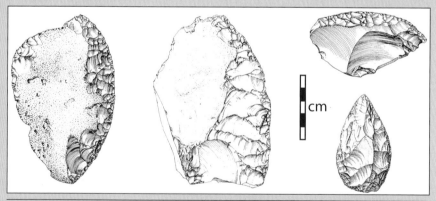

FIGURE 2
A selection of scrapers from the classic High Lodge Industry. (After Ashton et al. 1992 © Trustees of the British Museum.)

Text Box 3.12

certainly associated with the 'classic' High Lodge industry there are reports that such did exist (Wymer 1985). A possible handaxe and handaxe-thinning flake were recovered by the British Museum in association with the flake industry and handaxes and thinning flakes were found in the lowest stratum of the Mildenhall glaciofluvial sands (Ashton 1992, 162).

Recent interpretations (Cook et al. 1991; McNabb and Ashton 1995) suggests that the handaxes were originally contained within the High Lodge clayey-silts. The deposits containing them were also entrained *en masse* by the Anglian Ice but, unlike those containing the flake industry, did not survive intact. This interpretation is consistent with the condition of the artefacts which suggests that they have not been moved far but are certainly not *in situ.* Furthermore, the handaxes cannot be contemporary with the sedimentation which took place in front of a retreating ice sheet. Another important pre-Anglian site occurs only 2 km away at Warren Hill where a very rich handaxe assemblage has been found in deposits now believed to form part of the Bytham river system (Wymer et al. 1991).

prevailed. There is currently no evidence that hominins were present during the earlier climatic optima, suggesting that each represents a relatively brief pulse of occupation, perhaps the final terminus of the 'wave' of European colonisation ~600–500 ka BP (cf. Roebroeks 2006). Furthermore, despite claims to the contrary (Ashton and Lewis 2002), the quantity of artefacts within the Thames gravels of MIS12 age does not suggest dense populations in the Thames valley during MIS13 or MIS12. Indeed, the earlier MIS12 Winter Hill gravel is famously barren. A few isolated handaxes have been found on the surface of the Winter Hill and equivalent higher level gravels in Oxfordshire (at Kidmore End and between Gallowstree Common and Sonning Common), but as these are surface finds they could potentially date to any period within the Lower Palaeolithic (Wymer 1999, 174). The earliest secure artefacts come from the post-diversion Black Park gravel of late MIS12 age, with notable concentrations in the abandoned 'Ancient Channel' between Caversham and Henley (Wymer 1968, 1999), which includes several prolific sites at Highlands Farm Pit, Kennyland's and Farthingworth Green. The critical point is that artefacts derived from MIS13 (or earlier) land surfaces would be expected to have been incorporated into both the Winter Hill and Black Park terraces, leading Wymer to suggest that the material in the Ancient Channel and other Black Park gravels belongs to a hypothesised mid-MIS12 interstadial during which conditions became temporarily suitable for hominin occupation.

Evidence that hominins persisted into the early Anglian is also found in Unit 8 of the Eartham Formation at Boxgrove (Roberts 1999), associated with a warmer interstadial. Refitting artefacts were associated with a sparse mammalian fauna including red deer, bison and possibly horse, and a poorly humic soil with evidence of earthworm activity and rooting, suggestive of plant growth during an interstadial (MacPhail 1999). Human presence well into MIS12 has also been proposed on the basis of refitting artefacts from the 'head' gravel of unit 11, associated with mass-movement under periglacial conditions (Roberts 1999). These too show some evidence of short-lived soil formation with a slight amelioration in climate. Contrasts in handaxe shape between Unit 11 and the underlying beds were argued to reflect changes in raw materials caused by the burial of the chalk cliff. This might also suggest a brief return of hominins to England during an MIS12 interstadial, although whether the refitting archaeology here actually attests to mid-Anglian occupation or is in fact material moved *en masse* from interglacial deposits on the downland block and incorporated more or less intact into the cold climate gravels remains unclear (Roberts 1999, 384)

The record from MIS11 is far richer with numerous artefact accumulations within the fluvial archive, such as the Boyn Hill Terrace of the Thames, as well as a number of well-preserved primary context sites yielding valuable technological and behavioural data (see for example Wymer 1999). Figure 3.16 shows the modified White and Schreve phases plotted against the Indian Ocean core MD900963 (Bassinot et al. 1994) and Shackleton's (2000) reconstruction of sea levels for the past 450 ka. Some temporal mismatches aside (it should be remembered that Shackleton's reconstruction is just one of a number of alternative schemes and is used here simply for illustrative purposes), this suggests that most of MIS11 would have been ideal for hominin colonisation and settlement, with a generally warm climate (see Chapter 2) and prolonged terrestrial links to continental Europe separated by periods of insularity. We have not attempted to overlay key archaeological sites over this graph, as there is no agreed correlation between key sequences, but a tentative scheme is presented in Figure 3.16 and discussed below. As a caveat to these, the realisation that many of our classic sequences may pertain only to MIS11c (Ashton et al. 2008a), makes it vital to acknowledge that such correlations are predicated on the assumption of a single vegetation succession and one high sea level event, neither of which is supported by the oxygen isotope record or the same sea level reconstructions. We believe that some of these correlations may not be as secure as previously thought. Of what, for example, do the molluscan fauna and pollen of MIS11a actually consist? It is unclear whether one might expect a full forest succession and how this might differ from a similar phase of MIS11c. If there were really were two phases of high sea level, can one extrapolate the pollen evidence from one set of estuarine beds to another devoid of pollen? How secure can one be projecting the pollen zonation between sites based on a similarity in their molluscs? Equally, there is currently little agreement in sub-stage variation between MIS11 mammalian fauna (compare Schreve 2001a and b with Ashton et al. 2008a).

The evidence we do have, however, appears to show that, as expected from the model, hominins were present more or less 'throughout' MIS11 (that is to say during several parts of it). The Lower Gravels at Swanscombe, and Golf Course Site at Clacton attest to a Late MIS12/early MIS11 presence, during pollen zones Ian, HoI and IIa (Conway et al. 1996; Singer et al 1973; Ashton et al 2008a; but see McNabb 2007 who disputes this). Hominins were present in the later Phase I and Phase II deposits at Swanscombe (Lower Loam, Lower Middle Gravel, Upper Middle Gravel) during pollen zones HoIIb to HoII, and at Beeches Pit during HoIII–IV. According to Ashton et al. (2008a), these classic sequences – along with the lacustrine deposits at the Hoxnian stratotype at Hoxne – represent only the first sub-stage of the MIS11 interglacial (MIS11c) during which hominin presence is a fairly constant feature.[3] Terrestrial sequences belonging to MIS11b and MIS11a may therefore be found in the Phase III deposits at Swanscombe and Beds C–A at Hoxne (Ashton et al. 2008a). Primary context artefacts are found in the Upper Loams at the former (and its local correlates at Wansunt Pit, for example; White et al. 1995) and in the lower and upper industries of Beds A2iii and A2ii in the later (Ashton et al. 2008a), meaning hominins were present during both warm sub-stages at least. Thus, several extensive phases of access and occupation have left a very rich record (cf. Ashton and Lewis 2002).

Evidence of human occupation in the MIS9 archive is remarkably rich – the Lynch Hill Terrace of the Middle Thames alone boasts over 192 sites and findspots, and the equivalent terraces of the Solent system are equally well endowed (Wymer 1988, 1992, 1996a, 1999; Bridgland 1994; Hosfield 1999; Ashton and Lewis 2002; Ashton and Hosfield 2009). Most of these represent single find spots or derived assemblages, although some areas have yielded remarkable quantities of finds. One noteworthy example is the stretch between Cookham and Maidenhead on the right bank of the Thames and Burnham and Farnham Royal on the left bank, which is one of the most the prolific areas for Acheulean finds anywhere in Britain (over 2000 handaxes and other artefacts are known) and includes the important sites at Cannoncourt Farm Pit at Furze Platt and Bakers Farm Pit at Farnham Royal (Wymer 1968; Cranshaw 1983). Based on these statistics, Wymer (1999) suggested that human populations may have been at their greatest during this period, although the extent of quarrying, urbanisation and the presence of several avid collectors – Lewellyn Treacher and Alan Lacaille amongst them – suggests that the abundance of finds may be to an extent a product of collection opportunity and bias (cf. Ashton and Lewis 2002). Only five key sites can be identified for this period amongst the many 'dredgers' (Gamble 1996) – Wolvercote Channel, Stoke Newington, Cuxton, Globe Pitt at Little Thurrock and Purfleet (see Text Boxes 3.13, 3.7, 3.14, 3.15 and 3.8 respectively).

Figure 3.13 and 3.16 show that Britain may have been an island on three separate occasions during MIS9 (the warm sub-stages) with reconnection to Europe occurring during the intervening cold sub-stages. A paucity of suitably long sequences, and relatively recent acceptance of a distinct MIS9 interglacial in the terrestrial record (Bridgland 1994;

Text Box 3.13

WOLVERCOTE CHANNEL, OXFORDSHIRE

The Wolvercote Channel is situated approximately 3 km north of Oxford, on the west bank of the Upper Thames, south of its confluence with the River Cherwell. Discovered during brick-making operations around the turn of the last century, it consisted of a wide, 4.5 m deep channel infilled with calcareous sandy gravel and laminated silty clays, cut into Wolvercote Terrace gravels overlying Oxford Clay (see Figure 1). No excavations have ever been conducted into the channel, although several detailed examinations of the deposits were undertaken prior to the closure of the brickpit in the 1930s (e.g. Bell 1894, 1904; Sandford 1924, 1926). Subsequent attempts to relocate the sediments have been unsuccessful (Bridgland and Harding 1986) although a temporary exposure was opened on the eastern edge of the pit during the mid-1980s (Briggs et al. 1985; Tyldesley 1986b).

The gravel at the base of the channel contained artefacts and a temperate mammalian fauna comprising straight-tusked elephant (*Palaeoloxodon antiquus*), bear

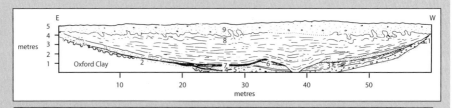

FIGURE 1
Section through the Wolvercote sequence. (Redrawn after Sandford 1924.)

(*Ursus* sp.), horse (*Equus ferus*), narrow-nosed rhinoceros (*Stephanorhinus hemi-toechus*), red deer (*Cervus elaphus*), aurochs (*Bos primigenius*) and possibly bison (Sandford 1924; Schreve 1997). Above these were a series of cross-bedded sand and gravels, sandwiched between two iron pans; the upper iron pan is followed by a break in deposition, represented by an erosion surface. Overlying this surface is the main silty-clay infill of the channel, indicating a very low-energy regime. At the base of these silty-clays, Bell (1904) identified a peat horizon, which yielded 30 species of flowering plants, 37 species of moss (Bell 1904; Duigan 1956), and 5 species of beetles (Blair 1923) all indicating cool temperate conditions. Pollen (probably) from the laminated silty-clay also showed a change from pine-dominated forest to more open conditions (Briggs et al. 1985). Overall, the sequence represents the transition from pine woodland to open temperate conditions during a period of climatic cooling, probably towards the end of an interglacial.

The majority of the artefacts from the Wolvercote Channel derive from the basal gravel or the overlying cross-bedded gravels. Some show considerable iron staining, and were most probably obtained from one of the iron pans. There is little evidence of human presence following the erosion event at the top of the upper iron pan, during which time the climate gradually deteriorated. There is some question over the precise number of artefacts from the Channel (cf. Roe 1981; Tyldesley 1986a), although an estimate of ~200 pieces, including 78 bifaces and 7 flake tools, may not be far wide of the mark (Tyldesley 1986b). Preservation is good with 86% of the surviving material being in fresh or mint condition. Most of the artefacts are made of flint although quartzite and greywacke was also used.

The handaxes from Wolvercote are predominantly pointed in planform, with a small sub-group of 'slipper-shaped', plano-convex pieces (see Figure 2). These exhibit differential treatment of the two worked faces – the flat surface is nearly always knapped first, and always far less intensively than the domed face. Roe (1968a) considered the Wolvercote handaxes to be so distinctive that he assigned them to their own sub-group, which he

Text Box 3.13

compared with the European Micoquian. On purely typological grounds he believed them to belong to MIS7 or 5e (Roe 1994). This is much younger than the MIS9 age for the Wolvercote Channel deposits suggested by Bridgland (1994) and accepted here. Wymer (1968) was less concerned with the plano-convex pieces and compared the whole assemblage to the Middle Gravels at Swanscombe, a far more realistic assessment of the Wolvercote Channel assemblage which, it must be said, actually contains ~90% unremarkable pointed handaxes.

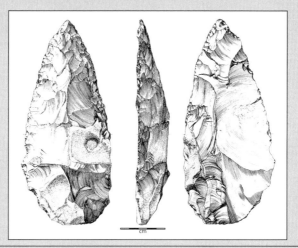

FIGURE 2
The classic Wolvercote-style handaxe. (After Roe 1981.)

Tyldesley (1986b) thought that the Wolvercote-type handaxes might all have been produced by a single knapper and could easily have been made in a single day given access to enough suitable flint. Others, however, have explained the character of these handaxes in the context of the paucity of flint in the Upper Thames. White (1998a) noted that many of the plano-convex handaxes had been made on flakes or naturally flat plaquettes, and might therefore simply represent the careful crafting of these forms out a few pieces of suitable local flint. Ashton (2001), however, proposed that they had been selectively transported into the Upper Thames from the flint-rich regions to the south-east. Large handaxes were preferentially transported, while weight considerations may help explain the plano-convexity (being half the weight of a biconvex handaxe). Flakes and plaquettes may have been selected deliberately to allow this. Reworking of the tips as they became blunt or broken through use could also explain the unique Wolvercote shape (Ashton 2001).

Text Box 3.13

CUXTON, KENT

The rich source of Palaeolithic artefacts at Cuxton, Kent, has been known since at least 1889 (Payne 1893, cited in Tester 1965). It has been the subject of three controlled excavations: by P.J. Tester at the Rectory Site between 1962 and 1963 (Tester 1965), by John Cruse (on behalf of the Maidstone Area Archaeology Group) on the southern side of the Rochester Road in 1984 (Cruse 1987), and by the Medway Valley Palaeolithic Project (MVPP) in 2005 (Wenban-Smith 2006).

Cuxton lies on the west bank of the River Medway, in a gap cut by the river through the North Downs. The underlying solid geology is Middle Chalk containing isolated flints and occasional bands of flint, with flint-rich Upper Chalk cropping out less than a mile to the west. The site itself lies in a small remnant of Medway terrace gravel, situated on a chalk spur between the Medway and a tributary valley once occupied by a north-west flowing stream (Wenban-Smith 2006).

Tester's excavations revealed a very thin Pleistocene sequence at the site (see Figure 1): 0.5 m of sand and gravel lying on Chalk and chalk breccia, overlain by 0.6 m of loam capped by chalk rubble. Cruse's excavations exposed a deeper sequence of over 3 m of fluvial sand and gravel, again lying on brecciated chalk; apparently Tester's trenches had exposed only the top feather edge of the terrace sequence. The MVPP trench at 21 Rochester Road, ~40 m south-west of Cruse's trench, also produce a very shallow sequence just 1 m deep, basically comprising three cycles of gravel and cross-bedded sands.

The terrace deposits at Cuxton have a surface height of ~18.5 m OD but unfortunately the site lies in a part of the valley where correlation with terrace deposits in the Upper and Lower Medway is difficult, and where altitude is a poor guide. Dines et al. (1954) placed Cuxton on the second terrace. Bridgland (in Cruse 1987) suggested that they were part of the Binney Gravel, the Medway equivalent of the Devensian Taplow/Kempton Park Formation, which would imply that the archaeology is all derived from older deposits. In later projections of the Medway terraces, Bridgland (1996) concluded that Cuxton actually lies on Terrace No. 3, which he suggested might correlate with either the Lynch Hill/Corbets Tey or Taplow/Mucking Formations of the Thames (MIS 10/9/8 or 8/7/6, respectively). As the Cuxton sequence represents a degraded and landscaped remnant (cf. Tester 1965, 33), the former age is preferred (D.R. Bridgland, pers. comm.). Recent OSL dates obtained by the MVPP suggest that the deposits they dated belong to MIS8 (Francis Wenban-Smith, pers. comm. 2011), in accordance with Bridgland's correlations.

Tester's excavations in the highest part of the outcrop produced a large Acheulean assemblage (657 artefacts, including 199 handaxes) mostly from the gravel and in fresh condition. Cruse's excavations in a deeper-channel exposure identified two separate artefact groups: a non-handaxe assemblage (n = 118) from the lower gravel and a handaxe assemblage (n = 102) from the upper gravel, separated by a depositional hiatus (Callow, in Cruse 1987). The latter is probably the lateral equivalent of Tester's gravel (see Cruse 1987, Figure 2.3).

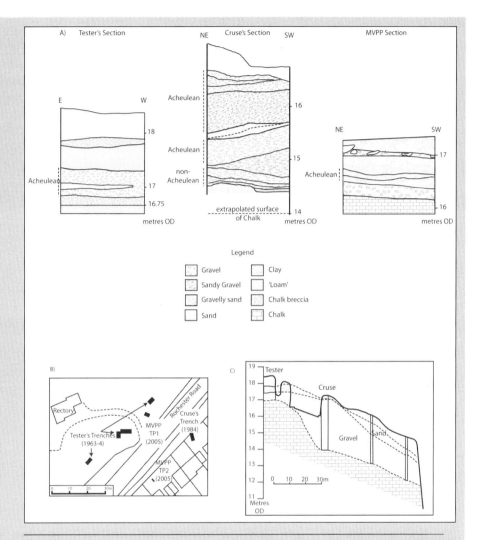

FIGURE 1
(a) Sections through the Cuxton deposits as recorded by Tester (1961), Cruse (1987) and the MVPP (Wenban-Smith 2004) (b) Location map showing position of various excavations (c) Longitudinal Section showing the positions of Tester's and Cruse's sections.

Wenban-Smith et al. recovered a further 20 handaxes from their trench (see Figure 2). The different locations of these trenches in relation to the terrace formation may explain the differences in the archaeology each contains, the shallow sequences towards the edge of the terrace containing a conflated sequence that conceals the separation of handaxe and non-handaxe assemblages found in Cruse's section. Tester (1965, 38) described the handaxe assemblage as being dominated by 'roughly made, pointed hand-axes with thick, crust covered butts', although some ovates and cleavers were present. This impression was confirmed by Roe (1968a) in his metrical analysis of 160 handaxes from Tester's

Text Box 3.14

Text Box 3.14

excavations, which showed a tendency towards elongated pointed forms (56.9%). He duly placed it in his Pointed Tradition, Group I (with cleavers). The MVPP excavations uncovered the second largest handaxe ever found in Britain (307 mm long), which Wenban-Smith has described as 'flamboyant'! Six proto-Levallois cores and flakes were reported by Tester (1965) from the Rectory Site, although this was questioned by Callow (in Cruse 1987). Organic preservation was poor throughout.

FIGURE 2
A very large and elegant ficron handaxe from Cuxton, discovered during the MVPP 2005 excavation. The piece is 307 mm long, making it the second largest handaxe ever found in Britain. (Courtesy of Francis Wenban-Smith.)

Text Box 3.15

GLOBE PIT, LITTLE THURROCK, ESSEX

Globe Pit, Little Thurrock is situated on the north side of the Thames at a lower terrace level than Swanscombe. It has been known as a source of Palaeolithic artefacts from the late nineteenth century (Spurrell 1892; Smith 1894), from which time the deposits have been the subject of numerous investigations (e.g. Kennard 1904, 1916; King and Oakley 1936; Oakley and Leakey 1937; West 1969; Hollin 1977; Bridgland 1994; Conway 1996). Archaeological excavations were carried out in 1954 by John Wymer (Wymer 1957), in 1961 by Andrew Snelling (Snelling 1964) and in 1983 by Phil Harding (Bridgland and Harding 1993). Much controversy has surrounded the age of Little Thurrock, particularly the reconciliation of its position in the Thames terrace staircase with its contained archaeology. As it contains a non-handaxe industry similar to that from the Lower Gravels at Swanscombe it should, according to cultural interpretations of the twentieth century, be of the same age (King and Oakley 1936; Oakley and Leakey 1937).

The basic sequence comprises ~1 m basal gravel (Beds 1 and 2), overlain by ~5 m brickearth (Bed 4), and capped by an upper sand and gravel (Bed 5; see Figure 1). The basal sand and gravel deposits are interpreted as either a single fluvial aggradation over two benches, the higher at 15 m OD on Thanet Sand and the lower at 6 m OD on Chalk (Bridgland and Harding 1993; Bridgland 1994); or two separate gravels (the higher = Bed 1, the lower = Bed 2), separated by a period of downcutting and solifluction (Bed 3). On the basis of altitude and local correlation, the deposits have most recently been assigned to the Lynch Hill/Corbets Tey Formation, correlated with late MIS10 and MIS9 (Bridgland and Harding, 1993; Bridgland, 1994). Although no faunal remains have been recovered from Globe Pit, the brickearths represent the lateral continuation of the fossiliferous brickearths at Grays

Thurrock, while the gravels have been equated with the Little Thurrock member at Purfleet (both of which have been attributed to MIS9; Schreve 1997, 2001a and b; Schreve et al. 2002). Aminostratigraphy placed this site in MIS11 (Bowen et al. 1989), clearly conflicting with other lines of evidence. A very poor pollen record from the site was able to demonstrate only temperate conditions, with a preponderance of tree pollen (mostly oak and pine) and grasses (West 1969).

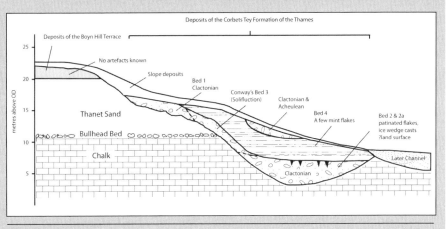

FIGURE 1

Section through the Globe Pit sequence, showing the relationship between the different beds and their contained archaeology. (After White 2000, modified after Wymer 1985 and incorporating data from Bridgland 1994 and Conway 1996.)

Clactonian flakes, cores and flake tools were recovered in primary context from Bed I at Globe Pit. Bed 2 also yielded flakes and cores, as well as two non-classic handaxes from Bed 2a. It has been claimed that Acheulean material was present in the gravel overlying the brickearth (Kennard 1916; Wymer 1985; Bridgland and Harding 1993). There is still some confusion regarding the relationship between Beds 1 and 2 that has important connotations for our understanding of the site's archaeology. Bridgland (1994; Bridgland and Harding 1993 and pers. comm. to MJW 1999) considered them to be part of the same gravel, but noted that the top of Bed 2 (2a) was marked by a heavily cemented and iron-panned erosional surface, making the relationship between the archaeology in Bed 1 and in the top of Bed 2 dubious. Conway (1996; cf. Wymer 1985) saw them as two discrete units separated by a period of erosion and subsequent slope degradation, in which case the material from Bed 2 may represent a mixture of older material derived from Bed 1 and younger material in primary context. In either case the material from Bed 2a is probably unrelated to the other archaeology. Most of the existing material appears to have been obtained from Bed 1 (the Wymer, Snelling and Harding collections; cf. Conway 1996).

Schreve 1997, 2001a and b; Schreve et al. 2002; Roe et al. 2009), means that what archaeology we have usually floats rather unconstrained in MIS9 time. However, the pits at Purfleet (Text Box 3.8) may preserve a more or less continuous record through MIS9, possibly showing that humans were present on at least three occasions during the beginning, middle and end of the interglacial, each time it seems with a different technological repertoire (White 2000; Schreve et al. 2002). This is again exactly what one would expect from the model of colonisation, residency and extinction we outlined above, with developments on Britain representing both *in situ* cultural evolution as well as contact and mixing with hominin populations on the continent.

Arks and lifeboats

The White and Schreve model conforms to the cogent reminder by Dennell et al. (2011) that Pleistocene hominins in Europe evolved under conditions that rarely allowed adaptations that were stable in the long term. Constant dispersal was the rule, and settlement was infrequent and intermittent; hominins were, it seems, 'dancing to the rhythms of the Pleistocene' (Gamble 1999, 125). As seen above, Britain and probably large swathes of Northern Europe were possibly abandoned for more than 50% of Middle Pleistocene time, and even further south local extinction and relocation was still frequent (Hublin and Roebroeks 2009; Dennell et al. 2010). The Pleistocene peopling of Europe, then, may be characterised as a pattern of 'expansion and contraction, abandonment and re-colonisation, integration and isolation' (Dennell et al. 2011, 1514).

Given these temporal and geographic discontinuities, Dennell et al. (ibid.) suggest that hominin populations probably consisted of a few core groups and a number of peripheral ones, with survival of the core only in a few refugia. It is critical here to emphasise that these refugia served as 'lifeboats' for European hominins, not arks or sanctuaries, and that when the going got tough it was regional extinction, not a southern exodus, that most groups faced. The warmer climes of southern Europe – particularly Iberia, the Balkans and Italy – form the most realistic refugia for core populations, but some cryptic refugia may also have existed north of the Alps, for example in southwest France (ibid.).

Such refugia preserved source populations for recolonisation, although the record is too partial to determine whether even these areas were continuously occupied; different refugia may have operated at different times based on the intensity and local effects of climatic cycles and evolving survivorship traits over time, such as enhanced fire use and cooperative hunting. As noted in Chapter 2, the early occupation of Iberia appears to be concentrated in warmer periods, which may suggest that core populations during the most severe events were actually situated further to the east, perhaps concentrated only in Western Asia (ibid.). If populations in the southern refugia did, from time to time, become extinct, then Europe would have become an empty continent. This possibility also serves to emphasise the fact that Europe was never a closed system, but subject to immigration from outside its modern political boundaries.

Dennell et al. (ibid.) suggest that during challenging climatic conditions European populations in these refugia may have fallen to as few as 1500–2500 individuals, with perhaps only 60–100 surviving in more northerly cryptic refugia. These figures are, of course, informed guesstimates, but they do serve to remind us that hominin population density was incredibly low, with small social and mating networks and mates drawn from a very limited pool. According to these authors, extinction, recolonisation, integration and recombination present the only manner in which Eurasian populations could maintain genetic viability because, given such small populations, inbreeding was almost inevitable. Movements out of refugia during phases of climatic ameleoration would have been highly variable, and major geographical features such as the Alps and Pyrenees may have acted as permeable barriers. Dennell et al. illustrate this using Hewitt's (1999, cited in Dennell et al. 2011) three main patterns of expansion in animals, based on the behaviours of three key species: 1) the grasshopper, from the Balkans; 2) the bear, from Iberia and the Balkans; and 3) the hedgehog, from Iberia, Italy and the Balkans. Other permutations are of course possible. The key here is that the recolonisation of Britain from proximal areas of northwest Europe may have originated in a variety of distal sources, each perhaps contributing a different cultural flavour to the mix. Such a pattern also explains why *Homo heidelbergensis* is such an ill-defined heterogeneous species showing wide regional and temporal morphological variation; if, as widely believed, this species formed an anagentic line to Neanderthals (Hublin and Stringer 2009), the evolutionary path was unstructured and contingent on the caprice of time and chance, not predictable, directional or linear (Dennell et al. 2011).

Whatever happened in the refugia, it is clear from both the White and Schreve and Dennell et al. models that Britain formed a 'sink' area, one that (as discussed in Chapter 1) needed to be filled by people originating from elsewhere; even during periods of occupation populations may have been reproducing below replacement levels and thus continuously 'topped-up' from outside. The British Lower Palaeolithic (and equally that of much of northern Europe) is thus a long record of abandonment and colonisation, and a very short record of residency. The sad but inevitable conclusion of this must be that Britain has little role to play in any understanding of long-term human evolution and its cultural history is largely a broken record dependent on external introductions and insular developments that ultimately lead nowhere. Britain, therefore, was an island of the living dead.

Habitat preferences

The sub-headings of John Wymer's last major work on the British Lower Palaeolithic (Wymer 1999) make it clear that when present, humans were active in a wide variety of Middle Pleistocene environments – along the river valleys, beside the sea, around lakes, on the downs, plains and hills, towards the fringes of the highlands and in caves and rock shelters. However, their distribution is uneven both between these landscape settings and across Britain.

As shown in Figure 3.15, the overwhelming majority of British Lower Palaeolithic sites and findspots occur in river valleys, with much smaller concentrations in other settings. This is partly an artefact of preservation and collection opportunities – Palaeolithic rivers readily buried artefacts in their sediments, modern societies accidentally dug them up again in their pits and quarries – although Ashton et al. (2006) have suggested that the dominance of human activity in riparian habitats is also a true reflection of human habitat preference. Using evidence from archaeological and geological sites belonging to MIS11 they conclude that humans were targeting river valleys, which provided a wide variety of plants, animals and lithic raw materials, and acted as landmarks and easily navigable corridors through forested environments. Wymer (1999) took this one step further, suggesting that the distribution of artefacts within river valleys reflects hominin preferences for certain nodes within them, such as the confluences of the main river and its major tributaries. These formed junctions between routeways, providing access to wide plains with an abundance of resources and access to different parts of the landscape. The interfluves might also have provided relatively safe havens from which the valleys could be monitored for game. Wymer (1999, 48) also suggested that the chalk hinterlands would have been favoured locations, providing access to raw materials, well-drained soils with attractive grazing for herbivorous prey (whose feeding habits would have kept the area relatively open) and easy access to the more heavily wooded clay-with-flint and tertiary uplands for shelter and cover.

Conversely, Ashton et al.'s (2006) critical examination of claims for the exploitation of lacustrine habitats, concluded that they were minimally used and that at many sites previously characterised as lake-side settings (Barnham, Elveden, Hoxne, Hitchin), hominin occupation actually occurred only after the lake basin had infilled and a fluvial drainage network had become established. In Britain, this pattern is particularly clear in previously glaciated areas. As noted above, the Anglian ice left a landscape peppered with kettle holes and over-deepened, sub-glacial valleys, and a heavily disrupted drainage system that took millennia to stabilise; the final establishment of river systems at the aforementioned sites possibly being related to increased precipitation and a rising water table recognised at several Hoxnian sites during the latter part of the Hoxnian, *sensu stricto* (Gibbard and Aalto 1977; Gibbard et al. 1986). Even where lake-side occupation might be reasonably supported – for example at Foxhall Road, Ipswich – it occurred around pools within sub-glacial valleys, joined into a wider network by feeder streams (Allen and White 2004).

This is not to say that hominins were actively avoiding lakes, but that most lakes were not well known or well used localities, being rather off the beaten track and lacking the local lithic raw materials that often propagated the manufacture of dense artefact scatters. Examples such as Hoxne, situated on wooded interfluves, may have effectively been 'forest oases', known about perhaps, but visited very rarely and around which raw materials were scarce (cf. White 1998a). At a number of other sites, such as Caddington, Round Green and Gaddesden Row on the chalk uplands of the Chilterns, humans *were* active around isolated pools (White 1997; Text Box 3.16). Here, however, the scant botanical and geological data hints at occupation only towards the end of interglacials, perhaps when the upland environment had become more open, thereby revealing the presence of these basins as visible features in the landscape (White 1997; cf. Sampson 1978). Local flint was also available at these locations, but its accessibility probably depended on exposure through sub-aerial weathering of the underlying clay-with-flints or solifluction down the slopes and edges of the doline during cool conditions (Ashton et al. 2006).

We know of only a handful of caves – Kent's Cavern and Brixham Cave in Devon being the most notable – that have produced Lower Palaeolithic archaeology, but these artefacts are unlikely to have been deposited directly in the caves by hominins and were

THE CHILTERN HILLS, HERTFORDSHIRE AND BEDFORDSHIRE (CADDINGTON, GADDESDEN ROW, ROUND GREEN AND WHIPSNADE)

A significant cluster of primary context Acheulean sites was discovered between 1887 and 1917 by Worthington Smith, in a series of brickpits all situated within a 10 km radius of Luton (W.G. Smith 1894, 1916; R.A. Smith 1918; see Figure 1). The sites sit on the north-eastern end of the Chiltern Hills, the chalk uplands forming the northern watershed of the Middle Thames basin, that are dissected by the rivers Lea, Colne, Gade and Ver (Catt and Hagen 1978). The Chalk here is overlain by a number of deposits, including *in situ* Reading Beds, although the most common are the superficial deposits mapped as clay-with-flints (Loveday 1962).

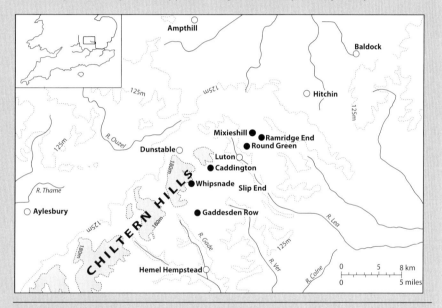

FIGURE 1

Map showing location of Worthington Smith's main sites on the Chiltern Hills (closed circles) and major modern towns (open circles). (After White et al. 1999a.)

Smith's sites all occurred in isolated patches of Pleistocene 'brickearth' mantling Tertiary deposits, which Smith interpreted as remnants of a once laterally extensive 'living floor', interrupted in places by lakes, ponds and swamps. Smith's interpretation of the formation and extent of the brickearths is no longer accepted (White 1997). The brickearths actually represent the separate infillings of individual funnel- or basin-shaped solution hollows (dolines) formed through the dissolution and collapse of the underlying Chalk (Avery et al. 1982; Catt 1978; Bridgland and Harding 1989). These most likely filled during warm periods subsequent to or contemporaneous with their creation, and over time formed semi-permanent ponds (Catt et al. 1978). The localised nature of the deposits,

Text Box 3.16

practically all now removed by quarrying, explains why all subsequent attempts to relocate Smith's archaeological horizons have met with failure (Sampson 1978; Wymer 1980; Bridgland and Harding 1989; White et al. 1999a).

Caddington (TL 055193) was Smith's flagship location in the Chilterns, and he monitored seven different pits around the village over a period of nearly 30 years. His major published work (1894) concentrates on the most prolific, Pit C or the 'Cottages Site'. Thousands of primary context artefacts were recovered from Caddington (see Figure 2). During his lifetime, Smith managed to conjoin over 500 pieces, including some virtually complete handaxe knapping episodes, suggesting that parts of the site were minimally disturbed. Smaller Acheulean assemblages comprising handaxes, flake tools, roughouts, cores and handaxe manufacturing débitage were recovered from brickearth deposits at Round Green (n = 340) Whipsnade (n = 201) and Gaddesden Row (n = 149), the latter assemblage apparently having been depleted by losses following Smith's death (Sampson 1978; see Figure 3). Derived, abraded artefacts were also found within the contorted drift capping the brickearth at each site.

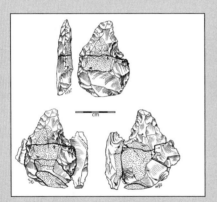

FIGURE 2
Broken handaxe and refitting flake sequence from Caddington. (After Smith 1894.)

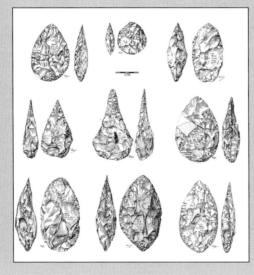

FIGURE 3
Handaxes from Worthington Smith's sites at Caddington, Round Green and Gaddesden Row. The handaxe from Caddington at top right is made of quartzite. (After Smith 1894, 1916.)

Text Box 3.16

Organic preservation within the brickearths is very poor. Excavations at Caddington by Sampson and Campbell in 1971 failed to locate Smith's Cottages Site, but did reveal an important Pleistocene sequence at the Rackley Site, 150 m to the south (Sampson 1978). Palynological analysis showed that during the infilling of this feature, temperate oak forests were declining and the environment was becoming more open, with increasingly higher proportions of open ground herbs, grasses and pine (Campbell and Hubbard 1978, 51). By the time the Cottages floor was laid down, the immediate locale hosted a mosaic environment with open grassland flanked by mixed woodland (Catt et al. 1978; cf. Campbell and Hubbard 1978). Insect-pollinated aquatic species were also noted in the Rackley sequence, further indication of marsh or pond conditions. Sedimentological analysis on samples from Wymer's (1980) excavation at Gaddesden Row (Avery et al. 1982) showed the segregation of ground ice occurred during the infilling of the doline at this site. These clay-filled voids were larger and more frequent in the mid-upper levels of the exposed brickearth (ibid. 166–170), suggesting a cool-cold climate towards the end of the doline's active existence, again that the surrounding landscape was open.

White (1997) suggested that all of the Chiltern sites were occupied briefly towards the end of interglacials, when the dolines had almost completely filled with sediment. During these periods, the landscape would have been more open and the ponds more visible features in the landscape (Ashton et al. 2006). As well as water and raw materials, humans may have been attracted to these sites for their high vantage points, from which they could scan the valleys below for hunting opportunities (see Figure 4.18. White (1997) also suggested that Smith's claims for several stratified floors at Whipsnade and Gaddesden Row did not result from repeated visits by humans over long periods of time, but from the excavations intercepting the same sloping surface of the doline edge at different depths throughout the brickpits. The limited use of these sites – as evinced by the small, discrete assemblages they contain – supports Ashton et al.'s (2006) suggestion that river valleys formed the focus of activity, upland ponds and lakes only being exploited during specific periods and possibly for specific purposes.

Precisely which Pleistocene interglacial or interglacials are represented is unclear. Typologically almost all of Smith's sites are Lower Palaeolithic, and presumably therefore date to MIS13, 11 or 9; with the exception of Caddington, which contains derived Anglian MIS12 loess and must post-date that event (Avery et al. 1982). A small Levallois assemblage from the 'South Site' at Caddington (Sampson 1978) may relate to later MIS8 or 7 occupation of another doline, showing that these uplands were visited during several cycles.

Text Box 3.16

almost certainly introduced from the plateaux above them by erosional activity and slope movement. The almost total absence of Lower Palaeolithic archaeology from caves probably reflects a mixture of the genuine infrequency with which Lower Palaeolithic people used caves compared to their Middle Palaeolithic counterparts and the removal of archaeology that was from time to time deposited in caves by the continuous cycle of renewal of cave sediments. In sum, almost all evidence for the British Lower Palaeolithic derives from river valleys, a bias that has significant implications for our understanding of human behaviour at this time (see below).

Geographical distribution: a journey through space

River valleys, then, provide the best approximation of the spatial distribution of Lower Palaeolithic hominins in Britain. Even here, though, their spread appears uneven and most finds, sadly, cannot be dated more precisely than to a broad Lower Palaeolithic attribution. Lower Palaeolithic sites are missing from areas covered by ice during the Last Glacial Maximum, the deposits that once contained them having been destroyed, creating an apparent lacuna in northern Britain. At present the known northern limit of Lower Palaeolithic occupation derives from two handaxes from Rudston and East Ayton on the Yorkshire Wolds (Wymer 1999, 179).

Most of the evidence for pre-Anglian occupation comes from the Bytham River system (e.g. Waverley Wood, High Lodge and Warren Hill), the Westbourne–Arundel Raised Beach (e.g. Boxgrove and The Valdoe; Pope et al. 2009) plus a handful of poorly dated sites in the Solent system (e.g., Corfe Mullen; Hosfield 2011). The handaxes from the Breccia at Kent's Cavern also provides unique evidence of pre-Anglian occupation in the south-west (Roe 1981; Lundberg and McFarlane 2007). As stated in Chapter 2, not a single convincing site has been located in the Kesgraves or the MIS12 Winter Hill Gravel of the Thames; the two claimed 'flakes' from the Kesgraves at Wivenhoe, Essex (Bridgland 1994) are simply too small to determine whether they are of genuine hominin authorship. There is, however, derived evidence of hominin activity north and south of the Thames during MIS13. The oldest terrace (Terrace A) of the Wey at Farnham in Surrey has produced a series of crude handaxes believed to be of at least Anglian age if not much older (Oakley 1939; Gibbard 1982; Wymer 1999). The hundreds of artefacts in the Wallingford Fan Gravels, situated on the slopes of the Chilterns about four miles from the modern river in Oxfordshire, also testify to occupation of the adjacent upland zone (Roe 1986, 1994). Horton et al. (1981) concluded that the majority of the Wallingford Fan Gravel accumulated under cold conditions during the Anglian, partly by solifluction from the Chilterns and partly by fluvial deposition in a tributary of the Thames; the finds must therefore represent the sweepings of MIS13 landsurfaces.

The greatest concentration of MIS11 archaeology is found in southeast England, particularly the rejuvenated landscapes of East Anglia and the newly diverted Thames valley. Keen et al. (2006) suggested that the destruction of the Bytham river system left the Thames as the main arterial route into and across Britain, an assertion that is supported by the wealth of sites and findspots contained in the Boyn Hill Terrace Formation, particularly in the Lower Thames, such as at Swanscombe. Curiously, however, evidence from the Upper Thames is remarkably sparse; Hardaker (2001), for example, reported just 1126 finds from the Upper Thames for the entire Middle Pleistocene. While no MIS11 sediments remain in the Solent system numerous artefacts occur in the MIS10 Old Milton Terrace, which must in part at least relate to MIS13 activity (McNabb 2007). During periods of low sea level the Solent probably acted as the southern corridor into Britain.

Moving clockwise around the country, MIS11 archaeology in the major river valleys of the South West and the Midlands is notably impoverished. Wymer (1999) suggested that the chert handaxes found in the gravels of the River Axe in Dorset (most famously the 1800 or more handaxes from the Broom Pits) relate to MIS11 activity, although this is not supported by recent OSL dates (Hosfield and Chambers 2002). Cornwall and Devon have produced only a scattered handful of surface finds, none of which can be dated; the same is true of South Wales (Wymer 1999; Green and Walker 1991) – the finds there are certainly Lower Palaeolithic but this leaves a 300,000 year window during which they were deposited. The Severn–Avon system apparently has no MIS11 deposits, and although the valleys appear to have existed earlier, both have terraces extending only as far back as MIS10 (Maddy et al. 1995; McNabb 2007). Evidence of Middle Pleistocene archaeology in these is limited, with no major sites and only isolated finds. Lang and Keen (2005) suggest that these were probably derived from Bytham deposits which would preclude an MIS11 age. Similarly, no MIS11 deposits survive in the Trent, this river having successfully obliterated all of its Middle Pleistocene deposits and having been affected by an MIS8 glaciation (Bridgland et al. in press; T. White et al. 2010). The main Fenland systems of the Ouse and Nene, potentially dispersal routes in and out of East Anglia, possess little or no evidence of MIS11 activity (Wymer 1999; McNabb 2007), although East Anglia has one of the richest MIS11 records including Barnham, Elveden, Hoxne, Beeches Pit and Foxhall Road, among many others.

The picture for MIS9 is largely the same, and is, in John McNabb's (2007) term 'rather gloomy'. Thousands of artefacts have been recovered from the Lynch Hill Terrace of the Thames, particular in the middle reach, yet the equivalent Wolvercote Terrace of the Upper Thames has a very poor record with only three known sites (Wymer 1999). The Solent system also possesses a number of terraces equated with MIS9 (Westaway et al. 2006; McNabb 2007; Ashton and Hosfield 2009), including Terrace 10 of the Stour, Terrace 9 of the Hampshire Avon, Terrace 4 of the Test and the Taddiford Farm/Ensbury/High Cliff/Beckton Farm Terrace of the Solent, which have also yielded thousands of artefacts. The artefacts are all heavily abraded and not a single primary context site has yet been located. Very little has been reported from the South West or Midlands. No *in situ* archaeology has been recorded in the temperate deposits in the Bushey Green Terrace of the Severn or Terrace 5 of the Avon, suggested to equate with MIS9 (Maddy et al. 1995; Bridgland et al. 2004), and no derived material was recorded for the overlying MIS8 gravel either (Wymer 1994, 1996a, 1999; McNabb 2007), although Lang and Keen (2005) have more recently reported four handaxes from relevant terraces in both rivers. There are no MIS9 deposits in the Trent (although heavily derived materials attest to perhaps both MIS9 and MIS11 occupation), while possible MIS9 deposits of the Nene–Ouse have failed to produce a wealth of evidence; only Biddenham, Bedfordshire can be considered a real candidate for a rich MIS9 site in the Great Ouse, and this may belong to MIS11 (Harding et al. 1992). Interestingly, for the first time in the Middle Pleistocene, there is a lack of rich sites in East Anglia (Wymer 1999; McNabb 2007), and while Wymer states that people were undoubtedly there during MIS9 there is in fact little evidence to support this (McNabb 2007). As John McNabb laments, there are handaxes and terraces aplenty, just none that can be firmly tied down to this period.

In summary, while the majority of evidence for MIS11 and MIS9 comes from the East Anglia, the Thames and the Solent, the general distribution of handaxes and other Lower Palaeolithic finds, most of which cannot be dated, at least show that Middle Pleistocene Lower Palaeolithic hominins ranged across much of England and Wales (at least where relevant deposits have survived subsequent glacial destruction). This is shown in Table 3.2, which repeats the data from Roe's (1968b) monumental gazetteer of Lower and Middle Paleaeolithic artefacts, which although now 40 years old, reveals a pattern still valid today. Fluvial sedimentation patterns and course morphology/bedrock have obviously played a major role both in geographical patterns and in the actual location and survival of dense artefact accumulations within river systems (Hosfield 1999; Wymer 1999). As noted above, the Trent completely re-worked its MIS11 and MIS9 deposits, leaving a very heavily abraded archaeological record in the MIS8 (Etwall/Eagle Moor/Martin) and MIS6 (Eggington Common/Balderton/Southrey) terraces (Bridgland et al. in press); recent finds of handaxes in Lincolnshire (Bee 2001) remain undated, but at least testify to hominin presence. As already mentioned, Keen et al. (2006) suggested that after the destruction of Bytham (a critical east–west conduit) the Midlands lay very much off the beaten track. McNabb (2007) has similarly suggested that the development of the major SW–NE trending Great Ouse and Nene basins, which flowed into a broad fjord-like embayment around the Wash, possibly acted as a barrier to humans moving west out of East Anglia and northwards from the Thames valley after MIS12. This would presumably pertain only to west bank deposits of the River Ouse, however.

As Wymer has long noted, the richest archaeological signatures all lie within the chalk hinterland; outside this zone, artefacts are considerably rarer. The Thames Valley provides a good example. The Lower and Middle Thames offered both chalk flint and flint-rich gravel, but upstream of the Goring Gap the Upper Thames flows through an area devoid of any good quality flint resources (MacRae 1988; Roe 1994). The low density of finds along this stretch suggests that raw material availability had a major structuring effect on human discard patterns, perhaps engendering more careful and prolonged curation and resharpening practises (Ashton 2001). Equally, the issues surrounding the preservation and recovery of non-flint artefacts – which are neither as durable nor

Table 3.2 List of Lower and Middle Palaeolithic findspots by county, including the historical counties of Huntingdonshire, Rutland and Middlesex (after Roe 1968b). Roe's original values, which are now 40 years old, have been converted into percentages to show the relative concentration of Palaeolithic activities across the British landscape. More recent excavations means that values for Suffolk, Norfolk, Kent and especially Sussex (Boxgrove) will have changed dramatically, although proportionally the regional picture remains remarkably similar. Collector biases are evident, for example in the flake percentages for Bedfordshire, which is largely due to the activities of a single man, Worthington G. Smith.

County	No. Sites	Handaxes	Cores	Flakes	Flake tools	Misc.	Levallois cores and flakes
Bedfordshire	65	3.09	6.90	13.36	3.15	10.48	4.94
Berkshire	184	9.64	1.22	1.81	3.91	2.37	0.84
Buckinghamshire	103	4.91	1.11	2.19	3.76	2.92	1.05
Cambridgeshire	61	1.17	0.11	0.77	1.25	0.83	0.26
Carmarthenshire	1	0.01	0.00	0.01	0.00	0.00	0.03
Cheshire	1	0.00	0.00	0.00	0.01	0.00	0.00
Cornwall	2	0.01	0.00	0.00	0.00	0.00	0.00
Denbighshire	1	0.01	0.06	0.04	0.10	0.00	0.03
Derbyshire	18	0.36	0.78	0.44	0.23	1.54	0.00
Devonshire	36	0.23	0.06	0.04	0.07	0.11	0.03
Dorset	99	6.61	0.33	1.31	0.79	1.60	0.52
Essex	156	2.17	30.88	12.95	23.96	15.77	3.82
Glamorganshire	2	0.00	0.00	0.00	0.00	0.00	0.03
Gloucestershire	29	0.08	0.17	0.02	0.06	0.50	0.00
Hampshire	471	14.19	1.17	2.68	2.65	6.12	1.99
Hertfordshire	107	2.26	1.78	1.14	4.97	5.02	0.26
Huntingdonshire	39	0.09	0.39	1.06	0.73	0.44	0.78
Isle of Wight	21	0.40	0.22	0.14	0.55	0.17	0.50
Kent	492	19.78	30.83	46.74	26.59	24.77	46.72
Leicestershire	5	0.01	0.00	0.00	0.01	0.00	0.03
Lincolnshire	17	0.03	0.00	0.01	0.03	0.00	0.00
London	158	2.55	2.56	4.10	8.29	4.25	0.99
Middlesex	198	6.84	0.89	4.18	6.57	3.36	32.70
Monmouthshire	1	0.00	0.00	0.00	0.00	0.00	0.03
Norfolk	153	2.88	0.45	0.89	1.82	1.05	0.65
Northamptonshire	31	0.15	0.06	0.05	0.10	0.28	0.34
Nottinghamshire	10	0.07	0.00	0.07	0.12	0.17	0.00
Oxfordshire	87	2.14	14.13	0.38	0.45	2.26	0.05
Rutland	1	0.00	0.00	0.00	0.00	0.00	0.00
Shropshire	1	0.00	0.00	0.00	0.00	0.00	0.00
Somersetshire	52	0.59	0.33	0.65	0.55	2.48	0.44
Suffolk	177	10.93	3.62	2.97	6.43	8.22	2.17
Surrey	124	2.81	0.22	0.36	0.89	0.83	0.52
Sussex	96	0.65	1.06	0.79	0.54	0.61	0.24
Warwickshire	15	0.05	0.00	0.00	0.08	0.06	0.03
Wiltshire	56	5.29	0.67	0.84	1.28	3.81	0.00
Worcestershire	8	0.01	0.00	0.00	0.03	0.00	0.00
Yorkshire	13	0.02	0.00	0.01	0.01	0.00	0.03
	3091	100	100	100	100	100	100

as easy to spot as their flint counterparts – must be considered (White and White in press; Morigi et al. 2011). Hardaker (2001), whose work with R.J. MacRae in the Upper Thames almost doubled the number of known non-flint artefacts there simply by looking for them, amply illustrates this issue. One is drawn, however, to the conclusion that human populations were densest in the southeast, and that in other parts of the country hominins were a rare sight indeed.

CHAPTER 4

Behaviour and society in Lower Palaeolithic Britain, ~ 550 ka–300 ka BP

A flint implement . . . is not a fact but an inference.

Samuel Hazzledine Warren, 1941

This chapter explores the Lower Palaeolithic record of Britain, in terms of the behavioural repertoires and societies of the archaic hominins who roamed the British Middle Pleistocene landscapes. This period preserves the richest record of hominin settlement in Britain and in contrast to many other European countries, which have also yielded evidence of intensive Middle and Upper Palaeolithic occupation, sites of this age are relatively scarce in Britain, as will be seen in Chapters 6, 7 and 8. This cannot entirely be explained as a function of its much longer duration, but appears genuinely to reflect more intensive and repeated occupation during the Middle Pleistocene cycles discussed in Chapters 2 and 3. Inevitably, most of our information derives from the two most durable forms of evidence: stone tools and animal bones, and their association in various landscape contexts; augmented in very rare instances by the preservation of more transient and perishable technologies (wooden tools and fire) that provide hints at a range of behaviours not usually preserved in the archaeological record. This partial record makes the task of interpreting what does survive extremely difficult and, as shown in the succinctly worded quotation from the father of the Clactonian above, much of what we think we know is mere inference. Like all archaeology, our evidence is always indirect, whether in the form of a handaxe, its position in the landscape or its inferred function: there simply is no 'smoking gun'.

Of the many thousands of sites and findspots, however, only a handful has any real integrity, and for each such well-preserved 'flagship site' (Gamble 1996) capable of revealing 'ethnographical' aspects of behaviour and society (Roebroeks 2006), there are hundreds of 'dredgers', secondary context sites derived from fluvial gravels. The complex taphonomic filters through which these sites have passed, in which all but the most basic of technological information has been obliterated, means that most of the artefacts are little more than clasts once modified by hominins. The fragmentary and biased nature of much of our data, and the vanishingly small samples of past landscapes that even the flagships represent, means that no single site will ever provide a full suite of evidence, and more than any other archaeological period the Palaeolithic relies on the art of 'cabling' (Gamble 2001), that is, pulling together the disparate and partial strands of information to produce a (hopefully) compelling and coherent narrative. Even then the evidence is rarely straightforward, and the problem of equifinality (where different inter-pretations account for all the observed data, with no real means of choosing between them) is commonplace. On the other hand, this does produce a very lively academic environment, full of rich and heated debates, many of which are discussed below.

As noted in Chapter 3, only two hominin fossils are associated with this very long period – the Swanscombe skull and the Boxgrove tibia and incisors, all of which have been referred to the taxon *Homo* (cf.) *heidelbergensis* (Figure 4.1). The rarity of hominin fossils,

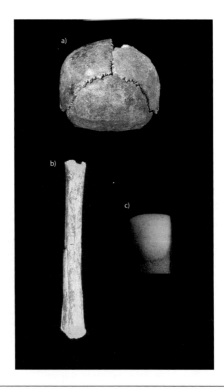

FIGURE 4.1
The complete corpus of Lower Palaeolithic human fossils from Britain. (a) The Swanscombe skull; (b) the Boxgrove tibia; (c) close-up of one of the Boxgrove incisors, showing cut-marks on the enamel. (All specimens have been referred to *Homo* cf. *Heidelbergensis*. Swanscombe © Natural History Museum; Boxgrove courtesy Mark Roberts.)

in Britain and on the continent, probably reflects the rarity of hominins in the landscape. Handaxes and other stone tools reveal only their presence, not their relative abundance (see Chapter 5).

THE BRITISH LOWER PALAEOLITHIC LITHIC RECORD

British Lower Palaeolithic lithic assemblages are traditionally divided into two main industries: those containing handaxes (Figure 4.2) alongside flake tools, cores/core-tools and débitage, invariably classified as Acheulean (de Mortillet 1873); and those containing flake tools, cores/core-tools and débitage but lacking handaxes, which are usually attributed or at least compared to the Clactonian (Warren 1926). This is a pretty blunt taxonomic tool, which takes into account few nuances within assemblages, but for almost a century British Lower Palaeolithic archaeology has been dominated by the struggle to understand the behavioural and cultural meaning behind these two broad assemblage types. This is a reflection not of the importance of the Clactonian in Britain, but the tyrannical hold a single tool form (the handaxe) has over the systematic, theoretical and popular understanding of the distant past.[1] When they are not arguing over the meaning of the Clactonian, many British Lower Palaeolithic specialists are engaged in

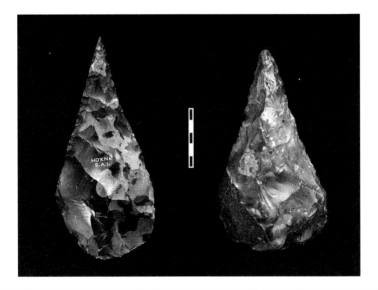

FIGURE 4.2
Two historically important handaxes from Britain. Left: Acutely pointed handaxe from Hoxne, found by John Frere in 1797. He described his finds as 'evidently weapons of war, fabricated and used by a people who had not the use of metals [living in] a very remote period indeed; even beyond that of the present world' (Frere 1800). Right: Handaxe found associated with elephant bones in gravel at Gray's Inn Road, London in 1679 by John Conyers. (© Trustees of the British Museum.)

another evergreen pursuit – debating the meaning of morphological variation and symmetry of handaxes, their patterns of discard and frequency within the landscape. With notable exceptions (for example the scrapers from High Lodge) other tool types are relegated to epiphenomena.

In some respects this situation stems from the fact that other tool types are rare and actually form only a small proportion of most assemblages, making meaningful analysis difficult. From a total of 3,091 sites and findspots, Roe's (1968b) gazetteer lists only 18 Acheulean localities with 50 or more scrapers or flake tools, which is still only half the number Bordes (1961) suggested should be required for formal typological analysis.[2] We know of no study that has systematically examined these collections but, intriguingly, there are grounds to assign many of them to MIS9, an issue to which we will return below. This means that, polemic posturing aside, much of what we think we know of the technical, behavioural and social landscapes of Lower Palaeolithic humans currently resides with handaxes and the Clactonian.

HANDAXE ASSEMBLAGES – THE ACHEULEAN

In Britain, as with most of Eurasia, the Acheulean comprises any assemblage containing handaxes or evidence for their manufacture (Goren-Inbar and Sharon 2006). No distinction is made between sites with many handaxes and those with a few (e.g. Leakey 1971) meaning that, while a range of behavioural, functional and taphonomic factors certainly control handaxe frequency, they rightly or wrongly remain the absolute marker fossil for recognising a socially mediated global technological phenomenon (e.g. Villa 1983; Hopkinson and White 2005).

Handaxes occur in many shapes, but in most assemblages they range around a modal form. Until recently three concepts developed from the theories and taxonomic systems of the nineteenth and early twentieth centuries have been used to explain this (Ashton and McNabb 1994; White 1998a):

1   Different handaxe shapes form discrete typological units that reflect mental templates in the minds of the makers.

2   Biases towards certain shapes within specific assemblages represent the inherited knapping traditions of different cultural groups.

3   There was a gradual evolution in handaxe morphology over time, from crude, unsophisticated pointed forms, often made using hard (stone) percussors to more elaborate, 'refined' ovate forms, made using soft (antler or bone) hammers.

Since the late 1980s the focus of Palaeolithic research has shifted away from this type of explanation. Few would really deny that the handaxe is a cultural object, in that it was socially maintained and socially transmitted down generations, but the emphasis is now squarely placed on explaining the variation evident in handaxes in the framework of dynamic technological organisation in the landscape, where factors such as raw materials (White 1998a; Ashton and White 2003), resharpening (McPherron 1994, 2006), function (Keeley 1980; Mitchell 1997) and site location (White 1998a; Pope 2002, 2004; Pope and Roberts 2005) played a prime role in variation. More recently, their role as part of a socially mediated technology predicated on personal relationships between individuals has also assumed prominence (Gamble 1998, 1999; Kohn and Mithen 1999; Pope 2002). While all of these studies have undoubtedly enhanced our understanding of handaxes within hominin social networks and behavioural systems, the pendulum may have swung somewhat too far from the ideas promulgated during the infancy of the discipline.

Equally, there are no longer any formally recognised or accepted temporal subdivisions within the British handaxe assemblages. Terms like Early, Middle and Late Middle Acheulean (e.g. Wymer 1968 and many others) – or indeed Chellean and Abbevillian – once used as a relative measure of age based on perceived sophistication, were largely abandoned decades ago, when independent chronological control began to reveal that, regardless of what archaeologists wished or thought to be true, no linear evolution in form or sophistication actually existed. The Swanscombe sequence (Smith and Dewey 1913, 1914 and see Text Box 3.1) in which cruder, pointed handaxes gave way first to better made points and ultimately to elegantly made ovates – once the yardstick for understanding the British Acheulean (McNabb 1996b) – was shown by discoveries of elaborate pre-Anglian ovates at Boxgrove (Roberts 1986) and a reversed sequence (i.e. ovates giving way to points) at Hoxne (Wymer 1983, 1985; Singer et al. 1993) to be of nothing more than local significance. No regional variants seem to exist either: there is no equivalent of Bordes' (1971) 'Northern Acheulean' of the Somme and Seine (with regular, refined handaxes) or 'Meridional Acheulean' of South-west France and Spain (with irregular, crude handaxes), although it is at least becoming clear that non-flint handaxes are more common outside the British chalk hinterland. We must, however, accept that, having spent two decades denying the possibility of cultural patterns, it is now clear that some non-linear, temporal patterning may exist which needs incorporating into our new social and behavioural frameworks (White 1998b; Wenban-Smith 2006).

The nature of handaxe variation

The classic Bordes' (1961) system is rarely employed formally in Britain (although see Lev 1973) and even the though the handaxe names Bordes employed have become fairly widely adopted, they sometimes take on different meanings, as in the case of the ficron. In Bordes' terminology a ficron is an elongated (lanceolate), pointed handaxe with less carefully crafted edges (Bordes 1961, 152), whereas in Britain, it is invariably used to describe pointed handaxes with well-worked *concave* edges (e.g. Wymer 1968). Instead of the *system Bordes*, two main systems of classification have been used in Britain over the past 50 years: John Wymer's (1968, 1985, 1999) typological system, which recognises 10 main types (labelled D–N) and numerous sub-types based around

overall shape, butt morphology, tip morphology and edge form (Figure 4.3); and Derek
Roe's (1964, 1968a, 1981) metrical system which employs a series of standardised
morphometric measurements and a form of graphical representation (the tripartite diagram – see Figure 4.3) to characterise whole assemblages without recourse to typological pigeon-holes. Roe's system divides handaxes into three metrically defined classes
– points, ovates and cleavers – with variation between and within each class indicated
by their position on the tripartite diagram.

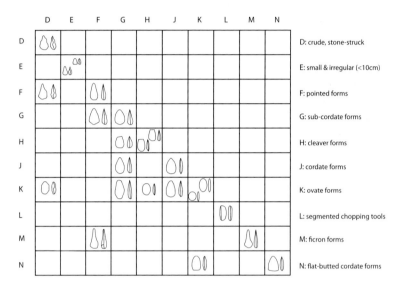

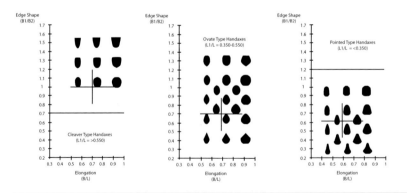

FIGURE 4.3
Diagrammatic illustration of the two main classification systems for handaxes used in Britain
since the 1960s. Top: Wymer's (1968) scheme (used with permission). Bottom: Roe's (1968a)
key to his tripartite diagrams (courtesy of The Prehistoric Society).

Both systems are capable of highlighting intra- and inter-assemblage variation but Roe's provides a more effective and subtle way of grouping sites together based on their dominant tool shape. The tripartite diagrams also provide a fairly refined method for examining the range of shapes within each assemblage, and largely overcome the problem that, typologically, handaxes are often difficult to categorise and usually form a continuum of variation, with one type grading into the next.[3] There is tendency amongst specialists (White included), however, to adopt the primary division into points, ovates and cleavers as a convenient shorthand, which only serves to mask variation and obscure the morphological nuances within each class.

Roe's (1968a; see Table 4.1) work on 38 handaxe assemblages from what we now recognise as spanning MIS13 to MIS7 revealed that, while there was considerable variation within each shape class, most sites showed a definite preference towards either pointed or ovate handaxes. Roe thus divided the British Acheulean into two main groups or traditions with a third 'intermediate' tradition lying between them (this in fact has little real meaning and reflects only the derived, mixed and poorly contextualised nature of these 'intermediate' assemblages). In essence, this constructed two Acheulean phyla, which were subsequently reinforced through multivariate statistical analyses (Graham 1970; Doran and Hodson 1975; Callow 1976 1986). These traditions were further divided into seven sub-groups on the basis of specific morphological traits. While the method could accommodate a cleaver tradition, cleavers made up only 2% of Roe's sample and no cleaver-dominated assemblages or groups could be defined (see below).

EXPLAINING HANDAXE VARIATION

As previously noted by White (1996, 1998a) Roe's work divided a collection of disparate and often poorly documented assemblages into a manageable framework that continues to provide a baseline for understanding the British Acheulean, in as much as nothing better has come forward to replace it (nor we suspect ever will). Roe interpreted the patterns he detected in cultural terms, reflecting different traditions of manufacture, with a complicating functional element thrown into the mix. Roe also tentatively posited an evolutionary trend in technique and form throughout the Middle Pleistocene although, at the time, he could find no clear temporal or geographical patterning. He was nevertheless convinced that this was not because none existed but that poor chronological resolution and incomplete evidence were obscuring the picture (Roe 1981). In this he may have been correct. Wymer (1968, 1985) favoured a similar explanation for the patterns he detected in the fluvial archive.

Over the past two decades a number of alternative, more behaviourally orientated explanations have been offered. The key questions these attempt to address revolve around both inter-assemblage variation (why different assemblages contain different handaxe forms or different frequencies of particular types) and intra-assemblage variation (the significance of variation in the form of handaxes within a specific assemblage). Here, we examine two of these – the so-called raw material model (White 1996, 1998a) and the

Table 4.1 British Handaxe traditions according to Derek Roe (1968a; sites in parentheses added after White 1996, 1998a; White and Plunkett 2004).

←	Pointed Tradition →		Intermediate →	←	Ovate Tradition →	
Group I (with cleavers)	Group II (with ovates)	Group III (plano-convex)	Group IV	Group V (crude, narrow)	Group VI (more pointed)	Group VII (less pointed)
Furze Platt	Swanscombe MG	Wolvercote	Broom	Fordwich	Elveden	Gaddesden Row
Bakers Farm	Chadwell St Mary		Santon Downham	Farnham terrace A	Allington Hill	High Lodge
Cuxton	Hoxne		Wallingford	Warren Hill worn	Caversham	Warren Hill fresh
Whitlingham	Dovercourt		Barton Cliff		Knowle Farm	Highlands Farm
Twydall	Hitchin				Bowman's Lodge	Croxley Green
Stoke Newington	?Foxhall Road				Tilehurst	Corfe Mullen
	(Foxhall Road Red Gravel)				Shide, Pan Farm	?Caddington
					Oldbury	(Boxgrove)
					?Round Green	(Foxhall Road Grey Clays)
					?Holybourne	
					?Swanscombe UL	
					(Wansunt)	

reduction model (McPherron 1994, 1996, 2006) – before returning to the issue of chronology, recast in the light of the settlement history model outlined in Chapter 3.

Handaxes in the landscape: the raw material model

In the early 1990s, Ashton and McNabb (1994) suggested that a key cause of variation in the British Acheulean related to the degree to which different raw material packages had affected the actions of the knapper. Using the position of residual cortex and natural surfaces on handaxes to reconstruct the dimensions and shape of the original nodule, they found that many pointed handaxes were made on thick and elongated blanks that guided the hand of the knapper (along a 'path of least resistance'), whereas many ovates and cordiforms were produced on large nodules or flakes, onto which the knapper was free to impose whatever shape they desired. Ashton and McNabb concluded that humans were guided not by a socially defined mental template for a specific shape, but by a generalised *mental construct* of a functional tool that was bifacially worked, had sharp durable edges and a basic level of symmetry (1994, 187). Morphological variation exists because different blank types either facilitated or demanded different technological approaches to the realisation of this construct. Building on this work, White (1995, 1996, 1998a; Shaw and White 2003; White and Plunkett 2004) examined ~1,500 handaxes from 23 assemblages. Based on technological and morphological characteristics of different handaxe types, he elaborated two basic knapping strategies, each designed to deal with different raw materials.

When knapping thick and elongated (sub-cylindrical) blanks, roughing out was attenuated and thinning concentrated at the tip. The butt was often left entirely unworked or partially worked in order to retain a robust 'handle' and to preserve a counterweight to the long tip, thus maintaining suitable prehensile properties and balance. This resulted in exaggerated reduction above the line of maximum width, causing the lateral margins to converge from a wide butt to a narrow tip. In other words, by minimising butt length to maximise the length of the lateral margins, a pointed form (where the line of maximum width sits low on the piece) was hard to avoid. The minimal working at the butt also resulted in handaxes with high levels of residual cortex, low scar counts, low refinement indices, a tapered cross section and relatively short cutting edges with acute angles only at the tip (see Table 4.2). The whole shaping of the piece was predicated on a strategy designed to exact the best result from the form of the original nodule.

In contrast, on large nodules roughing out and shaping were more intensive. Raw material conditioning was minimal, the form of the nodule having minimal effect on the finished handaxes, the shape of which was entirely humanly imposed. On both flakes and large nodules equal attention was given to the butt and the tip, meaning that lateral reduction occurred more or less evenly at both ends, leaving the point of maximum width towards the middle of the handaxe and creating a typological and morphometric ovate shape. Cordiforms emerged when the point of maximum width was slightly lower on the piece and two longer, sweeping margins were desired. Intensive reduction around the entire implement also facilitated all-round cutting edges with acute angles, low cortex

Table 4.2 Selected technological and morphological attributes on handaxes from 20 British assemblages (after White 1998a).

Site	Mean number of flake scars over 5mm (SD)	Mean residual cortex, %	Completely worked butts, %	all-round edges, %	Mean cutting edge length in mm (SD)	Mean refinement (thickness/width)	Conditioned by nodule shape, %
Furze Platt (n=106)	35 (16)	13.5	27	12	162 (61)	0.60 (0.13)	35
Whitlingham (n=132)	39 (18)	11.5	32	25	188 (76)	0.54 (0.11)	23
Cuxton (n=154)	no data	24	23	5	168 (69)	0.60 (0.13)	44
Stoke Newington (n=71)	36 (13)	18.5	27	15	147 (47)	0.57 (0.13)	34
Swanscombe UMG (n=120)	23 (11)	13.5	38	25	147 (55)	0.56 (0.12)	33
Dovercourt (n=117)	44 (16)	11.5	42	47	179 (67)	0.53 (0.12)	29
Hitchin (n=64)	50 (15)	10.5	46	42	218 (73)	0.50 (0.11)	22
Foxhall Road Red Gravel (n=18)	30 (23)	31	11	27		0.54 (0.12)	61
Wolvercote (n=51)	51 (16)	10.5	38	35	207 (93)	0.54 (0.14)	25
Fordwich (n=137)	38 (15)	16	37	24	219 (77)	0.68 (0.16)	34
Elveden (n=68)	56 (17)	3.5	82	82	251 (64)	0.46 (0.09)	4
Bowman's Lodge (n=29)	55 (15)	4	89	79	224 (64)	0.45 (0.07)	6
Round Green (n=16)	51 (18)	11.5	56	57	203 (64)	0.46 (0.08)	13
Holybourne (n=20)	48 (10)	4	95	75	175 (32)	0.45 (0.09)	0
Foxhall Road Grey Clays (n=19)	47 (22)	11	47	58		0.48 (0.14)	21
Wansunt (n=32)	56 (12)	2.5	79	73	212 (49)	0.39 (0.05)	3
Gaddesden Row (n=45)	50 (15)	12	62	70	200 (56)	0.41 (0.12)	17
High Lodge (n=67)	59 (16)	4.5	76	76	260 (67)	0.42 (0.10)	2
Caddington (n=31)	50 (15)	13	70	71	211 (62)	0.46 (0.12)	21
Boxgrove (n=82)	60 (16)	4.5	80	84	297 (67)	0.39 (0.05)	4

retention, higher scar counts and high refinement indices (Table 4.2).[4] While in some cases they appear to have followed a path of least resistance, in many they fashioned an intensively worked ovate with a sharp edge around the entire perimeter.

So, when unrestrained by the shape and size of raw materials, hominins produced ovate handaxes. White (1996, 1998a) offered two possible reasons why this might be the case. First, ovates can be seen to offer functional and operational advantages, having an all-round cutting edge and balance that allows the tool to be rotated during use, both to access new edges and in a sweeping motion whilst cutting (cf. Mitchell 1996). On points, the functionality, balance and use-mode are different. Sharp edges are restricted to the tip, the butt acting mostly to maintain good balance in the hand. Rotation and a gentle sweeping motion are barely possible, with pointed forms more suited instead to the sawing motion used in modern steel knives (ibid.). The various ovate forms can therefore be argued to have presented a greater amount of usable edge and a more efficient use mode than pointed forms. The second possibility, however, is that ovate handaxes represent nothing more than the inevitable result of complete circumferential knapping aimed at maximising edge and resharpening potential, 'rhythms of making' that were uncompromised by raw material considerations, or perhaps even the end result of a longer use-life (McPherron 1994;, 2006; Hayden and Villeneuve 2009).

White (1996, 1998a) also recognised a remarkable correlation between dominant handaxe shape and raw material sources (Figure 4.4). Point-dominated assemblages were almost

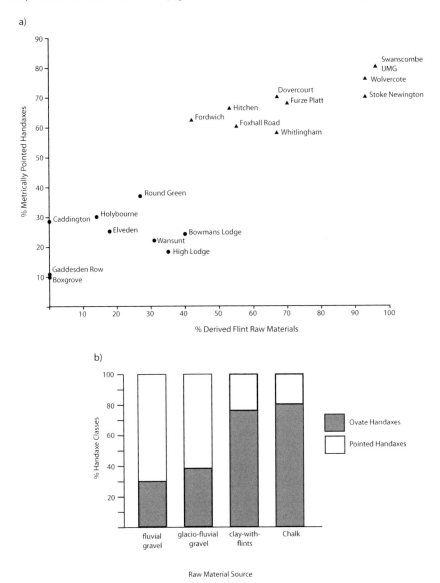

FIGURE 4.4
Graphs showing the relationship between dominant handaxe shape and raw material sources. (a) Percentage of pointed handaxes (y-axis) over percentage of derived raw materials (x-axis), showing that the two have a strong linear correlation. (b) Percentage of pointed and ovate handaxes for four different raw material regimes. Pointed handaxe dominate on material that had been fluvially transported and sorted.

always manufactured on cobbles from derived raw material sources, such as fluvial and glaciofluvial gravels. Ovate-dominated assemblages, by contrast, were always made on large nodules of fresh flint from primary chalk outcrops and clay-with-flints. Where no immediate source of raw materials existed, such as Wansunt Pit, Bowmans Lodge and the Foxhall Road Grey Clay assemblage, ovates tended to dominate, suggesting that, when faced with decisions about curation and transport, hominins preferentially carried well made, highly functional tools, or at least the blanks required to make them.

Changing raw materials through time at a site was also seen to have a structuring effect on the types of handaxes produced (White 1998a). At Swanscombe, the makers of the point-dominated Middle Gravel industries had access to raw material directly from the river beach (Wymer 1964), the diminutive size of many of the handaxes reflecting the size of the clasts within the gravels. However, the ovate industry in the Upper Loams, as well as at the nearby sites of Bowman's Lodge and Wansunt Pit, were produced after these gravels had been concealed by metres of fine-grained deposits (cf. Bridgland 1994; Dines 1964; Tester 1950; White et al. 1995), cutting off the previous source of raw material. Hominins therefore came to the locales equipped with finished ovates or suitable blanks derived from predominantly fresh flint sources. The reverse is seen at Foxhall Road, Ipswich, where an imported ovate industry on top of the Grey Clay was replaced by a locally made, point-dominated industry following the emplacement of the Red Gravel (White and Plunkett 2004).

Exceptions to this pattern have been noted, such as the site of Cuxton in Kent, where an assemblage dominated by pointed handaxes was manufactured on fresh flint (cf. Wenban-Smith et al. 2000). The flint available in this part of Kent, however, often takes the form of 'burrow' or 'pipe flint' (i.e. formed in burrows of Cretaceous marine animals) which, while often very long, is also narrow and thick (practically cylindrical in some cases). This has clearly influenced the choices made by the knapper in working the nodules (Shaw and White 2003); a similar situation is found at Fordwich, although here the handaxes are far cruder and almost exclusively worked with a hard-hammer (White 1998a and c). In fact, the differences between the crude, hard-hammer handaxes at Fordwich and the much better made series at Sturry, two sites situated on different terraces of the Kentish Stour, can be explained by the river downcutting into Chalk during the Sturry Terrace Level (Coleman 1952; Bridgland et al. 1998). This event introduced a new supply of nodules into the local gravels and exposed different strata of chalk flint, providing humans with a far greater range of technological options than the earlier 'pipe-flint' dominated deposits.

At Red Barns, Porchester, Hampshire a small, point-dominated assemblage (7 complete handaxes and 11 broken ones), was made on a source of fresh flint (Gamble and Apsimon 1986; Wenban-Smith et al. 2000). This flint, however, was riddled with frost fractures and of poor knapping quality: 61% of handaxe-manufacturing attempts had failed due to the quality of the material. Although the flint might have been large and its shape neutral, it was simply not of sufficient quality to allow knapping to progress in a completely unhindered fashion. Indeed, in an attempt to avoid breakage, hominins engaged in minimal shaping, followed by delicate finishing along the margins, mostly at the tip end.

Interestingly, the excavators suggested that the materials left behind at Red Barns were rejects left at the manufacturing location (Gamble and ApSimon1986), the flake assemblage showing that more handaxes were made at Red Barns than were found there and therefore that some had clearly been removed. This conforms to the suggestions of Pope (2002, 2004), who argued that handaxe assemblage composition is not only related to raw materials but also to discard and transport behaviour. According to Pope, handaxes in general were less likely to be discarded at one-off activity sites than at established, frequently used locales and, furthermore, the selective removal of better made (generally ovate) handaxes lead to them being under-represented at sites with poor raw materials. It is thus quite conceivable that better made ovate handaxes could have originally been present at Red Barns (and other point-dominated sites) but were selectively removed, leaving a signature dominated by partly worked and more pointed forms.

The raw material model does not suggest that hominin technical actions were controlled by raw materials. Rather, the packages in which they encountered flint at different places in the landscape influenced the decisions made in bringing forth a handaxe from a piece of flint. Lower Palaeolithic hominins are therefore cast as knowledgeable actors engaging intelligently and flexibly with the vagaries of a heterogeneous environment. Socially acquired practical skills were deployed in a range of situations; a hominin who at one site made a pointed form because of raw material considerations, would at another have been equipped with the knowledge and skill to make an ovate. In Schlanger's (1996) terms individuals used an 'enabling image in the course of situated action', the piece being shaped in hand according to context and circumstance.

The reduction model

A prevalent theme in Palaeolithic research during the past three decades has emphasised the changes imposed on tool morphology by the act of resharpening the working edges to extend an implement's use-life – the so-called 'reduction' models. Reduction models arose mainly from work conducted on New World bifacial points (e.g. Frison 1968) but have since been extensively applied to European and Near Eastern Middle Palaeolithic scrapers (Dibble 1987, 1995; Rolland and Dibble 1990; Dibble and Rolland 1992).

Reduction models argue that tool morphology is the product of complex reduction strategies in which a tool is repeatedly resharpened to rejuvenate the working edges. Artefacts at different stages of resharpening may appear to be discrete types yet, according to these models, are actually various expressions of the same tool at different points in their use-life, different forms occurring together on archaeological sites because of differential use, reuse and discard rates. With such an approach final form is de-emphasised, as the shape a tool takes when finally discarded may bear little resemblance to any original design. Indeed, rather than representing desired forms, tools may have been discarded because they were no longer considered suitable for reworking.

While most reduction models revolve around scrapers and other flake tools, a reduction model for handaxes has been developed and refined by McPherron (1994, 1996,

2006). This model postulated that when the bifacial edge of a handaxe dulled it was resharpened and this produced predictable effects on several key aspects of handaxe morphology. McPherron proposed that, since functional edges must be assumed to be more important than overall shape, resharpening would have focused on the longest arc of usable edge – the tip. This would create differential reduction to the tip length and total length and have major effects on the typologically key variables of elongation (i.e. length/width), refinement (thickness/width) and shape (the butt was expected to see minimal reworking). Furthermore, by assuming that raw materials at a site would be of a constant size and shape, McPherron argued that the sequence of resharpening would follow a regular pattern with predictable changes to the highlighted aspects of shape:

1   All handaxes began their use-life as elongated, pointed forms with long tips and poor levels of metrical refinement.

2   Through resharpening these were gradually transformed into smaller and less elongated cordiforms and ovates, with shorter tips and higher refinement.

3   The ultimate stages of resharpening saw the handaxe become discoidal in shape, at which time refinement may decrease, although the piece should display equal butt–tip length and very low elongation.

This process is summarised in Figure 4.5.

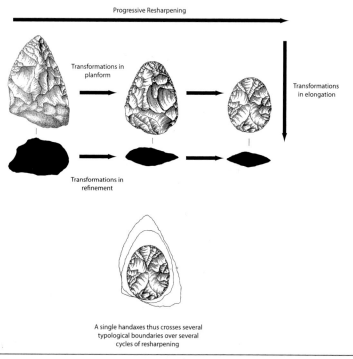

FIGURE 4.5
McPherron's model showing how handaxes may change in shape, elongation and refinement throughout a prolonged use-life. (Modified after McPherron 1994 and courtesy Shannon McPherron.)

White (1996) tested the predictions of the reduction model on handaxes from 22 British sites.[5] This showed that the patterns of change in elongation, refinement and shape predicted by McPherron's model were not particularly well developed. That is not to say that resharpening was not occurring; evidence from Boxgrove (Austin 1994) shows that handaxes were resharpened on the move (Figure 4.6), and a number of British sites contain recycled patinated or stained handaxes, showing that on occasion 'old' handaxes had been picked up, resharpened and reused (White 1996; Brumm et al. in press). It merely means that the regular and routine sequence of resharpening is hard to find, probably because the assumption that raw materials were of a constant shape and size is difficult to uphold and that handaxes started life in different sizes and forms. Resharpening was almost certainly happening and had a significant effect on handaxe shape and size; it is just very hard to measure.

Resharpening may, however, provide an explanation for the elusive British 'cleaver' (White 2006). As we noted above, Roe's method made provision for cleaver-dominated assemblages, as seen in Africa, India and the Levant, where distinct flake production methods designed to produce cleaver blanks were also employed (Kleindienst 1962; Gilead 1973; Isaac 1977; Roe 1994b; Petraglia 1998; Ranov 2001; Sharon 2007). And yet, in his analysis of 4,799 handaxes from 38 assemblages, he found just 122 metrically

FIGURE 4.6
Handaxe from Boxgrove with refitting tranchet removal. (Photo courtesy of Mark Roberts.)

defined cleavers, 2.5% of the total sample (Roe 1968a). Examples were found in both his pointed and ovate traditions and in all seven of his sub-groups, but they were rare and unevenly distributed, ranging from 0% to just 8.9% in frequency. Roe did, however, create one group (Group I) in which a slightly elevated frequency of cleavers was the defining feature, often in association with ficron-type handaxes (in the British sense; see above).

Using Cranshaw's (1983) data, White (2006) examined the metrical and technological properties of cleavers from these assemblages, finding that they differed only in the shape of the tip (Figure 4.7). He suggested that *in a British context* cleavers were not a discrete biface category, but rather a resharpened variant within the use-life of 'round-ended implements' (Cranshaw 1983), a form that occurred in an inverse proportion to

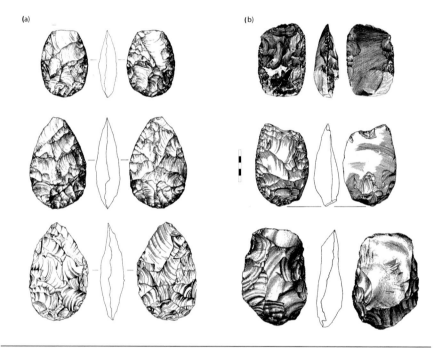

FIGURE 4.7
Selection of British 'cleavers' illustrating the effects of tranchet removals and the use of flake blank in accidentally creating this rare form in a British context (after White 2006). (a) handaxes from Boxgrove showing the different effects of tranchet removal orientation on biface shape. The top example shows one oblique tranchet, followed by a transverse tranchet, the latter removes the sharp lateral edge created by the former and also produces the cleaver shape. This action was quite deliberate, but the final shape was arguably just a by-product of this sharpening/resharpening practice. The lateral margins also show extensive retouch to strengthen and straighten the edges. Resharpening the bottom handaxe with a transverse blow would produce the same effect whilst retaining symmetry and overall shape, whereas another oblique blow would probably produce a more pointed form. (after Roberts et al. 1997 and courtesy of The Prehistoric Society). (b) Flake handaxes; top: Whitlingham (after Sainty 1927); middle: South Woodford (after Wymer 1985, reproduced with permission); bottom Baker's Hole (after Robinson 1986 and courtesy Penny Robinson.

cleavers at all these sites. He suggested that, when round-ended implements became blunt, they were often resharpened using a transverse tranchet removal. At Baker's Farm and Keswick over 90% of the cleavers had received at least one tranchet removal, either as the final flake or as an earlier blow followed by limited 'retouch', while the majority of cleavers from Furze Platt (75%), Whitlingham (68%) and Cuxton (53.9%) had at least one transversely orientated tranchet at the tip (Cranshaw 1983). This technical act had two effects: in some cases it created a genuine cleaver bit; and in all cases it preferentially removed material from the tip, affecting an unavoidable increase in relative butt size and decrease in relative tip length, thus producing a 'cleaver type' in Roe's terms (cf. McPherron 1994). There is thus a clear link between the cleaver form and transverse tranchet removals. Metrical analysis further suggested that at Cuxton, Keswick and Baker's Farm only the largest were selected for resharpening, whereas at the other two sites any suitable handaxe was reworked, showing that the practice was varied in its operation and outcome. All of these sites were situated in regions where raw materials were plentiful but often occurred in less than ideal packages, perhaps providing a reason why round-ended implements were resharpened here, but not everywhere. The few 'classic' cleavers found in Britain were argued to stem from the serendipitous use of large flakes with little functional or design intent (Figure 4.7). There is also an interesting chronological element to this pattern, which White (2006) summarily dismissed, but to which we will return below.

HANDAXES AND INDIVIDUALS

As exemplified in the two case studies discussed above, most attempts to examine variation in stone tools proceed from a functional and largely processual perspective. Features such as shape, symmetry, refinement, type, etc. are viewed in relation to how they impact on a human's ability to 'get the job done' (e.g. Ashton and McNabb 1994; McPherron 1994; White 1998a; Machin et al. 2007). Social life is usually regarded as intangible and unknowable, and only evident (if at all) as residual noise once functional, ecological and economic factors have been satisfactorily taken into account (e.g. Isaac 1972).

The past decade has seen a more explicit concern with social life and agency in Palaeolithic archaeology (e.g. Gamble 1998, 1999, 2007; Dobres 2000). For Clive Gamble (1998, 1999), who has undoubtedly been the leading figure in this movement, social factors are not simply noise. Instead, how individuals constructed their identity and defined their place in the social arena is fundamental to understanding the Palaeolithic, regardless of whether one is dealing with *Homo heidelbergensis* or *Homo sapiens*. This cannot be studied directly or in a stepwise processual manner, however, but requires a new theoretical approach to the Palaeolithic in which technology is seen as part of the social performances that helped create and bind society. Enacted in the context of 'gatherings' (Gamble 1999), the rhythms and gestures of Palaeolithic technology formed the routines by which individuals were known, relationships forged and networks maintained.

The actions were as important as the end products, and embodied the techniques (skills) and capabilities of agents through which they engaged with and understood the world, their place within it, and others (Ingold 1993). In the Lower Palaeolithic, the social networks formed through technology were principally intimate and effective, requiring continuous reaffirmation through copresence and interaction (Gamble 1999, 50–1). For Kohn and Mithen (1999) handaxes performed a different social role, used by males to signal their sexual fitness to prospective mates (see Text Box 4.1).[6] In both, artefacts had no active voice or symbolic meaning when they were not physically associated with the individual agent who made them.

Text Box 4.1

THE CLACTON SPEAR: A 400,000-YEAR-OLD WEAPON

The Clacton spear (Figure 1) is the only preserved wooden artefact from the Palaeolithic period in Britain. It was discovered in 1911 by Samuel Hazzledine Warren, who dug it out of an undisturbed part of the Freshwater Beds on the foreshore at Clacton-on-Sea (Warren 1911). These beds, and therefore the spear, date to an early part of MIS11c, that is ~400 ka BP. The fragmentary spear is constructed of Yew, with one end sharpened to a point, the other unevenly broken (Oakley et al. 1977). When found, the shaft and tip were almost straight and measured 38.7 cm in length and 3.8 cm in diameter, although it has subsequently suffered shrinkage and warping. Today it measures 36.7 cm and has a marked curve at the tip (Oakley et al. 1977). Andrews (in Oakley et al. 1977) suggests that the wood must have been dry and well-seasoned for the break to occur, as green yew wood is very flexible. Keeley (in Oakley et al. 1977) further suggested that a month of drying-out would have been sufficient, although this does not automatically imply that the object was maintained and used for that length of time.

FIGURE 1
The Clacton spear, discovered by
Samuel Hazzledine Warren at Clacton in 1911.
(© Natural History Museum.)

Keeley (ibid.) observed sets of striae on the surface of the spear, which he intepreted as manufacturing tool-marks, and noted that there was no evidence

Text Box 4.1

that the tip had been fire-hardened. Clark (in Oakley et al.1977) compared the Clacton spear with known archaeological and ethnographical wooden artefacts, noting that it was not as slender and tapered as throwing spears (the taper begins about 10 cm from the tip) or as rounded as a digging stick. He concluded that it was probably a thrusting spear.

In the past decade ~8 spears have been discovered from deposits overlying a brown-coal mine at Schöningen 13 II–4, Germany (Thieme 2005). Seven were made of dense, slow-growing spruce, and one of pine. The spears are up to 2.5 metres long and between 29 and 50 cm in diameter. They are constructed like a modern Olympic javelin, with the bulk of the weight in the spear's front third (Thieme 1997, 2005). Experimental reconstructions suggested that spears like this could be thrown up to 60 metres and still achieve good penetrative power (Rieder 2000, cited in Thieme 2005), and Thieme does not doubt that these were projectile weapons. Numerous other wooden objects were also recovered from Schöningen, including a 78 cm wooden stick, pointed at both ends, interpreted as a throwing stick; an 88 cm stick, stripped of all its bark and branches, one end showing polish from prolonged handling, the other charred from use as a fire-hook or roasting spit.

The Clacton and Schöningen spears serve to remind us of the perishable weapons and tools that rarely survive archaeologically.

These interpretations inject a welcome new perspective into the British Palaeolithic, although the question remains whether embedding technology into social life, or rather agency into technology, provides anything more than a new rhetorical device. It certainly allows more scope for discussion – highlighting aspects that Palaeolithic archaeologists have almost been afraid to talk about in open circles – and, judging by many conference presentations of the past ten years, has proved highly popular with postgraduate students. To help us explain and understand the Lower Palaeolithic, however, we need more than bald assertions that *all* technology *is* social mediation. Simply stating that humans used handaxes to negotiate their way in society doesn't actually make this real, and one runs the risk of creating axiomatic supra-individuals when one should be concerned with teasing out real individuals from the technological record. It is the former we see in the hundreds of thousands of handaxes from the fluvial archive, each one no doubt an instance of individual craftsmanship and skill. However, it is only through the actual observed individual – a very rare beast indeed – that the agency of the supra-individual can be validated.

White and Plunkett (2004) provided two instances where actual individuals may be evident in the Lower Palaeolithic record. At Foxhall Road, Ipswich, a cluster of eleven handaxes was recovered encircling a group focus, possibly a hearth (Layard 1903), around which a small group of perhaps four or five people sat. Similarities in the morphology of several of the handaxes suggested to White and Plunkett that each individual had their own style (or 'hand') of handaxe design (Figure 4.8). Another example can be found at Caddington (Catt et al. 1978) where *in situ* knapping scatters revealed the pres-

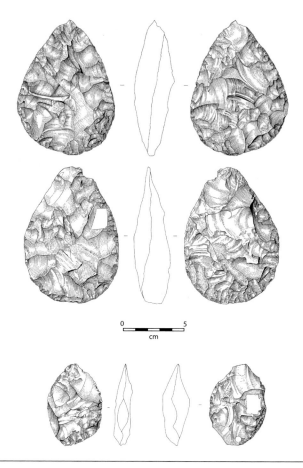

FIGURE 4.8
Paired handaxes from Foxhall Road, possibly representing the idiosyncratic styles of two Palaeolithic individuals. (After White and Plunkett 2004.)

ence of several individuals, each displaying their own technique, skill and experience in nodule choice and knapping trajectory. Some knappers produced closely matched shapes, others a variety of forms depending on the materials at hand (suggesting that each knapper really did have a varied repertoire of shaping available to them which they expressed in different contexts). The Caddington example expresses technique above form, but both were still testament to an individual flint-knapper's hand. Furthers examples may be evident at Boxgrove (Matt Pope pers. comm.).

A degree variation may of course be the unintended outcome of experience and motor skill. Yet there are imposed differences in the techniques employed (twisted and non-twisted edges, tranchet tips) and in the form of the end-product that may be more assertive, expressing more strongly the maker's identity. If this is the case, then at Foxhall Road the physical handaxe provided a lasting testimony that extended the significance of the object well beyond the original act of creating it. If, as Gamble suggests, technology was central to the construction of social identity, then the objects themselves were just as important as the technical actions of their manufacture and use, explaining to some degree why many handaxes show elaborate symmetry and refinement and why variation (within limits, see below), rather than standardisation, dominate most assemblages. The Caddington example, however, conforms more to Gamble's opinion that it was the *process* of creation as part of socially situated performances that helped create and affirm social roles.

THE FUNCTION OF LOWER PALAEOLITHIC TOOLS

What hominins actually did with the millions of stone tools they created appears to be the most basic of questions, yet it is noteworthy that functional analyses of British Palaeolithic stone tools have only rarely been undertaken. Granted, establishing the functions of stone tools is a difficult task, and beyond simple guesswork based on shape and historically received names (e.g. 'scrapers') the only objective method of establishing function/s is microscopic use-wear; a technique that has had a rather chequered history (Keeley 1980; Newcomer et al. 1986; Bamforth 1988). Microwear analysis is highly dependent on almost pristine preservational conditions, and very few British sites have proved suitable. Information exists only for Hoxne, Swanscombe, Clacton (Keeley 1980, 1993), Boxgrove (Mitchell 1996, 1997) and South Woodford (White et al. 1999b); recent attempts to study use-wear on the scrapers from High Lodge was unsuccessful (Nick Ashton pers. comm.). This is only part of the problem, however.

Theoretical splits within the British archaeological community have meant that Palaeolithic archaeologists in Britain – more so than in any other country we suspect – have run the gauntlet of the post-processual agenda.[7] With the flick of an –ist or an –ism, studies aimed at enhancing our understanding of the activities of ancient hominins or their responses to their heterogeneous and ever-changing environment have been cast as deterministic, wrong-headed and somehow inappropriate to enquiry (White 2008). We firmly reject these accusations. In the rush to use stone tools to understand what Neanderthal boys thought of their mothers, it is easy to lose sight of the fact that handaxes and other stone tools are not simply fossilised acts of social maintenance. They were fully functional objects, parts of complex webs connecting functional, ecological and social relationships through lifetimes and generations (Robb 2001; Hopkinson and White 2005). So, back to basics: what did Lower Palaeolithic humans do with all the stone tools they made?

Much of what we do know derives from the work of Lawrence Keeley (1980, 1993) and John Mitchell (1996, 1997, 1998; White et al. 1999a), both of whom conducted their studies under Derek Roe's guidance at the Baden-Powell Quaternary Research Centre in Oxford. Keeley (1980) examined material from the Lower Industry at Hoxne, the Swanscombe Lower Loams, South Woodford and the Clacton Golf Course site. Remarkably few artefacts preserved traces of use-wear – only 4 from Swanscombe, 28 from Hoxne and 50 from Clacton – reflecting both post-depositional alteration to their edges and the fact that the majority of débitage found in the archaeological record probably saw little or no use. The tasks to which tools had been put are summarised in Table 4.3 and Figure 4.9.

Table 4.3 Frequency of various uses (counting edges) of stone tools from Clacton and Hoxne Lower Industry (modified after Keeley 1980; 1993).

Use	Clacton Count	%	Hoxne Count	%	Swanscombe Count
Wood Whittling	10	20	2	5.9	1
Wood Chopping	4	8	1	2.9	
Wood Sawing	2	4	0		
Wood Scraping	5	10	2	5.9	
Wood Wedging	1	2	5	14.7	
Hide Scraping	3	6	4	11.8	
Hide Cutting	1	6	2	5.9	
Hide indet. Action	0		1	2.9	
Meat Cutting	10	20	10	29.4	1
Bone Chopping	0		2	5.9	
Boring	4	8	2	5.9	
Plant Cutting	0		3	8.8	
Other	10	20	0		2

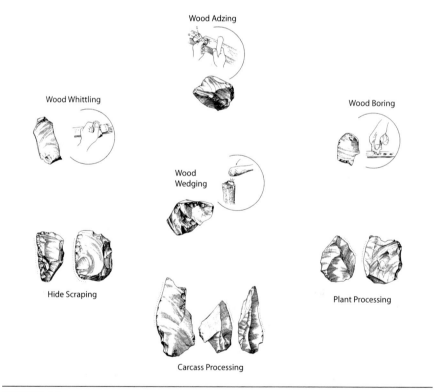

FIGURE 4.9
Artefacts from Hoxne and Clacton with functions inferred from microwear analysis. (After Wymer 1985 and reproduced with permission.)

It is clear from these figures that the majority of stone tools were used in processing wood or animal products, that is, hide working or butchery. That such activities were carried out is also directly shown by cut-marked bones and the rare preservation of shaped wooden artefacts, such as the Clacton spear (Warren 1911: see Text Box 4.1 and Figure 4.9). The stone tools successfully analysed appear to have played very little part in the processing of plant foods, perhaps because those plants exploited by ancient humans required little or no processing, because they played only a minor role in their diet beyond basic nutritional needs, and/or because they were unavailable during the seasons in which these sites were used. Indeed, Keeley (1993, 134) suggested that the plant processing activity he could detect was based round the collection of vegetal raw materials, not food.

The function of so-called 'chopper-cores' has been debated for almost a century (War-ren 1922; see Figure 4.10). Warren (e.g. 1923b, 1924) was convinced that those found in the Clacton assemblage, which possessed an alternately worked zigzag edge oppo-site a natural or cortical hand-grip, were genuinely tools, as the flakes produced during their manufacture would have been practically useless and much larger flakes had been

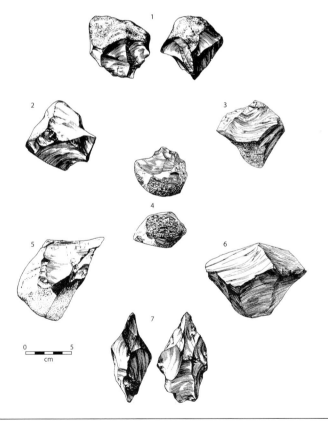

FIGURE 4.10
Clactonian Chopper Cores. (After Wymer 1985 and reproduced with permission.)

struck from other nuclei. Breuil (1932) and Ashton et al. (1992a), on the other hand, saw them simply as cores, with no inherent design intent or functional purpose (see also Toth 1985). Keeley (1980) found little evidence that cores were ever used as tools – of the 22 examined from Clacton only 2 bore traces of utilisation, both being employed to chop bone. Most evidence of chopping was encountered on large flakes. Keeley (1980, 116) also rejected claims that large numbers of chopper-cores from the Clacton Golf Course site showed macroscopic signs of wear (Singer et al. 1973), suggesting instead that this was the result of post-depositional spalling, a conclusion supported by the reduced frequency of 'use-wear' in the fine grained marls (20%) compared to the gravels (83%). While this supports the argument that choppers were cores, a much wider ranging microwear programme would be required to finally lay the problem to rest.

Hoxne and Clacton differed in the ratio of utilised flakes – 1:9 compared to 1:4 – which, according to Keeley (1980, 1993), reflected the fact that handaxes were being made and used at Hoxne, providing a bespoke cutting tool and generating an astonishing number of flakes and chips too thin and brittle to be of use. Indeed, flakes generated during handaxe manufacture seem to have been rarely used, with most utilised flakes being detached from cores deliberately selected for their production. Moreover, most tasks appear to have been accomplished with unretouched edges, although even these showed areas that had been modified to remove a spur or to blunt opposing edges to facilitate comfortable handling. The weakly developed wear patterns further suggested that these were rather *ad hoc* and rapidly discarded implements. Only pieces requiring a regular edge (for scraping) or a steep strong edge (for chopping) were retouched, and it is possible that the retouch found on hide-scrapers may be entirely the product of resharpening rather than intentional shaping, as scraping quickly dulls an edge (Keeley 1993, 131). Recent work by Brumm and McLaren (2011) on the High Lodge scrapers partly supports this statement. They concluded that the shapes seen in this celebrated scraper assemblage were not the result of intentional design, but the interplay of variation in original blank form and resharpening (see Pettitt 1992 for the same but unpublished conclusion). Contrary to the classic Dibble model (e.g. Dibble 1987, 1995; Rolland and Dibble 1990; Dibble and Rolland 1992), however, scrapers did not always change shape as they were resharpened. Keeley (1980, 175, 1993, 131) also noted that most hide-scraping edges were straight in shape, possibly because hides were processed over a round 'beaming post' (probably a log).

It is Keeley's analysis of the function of handaxes that is perhaps the most intriguing. Of the five handaxes he examined from Hoxne and the four from South Woodford, only three bore any evidence of use – all having been used to cut meat. Due to the small sample size, however, he leaned towards the received wisdom that they were multi-purpose tools, although he did emphasise their usefulness in a range of carcass processing tasks away from the home base, the simpler flake tools being used in central locations (possibly suggesting, therefore, that the site of High Lodge operated as a home base).

A re-analysis of the South Woodford handaxes by Mitchell (White et al. 1999a) failed to find any microscopic evidence of use-wear. He did, however, find a number of macroscopic signs that were not the result of post-depositional damage. Three of the handaxes had broken tips, probably due to a heavy-duty impact or twisting during use, perhaps to disarticulate carcasses. All three tips were subsequently retouched. Interestingly, a handaxe tip was also found at South Woodford, but does not appear to belong to any of the handaxes present. Large-scale damage to the edges of two of the handaxes also suggests heavy duty activity. Two of the handaxes also showed heavy duty damage to their faces, in the form of multiple incipient cones of percussion, suggesting that they were subject to repeated battering by or against a sharp object, resulting in a restricted area of impact (Figure 4.11). We assume that this was related to bone-cracking.

By far the most compelling evidence for handaxe function has come from Mitchell's work at Boxgrove (1996, 1997, 1998): 57% of the handaxes he examined bore traces of use-wear, all of them related to meat processing. Butchery experiments directed by Mitchell and conducted by a professional butcher found the Boxgrove style ovate handaxes to be a highly efficient tool (Mitchell 1996). Gripping the tool between thumb and fingers, thus avoiding any contact with the sharp edges, the butcher moved the piece in a gentle sweeping arc from butt to tip, using the free hand to push the flesh away from the active area and pull the meat taut as an aid to cutting. Use-wear on these experimental pieces extended around the entire working edge and was totally consistent with an archaeological sample from Boxgrove (Mitchell 1996 and pers. comm. to MJW). The butcher commented, however, that the bifacial edge of a handaxe was not an ideal tool to make an initial incision through skin: a flake or tranchet edge was far more effective for this purpose (Mitchell pers. comm. to MJW). Mitchell (1998) also noted damage patterns related to battering on several Boxgrove handaxes, which we again assume is related to the more heavy duty elements of dismembering a large animal.

FIGURE 4.11
Handaxe from South Woodford, showing area of incipient percussion cones resulting from repeated localised battering (inset = magnified image of percussion area). (Courtesy Jeff Veitch.)

These conclusions are largely in agreement with those of Keeley. The ubiquity of the handaxe may therefore be related to the fact that its bifacial margins provided a sturdy, resharpenable cutting edge, and that its weight and compact form made it usable as a chopper or a hammer; tips could also usefully serve for prising or stabbing. In this regard, they may be considered to have been versatile, reliable and maintainable (Bleed 1986; Ohel 1987), although judging by the vast quantities discarded close to their point of manufacture after seemingly little use and while still in perfectly serviceable condition, most do not appear to have been curated over long distances or for long periods of time. Equally, unlike their Middle Palaeolithic counterparts (see Chapter 6) they seem to have operated as tools per se, rather than as supports for other tools such as scrapers and notches (e.g. Boëda et al. 1990; Turq 2001; Soressi and Hays 2003).

One final piece of evidence for the function of stone tools (although not which stone tools) comes from the two human incisors from Boxgrove. These show a series of cut-marks running diagonally across the labial surfaces, suggesting that a large chunk of meat had been held taut between them (as a 'third hand') while the user sliced strips off for sharing or consumption. The direction of the cuts suggests that this particular human was right handed.

TEMPORAL TRENDS

To summarise much of what we have discussed: Palaeolithic archaeologists have long believed that handaxe shape variation among small and socially isolated groups should show regional and/or chronological patterning, in other words different 'traditions' that evolved through time. Most handaxe assemblages show a modal form, but until now this has been poorly correlated with either time or space. Roe (1968a, 1981) had entirely expected to find chronological patterning in the British handaxe assemblages he examined and, when this failed to emerge, understandably blamed poor and incomplete dating. As a result, more recent work has emphasised the role of reduction or raw materials in creating assemblage biases, with the probability that each individual hominid had their own 'hand' that expressed their social identity, encompassing a set of different styles that they drew upon in different ecological contexts. Recent advances in dating and in the correlation of Pleistocene deposits, however, provide tentative hints that temporal variation may be in evidence, but not at the scales most recent analyses employ.

In developing a raw material-driven explanation, White (1996; 1998a and b) noted that particular characteristics could not be explained by extra-somatic factors. The most prominent amongst these were incidences of tranchet removals, the unique burin-like removals on pointed handaxes at Whitlingham, Norfolk and frequencies of twisted ovate handaxes. The latter were noted to dominate assemblages belonging to later MIS11 and were offered as an example of endemic cultural variation occurring at a time when Britain was isolated from Europe (White 1998b). Twisted edges played no obvious functional role (although the predominant Z-twist rather than S-twist may reveal a predominance of right-handedness in Pleistocene humans). Later work at Foxhall Road (White and Plunkett 2004) showed that, within discrete clusters, only some individuals actually made this form, hinting at the possibility that individuals within a group adopted their own, highly specific style of handaxe as an expression of identity. The prevalence of such traits within an assemblage might therefore relate to the frequency with which these individuals made handaxes, or the role that these people played within a group. Assuming that the style developed by juveniles depended more upon their role model(s) than a collective ideal, then the choice of model was probably predicated on interpersonal relationships and social identities. The frequency of different forms within a group would therefore drift (cf. Isaac 1972) according to the players involved, the social and ecological context within which they acted and the time over which the assemblage accumulated.

The regional spread of such characteristics might therefore depend on inter-group networks or the size of a groups' local operational area (White and Pettitt 2011). In a 'sink' region such as Britain (see Chapter 2), however, they are equally likely to relate to characteristics introduced by colonising groups, which spread with them as they dispersed into empty or sparsely populated landscapes. Therefore, any chronological patterning will not just appear disjointed because of the poor temporal resolution and broken nature of the data, it will actually be disjointed because it records the ebb and flow of different groups over time.

All this is rather academic if no chronological patterning exists. Indeed, when viewed at the gross scales of point-dominated versus ovate-dominated groups (e.g. White 1998a) no patterning is evident and raw materials and reduction provide adequate explanations for assemblage biases. However, drilling down to smaller scales of Roe's sub-groups, a different pattern emerges. Table 4.4 shows the seven sub-groups defined by Derek Roe, alongside recent age-correlations based on biostratigraphy, lithostratigraphy and absolute dating. Sites for which no date estimate exists (mostly those with a vague provenence or from locations that have been destroyed before they could be re-examined using modern methods) have been removed from this table, as these are presently irrelevant to the question and serve only to obscure patterns. The intermediate group has also been removed, as these are all heavily derived and mixed sites containing artefacts from several different cycles.

Based on the correlations in Table 4.4, clear chronological patterning is evident in the British Lower Palaeolithic record. Group I sites all belong to MIS10–9–8, the absence of a strong Levallois element suggesting that they possibly belong to the earlier part of the cycle although this point is debatable. These sites contain ficrons and cleavers – the former probably a deliberately constructed form expressing the identity of the maker (see also Text Box 3.6), the latter reflecting a widespread resharpening practice at this time. Group III, of which Wolvercote is the sole member, also dates to MIS9 and Ashton (2001) has similarly made the case that resharpening practices in a region where raw material was poor was responsible for the shape of the handaxes there. Although not recorded in this table, it was noted above that Acheulean sites belonging to MIS9 also show much higher proportions of scrapers and flake tools, reflecting changes in the

Table 4.4 British handaxe traditions according to Derek Roe with inferred ages (1968a). Sites in paranthesis added after White 1996, 1998a; White and Plunkett 2004. Age attributions based on Preece et al. 1990 Ashton et al. 1992; Bridgland 1994, 1996 and personal communication; Boreham and Gibbard 1995; White et al. 1995; Schreve 1997, 2001a; Roberts and Parfitt 1999; Wymer 1999; White and Plunkett 2004; Wenban-Smith 2004; Ashton et al. 2005; Lundberg and McFarlane 2007; Ashton et al. 2008a; Hosfield 2011).

←	Pointed Tradition	→	←	Ovate Tradition	→
Group I (with cleavers)	Group II (with ovates)	Group III (plano-convex)	Group V (crude, narrow)	Group VI (more pointed)	Group VII (less pointed)
MIS9–8	**MIS11**	**MIS9**	**MIS13–15**	**MIS11**	**MIS13**
Furze Platt	Swanscombe MG	Wolvercote	Fordwich	Elveden	High Lodge
Bakers Farm	Chadwell St Mary		Farnham terrace A	Bowman's Lodge	Warren Hill fresh
Cuxton Farm	Hoxne UI		Warren Hill worn	Swanscombe UL	Highlands
Stoke Newington	Dovercourt		(Kent's Cavern Breccia)	(Wansunt)	Corfe Mullen
	Hitchin			(Foxhall Road Grey Clays)	(Boxgrove)
	(Foxhall Road Red Gravel)			Hoxne LI	
				MIS12–13	
				Caversham	
				MIS7	
				Shide, Pan Farm	
				Oldbury	

activities carried out at these sites and possibly demonstrating greater frequencies of hide-working and the development of more effective clothing.

Group II, dominated by squat, broad-pointed handaxes with a strong ovate element, all date to MIS11, as does the pointed ovate-dominated Group VI. Most of the Group VI sites, along with Hitchin from Group II, contain high proportions of twisted ovates. These groups are distinguished by raw material sources, Group II occurring on gravel raw materials, Group VI on fresh flint. That one period contains two dominant groups is another indication that different shapes had individual or cultural resonance according to different raw material contexts, hominins having more than one relevant style in their repertoire which they brought into action as needed. However, many of the 'twisted ovate sites' can now be argued to date from MIS11a. Groups IV and Group VII both date to pre-Anglian interglacials, the latter dominated by crude metrical 'ovates' that probably reflect raw material packages.

Although the assemblages that constitute each of these groups represent the actions of untold individuals over total spans of hundred or thousands of years (or generations) the patterns should actually come as little surprise. The conservatism of the Acheulean over one million years clearly shows that the technological systems of Middle Pleistocene humans were strongly rule bound. Variation in handaxe shape reflects constant modification to a basic formula but always within socially acceptable parameters and radical change is absent. Nowell and White (2010) described these processes as inventiveness and innovation, where inventiveness describe the ability to be creative within the technology at hand, and innovation those technological leaps to totally novel systems (Text Box 4.2). Rejecting the notion that cognitive deficiencies lie at the heart of this (e.g. Binford 1989a; Klein 1999; Mithen 1996), one must conclude that within archaic hominin societies the power of individual agents to express themselves through technology may have been strong, but their power actually to change the overarching structure of the Acheulean was limited (Hopkinson and White 2005).

GROWING UP IN THE MIDDLE PLEISTOCENE

One of the most intriguing aspects of the Lower Palaeolithic material record is its conservative nature. Despite a diverse range of variations on a theme – from the Acheulean, through Clactonian and other non-handaxe occurrences to the central European 'Lower Palaeolithic microlithic industries' – the underlying technological and typological foundations barely change for almost one million years. By contrast, in terms of human development and life histories, the Middle Pleistocene was one of the most dramatic periods in human prehistory.

Nowell and White (2010) have explored this decoupling of the biological and technological realms. Their starting point was modern human life history, the slowest of all the primates. Humans experience five phases of life: infant, child, juvenile, adolescent and adult, with childhood and adolescence apparent being unique to our species (Kennedy 2003; Bogin 2003). Human infants are relatively large at birth, and grow slowly during a long period of childhood, which provides time to develop behavioural experience and plasticity (Bogin 2003). Similarly, adolescence (which in humans is associated with a rapid growth spurt) provides additional time for humans to develop cultural, linguistic and social skills (ibid.). Humans also reach reproductive maturity later than other primates and have increased longevity, with a large proportion of a woman's life being post-reproductive (Hawkes et al. 2003; Kaplan 2002; Zimmermann and Radespiel 2007; Nowell and White 2010).

Although not fully modern in their adaptations, the life history of Middle Pleistocene hominins represents a substantial departure from those of the apes and earlier hominins, and more closely approaches that of Upper Pleistocene humans (Nowell and White 2010). It has been suggested that it was during the Middle Pleistocene that the life histories of *Homo* came to include, for the first time, either a childhood stage or a significantly expanded childhood (Bogin 2003; Krovitz et al. 2003). Skeletal evidence also indicates an adolescent stage had evolved in archaic *Homo sapiens* (Antón and Leigh 2003; Bogin 2003), although whether this stage was part of the life history of *Homo erectus* is debatable (Antón and Leigh 2003; Bogin 2003; Tardieu 1998). This is extremely important: for the first time in hominin history more time would have been available for individuals to learn social, ecological, and technical skills. A recent dental study, however, suggests they experienced a faster pace of development than modern

Text Box 4.2

humans, with shorter phases of childhood and adolescence (Dean et al. 2001),. Kennedy (2003) argued that Middle Pleistocene hominin species reached sexual maturity around age 13, with a mother's first birth occurring somewhere between 15 and 16.5 years of age, which is within the range of modern humans. *Homo erectus* may also have been the first hominin species with extended post-menopausal longevity (Aiello and Key 2002), leading some to suggest that grandmothers and great aunts became instrumental in teaching and provisioning the young – the so-called 'Grandmother Hypothesis' (Hawkes et al. 1997).

All of this biological turmoil is the genus and species' equivalent of adolescence. With hominin life history undergoing such transformations during the Middle Pleistocene, including the emergence of several aspects of growth and development that foreshadow the 'modern condition', why do we see such stasis in technological systems? Rejecting cognitive inadequacies as an explanation (and not particularly enamoured with the 'if it ain't broke, don't fix it' explanation) Nowell and White (2010) explore several socially driven possibilities.

Assuming that Palaeolithic hominins experienced their short childhoods in small groups, with cultural transmission predominantly vertical (down generations through parents and grandparents) and with few peers with whom to play and experiment, the existing technological system – a *status quo* – may have been indelibly imprinted on the impressionable young hominin mind. Subsequent life choices might then have operated only within the range of inherited possibilities, variations on a theme predicated on local circumstances. Similarly, if an adolescent phase was present, this may have been the period in which an individual developed and secured their relational and economic roles, with selective fitness and social ties binding hominins to do things in a certain way. If we entertain the various theories concerning the social resonance of handaxes and other stone tools (e.g. Gamble 1998, 1999; Kohn and Mithen 1999), then the small networks within which Middle Pleistocene hominins lived – where daily contact was only with familiar faces – may have limited the scope for deviancy in any realm.

Mathematical models have demonstrated that levels of cultural innovation and the promulgation of advantageous cultural traits increase with population size (e.g. Shennan 2001). Middle Pleistocene groups may simply have been too small and too widely dispersed for enduring change to arise and spread. Local innovations and transformations in existing technologies – which were in any case extremely limited given the level of technology in operation – may have had no effect outside the local hominin network, and would disappear if and when individual or group perished. Furthermore, small population densities, which may be assumed on the basis of high levels of hominin carnivory in Middle Pleistocene Europe (Roebroeks 2006), potentially have a negative impact on cumulative cultural development, with the degradation and even loss of more complex skills (Heinrich 2004; cf. Hosfield 2011). This may help to explain why changes in life history (alongside evidence for complex planning, hunting and transmission of technology and other life skills) did not kick-start a 'ratchet effect' (Mithen 1994) and failed to break the stasis (cf. Hosfield 2010). The result, globally and at scales of tens of millennia, is apparent stability with a lot of noise – exactly what we see in the Lower Palaeolithic record.

Text Box 4.2

Even this brief survey is too broad in its focus – once again being based on gross meas ures of shape – and we are convinced that an examination of the nuances within each of these groups will provide yet more individually and culturally significant characteristics. The obvious conclusion is that the scale of investigation has a massive impact on our deductions, and what is obvious and relevant at one scale is invisible at others. Attempt- ing to identify the 'prime mover' in handaxe variation is thus a rather fruitless task, that can only result in sterile debates where neither side can see the others point of view sim- ply because they are looking through different filters (e.g. White 1998a versus Wenban- Smith et al. 2000 versus Shaw and White 2003). When added to the chronology of the Clactonian (below) one can only conclude that there are significant cultural signatures within the British Lower Palaeolithic, over which a number of confounding factors are overprinted. It is also clear that, in order to understand these patterns, chronological and geographical variation in Europe must be brought to the same level of understanding.

THE CLACTONIAN

The Clactonian is a uniquely British core-and-flake industry first defined on the basis of collections of artefacts discovered at Clacton-on-Sea Essex during the 1900s (e.g. War- ren 1912). Recognised (or not, as the case may be) at just a handful of sites (Table 4.5,

Table 4.5 Key Clactonian occurrences.

Site	Context	Occurrences	References
Clacton on Sea, Essex	MIS12–11 Thames deposits of the Boyn Hill/Orsett Heath Formation	Lion Point Jaywick Sands West Cliff Golf Course	Warren 1922; 1923; 1924; 1951; Oakley and Leakey 1937; Singer et al. 1973; Bridgland et al. 1999 Butlin's Holiday Camp
Swanscombe, Kent	MIS11 Thames deposits of the Boyn Hill/Orsett Heath Formation	Lower Gravel, Barnfield Pit Lower Loams, Barnfield Pit	Smith and Dewey 1913; 1914; Chandler 1930, 1931, 1932; Conway et al. 1996;
		Lower Gravel, Rickson's Pit	
Ebbsfleet, Southfleet Road	MIS11 Thames deposits of the Boyn Hill/Orsett Heath Formation	'Elephant Site'	Wenban-Smith et al. 2006
Barnham, Suffolk	Early MIS11 fluvial deposits	Rolled series within and atop of cobble band	Paterson 1937; Ashton et al. 1998
Globe Pit, Little Thurrock, Essex	MIS10/9 Thames deposits of the Lynch Hill/Corbets Tey Formation	Bed 1	King and Oakley 1936; Bridgland and Harding 1993; Bridgland 1994
Purfleet, Essex	MIS10/9 Thames deposits of the Lynch Hill/Corbets Tey Formation	Coombe Rock Lower (Thurrock) Gravel	Wymer 1985; Schreve et al. 2002
Cuxton, Kent	MIS10/9 deposits of the Medway	Lower Assemblage	Tester 1965; Cruse 1987; Bridgland 1996

see also Text Boxes 3.1, 3.3, 3.4, 3.8, 3.15) it is the *bête noir* of the British Palaeolithic and over the past 100 years has been at the centre of heated and often acrimonious debate.[8] For a few it is nothing more than a fictional construct of archaeological sampling and systematics; others regard it is a parochial industry unworthy of study, and some as the key to understanding the British Palaeolithic in its wider European context. We outline in this section the present understanding of the Clactonian and critically synthesise some of the many attempts that have been made to interpret it. For fuller digests of the history and development of the Clactonian, the reader is referred to White (2000), on which the account below is largely based, and McNabb (2007). A brief timeline is also presented in Table 4.6.

Table 4.6 Key moments in the history of the Clactonian industry.

Date	Event
1890s	Kenworthy discovers flakes and cores in Pleistocene deposits at Clacton on Sea.
1900–1910s	Samuel Hazzledine Warren active at Clacton, amassing large numbers of artefacts including the tip of a wooden spear. Warren found it difficult to classify his finds within the prevailing Mortillean framework.
1913	Smith and Dewey discover a non-handaxe (Clactonian) assemblage at Barnfield Pit, Swanscombe.
1914	B.O.Wymer (father of J.J. Wymer) discovers a non-handaxe assemblage at Little Thurrock, Essex.
1922	Abbé Henri Breuil assigns material from Clacton to the Mesvinian.
1923–24	Warren (1923, 1924) suggests that Clacton-Mesvinian was a chopper-based industry that formed an entirely different cultural tradition to the Chellean-Acheulean, the two possibly being made by different races of human.
1926	Breuil (1926) retracts Mesvinian label following re-analysis of material at Mesvin. Warren (1926) proposes Clactonian as new cultural designation.
1930–32	Chandler finds Clactonian material at Rickson's Pit, Swanscombe, and sub-divides Swanscombe Clactonian into two evolutionary Stages, Clactonian I and II.
1932	Breuil (1932) introduces a new framework comprising several parallel cultural phyla of handaxe and non handaxe industries, plotted against the Penck and Bruckner (1909) Alpine glacial sequence. Two major substages of the Clactonian were identified, which finally evolved into early Levallois industries. Brueil reclassifies Clactonian as a core industry.
1937	Oakley and Leakey excavate at Jaywick Sands, Clacton, and introduce a four-fold division Clacton I, IIa (found at Swanscombe), IIb (found at Clacton) and III (found at High Lodge).
1939	Paterson (1937) presents details the Brecklandian Clactonian at Barnham St Gregory, Suffolk. He recognises five local variants separable by context, condition, and typology, which show a progressive development in technique uncontaminated by other cultures.
1940s	Ideas of cultural admixture filter into the Clactonian canon. Paterson and Fagg (1940), for example, suggest the assemblage at Elveden shows handaxe making groups adopting Clactonian core-and-flake techniques.
1949	Oakley (1949) formalises hypothesis that Clactonian is related to the pebble-tool cultures of East Asia, an interpretation readily embraced by Warren (1951).
1950s–1970	Notion that Clactonian represented earliest occupation of Britain takes hold (e.g. Oakley 1961, Wymer 1968), the culture later being assimilated into the incoming Acheulean groups.
1964	Oakley (1964) suggests that the Clactonian was a woodworking variant of the Acheulean, perhaps a seasonal or contextually specific activity facies.
1974	Wymer draws up the classic synthesis of the Clactonian.
1990s	Ashton and McNabb begin to argue that the Clactonian does not exist.

The Clactonian defined

The classic definition of the Clactonian, which is probably that most familiar outside of British archaeology, can be summarised using the magisterial work of John Wymer (1968, 1974):

1   It is a technologically distinct, primitive core-and-flake industry that contains chopper-cores and unstandardised flake tools (Figure 4.12) but definitively lacks handaxes. The use of the block-on-block or anvil technique is common (see Table 4.7 for past attempts to provide a template for what constitutes a Clactonian industry).

2   It thus represents the products of a habitually non-handaxe making culture group, related not to the Acheulean but to the chopper/chopping tool indus- tries of Asia.

3   It represents the earliest occupation of Britain, with little evidence of any chron- ological overlap with the Acheulean.

4   It entered Britain from the east, via central Europe and Asia, and was ultimately replaced by the Acheulean, which had a southerly origin.

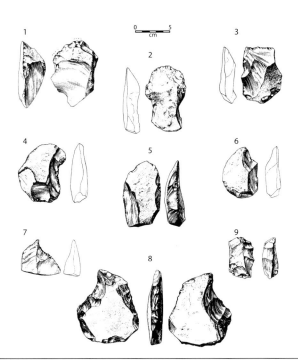

FIGURE 4.12
Clactonian flake tools. (1–3) end-scrapers; (4) 'bill-hook' form; (5) side scraper; (6) notched flake; (7) borer; (8) bifacially worked axe-shaped implement; (9) denticulate. (After Wymer 1985 and reproduced with permission.)

Table 4.7 Selected typologies for the Clactonian.

Warren (1922, 1923, 1924)	Paterson (1937)
large flakes	flakes
trimmed flakes	cores
cores, discoidal cores	choppers and hammerstones
choppers	pointed tools
pointed implements	side-scrapers
	single & double notches
	nosed scrapers
	tools made on cores
	multiple tools

Chandler (1932a)	Warren (1951)
flakes (wide and thick, high flaking angle, prominent bulbs, unfacetted platforms)	pointed nodule tools
cores	choppers
anvils with bruised edges	axe-edged tool
choppers	discoidal forms & flake discs
rough handaxes	side scrapers
strepy points	bill-hook forms
nodules with flakes from one or two ends	endscraper
peculiar tortoise cores	calscraper
	bulb-scraper
	sub-crescent forms
	proto-Mousterian flake points
	piercers
	flakes (broad platform, strong bulb, low flaking angle)
	cores
	anvil-stones
	notches

Oakley and Leakey (1937)	Wymer (1968)
flakes (as for Chandler)	flakes (as for Warren, 1951)
cores	cores:
nosed scrapers	pebble chopper-cores
trilobed hollow scrapers	bi-conical chopper-cores
discoidal and quadrilateral scrapers	proto-handaxe cores
triangular points	non-standardised flake tools
beaked points	
butt end scrapers	

They come to bury the Clactonian, not to praise it

The past 25 years has seen this definition eroded. McNabb (1992) comprehensively dismissed the notion that the Clactonian is a 'primitive' industry marked by inferior technology and skill. In a wide-ranging analysis of Clactonian and Acheulean core and flake working, McNabb found that no technological differences actually existed, and that no individual or group of features could be used to characterise Clactonian artefacts. He concluded that a single repertoire of core-working techniques, common to both handaxe and non-handaxe industries, persisted in Britain from the earliest occupation down to the introduction of Levallois (McNabb 1992; Ashton and McNabb 1992). The only sup-portable differences were typological – namely the presence of handaxes and, possibly, more standardised scrapers in Acheulean assemblages (which we might now under-stand to be a function of the age of some of the sites studied). Furthermore, sampling and collector biases (i.e. the preferential retention of handaxes) probably accounted for the apparent paucity of hard-hammer flakes and cores from many Acheulean assem-blages. This leaves the Clactonian defined entirely in negative terms – by the absence of handaxes – and lacking any characteristic markers. For McNabb (1992; Ashton and McNabb 1992), the Clactonian was thus largely an artefact of classification.

This position was bolstered by claims that handaxes do actually occur in Clactonian contexts. Crude, pointed implements have always been accepted as a feature of the Clactonian, sometimes described as poor imitations of handaxes by people unaccus-tomed to making them (Warren 1922; Chandler 1930). If these were found in Acheulean contexts, however, they would undoubtedly be regarded as rough handaxes (Warren 1951). But far from shaking the foundations of the Clactonian, these were seen as sup-porting it; such implements were always crude and poorly fashioned, totally unlike the elegant symmetrical handaxes found in the Acheulean. Ashton and McNabb (1994) argued that this perspective was based on a narrow definition of handaxes, which occur in a broad continuum of variation based not around a strict mental template but a loose mental construct (see above; cf. also Dibble 1989). At one end of this spectrum one finds the symmetrical, well-made, classic handaxe forms, while at the other sits rougher, irregular forms, which they termed 'non-classic bifaces'. This term described pieces that possessed a certain amount of bifacial thinning, had durable cutting edges and a basic level of symmetry, but which otherwise failed to demonstrate any deliberate and arbitrary imposition of a preconceived shape as implicit in the traditional concept of a handaxe. These were noted as being found in varying frequencies in virtually all Acheulean assem-blages, where they sit, unloved, among the classic forms, and in very small numbers in Clactonian ones.

This underlines yet another continuum in the actual frequency of handaxes, ranging from sites where handaxes and handaxe manufacture dominate to the exclusion of every-thing else, to those where they are a rare and minor component (Ashton and McNabb 1994). Accordingly, sites where handaxes are absent or occur only as rare, non-classic forms (i.e. those termed Clactonian) should be considered as the extreme end of this continuum, rather than a distinct assemblage type. This suggests that another of the defining characteristics of the Clactonian is based on erroneous archaeological sys-tematics and that the non-classic bifaces found in the Clactonian should be regarded as essentially identical to the more familiar classic handaxes of the Acheulean; several of which are, furthermore, also claimed to occur at some Clactonian sites (Ashton and McNabb 1994; McNabb and Ashton 1992; McNabb, 1996a; see Table 4.8 and Figure 4.13). Again, the Clactonian was argued to be an invalid taxon.

For those who reject the Clactonian as a distinct entity, chronology rings the final death knell. Since the 1980s, it has become abundantly clear that the Clactonian does not

Table 4.8 Handaxes in the Clactonian. Key to references: (a) Roe, 1968; (b) Wymer 1985; (c) McNabb and McNabb 1994; (e) McNabb 1996b; (f) Conway 1996; (g) Leeds 1930; (h) Warren archive BM; (j) Ohel 1979; (k) Newcomer 1979; (l) Conway et al. 1996; (m) Waechter 1969; (n) Ashton 1998.

Provenance	Type	Condition	Original Context	Problems	Location	Refs.
Clacton-on-Sea, 1903	point	rolled	unknown	unknown context; vague provenance	Ashmolean Museum	b,g
Clacton Foreshore, 1929	non-classic on pebble	very rolled	unknown	unknown context	Ipswich Museum	b
Clacton, Lion Point,	ovate	rolled	from foreshore, originally in channel?	? over context	Ipswich Museum	b, e
Clacton, Lion Point	non-classic	rolled	from foreshore, originally in channel?	? over context	BM (Warren)	a, c,
Clacton, Lion Point	?	rolled	from foreshore, originally in channel?	? over context	missing	a, c,
Clacton, Lion Point	non-classic	rolled	from foreshore – originally in channel?	? over context	BM (Warren)	a, c,
Clacton, West Cliff	'rude handaxe' (?non-classic)	?	'Freshwater deposits with E. antiquus etc.'	none, but no longer extant	missing	c, h
Clacton, West Cliff Foreshore	'pseudo-chellean form' (?non-classic)	?	unknown	? over context, no longer extant	missing	c, h
Clacton, West Cliff	'rude ovate' (?non-classic)	?	Elephas antiquus bed	none, but no longer extant	missing	c, h
Rickson's Pit, Swanscombe	non-classic	fresh	Lower Gravel	? over context	British Museum	d
Barnfield Pit, Swanscombe	ovate	fresh	?	contradictory reports regarding context, possibly genuine	BM (Marston)	e
Barnfield Pit, Swanscombe	non-classic	fresh	Lower Gravels	none	BM (Dewey)	d
Barnfield Pit, Swanscombe	non-classic	sl. rolled	Lower Gravels	none	BM (Chandler)	e
Barnfield Pit, Swanscombe	non-classic	sl. rolled	Lower Gravels	none	BM (Chandler)	e
Barnfield Pit, Swanscombe	non-classic	sl. rolled	?	? over context	BM (Chandler)	e

Barnfield Pit, Swanscombe	ovate	fresh	?	contradictory reports regarding context, ?fallen from Middle Gravel	BM (Waechter)	j, k, l, m
Little Thurrock	non-classic	fresh	Bed 2a	? over association with Clactonian in Bed 1	British Museum	f
Little Thurrock	non-classic	fresh	Bed 2	? over association with Clactonian in Bed 1	British Museum	f
Barnham	ovate	fresh	Cobble band	none, caused change in assemblage attribution	British Museum	n

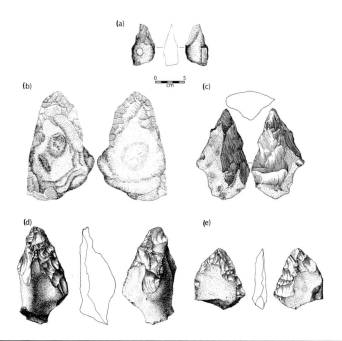

FIGURE 4.13
Handaxes in the Clactonian. (a) and (b) Bed 2a Globe Pit, Little Thurrock; (c) and (d) Lower Gravel, Barnfield Pit, Swanscombe; (e) (?) Lower Gravel, Rickson's Pit, Swanscombe. (From White 2000; (a) and (b) after Conway 1996 and courtesy of the Lithics Study Society; (c) after Chandler 1930, (d) and (e) after Ashton and McNabb 1994 and © Trustees of the British Museum.)

represent the earliest occupation of Britain. Acheulean assemblages are widespread in pre-MIS12 contexts at Boxgrove (Roberts and Parfitt 1999), High Lodge, Suffolk (Ashton et al. 1992), Warren Hill, Suffolk (Wymer et al. 1991) and Happisburgh I (Ashton et al. 2008b). The Clactonian cannot therefore be considered to mark the earliest (or pre-Acheulean) dispersal of humans into Britain, and links between the Middle Pleistocene non-handaxe occurrence and those 250–400 ka earlier at Pakefield and Happisburgh are difficult to sustain. As such, the Clactonian may be seen as little more than a randomly occurring non-handaxe variant of an elastic Acheulean (Rolland 1998), with only local, context-specific significance related to activities and resources.

Exhuming the Clactonian

By the late 1990s the Clactonian was a moribund concept with few supporters, especially among the 'young bucks' as Derek Roe would describe them. A few, however, were dissatisfied with the way in which the debate had progressed, feeling that the Clactonian had been explained away, not explained (e.g. Wenban-Smith 1998; White 2000). A different perspective was required.

Clearly, the old view that the Clactonian was a primitive industry could not be sustained, but concluding from this that it did not exist was a step too far. McNabb's work shows that simple core and flake working, and its resultant products, operates according to a rule of limited possibilities (Rolland 1981). Any technology based on single, parallel and alternate hard-hammer knapping episodes with multiple or migrating platform cores will be similar, whether they belong to Asia or Europe, the Lower Palaeolithic or the Bronze Age. Technological convergence is practically unavoidable, and similarities between Acheulean and Clactonian core and flake working are only to be expected, the frequency with which particular actions are expressed not dependent on cultural links but on skill, raw materials and context. That previous generations of archaeologists had not emphasised this inherent universality possibly stemmed from a desire to provide the Clactonian with a unique, reinforcing characteristic and to enhance its ancient credentials. Many had recognised it (e.g. Kelley 1937; Warren 1951; Wymer 1968; cf. Newcomer 1971) but this never led them to question its validity. It is a simple case of technological convergence.

The presence of handaxes in the Clactonian is equally problematic (Wenban-Smith 1996, 1998; White 2000). Table 4.8 lists some 19 handaxes claimed to have come from Clactonian contexts at Swanscombe, Clacton, Little Thurrock and Barnham. Almost all examples from Swanscombe and Clacton have question marks over their context or circumstances of their discovery, and those that do not are all non-classic forms. Only the two from Little Thurrock and one from Barnham derive from clear, excavated contexts, and even these are not unequivocally associated with Clactonian signatures.

At Little Thurrock, Clactonian material occurs throughout Bed 1 (Wymer 1957; Conway 1996), while the two non-classic bifaces came from within or immediately beneath Bed 2a, a ferrous hard-pan that may mark an erosional surface (Conway 1996; David Bridgland pers. comm.; see Text Box 3.7). At Barnham, handaxe manufacturing scatters, an ovate handaxe and a butt fragment were recovered from the surface of the cobble band, a lag deposit that formed a periodic land surface and the context from which both Wymer and Paterson recovered fresh Clactonian material (Paterson 1937; Wymer 1985; Ashton et al. 1994a, 1994b; Ashton 1998c; see Text Box 3.2). The Acheulean material, however, came from different parts of the cobble band, leading Wenban-Smith (1998) to suggest the two areas were exposed at different times, thus questioning the true contemporaneity of the two assemblage types. Establishing true contemporaneity – rather than geological contemporaneity – is a very real problem for Palaeolithic archaeology, and is really only possible for refitting material (see Conard and Adler 1997), but even if we reject Wenban-Smith's solution (which we do not), there is still a valid Clactonian presence throughout the body of the cobble band (White 2000).

The significance of non-classic bifaces is also not as clear as might be supposed. Biface shapes do form a continuum, but redefining the boundaries of what actually constitutes a handaxe does not solve the original problem, it merely moves the goal posts and changes the problem into one we feel we can answer. As John Wymer once sarcastically commented on one of our papers (White 1998a): 'have you heard of handaxes, Mark? They are like bifaces – only different'. This is true of the non-classics cited by Ashton and McNabb.

In Acheulean assemblages, non-classic pieces occur alongside a range of classic forms and are regarded as the work of novices, pieces made in a hurry, or on poor pieces of flint. The critical point is that larger numbers of classic handaxes always coexist with these 'rude' forms, demonstrating that the hominins responsible for these industries had a broad and flexible approach to the socially maintained and transmitted concept of exactly what a handaxe should look like, which could be modified to meet the contingencies of the situation (White 1998a; 2000). This is not true in the Clactonian. Classic forms are (arguably) completely absent and even non-classics very rare. They are bifaces only because they have seen a minimum of bifacial knapping to create a robust edge. They do not show deliberate imposition of form by shaping a volume. They do not prove that the makers of the Clactonian had a socially transmitted repertoire of handaxe shapes identical to that seen in the Acheulean, and may be nothing more than an accidental form predicated on the particular way a particular hominin decided to work a particular nodule on a particular day. Other authors interpret identical pieces as cores (see Vishnyatsky 1999, Figure. 3.11).

That a single handaxe can radically alter the industrial affinity of an assemblage serves to highlight just how fragile the systematics of British archaeology has become (White 2000). It is actually surprising that pure core-and-flake assemblages exist at all. When one considers that most assemblages are disturbed and mixed to various degrees and that handaxes are pretty ubiquitous in most terrace staircases (some now known to be much older than the Clactonian) it really is not surprising that the odd stray handaxe finds its way into alien contexts; the abraded condition of most 'Clactonian bifaces' alone should alert us to the fact that something may be amiss. Non-handaxe assemblages therefore survive only in a few fortuitous cases where later mixing did not obliterate the real signature; a situation that, in itself, suggests that handaxes were not made near these sites.

Finally, while the Clactonian categorically does not represent the archaeological signature of the earliest hominin occupation of Europe (although interestingly both Pakefield and Happisburgh both yielded a non-handaxe assemblage), White (2000) found an even more interesting chronological pattern (Table 4.9). Based on recent lithostratigraphical and biostratgraphical correlations (Bridgland 1994; Schreve 1997, 2001a and b; Parfitt 1998a) non-handaxe signatures occur twice within the British record. The first occurrence is at the end of MIS12 or beginning of MIS11, during pollen sub-zones HoI–HoIIb (Wymer 1974, 1985; Bridgland 1994). The Acheulean arrived later, perhaps no earlier than HoIIb–c, at which point the Clactonian apparently disappeared. At Beeches Pit, West Stow, Suffolk, the Acheulean occurs in sediments that may correlate,on the basis of molluscan faunas, with the Lower Loams at Swanscombe (Preece et al. 2006). A period of overlap may have occurred, although again the resolution is in the nature of thousands of years – enough time to witness the rise and fall of several empires and certainly sufficient time for one group of hominins to be replaced or assimilated by another. The second occurrence is during the same part of the next cycle; late MIS10/early MIS9. At Purfleet and Cuxton, the non-handaxe assemblages are replaced by handaxe industries, with the first appearance of Levallois occurring towards the end of the cycle (White

Table 4.9 Chronology of non-handaxe (Clactonian) assemblages in the British Isles.

Site	Age	Evidence	References
Globe Pit, Little Thurrock	late MIS 10/ early MIS 9	• Basal part of Lynch Hill/Corbets Tey Formation • Lateral equivalent of overlying brickearth (Grey's Brickearth) contains Posts-Hoxnian/pre-OIS 7 interglacial faunal suite	Bridgland & Harding 1993; Bridgland 1994;
Cuxton	late MIS 10/ early MIS 9	• Basal part of Lynch Hill/Corbets Tey Formation	Bridgland 1996
Purfleet	late MIS 10/ early MIS 9	• Basal Gravels of Lynch Hill/Corbets Tey Formation • Underlies Post-Hoxnian/pre-OIS 7 interglacial faunal suite	Bridgland 1994; Schreve 1997; Schreve et al. 2002
Clacton, Freshwater Beds	early Hoxnian (MIS 11)	• Lower Part of Boyn Hill/Orsett Heath Formation • Early Hoxnian mammal fauna • non-Rhenish molluscan fauna • Early Hoxnian pollen profile	Turner and Kerney 1971; Wymer 1974, 1985; Bridgland 1994; Schreve 1997.
Swanscombe, Phase I deposits	early Hoxnian (MIS 11)	• Lower Part of Boyn Hill/Orsett Heath Formation • Early Hoxnian mammal fauna • non-Rhenish mollusc fauna	Wenban-Smith et al. 2006 Bridgland 1994; Schreve 1997; Kerney 1971; Conway et al. 1996
Barnham (rolled series)	early Hoxnian (MIS 11)	• Conformably overlies Anglian till • Early Hoxnian fauna in associated lateral deposits	Lewis 1998; Parfitt 1998

et al. 2006, 2011). The chronological distribution of non-handaxe assemblages is therefore recurrent, appearing at the end of a major glacial phase or beginning of the succeeding major interglacial, where they appear to exist alone until eventually replaced by Acheulean assemblages towards the late-middle or end of the warm episode.

In from the cold: the Clactonian in the twenty-first century

The debates of recent decades have left the Clactonian bruised but not beaten. Even its most ardent critics have accepted that there is something to be explained although we still disagree on what, when and how (McNabb 2007; Nick Ashton pers. comm.). Here we offer a synthesis of what *we* understand the Clactonian to be (after White 2000):

1   A Lower Palaeolithic industry in which unprepared core and flake reduction dominates the lithic technology, and which contains relatively high levels of flake tools and very rare bifacially worked core tools that serendipitously resemble crude handaxes. The core and flake technology is inseparable from that seen in the Acheulean assemblages, but this reflects nothing more than a universal repertoire of basic, if not unavoidable, flint working techniques used throughout prehistory. Choppers may be present but are not unique identifiers.

Frequencies of tools and techniques vary according to context and recovery. Soft-hammer flaking is absent.

2   Only the presence/absence of handaxes can be used clearly to divide the Clactonian from the Acheulean. Differences in scraper morphology may be another marker although this contrast is as yet poorly defined.

3   The Clactonian does not represent the earliest occupation of the British Isles but has a recurrent occurrence. It first appeared at the end of MIS12, persisted through early MIS11, and was then replaced by assemblages that included handaxes. This pattern was essentially repeated during the following climatic cycle (MIS10–9) (Table 4.9). It has no proximal relationship to the Mode 1 industries at Pakefield or Happisburgh 3, which relate to a different phase of early colonisation, probably by a different hominin species.

THE CLACTONIAN EXPLAINED

If one accepts that the Clactonian is a genuine archaeological phenomenon that cannot be explained away, it therefore requires explanation. Over the past century each generation of archaeologists has recast the Clactonian according to prevailing theoretical trends. Although based on a small British non-handaxe phenomenon, this was not an entirely parochial endeavour, but mirrors and informs the many ways archaeologists have sought to explain variation in stone tool assemblages from Clacton to Cape Town. This section critically reviews the most significant of these interpretations before developing yet another explanation that emerges from the recent work of Dennell et al. (2011). The following text largely summarises the opinions of White (2000) which, despite a decade of arguing with John McNabb, have hardly changed at all.

Activity facies interpretations

One common explanation for the Clactonian views it as the localised or seasonal activity variant of the Acheulean, perhaps a special woodworking facies employed in heavily wooded environments (Warren 1922; Oakley 1964). More dynamically, Ohel (1979; Ohel and Lechevalier 1979) saw handaxe and non-handaxe assemblages as two extremes in a continuous sequence of reduction occurring across the landscape, with Clactonian signatures representing preparatory workshops where handaxes were roughed-out and then removed, and Acheulean ones places where handaxes were finished, used and abandoned. Yet another formulation regarded handaxes as problem-solving devices, their frequency within an assemblage reflecting how often humans encountered the 'problem' (McNabb 1992; Ashton and McNabb 1994). Clactonian sites therefore represent an extreme functional state where no handaxes were required. In some cases sampling biases may be operating at the intra-site level, with excavations randomly revealing only those parts of locales where handaxes were not present (Ashton and McNabb 1994). There are problems with all these variations.

At the most basic level, there is no convincing correlation between Clactonian sites and wooded environments, or vice versa. Although the resolution of our reconstructions is anything but fine-grained, most Clactonian and Acheulean locales show a mixture of flora and fauna indicative of mosaic environments comprising both forested and open habitats: the riparian landscape at Clacton, for example, has been interpreted as showing open grassland on the valley floor, flanked by woodland on the margins (Turner and Kerney 1971). The tasks conducted at each site type are also similar. As described above, Keeley's (1980, 1993) work at Clacton and Hoxne revealed a similar range of woodworking, hide preparation and meat processing, even though the small sample at Clacton was biased towards woodworking (Keeley 1993; Wymer 1985). That a range of carcass-processing activities, including bone chopping and butchery, was conducted at both site types would therefore seem to suggest that handaxes – apparently the ideal butchery tool (Mitchell 1997, 1998) – would have been quite a useful problem-solving tool in most Clactonian contexts. Even if one were to dismiss microscopic use-wear as a dubious technique, this is supported by the presence of cut-marked animal bones from Clacton, Swanscombe, Hoxne, Boxgrove and many other sites (Binford 1985; Stopp 1993; Roberts and Parfitt 1999; Simon Parfitt pers. comm.). To accept a functional argument we must accept that, over vast periods of time and in similar resource settings, human populations who had the capacity to make handaxes chose not to at certain locations, substituting other tools in their place, even though they were carrying out the same set of tasks inferred for those places where they did make them. We might also ask why, in some of the former situations, handaxes were later found to be necessary (i.e. Swanscombe and Barnham). Intensity of occupation rather than activity facies might be one solution for handaxe frequency (see Pope 2002; Pope and Roberts 2005) but cannot explain their absence from obviously well-used Clactonian sites.

The spatial separation of different technological phases also lacks empirical support. The total absence of roughouts, broken handaxes and thinning flakes does not support the notion that handaxes were roughed out at Clactonian sites, the claimed roughouts at Clacton and Swanscombe (Ohel 1979) are actually just cores (Bordes 1979; McNabb 1992). There is also no bias towards the early stages of reduction in Clactonian sites, as one would expect of roughing-out stations, both assemblage types having a similar range of dorsal cortex patterns suggesting that full reduction sequences were carried out (McNabb 1992). Moreover, there is no association between Clactonian assemblages and the availability of high quality raw materials, as one might expect at quarry sites (Wymer 1979; Roe 1979). At Clacton, Swanscombe and Barnham, hominins mostly exploited gravel flint, perhaps supplemented by fresh chalk flint introduced from elsewhere. They can hardly have operated as ideal workshops.

Any consideration of site function and activity facies must also take into account that, with very few exceptions, Clactonian sites are in secondary context and represent spatially and time-averaged segments of the diverse landscapes upon which humans enacted innumerable activity episodes. The widespread deposits that contain them have been very heavily sampled over almost a century. Had handaxes been made or finished anywhere in the vicinity one might expect to find evidence of them in the same gravel deposits (Newcomer 1979). Small-scale excavation of high resolution scatters, such as those within the Swanscombe Lower Loam or on the Barnham knapping floor (where handaxes were eventually discovered, see Ashton et al. 1994a and b; Ashton 1998a), may genuinely reflect sampling errors, but this cannot be true of the Swanscombe Lower Gravel or Clacton Freshwater Bed, derived contexts which have been sampled at different points over several square kilometres and which contain the sweepings of vast landscapes. Finally, the Clactonian and Acheulean do not appear to overlap chronologically. To accept them as two parts of the same knapping complex, they should occur throughout the Lower Palaeolithic on laterally continuous occupation horizons (cf. Roe 1979).

Raw material interpretations

Most of the raw material selected for use in the Lower Palaeolithic was locally available, often being situated directly at the knapping locality (see Féblot-Augustins 1997, 1999; White 1998a). Given this, the most obvious explanation for the lack of handaxes in Clactonian sites is that the available raw materials were simply too small or of inadequate quality to support their manufacture. Raw material differences may also explain some of the variation within the Clactonian, such as differences in flake size, or the frequency of different knapping techniques or tools. However, while the small, rounded flint pebbles at Clacton Golf Course and Jaywick Sands (Oakley and Leakey 1937; Singer et al. 1973) may not have been suitable for handaxe manufacture (McNabb 1992), this is not true of other non-handaxe sites.

The hominins who created the Swanscombe Lower Loam assemblage had access to flint from the river gravel and local chalk outcrops that were often larger than those used in the Lower Middle Gravel to make handaxes (Wymer 1964; White 2000). At Barnham, hominins had access to large nodules from the cobble band; while these are often of dubious quality they were shown in replication experiments to be (sometimes) adequate for handaxe manufacture some 400,000 years and three glacial cycles after their burial (Wenban-Smith and Ashton 1998). The makers of the MIS9 non-handaxe assemblage at Little Thurrock had access to large nodules from the local Chalk and the Bull-Head Beds in the Thanet Sand (Bridgland and Harding 1993); while those at Purfleet used flint from the local Chalk, Coombe Rock and river gravels (Schreve et al. 2002). Even at Clacton, artefacts >20 cm in maximum dimension are found, suggesting that nodules of sufficient size and shape to support handaxes were present. Indeed, these are far larger than most used to make handaxes from the Red Gravel at Foxhall Road, Ipswich (White and Plunkett 2004) or Lower Middle Gravel at Swanscombe (White 1996).

Even if immediately available raw materials were inadequate for handaxe manufacture, suitable raw materials would certainly have been available within a few kilometers and cannot be seen as a limiting resource on anything other than an immediate scale. At a number of British sites where raw materials were inadequate or absent from otherwise favourable locations, hominins imported flint or finished artefacts – as seen at

Bowman's Lodge and Wansunt, Dartford (White 1998a), and the Grey Clay assemblage at Foxhall Road, Ipswich (White and Plunkett 2004). If the raw materials at Clactonian sites were really inadequate for handaxe manufacture, and had the hominins there wanted or been able to produce handaxes, then this solution was readily available. Other materials could even have been substituted for stone, notable examples being the elephant-bone handaxes from lithic-poor locations such as La Polledrara and Castel di Guido, Italy (Radmilli 1984; Anzidei and Huyzendveld 1992; Gaudzinski et al. 2005). They did none of these things, and the truth is that we simply do not really know why.

Landscape interpretations

Ashton's (1998b) *static resource model* attempted to overcome the interpretative hurdles of the raw material and activity facies interpretations by merging their elements into a framework of flexible hominin behaviour in the landscape. He argued that valued static resources encouraged repeated visits to a particular locale, resulting in the build up of archaeological palimpsests. If lithic raw material was the resource being targeted, then the assemblage might be dominated by locally discarded material with varying but probably low levels of import and export; but if some other resource, for example vegetation, water, sleeping places or shady trees were targeted, then imported stone might accumulate there by accident and design. In contrast, the exploitation of mobile resources might lead to greater export and transport behaviour, with single discards or discrete activity areas occurring over a much wider landscape, which would be far less visible archaeologically.

Ashton (1998b) illustrated this using Barnham and Elveden, two sites suggested to be broadly contemporaneous along different parts of the same river. At Barnham, knapping was concentrated around a source of raw materials formed by coarse lag gravel. The uncertain quality of the available flint is suggested to have encouraged core and flake working, with only occasional handaxe manufacture on selected nodules. At Elveden, though, flint was available from both a similar gravel outcrop and from a chalk river bank. Core and flake working is therefore still common but handaxes are far more abundant. The rarity of handaxes at Barnham might therefore reflect, individually or in combination, the general unsuitability of the materials or a specific focus in activity, the latter perhaps even conditioned by the former. The presence of occasional handaxes in the brickearths overlying and concealing the cobble band at Barnham might show a dramatic alteration in the resource structure of the local landscape, the site no longer a focus of activity, but a place where isolated activities occurred.

Here, handaxe frequency depends on the resources available and the fashion in which humans organised themselves in the landscape. The model explains perfectly the primary context material at Barnham and Elveden, the archaeological situations it was constructed for, but fails when applied elsewhere. At Little Thurrock, an Elveden-type situation prevailed, but a Barnham-type assemblage resulted; while at Foxhall Road Red Gravel assemblage a Barnham-type situation seems to have prevailed, but an Elveden-type assemblage resulted. In the Foxhall Road Grey Clay assemblage we see neither resource situation, but an Elveden-type assemblage. The problem with the model is that is it not, in fact, a model but an extrapolated interpretation that appeals to functional, behavioural, material or social factors as necessary. It has no predictive power and in brings us no closer to an actual understanding of why handaxes are present at some sites and not at others, beyond the fact that Palaeolithic hominins sometimes did things for reasons we cannot fathom.

Wenban-Smith (1998) who, unlike Ashton and McNabb, accepts the Clactonian as a valid entity attempted to explain its character, chronological distribution and relationship to the Acheulean in terms of changing planning behavior in an evolving interglacial landscape. To him, the Clactonian was a simple *ad hoc* industry produced opportunistically in post-glacial landscapes that were littered with coarse fluvial and outwash gravel. Faced with such a material abundance, hominins had little need to plan ahead or create complex formal tools: flint could be procured and 'disposable' sharp-edged flakes and informal tools produced wherever and whenever necessary. As the landscapes matured, however, vegetation and fine-grained sediments deposited by quiescent rivers would have concealed most of these sources, rendering the landscape flint-poor. Under these circumstances, humans were forced to adopt a strategy that involved careful planning and the manufacture of formal tools that could be carried in anticipation of future use – that is, handaxes.

If hominins really responded to basic raw material availability in this fashion, one might expect such a response to local variations, with Clactonian assemblages found throughout an interglacial wherever raw materials were plentiful, but Acheulean ones where raw materials were scarce. This was, however, clearly not the case. Both handaxe and non-handaxe assemblages are situated around sources of abundant raw materials, either chalk exposures (e.g. Little Thurrock, Purfleet, Elveden, Boxgrove) or river gravels (e.g. Swanscombe Lower and Middle Gravel, Barnham, Stoke Newington). Both handaxe and non-handaxe assemblages are also found in sites apparently lacking a good-quality flint source and marked by fine-grained sedimentation (Wansunt Loam and Swanscombe Lower Loam) where a degree of planning and provisioning was required. It is therefore unclear why comparable resources (or lack of them) should elicit an *ad hoc* response during one period of time but demand a more carefully planned strategy in another.

The proposal that, at a regional scale, raw material availability would diminish throughout an interglacial is plausible, through both geological processes and hominin depletion of suitable nodules. The small windows we have into past landscapes, however, seem to show that Acheulean sites were usually places with abundant raw materials from fluvial systems, chalk outcrops and clay-with-flint exposures (White 1998a). The landscapes exploited by the makers of both Acheulean and Clactonian signatures also appear to have been equally vegetated with a shifting mosaic of woodland and grassland (Turner 1970; Kerney 1971; Conway et al. 1996; Schreve 1997). Whatever the precise composition of the mosaic, the very existence of a rich vegetation presupposes the widespread development of soils and fine-grained sediments over the British landscape from the early Hoxnian onwards. None of this conforms to Wenban-Smith's predictions.

There is also little to support the differentiation into planned and expedient technologies. We know little of the distances or time over which handaxes were transported and curated through the landscape and, judging by the density of handaxes and manufacturing débitage at many Acheulean sites, most appear to have been produced, used and discarded in the same broad location over short time spans (White 1998a; Ashton and White 2003; contra Hallos 2005). Equally, we know nothing of the time or distances over which *selected* cores or flakes were curated. Thus there are few empirical reasons to suppose that, other than the obvious differences in the technological procedures involved in their manufacture, handaxe use involved greater planning depth than cores and flakes. One might also ask why Clactonian societies, who under this interpretation had presumably historically made handaxes, would simply abandon this practice for a profligate *ad hoc* strategy, even if resources allowed it.

Habitats, hunting and social transmission

In a heavily criticised review of the chronology and environment of handaxe and non-handaxe assemblages across Western Europe, Collins (1969 and comments therein) suggested that the Clactonian and Acheulean represented contrasting subsistence adaptations predicated on different habitats. The Clactonian was cast as the tool kit of non-hunting populations living in heavily wooded environments, while the Acheulean was associated with big-game hunters on the open plains. Adopting this environmental dichotomy, Mithen (1994) constructed a model that explained the Clactonian and Acheulean not in terms of subsistence strategies but in how technology was socially transmitted between individuals and generations. According to his model, the dynamics of social learning within human groups varied as a function of group size, which is in turn correlated with the character of the environment within which they operated (ibid. 1994).

For Mithen, the complex and standardised bifacial technology seen in the Acheulean, and its persistence as a social tradition through time, can be explained by the way in which technology passes through groups living in non-temperate, open environments. Groups living in open environments tend to form large groups in response to higher predation risk and larger resource packages. Larger group size engenders stronger channels of social transmission. This is because individuals are exposed to many others and because factors such as predation, resources distribution and access, and interpersonal conflicts will foster strong kin-bonds and coalitions; the young will therefore tend to remain close to familiar adults, from whom they can learn. This leads to strong social transmission, especially imitation, which in terms of lithic technology will produce high levels of knapping skill and regular patterns in artefact form. Innovation tends to be low, however, as the constant proximity of learning young to adults discourages experimentation; conversely any innovation that did emerge would quickly spread through social channels.

By contrast, according to Mithen, the Clactonian, with its lack of complex formal tools, shorter knapping procedures and relative low skill requirements, reflects the impaired social transmission of smaller groups in temperate closed environments. Groups living in closed wooded environments form smaller social units because of low predation risk and small, patchy food resources and experience fewer inter-personal conflicts. Consequently they will be less cohesive with more independent young. Channels of social learning are weaker, with high levels of trial-and-error learning, resulting in weak social traditions and unstandardised techniques and forms. Individual knapping skills will be low and the ratchet effect – where skill increases cumulatively as it is passed through successive generations – will not operate. Innovation may be higher due to more experimentation but new developments will often fail to be transmitted.

This model offers a highly innovative solution to an old problem, but like Collins' original formulation lacks clear palaeoenvironmental foundations. There is little evidence that the Acheulean is exclusively or mostly associated with non-temperate open environments or the Clactonian with closed temperate woodlands. Indeed, the primary Acheulean context signatures at Boxgrove, Swanscombe, Elveden, Hoxne, Beeches Pit and Hitchin are all associated with a temperate climate (Roberts and Parfitt 1999; Conway et al. 1996; Ashton et al. 2005; Singer et al. 1993; Preece et al. 2006; Boreham and Gibbard 1995) while the non-handaxe assemblages at the Clacton Golf Course and the lower units at Purfleet are found in cool climate contexts (Singer et al. 1973; Schreve et al. 2002). During MIS11 the appearance of the Acheulean did roughly correspond with an episode of open conditions but forest regeneration took place within some 400 years (Turner 1970). As noted above, both Clactonian and Acheulean assemblages appear to have been produced in similar habitats: both are associated with temperate environments, both are found adjacent to water sources, and most sites show a mosaic of open and wooded environments; in a complete reversal of the expected pattern the Acheulean at Beeches Pit was produced during the height of the MIS11 interglacial during a period of dense forestation (Preece et al. 2006).

From a technological perspective, McNabb and Ashton (1995) counter-argued that similarities in core and flake working suggest few differences in social learning, although this does ignore the fact that handaxes show levels of skill and socially maintained repertoires well above the Mode 1 base line. If this were the case, then no differences in human social interaction or cultural transmission need to be envisioned from the earliest Oldowan until the advent of Levallois. Wenban-Smith (1996) has also noted that other workers see the opposite social problems in forests, difficulties involved in coping with heavily wooded environments would actually require strong and elaborate social networks, probably enhancing rather than suppressing social transmission (e.g. Gamble 1986, 1987).

Within his more recent 'Sexy Handaxe' theory (Kohn and Mithen 1999; see Text Box 4.3), however, the absence of handaxes from some contexts would presumably not depend on strong channels of social learning and environmental differences but would rather reflect social arenas where sexual fitness was not being overtly expressed or where another strategy was being used.

Text Box 4.3

YOU SHOW ME YOURS AND I'LL SHOW YOU MINE: WERE HANDAXES SEXY?

Handaxes are usually explained in functional terms, as butchery tools whose form is predicated on efficiency and material considerations. A very different perspective has been offered by Kohn and Mithen (1999) who pointed out that such perspectives fail to account for a number of factors. Key amongst these are the time and energy invested in handaxe manufacture when simple flakes would often suffice for the task at hand; the deliberate imposition of symmetry (which for some is functionally redundant (e.g. Machin et al. 2007) but for others a functionally advantageous design (White 1998a and b; Nowell and Chang 2009; Hayden and Villeneuve 2009)) and the occasional occurrence of 'giant' tools which clearly were non-functional in a 'normal' sense. Kohn and Mithen suggested that, rather than being purely functional objects, social factors were also at work in their manufacture, and they argued specifically that handaxes were products of Darwinian sexual selection, in which they expressed a male's reproductive fitness and were therefore integral to mate choice within complex and competitive human groups. In this sense they were, according to the argument, the Middle Pleistocene equivalent of a Ferrari.

In constructing their argument, Kohn and Mithen suggested that the time and effort invested in handaxe manufacture would serve as an obvious display of the knapper's intelligence and health, displaying to potential mates their knowledge of resource (raw material) distribution, the ability to plan (and therefore procure a variety of resources), technical *savoire-faire* and social awareness. Similarly, handaxes would often be made with symmetrical form because of an evolved psychological bias that was attracted to symmetry. In other words, females were attracted to males who could make symmetrical handaxes, because these sub-consciously signalled the males' sexual fitness. It follows that the giant handaxes from sites such as Furze Platt and Cuxton, might be explained as the material component of elaborate social displays, perhaps in poor raw material contexts. So, 'just as a peacock's tail may reliably indicate its success', so might the manufacture of a fine symmetrical handaxe have been a reliable indicator of a hominin's ability to secure food, find shelter, escape from predation and compete successfully within the social group. Such hominins would have been attractive mates, their abilities indicating 'good genes' (Kohn and Mithen 1999, 521). The obvious corollary of this is that elaborate handaxes were usually made by males, females making the irregular, less refined examples. Feminists, don't blame us.

To ensure that handaxes were a reliable signal of an individual's fitness (and not stolen from another) males would have had to make handaxes on a regular basis – practice in other words – even if there was no immediate physical task to which to put them. This would explain the large numbers recovered from the archaeological record in seemingly pristine condition. Others have subsequently taken this to mean that the handaxe was a 'lekking device', that is, an object used in a social display arena to make the individual more attractive to the opposite sex (Nowell and Chang 2009; Burriss 2009).

Shennan (2002) has commented that the 'sexy handaxe' theory is untestable. This is certainly true – the behaviour it seeks to understand are no longer observable – but it suffers in this no more than other socially orientated approaches (e.g. Gamble 1999, 2007), and hypotheses can certainly be evaluated in terms of how much of the disparate archaeological record they help weave together (cf. Mithen 2008). Others have rejected the theory outright, on the grounds of an absence of archaeological support, technological 'reality' or strong theoretical foundations (Nowell and Chang 2009; Machin 2008; Hayden and Villeneuve 2009). However, as Kohn and Mithen make absolutely clear, handaxes surely cannot have had one all-embracing explanation. Rather, over the expanses of Middle Pleistocene time and space in which they were made, they undoubtedly served multiple roles in the functional and social worlds. One of these possibly involved display and sexual signalling. In this, we are certainly sympathetic to Kohn's and Mithen's views.

Population dynamics and colonisation patterns

The foregoing interpretations view the Clactonian as a uniquely British phenomenon, ignoring the fact that for much of the past 500 ka Britain existed as a peninsula of Atlantic Europe, with only short periods of insularity during each interglacial (Preece 1995; White and Schreve 2000; cf. Dennell et al. 2011 and discussion above).

White and Schreve (2000, and see revised model above) suggested that the apparent temporal pattern of the Clactonian and Acheulean was related to phases of abandonment and recolonisation of Britain during two successive glacial–interglacial cycles. The Clactonian is seen as a signature of initial recolonisation with only the main, later occupation host to handaxe-making populations. The absence of this pattern from subsequent interglacials is argued to relate to the introduction of Levallois technique around MIS8. To explain this pattern, White and Schreve offer two suggestions. First, if the earliest settlers to recolonise after a major glaciation were characterised by small and relatively isolated groups, then they might have experienced social conditions that led to elements of their technology to phase out over a few generations (cf. Mithen 1994; Aldhouse-Green 1998; Toth and Schick 1993: Heinrich 2004). Later groups may have been larger and maintained larger networks, allowing them to disperse and settle with no deleterious effects on social learning or technology. Wenban-Smith (1996) offered a similar proposal, suggesting that social groups could have experienced environmental stresses and social splintering during glaciations, causing a breakdown in social learning and the loss of sophisticated handaxe technology. The Clactonian would, in this account, represent an impoverished variant of the Acheulean (cf. Narr 1979), a short-lived technical tradition in which the knowledge of handaxe manufacture had been lost.

Their second, and preferred option, was that the Clactonian and Acheulean reflect two waves of colonisation by different populations, from different regions of Europe, each with their own historically maintained technological repertoire (Breuil 1932; Wymer 1968; Roe 1981). In this case, earlier dispersals may have originated from the non-handaxe 'province' of north-west and central Europe, followed by the arrival of the Acheulean from more distant refugia to the south (Obermeier 1924; McBurney 1950; Svoboda 1989; Bosinski 1995). This advocates *fluctuating* local and regional populations whose material culture and technical traditions vary by virtue of social distance although, of course, one also has to bear in mind the possibility that Clactonian populations were not replaced but evolved *in situ* into Acheulean ones.

This suggestion conforms to Dennell et al.'s (2011) contention that the Lower Palaeolithic settlement of Europe was one of constant expansion and contraction, abandonment and dispersal, integration and isolation. After each cold episode, hominins would recolonise northern Europe from a number of southern European refugia (and possibly also western Asia or Asia), introducing different cultural elements in the process. Britain was thus a sink area, its material culture continuously renewed from elsewhere, the evident patterns reflecting not indigenous developments but alien ones. Taking this model to its extremes one might actually suggest that the Clactonian is not only the product of a distinct cultural tradition, one preserved in pockets and spreading into Britain when the opportunity arose, but actually the cultural signature of an entirely different hominin taxon, possibly one originating from the east and occupying central Europe for much of the Middle Pleistocene. This would return us to the suggestion of Warren (1924) that the Clactonian and Acheulean were the products of different human 'races'. Recent years have seen such opinions regarded as naïve and foolish (if not politically dangerous) and notions of a single, continental-scale technological complex (the Acheulean), with no cultural variation and only one hominin species, have taken hold. The discovery of *Homo floresiensis* and the Denisovans should make it abundantly clear that such opinions are somewhat limited in their vision.

LIFE BEYOND THE LITHICS: SURVIVAL IN THE LOWER PALAEOLITHIC NORTH

Fire

Fire is widely considered an essential prerequisite to the successful colonisation of north-western Europe, not only as a tool for surviving cold nights, but also as a source of light, protection, and a cooking aid (Dennell 1983; Gowlett 2006, Preece et al. 2006). Securely linking evidence of fire to human agency rather than to natural causes is extremely difficult, a situation not helped by the absence of constructed hearth features prior to the Late Middle Palaeolithic (James 1989; Gamble 1986, 1995; Roebroeks and Tuffreau 1999; Gowlett 2006). As John Gowlett (2006, Gowlett in Preece et al. 2006; see also Roebroeks and Villa 2011) has noted, evidence for fire use before ~400 ka BP is remarkably slim, with only a few disputed African examples (e.g., Koobi Fora ~1.6 Ma;

Chesowanja ~1.5 Ma and Swartkrans >1 Ma), and the more widely accepted evidence from Gesher Benot Ya'aqov in Israel (~790 ka BP) suggesting that humans were using fire before their spread into the temperate zone (Bellomo and Kean 1997; Gowlett et al. 1981; Brain and Sillen 1988; Goren-Inbar et al. 2004).

After ~400 ka BP the evidence for hominin use of fire is clearer. The best examples from the Middle Pleistocene are biased towards localities with exceptional preservation in tufa and travertine deposits, including the combustion zones at Beeches Pit, Suffolk (see Text Box 3.2 and 4.4; Gowlett et al. 2005; Gowlett 2006; Preece et al. 2006); the hearths and charred artefacts at MIS11 sites at Bilzingsleben II, Germany (Mania 1991; Mania and Mania 1995) and Vèrtesszöllös, Hungary (Vèrtes and Dobosi 1990); the MIS7 site at Weimer-Ehringsdorf, Germany (Kahlke et al. 2002); and the MIS5 site at Tau-bach, Germany (Bratlund 1999). Hearths are also present at other sites with exceptional preservation, such as the brown-coal mine at Schöningen 13 II–4, which has been inter-preted as a horse-hunting camp (Thieme 2005).

NO SMOULDER WITHOUT FIRE: BEECHES PIT AND FIRE USE AROUND 400 KA BP

Beeches Pit, West Stow, Suffolk has produced the only convincing evidence for the human use of fire in the Lower Palaeolithic. Evidence of burning was found in Areas AF and AH, in the form of burnt and fire-crazed flint, charred and calcined bone and sharply defined features with blackened fills and reddened edges (Gowlett 2006; Gowlett et al. 2005; Preece et al. 2006; Figure 1). Calcined shell, charcoal, clinker and heat-fused sediment was also found dispersed throughout Bed 3b.

FIGURE 1
Evidence of highly localised burning at Beeches Pit, Suffolk. Inset shows a 27 piece refitting series that records the roughing out of a handaxe that was subsequently abandoned. Sev-eral of the refits stand out for being burnt bright red; these having moved around 2 m down slope from the presumed knapping position and becoming in corporated within the limits of a hearth visible at the bottom left of the main picture. The site view shows an area 3 × 2 m, looking east. (Courtesy of John Gowlett.)

Text Box 4.4

Gowlett (2006; Gowlett et al. 2005) makes a strong case that these fires were created by hominins and not the result of natural burning:

1 The evidence of burning coincides with the first appearance of hominins at the site; it does not appear beforehand and is stratigraphically associated with the greatest concentration of artefacts. There is, therefore, a strong correlation between the evidence of burning and other indicators of hominin activity.

2 The spatial distribution of the artefacts respects the burnt areas. One handaxe roughing-out sequence of 27 pieces, for example, is unburnt except for three reddened flakes that strayed into the fire. The spatial patterning is consistent with a knapper sitting about 2.5 m from the fire.

3 Excavation demonstrated that the areas where burning was most intensive were located within shallow depressions, two of which intersect, implying a sequence of separate burning events in the same area of the site.

4 Burning has been recognised in three different beds (3b, 4 and 5) showing the repeated use of fire over a prolonged period during interglacial conditions and the ensuing cold stage.

5 Analysis of the burnt flint and charred and calcined bone indicate that the fires burned at temperatures of 400–800° C, which are typical of those seen in deliberately constructed camp-fires and well-above those of natural grassland fires (which burn quickly and only exceed 65° C for a few minutes) or forest fires (which seldom exceed 300° C). Burning tree stumps also tend to smoulder at low temperatures. Clearly, the Beeches Pit fires burnt bright, they didn't smoulder.

Gowlett interprets these features as ovoid hearths, ~1 m across and filled with a thickness of ~20 cm of burnt debris. To attain such a depth of fill, the hearths must have been reused several times, suggesting that the site was occupied or revisited for an extended period of time. This reinforces the notion that it represents a home-base.

Text Box 4.4

In most other landscape settings such evidence for fire that does occur cannot be directly associated with human agency. Evidence for charcoal at Swanscombe (Oakley 1964b), Hoxne (James 1989), High Lodge (Cartwright 1992) and Barnham (Cartwright 1998) probably represents nothing more than concentrations of charcoal from natural fires along the strand-line of major rivers (Nicholls et al. 2000; Villa 1982; White and Plunkett 2004). A claimed hearth at Foxhall Road (Layard 1903), marked by fire-cracked rocks, a carbonaceous discoloured area and burnt flint, may or may not have been a hominin-constructed hearth, and may or may not have even be a real combustion zone. That artefacts were spread around it in a semi-circular pattern suggests it was a group focus where people communicated face to face but this could equally have been a log or a carcass located in the sheltered lee of the channel margin.

The rarity of evidence for fire relates to several factors (Gowlett 2006). First, it is transient: burnt bones are susceptible to leaching and charcoal easily winnowed and floated by wind and water (Nicholls et al. 2000; Scott et al. 2002; White and Plunkett 2004). Most unstructured hearths would probably have consisted of little more than a few twigs and branches around which people huddled very closely. It is extremely unlikely that such features will survive intact in anything other than the most exceptional preservational environments (e.g. caves and travertine springs) and one certainly would not expect to find them in coastal marine situations such as Boxgrove or any of the fluvial margins discussed above. Secondly, fluvial contexts and marine lagoons were probably not the best place to build a fire at all, being exposed to the elements, predators and flooding and alerting any would-be prey to a hominin presence, or at least danger. Fires may have been preferentially constructed at home bases, such as the wooded sheltered spring locations of Beeches Pit and other European travertine sites (Gowlett 2006; Gowlett in Preece et al. 2006). And yet, fire is also absent from cave sites prior to MIS11, such as Arago, France, and Atapuerca Gran Dolina, Spain, leading Roebroeks and Villa (2011) to come to the 'surprising' conclusion that fire use was not widely practised, if at all, before this date.

Gowlett (2006) also raises the intriguing possibility that during the Lower Palaeolithic fire could not be kindled, based largely on the fact that Beeches Pit shows that fairly large fires were kept going at high temperatures for fairly long periods of time. This would suggest that strong social networks were required to ensure that, if lost, fire could be replenished from neighbouring groups either directly or by gaining information on local lightning strikes. It also suggests that humans would have had to carry fire with them from place to place – from valley to cave to coast – making it an even rarer commodity. We accept that fire use has social connotations; camp-fires make people sit in close proximity and communicate face-to-face. However, the notion that fire manipulation depended on luck more than control seems all too redolent of the 1981 cult B-movie *Quest for Fire*, and seems to us to be an extremely maladaptive gamble in northern latitudes where, even if there *were* neighbouring groups in relatively close proximity, just a few cold days without fire could decimate a group. If Beeches Pit can be regarded as a home base then the evidence for prolonged fire husbandry need not indicate an inability to kindle fire but the necessity for those who remain 'at camp' to maintain a fire through-out the day for warmth, safety and entertainment. Wood would certainly not have been limited in the forests around the site.

No hearth and no home? Searching for campsites and still missing the evidence (with apologies to Binford 1987a)

Panning out from the fire side to get a wider view of the campsite, we find ourselves faced with almost exactly the same problem – we don't see very much. The Lower Palaeolithic of Britain (or anywhere else) shows no well-structured sites that can be divided into different social and economic zones (although see Mania 1991); it has no hearths, no homes, no structures, no storage pits, no ditches, nor any apparent site furniture. Most sites are actually minimally altered natural settings – river valleys, lakesides, sea-shores and caves – the most noticeable thing hominins actually did at any of these places was to create and leave a lot of litter. Lower Palaeolithic sites are therefore interpreted as magnet locations, key and familiar places that offered more or less predictable access to the bare necessities of Palaeolithic life, both static and mobile – fresh water, plants (for food, cover and shade), animals (for food, blood, bones and hides), stone and wood (for tools), and, of course, other people. This has led some to suggest that Lower Palaeolithic occurrences were not continuously occupied camp sites, but simply locations where episodic and goal-oriented visits occurred over time, leaving palimpsests of unconnected activities (Binford 1987a; Gamble 1995b, 1996). Lower Palaeolithic hominins, Binford argued, did not construct technologically assisted cultural landscapes, but simply moved through the natural environment to areas of vital resources engaging nature as they found it (*niche* geography versus *cultural* geography; Binford 1987a, 424).

Most reconstructions of Middle Pleistocene hominin behaviour thus invoke highly mobile lives, groups constantly moving along well-worn paths between a number of critical resource patches (Gamble 1995b, 1996). This does not mean that hominins were not active in other parts of the landscape, just that our most important archaeological sites are nodal points in a wider hominin network, which facilitated a range of core activities and encouraged repeated occupancy (and which happened to coincide with sedimentary environments favourable to preservation) (White and Plunkett 2004). As we have seen in Chapter 3, by default or design most of these are situated alongside rivers where, if the microwear evidence at Hoxne and Clacton can be taken at face value, hominins conducted a wide range of production and extraction activities largely based around the exploitation of stone, animals and wood.

White and Plunkett suggested that one might therefore describe our archaeological sites as identical fragments of ancient 'landscapes of habit' (Gosden 1994): familiar and often frequented places around which humans carried on the 'unthoughtful flow of action' – the repeated, recursive routines that provide the basic shape of life. Impromptu foci for socialising they may have been (Gamble 1999) but as White and Plunkett (2004) have emphasised, they are still, effectively, *all the same place*. This is one of the key reasons why one always recovers similar artefacts, always gets the same basic archaeological signature, and always seem to find *Homo heidelbergensis* a cognitively challenged and monolithic species.

The critical question, then, is how much are we missing? Is the preserved record at all representative of Middle Pleistocene behaviour, or is it like trying to reconstruct the entirety of twenty-first century life by excavating only the remains of fishing competitions around private rivers – undoubtedly social events but nevertheless dominated by fishing tackle, thermos flasks and the odd wellington boot? The Lower Palaeolithic is a biased record based on preservation, recovery and excavation more than hominin behaviour. Away from these rich sedimentary basins chances of recovery are very slim indeed. Flukes of preservations such as the Clacton and Schöningen spears (Warren 1911; Thieme 1997), the oft maligned living floors at Bilzingsleben (Mania 1991), and the camp fires at Beeches Pit, offer small clues as to what we are missing – although even here they still seem to be carrying out the same activities.

The recovery of a genuinely well-preserved camp site sits like something of a grail-quest to Palaeolithic archaeologists. Learning our lessons from the African Lower Palaeolithic, it is clear that the open, waterside locations representative of most of our sites are not safe places to be, and are certainly not the types of places one would choose to build camps and tend children (e.g. Isaac 1978; Binford 1981a; Schick 1987; Potts 1988). Roberts (1996a and b) suggested that the humans at Boxgrove used the coastal plain as a hunting ground and situated their camps in the forested downland block; if so they sadly did not survive the effects of the Anglian glaciation that so serendipitously buried and preserved the Slindon Formation. Mark Roberts (pers. comm. to MJW) similarly suggested that the famous scraper assemblage at High Lodge represents the remains of a home base, a safe haven where humans leisurely processed the spoils of the hunt without the unwanted attention of other carnivores; and which only survives because it was picked up and shunted by a glacier (Ashton et al.1992). If originally situated in forests, most camp sites were probably not in favourable preservational environments.

And yet, even if one found the legendary 'Palaeolithic Pompeii' (Binford 1981b), would it provide the answers we are looking for? Would it show a wider range of activities, and enable us to recreate in fine detail complex social interactions? Or would it just comprise the similar ranges of bones and stones? The question remains: are camp sites 'absent without leave' (having never formed part of the Lower Palaeolithic behavioural package, 'home' simply being proximity to kith and kin) or are they just 'missing in action' (the biased nature of archaeological visibility meaning that we are never likely to find them or recognise them among the limited range of objects recovered) (White and Plunkett 2004)?

Landscapes of habit

By weaving together the evidence from the many 'normal' localities, a view of how hominins operated within their landscape comes into focus. As suggested above, most of our rich and primary context sites represent magnet locations to which groups repeatedly returned to conduct a variety of routine social, technological and economic activities. Through the connections made between these places, hominins created their 'local hominin network' (Gamble 1995b, 1996), which facilitated access to vital static and mobile resources (including 'things' and other people), buffered them from local disruptions, and formed the nexus for spatial, subsistence and social behaviour. The scale of these networks depended largely on the distance between different resource patches (i.e. sites), which varied according to latitude, longitude and relief (Gamble 1995a; Roebroeks 2001). In Britain, as in much of oceanic western Europe, a fairly fine-grained, open-woodland mosaic existed during most interglacials with the distance between patches relatively small compared to continental locations father east.

It appears that these networks were indeed rather small, at least so far as one can tell from transfers of raw materials and lithic objects. The modal distance for transport in the Lower Palaeolithic in western Europe is 0–5 km, but transport between 5 and 40 km and rarely up to 80 km has been reported (Féblot-Augustins 1997, 1999; Wilson 1988). These data have been used to model the spatial scale of the local hominin network. Gamble (1995b; Gamble and Steele 1999) suggested a network with a radius of 40 km, although this must be regarded as a minimum estimate only. The distance over which stone tools were moved probably reveals more about the dynamics of transport and curation (the time during which items remained mobile and functional) than the actual size of hominin ranging behaviour (Roebroeks 2001; White and Plunkett 2004).

Most British Lower Palaeolithic sites are located at a source of raw materials, and for those without an immediate source of flint this was usually available from chalk or clay-with-flint outcrops or gravel deposits within the surrounding 5–10 km (White 1998a). Given the current lack of petrographical studies and the difficulty of macroscopically distinguishing between different flints types in Britain, more distant movements are impossible to identify, and the scale of lithic transport and curation has probably been underestimated in this country. One notable exception to this is at Waverley Wood, where andesite originating in the Lake District was used (300 km from the site), although it is still open to question whether this represents direct hominin procurement or materials collected from glacially transported deposits (Lang and Keen 2005; Keen et al. 2006). The same is true of instances of white 'Lincolnshire' flint occasionally used to make handaxes in East Anglia, hundreds of kilometres from the source in the Lincolnshire Wolds. One should also be mindful of the fact that the geological occurrence of flint does not automatically mean it was readily available for hominin exploitation. Although large parts of south-east England rest on flint-bearing Middle and Upper Chalk, for example, flint is not uniformly present and the Chalk is generally covered by vegetation, soil and other superficial deposits, only cropping out in the few places where it is being actively eroded.

The British Lower Palaeolithic record thus clearly shows that hominins used the different locales in their network places in a pragmatic but flexible fashion. At locales where raw material was readily available, humans tended to use it, regardless of size and quality, although as argued in the raw material model these two factors do seem to have had a structuring effect on the morphology of some of the resulting tools. The presence of flint was probably one of the primary factors in drawing humans to a locale, the levels of technological activities so facilitated producing high archaeological visibility. The range of objects recovered and use-wear analyses both suggest that full *chaînes opératoires* were enacted, from raw material procurement, though manufacture, use and discard. That these sites are usually littered with both manufacturing debris and discarded tools suggests that most Lower Palaeolithic tools were made, used and thrown away in quick succession, with little to suggest the long term curation or transport of the vast majority of lithic objects (Binford 1989a).

The exceptional preservation of a Palaeolithic landscape at Boxgrove offers a fine-grained view of hominins within their landscape (see Text Box 3.4). Lithic scatters from the site show that hominins were obtaining and testing flint nodules adjacent to the chalk cliff face, before removing it to the coastal plain for further working (Roberts and Parfitt 1999). Some knapping episodes (for example Q1D and GTP17) saw the complete reduction from nodule to handaxe; in some (e.g. Q1A) roughing out and finishing took place in different locations. Some handaxes saw further modification in the context of use and transport (Austin 1994), others were removed from the manufacturing area for continued use elsewhere (e.g. GTP17). Using this exceptional landscape-scale data, Pope (2002, 2004; Pope and Roberts 2005) has argued that deposition around the landscape was subtly structured around things and other people, and were mutable entities driven by long-term contextualised decisions made by hominin agents. Selective discard practices were thus important in creating variation in the archaeological record.

The knapping scatters at Caddington (Smith 1894; Sampson 1978) reveal a similar pattern, the only handaxes remaining with their débitage being those that were bro-ken during manufacture. Lithic scatters in the Swanscombe Lower Loams also show small-scale movement and localised separation of knapping episodes. Here, at least nine nodules were introduced, some cores having seen prior working elsewhere and others later removed from the site (Ashton and McNabb 1996). The same is found at Beeches Pit (Hallos 2005). In none of this, however, is one left with the impression that many handaxes or any other tools were curated over long distances or for long periods of time. Humans are not sessile and objects moving in and out of sites do not testify in any way to long-term or long-distance activities. As Boxgrove has shown, the knapping of the imported objects could have been started, and the missing ones dropped, just a few metres outside the excavated area.

On the other hand, at attractive locations where flint was not immediately available (for example the assemblages in the loams of Wansunt Pit and Bowman's Lodge, Hoxne Beds A2 and the Foxhall Road Grey Clay) hominins imported well-made tools or high quality stone to make tools (cf. Féblot-Augustins 1999). These considerations had a major impact on the types of stone tool found at a site which, in the case of handaxes, tend to be ovates, indicating that hominins carefully selected the pieces they carried with them. An exception to this pattern might be found at South Woodford, Essex, where large, pointed handaxes were introduced to a supposed butchery locale (White et al. 1999b), although even here it has been suggested that large clasts were grubbed from the local gravel. These transported tools may have formed part of a personal toolkit but the fact that many 'pristine' and apparently minimally used handaxes were eventually discarded in these locations again suggests that most Lower Palaeolithic stone tools were eminently disposable and replaceable; the need to carry other things often taking precedence. Having said that, the Wansunt Pit assemblage does contain three of the smallest, possibly heavily reduced, handaxes known in the British Lower Palaeolithic (Smith and Dewey 1914), indicating that some pieces may have had much longer use lives and that humans acted in a manner appropriate to their situation not in a formulaic fashion (Figure 4.14). Similar, diminutive pieces (although this time made on small peb-bles) were found at Foxhall Road, which Miss Layard considered to have been childrens' toys.

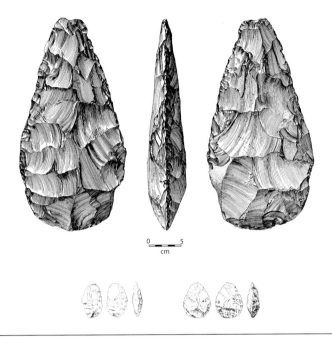

FIGURE 4.14
The Furze Platt Giant and the Wansunt Pit Miniatures, the largest and some of the smallest handaxes in the British Palaeolithic. (Furze Platt after Lacaille 1947; Wansunt after Smith and Dewey 1914.)

These patterns of raw material exploitation suggest that lithic transfers operated along a continuum that depended on knowledge about the resources available in different parts of the landscape (White and Plunkett 2004). The information flowing through the local hominin network included knowledge of what resources could be found where, when it was necessary to transport lithics, and when it was not. Although flint is not a limiting resource over large parts of southern Britain, it is not available everywhere, and while a skilled knapper can make a handaxe in about ten minutes, they cannot do this without suitable materials. Rather than representing an *ad hoc* technology created on the spot in response to an immediate stimulus, Lower Palaeolithic technology shows a high degree of planning depth. As White and Plunkett (2004) suggest, the once-dominant image of limited cognitive skills and simple unplanned behaviour (e.g. Binford 1979, 1985) can now be seen to have been formed through a misreading of the signatures found on most 'normal' Palaeolithic sites, where abundant resources encouraged repeated visits to places where hominins simply did not need to take much with them. The recent proposals of Brumm et al. (in press) that hominins routinely 'scavenged' previously discarded objects, may even hint at the provisioning of places with the anticipation of future need. Evidence for the regular transport of lithic artefacts over 5–40 km, much easier to see in Europe where different raw materials were used (e.g. Wilson 1988), also suggests that hominins routinely carried a small toolkit as they moved through the landscape, again hinting at greater planning depth. The overall pattern of immediate gratification, small-scale movement and rapid turnover does support the notion that Lower Palaeolithic life was local and episodic (Gamble 1986, 1995b, 1996), but this does not imply that Palaeolithic hominins were incapable of operating in other ways.

It is in non-flint technology that more evidence of long-term curation in the landscape is found, but not the wooden element. The Clacton spear is broken, possibly a flexion break during use (see Text Box 4.1), but the Schöningen spears are all complete and in perfect working order. Despite the effort that went into making them, they seem – at this time and in this place – to have been treated in the same fashion as stone objects. Tools to make tools, however, were treated very differently. Boxgrove has produced a number of soft hammers of antler and bone (Pitts and Roberts 1997) (Figure 4.15). The hammers, made of bison and elephant bone, were clearly used intensively, although several possess scrape marks produced when removing membranes and gristle, suggesting they were made of fresh bone at butchery sites. It is difficult to tell whether they were made opportunistically on the spot or whether they had been manufactured earlier in the anticipation of use. The antler hammer, made from the stem of an antler of the giant deer *Megaloceros dawkinsii*, tells a different story. According to Pitts and Roberts, this piece had been laboriously shaped long before it was actually needed, and had then been used so intensively – perhaps to make over a hundred handaxes – that the wear had rendered the end almost unrecognisable. This was clearly a tool that had formed part of a

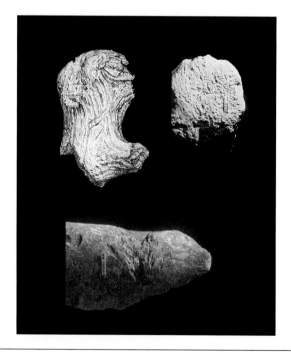

FIGURE 4.15
Soft-hammers from Boxgrove. Top: antler soft hammer with photograph of percussion scars on the pedicle. Bottom: bone hammer showing scars from repeated contact with the edge of a stone implement. (Courtesy of Mark Roberts.)

knapper's personal equipment, a tool to make tools that was carried around the landscape over long periods and which rendered the owner ready for action and able to produce a range of stone implements whenever opportunity required. A degree of forward planning is clearly demonstrated, showing that the long-held view that archaic hominins acted in the 'here and now' and had limited planning abilities (e.g. Binford 1979, 1985, *inter alia*) was unfounded. Another interesting aspect of these hammers is that they are mostly squat pieces that fitted in the palm of the hand – rather like a stone hammer – providing a firm grip and subtle control. This is unlike those favoured by modern knappers, which usually take the form of a bar held at one end and swung like a baton in use.

Hunters in the British landscape

Opinions regarding the hunting capabilities of Lower Palaeolithic humans have changed dramatically since the 1980s and 1990s, when most people accepted the view that they were little more than obligate scavengers (e.g. Binford 1981a, 1985; Gamble 1987; Stringer and Gamble 1994; Villa 1990). The empirical basis for this view stemmed largely from an examination of faunal remains and the absence of any convincing 'smoking gun' hunting sites. Binford's (1985) examination of anatomical part frequencies of faunal remains at Swanscombe led him to conclude that much of it was a 'background' scatter of natural deaths that accumulated at a waterside. Only six bones exhibited tool-inflicted cut-marks, related in equal proportion to meat removal and disarticulation. Overall, Binford concluded that hominins were clearly interested in meat, but that they had played little role in the deaths of the animals and simply scavenged at the source of the carcasses. At Hoxne, Binford found only ten bones bearing cut-marks, related to both disarticulation and meat removal, although he also found evidence for systematic processing of bone marrow. The frequency of different anatomical parts, particularly of horse and red deer, led him to the conclusion that the Hoxne fauna represented a transported, scavenged assemblage where heads and marrow-rich bones were targeted. He did, however, suggest that fallow deer, represented by the most meaty limb bones, may have been 'rarely killed for meat' (Binford 1985, 322). Stopp's (1993) analysis of fauna from the undisturbed West Cutting site at Hoxne, found 27 definite and probable cut-marked bones – again, clearly showing that humans had interfered with animal carcasses; 23 bones had been gnawed by other carnivores. Red deer and horse were the most frequently processed animals but the skeletal representation and mortality profile of this small sample led Stopp to conclude that the manner in which humans had obtained the carcasses was indeterminable. Binford also dismissed human hunting at Torralba and Ambrona, Spain (1987b), Zhoukoutian, China (Binford and Stone 1986), and a host of other pre-modern human sites (e.g. Binford 1981a, 1985). These far-reaching papers, along with his conclusions of limited planning depth noted above, created an enduring image of Lower (and Middle) Palaeolithic humans as hapless creatures ekeing out a living from scraps of meat that the lions left behind.

This picture has been eroded by new analyses and discoveries over the past 15 years. As we have seen in Chapter 2, high levels of carnivory with routine and unhindered access to meat resources is regarded as one of the prerequisites for successful colo-nisation of northern latitudes (Roebroeks 2001). This, we assume, must indicate active and successful hunting. Direct evidence for hunting is also growing. The spears from Schöningen 13 II–4 – made of dense, slow-growing spruce, up to two metres long and weighted like an Olympic javelin (Thieme 1997, 2005) – can hardly be considered to be snow probes (Gamble 1987). Experimental reconstructions suggested that these could be thrown up to 60 m with good penetrative power (Rieder 2000, cited in Thieme 2005), but whether they were throwing spears or thrusting weapons is irrelevant to the main point – these were objects designed and executed to kill large animals. They were cre-ated in advance of, and in anticipation of, hunting. There can be no clearer evidence of planning or the ability and prior intention to hunt. Although the fauna has yet to be fully published, these spears were used to hunt at least 20 horses along the shoreline of an 800 m long lake, possibly in a single event during the autumn when lake levels were low (Thieme 2005). Hearths and possible roasting spits were also found; the whole interpreted as a briefly occupied hunting camp. This clearly contradicts Gaudzinski's (1996, 1999a) contention that mono-specific faunal accumulations (as clear evidence of organised hunting) only appear from MIS7 onwards.

In Britain, evidence of a horse-hunting event is found at Boxgrove GTP17 (Roberts and Parfitt 1999) (Figure 4.16). Although only partially preserved, the surviving elements sug-gest that a single adult individual was originally present. Evidence of butchery exists in the form of cut and scrape marks, the location of which shows evidence of skinning, dis-articulation and filleting, as well as bone breakage for marrow processing. One scapula exhibits a semi-circular wound, probably a spear puncture. The archaeology associated

FIGURE 4.16
Horse scapula from Boxgrove GTP17. The bone shows a circular area of damage believed to have been caused by a spear penetrating the horse's shoulder. (Courtesy Mark Roberts.)

with the horse show that six or seven nodules of flint had been brought from the cliff 40 m away and were reduced on the spot to make handaxes. These were used to butcher the horse in a leisurely fashion over several hours showing that hominins had complete mastery over the situation (Roberts and Parfitt 1999). The handaxes were subsequently removed, presumably to further process the fillets sliced from the horse. This event provides an explanation for why humans often treated their stone tools in a seemingly cavalier fashion at Boxgrove (where several hundred were found accumulated around the waterhole of Quarry 1 – Pitts and Roberts 1997). While hunting a fast-moving animal on the coastal plain, hominins really didn't need the encumbrance of several kilograms of flint, especially when it could be procured quickly once the animal was killed.

Butchery traces on almost-complete rhinoceros skeletons at Boxgrove have been forwarded as evidence that humans were also hunting these animals at the waterhole, perhaps trapping them there (Pitts and Roberts 1997; Figure 4.17). In excess of half a ton of edible parts would have been available, leading Roberts (1996a and b) to suggest that, either hominins were taking this back to a camp site where they were storing it, or sharing it with groups far larger than previously thought. Alternatively, their methods may simply have been wasteful. Accepting the conclusion that these were hunted animals, however, would also lead us to suppose that many of the other cut-marked animal bones found at Boxgrove – which include bear, red deer, fallow deer, roe deer, badger and bison – were also the remains of hunted individuals. Cut-marked bones from a bear

FIGURE 4.17
Rhino butchery area from Boxgrove Q1, showing rhinoceros pelvis and handaxes. (Courtesy Mark Roberts.)

paw have also been identified at Grays Thurrock, Essex (Simon Parfitt, pers. comm.). Although much younger than the MIS13 site at Boxgrove and MIS9 site at Grays, hunting of both rhinoceros and bear are well documented at Taubach, Germany, dated to MIS5e (Bratlund 1999).

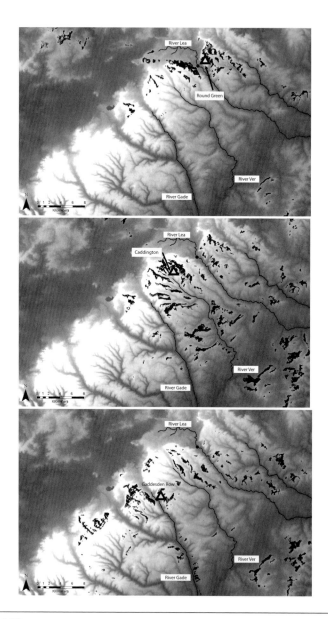

FIGURE 4.18
Viewsheds from three upland sites in the Chiltern Hills; Round Green, Caddington and Gaddesden Row. Clearly, when situated on top of these hillsides hominins had excellent views down the river valleys and across to adjacent hillsides (areas marked in black). (Courtesy Helen Drinkall.)

In the case of Boxgrove, the downland block would have provided an ideal vantage point for scanning the coastal plain for herds. The upland sites of Gaddesden Row, Caddington and Round Green (Figure 4.18), all situated in the Chiltern Hills, might similarly have served as focal points for scanning the valleys of the Lea, Ver and Gade (Smith 1894, 1916; White 1997; Drinkall in prep.). While monitoring the landscape, hominins could have geared up using the local flint sources exposed around these upland ponds, and when opportunities arose quickly moved into the valleys to hunt.

Tools, language and cognition

The Lower Palaeolithic of Britain, like the rest of the Old World, has no convincing evidence for symbolism or symbolic objects (Dibble 1987; D'Errico et al. 2003; D'Errico and Nowell 2000). A few handaxes contain natural fossils that have been carefully preserved despite the shaping of the final object, as seen at Swanscombe and West Tofts, while two flakes of coral-bearing chert ('starry stones') occur at Swanscombe, some 120 miles from its source in Wiltshire (Oakley 1981; Figure 4.19). These may have been prized objects, even long distance manuports in the latter instance, but these at best indicate an aesthetic sense or curiosity for the unusual. Outside Britain, the single handaxe (Excalibur) found thrown into the necropolis at Sima de los Huesos, Atapuerca, has been argued to have been a votive-style offering (Carbonell and Mosquera 2006), although in our opinion it is more likely to be a chance inclusion, perhaps originally a possession of one of the individuals who came to be deposited at the site. Several recent studies have suggested that symbolism may not have resided in objects, but in the body (e.g. Gamble 1998, 1999), objects, once discarded, having little more significance than any other pebble on the river beach. This is, of course, impossible to demonstrate conclusively and one must consider the fact that Middle Pleistocene hominins lived in small and probably isolated groups, meaning the type of signalling associated with later prehistoric material culture may simply not have been required. As Nowell and White (2010) note, there is little point in using artefacts to symbolise group ethnicity or personal identity when no one else is watching, or when everybody around you is kith and kin – this latter would rather equate simply to display.

The presence of language in the Lower Palaeolithic is equally moot. The anatomical evidence from fossil materials outside Britain is decidedly ambiguous, although numerical modelling of the relationship between brain size, group size and grooming behaviour suggests some form of vocal communication by at least ~500 ka BP (Aiello and Dunbar 1993). Artefacts may provide further clues. Wynn (1995) suggests that the process involved in learning and sharing and idea about handaxe shape requires not only observation of another individual, but also the ability to understand what others deem appropriate, to 'see' things as they see them. From the point of view of Dunbar's (1998, 200) Social Brain hypothesis and *theory of mind*, this would indicate that *Homo heidelbergensis* had achieved the fourth level of intentionality, the minimum requirement for mutually understood social signals to be evident in material culture (McNabb 1997). This would leave *Homo heidelbergensis* very close to modern humans in terms of in terms

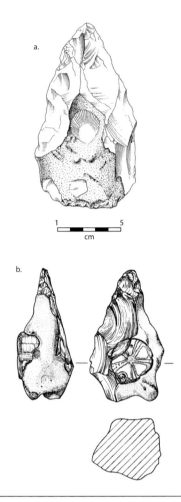

FIGURE 4.19
Handaxes retaining fossils that hominins appear to have deliberately preserved during manufacture. Top: West Tofts, Norfolk. Bottom: Middle Gravels, Swanscombe. (After Oakley 1981, Figures 2 and 3 and © The Royal Society.)

of intentionality and may grant them a linguistic capacity. The scale of the hearthside gatherings may also suggest that language was in place by this time. At Beeches Pit and Foxhall Road (if the latter is a hearth) the area of burning and artefacts is less than ~2 m² and could have sat no more than five or so people, spatially and socially reminiscent of Dunbar's (1996) small conversation groups, well acquainted people sitting together chatting in a social gathering. Roberts (1996b) has also argued that the levels of cooperation required to hunt horses and rhinoceroses on the Sussex coastal plain demanded linguistic communication, although one must ask why this is not also true of lions. Given the complexity seen in modern primates some form of linguistic communication is certain and, if Lower Palaeolithic hominins had actually complex language, we wonder how many of those conversations involved handaxes!

CHAPTER 5

Neanderthals of the forest steppe

The Early Middle Palaeolithic, ~325–180 ka BP

INTRODUCTION

Archaeologically, the Early Middle Palaeolithic (EMP) is most readily differentiated from the Lower Palaeolithic by the widespread and persistent use of Levallois technology often, but not invariably, accompanied by the disappearance of handaxes and an increase in flake tools (papers in Ronen 1982; Gamble and Roebroeks 1999). Although instances of much earlier Levallois technology are documented (see below) these are rather precocious flourishes that do not constitute a lasting shift in technological practices, but rather random or situational convergences on Levallois from a common Acheulean root (White and Ashton 2003; White et al. 2011). Furthermore, they exist among a typically Lower Palaeolithic suite of behaviours, whereas the persistent change that occurred ~330 ka BP was accompanied by changes in other hominin adaptive, social and cognitive structures (White and Ashton 2003; Gamble 1999), discussed below.

Sites assigned in this book to the EMP span the period from late MIS9 to late MIS7, and provide evidence for hominin occupation of Britain during two previously unrecognised interglacial periods between the Hoxnian (MIS11) and the Ipswichian (MIS5e), namely the Purfleet (MIS9) and Aveley (MIS7) interglacials. As discussed by Scott (2010) and White et al. (in prep.), for most of the twentieth century the compressed chronological frameworks available actually left little time for a discrete EMP, which was instead compacted into a handaxe-rich late Lower Palaeolithic with Levallois as a technological option (e.g. Wymer 1968; Roe 1981). In this account, the Middle Palaeolithic was restricted to a handful of Upper Pleistocene occurrences, discussed in the next chapter. Because of a strong tradition of multidisciplinary and interdisciplinary Quaternary studies, there are now a relatively large number of sites in the British terrestrial record that be firmly attributed to this newly defined period on a number of lithostratigraphical (Bridgland 1994;

Schreve et al. 2002, in press), biostratigraphical (Schreve 1997, 2001a and b; Keen 1999) and chronostratographical (Penkman 2005; Briant et al. 2006) grounds. Here we accept these attributions, and will not repeat the long debates regarding the ages of the various deposits concerned (e.g. Bridgland 1994; Gibbard 1985, 1994; Schreve 1997, 2001a and b; Schreve et al. 2002; Schreve et al. 2006; Candy and Schreve 2007).

This chapter presents the first general synthesis of environments, landscapes and archaeology of EMP Britain. It concentrates on a number of key sites (Figure 5.1) that have been attributed on non-typological grounds to late MIS9–7, setting them in their environmental and landscape context, and subsequently discusses their significance for an understanding of Neanderthal technical organisation, settlement history, societies and demography.

FIGURE 5.1
Major British sites discussed in Chapter 5.

THE SAALIAN COMPLEX: MIS9–7

The termination of MIS 9 and the climatic deterioration marking the onset of the MIS8 glaciation began ~300 ka BP (Figures 5.2 and 5.3). On the basis of the global oxygen record, MIS8 appears to have been less severe than most other Middle Pleistocene glaciations, being similar in magnitude to MIS4; although at ~50,000 years duration it lasted much longer. Two distinct warm peaks are evident, with a significant warming event towards the latter end of the glaciation related to an increase in insolation (Toucanne et al. 2009). Unlike MIS12 and MIS2, terrestrial evidence for an extensive lowland glaciation during MIS8 has been elusive; according to Kukla (2005) high levels of solar radiation in northern latitudes from late MIS9 prevented the formation of extensive ice sheets. However, recent work in eastern England has provided evidence for ice sheets advancing at least as far as Lincolnshire (T. White et al. 2010), while offshore boreholes have established MIS8 deposits well into the Southern Bight of the North Sea (Beets et al. 2005).

The warming limb initiating MIS7 began about ~245 ka BP, but was interrupted by a brief (*c.* 2 ka) reversion to colder conditions (Desprat et al. 2006). Thereafter, the climatic structure of the MIS7 interglacial shows that it was characterised by at least three warm peaks of more or less equal magnitude and duration (MIS7e, 7c and 7a) and two climatic deteriorations (7d and 7b) (Bassinot et al. 1994; Candy and Schreve 2007), refining previous studies where only two warm peaks and a single cold episode were emphasised (e.g. Zazo 1999). As such, the development of the British landscape, and changes throughout the interglacial, are now seen as far more complex than previously thought, with major implications for hominin colonisation, settlement and behaviour.

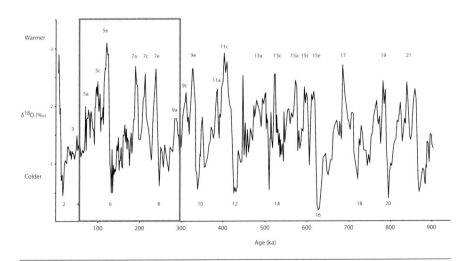

FIGURE 5.2
The Marine Isotope Curve from MIS1 to MIS21, with the period covered in this chapter highlighted. (Data from Bassinot et al. 1994.)

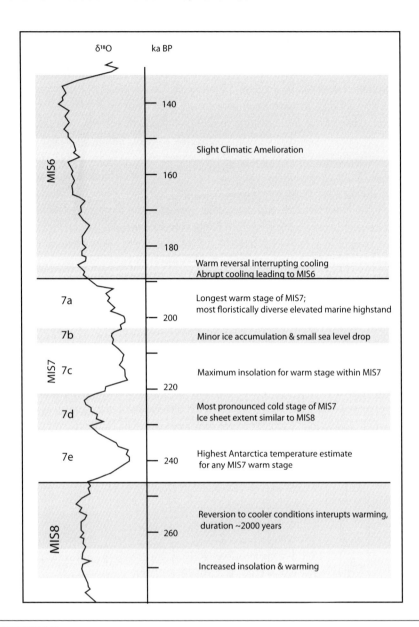

FIGURE 5.3
Key features of Marine Isotope Stages 8, 7 and 6. (After Scott and Ashton 2010 and courtesy Beccy Scott.)

Abrupt climatic deterioration began *c.* 180,000 years ago, marking the start of MIS6, with MIS7 therefore lasting some 60 ka years. There is evidence of an equally abrupt return to warm conditions in MIS6.5, possibly of equal magnitude to MIS7a. The remainder of the period, however, was extremely cold, with British and Scandinavian ice sheets extending into and blocking the northern North Sea (Toucanne et al. 2009).

PALAEOGEOGRAPHY AND SEA LEVELS OF THE EARLY MIDDLE PALAEOLITHIC

Sea level modelling

Waelbroeck et al. (2002) derived relative sea level (RSL) estimates based on high resolution $\delta^{18}O$ records – combined with evidence of high sea-level stands based on corals and low sea-level stands from salinity records (Rohling et al. 1998) – to reconstruct a composite RSL estimate for the past four climatic cycles, with an estimated error margin of +/−13 m (Figure 5.4). During MIS8 RSL was depressed by as much as 110 m, creating terrestrial

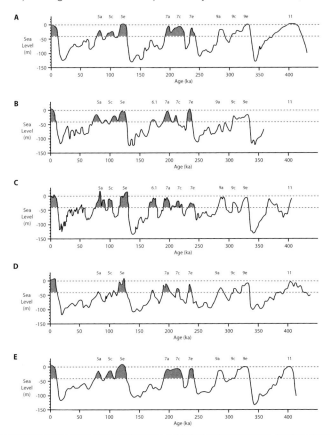

FIGURE 5.4

Sea level estimates from the benthic isotope record and other sea-level indicators, with periods during which Britain was an island during MIS7 and MIS5 indicated. Top dashed line: modern sea-level. Lower dashed line: −40m below modern sea-level, above which Britain is assumed to become an island. Shaded area: periods of high sea level and island status as described in this chapter. (Reconstructions based on data from A: Waelbroeck et al. 2002, based on North Atlantic and equatorial Pacific benthonic isotopic record; B: Lea et al 2002, based on foraminiferal Mg/Ca and planktonic oxygen isotopes; C: Shackleton 2000, based oxygen isotope data from equatorial Pacific (V19–30) and Vostock air oxygen isotope ratio; D: Siddall et al. (2003), based on Red Sea salinity and oxygen isotope record; E: Cutler et al. 2003, based on scaled data from benthic isotope record of core V19–30.)

conditions in both the Channel and North Sea. Three high sea-level stands were detected in MIS7, corresponding to the warm sub-stages 7e (c. −10 m OD), 7c (ca −5 m OD) and 7a (ca −11 m OD), but during none of these did RSL quite reach modern levels.

Waelbroeck et al. (2002) note that their results largely agree with estimates from corals and geochemical data on submerged speleothems from Argentorola Cave, Italy (Gallup et al. 1994; Bard et al. 1996, 2000), although more recent work on these speleothems have indicated that sea level in MIS7a was actually much lower, probably reaching no higher than −18 m OD (Dutton et al 2009a and b). These are similar to the estimates derived from Shackleton's (2000) $\delta^{18}O$ data, which project generally lower sea levels for all MIS7 warm peaks. On the other hand, estimates by Lea et al. (2002) using planktonic Mg/Ca and $\delta^{18}O$ found even higher sea levels, with MIS7e and MIS7a possibly exceeding both modern and MIS5e RSL.

For the cold sub-stages of MIS7d and MIS7b, most estimates produced the expected reduction in sea levels, but again there are some discrepancies. Waelbroeck et al.'s (2002) results show that, during MIS7d, RSL plummeted to c. −85 m OD, but MIS7b showed only a marginal fall to c. −25 m OD, some 35 m higher than projections derived from Shackleton's data. Interestingly, the Italian speleothem data, Shackleton's $\delta^{18}O$ reconstructions, Red Sea salinity (Siddall et al. 2003) and coral dating (Thompson and Goldstein 2005) all show a period of high RSL during the early part of MIS6 (MIS 6.5), when levels appear to have risen to <−19m OD, although the combined RSL data show lower levels well below ~−50m OD.

Despite inconsistent and contradictory reconstructions, it would still appear that sufficiently high sea levels existed for Britain to become an island during the warmer phases of MIS7, although it would have been a peninsula during periods of depressed sea levels in MIS8 and probably MIS7d. As noted in Chapter 3, Keen (1995) suggested that past sea levels at or above modern ordnance datum would have been sufficient to separate Britain from Europe, given the present critical depths of c. −50 m in the Dover Strait and −40 m in the North Sea; although he acknowledged the confounding problems of not knowing the Middle Pleistocene bathymetry of these basins, the absence of any telltale deposits and the fact that the North Sea is progressively downwarping and was probably shallower in the past.

EVIDENCE OF MARINE TRANSGRESSIONS IN THE TERRESTRIAL RECORD

There are a number of deposits along the coast from Essex to Cornwall (and also along the opposite French coast) that provide direct evidence for marine transgression and an open Dover Strait during MIS7. Where fossils are preserved, these generally show deposition during warm phases, although some preserve far-travelled cobbles and boulders that may be ice-rafted erratics emplaced during cold periods with high sea levels (Bates et al. 2000, 2003).

Extensive evidence for marine conditions during MIS7 has come from the Norton–Brighton Raised Beach on the Lower Coastal Plain at Sussex (Bates et al. 1997; Bates 1998; Bates et al. 2000, 2003). Relict beach deposits at Black Rock, Brighton, consisting of flint and chalk cobbles and pebbles with a base height of 8.5 m OD, have yielded AAR estimates consistent with an MIS7 correlation (Davies 1984). These are overlain by 20–25 m of 'coombe rock' (a rubbly, chalky solifluct) yielding a mammalian fauna similar to those from cold-climate deposits immediately predating the last interglacial (MIS5e) deposits at Marsworth, Buckinghamshire (Murton et al. 2001), and Bacon Hole, Gower (Stringer et al. 1986), and presumed to represent MIS6.

The Norton–Brighton Raised Beach has been extensively investigated at Norton Farm, where marine sands and gravels have been recorded between 5 and 9 m OD (Bates et al. 2000). Age estimation based on AAR, lateral correlation with other dated raised beach deposits, as well as the presence of both a small caballine horse and specific M1 morphology in northern voles, all suggest that the site belongs to late MIS7/early MIS6 (Bates et al. 2000; Bowen et al. 1989; Parfitt 1998b). Ostracods and foraminifera from Norton Farm revealed a marine regression, with fully marine conditions being replaced by intertidal mudflats, the foraminifera becoming stressed and reduced in size as tidal links receded to zero (Bates et al. 2000). Overall the invertebrate faunas showed a mixture of cold and warm species, perhaps suggesting that more continental conditions prevailed; the sparse pollen record also indicates an essentially open environment. The whole sequence was suggested to represent a high sea level event during deteriorating cold conditions (Figure 5.5), followed by a full marine regression at the MIS7/6 boundary (or conceivably a transition between one of the warm-cold sub-stages, or even MIS6.5). Similar evidence for cool-cold water conditions and high sea levels was noted on the other side of the channel, at Tancarville and Tourville (Bates et al. 2003).

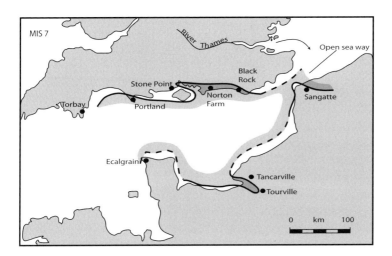

FIGURE 5.5
The palaeogeography of eastern England during MIS7. (After Bates et al. 2003 and Wiley, with permission.)

Further Raised Beach deposits at West Beach, Portland Bill, Dorset, lying at 10.5 m OD (Davies and Keen 1985), and at Hope's Nose, Torbay at 9–12 m OD (Davies 1984; Bowen et al. 1986) have also been correlated with MIS7 based on AAR estimates. Similar age estimates have been obtained from the sea caves at Berry Head (Figure 5.6), Torbay, from both AAR (Mottershead et al. 1987) and Uranium-series dates of 210 + 34/−76 ka BP and 226 + 53/−76 ka BP (Proctor and Smart 1991; Baker and Proctor 1996) on speleothem formed in regressive phases that seal intertidal brown loams. The molluscan faunas from these Devon and Dorset raised beaches, in contrast to Norton Farm, testify to warm sea temperatures similar to those of today and must, therefore, belong to different and probably earlier parts of the interglacial. Other sites with evidence for early interglacial marine conditions come from Selsey Life Boat Station (LBS), where brackish molluscs appear at −1.76 m OD, heralding a full marine transgression with deposits up to 7.5 m OD (West and Sparks 1960). As discussed below, the Selsey sequence probably represents the earliest part of MIS7.

The westernmost evidence comes from raised beaches of the Godrevy Formation in West Cornwall, which has produced TL and AAR estimations of both MIS7 and MIS5e age (Scourse 1999). At Fistral Bay, raised dunes attributed to both MIS7 and MIS5e show different prevailing wind directions, with MIS7 being dominated by northerly winds but MIS5e by southeasterlies. This may indicate very different climates during MIS5e and whatever part of MIS7 is represented here. Scourse tentatively suggested that the northerly winds may represent changing wind direction at the beginning of a cold stage. The Godrevy formation also contains non-local clasts within a muddy matrix, which Scourse (ibid.) suggests represent erratics deposited by ice floes during high sea-level stands during a cold period.

FIGURE 5.6
Raised beaches and sea caves in the Torbay area. Top: Raised beach at Shoalstone. Bottom: Berry Head. (Photographs courtesy Chris Proctor.)

A few sites within the Mucking Formation of the Thames (Bridgland 1994) also reveal high sea levels in the North Sea. At Aveley, brackish water molluscs and ostracods have been noted in the Lower Brickearth, suggesting a marine transgression during this early part of the interglacial (Allen and Robinson, cited in Sutcliffe 1995; Cooper 1972; Holyoak 1983). Similarly fine-grained, laminated sediments from Lion Tramway cutting, West Thurrock, have also been interpreted as representing intertidal or estuarine conditions (Schreve et al. 2006 see Text Box 5.1).

Text Box 5.1

LION PIT TRAMWAY CUTTING, WEST THURROCK, ESSEX

First discovered by A.S. Kennard in the early twentieth century (Dibley and Kennard 1916), the Lion Pit Tramway Cutting preserves a primary context Levallois knapping floor, potentially one of the most important MIS7 sites in Britain. However, although the site has been recently reinvestigated (Bridgland 1994; Bridgland and Harding 1995; Schreve et al. 2006), an area of only 5.25 m^2 was excavated, the narrow cutting within which the deposits are exposed (first cut to remove Chalk from the Lion Pit via a double track) and the sheer depth of sediment overlying the archaeology severely limiting the scale of any investigation.

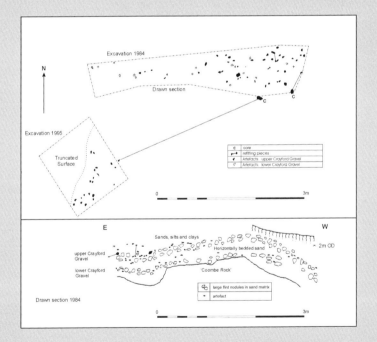

FIGURE 1
Excavation plan and geological section through the archaeological levels exposed in the recent excavations at the Lion Tramway Cutting, West Thurrock. (After Schreve et al. 2007.)

Text Box 5.1

The Pleistocene deposits exposed in the Lion Pit Tramway Cutting form part of the Taplow/Mucking Formation of the Thames; the basal 'Crayford Gravel' dating to the MIS8–7 transition immediately following downcutting to this terrace level. The sequence rests on chalk breccia containing sparse flints, with the main archaeological horizon occurring just above this, in the upper division of the coarse Crayford Gravel. These are overlain by *c.* 10m of fine-grained sediments, including fossiliferous sands and silty clay, and laminated beds of possible estuarine origin.

FIGURE 2
Levallois cores from the Lion Tramway Cutting, showing two different operational schema. (Top: lineal centripetal; bottom: recurrent unipolar.)

FIGURE 3
Photograph of the 1984 excavations at the Lion Tramway Cutting, showing the depth of sands and silts overlying the Levallois knapping floor. John McNabb provides a human scale. (Courtesy of David Bridgland.)

Molluscan and mammalian remains from the silts and clays above the archaeological horizon – including *Corbicula fluminalis*, *Bithynia tentaculata, Palaeoloxodon antiquus* (straight-tusked elephant) and *Stephanorhinus kirchbergensis* (Merck's rhinoceros) – attest to deposition in a slow-flowing river under wooded, fully temperate conditions, although the majority of the mammalian fauna favour open-grassland, which presumably occurred on the Thames floodplain (Schreve et al. 2006). Pollen from the site also revealed a wooded environment dominated by

Text Box 5.1

alder, hornbeam and hazel with lower frequencies of pine, oak, lime and ash (Hollin 1977). Samples from another exposure 0.9 km west of the Tramway Cutting showed two pollen biozones, the lower (correlated with pollen from the Tramway itself) being dominated by thermophilous woodland taxa, the upper showing the spread of local grassland (Gibbard 1994). No artefacts have been recovered from these beds, but human presence is attested by a cut-marked pelvis of a narrow-nosed rhinoceros (*Stephanorhinus hemitoechus*), with incisions concentrated around the obdurator foramen, an area where butchery and detachment of muscle blocks leaves these characteristic traces (Schreve et al. 2006).

The 'Levallois floor' occurs on a gravel 'beach' at the foot of a chalk river-cliff, both of which provided raw material for knapping activities. Including both recently excavated material and the earlier collections made by Warren (Warren 1923a and b), this site has produced some 250 artefacts, including Levallois cores, Levallois flakes and a range of associated débitage. Large flint nodules from the gravel and chalk cliff were used to execute full Levallois reduction sequences, from raw material acquisition, though preparation, exploitation and discard of the cores and waste flakes on the river beach, to the export of selected blanks for use elsewhere. How far the knapping floor extends laterally is unknown, but given the richness of the small area so far investigated a major spread seems likely. The relatively undisturbed nature of the site is demonstrated by refitting, although some vertical displacement has occurred and, despite sieving, finer débitage is underrepresented, presumably winnowed out (Schreve et al. 2006). Environmental indicators directly associated with the Levallois floor are practically non-existent but given the geological context a cool climate and fairly open conditions probably prevailed during the MIS8–7 transition.

In summary, as the climate ameliorated into early MIS7, rising sea levels led to a marine transgression. Data from the French side of the Channel, along with evidence from oceanographic and sedimentological source patterns, suggest an open Dover Strait during MIS7, and we can track evidence of high sea levels around the south coast from Cornwall to Essex. It would therefore seem extremely probable that Britain was cut off from Continental Europe during these periods, and that both hominin and animal populations were isolated or, if absent, perhaps faced insurmountable cognitive or technical barriers to seaborne dispersal (White and Schreve 2000). Furthermore, while the evidence from Portland Bill and Torbay show that high sea levels existed during fully temperate conditions, Norton Farm indicates the continuation of such conditions into a cold period. Whether this is the onset of MIS6, or one of the cold sub stages of MIS7, is currently unclear (Bates et al. 2003). This distinction is very important for understanding the movement of animals in and out of Britain for, although it is widely assumed that during cold sub-stages Britain may have been reconnected to Europe, the evidence presented above hints that this may not have always been the case. This may have significant implications for the EMP settlement history of Britain (White and Schreve 2000; Ashton and Lewis 2002; White et al. 2006).

LANDSCAPE EVOLUTION AND ORGANIC COMMUNITIES

The environments and environmental history of the EMP associated with MIS7 can be reconstructed at different scales through several proxies, including pollen, plant macrofossils and the dietary or habitat requirements of contemporary animals. MIS8 occupation is evident at a number of sites, notably Purfleet and Baker's Hole, but beyond sedimentological evidence for deposition under cold condition and cold-tolerant species such as mammoth and horse (which also occur in the proceeding interglacial) little can be said. Very few good palaeoenvironmental records exist for MIS7 and even fewer can be directly related to significant archaeological assemblages. As such, we cannot associate EMP hominins within a particular type of habitat, although the fact that most significant archaeological sites occur in similar fluvial settings allows the assumption that hominins were active in the same types of landscapes and habitats. This section will therefore describe the landscapes available for hominin exploitation during MIS7, had they been present or left visible traces, and provides for the first time a synthetic overview of the environmental history of the period (cf. Murton et al. 2001).

Vegetation history

Good evidence for the vegetation of MIS7 comes from pollen and plant macrofossils from just a handful of published sites: Aveley, Essex (West 1969), Marsworth, Buckinghamshire (Murton et al. 2001), Stoke Goldington, Bedfordshire (Green et al. 1996) and Selsey LBS, Sussex (West and Sparks 1960), each of which preserves evidence for vegetation development throughout parts of MIS7. This can be augmented by data from some very habitat and diet specific beetles. The majority of plants found in MIS7 sites still occur in southern Britain today, suggesting the existence of some analogous plant communities and implying an MIS7 environment very similar to the present day (Murton et al. 2001), even if populated by an exotic suite of animals and not controlled by modern land management practices.

At the Selsey LBS site, Sussex, West and Sparks (1960) described a succession of freshwater silts (Bed 1), detrital muds (Bed 2) and estuarine clays (Bed 3), filling a channel incised into Eocene Bracklesham Beds. Pollen and plant macrofossils were recovered from all major stratigraphical units and were divided into several zones showing successive vegetation change over time (Table 5.1). The site also produced a sparse archaeological assemblage from the detrital muds of Bed 2, including a Levallois core (Nick Ashton pers. comm.).

The pollen from the basal Freshwater Beds (Table 5.1) was characterised by high frequencies of non-arboreal pollen, dominated by grasses, sedges and other herbaceous plants. Other than birch and pine, tree pollen was sparse, with sporadic records of lime, oak, and hornbeam. West postulated that the thermophilous tree species were derived from older Pleistocene deposits, and that much of the pine pollen was probably far

Table 5.1 Summary of the pollen evidence from Selsey LBS (after West and Sparks 1960).

Bed	Zone	Characteristics
Bed 2–3	Zone F	– Extensive deciduous forest with very high frequencies of oak and hazel – Consistent presence of pine and birch. Maple, alder, lime and spruce also present. – Herbaceous pollen low.
Bed 2	Zone E	– Oak dominant (50% AP), ash and ivy appear; extensive regional deciduous forest cover – Herbs very low, grasses and sedge continuously present
Bed 2	Zone D	– Continued spread of pine and birch, oak first appears in significant numbers – Aquatics decline but sedge increases – Herbs in very low numbers reflecting increased forestation
Bed 2	Zone C	– Pine and birch dominant – Herbs persist in low numbers
Bed 1	Zone B	– Grasses dominant, herbaceous plants common – Sparse pine and birch

travelled, although macroscopic remains of several birch species unequivocally demonstrates that trees were present. The regional vegetation at this time was thus dominated by open grassland with some isolated stands of trees and shrubs. West suggested that this was a flora typical of Zone B of the Ipswichian (i.e. MIS5e) and, although this attribution is not accepted here, the notion that this flora represents the earlier part of an interglacial may still be valid. However, there is no evidence that this period was particularly cold. No arctic or subarctic plants were present and while the majority of the macrofossils are today distributed throughout Scandinavia, some have a more southerly distribution (West and Sparks 1960, 104). High frequencies of *Typha latifolia*, which is not found beyond the 14 °C isotherm, also suggest mild conditions and rapid warming.

The pollen spectra contained within the deposits of Bed 2 (the organic muds) and Bed 3 (grey silty-clay with evidence of incipient salinity) were divided by West into a further four Zones (C–F). These showed progressive forestation, and a concomitant decline in herbaceous species; by the end of the sequence regional forest cover was extensive (see Table 5.1). Thermophilous terrestrial plants such as ivy (*Hedera helix*), dogwood (*Cornus sanguinea*), and aquatic species including Eurasian water nymph (*Najas minor*) and soft hornwort (*Ceratophyllum* cf. *submersum*) also show warm summer conditions. Seeds of frogbit (*Hydrocharis morsus-ranae*), water-soldier (*Stratiotes aloides*) and duckweeds (*Lemna*), plants which rarely or never fruit in Britain today, may indicate higher summer temperatures than at present during Zone F (West and Sparks 1960, 113), while firethorn is presently a native of southern Europe. The high frequencies of hazel and the presence of holly (*Ilex*) and ivy suggest some degree of oceanicity, as the latter two in particular are frost-sensitive and will not tolerate average winter temperatures below 1.5 °C. The climate during Zones E and F was therefore one with warm winters and warm summers.

The pollen profiles from Marsworth (Figure 5.7) and Aveley reveal an entirely different succession. At the old Bulbourne Quarry, Marsworth (SP933143, now College Lake Wildlife Centre), botanical remains have been recovered from the fluvial sands and organic muds filling the Lower Channel, and from tufa clasts within these (Green et al.

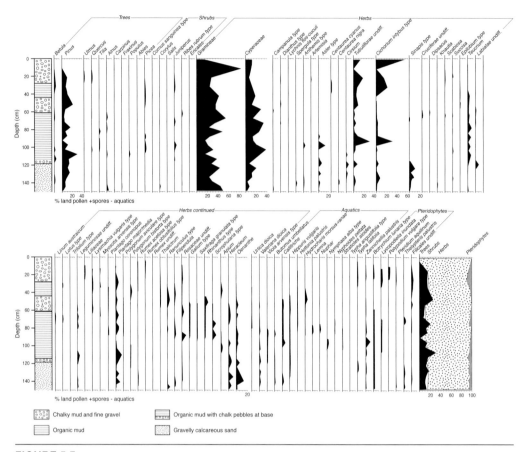

FIGURE 5.7
Pollen Profile from the Lower Channel Deposits at Marsworth. (After Murton et al. 2001 and Elsevier, reproduced with permission.)

1984; Murton et al. 2001). The latter represent the fragmented remains of deposits laid down in an earlier calcareous spring at this location; uranium-series dating of tufa clasts gave age estimates ranging from 254,000–208,000 ka BP, suggesting that the tufa was originally emplaced during MIS7e–c, and that the temperate conditions of the Lower Channel deposits represent MIS7a (cf. Candy and Schreve 2007).

Pollen from the tufa showed high frequencies of ash and pine with lesser quantities of oak, birch, elm, lime, alder and hornbeam. Leaf impressions of willow, hazel, maple, and rowan were also present. A local environment covered in temperate woodland similar to that found on the limestones of southern England today was inferred, although open ground herbs and high frequencies of grass pollen indicated that open grassland existed in areas away from the tufa spring (Murton et al. 2001). This may have been maintained by the contemporary herbivores who may even have been responsible for breaking up the tufa (ibid.).

In contrast, the botanical remains from the organic muds of the Lower Channel deposits were characterised by low quantities of tree and shrub pollen (<10%) but a dominance of open herbaceous taxa. Low frequencies of trees and shrub pollen (including alder, oak, elm, poplar, lime, hornbeam, hazel and juniper) were argued to represent individual or small clumps of trees and tall shrubs growing on the channel sides, existing in an otherwise open landscape dominated by grasses, sedge, and other common herbaceous plants. Nothing in the pollen indicated that the climate was significantly warmer or colder than today, except in the uppermost sample from the 'coombe rock' above the channel. This deposit, the formation of which is often triggered by cold conditions, contained sparse fossils of species characteristic of montane habitats in northern Europe today.

The picture provided by the Aveley pollen profile (see Text Box 5.2) conforms to that seen at Marsworth (West 1969; Bridgland et al. 1995). West (1969) divided the Aveley pollen profile into two major zones of an interglacial:

1   Early Temperate/Zone IIb, from the clays and silts of Bed 2[1] and the lower part of the Detritus Muds of Bed 3 (associated with the remains of straight-tusked elephant (*Palaeoloxodon antiquus*). This zone was dominated by pine, oak and hazel, with low frequencies of other tree taxa. Towards the end, the frequency of hazel falls as lime, hornbeam and spruce rise, accompanied by an increase in open ground pollen.

2   Late Temperate/Zone III, from the top of the Detritus Muds of Bed 3 and the mammoth area within Bed 3. This zone saw the continued fall in arboreal pollen with communities becoming more open. Oak and hazel decline significantly while hornbeam assumes dominance and pine continues to be well represented. Birch, alder and spruce also increase in significance.

Text Box 5.2

SANDY LANE QUARRY AND PURFLEET ROAD, AVELEY, ESSEX

The site of Aveley was instrumental in the recognition of the MIS7 interglacial in the terrestrial record (Schreve 2001b and references therein). First discovered in 1964, the fossiliferous temperate deposits at Aveley, along with those at Trafalgar Square and Ilford, were originally assigned to the Ipswichian (MIS5e) interglacial on the basis of its pollen record (West 1969; Mitchell et al. 1973; Hollin 1977). Aveley and Ilford, however, are situated at a higher terrace level than Trafalgar Square and contain different mammalian assemblages. This led Sutcliffe (1975) to question the notion that all these sites were of the same age and he concluded that, while the Trafalgar Square deposits were genuinely Ipswichian, the Aveley and Ilford deposits belonged to an older, post-Hoxnian, pre-Ipswichian temperate period (i.e. MIS7). This has since been supported by Bridgland's Thames terrace model (Bridgland 1994 and see main text) which places Aveley within the third (Mucking/Taplow) post-Anglian terrace formation, as does a range of biostratigraphic schema (Schreve 2001b; Keen 2001; Coope 2001) and aminostratigraphy (Bowen et al. 1989; Schreve et al. 2006). By contrast, the pollen signatures from the Ipswichian and MIS7 interglacials cannot, as yet, be separated.

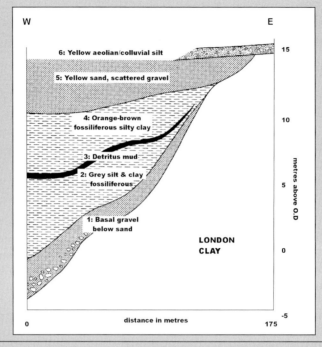

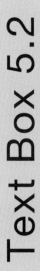
Text Box 5.2

FIGURE 1
Schematic section through the Mucking formation deposits at Sandy Lane, Aveley. (After White et al. 2006, modified after Bridgland 1994.)

FIGURE 2
Photo of 1997–8 investigations at Aveley. (Courtesy of David Bridgland.)

FIGURE 3
Levallois core from Aveley. (Photo Mark White.)

Text Box 5.2

The sediments at Aveley record a complex climatic signal with at least two temperate episodes separated by breaks in deposition. As noted in the main text, the mammalian faunas from the upper (Bed 2) and lower units at Aveley both represent fully temperate conditions but differ substantially in composition and environmental range. The Ponds Farm MAZ belongs to the older part of the sequence and is characterised by temperate woodland species such as straight-tusked elephant and fallow deer, alongside obligate thermophiles such as European pond terrapin (*Emys orbicularis*) and white-toothed shrew (*Crocidura* cf. *russula)* (Schreve 2001a and b). Molluscs from this part of the sequence indicate a slow-flowing, well-oxygenated river with water depths of 1–5m but also some areas of shallower water with a muddy substrate and surrounding marshland (D. Keen, pers. comm.). The proximity of more open grassland conditions is indicated by the presence of horse and bison. The Sandy Lane MAZ belongs to the later part of the sequence, and is separated from the Ponds Farm MAZ by a depositional hiatus. It is characterised by a reduction in woodland-favouring forms and an increase in herds of large grazers including a late form of steppe mammoth and horse; fallow deer is a notable absentee. The pollen evidence from Sandy Lane (West 1969) also records an opening up of the environment at this time, recording the transition from woodland to grassland in this part of the sequence; this is also in accord with the molluscan and beetle evidence.

The faunal turnover between the Ponds Farm and Sandy Lane MAZs may provide evidence for a marine regression. Slightly brackish molluscs in the upper silts testify to high sea levels during this period of deposition but a period low sea levels, presumably during a cold sub-stage marked by the deposition hiatus between the two MAZs, must have prevailed to allow this influx of new species from mainland north-west Europe. The timing of the suggested reconnection has previously been proposed as sub-stage 7d of the marine isotope record (Schreve 2001b), when increased global ice volume probably lowered sea level enough to rejoin Britain to mainland Europe, although new uranium-series dating from the correlative site at Marsworth has also suggested sub-stage 7b (Candy and Schreve 2007: see Text Box 5.3).

Until recently, Aveley had produced no evidence of human occupation but in 1996 salvage excavations at Purfleet Road during the upgrading of the A13 dual-carriageway (Schreve et al. in prep.) produced five flakes from the lower part of the Aveley sequence (Ponds Farm MAZ), while a further three flakes and a Levallois core were found in the upper part of the Aveley sequence (Sandy Lane MAZ). Although a very small collection, these artefacts are nonetheless valuable in helping to show hominin presence during both the early and later parts of this interglacial in association with different environmental regimes.

More recent work by Bridgland et al. (1995, 212–215) detected five pollen zones at Aveley (Table 5.2) which, despite some specific differences in representation and seriation, again shows a transition from an essentially wooded to an open landscape over time. Blezard (1966) proposed a considerable hiatus between the lower and upper parts of the

Table 5.2 Pollen zones from Aveley (after Bridgland et al. 1995).

Zone	Bed	Characteristics
5	Bed 5	– poor preservation, some saline indicators.
4	Bed 4	– Open conditions dominate – Grasses >50% total land, pollen and herbs dominate throughout – AP pollen low, maple and pine most common but still low frequencies. Alder, hazel, lime, elm, yew and spruce disappear.
3	Top 3 Base 4	– Grasses decline to <30% TLP, sedges increase – Alder dominant, hazel almost disappears, pine, oak, hornbeam reduced
2	Top 2 Base 3	– Hazel and oak decline, replaced first by willow and sedge and then by grasses (>50% total land pollen) – High charcoal concentrations, possibly suggestive of a catastrophic forest fire
1	2	– Well-developed deciduous woodland – 65% tree and shrub pollen dominated by pine, oak and hazel, with low frequencies of birch, alder, lime, maple, willow, elm, hornbeam, ivy, yew, ash – Herbs present, especially grasses

sequence and more recent work (Schreve et al. in prep.) has indicated that Bed 3 contains two organic horizons separated by a minerogenic sequence. As such, the Aveley deposits may contain a punctuated rather than gradual change in vegetation. Schreve et al. (ibid.) argue that this implies two warm phases separated by a cold phase that is poorly represented in the pollen record although there is little in the pollen that shows either an initial cooling or subsequent warming to support this. A similar transition from wooded to open conditions has been described at West Thurrock (Gibbard 1994).

The data summarised above provides three short snippets through different sub-stages of the MIS7 interglacial from which it is possible to make some tentative statements about the overall vegetation history of the period. On the basis of flora, fauna and sedimentology, the deposits at Selsey LBS, as well as the nearby site at West Wittering, have been assigned by several workers to the earliest part of an interglacial, previously MIS5e but now generally accepted as representing the earlier part of MIS7 (Parfitt 1998b; Preece et al. 1990; West and Sparks 1960). The data, not unexpectedly, show a familiar pattern of vegetation development after a glaciation, commencing with open grassland conditions and a relict cool fauna, which progressively gave way to extensive dense woodland vegetation and associated faunas, presumably MI7e. This period coincides with a marine transgression. The tufa samples from Marsworth have provided Uranium-series dates that suggest correlation of the woodland phases of MIS7 with sub-stages 7e *and* 7c. By extrapolation this would date the later open temperate conditions inferred from the pollen in the organic muds of the Lower Channel at Marsworth to MIS7a, with the cold-stage deposits above marking the onset of MIS6 (Candy and Schreve 2007). The long sequence from Aveley, which shows the same transition from wooded to open conditions and a similar faunal change, is believed to span the same period (Candy and Schreve 2007; Schreve 2001b). In summary, at a regional scale the interglacial began and closed with open phases, the middle largely dominated by dense coniferous and deciduous woodland during temperate interstadials.

The faunal landscape

Unlike pollen, fossil vertebrates and invertebrates that once populated these MIS7 grass-lands and woodlands are preserved at a relatively large number of sites. Table 5.3 presents the 49 species of mammal currently known to have been present in Britain during MIS7. As for all other Pleistocene periods, the MIS7 mammalian community was far richer in megafauna than today, providing a wide range of potential prey for hominins, with abundant herds of large herbivores existing in the open river valleys and beyond. Early Neanderthal occupants would also have faced stiff competition from the carnivore guild, which

Table 5.3 Mammalian fauna of MIS7 Britain (data from Schreve 1997; Parfitt 1998a; Wenban-Smith 1995).

Insectivora		Carnivora *(cont)*	
Erinaceus europaeus	Hedgehog	*Ursus arctos*	Brown bear
Sorex araneus	Common shrew	*Mustela putorius*	Polecat
Sorex minutus	Pygmy shrew	*Mustela nivalis*	Weasel
Neomys fodiens	Water shrew	*Meles meles*	Badger
Crocidura cf. *russula*	White-toothed shrew	*Cyrnaonyx antiqua*	Clawless otter
Lagomorpha		*Crocuta crocuta*	Hyaena
Ochotona pusilla	Steppe pika	*Felis chaus*	Jungle cat
Lepus timidus	Hare	*Felis sylvestris*	Wild cat
Chiroptera		*Panthera leo*	Lion
Barbastella barbastellus	Barbastelle bat	*Panthera pardus*	Leopard
Rodentia		**Proboscidea**	
Castor fiber	Beaver	*Palaeoloxodon antiquus*	Straight-tusked elephant
Scurius vulgaris	Squirrel	*Mammuthus primigenius*	Woolly mammoth
Citellus citellus	Ground squirrel	*Mammuthus trogontherii*	Steppe mammoth
Allocricetus bursae	Dwarf hamster	**Perissodactyla**	
Dicrostonyx torquatus	Collared lemming	*Equus ferus*	Horse
Lemmus lemmus	Norway lemming	*Stephanorhinus hemitoechus*	Narrow-nosed rhino
Clethrionomys glareolus	Bank vole	*Stephanorhinus kirchbergensis*	Merck's rhinoceros
Arvicola cantiana	Water vole	*Coelodonta antiquitatis*	Woolly rhinoceros
Microtus agrestis	Field vole	**Artiodactyla**	
Microtus arvalis	Common vole	*Sus scrofa*	Wild boar
Microtus gregalis	Narrow-skulled vole	*Megaloceros giganteus*	Giant deer
Microtus oeconomus	Northern vole	*Dama dama*	Fallow deer
Apodemus maastrichtiensis	Extinct small mouse	*Cervus elaphus*	Red deer
Apodemus sylvaticus	Wood mouse	*Capreolus capreolus*	Roe deer
Carnivora		*Bos primigenius*	Aurochs
Canis lupus	Wolf	*Bison priscus*	Bison
Vulpes vulpes	Fox	*Ovibos moschatus*	Musk ox

included lion, wolf, leopard and hyaena; some of these species, along with the bear, may also have been sitting tenants in the few desirable caves available in Britain.

The species list in Table 5.3 has been derived from some 30 stratigraphic horizons from 22 archaeological and palaeontological sites. Regardless of where they fall within the period they show a range of ecological and climatic preferences and most sites show a range of local environments. However, based on abundance (measured as either number of identified specimens (NISP) or minimum number of individuals (MNI)) the majority of sites show a dominance of animals adapted to open grassland habitats. The most common taxa are horse, woolly mammoth, the smaller 'Ilford-type mammoth' (now believed to be a form of *Mammuthus trogontherii*, the steppe mammoth; Lister and Sher 2001; Scott 2007), bison, narrow-nosed rhinoceros, woolly rhinoceros and giant deer, all open-dwelling grazers or grazers/browsers that required large quantities of daily forage. A suite of small mammals with similar grassland or shrubland associations is also evident, most notably the northern vole, field vole, hedgehog, hare, steppe pika, common shrew, lemming and ground squirrel. Of the carnivores, lion and hyaena are also predominantly open grassland predators, as is the jungle cat, which today hunts small mammals and waterbirds in marshy and grassland habitats (Schreve 1997; 2001b). Red fox and weasel are able to exploit a wide range of habitats, depending on the presence of small prey, while the red deer can adapt its feeding behaviour and rumen to suit its environment (Lister 2004; Stewart 2005), and all are thus not good indicators of habitat.

Contemporary with these predominantly open landscape species occurs a smaller woodland element, suggesting that the wider landscape was a mosaic of open/closed habitats, familiar from many Pleistocene localities (Gamble 1995a). Typical large woodland indicators include bear, straight-tusked elephant, Merck's rhinoceros, wild boar, roe deer and fallow deer, while among small mammals badger, beaver, woodmouse, white-toothed shrew and squirrel have similar associations; the polecat also favours forested locations today (Schreve 1997). Several species are also dependant on slow-running fresh water, such as water vole and beaver, perhaps unsurprising given the predominantly fluvial contexts from which they were recovered.

While most MIS7 assemblages are dominated by open-dwelling species, a small number of assemblages have higher frequencies of woodland animals, the most important being that from Bed 4 at Aveley (Schreve 1997). This observation formed the basis for the two MIS7 mammalian assemblage zones (MAZ) defined by Schreve (1997, 2001a and b): the Ponds Farm MAZ and the Sandy Lane MAZ (Table 5.4; see Text Box 5.3). The Ponds Farm MAZ is dominated by species representing heavily wooded environments such as straight-tusked elephant and white-toothed shrew and is argued to belong to earlier MIS7. The presence of *Emys orbicularis* (European pond terrapin), which requires average summer temperatures of 18 °C to hatch its eggs, indicates summer temperatures hotter than today. In contrast, the Sandy Lane MAZ is dominated by open-dwelling species such as steppe mammoth, narrow-nosed rhinoceros and horse, and is argued to belong to late MIS7. Schreve (2001b) tentatively suggests that an unconformity in the lower sands and silts at Aveley may indicate a further subdivision of the Ponds Farm MAZ.

Table 5.4 The characteristic faunas of the Ponds Farm and Sandy Lane MAZs

	Ponds Farm MAZ	Sandy Lane MAZ
Insectivora		
C. cf. leucodon		
C. cf. russula	*	
D. moschata		
T. minor		
Primates		
M. sylvanus		
Lagomorpha		
O. pusilla		*
O. cuniculus		
Rodentia		
C. citellus		*
C. fiber		*
T. cuvieri		
D. torquatus		*
L. lemmus		*
A. t. cantiana [1]		
A. t. cantiana [2]	*	*
M. gregalis		*
M. oeconomus		*
M. subterraneus		
A. maastrichtiensis		*
Carnivora		
U. spelaeus		
U. arctos		*
C. antiquus	*	
C. crocuta		*
P. leo		*
P. pardus		*
Proboscidea		
P. antiquus	*	*
M. primigenius		*
Perissodactyla		
E. ferus	*	*
E. hydruntinus		*
S. hemitoechus		*
S. kirchbergensis		*
C. antiquitatis		*
Artiodactyla		
D. d. clactoniana		
D. dama ssp. indet.	*	
B. primigenius	*	*
B. cf. priscus	*	*

THE BIOSTRATIGRAPHY OF MIS7

MIS7 comprised three warm events (7e, 7c and 7a), interrupted by two cold sub-stages (7d and 7b). Although well established in the marine isotope record, MIS7 has only recently been recognised as a distinct and valid interglacial in the terrestrial record. Key marker species include the 'Ilford-type' mammoth, the freshwater clam *Corbicula fluminalis* (which is absent from all later interglacials; Keen 1990) and the beetle *Oxyletus gibbulus* (which occurs in large numbers only during MIS7; Coope 2001). No formal attempt has yet been made to provide a pollen zonation for the period. Attempts have been made, however, to construct a finer resolution (sub-Milankovitch level) chronology for MIS7 using mammalian biostratigraphy.

Schreve (2001b) was initially undecided which MIS7 sub-stages her Ponds Farm and Sandy Lane MAZs represented (Table 5.4) but argued that the observed faunal turnover was probably climatically driven, with reduced sea levels required to allow the incursion of a new suite of animals from the continent. Such an event must have occurred during a cold sub-stage, either 7d or 7b. More recent work on the dating of tufa deposits from the Lower Channel at Marsworth has allowed some refinement of this observation (Candy and Schreve 2007). The brecciated tufa from the Lower Channel produced two clusters of dates, ~254 to 234 ka BP (correlated with MIS7e) and ~219 to 208 ka BP (correlated with MIS7c), suggesting two distinct phases of tufa development, separated by a cold event (MIS7d) during which deposition ceased. The youngest date for the tufa, ~208 ka BP, implied that the fossiliferous Lower Channel fill itself post-dates MIS7c and being fully interglacial and open in character it was assigned to MIS7a (ibid.). Drawing on these dates and their subdivisions of the Aveley fossil material, Candy and Schreve (2007) concluded that the wooded phase represented by the Ponds Farm MAZ belonged to both MIS7e and MIS7c and the open phase signalled by the Sandy Lane MAZ to MIS7a. This would place the climatic deterioration that reconnected Britain to Europe in MIS7b.

One difficulty here is that 7b was less severe than 7d, and sea levels may have fallen to only 25 m bmsl. At these sea levels, Britain is likely to have remained an island. Further complications with the mammalian biostratigraphy arise when the vegetation history is considered. The wooded conditions apparent from the flora at Selsey LBS (as well as West Thurrock (Gibbard 1994) and Stutton (West and Sparks 1960)) seems to suggest that the animals from these sites are placed in one or more of the forested phases, probably MIS7e and/or MIS7c. However, Schreve (1997; Candy and Schreve 2007) assigned the faunas from each of these sites to the Sandy Lane MAZ. The apparent contradiction at West Thurrock and Stutton could be explained by the fact that the flora and fauna from these sites is not firmly associated and might relate to different parts of the interglacial but Selsey LBS cannot be explained in these terms.

The floral sequence at Selsey LBS shows open conditions giving way increasingly to forested habitats, while the mammals of Bed 1, which included the steppe (Ilford-type) mammoth and narrow-nosed rhinoceros along with some cold indicators such as lemming, give way to a fully temperate fauna including straight-tusked elephant in Bed 2 (Parfitt 1998b).

Text Box 5.3

It is therefore difficult to see how Selsey LBS could equate with MIS7a as it shows the reverse of the pattern expected by Candy and Schreve. Even if one were to suggest that the open conditions and marine transgression at this site represent rising sea levels and vegetation developments following the cold conditions of MIS7b (White et al. 2006), no heavily forested phase should be expected to follow. An alternative explanation, following the argument for Marsworth, could be that Selsey LBS represents forest recovery in MIS7c after the colder conditions of MIS7d, but again this period is associated with the Ponds Farm MAZ, meaning that mammoth and narrow-nosed rhinoceros should not occur, only straight-tusked elephant (see Table 5.4). Other sites along the Sussex coast, at East Wittering and West Street, both near Selsey (Parfitt 1998b, 135), produced a faunal suite similar to the Sandy Lane MAZ, which Parfitt placed in a later phase of the same interglacial seen at Selsey LBS, when a mosaic of open and forested conditions prevailed.

Another exception is the site of Strensham which Schreve (1997) assigned to the later part of MIS7 (i.e. MIS7a) due to the presence of mammoth. In contrast, Bridgland et al. (2004) argued that it lies on the earlier of two MIS7 terraces in the Severn–Avon system, the later part of MIS7 being represented by the terrace at Ailstone.

A more complex situation can be proposed:

1 An early phase with a suite of open-dwelling species in which mammoth is the only elephant (of Ilford-type according to Schreve's 1997 analysis).
2 A subsequent, more wooded, phase characterised by straight-tusked elephant and other forest specialists.
3 A late phase characterised by a mosaic of predominantly open landscapes with significant woodland and a mixed fauna dominated by mammoth (by this time possibly only *Mammuthus primigenius*, see Scott 2007) and including straight-tusked elephant.

Much more data is required to test this proposed sequence. But, at sites with only a single biozone (most of them), the problems discussed above mean that the fauna (and archaeology) could feasibly date to several parts of the interglacial. Exactly where many of the other 'late MIS7' sites (e.g., Ilford, Stanton Harcourt, Stoke Goldington) actually fit within the sequence must therefore now be considered open to question, with no independent or unequivocal means of determining whether they are late, early or even middle MIS7. As such, we would

Text Box 5.3

Sampling biases complicate this picture. In some cases faunal variation may simply represent localised vegetation structure. Context is key when reconstructing environments on the basis of animal frequency: if we were to interpret sites at face value it would be easy to infer that the majority of MIS7 mammals operated close to water in open environments. But it is necessary to remember that some large 'keystone' herbivores probably helped create and maintain their own open habitats (such as elephant), and that the predominance of fluvial or lacustrine contexts in MIS7 sites (in Schreve's 1997 study 20/26) probably indicates the greater preservational potential of these settings rather than the clustering of animals solely in these locales. Large tracts of woodland may have existed not far from these open valleys, the lower proportions of woodland animals in the record a reflection of the frequency with which they entered these open habitats or other preservational basins, not the relative proportion of regional woodland cover at any given point in time.

A hint that this might be the case comes from the caves of the south-west of England, such as Bleadon Cave and Oreston Cave, which show micro-habitat variation and a complex vegetation mosaic. Within these caves, wild boar occurs in relatively high frequencies alongside other woodland species such as roe deer and open environment indicators. Outside the caves, however, not a single example of wild boar has been found (Schreve 1997). This presumably reveals the presence of dense forest on top of Mendip and the limestone hills of Plymouth (ibid.). Were it not for the preservation of wild boar and roe deer in these caves – which, after all, they were not actually living in – we would not see this forested element of the landscape. Carnivores, which always occur at much lower densities than their prey (Guthrie 1990) and who are thus less likely to die and be preserved in significant number at fluvial sites, are also best represented in the cave sites of south-west England where they probably denned and weaned their young (NISP data from Schreve 1997 shows that 84% of wolf remains, 96% of hyaena remains and 82% of lion remains come from just three sites). The presence of leopard at only Bleadon and Pontnewydd caves (see Text Box 5.4) similarly reflects the rarity of this animal and its fondness for cave localities, while the absence of hominin fossils from the archaeological record might equally reflect their rarity in the landscape and position on the trophic pyramid. Scott (2007) has made similar observations regarding the absence of rhinoceroses from central England, suggesting that this either represents a difference in regional habitat, or a different phase within MIS7 for these sites.

Text Box 5.4

PONTNEWYDD CAVE, CLWYD, NORTH WALES

Pontnewydd Cave is situated in Carboniferous limestone in the Elwy Valley about 50 m above the modern river. The first recorded excavations were by William Boyd Dawkins, the Rev. D. Thomas and Mrs Williams-Wynn in the 1870s (Dawkins 1874, 1880; Hughes and Thomas 1874) although by this time a substantial amount of deposit had already been removed. Between 1978 and 1996 systematic excavations were undertaken at the cave by Stephen Green which confirmed the stratigraphic sequence described by previous workers (see Table 1). This demonstrated that the cave system preserves a fragmentary record of infilling and erosion spanning at least 300 ka, and amassed significant collections of artefacts, fauna and 23 human teeth, comprising 4–7 individuals showing Neanderthal affinities (papers in Green 1984; Aldhouse-Green 1995).

FIGURE 1
View of the entrance to Pontnewydd Cave.
(© National Museums and Galleries Wales.)

FIGURE 2
Hard stone bifaces from the Early Middle
Palaeolithic of Pontnewydd Cave.
(© National Museums and Galleries Wales.)

Table 1 Stratigraphic sequence at Pontnewydd (after Green 1984; Aldhouse-Green 1995)

Bed	Interpretation
Laminated travertine	Calcareous precipitate
Upper clays and sands	Fluvial
Upper Breccia	Debris flow, dated to ~35–25 ka BP, containing derived artefacts and fauna
Silt	Fluvial, dated to >25 ka BP
Stalagmite	*In situ* precipitate, dated to ~220–80 ka BP
Lower Breccia	Debris flow, dated to >220 ka BP, containing artefacts, fauna and Neanderthal remains
Intermediate Beds	Debris flow, containing artefacts, fauna and a Neanderthal tooth
Upper sands and gravel	Debris flow, dated to >245 ka BP
Lower sands and gravels	Debris flow and fluvial sediments, dated to >245 ka BP

The site has produced over 600 artefacts, including handaxes, scrapers, Levallois pieces and a number of discoidal cores that may represent recurrent centripetal Levallois technology (Aldhouse-Green 1995, 1998). The artefacts are predominantly made from local volcanic raw materials with a few from sandstone and flint. The volcanics are noted as being difficult to work, a fact reflected in the crude, pointed nature of the handaxes and the 'inept' Levallois technique found at the site (Newcomer 1984; Aldhouse-Green 1988, 1995). The majority of the artefacts (and the human remains) come from the Lower Breccia with a smaller

Text Box 5.4

number originating from the Intermediate Beds. Both are allochthonous debris flow deposits. Consequently, the artefacts are thought to have originated outside the cave and show damage consistent with exposure in a cold climate prior to their introduction. Aldhouse-Green (1995) suggested that the cave – which is large enough to comfortably hold 6–12 people – may have been incidental to the human occupation, most of which occurred outside. However, the range of activities inferred from the artefacts suggest that it was more than just a transitory camp. Traces of butchery have also been noted on remains of horse and bear from the Lower Breccia (Aldhouse-Green 1995) and the presence of burnt flint hints at the erstwhile presence of hearths.

Thermoluminesence and Uranium-series dating programmes provided a minimum age estimate of ~220 ka BP for the Lower Breccia (Aldhouse-Green 1995). This is in agreement with the MIS7 attribution for the mammalian fauna from this bed which contains a mixture of open/closed and warm/cold adapted species – including lemming, horse, narrow-nosed rhinoceros, beaver and roe deer – probably representing different cold and warm sub-stages (Aldhouse-Green 1995; Schreve 1997). The fauna from the underlying Intermediate Beds is dominated by temperate woodland elements, potentially reflecting an earlier wooded phase of the same interglacial. Dates for the deposits in the 'New Entrance', which produced >100 artefacts, suggest that this phase of occupation took place ~175 ka BP, at the close of MIS7, although the dates range from ~225–175 ka BP and overlap at 2σ with estimates from the Main Entrance. The artefacts show a range of similar types but differ in frequency of representation. Given their secondary context, it is probably unwise to read too much into this. In sum, the occupation may predate the ages of all the deposits by several millennia, and may have spread across several warm and cold events throughout MIS7.

Text Box 5.4

Another notable element of the MIS7 fauna is the mixture of ostensibly warm and cold-adapted animals in the same assemblage, for example woolly rhinoceros and red deer at Ilford, or more famously temperate molluscs (*Corbicula fluminalis*) and red deer alongside musk ox and lemming at Crayford (see Text Box 5.5). There are several possible explanations. It may be entirely taphonomic, with elements of cold (sub-)stage and warm (sub-)stage faunas mixed in the same deposit. It may be a collection issue, with poor recording leaving animals that actually belonged to different contexts of very different ages and depositional environments now combined into a single collection (a particular problem at Crayford and Baker's Hole). Indeed, Scott (2007) has argued that the association of woolly rhinoceros with an otherwise warm fauna reflects stratigraphical uncertainties, and cannot be seen as indicating the beginning of MIS6 as suggested by Stuart (1976). She further argues that only the smaller 'Ilford-type mammoth' was actually present in MIS7, with the woolly mammoth not arriving until very late in the interglacial, or even early in MIS6, as indicated by recent dating programmes (Lister et al. 2005). For Scott (2007, 129), claims of woolly mammoth earlier in the interglacial are based on misidentifications. This would certainly help explain the paradox of such a classic cold climate indicator living in a warm temperate environment, although others see the MIS7 faunas as representing genuine communities and not taphonomic jumbles; Schreve (1997, 2001b) suggests the mixture highlights a more continental regime – with warm summers but much colder winters than at present – and a significant seasonal turnover in migratory species.

THE CRAYFORD BRICKEARTHS (STONEHAM'S PIT, NORRIS'S PIT, RUTTER'S PITS, FURNER'S PITS, SLADE GREEN)

The deposits once exposed in a number of pits at Crayford and Erith potentially hold a valuable key to our understanding of the EMP occupation of Britain. The deposits rest on Chalk/Thanet Sand with the basic sequence comprising a basal gravel overlain by brickearth and capped with 'trail'. The brickearth is subdivided into a lower fluviatile and an upper colluvial component separated by the highly fossiliferous *Corbicula* Bed. They have been assigned to the Taplow/Mucking Formation, correlated with OIS8–7–6 (Bridgland 1994), an attribution supported by an AAR ratio on *Bithynia* (Bowen et al. 1989). Precisely where they belong within this long period is a contentious yet important issue. Currant (1986a) and Sutcliffe (1995) preferred an OIS6 age because several cold-climate species are present, including lemming and musk-ox. Bridgland, however, suggested the main archaeological horizons were of late OIS8/early OIS7 age, with the sparser higher occurrences showing persistent human presence throughout 7. Schreve (1997) offers a solution: that the deposits date to terminal OIS7, as evidenced by similarities to the upper faunal suite at Aveley, the presence of cold-adapted species, and the dentition of the northern vole *Microtus oeconomus*, which shows a transitional morphotype between the fully temperate OIS7 specimens and those from sites assigned to OIS6. The abrupt warming during MIS 6.5 provides another possibility.

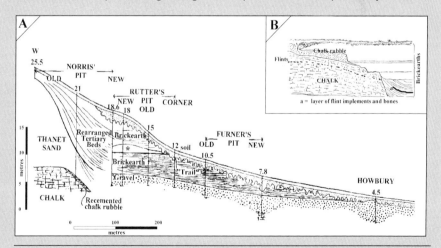

FIGURE 1
(a) Composite section through the Crayford and Erith brickpits (b) Spurrell's original section showing position of main archaeological horizon and band of flint at Stoneham's Pit. (After Spurrell 1880a.)

Text Box 5.5

Text Box 5.5

The archaeology from Crayford has proved similarly enigmatic. At Stoneham's Pit, Spurrell (1880a and b, 1884) found large numbers of *in situ*, conjoinable, laminar Levallois artefacts at the base of a chalk river-cliff in association with animal bones. Similar finds were later made in adjacent pits (Chandler 1914, 1916). Most of the artefacts came from the Lower Brickearth. Spurrell's main 'floor' was a sandy horizon within the Lower Brickearth, illustrated as occurring well above the base (1880a, Figure 1), while Chandler found refitting material in a similar position 'at the base' of the Brickearth in Rutter's New West Pit (Chandler 1916, 241–2). Others were recovered at various levels with at least one from just above the *Corbicula* bed at Erith (Kennard 1944). Spurrell also mentions artefacts in a different preservational state from the surface of the underlying gravel and Chandler reported workmen's tales of 'knives' (probably laminar Levallois) from here. Kennard supposed that the surface of the gravel had formed an older land surface related to the initial downcutting to this terrace level. Much has been made of the laminar, blade-line qualities of some of the Crayford material (Cook 1986; Révillion 1995), inviting comparisons with continental Middle Palaeolithic sites such as Seclin and notions that it anticipates the Upper Palaeolithic (cf. Mellars 1996).

The prevailing environments during the deposition of the Lower Brickearth and *Corbicula* bed were essentially similar (Kennard 1944). The molluscs reveal a slow-flowing river with little aquatic vegetation and non-marshy banks set in dry, open grassland; woodland and semi-aquatic species are sparse. The western edge of the river was set against Chalk and Thanet Sand that provided abundant flint (Spurrell 1880a and b; Chandler 1914, 1916). The mammals show a similar range of environments; dominated by open grassland species they famously contain a mixture of cold- and warm-loving species. The faunal composition, which includes the first occurrence of ground squirrel since the Anglian, suggested to Schreve an eastern European 'feel' testifying to more continental temperate conditions in Britain at this time, with warmer summers but harsher winters. The presence of *Corbicula fluminalis*, however, would seem to point to both warm summers and mild winters, the size distribution showing optimum rather than stressed conditions (Kennard 1944), although its recent southerly distribution may be masking wider tolerances (Keen, in Schreve et al. in prep). So, in all respects, a clear understanding of Crayford remains elusive.

Rich insect assemblages have been published from five MIS7 sites: Aveley (Schreve et al. in prep; see Text Box 5.2); Stoke Goldington (Green et al. 1996); Marsworth (Murton et al. 2001); Strensham (Rouffignac et al. 1995) and Stanton Harcourt (Briggs et al. 1985 see Text Box 5.6). Although the majority of remains recovered and published from these sites are beetles, other orders have been noted. Spiders and mites were reported at Stoke Goldington (Green et al. 1996), while Trichoptera (caddisflies), Dermapotera (earwigs), Megaloptera (alderflies), Diptera (flies/midges), Hymenoptera (wasps/bees/ants) and Hemiptera (aphids/shield bugs/cicadas) were found at Stanton Harcourt (Briggs et al. 1985).

THE STANTON HARCOURT CHANNEL (DIX'S PIT), OXFORDSHIRE

The Stanton Harcourt Channel deposits form part of the complex Summer-town–Radley Formation of the Upper Thames which subsumes sediments dating from MIS8 to possibly MIS2. The lower channel deposits of this group are highly organic with rich floral and faunal assemblages indicative of fully interglacial conditions during MIS7 (Briggs et al. 1985; Buckingham et al. 1996; Bridgland 1994); Schreve (2001b) assigns the site to the later part of the interglacial. The MIS7 channel deposits comprise silts, sands and gravels with a basal boulder bed, occupying a shallow SW–NE trending, single-thread channel incised into Oxford Clay (Briggs et al. 1985; Bridgland 1994; Buckingham et al. 1996). The 'Ilford-type' mammoth (a late form of *Mammuthus trogontherii*) dominates the mammalian assemblage, accompanied by large numbers of horse (*Equus ferus*) and straight-tusked elephant (*Palaeoloxodon antiquus*). Brown bear (*Ursus arctos*), red deer (*Cervus elaphus*), lion (*Panthera leo*) and spotted hyaena (*Crocuta crocuta*) are also present in smaller numbers. Pollen preservation is poor, although 30 taxa have been recorded, mostly aquatics and marginal plants (Buckingham et al. 1996; Scott and Buckingham 2001). Arboreal pollen includes alder, birch, pine, blackthorn and elder with oak and other thermophilous species being represented by abundant and often very large pieces of wood. However, despite the presence of large tree trunks, the local environment was predominantly herb-rich grassland. Molluscs from the channel indicate an absence of dense forest in the local vicinity while the beetles are largely inhabitants of thinly vegetated, sunny ground, only a few shade-loving species being present. The occurrence of the molluscs *Corbicula fluminalis* and *Potomida littoralis* suggests warm conditions (Keen 1990), as does the insect fauna, which is dominated by species that today have a mainly southern distribution, suggesting a climate as warm or warmer than the present (Buckingham et al.1996). Fish remains have also been recovered from the channel, including stickle-back, pike, perch and eel, together with specimens of frog and bird.

To date the channel deposits have produced just 27 artefacts, including 11 handaxes, a Levallois-like core and 2 chopping tools (Buckingham et al. 1996; Scott and Buckingham

FIGURE 1

Photograph of the site under excavation. Top photograph shows mammoth tusks and limb bones; bottom photograph shows mammoth tusks and bones, alongside large fragments of wood, including oak. (Courtesy Kate Scott.)

Text Box 5.6

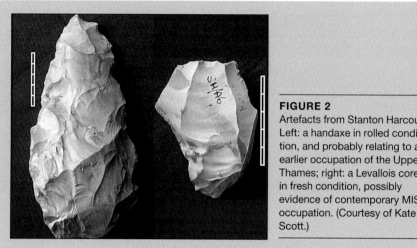

FIGURE 2
Artefacts from Stanton Harcourt. Left: a handaxe in rolled condition, and probably relating to an earlier occupation of the Upper Thames; right: a Levallois core in fresh condition, possibly evidence of contemporary MIS7 occupation. (Courtesy of Kate Scott.)

2001; Kate Scott pers. comm. 2004). Although most are in an abraded condition, the core and some of the flakes are practically mint and may represent a human presence contemporary with the channel deposits (Buckingham et al. 1996). Raw materials are locally very poor and this is exactly the type of situation where one might again expect humans to have come prepared with a tool-kit that they subsequently took away with them; hence the large quantities of tools and knapping waste seen in the Lower Thames are absent. The abraded and derived material on the other hand is probably of pre-MIS7 origin, possibly the same source as the large collections of abraded material from the overlying (MIS6) Stanton Harcourt Gravel at Gravelly Guy/Smith's Pit, Stanton Harcourt (MacRae 1982, 1991). According to Lee (2001) the Gravelly Guy/Smith's Pit artefacts are very similar in condition and form to those from the channel deposits at Dix's Pit (Buckingham et al. 1996), suggesting that they may *all* be earlier than the oldest deposits in which they were found and all derive from eroded, older pre-MIS7 landsurfaces (Hardaker 2001; Scott and Buckingham 2001).

The Stanton Harcourt Gravel is also the most probable source of the artefacts from Mount Farm Pit and Queensford Pit at Berinsfield (MacRae 1982; Lee 2001) which produced over 200 artefacts of both flint and quartzite. These are mostly abraded and frost-damaged handaxes but some flakes (including handaxe thinning flakes) and, most notably, two Levallois cores and seven Levallois flakes, were also recovered. The rolled condition of the artefacts again suggests derivation from older deposits but Roe (1986) makes the important point that the Levallois material is fresher than the handaxes and may therefore be younger. The lack of any decent raw material in this area (the closest primary source is the Chiltern foothills six miles to the south) led Wymer to infer that, the handaxes manufacturing flakes notwithstanding, hominins must have been importing finished handaxes (as well as perhaps roughouts and other blanks) into the area. Indeed, preferential transport may explain why a region apparently so lacking in flint and decent archaeological assemblages has managed to produce a number of very large finished handaxes and a small amount of Levallois material (Roe 1994).

Text Box 5.6

As stated in Chapter 2, at a regional scale beetle data are very useful for reconstruction of palaeoclimates, because many are highly habitat and temperature specific and because beetles respond to climate change, not by evolving in the Darwinian sense, but by altering their geographic ranges (Coope 2002). This is often achieved much faster than other terrestrial biota, which may lead to beetle faunas apparently being out of phase with other proxies (ibid). The beetle faunas from these five assemblages were made up of species that could occur today in southern England, with a few notable exotics. At Stanton Harcourt (Briggs et al. 1985) and Strensham (Rouffignac et al. 1995) the beetles were described as fully western European in aspect and possibly indicative of an oceanic type climate. July temperatures at Stanton Harcourt were suggested to be between 16 and 18° C, with those at Strensham slightly lower at 16° C; average winter temperatures were argued not to have been much below 0° C. At Stoke Goldington (Green et al. 1996) and Marsworth (Murton et al. 2001), however, a number of exotic species with ranges south and east of Britain, and some cold tolerant (but not obligate) species, are present, from which a more continental type climate has been inferred. At Stoke Goldington summer temperatures 1–2° C hotter than modern values were proposed, while at Marsworth the mutual climatic range (see Elias 1994) suggested maximum temperatures of 15–17° C, and a minimum temperature falling somewhere within the range of –9–1° C. As noted above, a number of floral and faunal elements have also suggested greater continentality during MIS7, but if the beetle record is taken at face value, then the climate may have fluctuated between oceanic and continental. In this case, these sites may belong to different parts of the interglacial, although it must be stressed that only a 'hint' of continentality really exists.

SUMMARY

The humans who visited and moved through these MIS7 river valleys and surrounding plateaux would have thus been enveloped in a lush landscape that offered a variety of affordances (Text Box 5.7). Trees and shrubs would have provided both edible fruits and materials to make spears and other implements. Many of the herbaceous plants also had edible elements. The rich vegetation attracted a range of large herbivores, prey for hominin and non-human carnivores. Romantically we might see this as an unspoilt, giving environment, with bountiful animal and vegetal resources and very mild climate ideally suited for hominin interaction. In a sense it is surprising, therefore, that most of the sites that have provided detailed palaeobotanical or invertebrate evidence reveal very little evidence of hominin presence. It may be that the types of environment that provided preservational opportunities – swampy and perhaps stagnant areas – were simply not attractive to humans. Hominins may have focused their activities on more sandy or gravely substrate, or the drier grassy slopes, which would not have acted as such a hindrance to mobility and hunting. However, as we will see below, hominin occupation during MIS7 appears to have been surprisingly sparse and intermittent whatever the local conditions.

A RICH TAPESTRY OF MIS7 ENVIRONMENTS[1]

The various channels and floodplain pools found at MIS7 sites were heavily vegetated, with deep-water floating plants including water lily, floating heart and duckweed; and shallow-water floating plants like water violet, water soldier and mare's tail. Other aquatics included water crowfoots, various 'pondweeds', and watercress. At many sites, the aquatic plants have suggested water that was generally still or slow moving, poorly oxygenated, and in Chalk areas highly calcareous. This is complemented by the coleoptera. Of the five insect-rich sites available, only Stanton Harcourt has a significant frequency of species indicative of free-flowing water, including *Orectochilus villosus*, a night hunter that preys on drowning animals trapped on the surface, and *Esolus parallelepipedus*, which lives amongst stones in vigorous streams (Briggs et al. 1985). *Oulimnius tuberculatus*, which inhabits shallow, well-oxygenated riffles in free flowing rivers, was present in Aveley Bed 3i, but otherwise the dominant insect signature from this and all other sites shows sluggish or stationary water and mats of decomposing material. Such environments are strongly indicated by a number of dyticid and hydraenid water beetles typical of grassy pools or backwaters and the majority of the Hydrophilidae which live off rotting vegetation. As these sites generally represent the deposits of significant Pleistocene rivers – the Thames and the Great Ouse – it seems likely that only marginal floodplain pools and cut-offs are represented in the fossil record, the main rivers not preserving high concentrations of coleopteran or plant remains.

The pollen and macrofossil records also reveal a variety of wetland plants that grew around the water margins including sedges, rushes, bulrush, watercress and wild mustards. Moving further onto the floodplains, the vegetation blends into a rather marshy, herb-rich grassland which Coope (in Ruffignac et al. 1995) reconstructs as lush water meadow, evocative of a warm summer's day on the banks of the River Cam at Grantchester. Abundant herbaceous plants that grew in such places are found throughout the interglacial and included such familiars as ferns, valerian, marsh violet, teasel, forget-me-nots, meadowsweet, and several members of the buttercup and daisy families. Areas of base-rich marshland were also host to mosses and lichens. Several species of ground beetle indicate more open, meadow-like country shaded by weedy vegetation. This community – represented at different sites by a number of ground beetles such as *Bembidion obtusum*, *Calathus melanocephalus* and *Patrobus atrorufus* – is today found together on agricultural land, which Coope (in Murton et al. 2001) sees as mimicking these ancient habitats. In places, the marshy vegetation around all of these sites was more open, with bare patches of humus rich soil (e.g. Murton et al. 2001). *Clivina fossor*, found in four of the beetle assemblages, lives in patchy and open grassy vegetation where it excavates tunnels in damp, clayey or humus-rich soils (Murton et al. 2001).

On the valley sides dry, herb-rich grassland existed with many species evocative of southern England today, including several species from the daisy–dandelion family, thistles, pinks, bellflowers, Jacob's ladder, flax, gentian, and field pansy.

Cornflowers, goosefoot, knotweeds, wormwood and various plantains grew on disturbed or sandy areas along the riverbanks or steepest slopes alongside stinging nettle and dock. The beetles also indicate some drier sandy/gravelly ground with sparse vegetation, such as *Calathus* and *Agriotes*, whose larvae feed on roots and grass. Such taxa are rare, however, probably indicating that these habitats occurred at some distance from the main catchment at the sites in question.

Dung beetles are found in some abundance, including both dung feeders (e.g. *Aphodius*) and dung predators (e.g. *Oxytelus gibbulus* which feeds on arthropods and worms in dung). This demonstrates that the large, herbivorous mammals found in the fossil record were active around the watercourses, their feeding behaviours helping to construct and maintain their own niches and to explain the apparent rarity of trees locally at many riverine sites (cf. Coope et al. 1961; Green et al. 1996). Carrion beetles show that these animals also died in these locations. At times and places these rather idyllic meadows must have resembled killing fields. Although humans are only minimally represented, if at all, the fossils of other large carnivores show that they were active in these environments in MIS7.

The pollen and macrofossils both record a variety of trees and tall shrubs with most of the modern 'British' deciduous and coniferous trees being present. Depending on which part of the interglacial is represented, these would have occurred as dense woodland, small clumps or even individual trees. Various woodland understorey plants have also been recorded from this interglacial including hazel and juniper, alongside bracken, ivy, fern, anemone, geranium and stitchwort. Such woodland probably stood on the interfluves and valley sides rather than in the valley bottoms. Within the beetle faunas only Aveley and Stanton Harcourt yielded obligate woodland species with most of these being dependant on deciduous trees. At Stanton Harcourt two species were found that are dependant on oak: the weevil *Rhynchaenus quercus*, whose larvae mine oak leaves, and *Xyleborus dryophagus*, a scolytid beetle that drills galleries in oak wood (Briggs et al. 1985). The Anobiid beetle *Docatoma chysomelina*, which inhabits fungi on dead or dying trees, was also recorded. Similarly, Aveley (Schreve et al. in prep) yielded two oak-dependant species, *Curculio venosus*, which lays its eggs in acorns, and the aforementioned *R. quercus*. A wider range of deciduous species is indicated by *Scolytus multistriatus*, a bark beetle that feeds on trees such as oak, elm, prunus and poplar, and *Cerylon histeroides*, which lives under dead bark on many species. The elaterid beetle *Prosternon tesselatum*, the larvae of which develop in rotting coniferous stumps, also implies the local presence of conifers; demonstrating that not all coniferous pollen is necessarily far travelled.

At the other sites, we can only assume that any trees that existed were outside the range of the beetle catchment. Recent studies (ibid.) have shown that the representation of 'tree' insects falls off very sharply with distance from trees,

Text Box 5.7

compounded by the fact that the migratory capacity of many woodland insects is limited. While a number do undertake flights to new feeding stations or to find mates, their preservation in the archaeological record depends highly on their flight (and death) paths intercepting suitable preservational deposits. So, archaeological deposits lacking woodland beetles do not automatically indicate a landscapes lacking in woodland vegetation, just that no trees were in the near proximity of the sampled area. Indeed, *Bembidion gilvipes*, which is usually found in moss and leaf litter in deciduous forest, is found at Strensham and Stoke Goldington, perhaps a small indication of some local woodland at these otherwise apparently open grassland sites.

NOTE

1 This section draws heavily on the work of Russell Coope, using the references cited in the main text.

THE ARCHAEOLOGY OF EARLY MIDDLE PALAEOLITHIC BRITAIN

Using only dated sites, White and Jacobi (2002) divided the British Middle Palaeolithic into two chronologically and technologically discrete entities: an Early Middle Palaeolithic (EMP) and a Late Middle Palaeolithic (LMP) (see Chapter 6 for the latter). This bipartite division recognised the EMP as a period in which Levallois technology dominated the lithic repertoire. Handaxes were practically absent and it can now be shown that the co-occurrence of handaxes and Levallois technology that so exercised the cultural sequences of Wymer (1968, 1985) and Roe (1981) is largely due to taphonomic mixing. In most cases, it is possible to demonstrate differences of preservational state, with the handaxes usually more worn and probably belonging to an earlier phase of occupation in the same location (Scott 2006; 2010; see below). This technological pattern stands in contrast to the Late Middle Palaeolithic, which is dominated by handaxe manufacture and discoidal core technology, but which has so far produce limited, if any, evidence of contemporary Levallois technology. The absence of chronological control over most occurrences of both Middle Palaeolithic handaxes and Levallois technology means that this pattern remains provisional, and could potentially be overturned by a single new discovery. However, for present purposes, it provides a useful heuristic, which enables us to use the occurrence of Levallois technology to gauge the distribution and extent of EMP occupation of Britain.

The English Rivers Project (Wymer 1992, 1993, 1994, 1996a, 1996b, 1997) listed some 250 findspots in England from which Levallois material has been reported (as well as another two from Wales), almost all situated in the southern half of the country, almost all found in fluvial deposits of major rivers and their tributaries, and nearly 50% located in the Thames Valley (Figure 5.8 and 5.9). This pattern is certainly an artefact of three controlling factors:

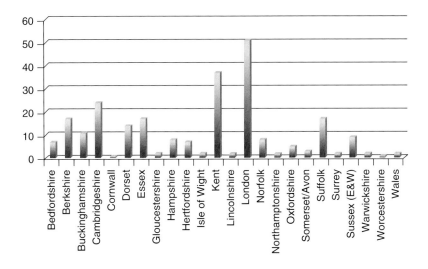

FIGURE 5.8
Number of known British Levallois sites and find spots, by modern county.

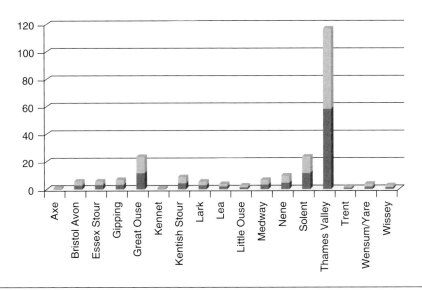

FIGURE 5.9
Number of known British Levallois sites and find spots, by river valley.

1   Most sites are located south of the maximum ice advance of the Last Glacia-
     tion (MIS2) and therefore safe from the direct effects of glacial destruction.

2   Regardless of the proportion of hominin activity that actually took place in and
     around river valleys, they provide ideal burial environments in which lithic mate-
     rials are frequently preserved in primary and secondary contexts.

3   The extent to which major commercial quarrying activity and/or major urban
     expansion during the late nineteenthh and early twentieth centuries, combined
     with the energies of particular local collectors, provided opportunity for discov-
     ery and recovery of lithic collections.

It thus seems unlikely that either the distribution of Levallois findspots or frequency of
Levallois artefacts provides a true impression of hominin settlement or activity during MIS7
(see below). They do, however, serve to demonstrate that, whenever they were present,
Neanderthal groups utilising Levallois technology were ranging widely across the British
landscape from the till plains of East Anglia to the rugged broken uplands of the west.

To gain a fuller understanding of the hominin societies that occupied Britain during this
period, it is necessary to concentrate on those sites that can be reasonably securely
dated, have good contextual information, and which have yielded a lithic assemblage.
Fewer than 20 such sites presently exist, providing a mixture of high- and low-resolution
signatures (see Table 5.5). Sadly few have been excavated to modern standards and for
various historical and/or taphonomic reasons, most lack the ethnographically orientated
behavioural information that can be gained from a single, well-preserved and well-excavated site such as Boxgrove (Roberts and Parfitt 1999) or Maastricht-Belvédère (Roebroeks 1988, *inter alia*). Only one extensively refitting assemblage is known (Stoneham's
Pit, Crayford), although some of the other sites probably represent primary context, though
not *in situ*, occurrences. However, taken together they do permit a certain amount of
cabling (Gamble 2001), the individual strands coming together to tell a story that operates
at various scales and beyond the level of an individual site, and recent detailed technological analyses have begun to add rich texture to the ways in which Neanderthals organised
themselves in the landscape (Scott 2006, 2010). The basic information for these sites is
summarised in Table 5.5, and details of key sites are presented in Text Boxes.

TRANSITIONS BEFORE *THE* TRANSITION: THE EMERGENCE AND SIGNIFICANCE OF LEVALLOIS TECHNOLOGY

Temporal roots: a permeable marker

While the widespread appearance of Levallois technology is commonly used to mark the
beginning of the Middle Palaeolithic, Levallois and other 'prepared core' or Mode 3 technologies actually have much older roots (White and Ashton 2003; White et al. 2011; see
Text Box 5.8). Hints of prepared core technology have been found in otherwise Oldowan
assemblages at Nyabusosi, Uganda, dating to *c.* 1.5 ma BP, and the ST Site Complex at

Table 5.5 Summary of main archaeological sites from MIS8-7.

Site	Dating Method	White et al. (2006) attribution	Assemblage Size	Industry	Context and Integrity	Environment	Raw Materials
Purfleet, Botany Pit, Essex	Lithostratigraphy, biostratigraphy, OSL	Early MIS 8	3800	Proto-levallois, bifaces	Fluviatile sands and gravels of Lynch Hill/Corbets Tey Formation. Primary and secondary context	Riverine, cool-cold.	Immediate: chalk flint eroding directly from channel edges
Cuxton, Kent	Lithostratigraphy	?Early MIS8	Few	Proto-Levallois	Fluviatile sand gravel of Medway, probably Lynch Hill/Corbets Tey equivalent. ?Primary and secondary context	Riverine	Immediate: Medway Flint Gravel and local chalk outcrops
Northfleet, Kent (Coombe Rock)	Lithostratigraphy, biostratigraphy	Late 8	1400	Levallois	Within chalk rubble at base of Mucking/Taplow Formation. Minimally reworked	Riverine. Cold, open	Immediate: chalk flint accessible at channel edge
West London; between Slough and Acton	Lithostratigraphy	MIS 8–7	750	Levallois	On top of Lynch Hill Gravel, below solifluction gravel and brickearth. Integrity unclear, minimally reworked	Riverine	Immediate: from local gravel
Creffield Road, Acton, London	Lithostratigraphy	MIS 8–7	500	Levallois (point dominated)	On top of Lynch Hill Gravel, below brickearth and periglacial gravel. Primary context	Riverine	Immediate: from local gravel
West Thurrock, Essex	Lithostratigraphy, biostratigraphy	Late MIS 8–Early MIS 7	~250	Levallois	*In situ* on top of Crayford Gravel of Mucking/Taplow Formation. Primary context	Riverine. Cool; open? wooded fully temperate deposits immediately above archaeology	Immediate: chalk flint from channel edge and lag gravel of large, minimally worn nodules
Aveley, Essex (Aveley Member sands)	Lithostratigraphy, biostratigraphy	Early MIS 7	5	flakes	Fluviatile sands of Mucking/Taplow Formation overlying London Clay. Primary context.	Riverine, possible estuarine influence. Warm, heavily wooded.	Local: geology is London Clay and fine-grained fluvial deposits
Ebbsfleet, Kent (fluviatile gravel)	Lithostratigraphy, biostratigraphy	Early MIS 7	750	Levallois	Within gravel of Mucking/Taplow Formation. Primary and secondary context	Riverine. Warm, open grassland, woodland present.	Immediate: large clasts from banks and bars of river
Selsey, West Sussex	Lithostratigraphy, biostratigraphy	Early MIS 7	4	Levallois	Detrital muds infilling channel incised into Bracklesham Beds. ?Primary context	Riverine. Warm; open grassland with woodland present	Local: chalk outcrops within a few kms

Site	Dating methods	MIS stage	No.	Technology	Context	Environment	Geology
Pontnewydd, Clywd, Wales	Biostratigraphy, U-series, TL	Mid MIS 7	1500	Levallois, bifaces	Lower Breccia of cave sequence. Secondary context	Cave/river. Warm/cold; still or slow-moving water nearby. Open/wooded	Immediate: igneous and sedimentary rock, with small flint component
Aveley, Essex (Aveley Member silts)	Lithostratigraphy, biostratigraphy	Later MIS 7	3	Levallois	Fluviatile silts of Mucking/Taplow Formation overlying London Clay. Primary context	Riverine. Warm; open, with marshy areas.	Local: geology is London Clay and fine-grained fluvial deposits
Brundon, Suffolk	Lithostratigraphy, biostratigraphy, U-series	Later MIS 7	~250	Levallois	Below and within gravel (Bed 3) of Stour. Primary and secondary context	Riverine. Warm; open grassland, woodland present	Immediate: large clasts from gravel bedload
Crayford, Kent	Lithostratigraphy, biostratigraphy, AAR	Later MIS 7	500	Levallois, laminar	Within Lower Brickearth of Mucking/Taplow Formation. *In situ.*	Riverine. Warm/cold; open grassland, sparse woodland	Immediate: Bullhead and chalk flint eroding from channel edges
Holbrook Bay, Suffolk (Stutton and Harkstead)	Lithostratigraphy, biostratigraphy	Later MIS 7	~100	Levallois	Sand and brickearth overlying gravel and London Clay. ?Primary context.	Riverine. Warm. Open grassland, woodland present	Local: range of glacial/fluvial gravels; Chalk possibly outcropping within 10–15 km to north
Stanton Harcourt, Dix's Pit, Oxfordshire	Lithostratigraphy, biostratigraphy	Later MIS 7	27	flakes, cores	Within channel deposits of Summertown-Radley Terrace. Secondary context	Riverine. Warm; open grassland, deciduous woodland. present	Exotic: Upper Thames generally poor in flint. A few poor quality local resources with nearest fresh flint from Chiltern Hills
Stoke Tunnel and Maidenhall, Ipswich, Suffolk	Lithostratigraphy, biostratigraphy	Later MIS 7	20	Levallois	Within 'Bone Bed' and purple clays of Gipping/Orwell. ?Primary context	Riverine. warm; open grassland, woodland present.	Local: range glacial/fluvial gravels; chalk outcropping within 5–10 km to north

Peninj, dating from 1.6–1.4 ma BP (Texier and Francisco-Ortega 1995; Torre et al. 2003). In South Africa, various forms of prepared core technology are documented in Lower Pleistocene contexts, while Levallois *sensu stricto* is claimed as early as 1.1 million years ago at Canteen Koppie, Stratum 2a, and is apparently widespread by 600–500 ka BP at Wonderwork Cave MU4, Kathu Pan 1:4a and Rooidam 2 and 3 (Beaumont and Vogel 2006). For East Africa, Tryon (2006) makes it clear beyond doubt that Levallois is an Acheulean phenomenon and that the MSA is marked by a diversification of techniques rather than their origin (ibid., 373). Levallois technology can be found in East African Acheulean assemblages from at least as early as ~510 ka BP (Tryon 2006; Tryon et al. 2006), while in North Africa it occurs in contexts dating to ~500–320 ka BP in the famous quarry sites around Casablanca, Morocco (Raynal et al. 1995, 2001, 2002).

Text Box 5.8

LEVALLOIS TECHNOLOGY: A BRIEF HISTORY AND MODERN DEFINITIONS

Levallois can be broadly defined as a lithic technology in which the parent core is carefully prepared and configured in order to control the size and shape of a limited number of 'desired' flake products (Figure 1). It was named after a suburb of Paris (Levallois-Perret) where distinctive products were first recognised during the late 1800s although, as early as 1861 (just two years after the events at Amiens), John Evans (1862) recognised a series of flakes from the lower gravels of the Somme that showed evidence of shaping prior to removal from their parent core. For much of its history since, the study of Levallois technology has been

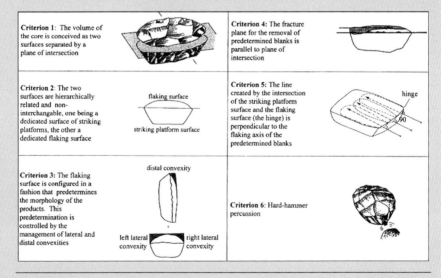

FIGURE 1
Boëda's technological criteria that is now accepted as identifying and conceptually underwriting Levallois reduction. (After White and Ashton 2003, original drawings modified after Boëda 1995.)

plagued by problems concerning cultural significance, definition and technological attributes, and degree of pre-determination.

For much of the nineteenth century, Levallois was recognised as yet another element of Palaeolithic assemblages with or without handaxes. By the early twentieth century, however, Commont (1908, 1909, 1912) had adopted Levallois as the index fossil for the Mousterian, a measure prompted by the need to distinguish the Mousterian from the Chellean and Acheulean, all of which contained flake tools and handaxes (Monnier 2006). Commont saw Levallois flakes as essentially serving the same role as handaxes, which diminished and disappeared through time, providing a further distinction between the ancient Mousterian and the upper Mousterian. Commont's untimely death meant that, by the 1920s, his reading of Levallois as a technique used within a Mousterian cultural setting was being unravelled by Breuil (1926, 1932; Breuil and Koslowski 1931, 1932, 1934) who erected two parallel cultural phyla for the Palaeolithic of Europe – a flake tool phylum and a handaxe phylum. The Mousterian and Levalloisian both belonged to the flake tool phylum, having emerged from a common ancestral route in the Clactonian and from there followed separate evolutionary trajectories. Breuil thus gave Levallois independent cultural status, subsuming seven evolutionary stages, even though it was a well-known element of otherwise typical Mousterian scraper assemblages. Although not without severe theoretical and operational difficulties (Oakley and King 1945, 1948; White et al. in prep.), this model was widely implemented in Britain for several decades.

Brueil's framework was ultimately replaced by that of Francois Bordes, a name almost synonymous with the Middle Palaeolithic during the later twentieth century (Pettitt 2009). Early in his career Bordes provided the first formal definition for the Middle Palaeolithic (rather than the Mousterian) which included the presence of the Levallois technique (Bordes 1950a and b). He emphatically rejected parallel phyla (as well as most other tenets of Breuil's theoretical position) and posited instead a more branching evolution. Still, confusion persisted as to whether Levallois was a culture per se or a technique widely used in many cultures (cf. Wymer 1968; Roe 1981). Since the 1982 publication of the Haifa conference (Ronen 1982), Levallois has come to be seen as a marker for the beginning of the Mousterian/Middle Palaeolithic in Europe – what goes around comes around.

Bordes also provided the classic *typological* definition of Levallois which depended on specific flake properties and the presence of tortoise (or blade) cores. Although widely adopted, a lack of clarity in definition and identification soon emerged, with no two researchers apparently in agreement regarding precisely what were and what were not Levallois cores (Perpére 1986). Over the past three decades, something of a consensus has emerged around the *Levallois concept* of Eric Boëda (e.g. 1986, 1995), in which Levallois is conceived as a way of managing the volume of the core in order to exploit one of its surfaces. Boëda has identified six technical and geometrical principles that absolutely underwrite Levallois production. His scheme emphasises technology above typology and has significantly increased the range of methods subsumed within Levallois. It recognises two principal schemes of reduction: *recurrent*, in which there is more than one 'priviledged'

Text Box 5.8

Text Box 5.8

removal per prepared flaking surface; and *lineal*, in which each prepared flaking surface produces only one preferential removal. These two basic schema can be manifested in many different ways, depending on the manner in which cores are prepared and exploited, which may be centripetal, convergent, unipolar or bipolar.

Issues regarding the degree of predetermination of Levallois flakes still plague Middle Palaeolithic research, often for other agenda-driven reasons. For Bordes, (1961) predetermination was of the essence, for Van Peer (1992) Levallois was an intentional set of actions intended to provide large flakes, while for Boëda the notion of pre-determination is folded into the Levallois concept. Dibble (1989), on the other hand, saw Levallois as a continuous reduction strategy in which the lack of standardised products belies the idea of predetermination, although this approach confuses standardisation with predetermination (White et al. 2011). We follow here Chazan (1997) in that we do not claim to understand the knappers' exact expectations but believe each Levallois episode was conducted according to a specific plan of action designed to better control the final end product.

Some of the earliest evidence of Levallois outside Africa can be found at Gesher Benot Ya'aqov, Israel, where a range of prepared core techniques coexist from about ~750 ka BP. (Goren-Inbar 1992; Goren-Inbar et al. 2000; Madsen and Goren-Inbar 2004). Not only does this show an intriguing blend of different methods, it also underwrites the observation that prepared core technology, in one form or another, is a routine feature of Acheulean core working throughout the Lower Palaeolithic in the Levant (cf. Goren-Inbar 1992; Copeland and Hours 1993; Shaw 2008). By comparison Levallois – and only Levallois – came late to Europe, although its does occur sporadically almost as soon as handaxe-making populations arrive ~600 ka BP. Among the earliest finds are two lineal Levallois cores from the MIS14 Fréville Terrace deposits at Rue Marcellin Berthelot, St Acheul (Tuffreau and Antoine 1995; Tuffreau 1995) and the large collection of flakes and cores from MIS12 Somme terrace. In Britian, examples of early Levallois cores have been recovered from MIS11 deposits at Rickson's Pit, Swanscombe (Roe 1981; Bridgland 1994) and Bowman's Lodge, Dartford (Tester 1950).

Precocious occurrences of Levallois become more frequent after ~400 ka BP perhaps simply a reflection of the larger number of artefacts that can be assigned to this period rather than a genuine cultural practice. Levallois is found in MIS11 or MIS9 deposits at Atapuerca TD10 (Carbonell et al. 1999a; Falguères et al. 2001) and in the Upper and Lower Members at Ambrona, suggested to be older than ~350 ka BP (Villa and Santonja 2006; Pérez-González et al. 2001). MIS10–9 dates have also been proposed for Levallois material from Korolevo L15–17, Ukraine (Adamenko and Gladiline 1989); Wallendorf, Germany (Mania 1995); Orgnac 3, France (Moncel and Combier 1992; Moncel et al. 2005); Rosanetto, Italy (Mussi 1995); Aridos, Spain (Santonja and Villa 1990) and Purfleet, England (White and Ashton 2003).

While this pattern does not exactly support an exclusive association of Levallois with the Middle Palaeolithic, it should be emphasised that most sites >300 ka BP lack

Levallois, suggesting that while it was an option for Lower Palaeolithic hominins, it was only infrequently employed. It is only after ~300 ka BP that Levallois technology becomes a common and lasting technological practice, indicating to us that it represents not a major cognitive leap among hominins (*sensu* Gowlett 1984), but a change in other social, behavioural or adaptive structures. This brief global conspectus does, however, serve to illustrate that Levallois technology did not originate in north-west Europe as suggested by Clark (1977) nor was it a Middle Pleistocene African invention that spread into Eurasia ~300 ka BP during a dispersal event involving the speculative *Homo helmei* (Foley and Lahr 1997). In fact, the underlying rationale of this latter 'Mode 3' hypothesis – the common use of Levallois technology by both Neanderthals and anatomically modern humans (at Skuhl and Qafzeh) in the Levant ~100 kya – might, in the light of the recent sequencing of the Neanderthal genome, be better explained as just one more result of their intersecting social and biological worlds (cf. Green et al. 2010). Bordes (1971) saw Levallois as a technology that developed more than once and in more than one place, a view shared by Otte (1995), Rolland (1995), Villa (2001), White and Ashton (2003) and Sharon (2007). The latter saw no reason to assume cultural links between technologies in North and South Africa separated by ~700 ka and 5,000 miles. Indeed, given the diversity and spatio-temporal patterns outlined above, it is difficult to talk of an 'origin' for Mode 3, but rather multiple and independent invention from local antecedents in different places and at different times to service local technical requirements; and in some instances simply chance (White et al. 2011).

Technological roots: a technology of convergence

White and Ashton (2003) and White et al. (2011) have suggested that the link between Levallois and other prepared core technologies lies in the technological concepts that underpin the Acheulean. They see Levallois as an immanent property of the Acheulean, a core reduction option that could be exercised at any point in time and space depending on need or opportunity (White et al. 2011). For Rolland (1995) the manufacture of finely made handaxes in Europe resulted in the inevitable but accidental discovery of Levallois through the removal of large, axial thinning flakes, and examples of such detachments – termed 'pseudo-Levallois' by Callow (1976) and 'biface acheuléen ayant servi de nucléus Levallois' by Bordes (1961) – are fairly commonplace. Another example of Levallois technology emerging from handaxe manufacture comes from Cagny-la-Garenne, France. Here, large axial flakes, detached from handaxes broken during manufacture and very thick handaxes, have resulted in cores approximating (or in fact representing) lineal Levallois (Tuffreau 1995). In such cases, Levallois can be seen to emerge as a mutation of handaxe manufacture by co-opting existing technology and refocusing the aim of manufacture away from the core tool and towards the large flakes that could be detached from it, although it should be noted that recurrent bipolar Levallois cores have also been noted at Cagny (Lamotte 1991, cited in Tuffreau 1995), suggesting that the occurrence of Levallois here is far more than fortuitous or accidental (Figure 5.10)

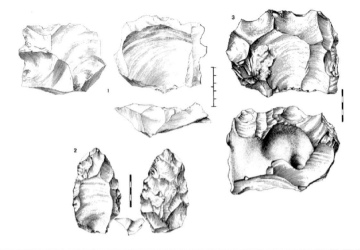

FIGURE 5.10
Pseudo Levallois cores. 1 and 2 Cagny la Garenne (after Tuffreau and Antoine, 1995, courtesy Wil Roebroeks); 3 Rickson's Pit, Swanscombe (from Burchell, 1931). Scales in centimetres.

In other cases, however, Levallois appears to have emerged, not directly from handaxes, but from an elaboration of core working and migration of technological principles across different schema (White and Ashton 2003; White et al. 2011). Occurring within the context of 'typical' Lower Palaeolithic MPC working, Botany Pit, Purfleet, also contains 'proto-Levallois cores' that show two hierarchically organised surfaces – a striking platform surface and a flaking surface – separated by a plane of intersection (Figure 5.11; see Text Box 5.8). Flakes were detached more or less parallel to this plane and removed material from the surface of the nodule. These cores show very little preparation to either surface, the striking platform often formed by one or more bold removals, the flaking surface often exploiting existing convexities that are then 'managed' by a series of long, elongated flakes across the longer axis. Classic lineal Levallois cores were also recovered from this site, making up about 8% of the total. Proto-Levallois flaking has also been observed at Frindsbury (Cook and Killick 1924) and Cuxton, Kent (Tester 1965; White et al. 2006), although the dating of these occurrences is less secure.

At Orgnac 3, France, Moncel and Combier (1992) have described the *in situ* evolution of Levallois throughout 10 levels, dating from ~350–300 ka BP. The basal levels (8–6) show a variety of methods, including a hierarchically organised centripetal technique designed to exploit small plaquettes that, although termed non-Levallois by Moncel and Combier, is conceptually very similar to proto-Levallois cores at Purfleet (White et al. 2011). Knapping was structured around two hierarchically organised surfaces divided by a plane of intersection; the striking surface was often prepared first and more intensively, with the flaking surface taking advantage of the natural morphology of the plaquette. The method appears to have followed fixed rules aimed at controlling variability while residual cortex patterns suggest that reduction intensity increased over time. Levallois cores, mostly unipolar and bipolar, appear in Level 5b, their earliest forms suggesting to the

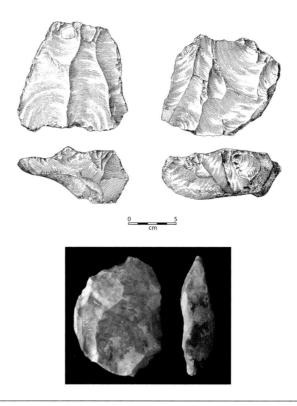

FIGURE 5.11
Two proto-Levallois cores from Botany Pit, Purfleet (after White and Ashton 2003) alongside a classic linear Levallois core from the same pit. (Photograph Mark White.)

excavators a method that was controlled but whose rules were not fully standardised. By Levels 4a and 4b, fully fledged and formalised Levallois technology is seen, with a diversification in the method to include most of the variants identified by Boëda, as well as the complete re-preparation of Levallois surfaces between exploitation phases (Moncel et al. 2005). At Orgnac 3, then, we see the gradual emergence, diversification and standardisation of an evolving technological practice.

The slow development of controlled core working has also been found in Rhine terrace deposits at Achenheim, Germany (Vollbrecht 1995). Levels attributed to the beginning of the early Saalian (MIS9–8 transition) have yielded cores deliberately prepared to allow the exploitation of a hierarchical flaking surface. Levallois flaking *sensu* Boëda first appears in Layer 20a, dated by TL to between 278 ± 36 and 244 ± 31 ka (Buraczynski and Butrym 1987), and is the most highly represented mode of flake production by Levels 20–18 (Junkmanns 1991, 1995). Similar approaches to core technology have been reported in many other MIS9–8 sites in Europe, including Markkleeberg, Germany (Baumann and Mania 1983; Svoboda 1989); Mesvin IV, Belgium (Cahen and Michel 1986); Argoeuves and La Micoque, France (Tuffreau 1982, 1995; Rolland 1995) and Korolevo, Ukraine (Adamenko and Gladiline 1989).

In sum, the emergence of Levallois technology appears to have been a rather disjointed affair involving in the first instance the precocious and ephemeral exaption of handaxes. This was followed by a separate, more gradual process, involving the elaboration, reorganisation and recombination of core technology to establish a basic level of controlled flaking, followed by refinement, elaboration and diversification towards a full Levallois concept. By late MIS8–early MIS7 at the latest, a fully formalised and full suite of Levallois methods were evident in Britain and across Europe, and could be said to have begun to dominate technological systems.

Conceptual roots

One might dismiss these earliest examples as little more than random and ephemeral convergence driven by local contingencies: large, broken handaxes at Cagny, the centripetal working of plaquettes at Orgnac 3, and natural convexities at Purfleet that became self-managing. But this would miss a fundamental point: that in all cases, and regardless of whether knapping strategies were demanded by external forces such as raw materials or were moments of creative genius, we see the intelligent application of existing technological concepts in novel ways, designed to enhance control over flake production and form.

In doing so, hominins were creating a third operational schema that merged key principles from two much older, previously discrete systems: débitage and façonnage (White and Pettitt 1996; White and Ashton 2003). Débitage, or systems of flaking, are primarily aimed at dividing a volume of material into small functional units – flakes and blades. During the Lower Palaeolithic, débitage was most frequently manifest as simple migrating platform cores showing many varied and interchangeable platforms, no fixed plane of intersection, no hierarchically organised surfaces, little control over flake dimensions and the working of a volume rather than a surface. More rarely, radial or discoidal cores were produced, which did employ a plane of intersection but one that was largely created by (potentially blank-driven) alternate flaking practices around a perimeter and not designed to service flake production.

Façonnage, or systems of shaping, are primarily geared towards reducing a mass of material using a complex of interrelated flake scars on the surface so that the remaining volume conforms to a desired form (cf. Boëda et al. 1990; Baumler 1995). In the Lower Palaeolithic this was employed almost exclusively to produce various bifacial tools. Inherent in most systems of bifacial façonnage is a plane of intersection separating two interdependant surfaces that may be hierarchical or non-hierarchical, biconvex or planoconvex, depending on the precise operational chain and blank type used (Boëda et al. 1990). There is no distinction between predetermining and predetermined flake removals but the important point is that the two surfaces are organised in relation to each other. Reduction is orientated towards the removal of flakes from the surface of the piece so as to thin and shape an inner volume. This also applies to handaxes produced on flake blanks, which Boëda et al. (1990) regard as débitage, but which White and Ashton consider purely façonnage. While the initial act – the striking of the flake blank – is débitage, all subsequent actions equate to façonnage, and the two are separate, distinct and non-reflexive steps in the biography of the object (White and Ashton 2003).

Levallois represents the intergration of these two systems into a new reflexive dynamic. As White and Ashton (2003) note, while the goal of each Levallois sequence may have been the production of flakes from a core, it cannot be considered exclusively 'débitage' because it contains an elaborate shaping phase clearly aimed at controlling the form of an inner volume by organising two hierarchical surfaces, divided by a plane of intersection. But neither is it a system of 'façonnage' as the shaping of the core is only a means to producing desired flake blanks and not the releasing of an inner core tool. Levallois thus creates a reflexive exchange between the two schema, twisting and turning between structured shaping phases to production phases. The rigid distinction between operational schemas of earlier periods collapses in Levallois, and constructs that had been conceptually separate merge into one unified and highly flexible concept (White and Ashton 2003). As a fusion of the principles of both débitage and façonnage, Levallois offered a more flexible and controlled range of outcomes than the systems from which it emerged. Rather than being constrained by the design of a 'tool', Levallois products provided flexible 'supports' for a range of other tools on the same blank (cf. Boëda et al. 1990). This represents a conceptual as well as an operational change in archaic human technology.

The (temporary) demise of the handaxe

Returning to the assertion made above – that Levallois was immanent within the Acheulean – it is clear that, as soon as hominins equipped with an Acheulean technology that included both bifacial 'façonnage' and migrating plane 'débitage' (which they *all* do) gained a firm foothold in Europe, Levallois was an option waiting to be used, even if only as single, unique examples.

It is therefore perhaps unsurprising that at most British sites where Levallois is evident, handaxes are generally absent, or present only in very small numbers. Although previous generations viewed Levallois and handaxes as contemporary, coexisting technologies (Roe 1981; Wymer 1968), we suspect that this was the result of using a compressed chronological framework that forcibly merged materials of different ages. In her recent re-evaluation of nine sites, Scott (2010) concluded that not one of the claimed handaxes from an EMP context could be substantiated, all belonging to earlier or later occupation. For example, the large collections of handaxes known from the London Borough of Hillingdon (see Text Box 5.9) are in a different preservational state to the Levallois material and derive from different archaeological horizons; as are those from Baker's Hole, Kent, which probably derive from Boyn Hill deposits at nearby Swanscombe. Similarly, the two handaxes listed by Roe (1968b) as coming from Creffield Road, Acton, were not from the pits in which Brown found the Levallois material (White et al. 2006), while stratigraphical uncertainties at Purfleet leaves it unclear whether the handaxes from Botany Pit (see Text Box 5.10) actually belong with the Levallois material in the Botany Gravel or equate with the final Acheulean in the Blueland's Gravel at Greenlands/Bluelands Pit at Purfleet – the most parsimonious reading favours the latter.

WEST LONDON, BETWEEN HILLINGDON AND ACTON

Large quantities of handaxes and Levallois material have been recovered from localities on the Lynch Hill Terrace of the Middle Thames across West London, from Slough in the west through to Creffield Road, Acton in the east (Brown 1887a and b, 1895; Lacaille and Oakley 1936; Lacaille 1938; Collins 1978; Bazely et al. 1991; Ashton et al. 2003). The English Rivers Project (Wymer 1996a) recorded 28 findspots along this stretch although just five – Boyer's Pit, Sabey's Pit, Clayton's Pit and Eastwood's Pit in the Yiewsley/West Drayton area and Creffield Road, Acton – produced the vast majority of the material. Most was collected by John Allen Brown and Robert Garroway-Rice between 1890 and 1929 from fluvial gravel overlain by a solifluction/coombe rock and brickearth (Brown 1895; Collins 1978; Ashton et al. 2003).

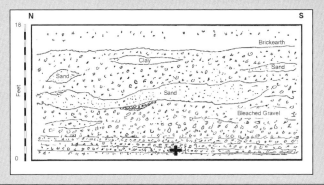

FIGURE 1
John Allen Brown's section from Eastwood's Pit, Yiewsley. (After Brown 1895.)

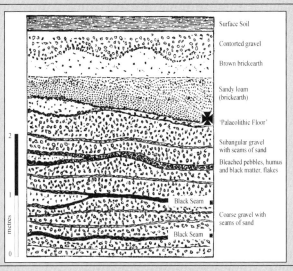

FIGURE 2
John Allen Brown's Section from Pit 2 at Creffield Road. (Modified after Brown 1887a.)

Text Box 5.9

FIGURE 3
Artefacts from the Hillingdon Pits.

Precise contextual information is largely lacking for the Yiewsley materials and, while both collectors did record the discovery date and the pit from which artefacts were recovered, only Brown noted find-depth. However, given the complex history of quarry ownership and expansion this information is often meaningless, especially given the absence of any useful sections (Scott 2006). Brown did at least note that 'implements of later age, consisting of long, sharp spear-heads, knives, etc' (i.e. Levallois products) were recovered from higher up in the sections than the handaxes and always under the unstratified deposit (i.e. soliflucution gravel and brickearth) (Brown 1895, 163), suggesting that the handaxes came from within the terrace gravel but that the Levallois material came from on or near the gravel surface, variations in recovery depth reflecting undulations in this surface (Scott 2006). More recent work recovered a small quantity of pollen from the Hillingdon deposits but this was insufficient to convincingly characterise the contemporary environments (Hubbard in Collins 1978); no other proxies were recovered. In sum, although large and of technological interest, the interpretative value of the Hillingdon sites has been sadly compromised by their collection history.

The same is not true for the Creffield Road locality, where a number of gravel pits in the grounds of 83 Creffield Road and the Haberdashers' Aske Girls' School were investigated and described by J. Allen Brown from 1885 to 1901 (Brown 1887a and b; Scott 2006, 2010). Like the Hillingdon sites, the sediments exposed in these pits comprised coarse fluvial gravel overlain by brickearth and mantled with contorted (solifluction) gravel. The fluvial gravel was interrupted by three black seams, which Brown believed to be ancient landsurfaces. These were situated at depths of 11–12 ft, 8 ft and 6 ft, each producing a quantity of artefacts (2, 8 and 500+ respectively), with the uppermost representing a major accumulation on the surface of the gravel immediately beneath the brickearth (Brown 1887, 55–61). The main assemblage is characterised by Levallois points and flakes, plus a small number of heavily reduced cores, but handaxes are absent. Brown believed the site to represent a flint workshop and noted the presence of flint nodules >30 cm diameter, but recent work favours a more nuanced interpretation (White et al. 2006; Scott 2010; see main text). Excavations in the grounds of the school in 1988 revealed a similar geological sequence and produced a further 124 artefacts (Bazely et al. 1991; Scott 2010).

Available descriptions show that the Levallois industries in West London lie *on top* of the Lynch Hill Terrace gravel, underlying brickearth. The absence of

Text Box 5.9

Levallois artefacts from similar contexts in the Taplow Formation suggests that these artefacts were deposited after the final aggradation of the Lynch Hill gravel but before the final aggradation of the Taplow gravel, suggesting that the archaeology dates to between these two events, that is, within later MIS 8 and earlier MIS 7 (Ashton et al. 2003). That the artefacts are in fresh condition suggests that they were buried without much movement shortly after discard. The brickearths overlying the Lynch Hill (as well as Taplow and Kempton Park) terrace in the Middle Thames are generally assigned to the polygenetic Langley Silt Complex, produced by a variety of alluvial, fluvial and aeolian processes (Gibbard 1985; Gibbard et al. 1987). Collcutt (in Bazely et al. 1991, 23) saw these basal, fine-grained deposits (brickearths) at the Creffield Road School Site as the final phase of the Lynch Hill terrace, although Green and McGregor (in Bazely et al. 1991, 27) favour a later deposit related to small-scale channel development, ponding and colluvial deposition on the terrace surface. TL dates on the fine-grained sediments in the pit investigated by Collins (1978) at Yiewsley showed that they began to cover the Lynch Hill gravel by at least 150 ka BP, showing that deposition commenced during MIS6. This does not contradict the MIS8 or early MIS7 date suggested for the Levalloisian material on top of the terrace gravel.

EARLY LEVALLOIS TECHNOLOGY AT BOTANY PIT, PURFLEET

Since the 1960s a series of commercial pits have been opened at Purfleet, Essex, located in the Lower Thames Valley some 20 km east of central London. These have exposed a complex sequence of Pleistocene deposits, representing an abandoned meander loop of the Lynch Hill/Corbets Tey Formation of the River Thames, which span the period from terminal MIS10 to early MIS8 (Bridgland 1994; Schreve et al. 2002). The most complete sequence is found in Bluelands and Greenlands Pits, comprising a 7–8 m thick, tripartite aggradation of three broadly fining-upward sequences, each containing a different archaeological industry (Wymer 1985; Schreve et al. 2002; see Chapter 3 and Text Box 3.8).

The sediments at Botany Pit consist of some 3.4 m of sand and gravel banked up against a chalk river-cliff at 10 m OD, and are interpreted as the upper part of the overall Purfleet sequence, dating to late MIS9/early MIS8 (i.e. >300 ka BP). Equivalent deposits in the neighbouring Greenlands Pit have provided an averaged age of ~324 ka BP by OSL (Eddie Rhodes, pers. comm.). The Botany Pit sediments contain evidence for the first 'routine' use of prepared core technology in Britain. The substantial, slightly rolled assemblage found by Andrew Snelling in 1961 (Wymer 1968, 1985) is essentially a core-and-flake assemblage with much primary flaking but few formal tools. The industry shows an 'undeveloped' form of prepared core working, described by Wymer (1968, 1985) as Proto-Levallois and by Roe (1981, 228) as a reduced Levallois with simplified preparatory stages. The size and character of the Botany Pit assemblage led Wymer (1968, 1985) to conclude that the site was a 'quarry or workshop'; local topography undoubtedly played a part as the

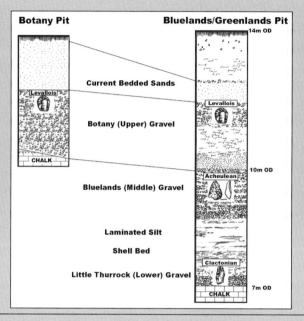

FIGURE 1
Proposed correlation of the botany sediments with the sequence recorded at Bluelands/ Greenlands Pits. (Modified after White et al. 2006.)

Botany Pit site was situated near the inside of a large bend with very gently inclined margins that cut through the flint-bearing seam in the Chalk that probably presented a wider and more inviting riparian plain with easier access to raw materials than Bluelands/Greenlands at this time (Peter Allen pers. comm. 2003).

Included in the Botany Pit material is a small number of fresh handaxes, recorded by Snelling as coming from the base of the Botany sequence, reportedly resting directly on Chalk. They thus occur below the main Botany industry and, although a case may be made to associate the two elements, it seems most likely that the handaxes pre-date the core-and-flake assemblage and represent the final, lateral extension of the Acheulean industry from the Middle Gravel (cf. Wymer 1985; Bridgland, 1994). If so, the Botany deposits would correlate with the final middle cycle and upper cycle of the overall Purfleet sequence (Schreve et al. 2002). This places the flint assemblage from Botany Pit among the earliest examples of prepared core technology in Europe, dating to ~300 ka BP.

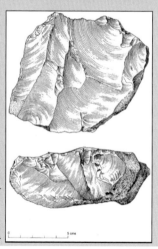

FIGURE 2
A Proto-Levallois or simple prepared core from Botany Pit. (After White and Ashton 2003.)

Text Box 5.10

This pattern conforms to a more widespread trend seen at this time, whereby Levallois technology largely replaces handaxes over large swathes of the 'Acheulean world' (cf. Goren-Inbar and Belfer-Cohen 1998). This may reflect the fact that Levallois products served as large multipurpose knives (e.g. Beyries 1987; Plisson and Beyries 1998) the role previously performed by handaxes (Keeley 1980; Mitchell 1996, 1997). Indeed, many large Levallois flakes strongly resemble unifacial handaxes, although are much thinner and lighter – an obvious advantage in a mobile toolkit (White and Pettitt 1996). Baker's Hole contains a number of very large lineal Levallois flakes retouched using limited bifacial/alternate retouch that are to all extents and purposes 'pseudo-handaxes' (White et al. 2006; Figure 5.12); although attempting to reduce a core tool to such dimensions through façonnage would generally have ended in failure and endshock. Furthermore, the range of Levallois methods was capable of yielding a variety of fairly regularised medium to large cutting instruments that had greater potential for mainte-nance and transformation into tools. Most of the larger British assemblages also show some use of recurrent Levallois methods, with several episodes on a single core. Not only do these show a more economical use of lithic resources, one core capable of replacing numerous large cutting tools (i.e. handaxes), but also allows the production of varied forms, emphasising flexibility and versatility.

There are three MIS8–7 sites that apparently contradict this tidy pattern. At Pontnew-ydd, numerous handaxes and Levallois products appear to occur in the same context

FIGURE 5.12
Retouched Levallois flake from Baker's Hole, essentially a unifacial handaxe. (Courtesy Beccy Scott.)

(Green 1984; see Text Box 5.4). This has previously been argued to be a function of local circumstances. The Levallois from this site has been described as crude and inept (Aldhouse-Green 1995), possibly due to the quality of the raw materials, leading White et al. (2006) to suggest that hominins may have reverted to handaxe manufacture to compensate. We now see this as rather special pleading, and a more parsimonious explanation for their co-occurrence is that the handaxes and Levallois material, both of which are allochthonous to the cave deposits within which they are found, actually relate to different phases of occupation outside. At Broom, Dorset, thousands of handaxes in a generally rolled condition have come from deposits of the River Axe dated to ~250–270 ka BP by OSL (Hosfield and Chambers 2002; Hosfield 2005; Wymer 1999 had other ideas regarding the date of this assemblage). Several Levallois pieces have previously been reported (Roe 1968b) although these can no longer be verified (Ashton and Hosfield 2009). At Harnham, Wiltshire, handaxes and manufacturing debris has come from fluvial sands and gravels and overlying solifluction deposits. OSL and AAR on silts separating the gravel and solifluction unit have produced age estimates of ~250 ka BP, that is, early MIS8 (Whitaker et al. 2004).

Based on these data, Ashton and Hosfield (2009; Ashton et al. 2011) have postulated an east–west divide in the EMP settlement of Britain, with differential access across the North Sea and Channel basins by populations with different technological repertoires. Access from the east, they contend, would have required a reduction in sea level of *c.* 20 m, but a drop of at least 30 m in the Dover Strait and 60 m in the Channel would have been necessary for people to cross from the south. These contrasting geographies are thus suggested to have led to colonisation in the east and west of Britain during different climatic and environmental phases with populations originating from different areas of Europe.

However, the summary distribution of Levallois material provided in Figures 5.8 and 5.9 shows this pattern to be entirely illusory. When present, Levallois-using hominins span most of southern England at the very least, and were present across the entire south-west coast from Devon to the Isle of Wight. Even if we accept the OSL dates (and at this time depth this is debatable) we consider it most likely that the handaxes from Broom and Harnham are perfectly valid examples of the MIS9 Acheulean. The material below the early MIS8 silt at Harnham is obviously older (i.e. MIS9) while the conjoinable material in the solifluction unit above has potentially moved *en masse* from these older deposits. The material from Broom is not *in situ*, meaning the date on the terrace gravel only provides a *terminus ante quem* for their manufacture. Sadly, then, we suspect that the poorly understood taphonomy of these deposits lies behind these apparent exceptions, rather than an interesting cultural geography. Furthermore, given the topography of the Channel River and its tributaries (Gupta et al. 2007), access from the south would have been difficult even during periods of very low sea level, and the general distribution bias to the east, with a dominance of finds in East Anglia and the Thames Valley is unsurprising – this is in fact the pattern in almost every interglacial from MIS13 onwards. We return to the issue of the Channel barrier from the context of modern humans in Chapters 6 and 7.

LITHIC TECHNOLOGIES

The sites outlined in Table 5.5 and the text boxes in this chapter represent the corpus of the better-contextualised, securely age-constrained EMP sites in Britain. They are all characterised by the use of Levallois, often amongst a number of other non-Levallois techniques, but as suggested above almost never accompanied by handaxes. While other large Levallois collections do exist, these have been excluded from recent studies aimed at developing the validity of an early Middle Palaeolithic period (e.g. White et al. 2006; Scott 2006, 2010; Scott et al. 2011) due to concerns over their integrity. For example, some 46 Levallois pieces have been reported from New Hythe, Kent, within an assemblage of some 456 artefacts including cores, flakes, handaxes and at least one bout coupé handaxe (Wymer 1993, 1999; Roe 1981; Tyldesley 1987; Coulson 1990). The site is situated on Terrace 3 of the Medway, correlated with the MIS8–7–6 Mucking/Taplow Formation of the Thames (Bridgland 2003), but only minimal contextual information is available (Hinton and Kennard 1905) and an examination of existing collections failed to isolate a valid sample (Scott 2010). Similarly, the relatively large Levallois samples from Barnham Heath, Suffolk (Wymer 1985), Bramford Road, Ipswich (Moir 1931; Wymer 1985) and Bapchild, Kent (Dines 1929; Roe 1981), all occur within heavily derived and mixed assemblages of diverse ages and possess little interpretative significance. It is a sad indictment of the state of the British Palaeolithic that no significant new sites have been discovered for over 50 years largely, we feel, due to an over concentration on existing museum collections and little real appetite for prospection and excavation.

Unpacking Levallois

As discussed above, the oldest EMP site in Britain occurs in the Botany Gravel at Purfleet. This is dominated by a simple prepared core technology or 'proto-Levallois' method argued to show the *in situ* emergence of Levallois from earlier European core technologies (White and Ashton 2003). By late MIS8, a suite of fully formed lineal and recurrent Levallois strategies are evident, aimed at producing a variety of target end-products (White et al. 2006; Scott 2006, 2010; cf. Boëda 1995; Boëda et al. 1990).

Detailed technological analysis of nine securely dated EMP assemblages by Beccy Scott (2006, 2010) showed that a wide range of Levallois methods occurred in Britain during MIS9–7, with most sites having evidence for a number of different methods (Figures 5.13 and 5.14). At Creffield Road, Acton, heavily reduced and often exhausted Levallois point cores showed evidence for unipolar, bipolar and convergent preparation, and both lineal and recurrent exploitation (Figure 5.15). Some cores showed evidence of cyclical re-preparation between discrete phases of exploitation, sometimes with a change in reduction schema from bipolar to unipolar, to facilitate the continued production of points. This falls into a continent-wide appearance of lithic points at this time. Scott (2010) also notes one unique example where the flaking and striking surfaces switched function during re-preparation, but still retained, within each discrete phase of

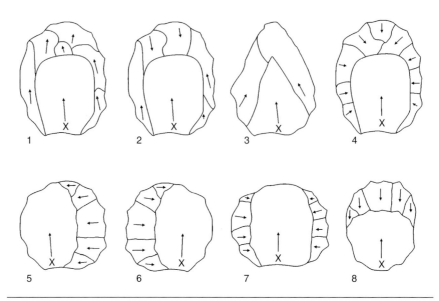

FIGURE 5.13

Diagrammatic representation of the variety evident in Levallois surface preparation, based on the location of flake scars. Key: 1. Unipolar; 2. Bipolar; 3. Convergent unipolar; 4 centripetal; 5. Unidirectional right; 6. Unidirectional left; 7. Bipolar lateral; 8. Unipolar distal. NB. Numbers 5, 6, 7 and 8 may reflect centripetal, unipolar or bipolar preparation for which no evidence is retained, or genuinely represent the type of preparation named above. (After Scott 2006 and courtesy Beccy Scott.)

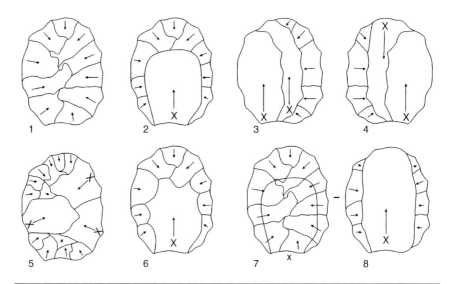

FIGURE 5.14

Diagrammatic representation of the variation evident in Levallois exploitation methods. Key: 1. Unexploited; 2. Lineal preferential; 3. Unipolar recurrent; 4. Bipolar recurrent; 5. Centripetal recurrent; 6. Re-prepared but unexploited; 7. Failed lineal; 8. Overshot lineal. (After Scott 2006 and courtesy Beccy Scott.)

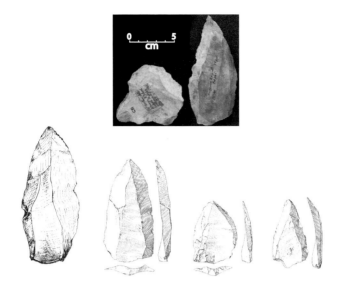

FIGURE 5.15
Levallois points and an exhausted core from Creffield Road, Acton. (Line drawings after Roe 1981 and photographs courtesy Beccy Scott.)

exploitation, their hierarchical relationship. A similar approach to Levallois technology, with a notable proportion of Levallois points and exhausted cores, was also observed in the nearby Hillingdon sites (see Text Box 5.9).

Perhaps more surprisingly, similar technological variation was observed at Baker's Hole and the Ebbsfleet Channel, Northfleet (Scott 2010, 89; see Text Box 5.11). The late MIS8 Levallois material from the classic Baker's Hole site mostly comes from the Coombe Rock, a continuously developing chalk rubble deposit that incorporates artefacts reworked to varying degrees from Neanderthal knapping areas on the active slope margins, which also provided a source of very large raw materials.[2] Internationally renowned, the assemblage from this site is often cast as showing the profligate use of locally available flint, a view which emphasises the occurrence of very large 'tortoise-cores' bearing a single privileged flake (Wymer 1968; Roe 1981; Coulson 1990; Figure 5.16); in Boëda's terminology centripetally prepared, lineally exploited cores. While acknowledging that centripetal preparation does indeed dominate, Scott (2010) also highlights greater variation in both preparation and exploitation, with some evidence for the use of recurrent techniques as well as the re-preparation of flaking surfaces to extend the productive life of some cores. The key concern of the Baker's Hole knappers appears to be the production of very large, broad flakes, a requirement facilitated by the ubiquity and size of the local raw materials, which were quickly abandoned once flakes of the desired size could no longer be achieved (Scott 2010, 97). Several large Levallois products show evidence of retouching into flake tools. Some show intensive working to both edges, into forms that should strictly be termed double sidescrapers, while others show bifacial or alternate retouch. A number resemble handaxes in form (White et al. 2006; Scott 2010) and may have served a similar function as these large cutting tools; indeed, Scott sees the retouch to these tools as accentuating the cutting edges rather than transforming them. Overall, Baker's Hole appears to be a place where Neanderthals equipped themselves with a series of very large knives; cores were abandoned in an unexhausted state because the prime concern was the size of the resultant tool, the cores themselves being just too large for transportation.

THE EBBSFLEET VALLEY, NORTH KENT

Since the late 1900s, Pleistocene deposits in the Ebbsfleet Valley – within which lies the famous site at Baker's Hole – have produced vast quantities of Levallois material. The overall sequence comprised a basal coombe rock filling a channel cut into the Chalk, overlain by fluvial gravel and a sequence of fluvial and colluvial silts, which sometimes interdigitate at the margins (Abbott 1911; Smith 1911; Burchell 1935, 1936a and b, 1957; Carreck 1972; Kerney and Sieveking 1977; Bridgland 1994; Wenban-Smith 1995). There is considerable lateral variation within the deposits, which has often caused difficulties in correlating the various exposures, although a recent reassessment of materials and archives relating to the various investigations has greatly clarified the stratigraphical and archaeo-logical situation and is preferred here (Scott et al. 2010 and see Table 1).

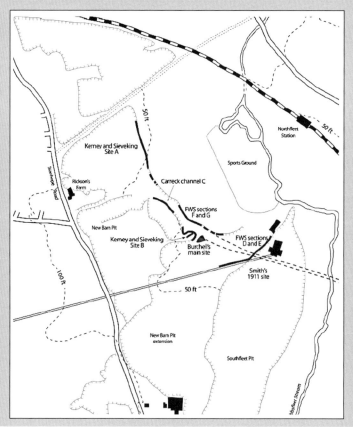

FIGURE 1
Location map of sites located in the Ebbsfleet Valley. (After Scott et al. 2010b.)

Text Box 5.11

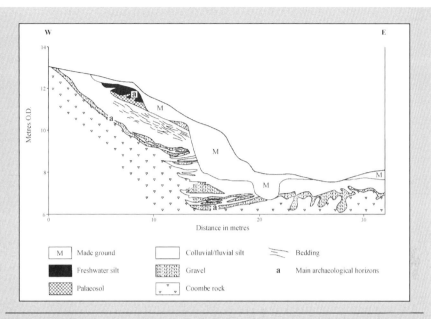

FIGURE 2

Section through the Ebbsfleet Channel deposits excavated by the British Museum. (After White et al. 2006, modified after Kerney and Sieveking 1971 and Bridgland 1994.)

Table 1 Correlation of key stratigraphical sequences from Ebbsfleet with interpretation and archaeology (modified after Scott et al. 2010)

Scott et al. (2009)	Burchell (1935, 1936a and b, 1957)	Kerney and Sieveking (1977)	Bridgland (1994)	Interpretation	Archaeology
Phase V (Cool)	Coombe rock and trail		12	Solifluction	Derived handaxes
	Uppermost Loam		11	?Fluvial	
	Calloutis		10	?Fluvial	
Phase IV (Warm)	Upper Loam (Temperate Bed)	Freshwater silt	6	Fluvial	Derived handaxes
	Weathered surface	Weathering	5a	Soil	
	Middle Loam	aeolian/ soliflucted silt and solifluxion gravel	8	Colluvial	
	Coombe rock and trail		7	Solifluction	Derived handaxes
Phase III (Cool)	Middle Loam		5	Colluvial	
	Lower Loam		5	Fluvial	
	Gravel		4	Fluvial	Levallois
	Lowermost Loam		3	Fluvial	
Phase II (Warm)	Meltwater Gravel		2	Fluvial	Levallois
Phase 1 (Cold)	Main Coombe Rock	Coombe rock	1	Solifluction	Levallois

Text Box 5.11

According to Scott et al. (2010), Levallois material is restricted to two discrete levels. Thousands of artefacts in fresh condition came from the main coombe rock (Phase I), including large Levallois cores and flakes alongside other débitage (Smith 1911; Abbott 1911). A similar assemblage of several hundred pieces was collected from the fluviatile gravels above this (Burchell q.v., Kerney and Sieveking 1977). Some material from the gravel has been refitted (Wenban-Smith 1995), showing it is in primary context, although a degree of spatial relocation seems probable given its condition. Both assemblages are based around the exploitation of recurrent Levallois cores manufactured on the most immediate source of materials: the exposed and eroding chalk cliff in Phase I and the clasts from the gravels in Phase II. The material from the upper deposits (including the handaxes) is rolled and has all presumably been derived from the sediments of the MIS11 Boyn Hill terrace above.

Five alternating warm–cold episodes are recorded in the Ebbsfleet Valley, all correlated with MIS8–7 on the basis of lithostratigraphy, biostratigraphy and aminostratigraphy (Bridgland 1994, Schreve 1997; Wenban-Smith 1995; Scott et al. 2010). Hominins were certainly present during at least two of these. The incision of the channel and the emplacement of the coombe rock and the 'Baker's Hole' industry it contains is attributed to late MIS8/early MIS7. The sedimentology and elements of the fauna (woolly rhinoceros) from these basal units indicate cool and open conditions. The primary-context archaeology from the overlying fluvial deposits of Phase II, however, is associated with a fauna dominated by 'Ilford-type' mammoth, woolly rhinoceros and horse, together with *Bithynia tentaculata*, revealing temperate but still open conditions, with nearby woodland and running water (Wenban-Smith 1995; Schreve 1997; Scott et al. 2009). Human use of the gravel surface apparently extended throughout the warming limb of the interglacial. An episode of cooling, followed by a return to full interglacial conditions, is shown by the fossils and micromorphology of the colluvial and freshwater silts of Phase III (Scott et al. 2010; Burchell 1957, Kemp 1995; Wenban-Smith 1995), probably representing sub-stages of MIS7. These units are also much more extensive than the underlying fluvial beds (Bridgland 1994) and probably masked the gravels originally targeted by hominins as a source of raw material.

Wenban-Smith (1995) proposed two warm phases (II and IV) and one cold phase (III) which he correlated with MIS7c–7a, although Schreve (2001b) suggested that all the interglacial sediments at the site belonged to the Sandy Lane MAZ and therefore the end of the interglacial. Such an interpretation would require a major hiatus between the incision of the channel and deposition of the coombe rock and the accumulation of the fluvial sediments (Scott et al. 2010).

Text Box 5.11

A similar range of forms, methods and rejuvenation techniques was recorded in the early MIS7 assemblage from the Lower Gravel in the adjacent Ebbsfleet Channel, the minor variations designed to deal with changes in raw materials; the source of large nodules exploited earlier at Baker's Hole having been silted over and large cobbles from gravel used instead (Scott 2010, 106–118). However, while still aimed at the production of large (and sometimes elongated) Levallois flakes these were now retouched

FIGURE 5.16
Cores from Baker's Hole. (Courtesy Beccy Scott.)

in ways that transformed the edges to a greater degree than previously (Scott 2010, 118). While MIS8 hominins preserved the handaxe-like properties of Levallois flakes – regarding them essentially as tools in themselves – for MIS7 hominins Levallois flakes were supports for other tools (cf. Boëda et al. 1990). This represents a transformation in conception of how Levallois flakes operated in the technological system, presenting a greater number of opportunities and equipping people for more flexible action in the wider landscape (White and Pettitt 1996).

In contrast, the assemblage from the Lion Tramway Cutting, West Thurrock, Essex, (Figure 5.17) shows no evidence of cyclical re-preparation and little evidence for recurrent techniques (see Text Box 5.1).[3] Most of the material from this site was originally deposited on a coarse gravel beach formed by the upper Crayford Gravel, some pieces having post-depositionally worked their way down to lower layers (Schreve et al. 2006). The material demonstrates the use of centripetal, convergent, unipolar and bipolar preparation (Schreve et al. 2006) but only two cores and two flakes bear evidence of recurrent exploitation, the remainder being lineal. Within the small areas excavated there is a flake deficit, suggesting that more flakes were selected and transported away, only the failed or broken examples being left on site. The site also produced very few retouched tools (only two from an assemblage of ~250). The different approach to the use of Levallois technology here is unlikely to relate to raw material abundance, as other sites on or adjacent to a source of material (e.g. Ebbsfleet, Creffield Road, the Hillingdon Sites; see Text Boxes 5.9 and 5.11) reveal ample evidence for recurrent exploitation and cyclical re-preparation. It might therefore be suggested that the Lion Tramway Cutting site was a focus for a different and perhaps attenuated set of hominin activities (see below), although any conclusions must be treated with caution given the very small area currently investigated. The same is true of Jordan's Pit, Brundon (see Text Box 5.12), again situated near a source of very large flint gravel, but lacking in strong evidence for recurrent techniques or re-preparation, although for this site the integrity of the sample has been strongly compromised by both collection and storage history.

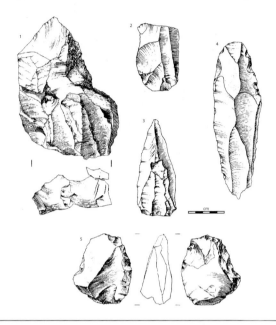

FIGURE 5.17
Levallois artefacts from the Lion Tramway Cutting, West Thurrock. (After Schreve et al. 2007.)

THE VALLEYS OF THE RIVERS GIPPING AND STOUR, SUFFOLK

Text Box 5.12

Four localities assigned to the Early Middle Palaeolithic of MIS7 occur in fluvial deposits of the Gipping and Stour, Suffolk. Perhaps the best known is the Stoke Bone Bed – seen in exposures in Ipswich at Stoke Tunnel, Maidenhall and Halifax Junction Pipeworks (Layard 1912, 1920; Wymer 1985) – which represent part of a 30 m sequence of Pleistocene sediments of the River Gipping/Orwell, banked-up on their south-east side against an eroded slope of London Clay. These deposits are richly fossiliferous, yielding a suite of mammals regarded as typical of later MIS7 (Schreve 1997), a position within the interglacial that does not conflict with Turner's post-temperate pollen spectrum (in West 1977). Archaeology from the Bone Bed is sparse, with only 20 or so pieces coming from within or just above the main fossiliferous horizon (Wymer 1985, 232), but these include two or three classic Levallois cores and some Levallois flakes, many in fresh condition. Environmental indicators suggest fully temperate conditions, with high insolation and summer temperatures of at least 17° C attested by *Emys orbicularis*. The local landscape was dominated by open grassland with an important woodland component; a body of slow-flowing freshwater ran nearby. Sections opened close to Wymer's 1976 Maidenhall excavations in 2002 failed to expose the Bone Bed (MJW pers. obs.).

Jordan's Pit, Brundon lies on the south bank of the River Stour at about 30 m OD. Here, Moir and Hopwood (1939) described some 14 metres of glacial, fluvial and colluvial deposits, the fluvial gravel of Bed 3 yielding a moderate lithic assemblage of over 250 objects including handaxes and Levallois

FIGURE 1
Levallois core from the Stoke Bone Bed. (Courtesy of Beccy Scott).

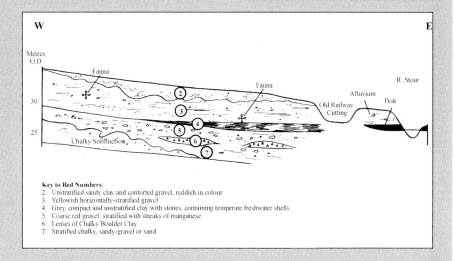

Key to Bed Numbers:
2. Unstratified sandy clay and contorted gravel, reddish in colour
3. Yellowish horizontally-stratified gravel
4. Grey, compact and unstratified clay with stones, containing temperate freshwater shells
5. Coarse red gravel, stratified with streaks of manganese
6. Lenses of Chalky Boulder Clay
7. Stratified chalky, sandy-gravel or sand

FIGURE 2
Section through the deposits of the River Stour at Brundon. The archaeology was principally associated with Bed 3. (After White et al. 2006, modified after Wymer 1985, with permission.)

products. The gravel is, in places, remarkably coarse (MJW pers. obs.). The reports of Moir and Hopwood (ibid.) and Wymer (1985) both stated that the artefacts from Bed 3 were in mixed preservational state, although they differed on whether it was possible to separate the handaxes and Levallois material into two industries on this basis. A smaller collection of fresh Levallois material in association with mammalian and molluscan remains was also recovered from a manganese-stained gravel horizon above organic temperate beds at the base

Text Box 5.12

Text Box 5.12

of Bed 3, which Moir considered to be a palaeo-landsurface. A mixture of two or more assemblages is probably present within the gravel with a more coherent assemblage in the stained horizon at its base.

The environmental evidence from Brundon showed a fast-flowing river situated in a dry, open grassland landscape with some woodland and scrub vegetation. The molluscs and mammals were compared with those from the MIS7 site at Ilford (Kennard, in Moir and Hopwood 1939), while Schreve stressed the similarities with the later MIS7 upper deposits at Aveley. Neither attribution contradicts the early Uranium-series dates from the site which provided estimates of 230 ± 30 ka BP and 174 ± 30 ka BP (Szabo and Collins 1975).

Artefacts and organic remains have also been collected from the foreshore and cliffs of the Stour Estuary at Stutton and Harkstead, Holbrook Bay, Suffolk (Whitaker 1885; Evans 1897; Spencer 1958, 1962, 1970; Wymer 1985). The sequence exposed in the low cliff section shows 5 m of Pleistocene sand and bedded silts (brickearth) with infrequent gravel, predominantly resting directly on London Clay but occasionally on gravel. About 100 artefacts in a variety of preservational states are recorded from here, including ~10 rolled handaxes, a Levallois core and several Levallois products (Wymer 1985, 210 and 236). Most were recovered out of context, with only one Levallois flake and a fresh partial handaxe (made on a flake) recorded as definitely coming from the brickearth (Wymer 1985). According to Wymer's (1985) observations, the rolled handaxe assemblage is probably eroding from the basal gravel, with the brickearth containing a sparse Levallois industry.

Schreve compared the fauna from both the Stutton and Harkstead localities with that from the upper part of the Aveley sequence, a position within the interglacial compatible with the Zone III pollen spectrum identified by Sparks and West (1963) from sediments beneath the foreshore. The organic proxies show a local environment dominated by open grassland adjacent to a slow-flowing stream with patches of local woodland. Some species are indicative of high summer temperatures (e.g. *Emys orbicularis*) although more continental climatic indicators are also represented (Schreve 1997; Sparks and West 1963).

Of all the assemblages assigned to the British EMP few have received as much attention or been as poorly understood as the *in situ* laminar Levallois material recovered from fine-grained sediments at the base of a flint-bearing, chalk river cliff at Crayford (see Text Box 5.5 and Figure 5.18). Mellars (1974) emphasised the Upper Palaeolithic qualities of the Crayford material, later comparing it to other examples of laminar Levallois at Seclin (Mellars 1996); while Roe regarded it as evolved Levallois (Roe 1981), the laminar 'flake-blades' testament to a later and more refined technique. On the other hand, Cook (1986), who failed to find any evidence of predetermination in the Crayford material, suggested it was not Levallois at all; a conclusion endorsed by Révillion (1995) whose

FIGURE 5.18
Refitting laminar flakes from Crayford found by Spurrell. (Photograph courtesy Beccy Scott and material © Natural History Museum.)

application of Boëda's *Levallois concept* saw the properties of the flakes as fortuitously emerging from the 'convergent, direct non-Levallois flaking' directed at exploiting cylindrical nodules.

Historically, the problem with analysing and understanding the Crayford material has been that ever since Spurrell's pioneering work (Spurrell 1880a and b, 1884) the refitting groups have been firmly conjoined. This obstacle was finally overcome by a complete re-analysis under the auspices of AHOB2, which involved the dismantling and rejoining of Spurrell's refitting sequences (Scott et al. 2011). This clearly showed that some of the material from Stoneham's Pit, at least, relates to Levallois point production that conforms fully to Boëda's criteria, although most represents on-site decortication of nodules taken from the chalk cliff and Crayford gravel. Some cores were further prepared, their volumetric properties being deliberately adjusted to create a Levallois flaking surface, and Levallois products were produced on site. Despite the popular impression of vast knapping scatters at Stoneham's Pit, only three fairly complete reduction sequences are in fact present. Two are on cylindrical nodules that 'conditioned' the knapping trajectory employed and prompted the removal of laminar products aimed at reducing the rounded core forms and transforming them into a flattened Levallois flaking surface (Scott et al. 2011). One was subsequently re-prepared and exploited again. The Levallois flakes are missing from both sequences (Scott et al. 2011), and therefore can be regarded as the desired result of a technical sequence intended from the outset for a purpose, and exported at least from the immediate site for that very purpose – in other words, predetermined in both form and function. Most of the sequences from Stoneham's Pit, however, are incomplete and comprise heavily cortical flakes – whether part of a Levallois sequence or not is unclear. There is also a highly noteworthy paucity of cores. Given the almost completely undisturbed nature of the finds from this location the cores were presumably removed from the beach beneath the chalk cliff for exploitation elsewhere (Scott et al. 2011).

Technology unchained

The different approaches to Levallois seen in EMP assemblages did not represent conceptually discrete plans of action (contra Boëda 1986) but interchangeable options within a general technological repertoire which Neanderthals called upon as and when necessary (White et al. 2006). Not only do different exploitation and preparation schema coexist within assemblages, but knappers also shifted between them during re-preparation phases on individual cores, as seen for example in the switch from bipolar to centripetal Levallois at Baker's Hole, and from bipolar to unipolar at Creffield Road to allow the continued production of points from increasingly smaller cores (Scott 2010; for European and Levantine examples see Dibble 1995; Bietti and Grimaldi 1995; Texier and Francisco-Ortega 1995; Jaubert and Farizy 1995; Schlanger 1996). Thus, the different methods identified by archaeologists represent a set of options and skills – Pelegrin's (1990) connaissance (knowledge) and savoire-faire (know-how) – rather than rigid formulae. The selection of different techniques depended largely upon situation or need. In some cases, knapping was geared towards the deliberate production of certain end-products – blades at Creffield Road, long broad 'knives' at Crayford and 'pseudo-handaxes' at Baker's Hole – proof if it were ever needed that Levallois products were intended and to a large degree predetermined (Scott 2010, contra Dibble 1989). In other situations, knapping was geared towards maximising the productvity of the flaking surface through recurrent techniques.

Scott's highly detailed analysis has also shown how individual knapping sequences subtly responded to the form of the raw material and the configuration of the core as it evolved 'in hand' (cf. Schlanger 1996). However, once a particular form of preparation and exploitation had been selected, and knapping commenced, Neanderthals were apparently unable to change tack (Scott 2010). This was not due to inflexible cognitive pathways but the fact that the evolving form of the core, as created by previous removals, structured the overall knapping trajectory. Levallois technology thus provided Neanderthals with a set of technological principles that both enabled and constrained action. This action extended into the landscape.

Across Europe, Levallois formed part of a highly mobile, curated tool-kit involving the movement of both flakes (as blanks and retouched tools) and cores (as the sources of such flakes) (Geneste 1985, 1989; White and Pettitt 1996, Roebroeks et al. 1988). Both practices offered solutions to the anticipated, but largely unpredictable, future need for cutting edges and represent the extension of the *chaîne opératoire* in time and space (White and Pettitt 1996). This was accompanied by a greater differentiation of place with different discard patterns responding to planned/anticipated use of fixed and mobile resources (White et al. 2006; see below). It is interesting to note, however, that while the continental evidence suggest that Levallois products were preferentially selected for transport, and are more likely to occur on intermediate (>5 km) and exotic materials (>30 km) (Geneste 1985, 1989), the maximum transport distances of artefacts and raw materials shows little change between the Lower Palaeolithic and the EMP (Féblot-Augustins 1999). So, while the EMP testifies to more varied and sophisticated integration, planning and curation of technology in the landscape overall ranging (and/or drop-out) patterns seem to have remained similar to those of the following *Homo heidelbergensis* societies. This might be taken as evidence that the changes seen in the EMP were small steps rather than giant leaps. Indeed, recent work (Clinnick 2010, cf. Gamble and Steele 1999) suggests that maximum raw material transfers do not reflect cognitive clout but the minimum predatory range needed to sustain healthy bodies and healthy social relationships amongst large-brained, carnivorous hominins living in fission–fusion societies.

The sites summarised in Table 5.4 show how EMP Neanderthals carried out different activities at different points in the landscape, part of the aforementioned complex pattern of landscape use and technological organisation. The largest assemblages are usually situated adjacent to a source of accessible raw material in the form of chalk outcrops or coarse gravels and probably served as 'extraction and production sites' or 'mixed strategy sites' (Turq 1988, 1989). These were familiar places – presumably nexus points in the Neanderthal cognitive landscape – to which they returned repeatedly, leading to the accumulation of large artefact assemblages, including much débitage. The chaîne opèratoire evident at these sites extends from raw material procurement, through primary reduction to tool manufacture. The absence of any use-wear or dedicated cut-mark analyses makes it difficult to determine if any tools were used at these sites, thus making it difficult to differentiate between Turq's site categories, but we assume that these riverside locations offered a range of affordances other than just flint. Furthermore, as shown above, there is technological variation that probably reflects how these sites were regarded and used by Neanderthals throughout space and time – the absence of recurrent techniques at West Thurrock and Brundon compared to most other sites, the differential retouch practices at Baker's Hole compared to Ebbsfleet – although precisely how and why this is the case remains elusive. At West Thurrock there is a deficit of Levallois flakes, while at Crayford both cores and their products are lacking, suggesting that whatever activities took place at these sites, they also served as 'gearing-up' stations for action that extended out into the landscape.

Sites with small assemblages, however, are situated in locations lacking a source of raw material and correspond most closely with Turq's 'episodic sites': ephemeral occupations reflecting specific episodes during which a mobile tool-kit was brought into play and after which a few elements dropped out of circulation. These small assemblages generally comprise a few Levallois cores, flake tools and Levallois flakes – precisely what would be expected in a curated, Levallois-based tool-kit. So, from the earliest Middle Palaeolithic the British record shows evidence for varied but logistical use of technology with clear levels of future planning and anticipation of action in the landscape.

Further hints at the complexity of technological organisation are found at Creffield Road, Acton (White and Jacobi 2002; White et al. 2006; Scott 2010). Material from this site is characterised by a small number (n=15) of heavily reduced and exhausted Levallois cores, but a large number of Levallois products (n=123), of which nearly 50% are Levallois points (Scott 2010).[4] Most of the Levallois products are too large to have been struck from the cores in their discarded state and about 20% are larger than the cores themselves, suggesting extensive reduction over several re-preparation cycles (Figure 5.18). The lack of debordant flakes, which would have been produced during these re-preparation cycles, suggests that the cores may have been worked elsewhere and brought to Creffield Road only at the end of their use-life; although the presence of large cortical flakes also shows that primary reduction took place at the site, utilising large clasts from the local gravel. It is worth noting that, at other sites situated on a source of raw material, cores were rarely if ever used to exhaustion but were usually abandoned in a potentially exploitable condition (Scott 2010).

These features suggest that Creffield Road was a gearing-up station, frequently visited to manufacture cores and points that were then taken away and extensively used elsewhere (White et al. 2006; Scott 2010). The cores found at Creffield Road therefore represent material finally discarded there after an extensive, mobile use-life as part of a curated tool-kit, once Neanderthals had access to new supplies. The Levallois points – which fall within the limits of projectile points defined by Shea (1993; Shea et al. 2001) – were suggested to have had a similarly complex life history and to have served as weapon heads (Scott 2010). Three examples show deliberate thinning at the butt, presumably to facilitate hafting, while the prevalence of proximal fragments among the broken examples might testify to the removal of snapped projectile heads from armatures once replacements were procured (Scott 2010, 56). The location of Creffield Road, on the surface of the Lynch Hill Terrace, would have presumably overlooked the Thames Valley following the fluvial down-cutting to the Taplow Terrace level at the end of MIS8, making the site not only an ideal spot for re-tooling but also a good vantage point for hunters (White et al. 2006).

Creffield Road was obviously just one part of a much wider Neanderthal *local operational area* (White and Pettitt 2011 and see Chapter 6). Similar technological characteristics were also noted at the nearby Hillingdon sites (see Text Box 5.9), perhaps suggesting that these sites also served as gearing-up stations on higher ground. These sites therefore show Neanderthals ready for action, equipped with maintainable tools and cores to makes new tools, and possessing a thorough knowledge of resources in the landscape. These presumably linked with a number of other 'action stations' in the valley below, episodic sites that Neanderthals exploited for a number of economic and social activities, before returning to discard and replace exhausted tool-kits. Precisely this type of relationship has been postulated to explain technological contrasts between lowland sites in the Maas Valley – notably Maastricht-Belvédère – and upland, valley-side sites on the Southern Limburg plateau, where heavily retouched tools and exhausted cores were discarded in locations adjacent to a source of raw material (Kolen et al. 1999).

DESERTING BRITAIN: EARLY MIDDLE PALAEOLITHIC SETTLEMENT HISTORY AND DEMOGRAPHY

Artefacts as people

Compared to the Lower Palaeolithic record, the corpus of EMP sites and materials appears remarkably slight, even accounting for the much shorter time period involved. Over the past decade, several workers have attempted to quantify this impressionistic view (Hosfield 1999; Ashton and Lewis 2002; Ashton and Hosfield 2009). In their influential study, Ashton and Lewis (2002) produced estimates of relative artefact density over time, taking the absolute number of handaxes and Levallois pieces known from different terrace levels of the Middle Thames and adjusting them to account for:

1   Biases in collection opportunities presented by differences in surviving terrace surface area.

2   Biases in collection opportunities presented by the extent of quarrying (prior to mass mechanisation).

3   Biases in collection opportunities presented by differences in urbanisation.

4   The period of time represented by each terrace unit.

They saw in their data an interesting pattern with a maximum peak in artefact density in MIS13 which gradually reduced through MIS11 and 9 (Figure 5.19). This was followed by a major collapse in artefact numbers in MIS7 and a virtual absence from MIS6 onwards. A similar pattern was found in the Solent Basin (Ashton and Hosfield 2009) with peaks in the Bournemouth area and the Test Valley between MIS13 and MIS8; although as the authors admit the cogency of these patterns and their ability to interpret them are severely curtained by the poorly understood dating, the poor preservational state of the materials and the paucity of environmental or landscape evidence. While most British Palaeolithic archaeologists would probably accept that some variation on this pattern exists, it is almost as certain that no two of them would agree on its meaning.

For Ashton and Lewis, artefact density is a proxy for population density, although we wonder how useful such an analogy is in the absence of any quantification of actual population numbers (see below). In their interpretation, hominin populations were highest during the Lower Palaeolithic but each successive interglacial saw reduced population density. The relatively low numbers of artefacts from MIS7 was interpreted as reflecting a major decline, followed by a population 'crisis', that ended with local extinction or

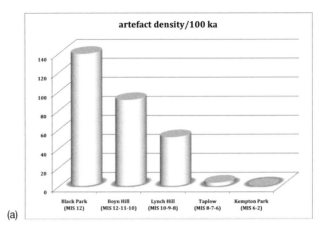

(a)

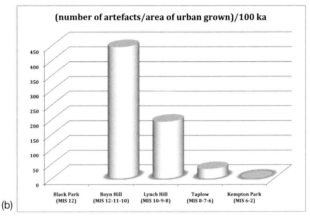

(b)

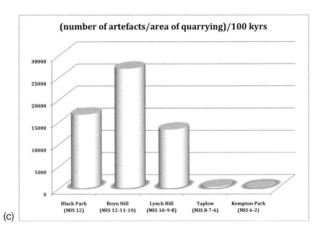

(c)

FIGURE 5.19

The gradually declining numbers of artefacts over time in the terraces of the Middle Thames. (a) Artefact density per 100,000 years of terrace formation; (b) Number of artefacts/area of quarrying per 100,000 years of terrace formation; (c) Number of artefacts/area of urban growth per 100,000 years of terrace formation. (Data after Ashton and Lewis 2002.)

abandonment during MIS6. They interpreted this pattern as a function of two related parameters. First, the demographic events of MIS8/7 were seen as evidence of changing hominin habitat preferences, away from the warm maritime west favoured before ~300 ka BP and towards the cooler continental east, as the Mammoth Steppe matured into a rich hunting ground (Gamble 1995a). Second, they suggested that over time access to Britain had become more difficult, possibly revealing that the breach of the Weald–Artois anticline that created the Strait of Dover, occurred during MIS8 or MIS6, later than the MIS12 date commonly accepted (cf. papers in Preece 1995; White and Schreve 2000; Bates et al. 2003; see Chapter 3). As a result, in the event of local crashes, immigrants from adjacent parts of Europe could not replace the previous populations, meaning fewer people making fewer artefacts and thus leaving an impoverished archaeological record. As discussed in Chapter 3, while more recent evidence has supported the consensus that the initial breach probably did occur during MIS12, a second catastrophic event that significantly widened it (possibly related to overspill from a moraine-dammed lake) has been proposed for MIS6 (Gupta et al. 2007; Gibbard 2007; but see Toucanne et al. 2009 and discussion in Chapter 3). Following on from this Ashton and Hosfield (2009) and Ashton et al. (2011) hypothesise that as the North Sea is a subsiding basin, colonisation would have become increasingly difficult with successive interglacials, implying that during earlier post-Anglian interglacials hominins could have simply waded across. It bears repeating that, according to Ashton and colleagues, the height of the southern North Sea floor during MIS11 must have been close to modern sea levels, even if only to allow the invasion of the 'Rhenish' fauna at Swanscombe and Clacton (Kerney 1971; White and Schreve 2000; Ashton et al. 2008a; see Chapter 3). By MIS5e, in contrast, a major drop in sea level of perhaps 30 m would have been required to gain easy access from the east (Ashton et al. 2011). These changes in palaeogeography are offered as a clear explanation for the decline in Middle Thames and Solent artefact numbers and arguably hominin population over time, although the impact of the major overspill of MIS12, massive discharges through strait into the Channel River, successive glaciations and other erosional events in the North Sea Basin and fact that downwarping rates are unknown renders this total speculation.

We have already commented upon these sea-level reconstructions in Chapter 3. An alternative is shown in Figure 5.4, which correlates Shackleton's (2000) sea-level estimates correlated with the Indian Ocean Stack MD900963 (Bassinot et al. 1994). Compared to Figure 3.13, it is clear that even with a breach during MIS12, MIS7 is notable for having far fewer opportunities for entry to Britain than previous interglacials. According to three of the reconstructions in Figure 5.4, Britain was an island for MIS7e and MIS7c–7a. A local extinction event after MIS7d would therefore have left an uninhabited island with no possibility of recolonisation until the beginning of MIS6, at which point humans may be present at Crayford. There is no need to posit changing habitat preferences, nor declining populations. The majority of the Taplow Gravels, therefore, would be expected to contain no artefacts because there were actually no hominin populations, not smaller ones. This is, admittedly, something of a variation on Ashton and Lewis's original claims, but here we do not equate number of artefacts with number of people, but rather duration and presence of settlement.

Artefacts as clasts

The question that now needs to be asked is how far the lack of archaeological visibility is not a reflection of population size but entirely due to the duration of occupation. The gravels underlying the Taplow Terrace and its correlates were aggraded between terminal MIS8 and MIS6, with the strongest evidence of hominin presence coming from MIS8 and early MIS7 contexts at sites such as Baker's Hole, West Thurrock and Crayford (Ashton and Lewis 2002).[5] As it is widely accepted that hominins were absent from Britain during most of MIS6, the cold climate deposits belonging to this period at the top of the Taplow Terrace would therefore be expected – a priori – to contain very few or no artefacts.[6] For all other terraces, it can be assumed from sites such as Swanscombe and Purfleet that hominins were present throughout the warming limb, the full interglacial and the cooling limb, being absent only during the glacial optima.

In Ashton and Lewis's calculations no adjustment is made to the estimated duration of the Taplow deposits to account for this known absence. They do, however, reduce the formation period of the Black Park Terrace, even though this is obviously an heuristic for the whole of the much longer MIS13 and MIS12 cycle from which the artefacts in these deposits were probably derived. Indeed, most extant and/or exploited Taplow deposits actually belong to the MIS6 aggradation phase (White et al. 2006; Bridgland 1994 and pers comm. 2005), the MIS7 interglacial and late MIS8 glacial deposits having been removed by the Thames over large areas. This means that artefacts will only be found in fortuitously preserved pockets of interglacial sediment, not the entirety of the Taplow Terrace, making all calculations based on terrace area utterly spurious. This of course totally begs the question as to why surface area rather than terrace volume or quarried volume is used at all. The latter would give a much fairer representation of artefact density, although even then the precise channel context exploited by quarrying needs to be understood; as has often been observed, channel edge situations contain vastly greater number of artefacts than deep, channel bed deposits.

In all, by failing to adjust for the known spatial and temporal distribution of suitable deposits we may in fact only really be learning what we already know – that hominins were absent for most of the period. However, one still needs to ask precisely how and why OIS6 differs from previous cooling limbs, when hominin presence seems to have persisted, and why they left Britain at a time when their 'preferred' conditions once more prevailed.

Artefacts in action

Following on, for many researchers, the greatest objection to such models lies in their simple equation that 'more' artefacts = 'more' people. Just how representative are samples of handaxes from largely secondary context sites? How many people are we dealing with? What formal relationship is there between numbers of handaxes and numbers of people on the ground? How many handaxes an individual hominin or group of hominins produced over time and space is a complete unknown and probably varied according to changes in tool 'husbandry' – the conservation and management of lithic resources, which subsumes curation – both over time and in relation to different resources in the landscape. Until these questions can be answered clearly, this must surely remain pure speculation. Furthermore, comparing handaxes and Levallois may also be like – to marshal an old cliché into service – comparing apples and oranges.

As noted in the introduction to this chapter, the EMP was a period of increasing behavioural complexity, heralding a number of changes in hominin behaviour that are critical to our understanding of Neanderthals (White et al. 2006). As described above, Levallois technology was part of a more sophisticated repertoire of stone tool husbandary. Despite recent arguments concerning the role that Lower Palaeolithic handaxes played in mediating social relationships and creating social geographies (Gamble 1999; Pope 2002, 2004; Pope and Roberts 2005), they still appear to be somewhat 'monolithic', if not physically then conceptually, for their makers. They appear to have had a limited function, predominantly involving butchery tasks (Keeley 1980; Mitchell 1996, 1997; Austin et al.1999), provided a limited range of future possibilities and subjected to a restricted pattern of edge modification; they also appear to have been largely used close to the place they were made (Chapter 3). This conception of resource affordances in the landscape we refer to as *unilocal* and we suggest can be said to define the behaviour of the pre-EMP world. Levallois technology, by contrast, was far more versatile (many different products could come from one core), maintainable (cores and flakes could be reworked following 'failure') and flexible (products were turned and retouched to perform many tasks). Furthermore, evidence from across Europe also shows that, with the advent of Levallois, the lithic chaîne opératoire was extended in time and space. In this sense it is *multilocal* in organisation. Although maximum transfer distances did not increase dramatically (Féblot-Augustins 1999), the selective curation and transport of Levallois products is marked; in south-west France, Geneste (1985, 1989) demonstrated that when products move they are mostly doing so in the form of Levallois. Therefore, the products of one Levallois core could potentially replace many handaxes and other tools, while increased mobility and reduced discard would mean fewer would enter the archaeological record. Thus, low archaeological visibility in Britain throughout the EMP relates clearly to changes in technology and more importantly the ways in which technology was used within the wider landscape, rather than the number of people making stone tools. In the wider context, we are seeing at this time the shift from unilocal to multilocal conceptions of the landscape.

At about the same time the rich, semi-arid grassland environments of the mammoth steppe appear to have been maturing across northern Europe, with the first solid evidence for occupation of north-east Europe (Gamble 1995a). The distribution and movement of herds on these vast grasslands necessitated multilocal approaches to resource procurement and technology, manifest in greater planning and mobility, more flexible technologies and new hunting strategies. Based on the European evidence, Gaudzinski (1999a) sees MIS7 as the period during which strong evidence for sophisticated and specialised hunting emerges, with the appearance of mono-specific faunal assemblages and repeated use of natural traps and ambush sites (Gaudzinski 1995, 1996, 1999a; Scott 1980; Jaubert et al. 1990; Stiner 2002). This can be further linked to the isotopic evidence for hyper-carnivory in Neanderthals (Bocherens et al. 1999, 2001, 2005; Richards et al. 2000).

The British evidence cannot at present reveal much about how Neanderthal technologies interfaced with their wider subsistence practices; many larger assemblages are poorly contextualised, decent kill or butchery sites have yet to be found, and what is available has not been systematically studied for cut-marks. However, the pointed morphology of some Levallois products backed or proximally thinned to aid hafting, indicates that they operated as spear points, presumably in similar hunting situations (Scott 2006, 2010; see also Shea 1993; Shea et al. 2001). When linked to Scott's evidence for more complex landscape use and technological practices discussed above, the British evidence might thus show fully tooled-up Neanderthals moving through the landscape targeting herds and individual animals where they were most susceptible. Examination of cut-marks on faunal sites, showing hominins were present but left little evidence in the form of lithic refuse, may take on added significance here and is sorely required.

Ashton and Lewis also suggest that most of the larger EMP sites belong to the early part of the period, during the MIS8–7 transition, and that no evidence exists for hominin presence during later MIS7. Based on Schreve's (2001a and b) biostratigraphic framework for MIS7, White et al. (2006) disputed this, insisting that hominin settlement could be detected throughout MIS7 (see attributions in Table 5.3 and 5.4). However, as discussed in Text Box 5.3, it now seems that distinguishing different parts of the MIS7 interglacial is more difficult than White and colleagues believed, although the evidence of occupation in both the lower and upper parts of the Aveley sequence clearly shows that hominins were present during at least two different parts of MIS7 (see Text Box 5.2).

What is abundantly clear, though, is that most of the larger assemblages certainly can be attributed to late MIS8–early MIS7, on lithological and non-mammalian evidence. As first suggested by White et al. (2006), we contend that this has more to do with landscape affordances over time than with regional population size. During the initial, colder parts of the EMP, highly erosive and gravel-laden rivers provided large reservoirs of raw materials in the form of coarse gravels and Chalk exposed during downcutting. During the relatively quiescent later interglacials and other periods of low-energy deposition finer silts and sands were deposited that increasingly covered these sources. If lithic raw materials were increasingly hidden one might expect an increasing concern with curating material in the landscape. So, hominins may have created richer, highly visible signatures during the colder and early interglacial phases, simply because raw material was more plentiful and easily available. Concomitantly, there are relatively fewer rich sites later in the interglacial, in part because these opportunities no longer existed; so episodic occupation restricted to just a few artefacts occur, hard-to-recover evidence of Neanderthals moving through an area but leaving little litter as evidence that they had been there at all.

This picture is supported by evidence from Ebbsfleet, Crayford and West Thurrock, where the rich archaeological horizons coincide with the availability of a source of raw material, the sites therefore acting as extraction locales (Figure 5.20). Once these sources became concealed by further deposition, evidence of hominin presence diminished to just a few pieces, or even just a single cut-marked bone as in the case of West Thurrock (Schreve et al. 2006). At sites lacking in adequate raw materials, large assemblages simply do not occur at any point during the cycle, as seen at Aveley.

Returning to the questions posed above, it is almost certain that hominin populations throughout the entire Pleistocene were vanishingly small. Gamble's (2002) attempt to model hominin populations based on observed hunter-gatherer densities and the surface area of Britain (Table 5.6), produced an estimate for Pleistocene populations in England and Wales, the known distribution of Neanderthal settlement, of just 3,000 to 13,500 people. This is probably a massive overestimate. Figures provided by Hublin and Roebroeks (2009) suggest that, at any given point during MIS3, the makers of the Central European Micoquian numbered just 1,240–1,940 and the MTA a mere 470–750. Even Upper Palaeolithic populations in Europe have been estimated to have been as few as 4,400–5,900 (Bocquet-Appel et al. 2005). Given such remarkably low population estimates for the whole of *Europe*, it is clear that estimates of population declines in *Britain* based on artefacts such as those discussed above, are virtually meaningless. Humans were simply never common in the British landscape, so at best they are modelling presence, absence and time.

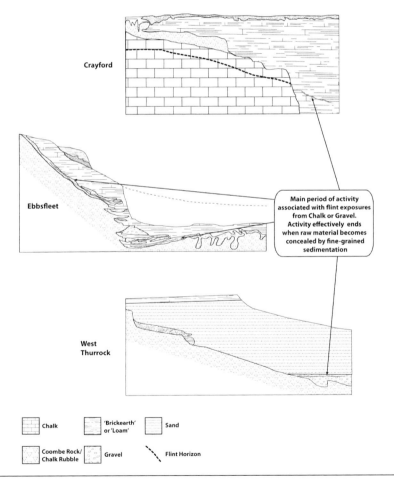

FIGURE 5.20
Geological sequences at Crayford, Ebbsfleet and West Thurrock, illustrating how hominin activity persisted only as long as a source of raw materials was available at each site.

Table 5.6 Population estimates for Pleistocene Britain based on different ethnographically observed densities (after Gamble 2002).

Ethnographic densities	Persons per km²	England 130,000 km²	Wales 20,000 km²	Scotland 78,000 km²	Total Population
High	0.09	11,700	1,800	7,020	20520
Low	0.05	6,500	1000	3,900	11400
Sparse	0.02	2,600	400	1,560	4560

Nevertheless, some of the larger assemblages may testify to larger gatherings, although not necessarily to larger populations. It has been suggested that some of the Neanderthal multiple kill sites on the continent, such as Mauran, acted as focal points for relatively large (seasonal) aggradations of people (Farizy and David 1992). This may be equally true of the lithic record, with the richest sites such as Purfleet and Baker's Hole suggesting either frequent repeat visits to key resources or exceptionally large gatherings (for Boxgrove in this light see also Chapter 3). If the latter, then Levallois technology might have operated just as much in the social world as in the functional one (Gamble 1999; *contra* Kohn and Mithen 1999).

The beginning of the Middle Palaeolithic was therefore not simply a technological change. Formally it can be seen as the lithic manifestation of a multifaceted transformation of hominin societies and their organisation at this time (White and Ashton 2003). What Ashton and Lewis (2002) saw as growing adaptation to cooler eastern-type environments, might better be viewed as range expansion enveloping and exploiting new opportunities and transformations. It should be recalled that EMP Britain may have had a more continental climate and towards the close of MIS7 had a fairly open environment. Thus, one should see the EMP landscape as unfamiliar from a lithic perspective. The increased mobility demanded by the unfolding mammoth steppe community could only be exploited by the integration of multilocal technology using lithic materials that were increasingly difficult to find.

Why Levallois and why MIS9

Until MIS9, Levallois had an ephemeral and sporadic occurrence within an otherwise fairly monotonous Lower Palaeolithic square dance, whereby whatever diversity is observed the net result is stasis (Chapter 3). For almost ~500 ka years lithic technology in Europe fluctuated without any lasting or directional change, always ending up at effectively the same common denominator – the handaxe. We have already rejected the notion that Levallois technology spread with *Homo helmei* as part of a late Middle Pleistocene dispersal event which, alongside a total absence of any supporting fossil evidence and consensus view that Neanderthals evolved *in situ* from earlier populations of *Homo heidelbergensis* (Stringer and Hublin 1999), is refuted by the temporal and spatial distribution of Mode 3 technologies through time. So the question remains: why Levallois and why now?

As argued above, Levallois technology was an immanent property of the Acheulean, occasionally used as a flaking option. In essence it restructured and elaborated existing technological systems, making them more flexible, versatile and multilocal. In other words, the Middle Palaeolithic did not see a major restructuring or development of hominin technology, but rather small and perhaps incremental intensifications of existing technologies in the context of wider behavioural changes in the landscape that also included the organisation of hunting. As White et al. (2011) observe, this fits with Kuhn's (2006) notion of rugged fitness landscapes. When depicted topographically, successful adaptations appear as peaks, unsuccessful ones as troughs and, during periods of change, populations tend to move towards adaptive positions nearest to the ones they already occupy and avoid crossing troughs to reach distant and advantageous peaks. Levallois is one such small step for mankind.

Rolland's (1999) perspective is sensible in this light. He saw the Lower-Middle Palaeolithic transition not as an *event* but a *process* involving protracted and piecemeal change in various technical, economic and social realms, stretching back to ~400 ka BP and earlier (Rolland 1999). These do not necessarily represent novel patterns of behaviour, but rather an intensification of much older practices; in effect the arrival of handaxe-making hominins throughout Europe around MIS15 actually marks the beginning of the transitional process. Non-technological behavioural changes similar but not identical to those in Europe are also seen at the Early Stone Age–Middle Stone Age boundary in Africa (Tryon 2006), again the culmination of long-term change. What we need to explain, then, is not why prepared core technologies are found sporadically on most continents from an early date – this is a function of a shared common technology in which they are plesiomorphic – but why they should become the dominant mode of production across different parts the Old World when they did.

The beginning of the Middle Palaeolithic in Europe coincided with the cooling limb of MIS9–8, a period that also saw the emergence of Mammoth Steppe communities spreading westwards from Beringia (Guthrie 1990; Gamble 1995a; Rolland 1999). In terms of animal communities this change would produce larger herds of widely and patchily distributed prey animals. Humans responded in a number of ways, outlined above. While Levallois technology becomes more visible in the record at this time, it is by no means universal and appears to be limited to a few isolated occurrences within an apparently Acheulean landscape. Nevertheless, the fact that it does now become more evident suggests that it was more widely used, in contrast to the isolated and ephemeral pre-MIS9 instances, which may simply represent moments of innovation that failed to spread beyond a single group or even individual.

Hosfield (2005) tentatively suggested that the higher populations postulated for MIS9 facilitated the necessary channels of cultural transmission for Levallois technology to develop and spread (cf. Shennan 2001). If we elaborate on this suggestion, one can imagine how larger populations ranging extensively over the newly matured grasslands to exploit the disparate biomass might have created the fertile cultural conditions and demographic networks through which cultural manipulations such as Levallois could spread (cf. Shennan 2001). However, following Dennell et al. (2011) who suggested that during most Middle Pleistocene glaciations hominins survived only in a few isolated refugia – in Iberia, the Italian Peninsula and the Balkans – the events of MIS9 cannot be seen as an instance of *in situ*, linear evolution leading to long-term technological change.

Rather it must be viewed over most of northern Europe as an example of arrested development that ended with the extinction of most populations during the MIS8 glacial maximum. It does, however, emphasise the fact that Levallois was an emergent property of the Acheulean. Moreover, if the Dennell refugia model is correct, then the continent-wide appearance of Levallois technology might be explained simply by its survival or development within one or more of these refugia (or even in western Asia) – where cultural transmission and social networks may have been equally fertile – followed by subsequent dispersal across Europe as hominins recolonised previously abandoned landscapes during the warming limb of MIS8–7.

A subtly different yet complementary situation can be seen in Africa. Marean and Assafa (2005) have suggested that the climatic cycles of cold–dry and warm–wet during the Middle Pleistocene in Africa produced a 'recurrent and amplifying cycle of vegetation change and habitability'. During cold–dry stages the present grasslands became increasingly arid, the forested areas in Equatorial Africa became more open, and reduced sea levels extended the coastal platforms. Vast areas of north and south Africa became inhospitable except near coasts and fluvial corridors, with the majority of populations concentrated in two areas: (1) the grassland and wooded grassland of Equatorial Africa, and (2) small, fragmented populations along coasts and other isolated refugia. So, climatic fluctuations caused African populations to shrink into the centre during cold and dry episodes and to swell into the extremities during warm, wet ones. East and central Africa thus acted as something of a culture pump, spreading novel technologies beyond their points of emergence. The MSA originated in one of these more densely populated areas, whence it spread during a later expansion phase, the pattern of expansion and contraction leaving a patchwork pattern in the record, with those abandoned areas showing sudden rupture, continuously occupied areas showing technological diversity and areas of transition blurred between the two. In other words, Mode 3 technologies, of which Levallois is one part, is a technology of convergence on a global scale predicated on a few founder populations in refugia and the exploitation of more open environment engendered by the higher biomass these supported.

A LAND FIT FOR . . . APPARENTLY NOBODY

While the meaning and validity of the patterns proposed by the 'Deserted Britain' model are open to question, the close of MIS7 does appear to have seen a total population collapse, with all hominin groups either abandoning Britain or suffering local extinction. Britain was subsequently a human wasteland for some 120,000 years with no evidence of hominin presence during the late Saalian glaciation (MIS6) the Ipswichian interglacial (MIS5e), the early Devensian stadials and interstadials (MIS5d–a) or the main Devensian glaciation (MIS4).

Previous claims for intensive hominin occupation during the Ipswichian and Early Devensian were largely founded on the Geological Society's simplified and compressed 1973 chronological framework (Mitchell et al. 1973). This recognised only two post-Anglian warm events and two cold events, resulting in genuine archaeological occurrences, now known on the basis of lithostratigraphy, biostratigraphy or direct dating to be of MIS7, MIS9 and even MIS3 date, being erroneously assigned to the Ipswichian. Moreover, while some sites genuinely belonging to this interval do contain artefacts or other claimed evidence for hominin presence, none of these has archaeological merit. In separate reviews, Ashton (2002) and Currant and Jacobi (2002) and Lewis et al. (2011) have systematically rejected all the claims for occupation of Britain during the period MIS 6–3, finding that artefacts from sediments of this age were generally in rolled condition and unlikely to be contemporaneous with the deposits in which they were found, had very uncertain provenances and associations or were not, in fact, anthropogenic at all (see Table 5.7).

Taphonomy presents some of the greatest challenges to understanding the settlement history of this, or any other period, as illustrated by the relatively large collections of handaxes and associated materials at two sites in the Upper Thames – the MIS6 Stanton Harcourt Gravel at Berinsford and Gravelly Guy (MacRae 1982, 1991; Scott and Buckingham 2001; see Text Box 5.6) and the MIS5a gravel at Cassington (Maddy et al. 1998; Hardaker 2001). The latter yielded over 100 artefacts, 90% of which were on quartzite, with a small flint (n = 8) and andesite (n = 1) component. All were in an abraded condition and all clearly derived from earlier occupation elsewhere; in fact the spatial distribution of artefacts on the different raw materials further suggested that they were introduced by different rivers, the flint derived from the west and transported by the Thames, the quartzites coming from the North Down and Cherwell/Rowell Brook tributary system (Hardaker 2001).

Dismissing such claims of occupation during this interval will of course only serve to perpetuate the abandonment model and we predict that the next decade will see an increased concern with demonstrating hominin presence during MIS5. As Roebroeks and Van Kolfschoten (1994, 500; Roebroeks 1996) remind us, absence of evidence is not evidence of absence, and negative evidence has rarely proved durable (as was amply illustrated by the demise of their own short-lived 'Short Chronology' for the earliest occupation of Europe). However, Britain is one of the most extensively researched areas of the Pleistocene world, boasting 150 years' history of archaeological endeavour and a large number of sites firmly attributed to the period concerned. Nothing convincing has yet been found to plug the hiatus and claims must be based on very firm foundations. The model certainly should not be rejected on the basis of recent OSL dates of ~100 ka BP (MIS5d–5b) from colluvial sediments from Kent. These dates – for two genuine flakes from the weathered top of a solifluction gravel at Dartford (Wenban-Smith et al. 2010) and a collection of material from an infilled doline at Westcliffe St Margarets, Kent (MJW, unpublished data), are not necessarily wrong, they just date the sediment, not the artefacts. As Kent has one of the richest Palaeolithic records in the country, and colluvial sediments are likely to pick up artefacts from older surfaces by entrainment or deflation, more robust evidence is required.

With such a large gap in the record, Britain has very little to contribute directly to our understanding of European Neanderthals for much of their 'classic' chronology. However, a small cottage industry has nonetheless emerged around explaining this hiatus, involving a variety of ecological, geographical and social factors operating over multiple climatic fluctuations of different magnitude. Three principle but largely overlapping hypotheses will be considered here in terms of the major explanations forwarded by specialists.

Table 5.7 Claimed human presence during MIS6 to MIS4 with reasons for their rejection. (After Schreve et al. 2011. Data principally taken from Ashton 2002 and Currant and Jacobi 2002, with additions.)

	Archaeology Present	Reason for rejection (see key)
MIS 6		
Taplow Gravel	stone artefacts	1
Stanton Harcourt Gravel	stone artefacts	1
Warwickshire Avon Terrace 4	stone artefacts	1
River Trent, Egginton Common Sands and Gravels	stone artefacts	1
MIS 5e		
Barrington, Cambridgeshire	small flint core	2
Cardo's Pit, Barrington	flake	2
Lavenham, Suffolk	stone artefacts	2
Newmarket Railway Station, Cambs	flints	3
East Mersea	flake	2
Victoria Cave	handaxe	4
Milton Hill Fissure	butchered and burnt bone	5
MIS 5d-a		
Kempton Park Gravel	stone artefacts	1
Cassington, Unit 1	stone artefacts	1
Bacon Hole, grey clay, silts and sands	split and polished bone	3
MIS 4		
Banwell Bone Cave	modified bone and antler	3
Banwell Bone Cave	human tooth	2 (modern)
Bosco's Den	split pebble	3
Steetley Wood Cave	human mandible	2 (modern)
Tornewton Cave, Reindeer Stratum	stone hammer	3
Windy Knoll	stone artefacts	4 (from Creswell)
River Trent, Beeston Gravel	stone artefacts	1
Kempton Park Gravel	stone artefacts	1

Key to Rejection codes: (1) Derived, abraded artefacts clearly not contemporary with deposits in which they were found and likely to have originated from older deposits in the region; (2) Finds of late or post-Pleistocene type and/or other evidence that they came from deposits of different age; (3) Non-anthropogenic; (4) Do not actually belong at the site to which they have been attributed (based on preservational state, archival records etc.); (5) Re-examination failed to verify.

Neanderthals were unable or unwilling to cope with the climatically severe or glacial environments of MIS6 and MIS4, suffering local extinction or abandoning Britain in favour of warmer refugia elsewhere.

Glacial climatic conditions and associated cold tundra environments during MIS6 and MIS4 comprise over 50% of the entire period of absence. The recurrent abandonment of Britain during hostile glacial maxima has been hypothesised for the entire Middle Pleistocene (White and Schreve 2000), and other than a few occasional forays into the west (e.g. Paviland, see Chapter 6) even *Homo sapiens* shunned Britain for much of the Upper Palaeolithic (MIS3 and MIS2) (Housley et al. 1997; Gamble et al. 2004; Pettitt 2008; Blockely et al.

2006). Other than a period of amelioration near to its beginning (MIS6.5), MIS6 appears to have seen some 50,000 years of sustained cold and was certainly one of the more severe glaciations of the past 500,000 years (Shackleton 1987). In The Netherlands MIS6 ice sheets extended further than those of MIS12, although evidence for a terrestrial MIS6 glaciation in Britain is more muted. Possible MIS6 glaciogenic deposits have been identified in the Welton Member at Welton-le-Wold (Bowen et al. 1986; Bowen 1999), the Sandy Till along the Durham and Northumberland Coasts (Francis 1974; Bowen 1999), the Bridlington Member of the East Riding of Yorkshire (Catt 1991) and the Briton's Lane Formation of north Norfolk (Hamblin et al. 2000; see Schreve et al. in press for longer descriptions of these sequences). None however have an unequivocal MIS6 date.

Despite the uncertain evidence for actual terrestrial ice, the flora and fauna from MIS6 deposits do testify to severe climates and harsh environments on mainland Britain (Schreve et al. in press). Although generally sparse, a fact that in itself suggests low biomass, mammalian faunas recovered from MIS6 deposits notably contain musk ox, lemming, woolly mammoth, woolly rhinoceros, a very small caballine horse, (Figure 5.21) a large form of northern vole, brown bear, bison, and reindeer (Schreve 1997; Schreve et al. 2011; Brandon and Sumbler 1991). These are all indicative of cold, open environments. Pollen from the Balderton sands and gravels between Newark and Lincoln also showed an essentially treeless environment dominated by open herbaceous vegetation (Brandon and Sumbler 1991) while beetles from this region indicate cold continental conditions, with mean July temperatures of about 10° C and January temperatures of –20° C.

The Early Devensian glaciation (MIS4), and cold sub-stages of MIS5d and MIS5b show similar conditions. Again, while evidence for ice-sheets on the British mainland is lacking (see Chapter 6), the faunal record is characterised by a suite of Arctic-adapted mammals, formally assigned to the Banwell Bone Cave MAZ (Currant and Jacobi 2001; Schreve et al. 2011; Table 5.8). This MAZ shows extremely low bio-diversity, dominated largely by bison and reindeer, with arctic hare, wolf, arctic fox, a large-bodied brown bear, wolverine and northern vole. The dating of the Banwell Bone Cave MAZ is somewhat uncertain but certainly post-dates the Ipswichian (MIS5e). Recent uranium-series dating of mammalian remains from Stump Cross Cavern, North Yorkshire, and Wood Quarry, Nottinghamshire, have produced ages of 79.2 ± 2.4 ka BP (SC-90–6A: Baker et al. 2007) and 66.8 ± 3.0 ka BP (Pike et al. 2005a) respectively, suggesting that these faunas and the associated arctic conditions prevailed throughout both late MIS5 and MIS4.

In northern France, occupational gaps are known from MIS6 and 4 despite the favourable preservational conditions that prevailed during the accumulation of loess and lack of subsequent glaciations in the area, suggesting a real absence of Neanderthals (Roebroeks et al. 2011, 115); a similar conclusion was reached by Lewis et al. (2011) after a critical review of potential MIS5 archaeological sites. A similar gap in occupation is apparent during MIS4 despite a faunal assemblage from Brean Down in Somerset including species absent from Britain during MIS5 and therefore implying dispersals over dry land, such as horse and the collared lemming *Dicrostonyx torquatus* (Currant and Jacobi 2011).

For at least parts of MIS6, MIS4 and the stadials of MIS5 we can thus infer polar desert

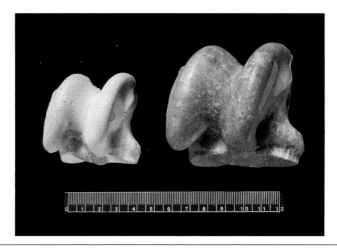

FIGURE 5.21
Major size differences of astragali between MIS6 caballine horse (left) and MIS7 caballine horse (right). (Courtesy of Danielle Schreve.)

and semi-barren tundra stretching across much of Britain. These conditions were almost certainly totally inhospitable to humans, making at least part of the hiatus in occupation readily explainable. However, extreme glacial environments only existed for c. 8% of the time (Gamble 1986, 1987, 1992), the majority representing either the cooling or warming limbs of climatic cycles during which arguably 'favoured' intermediate conditions prevailed. Evidence from Boxgrove (Chapter 3), Purfleet and Baker's Hole (above), among others, shows a recurring pattern of occupation throughout earlier warming and cooling limbs, leaving the failure of hominins to exploit transitional episodes of MIS6 and 4 somewhat intriguing.

Continued hominin absence from the more genial climates of MIS5 was caused by the rapid onset of island insularity at the end of MIS6

The sudden termination of MIS6 around 130,000 years ago resulted in mass melting of the global ice sheets and major sea-level rise, flooding of the Channel and North Sea basins and isolating Britain from Europe in as little as 3,000 years (Shackleton 1987). This 'rapid' event is suggested to have occurred too quickly for hominins to make the distance from their southern (Mediterranean) and eastern (steppe) refugia and were thus unable to re-enter Britain before it was cut off (Von Koenigswald 1992; Ashton 2002). Most sea-level estimates for MIS5c and 5a suggest that Britain was also an island during these periods (a critical depth of just 20 m produces the same pattern). During the stadials of MIS5d and 5b, sea levels were reduced (e.g. Shackleton 2000; Waelbroeck et al. 2002; Lea et al. 2002, Siddall et al. 2003; Cutler et al. 2003) but the different reconstructions vary enormously in their estimates of the magnitude of these events, which may have been as little as –10 m below msl or as much as –80 m. Most estimates appear to hover around ~–40 m below msl, but this excludes any error-ranges and represents the low-stand of a progressive process which, judging from the reconstruction graphs,

Table 5.8 Upper Pleistocene mammalian assemblage zones (after Currant and Jacobi 2001, 2010).

Taxon	Common name	Joint Mitnor MAZ (MIS 5e)	Bacon Hole MAZ (MIS5c)	Banwell Bone Cave MAZ (MIS5a?)	Brean Down MAZ (MIS4)	Pin Hole MAZ (MIS3)	Dimlington Stadial MAZ (MIS2)	Goughs Cave MAZ (Late MIS2)
Homo						*	*	*
Sorex minuteus	Pygmy shrew	*						
Sorex araneus	Eurasian common shrew	*						
Dicrostonyx torquatus	Collared lemming				*		*	
Lemmus lemmus	Norway lemming							*
Lepus timidus	Arctic hare	*		*	*	*		*
Spermophilus major	Red-checked souslik					*		
Microtus agrestis	Field vole	*	*					*
Microtus gregalis	Narrow-skulled vole				*			
Arvicola cantiana	Water vole	*	*					*
Clethrionomys glareolus	Bank vole	*	*					
Microtus oeconomus	Northern vole		*	*				*
Apodemus sylvaticus	Wood mouse	*	*					
Canis lupus	Wolf	*	*	*	*	*		*
Vulpes vulpes	Red fox	*	*	*	*	*	*	*
Vulpes (Alopex) lagopus	Arctic fox			*		*		*
Ursus arctos	Brown bear	*		* (large form)		*	*	*
Mustela erminea	Stoat					*		
Mustela putorius	Polecat					*		
Meles meles	Badger	*	*					

Gulo gulo	Wolverine				*			
Crocuta crocuta	Spotted hyaena	*		*	*			
Panthera leo	Lion	*		*	*	*		
Lynx lynx	Lynx							*
Palaeoloxodon antiquus	Straight-tusked elephant	*	*	*				
Mammuthus primigenius	Woolly mammoth		*		*	*	*	*
Equus ferus	Horse		*		*	*		*
Coelodonta antiquitatis	Woolly rhinoceros			*	*			
Stephanorhinus hemitoechus	Narrow-nosed rhinoceros	*	*					
Hippopotamus amphibius	Hippopotamus	*						
Cervus elaphus	Red deer	*	*		*	sp		*
Dama dama	Fallow deer	*						
Capreolus capreolus	Roe deer	*						
Megaloceros giganteus	Giant deer	*			*			
Rangifer tarandus	Reindeer		*	*	*	*		*
Ovibos moschatus	Musk ox					*		
Bison priscus	Bison	*	sp	*	*			
Bos primigenius	Aurochs							*
Saiga tatarica	Saiga antelope		*		*			*

only pertained for a very short period, perhaps only centuries (see Figure 5.4). Current and Jacobi (2011) note several key absences from later MIS5 faunas which they tentatively explain as species that could not swim particularly well or were unable to make the crossing over sea-ice, implying that sea levels remained a barrier throughout, other than at a few brief episodes when hominins do not appear to have been present in northern France. As such, Britain may have been effectively isolated from Europe for most of MIS5, with very limited windows of opportunity during periods of climatic deterioration when other barriers within the Channel and North Sea basins came into operation (see Chapter 7). The high sea levels reconstructed for parts of MIS6, as seen for example at Norton Farm (Bates et al. 2003), might also show that opportunities for access were limited throughout this period. Taken together, the avoidance of extremely cold environments during MIS6 and MIS4 and the effect of rapidly occurring, sustained (quasi-)insularity during MIS5, provide a simple and effective answer to this prolonged period of hominin absence. However, this did not prevent other animals from exploiting the 3,000 year 'window of opportunity' and successfully colonising the British landscape, including the European pond terrapin and hippopotamus, animals of two extreme sizes.

Absence during the Ipswichian Interglacial (MIS5e) reflects an absence of hominin populations from NW Europe as a whole, with Neanderthals avoiding fully temperate deciduous forests for a number of ecological and social reasons.

The Ipswichian interglacial was one of the warmest episodes of the last half a million years, with beetle faunas indicating mean July temperatures some 4° C above those in southern England at the present day (Coope 2000a). Pollen spectra indicate that dense, deciduous forest comprised largely of oak, maple, ash and hazel dominated the landscape, accompanied by some dry grassland and areas of disturbed ground (Gibbard 1985; Turner 2000). Frost-sensitive species such as holly, ivy and mistletoe indicate that winters were mild, mean January temperatures perhaps only dropping to 1–2° C. The Ipswichian mammalian fauna was also dominated by thermophilous species, including straight-tusked elephant, fallow deer, giant deer, narrow-nosed rhinoceros, wild boar, wood mouse, red deer, aurochs, and, famously, hippopotamus (Currant and Jacobi 1997).

Why was nobody at home in this Garden of Eden, not just in Britain, but north-west Europe as a whole? Gamble (1986, 1987) has suggested that the deciduous forests characteristic of interglacial maxima were not well-stocked larders affording easy pickings, but rather difficult places to make a living, with unevenly spaced plant resources in inedible or inconvenient packages and scattered, small groups of animals. Success in such environments depended upon complex solutions involving technical and planning skills, extended alliance networks and sophisticated channels of information exchange. Neanderthal societies were ill-equipped to deal with such conditions and much better suited to life on the open wooded grassland of the Mammoth Steppe (Guthrie 1990) which was ecologically more varied and provided localised access to a range of resources of different size and character (Gamble 1986, 1987). The spatial structure of these mosaics also rendered them more resilient and quick to recover from disruption through fire or overgrazing, as any local perturbations would be rapidly repaired, filled by resources in adjacent areas

(Gamble 1995). As discussed above, Ashton (2002; Lewis and Ashton 2002) suggests that hominins became progressively more specialised to open (and often cool) grassland environments throughout the Middle Pleistocene, so during the more recent forested inter-glacials (including MIS7 and 5e) the focus of occupation would have been in the east, the west only being colonised during cooler periods when more continental steppic conditions prevailed as far as the Atlantic Seaboard (Currant and Jacobi 2001)

In a broader context, then, the absence of hominins from Britain may simply reflect the fact that there were no hominin populations in adjacent areas of north-west Europe either, and thus no one to colonise this empty landscape. However, while the absence of hominins in Britain has not yet been seriously challenged, the wider pattern Gamble detected over 25 years ago may actually be an artefact of preservation bias and collection opportunity (Roebroeks et al. 1992; Speleers 2000; Roebroeks and Speleers 2002). The contexts where hominin occupation has been detected in central and Eastern Europe – thick tra-vertines and deep glacial landforms exposed over vast areas in huge quarries – are virtu-ally absent in the west (Speleers 2000). Fluvial deposits of relevant age are usually deeply buried under modern floodplains and accessed only through small exposures, while in Northern Germany, the Netherlands and Western Belgium the MIS5e deposits are overlain by marine deposits and generally unexposed. There is also the complication that many MIS5e landsurfaces, such as those on the raised beaches of northern France (Speleers 2000), underwent erosion during MIS5d. The recent report of a Last Interglacial Palaeo-lithic occupation site from tufa deposits at Caours in the Somme valley of northern France (Antoine et al. 2007) has furthermore demonstrated north-west Europe was successfully occupied during MIS5e and that suitable founder populations did exist. Perhaps hominins arrived just too late to make the crossing. Hominin presence is also well attested during the later phases of MIS5 including a number of locations across northern France (Cliquet et al. 2001; Locht and Antoine 2001) and Maastricht Site J in the Netherlands (Roebroeks et al. 1997) but by this time Britain was probably already an island.

It should also be noted that, in fact, very good evidence exists for Neanderthals suc-cessfully using densely forested environments during MIS5e at, for example, Lehringen, Gröbern and Taubach in Eastern Germany (Roebroeks et al. 1992; Bratlund 1999), where individual straight-tusked elephants, forest rhinoceroses and bears were hunted. Even if this were not the case, and there were social, ecological and behavioural reasons that Neanderthals avoided forests, it would appear that MIS5e environments were not blanket forests, but actually a mosaic of forested and open habitats just like any other interglacial (see Stuart 1995; Gao et al. 2000). Indeed, as Schreve et al. (2011) point out, the very presence of hippopotamus – the classic MIS5e indicator species for Britain and a heavyweight grazer – is indicative of open grassland, and plays an active role in creat-ing and maintaining such open environments, particularly in river valleys.

So, even though it may be less intellectually satisfying, it would appear that the rather prosaic factors of inhospitable cold and island status may be all that were required to explain the absence of hominins between ~180 and 60 ka BP. They would return only when these obstacles had been removed.

The Neanderthal steppe

Landscapes and human environments of the Late Middle Palaeolithic, ~60–35 ka BP[1]

INTRODUCTION: DISPERSED POPULATIONS OF THE NEANDERTHAL STEPPE

By ~180 ka BP Britain was a human desert once more. Early Neanderthals had abandoned the region, probably as part of a wider depopulation of north-west Europe. When they returned, they did so as part of a taxonomically rich mammoth-steppe faunal community, an adaptation to the grasslands of northern latitudes that characterised large parts of MIS3. Surviving on the Neanderthal steppe required the Neanderthals to be adept hunters, given that most available protein and many nutrients took animal form. Stable isotope analyses have, not surprisingly, shown ubiquitously high levels of meat protein in the Neanderthal diet (Bocherens et al. 1999; Richards 2007) and one might expect exceptionally low population densities for a Pleistocene hunter-gatherer dependent almost entirely upon meat for survival (Binford 2001). The British Late Middle Palaeolithic archaeological record certainly seems to reflect such small groups, present, probably intermittently, between ~60 ka and 42 ka BP.

THE LANDSCAPES, ENVIRONMENTS, AND RESOURCES OF BRITAIN AND DOGGERLAND

Marine Isotope Stage 3: a 'failed' interglacial

All Neanderthal activity in Upper Pleistocene Britain appears to fall within MIS3 (broadly ~59–25 ka BP; Figure 6.1). The structure of this highly complex period is thus critical to

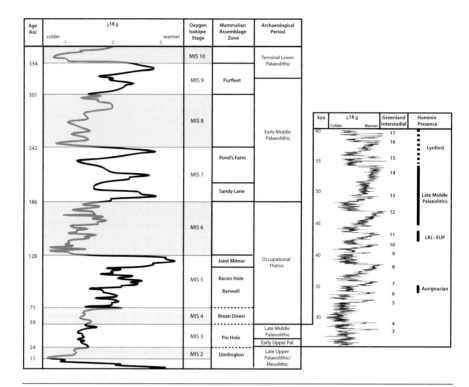

FIGURE 6.1

Chronology of the British Middle Palaeolithic and Early Upper Palaeolithic, shown relative to the Marine Ice oxygen isotope records, Mammalian Assemblage Zones, and Greenland interstadials. (Marine Isotope Curve and ages based on Indian Ocean Core MD900963, after Basinnot et al 1994; Mammalian Assemblage Zones after Schreve 2001 and Currant and Jacobi 2010; MIS3 isotopic curve and Greenland interstadials based on annual layer counting of the North-Grip Greenland ice core after Svenson et al. 2008.)

understanding the rhythm of 'classic' Neanderthal settlement of Britain and northern Europe. Climatically, MIS3 stands out from other 'warm' episodes such as MIS5 as it was relatively cold and extremely unstable (although, in fact, it appears that many other cycles may also show abrupt climatic oscillations of similar wavelength (Oppo et al. 1998; McManus et al. 1999), the signal being muted by the much greater depth and age of the sediments concerned). The Greenland Ice Cores (GRIP: Dansgaard et al. 1993; Bond et al. 1993; GISP2: Grootes et al. 1993; NGRIP: Anderson et al. 2006; Svensson et al. 2008) record 15 high-frequency, high-amplitude 'Dansgaard–Oeschger' (D–O) oscillations between ~60 ka BP and ~25 ka BP, each of ~500–2000 years duration. These typically consisted of an abrupt warming of ~5–8°C within 10–50 years, followed by a slower cooling (Figure 6.1 and Table 6.1). Thus, MIS3 was neither an interglacial nor a glacial, but a series of alternating warm and cold events occurring over millennial timescales (Hopkinson 2007).

Six distinct cold episodes – Heinrich events – are also registered in the marine sediment record by layers unusually rich in ice-rafted debris, the sediment trail of massive ice discharges from the North American Laurentide ice sheet into the North Atlantic and corresponding episodes of calving of the Scandinavian ice sheet (Heinrich 1988; Baumann et al. 1995; see Table 6.1). Such iceberg 'armadas' seem to have reduced sea-surface salinity and sea-surface temperature and thus affected the circulation of North Atlantic Deep Water, perhaps shutting it down entirely (Bond et al. 1993; Ganopolski and Rahmstorf 2001).

D-O events are relatively muted in the marine record due to their relatively short duration and are extremely difficult to detect in fragmentary terrestrial records. Where they are visible, however, they possess a good degree of synchrony between the ice core data and terrestrial proxies (Fletcher et al. 2010). A number of both colder and warmer events are recorded in the British Devensian/Upper Pleistocene record (Table 6.2) although actual climate change is evident at only two sites. At Kempton Park in Surrey a relatively warm climate gave way to colder conditions; by contrast a transition from cold to warm is seen at the Ismaili Centre, Kensington, London; together, therefore, these record at least three distinct climatic episodes (Table 6.2). Devensian coleoptera, however, reveal greater variation in reconstructed temperature estimates, suggesting that a number of different climatic episodes are recorded in the British geological data (see Table 6.3).

Table 6.1 Suggested ages (ka cal BP) of Heinrich events, Greenland stadials and Greenland interstadials. 'Consensus' represents, in our opinion, the most likely age of events and Greenland stadials and interstadials.

Event	NGRIP Svensson et al. 2008	Hemming 2004	Vidal et al. 1999	Sanchez-Goñi et al. 2000	Sanchez-Goñi et al. 2002	GRIP	Bond and Lotti 1995	Consensus
H3		~31 kyr		30.1–29.1 kyr			29 kyr	31–29 kyr
IS5	~32.5 kyr					32 kyr		32 kyr (Denekamp?)
IS6	~33.7 kyr					33.5 kyr		33.5 kyr
IS7	~35.4 kyr					36-35 kyr		36–35 kyr (Hengelo?)
IS8	~38.2 kyr					38–37 kyr		38–37 kyr (Hengelo?)
H4		38 kyr	35 kyr	39.8–38.5 kyr			37 kyr	40–37 kyr
IS9	~40.1 kyr			40.5–40 kyr		40 kyr		40.5–40 kyr
S?				40.6 kyr				40.6 kyr
IS10	~41.4 kyr			41.5–40.6 kyr				41.5–40.6 kyr
S?				41.5 kyr				41.5 kyr
IS11	~43.3 kyr			42.5–41.5 kyr				42.5–41.5 kyr
S?				43.1–42.5 kyr				43.1-42.5 kyr
IS12	~46.8 kyr			45.5–43.2 kyr				45.5–43.2 kyr (Moershooft? Upton Warren?)
H5		45 kyr	45 kyr	46.5–45.4 kyr				46–45 kyr
IS?								51–48 kyr (Glinde?)
IS?								58–54 kyr (Oerel?)
H6		~60 kyr						~60 kyr

Table 6.2 Multi-proxy climatic conditions at selected British Devensian sites. Asterisks indicate from which level particular proxies were found.

Site	Flora	Insects	Molluscs	References
Brandon, Warwickshire, Avon Terrace 2	Alpine-Arctic	–	1 or more arctic species	Shotton 1968, Kelly 1968
Four Ashes, West Midlands, Group 3	–	Cold	–	Morgan 1973
Ismaili Centre, Central London (ICa lower part of clayey silts*, Bed E2** and Lower Units D***)	Alpine Arctic*	Cold**	No obligate cold species*** (low species richness, n= 6)	Coope et al. 1997
Kempton Park, Surrey: Upper Samples	Alpine-Arctic	Cold	No obligate cold species	Gibbard et al. 1982
Latton, Wiltshire	Alpine-Arctic	–	–	Lewis et al. 2006
Oxbow open coal mine, West Yorkshire	Alpine-Arctic	–	–	Gaunt et al. 1970
Sandy, Ivel Valley, Bedfordshire	Alpine-Arctic	Cold	1 or more arctic species	Gao et al. 1998
Syston Terraces, Leicester	Alpine-Arctic	Cold	No obligate cold species (low species richness, n=7)	Bell et al. 1972
Whitemoor Haye	Alpine-Arctic	Cold	–	O'Brien unpublished 2006, Buteux et al. unpublished report
Upper Thames: Queensford, Sutton Courtenay*, Standlake	–	Cold	1 or more arctic species*	Briggs et al. 1985
Earith, Cambridgeshire, E4/E9	Temperate	Cold	–	Bell 1970
Earith, Cambridgeshire, E5/E7	Temperate	Warm	–	Bell 1970
Four Ashes, West Midlands, Group 2	–	Warm	–	Morgan 1973
Ismaili Centre, Central London (ICb upper part of clayey silts* and Bed C2**)	Temperate*	Warm**	–	Coope et al. 1997
Kempton Park, Lower Samples	–	Temperate	No obligate cold species	
Lynford, Norfolk	Temperate	Warm	1 or more arctic species	Boismier et al. 2003; Green in press, Coope in press, Keen in press
Marlow, Buckinghamshire	Temperate	–	–	Bell 1969
Upton Warren, Worcestershire	Temperate	Warm	1 or more arctic species	Coope et al. 1961

In the terrestrial record, five non-forested MIS3 interstadials have been identified from Dutch and German organic deposits, from oldest to youngest the Oerel, Glinde, Moershoofd/Moershoofd Complex, Hengelo and Denekamp interstadials (Zagwijn 1989; Behre 1992; see Table 6.1). It is important to note that these episodes were originally detected in localised and fragmentary peats and humic silts and are differentiated almost

Table 6.3 Published temperature estimates for Devensian beetle assemblages.

Site	Mean warmest month temperature (°C)	Mean coldest month temperature (°C)	MCR method	Reference
Colder beetle Assemblages				
Brandon	10	As low as –20	No	Coope 1968
Four Ashes Group 3	10	None given	No	Morgan 1973
Earith Bed E4 & E9	8	–22	Yes	Coope 2000
Ismaili Centre E2	7–11	–12 to –32	No	Coope et al. 1997
Ivel Valley	8–11	–10 to –28	Yes	Gao et al. 1998
Latton, Wiltshire	9–14	–14 to –26	Yes	Lewis et al. 2006
Oxbow	10	None given	No	Gaunt et al. 1970
Syston Terraces	10	–5 to –20	Yes	Bell et al. 1972
Whitemoor Haye	10	–15	Yes	Buteux et al. unpublished
Upper Thames Floodplain	10	None given	No	Briggs et al. 1985
Warmer beetle assemblages				
Earith Bed E5 & E7	16	–5	Yes	Coope 2000
Four Ashes Group 2	15–16	None given	No	Morgan 1973
Ismaili Centre C2 and South Face	16–18	–1 to –6	Yes	Coope et al. 1997
Lynford	12–14	<–10	Yes*	Coope in press
Upton Warren	16–18	–1 to –11	Yes	Coope 2002 (estimated from Figure 1)

* Because Lynford contains a high number of Asiatic species the MCR method showed no climatic space in which 90% of the species overlapped. The data presented represent Coope's most likely estimate.

entirely on the basis of radiocarbon dates; a full sequence has never been found in stratigraphical succession at any one site. As Hopkinson (2007) points out, using these data to make continental-scale correlations is fraught with difficulties, involving Europe-wide extrapolation of climatic histories from vegetation patterns that may relate entirely to localised factors. Such correlations further rely very heavily on radiocarbon dates that are not precise enough for the job and which may in fact be seriously inaccurate. The same certainly applies to attempted correlations with the ice core data where the error ranges of radiocarbon determinations are often longer than the duration of individual climatic episodes (Huntley and Allen 2003). Equally, while the coleoptera may provide a more sensitive record as they can respond far more rapidly to climatic change (Coope 2002), the data tend to derive from isolated pods of organic sediment that are difficult to seriate into a coherent biostratigraphy without recourse to the same radiocarbon dates. Because minimal, if any, vegetation succession is evident in any of these periods (other than during the Oerel), and none show any forest development, it has been suggested that they do not qualify as interstadials, but should be classed as intervals (Casper and Frund 2001). Recent studies of high resolution pollen records from terrestrial and marine sources, however, have shown that millennial-scale variability is evident in the vegetation record across Europe during the last glacial, the precise vegetational response in any given region being conditioned by the character of the D-O event, latitude and historical factors such as the nature of the preceding event, the location and size of refugia, migration lags, etc. (Fletcher et al. 2010). These findings are particularly relevant because they track climatic conditions impacting upon terrestrial ecosystems in regions immediately adjacent to Britain, although only one probable interstadial – the Upton Warren ~42–44 ka BP (Coope et al. 1961) – has so far been identified in the British sequence.

These problems associated with 'wiggle matching' mean that, despite the very high resolution data derived from the isotope record, the terrestrial sequence cannot be so tightly constrained and most signatures will remain drifting between one of a number of possible warm-cold events. For this reason, the approach adopted by the *Stage 3 Project* (Van Andel and Davies 2003) is perhaps the most useful present heuristic for conceptualising the British data. This divided the jagged, saw-toothed pattern of climatic fluctuations into three broad sub-phases:

1   an early mild phase ~59–43 ka BP

2   a period of climatic deterioration, ~42–37 ka BP, showing more tightly spaced clusters of cold D-O oscillations

3   a cold phases commencing ~37 ka BP during which conditions were similar to those of the last glacial maximum (MIS2).

AN IDEAL HUNTING GROUND BUT NOT A GREAT PLACE TO LIVE: LANDSCAPES AND ENVIRONMENTS OF MIS3 BRITAIN AND DOGGERLAND

A major growth of continental ice occurred in MIS4, with the margins of the Scandinavian ice sheet advancing south, south-east and south-west into Denmark, Poland and the continental shelf (Lowe and Walker 1997, 338). The presence of ice-rafted sediments in the Norwegian Sea indicates that the beginning of MIS3 saw a major collapse of the ice sheet (Baumann et al. 1995) and, for much of MIS3, global ice volume was reduced to local caps (Shackleton 1987; Arnold et al. 2002). Recent modelling reinforces the view that much of Scotland, and by implication the whole of the British Isles, was probably ice-free, with only local pockets of ice surviving in the western highlands and no glacial advance until after ~34 ka BP and the onset of MIS2 (Brown et al. 2007; Sejrup et al. 2009; Hubbard et al. 2009).

As a result of these fluctuations MIS4 sea levels dropped to a low of 100 m below modern sea level (bmsl), with a subsequent rise to -50m bmsl with the onset of MIS3 (Shackleton 2000; Waelbroeck et al. 2002). After ~50 ka BP, sea levels fluctuated between –60 m and –80 m bmsl, with a general downward trend through time, in which each successive rise failed to reach the levels of the previous high stand. Combining these sea levels with the bathymetry of the North Sea and the Channel (Keen 1995), it can be presumed that throughout the entirety of MIS4 and MIS3 Britain formed a western peninsula of the European landmass.

As noted above, large parts of what is now the eastern coast of Britain, from the Scottish borders in the north to Kent in the south, were connected to the vast plains lying under the central and southern North Sea, an area which Coles (1998) termed 'Doggerland'. Faunal remains and artefacts dredged up from the submerged sand and gravel banks forming shallows in the North Sea, such as Leman and Ower, Dogger and Brown (which during the Pleistocene formed the hills of Doggerland), have demonstrated that this was rich in herbivorous and avian resources, and from the point of view of hominin dispersals one can regard Britain as the upland peripheral remnant of an area originally three times its present size, drained by river systems ultimately linked to those of the continent. Predictably, the recovery of Middle Palaeolithic archaeology and Neanderthal remains from the North Sea (Glimmerveen et al. 2004; Verhart 2004; Hublin et al. 2009) has demonstrated that Neanderthals were active on Doggerland. From a demographic perspective, one should not view the vast area across which Britain was connected to the continent as a continuous area of potential population dispersal. The river valleys of Doggerland presumably afforded a number of easy opportunities for movement but, given the relatively sparse Middle Palaeolithic archaeology from adjacent areas of the European continent, such as Belgium and the Netherlands, it is likely that Neanderthal occupation of Doggerland was also sporadic and perhaps restricted to interstadials.

For much of the Pleistocene the present English Channel took the form of a fluvial basin occupied by a vast east–west flowing river and its tributaries – the Channel River or Fleuve Manche – with no evidence of marine transgression during MIS3 (Lagarde et al. 2003; see Figure 3.12). The modern submarine relief of this basin is incised with a complex network of channels which represent extensions of the river valleys of southern Britain, such as the Solent and Arun, and those of northern France, such as the Seine, Somme and Béthune (Gibbard and Lautridou 2003). During the low sea level of MIS3 these rivers drained into the Channel River, which in turn drained into the Atlantic Ocean around the −100 m isobar located to the south of modern Penzance, Cornwall. The Channel basin would have been dominated by the Channel River, a huge anastomosing system (possessing a network of linked streams) with valleys typically 10–20 km wide. A number of high-energy, multi-channelled or braided rivers flowed into this from northern France and southern Britain, many of which still exist, their lower reaches flooded by subsequent marine transgression but recognisable as submarine valley systems (Antoine et al. 2003). One such English tributary was the (now extinct) palaeo-Solent, which flowed south through the Hampshire basin, receiving tributary waters from the Arun, Test, Stour and Itchen before flowing southeastward to the east of the Isle of Wight, then turning south to flow into the Channel River some 10 km south of modern Portsmouth. The scale of the Channel River should not be underestimated; from at least 250 ka BP it carried drainage from almost half of western Europe, which included meltwater from the Alpine and northern European ice-sheets (Bourillet et al. 2003). Given its scale, the Channel River system likely constituted a major barrier to northwards dispersal by Neanderthals, as with the succeeding Upper Palaeolithic, dispersal into Britain coming instead from the east, that is, the Low Countries (Pettitt 2008). The nature of this barrier presumably varied over seasonal and millennial times-cales in terms of discharge variations and the location and size of braided reaches.

North of the Channel basin, southern England was high ground. Today, this is an erosional coastline characterised by cliffs that in many areas stretch up to 80 m high. Using the Hurd Deep as a referent (which is today at 200 m below mean sea level, that is −200 m bmsl), cliff and plateaux heights would have reached up to 800 m above modern sea level (amsl) for the area of Dartmoor. The character of these southern uplands differed from west to east: Cornwall, like Brittany, was a rugged landscape of steep slopes and short, southern-draining rivers incised into deep valleys which contrasts with the east where gently rolling, smooth slopes, dry valleys and long rivers gave way to the plains and hills of Doggerland.

Most British Middle Palaeolithic data derive from caves with frustratingly poor palaeoecological information (Table 6.4) while most of the environmental proxies we have for MIS3 derive from open-air sites which lack firmly associated archaeology (Table 6.2). All data from both types of site nevertheless show a remarkably consistent and persistent set of environmental conditions: species vary according to climate (see Text Boxes 6.1 and 6.2) but the structure of the British landscape remains unaltered despite the long periods of time and climatic fluctuations involved. Consequently, it is possible to provide a time-averaged, generic palaeoenvironmental reconstruction for MIS3 Britain and justifiable to use it. Obviously this is a coarse generalisation and does not account for the complex interplay of geography, geology, climate and meteorology that would vary across the 1,350 km length of Britain from Land's End, Cornwall to Dunnet Head, Caithness.

Lack of regional variation aside, all molluscan and insect faunas currently known indicate the ubiquity of an open, treeless environment, with taxa characteristic of rich grassland, and local patches of marsh, acid heath and bare, sandy ground (see Text Box 6.3). Using data from 27 insect assemblages, Coope (2002) suggested that in the warmest months temperatures averaged just ~10° C, with the coldest months seeing lows of −20 to −27° C. If these data represent only the warm D-O events such estimates are probably extremely conservative (Coope 2002, 405–6). One marked warm period was evident at ~42–44 ka BP, when temperatures approached modern values (for Coope representing the Upton Warren Interstadial), but the structure of the environments inferred from the insects remained the same (Coope et al. 1997; Coope 2002).

Pollen has been recovered from both cave and open-air sites and also indicates a landscape dominated by rich herbaceous grassland. Arboreal pollen counts are generally very low for MIS3 and while species such as pine, alder, spruce, birch and willow are sometimes present, they are usually considered as being very far-travelled, or representative of dwarf species. At Lynford, Norfolk, Boismier et al. (2003) proposed that localised patches of woodland probably existed away from the floodplain environments that are normally sampled for palaeoecological remains, although this has been disputed on the

Table 6.4 Key British Late Middle Palaeolithic sites.

Site	Open/Context Cave	No. of artefacts	Types of artefacts	Raw materials	Fauna	Palaeoecology	Dates	References	Notes
Aston Mills and Beckford, Hereford and Worcester	Open	Carrant Gravels, Terrace 2 of the Worcester Avon and Carrant Brook	c. 50	handaxes, knives, chopping tools, points, bifacial points, débitage	flint	Pin Hole MAZ	steppic grassland fauna open steppic molluscs arctic beetles treeless grassland flora	¹⁴C: 38,000+/ −700 although with unreliable archaeological association	Whitehead 1977	
Ash Tree Cave, Whitwell, Derbyshire	Cave	Stony Cave Earth	Min. 30	scrapers, handaxe thinning flakes, débitage, some conjoins	flint, clay ironstone, quartzite	Pin Hole MAZ	cool steppic grassland fauna	¹⁴C: 40,900 +/ −1,800 (OxA–4103)	Armstrong 1956, Dudley 1993, Hedges et al. 1994	Problems with assigning Armstrong's material to context.
Beedings, Pulborough, West Sussex	Open	Infilled fissures in the Greensand	82 retouched MP and EUP tools plus débitage	Leafpoints, endscrapers, burins, Kostenki knives, denticulates, débitage	flint			TL date of 31,100 +/−5,700 on fragment of burnt leafpoint	Jacobi 2006	
Coygan Cave, Laugharne, South Wales	Cave	Brown Cave Earth of Bed 4	5	3 handaxes, 2 flakes	igneous rocks	Pin Hole MAZ	cool steppic grassland fauna	¹⁴C: 38,684 +2713/ −2,024 (BM–449) Uranium-series on flowstone inclusions gives TPQ of 64 kya	Aldhouse-Green et al. 1995	
Creswell Crags, Nottinghamshire, Church Hole.	Cave	Mottled Cave Earth and Red Sand	c. 37	scrapers, denticulates, backed knives, choppers, discoidal cores, hammerstones, débitage	quartzite, flint	Pin Hole MAZ	cool steppic grassland fauna	No absolute dates	Dawkins 1877; Mello 1877; Jenkinson 1984; Coulson 1990; Current and Jacobi 2001	Dawkins (1877) also lists a number of unworked quartzite pebbles as part of the MP assemblage

Table 6.4 Continued

Site	Open/Cave	Context	No. of artefacts	Types of artefacts	Raw materials	Fauna	Palaeoecology	Dates	References	Notes
Creswell Crags, Derbyshire, Mother Grundy's Parlour	Cave	Yellow Cave Earth	c. 10	chopping tools, ?handaxe, débitage	quartzite	Pin Hole MAZ	cool steppic grassland fauna	No absolute dates	Mello 1877; Dawkins and Mello 1879; Armstrong 1925; Jenkinson 1984	Mello and Dawkins record an ironstone 'hache' and quartzite chips from red sandy cave earth, above Armstrong's Mousterian context
Creswell Crags, Derbyshire, Pin Hole Cave	Cave	Lower Cave Earth	c. 118 extant. Claims for 2 or 3 separate horizons.	handaxes, scrapers, choppers, cores, débitage, EUP leafpoint	quartzite, flint	Pin Hole MAZ	cool steppic grassland fauna	Dates for fauna and speleothem overlapping with the distribution of MP artefacts: 14 UF ^{14}C measurements spanning 40,650 +/−500 to 55,900 +/−4,000 (reindeer antler) (woolly rhino calcaneum). OxA-11980 (37760 ± 340) provides *terminus ante quem* for Middle Palaeolithic archaeology. ESR 39,000 +/−2,000 to 51,000 +/−8,000 TIMS youngest date of 63,700 +/−400 for speleothem clast providing *terminus post quem* for Middle Palaeolithic archaeology	Mello 1875, 1877; Armstrong 1925, 1931–2, Jenkinson 1984; Coulson 1990; Jacobi et al. 1998, 2006	The Mousterian assemblages have been reconstructed by various authors by replotting the finds according Armstrong's co-ordinates (depth into cave and depth below stalagmite floor) and raw material type

Site	Cave/Open	Deposit	Number	Artefact types	Raw material	MAZ	Environment/fauna	Dates	References	Notes
Creswell Crags, Derbyshire, Robin Hood Cave	Cave	Lower Cave Earth	c. 500, 88 extant	Handaxes, choppers, scrapers, cores, debitage	quartzite, ironstone, flint	Pin Hole MAZ	Cool steppic grassland fauna	No absolute dates	Dawkins 1876, 1877; Jenkinson 1984, Coulson 1990	Exact figures for the RHC assemblage are difficult to determine from Dawkins' published accounts (1876, 1877), and the assemblage is now impossible to reconstruct in its entirety due to lack of contextual information.
Fenstanston, Cambridgeshire, West End Farm and Woolpack Farm Pits, Middle Devensian Units 3–5	Open	Terrace 1/2 Gravels of the River Great Ouse	c. 30	Handaxe, debitage	flint	Pin Hole MAZ	cool steppic grassland fauna. Terrestrial molluscan assemblage showing open grassland environment but no extreme cold indicators Braided river sediments laid down under cold conditions with sparse vegetation	No absolute dates	Gao et al. 2000	The artefacts were recovered from West End Farm Pit, in beds considered laterally equivalent to those 100 m to the west at Woolpack studied by Gao et al. Other Middle Palaeolithic artefacts have been recovered from pits exploiting Terrace 1–2 gravel at Fen

Table 6.4 Continued

Site	Open/Context Cave	No. of artefacts	Types of artefacts	Raw materials	Fauna	Palaeoecology	Dates	References	Notes
									Drayton, Hemingford Grey, Earith, Willingham and Over, all within a 5–10 km radius of West End Farm
Fisherton Brick Pits, Salisbury, Wiltshire	Open	Low Terrace deposits of the River Nadder, 50 m OD, 4–5 m above modern floodplain	At least two	handaxes	flint	Pin Hole MAZ	Cool steppic grassland fauna. Mixed molluscan assemblage indicating a cool climate and open marshy environment Cool-cold ostracods	No absolute dates	Delair and Shackley 1978, Green et al. 1983	This area was exploited for brick-making from the 1700s, the first mammalian fauna being recorded the 1820s, the first artefact in 1870. From about 1870 brickmaking declined here as the pockets of brickearth were exhausted. Other artefacts may have gone unrecognised in the decades prior to 1859.

Site		Deposit	Number of artefacts	Artefact types	Raw material	Fauna zone	Environment	Dating	References	Notes
Hyaena Den, Wookey Hole, Somerset	Cave	Cave Earth	11 definitive (others typologically ambiguous) plus 2 EUP bladepoints	Handaxes, thinning flakes; EUP blade points	flint, greensand chert	Pin Hole MAZ	Cool steppic grassland fauna. Small pollen assemblage from upper sequence that has a questioned association with the MP assemblage. Indicates open grass-herb landscape with some trees	UF ^{14}C on faunal remains from the cave earth: 45,100 +/−1600 to 48,600 +/−1000 AMS ^{14}C date of 37,700 +/−1200 from horse bone at base of Upper Sequence (OxA-5703)	Dawkins, 1862, 1863, 1874; Balch 1914; Tratman et al. 1971; Jacobi and Hawkes 1993; Currant and Jacobi 2004; Jacobi et al. 2006;	Dawkins listed a total of 35 artefacts from Hyaena Den, while Tratman identified 42. Dawkins noted 4 discrete occurrences: a) within the bone bed; b) near the northern part of the entrance; c) 3–4 ft [0.9–1.2 m] below the bone bed resting on bedrock and; d) on a ledge at the rear of the cave
Kent's Cavern, Torquay, Devonshire	Cave	Loamy Cave Earth	>50, plus EUP industry	Handaxes, scrapers, cores, Levallois flakes, awls, debitage EUP leafpoints	flint, greens and chert	Pin Hole MAZ	Cool steppic grassland fauna. Small pollen assemblage showing cold open shrub grassland with small amount of tree pollen	UF ^{14}C on fauna associated with EUP materials provided a TAQ of 37,200 +/−550 for subjacent MP material. U-series on crystalline stalagmite beneath suggests TPQ of <74,000	McEnery, Pengelly and Ogilvie McEnery and Vivian 1859; Pengelly 1884; Campbell and Sampson 1971; Proctor 1994; Straw 1996; Jacobi et al. 2006	all recovered Middle Palaeolithic artefacts, but precisely how many is unclear because the original collection of >1400 pieces has been widely disbursed or lost. Campbell and Sampson identified 45 MP artefacts from

Table 6.4 Continued

Site	Open/Context Cave	No. of artefacts	Types of artefacts	Raw materials	Fauna	Palaeoecology	Dates	References	Notes
									the Pengelly and Ogilvie excavations, to which must be added the handaxes found by McEnery. Coulson is strongly critical of Campbell and Sampsons reconstructions. Rogers (1955) lists at least 42 typologically definitive MP artefacts in the extant collections.
Riverside Pit, Little Paxton, St Neots, Cambridgeshire	Open	Terrace 1–2 of the River Ouse, basal gravels of Bed 1	c. 210	handaxes, bifacial scrapers, cores, debitage (indicative of complete reduction sequences)	flint	Pin Hole MAZ	Cool steppic grassland fauna	No absolute dates	Tebbutt et al. 1927; Paterson and Tebbutt 1947; Wymer 1985; Letter from Tebbutt to RM Jacobi 28/12/1982	Contrary to the 1947 account, which states that the artefacts came from a unit above the fossiliferous bed, Tebbutt in his letter to Jacobi is clear that both actually came from the basal gravel.

Site		Context	Number	Lithics	Material	Fauna/MAZ	Environment	Dating	References	Notes
Little Cressingham & Saham Toney, Norfolk	Open	Pleistocene channel deposits under the floodplain of the River Blackwater	3	Handaxes, debitage	flint	none	A very small pollen assemblage ostensibly showed open grassland with betula & salix. Cool steppic grassland fauna. Insects indicative treeless steppic environment with annual T° range 13 to–10°C or below	No absolute dates	Lawson 1978; Wymer 1985; West et al. 1974	The deposits and Little Cressingham and Saham Toney have been correlated with Devensian deposits at Wretton which showed similar vegetation with a cold molluscan suite
Lynford Quarry, Mundford, Norfolk	Open	Fine grained organic palaeochannel deposits incised into the low terrace of the River Wissey	c. 2700	Handaxes, bifacial scrapers, scrapers, notches, hachoir, cores, debitage	flint	Pin Hole MAZ	Sub-arctic molluscan suite. Pollen and plant macrofossils show open grassland, with areas of march and acid heath, some tree pollen (10%). Sedimentology shows no micromorphological evidence for permafrost	OSL: 64,000±5000 – 67,000±5000	Boismier et al. 2003; Gamble and Boismier (eds, in press)	
Oldbury, Ightham, Kent	?	Slope deposits adjacent to a rock overhang	>500, both derived and fresh, some of doubtful provenance	Handaxes, partially bifacial handaxes, scrapers, naturally backed knives, notches denticulates, debitage,	Flint	None	–	No absolute dates	Harrison 1892; Collins and Collins 1970; Cook and Jacobi 1998	

Table 6.4 Continued

Site	Open/Context		No. of artefacts	Types of artefacts	Raw materials	Fauna	Palaeoecology	Dates	References	Notes
Picken's Hole, Compton Bishop, Somerset	Cave	Sandy Loam of Bed 3	c. 50	Cores, possible handaxe thinning flake, possible handaxe fragment, debitage (all <50mm)	Flint, carboniferous chert	Pin Hole MAZ	Cool steppic grassland fauna	¹⁴C: 34,365+2600/−1900 (BM-654) and 27,540 +/−2440 (BM − 2117) unreliable; new UF measurement of 40,200 ± 700 (OxA−10804).	Apsimon 1986. Jacobi 2007.	
Rhinoceros Hole, Wookey, Somerset	Cave	Compact clayey silts (Bed 6)	4	handaxe, thinning flakes	flint	Pin Hole MAZ	Cool steppic grassland fauna	Problematic U-Series dates on flowstone clasts produced a TPQ for entire sediment sequence of <50,000 BP	Balch 1914; Tratman et al. 1971; Tratman 1975; Hawkins and Tratman 1977; Proctor et al. 1996	
Uphill Quarry Caves, Weston-Super-Mare	Cave		Min. 10	Handaxe, naturally backed knife, thinning flakes	Flint	Pin Hole MAZ	Cool steppic grassland fauna	No absolute dates	Harrison 1977	
Windmill Cave, Brixham, Devon	Cave	Cave Earth	<5	Scrapers, debitage, EUP leafpoints	Flint	Pin Hole MAZ	Cool steppic grassland fauna	No absolute dates	Pengelly 1873	

MIDDLE DEVENSIAN FLORAS WITH TEMPERATE AFFINITIES: A CASE STUDY FROM EARITH, CAMBRIDGESHIRE

A number of Devensian sites have yielded an essentially temperate vegetation comprising a mixture of 'northern' (arctic and alpine) and 'southern' plants. Bell (1969) considered this type of flora to be perfectly typical for the Devensian, although he noted that earlier workers who viewed the 'ice age' as a singular hostile environment regarded them as problematical and attempted to explain away their deviant nature.

At Earith, Cambridgeshire, plant macrofossils and pollen were recovered from a number of sporadically occurring organic lenses within a 5 m sequence of sand and gravel, at least one lens being cut by a later ice wedge cast (Bell 1970). These deposits are part of the low Terrace 1–2 of the River Ouse, from which a number of uncontextualised later Middle Palaeolithic artefacts have since been recovered (examples are known from Earith, Somersham, Colne Fen, Fen Drayton, Over and Needingworth). The flora from Earith can be divided in into two groups: one comprising Plant Beds E4 and E9, the other Plant Beds E5 and E7. This was prompted by the climatic differences identified in the beetle fauna (Coope 2000b, see below), although Bell identified very few significant differences in the flora. Radiocarbon assays on plant debris from Plant Bed E7 yielded a finite date of 41,140 + 1,890/−1,530 (Birm-88).

The flora from Earith was dominated by taxa characteristic of open herbaceous grasslands, essentially similar to modern British examples, but with the noted mixture of northern and southern elements. Six species were considered to be distinctly northern in their modern day distributions, usually being associated with mountainous habitats: fringed sandwort (*Arenaria ciliata*), hoary whitlow-grass (*Draba incana*), Alpine bistort (*Polygonum viviparum*), purple saxifrage (*Saxifraga oppositifolia*), Alpine cinquefoil (*Potentilla crantzii*) and Alpine meadow-rue (*Thalactrum alpinum*). Several species of aquatic plants, however, including slender water-nymph (*Najas flexilis*) and opposite-leaved pondweed (*Groenlandia densa*), have a mean July temperature requirement of 16° C, while the bulrush *Scirpus* needs July temperatures of 13° C in order to fruit. Earith also produced a number of halophytic (salt tolerant) plants with sea milkwort (*Glaux maritima*), saltmarsh rush (*Juncus gerardii*) and sea arrowgrass (*Triglochin maritime*) being obligate halophytes. These species must have grown in damp, salty areas, according to Bell (1970) depressions where high winds caused rapid evaporation and general upward movement of ground water prevented leaching, resulting in high soil salinity.

Some tree pollen was present in Beds E5/E7, mostly pine and spruce. Bell (1970) commented that in cold environments with generally low pollen productivity, buoyant, far-travelling grains such as pine and spruce were often greatly exaggerated in importance. Indeed, it is generally assumed that values of <10% tree

Text Box 6.1

pollen certainly indicate long distance transport (Faegri and Iverson 1989), an assertion usually supported by data from the Canadian High Arctic, where 60% of the pollen rain was tree pollen that had been transported some 1,500 km from the nearest tree (Ritchie and Lichti-Fedorovitch 1967, although arboreal pollen was much less significant in the Low Arctic, suggesting circulation patterns play a significant role in pollen dispersal). Bell does, however, raise the imperative question of how far the vegetation of river environments reflect that of the whole countryside and whether the pollen and plant macrofossil record is showing us only those pioneering plants capable of rapidly colonising unstable braided environments.

Overall the vegetation from Earith was compared with the steppe vegetation of the Lena valley of Siberia which has a continental climate that satisfies both warm and cold requirements. This requires the northern elements to tolerate high summer temperatures and the southern elements winter cold, leading Bell (1969) to wonder whether the distribution of some plants reflects not climate but other excluding factors such as competition, ground conditions, human impact or just chance.

THE FLORAL LANDSCAPE OF AN MIS3 COLD EPISODE

Eight of the sites listed in Table 6.2 contain a suite of plants that have collectively been described as arctic floras (e.g. Gibbard et al. 1982; Gaunt et al. 1970; Kelly 1968), characterised by taxa that are today distributed in the arctic–alpine or northern montaine zones. This is perhaps what most early scholars would have expected from an ice age flora. There is overlap: a number of the northern elements are shared with the essentially temperate Devensian floras but this group of sites differs in having a *total absence* of any southern or thermophilous plants. These sites again show an open, steppic landscape with very limited, if any, evidence for trees.

These sequences are typified by dwarf birch (*Betula nana*) and dwarf willow (*Salix herbacea*) both of which are snow patch vegetation, the latter in particular favouring areas were snow falls well into the summer (Gaunt et al. 1970). Dwarf birch today reaches 78° N and, while it is found as far south as northern England and Scotland, it occurs there only at altitude (Gao et al. 1998). Typical alpine–arctic plants have been identified in all of these sites, including:

- Alpine cinquefoil (*Potentilla crantzii*) – Sandy, Oxbow, Syston, Kempton Park, Brandon
- Alpine meadowrue (*Thalictrum alpinum*) – Oxbow, Syston, Brandon
- Mountain avens (*Dryas octopetala*) – Whitemoor Haye, Latton

- Cloudberry (*Rubus chamaemorus*) – Latton
- Perennial wall rocket (*Diplotaxis tenuifolia*) – Sandy, Ismaili Centre, Kempton Park, Marlow
- Blue flax (*Linum perenne*) – Whitemoor Haye, Ismaili Centre, Syston, Kempton Park, Brandon
- Fringed sandwort (*Arenaria ciliata*) – Oxbow, Syston, Kempton Park, Brandon
- Alpine bistort (*Polygonum viviparum*) – Sandy, Syston, Brandon

Of these, mountain avens has a particular resonance for Palaeolithic archaeologists, as this plant is the type fossil for the three *Dryas* phases of the terminal Pleistocene (see Chapter 8). Significantly none of these sites have any directly or indirectly related archaeology, possibly suggesting that Neanderthals were absent from Britain during the colder stadials of MIS3. However, if Iverson's (1954) statement that sea thrift (*Armeria maritime),* which is found in many warmer and colder Devensian sites, demands winter temperature above –8° C, is correct, then the winters may not have been markedly colder than the essentially temperate group of sites.

WHY WAS MIS3 TREELESS?

One of the most remarkable facets of the MIS3 environment is that, regardless of climate, the overriding environmental signature from all available proxies shows that a treeless, herb-rich grassland prevailed throughout, with trees apparently absent even during periods when beetles and plant macrofossils indicate that conditions were perfectly favourable for their growth. It has been noted in the main text that some specialists now challenge this assumption but it is still worth discussing the possible explanations of this situation.

Contemporary factors

Coope (2002) suggested that humic- and nutrient-poor soils may have inhibited tree growth. Coleoptera from the period immediately preceding his key warm interlude (the so-called Upton Warren interstadial) are characteristic of arctic tundra conditions which were not conducive to soil formation. Given the high frequency of climatic change during MIS3, soils would not have had sufficient time to mature during the warm interstadials, leaving them depleted in nutrients and humus content. The absence of suitable mycorrhiza (fungi which live in symbiosis with plant roots by helping them to absorb nutrients) may also have inhibited tree growth. Coope dismisses the notion that steppic dryness was an inhibitive factor because the coleoptera and mollusca show the presence of permanent streams.

The presence of large herbivores may, additionally, have prevented the colonisation of trees and woodland regeneration simply by grazing young saplings as they emerged further south, thus preventing their spread northwards (Coope et al. 1961).

Historical factors

The high-frequency of climatic change could have created a situation in which a migration lag occurred, there simply not being enough time for trees to spread into north-west Europe from their southerly refugia before the onset of renewed cold conditions (Coope 2000b, 2002). Invertebrate faunas could react much faster and throughout MIS3 the biota may have been out of equilibrium, leaving a warm fauna within an open environment that mimics cold conditions.

Huntley and Allen (2003) questioned this appeal to long lag times. They argued that the duration of the warm events, particularly between ~60 and 40 ka BP, was sufficient to counteract any migration lag. Based on evidence from the early Holocene, European trees moved out of their refugia at rates of 0.2–2 km yr^{-1}, meaning that some taxa advanced 2,000 km in 1000 years. From a British point of view this is well within the range of most of the proposed glacial refugia: the western Balkans, Italy, the Alps, the Carpathians, upland and montaine regions of Spain, and, during certain periods, south-west France (Hopkinson 2007a and references therein). It is possible that these rates do not apply, however, and that MIS3 trees failed to reach the north due to a 'population lag' (Huntley and Allen 2003, 93), that is, if trees survived in such small and isolated pockets then there may have been no source population capable of generating the rates of reproduction, survival and spread needed for long distance dispersal to be successful. However, evidence from southern Europe reveals very rapid response rates to changing conditions implying that, whatever the size of the relict populations during glacials, they were sufficient to allow larger populations to build up quickly, producing in the space of a few centuries populations capable of rapid, large-scale dispersal (ibid.). Indeed, one of the key aspects in which Stage 3 Project's computer models deviated from the observed pattern was in tree cover, the models predicting larger tree populations than are actually apparent in the palaeoenvironmental record (Huntley and Allen 2003).

It is therefore unclear why the environment of MIS3 Britain was treeless, assuming, of course, that it truly was. It is important here to return to the fact that not all palaeoenvironmentalists or Palaeolithic archaeologists subscribe to this view and some now favour the presence of trees at least in a few cryptic refugia (Stewart and Lister 2001). From the perspective of Neanderthal survival strategies, the alternative is an unforgiving environment stocked with little other than stone as a material resource (White 2006). Some of the issues are discussed in the main text but it is important to reiterate that the range of habitats for which data exist are limited and fairly uniform. This situation is largely caused by the fact that almost all the open-air sites offer very small, localised and largely identical sampling opportunities, that is, the environs around small pools, ponds and backwaters on the braidplains of fast-

Text Box 6.3

Text Box 6.3

flowing rivers. Bell et al. (1972) noted that many of the plants evident in the Syston Terraces were examples of pioneer vegetation capable of rapidly colonising these ever-changing land surfaces within one season, which of course trees are not. The records available do not necessarily reflect what was happening on the watersheds or beyond and in many cases the main braided channels themselves are not even signalled in the environmental record. Hicks's (2006) review of apparently tree-less pollen profiles suggested that these may in fact relate either to the presence of few scattered trees, or climatic situations that were unfavourable for trees to produce pollen and which instead reproduced vegetatively (Koop 1987). In *Pinus*, the latter occurs when mean July temperatures do not exceed ~11° C, exactly the types of temperatures reconstructed for MIS3. Compounding the problem, tree pollen, where present, is usually dismissed as far travelled, supporting the idea of a treeless landscape simply by a particular reading of the data. Plant macrofossils in Devensian channel deposits, such as the tree birch twigs from flood debris at Cassington (Maddy et al. 1998), which provide the strongest hint that trees were present, are ignored or assumed to derive from older deposits. Given the tiny window offered by coleoptera and molluscs, and the paucity and problems of pollen, we actually have no idea what was happening in the rest of the landscape and should perhaps be a little more circumspect in reconstructing the ecology of MIS3 Britain and Doggerland from a few dozen organic ponds in river valleys.

basis of the molluscs and insects, neither of which show any obligate woodland species (D. Keen pers. comm. to MJW 2003).

The Hyaena Den at Wookey Hole, Somerset, and Kent's Cavern, Devon, have produced sparse pollen profiles from contexts associated with human occupation (Campbell in Tratman et al. 1971; Campbell and Sampson 1971). While the low counts (129 grains at Hyaena Den and 104 grains at Kent's Cavern) and complex dispersal, transport and deposition mechanisms within cave environments demand caution (Turner 1985; Coles et al. 1989), both are consistent with a cool, steppic, grassland environment. However, both sites also revealed up to 15% tree and woody shrub pollen. If accepted, these are most likely to reflect conditions directly outside the caves: experiments at Creswell Crags established that most pollen introduced into the caves was airborne, and that 90% of the airborne pollen was from taxa that grew within the gorge, often within 500 m, with all the tree species present being found within 5 km (Coles et al. 1989; Coles and Gilbertson 1994). Pollen adhering to a reindeer antler fragment excavated from the southwestern chamber of Robin Hood Cave was of grassland type, with rich herbaceous vegetation and some birch (*Betula* cf. *nana*, which has been equated with the Upton Warren Interstadial: Jenkinson et al. 1986), although the antler is undated and was stratigraphically associated with a human mandible of Holocene age. Thus the antler and pollen are not reliably placed within MIS3.

Most recently, Caseldine et al. (2008) examined pollen contained within speleothem deposits in British caves which were dated using high precision thermal ionisation mass spectrometric (TIMS) and ICP-MS Uranium-series dating (U-Th). Two samples from Lancaster Hole, Lancashire, were dated to MIS3. The limited pollen obtained produced an unexpected result, being dominated by tree species including pine, oak, alder and hazel and suggesting the presence of thermophilous trees. Some circumspection is required when evaluating these results and Caseldine et al. (2007) acknowledge that there are other taphonomic issues that need to be addressed. Most critically, the tree pollen may reflect the storage of grains in the groundwater system from the previous interglacial (or reworking into the groundwater), or result from long distance transport in cold periods with minimal vegetation. These possibilities, though, were all considered and strongly rejected on the basis of excellent preservation demonstrating rapid transport and incorporation into the speleothem, the lack of speleothem growth during extremely cold periods and the absence of modern day analogues for flowstones being fed by water with residence-times measuring thousands of years.

These results clearly challenge the view derived from molluscs and insects of a completely treeless environment, leading to the suspicion that, by concentrating almost exclusively on data from microhabitats in river floodplain/braidplain situations, our environmental reconstructions have missed a critical element of microclimatic variation within the British Pleistocene. This supports the view expressed by Campbell (1977), greatly elaborated by Stewart and Lister (2001), that trees survived in sheltered locations that provided isolated 'cryptic refugia', such as the southern flanks of Mendip and the Ilsham Valley, and protected gorges like Creswell Crags (Derbyshire/Nottinghamshire). In this regard, it may be no coincidence that these areas also saw perhaps the greatest incidence of Neanderthal settlement in Britain, with Neanderthals using them as relatively resource rich locales from which to conduct logistically organised activities.

The Stage 3 Project reconstructions

The site-derived proxies discussed above can be augmented by the palaeoclimatic models generated by the Stage 3 Project (Van Andel and Davies 2003). This project, which involved 34 specialists in Pleistocene archaeology, palaeontology, geology and ecology, undertook high-resolution computer simulations of the palaeoclimate of MIS3 on a European scale. As the models were generated using input-data derived from almost all dated sites across Europe, the projections yield familiar results, although a number of variables not directly evident in the terrestrial record could also be reconstructed. While the project succeeded in modelling a 'typical' warm event, however, it failed to generate an adequate model for any cold event of MIS3, simulations for which generally indicated conditions far warmer than the actual data indicate. To overcome this problem, the MIS3 project substituted data from MIS2 (Barron et al. 2003). These cold event simulations are excluded from consideration here, because during MIS2 ice advanced over mainland Britain, reaching as far as Lincolnshire in the east and South Wales in the west, with the unglaciated areas subject to severe periglacial conditions, with greater aridity, loess formation (wind-blown silt deposits) and large areas subject to continuous permafrost (cf. Ballentyne and Harris 1994; Lowe and Walker 1997, 108–9). As noted above, MIS3 saw no continental ice on mainland Britain. Moreover, while some MIS3 cold events are isotopically heavier and perhaps therefore more severe than parts of MIS2, the latter also differed in having far fewer and more attenuated climatic fluctuations, which suggests it was a period of more sustained cold. In sum, MIS2 is not a good analogy for MIS3 and hence only the warm event modelling is used here, with the obvious extrapolation that cold events would have been significantly harsher (Text Box 6.4).

The Stage 3 Project warm event simulation was based on conditions ~45 ka BP, which was taken to represent all such events between ~60 and 42 ka BP. Given the apparent gradual deterioration throughout MIS3, these were probably the most favourable conditions Neanderthals would have experienced during this period. Modelled temperatures show average warm event values at least 7–10° C lower than present. Summer temperatures would rarely

AN MIS3 COLD INTERVAL AT SANDY, BEDFORDSHIRE

The organic lenses in the fluvial sands and gravel of Unit 2 at Sandy, Bedfordshire, were interpreted as being deposited in pools on the braidplain of the River Ouse, with slow or still water conditions (Gao et al. 1998). The pools at Sandy were only sparsely vegetated, with only pondweed and mare's tail represented by the plant macrofossils, although other cold-climate sites had a more diverse aquatic and emergent-aquatic vegetation, including water milfoil, bogbean and bulrush as well as several species of pondweed. Edible species including perennial wall rocket and silverweed were also present on patches of bare ground, possibly around the river bank.

Whether the pools at Sandy were permanent or seasonal is unclear. The molluscs, which included the European stream valvata *Valvata picinalis*, the smooth ramshorn snail *Gyraulus laevis* and wandering snail *Lymnaea peregra,* would appear to show permanent water, although the beetles reveal little evidence of permanent water. The dominant water beetles present are amongst the least aquatic (the inaptly named *Helophorus aquaticus*), preferring instead swampy grassland, while the others usually inhabit shallow ephemeral puddles (e.g. *H. sibericus* and *H. grandis*; Gao et al. 1998, 133). Occasional drying-up of these stadial water bodies is also suggested by the regular occurrence of halophytic plants and animals at sites such as Brandon (Coope 1968), Latton (Lewis et al. 2006) and Earith (Bell 1970), although some may have been more permanent. This may suggest that greater aridity and stronger winds made these habitats more precarious. Ice wedge casts and patterned ground have also been noted from Brandon, Earith and other sites reflecting periglacial activity and suggest that during the stadial events, the ponded environments and surrounding ground would have been frozen for much of the year, providing very restricted resources for animals or hominins if they were present. There are hints of faster channels flowing nearby, as the beetle assemblage contained the ground beetles *Bembidion fellmanni* and *B. hastii*, which are characteristic of the gravelly margins of running water courses, where they live on the dead insects washed up among the stones (cf. Coope 1968).

Text Box 6.4

Like their interstadial counterparts, these cold climate pools were immediately surrounded by marshy ground, where sedges, rushes and reeds grew, accompanied by the phytophagous weevil *Notaris bimaculatus* and several species of the leaf beetle *Donacia* that fed on them. Several marsh snails, including the button ramshorn snail *Anusis leucostoma*, the dwarf pond snail *Lymnaea trunculata,* and the small amber snail *Succinea oblonga,* also exploited these habitats. Areas of drier grassland were also close by, on which grew many of the open ground arctic plants identified above, including hoary whitlowgrass, Alpine bistort, Alpine cinquefoil and Alpine meadowrue. Similar environments are indicated by the molluscs *Pupilla muscorum* and *Columella columella* and by the beetles *Amara alpina* and *A. quensili* which are often found together on dry alpine heath. Many of the herbaceous plants require base-rich conditions, showing that the soil conditions here were rather acidic, an observation that can be extended to several other sites where these plants grew. Birch and Willow were also found but again these were exclusively the cold-climate, dwarf forms including *Betula nana* and *Salix herbacea*. Osier (*Salix viminalis*) can today grow to tree height but this is doubted for the Devensian specimens which have smaller leaves (Bell 1970).

have exceeded 8–12° C, while winter temperatures would fall to –8° C and far lower (Barron et al. 2003). Winters would have been long and the spring thaw late; temperatures are unlikely to have exceeded zero until April had passed (Barron et al. 2003, 70). These surface temperatures would have been further reduced by wind chill. Atmospheric circulation models projected strong westerly airflow over Europe, creating strong zonal winds north of the transverse European mountain ranges (Barron et al. 2003, 63). In Britain, wind-chill reduced the effective temperatures to at least 8° C in summer and at least –13° C in winter (Aiello and Wheeler 2003, 59) and these values are probably underestimates (cf. Coope 2002).

In terms of precipitation, the MIS3 project found that the period was probably not extremely dry and arid, in concord with the direct proxies above. Based on projections of sea surface temperatures, sea-ice coverage and atmospheric circulation patterns, Barron et al. (2003, 68) concluded that onshore airflow over northwestern Europe may have delivered annual precipitation levels similar to those of today, although summers may have been drier. During the long winters on the Neanderthal steppe much of the precipitation would have fallen as snow. Snow cover probably lasted between 3 and 6 months each year, reaching depths of 10–50 cm, although again drifting is presumed to have left much of the landscape with a minimal cover. However, the models also suggest that substantial winter snowfall was preceded by heavy autumn rains (Barron et al. 2003, 72), falling just as temperatures began to drop. Given this level of precipitation, cloud cover, precluding much in the way of direct heating by insolation, was presumably another key factor in a grey, cold and wet landscape.

The steppe tundra environments that Neanderthals encountered when they returned to Britain during MIS3 thus differed greatly from the temperate woodland and grassland mosaic their predecessors had abandoned over 100,000 years earlier. Previously, Devensian landscapes have been characterised as arctic tundra (e.g. Bell 1970), but they are actually better described as part of the so-called 'mammoth steppe' (Guthrie 1982, 1984, 1990). This type of environment has no modern analogue, differing from modern Eurasian steppes by virtue of the unusual mixture of species living in the same communities, although in this period it was widespread across northern latitudes from the Atlantic seaboard into Eurasia and across Beringia into continental North America (Guthrie 1990). The name was coined to capture the two key essences: a northern, cold-tolerant fauna, and a low, rich sward; in basic terms it can be described as a rich xeric grassland with a diverse array of herbaceous plants capable of sustaining large herds of heavy-weight grazers such as mammoth, woolly rhinoceros, horse and bison (Guthrie 1990, 270). As Guthrie states (1990, 227), the Mammoth Steppe was a great hunting ground but not an ideal place for people to live.

Unlike modern plant communities, which Guthrie characterises as zoned or striped, those of the Mammoth Steppe are described as being similar to the chequered pattern of tartan or plaid textiles. Vegetation thus occurred in more fine-grained mosaics, providing a diverse range of resources in close proximity. This rendered the Mammoth Steppe more resilient to disruption through fire, storms and overgrazing because any ruptures in the fabric could be quickly recolonised and repaired by organisms from adjacent patches (Gamble 1995a). Hominins and other animals could also cope easily with such disruptions by simply migrating short distances to another part of their range. Gamble (1995a) sees these concepts as critical to an understanding of the dynamics of hominin interactions with their environment.

MIS3 faunal communities: the Neanderthal steppe

The MIS3 mammalian fauna has been designated the Pin Hole Mammalian Assemblage Zone (MAZ; Currant and Jacobi 1997, 2001, 2011; see Table 6.5). This faunal suite, characterised by mammoth, horse, woolly rhinoceros, bison and reindeer, is considered typical of most assemblages of this age over much of central Asia north of the Himalayas (Currant and Jacobi 2001, 1712). Although some browsers are present, none is considered an obligate forest species, and the whole has again been taken to show the dominance of rich, open grasslands with abundant but low quality/high fibre graze (i.e. the Mammoth Steppe of Guthrie 1990). The 'Pin Hole' type fauna is classically described as having a curious mixture of ostensibly warm-adapted (giant deer, red deer) and cold-adapted animals (woolly rhinoceros, reindeer, arctic fox, arctic hare, lemming), both apparently occurring in warmer and colder events. Some species, such as the souslik (ground squirrel), today have an eastern distribution (Stewart 2005). This admixture of warm-cold and eastern faunas has been argued to indicate the existence of highly continental conditions as far west as the Atlantic seaboard, with warmish summers but very harsh winters (Currant and Jacobi 2001). It should be remembered that this MAZ represents a formal biostratigraphic zone, not a reconstruction of precise faunal communities, which were presumably geographically varied and continuously remodelled in response to the highly unstable climates of the period. The mixed nature of the fauna may thus reflect seasonal variations within the faunal communities or overlapping tolerances. However, they might also in part reflect rapid faunal turnovers induced by the millennial-scale climatic fluctuations of MIS3, these turnovers being rendered archaeologically

Table 6.5 Taxa attributable to the MIS3 Pin Hole Mammalian Assemblage Zone (Currant and Jacobi 1997, 2001, 2011)

Taxon	Common Name	Taxon	Common name
Insectivora		**Perissodactyla**	
Sorex sp.	Shrew	*Equus ferus*	Wild horse
Rodentia		*Coelodonta antiquitatis*	Woolly rhino
Apodimus sylvaticus	Field mouse	**Proboscidae**	
Arvicola terrestris	Northern water vole	*Mammuthus primigenius*	Mammoth
Microtus agrestris	Field vole	**Carnivora**	
Microtus gregalis	Narrow-headed vole	*Panthera leo*	Lion
Microtus gregaloides	Vole	*Felis sylvestris*	Wild cat
Microtus nivalis	Snow vole	*Crocuta crocuta*	Spotted hyaena
Microtus oeconomus	Northern vole	*Canis lupus*	Wolf
Clethrionomys glareolus	Bank vole	*Machairodus latidens*	Sabre tooth tiger
Lemmus lemmus	Norway lemming	*Vulpes vulpes*	Red fox
Dicrostonyx hintoni	Lemming	*Alopex lagopus*	Arctic fox
Dicrostonyx torquatus	Collared lemming	*Ursus arctos*	Brown bear
Spermophilus major/ Citellus superciliosus	Red-cheeked souslik	*Ursus spelaea*	Cave bear
Lagomorpha		*Mustela ermine*	Stoat
Lepus timidus	Arctic hare	*Mustela nivalis/ermina*	Weasel/stoat
Ochotona pusilla	Steppe pika	*Mustela putorius*	Polecat
Artiodactyla		*Mustela putorius robusta/ M. eversmanni*	Large polecat
Cervus elaphus	Red deer	*Martes sp.*	Marten
Rangifer tarandus	Reindeer	*Gulo gulo*	Wolverine
Megaloceros giganteus	Giant deer		
Bos sp./B. primigenius	Aurochs		
Bison sp./B. priscus	Bison		

invisible by the stratigraphical and chronometric resolution available. More prosaically it may just reflect stratigraphical uncertainties associated with old excavations. One way in which this may be resolved is through the use of oxygen isotope analysis to determine whether the different elements within the Pin Hole MAZ are really occupying the same climatic phase, data which is not currently available.

The mega-herbivores that lived on the Mammoth Steppe probably played a key role in maintaining its nature by browsing, trampling, digging, and fertilising, thereby symbiotically acting as 'ecosystem engineers' for the very environment that supported them (Haynes 1991; Owen-Smith 1988). A suite of small mammals have similar grassland associations, notably the northern vole, field vole, hare, steppe pika, shrew, lemming and souslik. Lion and hyaena are also predominantly open grassland predators. In temperate contexts red deer are often considered to be browsers but actually exhibit significant phenotypic plasticity; their rumens develop according to the dominant vegetation available during growth so they can easily cope with browse or graze (Lister 2004). Its presence on this steppic environment is therefore not an insurmountable anomaly although its distribution may hint at greater micro-habitat variation (Stewart and Lister 2001).

In their study of the Mammoth Steppe faunas of unglaciated areas of Upper Pleistocene Siberia, Vereshchagin and Baryshnikov (1982) summarised the ecology of several species of relevance to MIS3 Britain. The dietary preferences of these species (Table 6.6), inferred directly from the gut contents of frozen carcasses and plant debris recovered from tooth alveoli or indirectly from modern living examples, also indicates the presence of a rich herbaceous grassland. The climate was clearly much colder than at present, but also probably drier and more continental, as the thick, skirt-like coats of mammoth, rhinoceros, bison and possibly horse would have been susceptible to 'lethal wetting and freezing' in cold, damp maritime climates (Vereshchagin and Baryshnikov 1982, 277). Snow cover was therefore probably quite thin, with strong winter winds blowing areas clear, contrary to the popular image of ice age mammals wading through deep blanket snow cover. Critically, this would have made dead winter vegetation accessible; according to Guthrie (1990) it was the availability of winter forage, and not cold temperatures, that formed the principal stress factor for the large herbivores of the Mammoth Steppe. Among the fauna only reindeer are truly adapted to snow, their broad feet and long legs allowing them to dig down to reach buried vegetation. The relatively short-legged, high-foot loaded bison, however, are not suited to snow movement or browsing although for short periods can tolerate snow depths of 60–70 cm, which they can sweep away with their heads (Guthrie 1990, 202).[2] The bevelled wear patterns seen on woolly rhinoceros horns and flattening of the underside of mammoth tusks also result from head-swipe movements in contact with the ground and may in part relate to sweeping away snow as well as other sexual and/or aggressive gesturing or simply accidental contact (cf. Guthrie 1990, 36; Lister and Bahn 1995). The presence of souslik and arctic fox, both of which dig underground burrows, also suggests that permafrost was absent for some of the time.

For the human populations of MIS3, Britain would have presented a rich hunting ground, and most of the megafaunal taxa present at this time are known to have been hunted by Neanderthals in adjacent areas of Europe (Gaudzinski 1996, 1999b; Gaudzinski and Roebroeks 2000). As rich as it undoubtedly was, however, Guthrie (1990) doubted whether the Mammoth Steppe played host to the density of game seen on the African or Asian savannah.

Fellow predators: Neanderthals and hyaenas

One characteristic of MIS3 Britain is the abundance of hyaenas (A. Currant pers. comm.). Radiocarbon dates for MIS3 British hyaenas are presented in Table 6.7. With few exceptions, in calibrated terms measurements predate 33 ka BP and stretch back beyond 45 ka BP. Three measurements on hyaenas from Creswell Crags originally appeared to show the persistence of hyaenas as late as ~28 ka BP, although recent re-measurement of these samples using ultrafiltration pretreatment has shown the original measurements to be gross underestimates, their age now in excess of 44 ka BP. It is therefore likely that most of the non-ultrafiltrated hyaena samples noted in Table 6.7 are also

Table 6.6 Dietary preferences of the mammoth steppe fauna (data compiled from Vereshchagin and Baryshnikov 1982; Guthrie 1990; note that Guthrie has questioned whether the gut contents of some of the frozen carcasses represent that animals normal diet or whether some indicate starving animals eating largely indigestible items or simply items ingested accidentally (such as twigs) alongside the target food)

Taxon	Dietary preferences	Habitat preferences
Mammoth	Frozen mammoths have been found to have eaten sedges, grasses and mosses, as well as woody plants and shrubs such as dwarf birch, willow and heathers. In winter many probably relied on dried grasses, supplemented by shrubs and twigs. It is estimated that a mammoth would have required 200–300 kg of forage daily.	Open landscapes of rich meadows and steppes. Mammoths may have migrated to different winter–summer feeding grounds, similar to modern African elephants.
Horse	Frozen examples have been found to have eaten up to 90% herbaceous plants, mostly grasses and sedges, plus some shrubs (dwarf birch, willow) and mosses.	Open grassland, tolerating some open woodland. Can cope with light snow cover of 50–60 cm.
Woolly rhinoceros	Grasses, cottongrass, sedges and asteraceae have been found in frozen specimens, while compressed woody remains of plants like alder, willow and birch have been recovered from teeth.	Cold steppe with only shallow winter snow cover.
Bison	Recent bison are predominantly grazers, feeding on coarse grasses.	Open steppe with low winter snow cover not exceeding 60–70 cm. May have undertaken massive seasonal migrations.
Reindeer	Grasses and semi-shrubs in summer and lichen which they dig from beneath snow in winter. Occasionally have been known to feed on small mammals and birds' eggs.	Open tundra and sparse coniferous forests. Reindeer undertake long winter migrations. Able to cope with greater snow depths than other Mammoth Steppe animals.
Souslik	Modern souslik feed on grasses, berries, mushrooms, mosses, insects and meat.	Lowland tundra and forest-tundra, found in areas where they are able to excavate their burrows and go into winter hibernation.
Collared lemming	Modern collared lemming in Siberia feed on shoots, leaves and bark of dwarf willow as well as cloudberry and crowberry.	Prefer dry, elevated parts of the tundra where they excavate their tunnels under stones and in hummocks.
True lemming	Modern animals predominantly feed on sedges, grasses and moss. In summer they also eat berries, mushrooms and shrubby plants.	Typical animals of the tundra, preferring swampy areas with herbaceous plants. They excavate shallow tunnels into dry, unfrozen ground and in winter build nests in snow.
Narrow-skulled vole	Legumes and grasses are their preferred diet, but in arctic conditions will eat sedges, cottongrass and willow. They store grass for the winter.	Open landscape ranging from semi-arid steppe, lowland tundra and alpine meadows. Also found in meadow glades in forested areas. In winter they excavate tunnel complexes at ground level beneath the snow.
Arctic fox	The arctic fox is an omnivore although its principal diet consists of lemmings and voles.	Open tundra, in winter may move north or south to polar arctic or southern forest zones. Poorly adapted to movement over deep snow.

Table 6.7 Direct and indirect AMS radiocarbon dates for MIS3 hyaenas in Britain. We have included two measurements from Ireland, as it presumably received its faunas from Britain.

Site	Identification	Laboratory number	Measurement	Range (2σ) uncal BP	Reference
Soldier's Hole, Cheddar	*Crocuta crocuta* atlas	OxA-10899	>36,800 BP	>36,800 BP	Jacobi 2007
Ash Tree Cave, Derbyshire	*Crocuta crocuta* right P4	OxA-5798	25,660 ± 380 BP	26,420– 24, 900 BP	Hedges et al. 1996. Possibly an underestimate (Higham et al. 2006).
Pin Hole, Creswell Crags	*Crocuta crocuta* partial left mandible	OxA-1448	42,200 ± 3,000 BP	48,200– 36, 200 BP	Hedges et al. 1989.
Pin Hole, Creswell Crags	*Crocuta crocuta* right pre-maxilla of neonate	OxA-4754	37,800 ± 1,600 BP	41,000– 34, 600 BP	Hedges et al. 1996.
Pin Hole, Creswell Crags	*Crocuta crocuta* left 3rd metacarpal	OxA-1206	32,200 ± 1,000 BP	34,200– 30, 200 BP	Hedges et al. 1988.
Pin Hole, Creswell Crags	*Crocuta crocuta* left 5th metacarpal	OxA-1207	34,500 ± 1,200 BP	36,900– 32,100 BP	Hedges et al. 1988.
West Pin Hole, Creswell	*Crocuta crocuta* left P2	OxA-5803	29,300 ± 420 BP	30,140– 28,460 BP	Hedges et al. 1996. An attempt to redate this with ultrafiltration pretreatment failed due to insufficient collagen yield (Higham et al. 2006); it may therefore be an underestimate.
Robin Hood Cave, Creswell Crags	*Crocuta crocuta* left C	OxA-5801	33,450 ± 700 BP	34,850– 32,050 BP	Hedges et al. 1996. An attempt to redate this with ultrafiltration pretreatment failed due to insufficient collagen yield (Higham et al. 2006); it may therefore be an underestimate.
Robin Hood Cave, Creswell Crags	*Crocuta crocuta* right P2	OxA-5802	31,050 ± 500 BP	32,050– 30,050 BP	Hedges et al. 1996.
Robin Hood Cave, Creswell Crags	*Crocuta crocuta* unspecified tooth	OxA-6114	22,980 ± 480 BP	23,940– 22,020 BP	Hedges et al. 1998. An attempt to redate this with ultrafiltration pretreatment failed due to insufficient collagen yield (Higham et al. 2006); it may therefore be an underestimate.
Robin Hood Cave, Creswell Crags	*Crocuta crocuta* unspecified tooth	OxA-12736	>52,800 BP	>52,800 BP	Ultrafiltrated measurement of sample previously dated OxA-6115 22,880 ± 240 BP. Higham et al. 2006.

Table 6.7 Continued

Robin Hood Cave, Creswell Crags (11)	*Crocuta crocuta* unspecified tooth	OxA-14944	>49,800	>49,800	Ultrafiltrated measurement of sample previously dated OxA-5802 31,050 ± 500 BP (Higham et al. 2006).
Church Hole, Creswell Crags (12)	*Crocuta crocuta* right I3	OxA-14926	>40,000	>40,000	Ultrafiltrated measurement of sample previously dated OxA-5799 26,840 ± 420 BP (Hedges et al. 1996; Higham et al. 2006).
Church Hole, Creswell Crags (13)	*Crocuta crocuta* left P4	OxA-5800	24,000 ± 260 BP	24,520– 23,480	Hedges et al. 1996. An attempt to redate this with ultrafiltration pretreatment failed due to insufficient collagen yield (Higham et al. 2006); it may therefore be an underestimate.
Bench Quarry	*Crocuta crocuta* dentary	OxA-13512	36,800 ± 450 BP	37,700– 35,900	Jacobi 2007b. Four measurements exist for this sample, each with different pretreatment and results. This sample was ultrafiltrated and 'is believed to be the most reliable estimate of age for the dentary' (Jacobi 2007b, 294)
Sandford Hill, Mendip	*Crocuta crocuta* cranium	BM-1526	36,000 ± 1,900 BP	39,800– 32,200	Stuart 1991.
Little Hoyle Cave, Dyfed, Wales	*Crocuta crocuta* tooth	OxA-1491	34,590 ± 1,500 BP	37,590– 31,590	Hedges et al. 1993.
Coygan Cave, Dyfed, Wales	Radius of *Coelodonta antiquitatis* from hyaena denning deposits.	OxA-2509	24,620 ± 320	25,260– 23,980	Hedges et al. 1994. Non-ultrafiltrated, probably an underestimate (Higham et al. 2006).
Coygan Cave, Dyfed, Wales	*Crocuta crocuta* C	OxA-14400	32,140 ± 250 BP	32,640– 31,640	Higham et al. 2006.
Coygan Cave, Dyfed, Wales	*Crocuta crocuta* C	OxA-14401	43,000 ± 2,100 BP	47,200– 38,800	Higham et al. 2006.
Coygan Cave, Dyfed, Wales	*Crocuta crocuta* M1	OxA-14473	32,400 ± 550 BP	33,500– 31,300	Higham et al. 2006.
Coygan Cave, Dyfed, Wales	*Crocuta crocuta* I3	OxA-14402	36,000 ± 500 BP	37,000– 3500	Higham et al. 2006.
Coygan Cave, Dyfed, Wales	*Crocuta crocuta* P3	OxA-14403	39,700 ± 1,700 BP	43,100– 36,300	Higham et al. 2006.
Castlepook Cave, Ireland	*Crocuta crocuta* scapula	OxA-4234	24,000 ± 300 BP	24,600– 23,400	Hedges et al. 1997.
Castlepook Cave, Ireland	*Crocuta crocuta*	OxA-4237	>45,200 BP	>45,200	Hedges et al. 1997.
Kent's Cavern	Digested bone fragment	OxA-10806	36,750 ± 450 BP	37,650– 35,850	Jacobi 2007b

underestimates. Taking these factors into account hyaenas appear not to have lasted beyond ~33 ka BP in Britain and extend to ages greater than 45 ka BP. As we shall see below, this is the apparent age range for the British Late Middle Palaeolithic. It certainly indicates that both Neanderthals and hyaenas were predators on the MIS3 Mammoth Steppe and raises the intriguing possibility that they were sympatric in Britain at the time.

The spotted hyaena has a ubiquitous distribution across Africa, where clans can comprise as many as 80 individuals (Kruuk 1972, 6–7). As hyaena populations appear to be governed by prey availability (ibid. 104) it is reasonable to assume that their relative abundance in MIS3 Britain reflects (despite Guthrie's contention) a relatively rich mammoth steppe fauna, which seems to have been the case for the taxonomically rich Pin Hole MAZ noted above. In modern Africa, human settlements attract hyaenas and can in fact stimulate a rise in hyaena population numbers, whereas in areas where human settlements are few hyaena populations can fall as low as individual numbers (ibid. 20). It seems possible, therefore, that hyaenas could have been attracted to Neanderthal territories where scavenging opportunities presented themselves, their population numbers rising accordingly. This fits with the palaeoenvironmental background discussed above; in Africa, hyaenas reach their highest densities in short grassland with few trees and with high ungulate biomass, environments very similar to those of MIS3 Britain.

It is easy to envisage how Neanderthals and hyaenas might coexist, sharing the niche of top predators and scavenging from each other's kills, leading to a mutually beneficial sympatry. As hyaenas consume organs and bone (Sutcliffe 1970; Skinner and van Aarde 1991), little may remain of their kills, although when parts are abandoned Kruuk found them frequently to be heads (Kruuk 1972, 126), a good source of fat. In Africa, hyenas routinely cache meat in shallow water, often failing to return to consume it. Such caches could provide useful scavenging opportunities for Neanderthals, at least when resources were scarce. As hyaenas are active almost entirely at night and spend the day in dens there would be little direct competition for resources. Although hyaenas have been known to attack humans, these events are generally restricted to the young or weak, and mostly take place when victims are sleeping (Kruuk 1972, 144). Furthermore, as other social carnivores such as lions and wild dogs can chase hyaenas away from their kills relatively easily, it seems that Neanderthals – with the benefit of cooperative action, weapons and fire – must certainly have been able to cope with these carnivores; although it is somewhat inconceivable that this suspected mutual tolerance would have extended to sharing the same cave.

In the Serengeti, the overall range of prey species of hyaenas and lions are very similar, although the two differ in their specific preferred prey, which probably has the effect of reducing the severity of competition (Mills 1990, 52). Such different prey selection with a shared set of available resources could provide a mechanism for sympatry; indeed recent isotopic analysis has highlighted differences in the main prey species of Neanderthals and hyaenas in Europe (Bocherens et al. 2005). Under such circumstances, Neanderthals might be actively drawn to hyaena territories. Hyaenas are relatively easy to find: their calls can be heard over vast distances at night and they have a tendency to follow specific paths (Kruuk 1972, 22). A sensible strategy, therefore, might be to operate on the edges of clan territories, where scavenging opportunities could be exploited after hyaenas had cached meat at night, while avoiding direct confrontation. Another strategy might be to target maternity dens, a good source of accumulated carcass parts. In the Ngorongoro crater, Kruuk (ibid. 39–40) identified seven permanent and contemporary clan territories, each typically some 6 × 4 km in extent, although Mills (1990, 150) noted that territories of African spotted hyaenas were highly variable, with a mean of 308 ± 39 km^2.

Modelling of hominin ranging patterns by Gamble and Steele (1999) suggests that, in northern latitudes, hominins would have had to adopt a carnivore-scale ranging pattern. Estimates of Neanderthal home ranges based on raw material movements fell between 2,025 km^2 and 5,000 km^2 (Gamble and Steele 1999, 403; Gamble 2002), clearly an order of magnitude larger than the ranges of African hyaenas. As noted above, Guthrie (1990) has suggested that even though it was a relatively rich hunting ground, the Mammoth Steppe would not have supported the density of prey found on the modern African savannah. As carnivore population density and range size is directly correlated to prey availability and distribution, it appears probable that the ranges of Pleistocene social carnivores were also much larger. The same factors presumably impacted upon both hyaena and Neanderthal range and group size.

NEANDERTHAL SURVIVAL STRATEGIES IN MIS3 BRITAIN AND DOGGERLAND

Forming the north-west uplands of Doggerland, Britain appears to have been a fairly rich resource of animal protein, home to herds of medium and large grazers and several species of top carnivore, such as the hyaenas noted above. However, given the prevailing view that Britain was a treeless grassland with short, cool summers and long, cold winters marked by blasting winds, frozen ground and persistent rain and snow, other resources, particularly wood from which to fashion hunting weapons and other raw materials with which to make artificial shelters and fire, were probably extremely scarce. Given inferred Neanderthal activity levels, metabolic rates and daily caloric requirements of ~5,500 kcal (Sorenson and Leonard 2001), coupled with the possibility that Neanderthal morphology did not provide a major thermal advantage in cold climates (Aiello and Wheeler 2003; Steegmann et al. 2002) and a persistent image of cultural ineptitude (Speth 2004) one has a considerable respect for the Neanderthals who clearly survived on the Northern European Plain during MIS3.

White (2006) explored a number of ways in which apparent tensions between the current behavioural, anatomical and palaeoenvironmental reconstructions might be reconciled in the British Late Middle Palaeolithic, concluding that current views require revision, particularly the environmental and cultural reconstructions, suggesting not only that trees probably existed in cryptic refugia (see above), but that Neanderthals must have had the ability and access to the necessary resources to create a number of survival prerequisites – notably clothes, fire, structures and hunting weapons – which are usually archaeologically invisible. Clearly Neanderthals were intermittently operating in Britain – the low level of occupation perhaps in itself testament to the difficulties they faced here – but the challenge is to understand how they solved these survival problems when they were present.

Scavenging may have been an important survival strategy in regions where weapons may not have been easily replenished. A strategy such as scavenging from hyaenas noted above may therefore have served as an emergency option. Alternative resources would have been available. Bone would presumably have been plentiful and could have been used for fuel and raw materials. To date, however, the Neanderthal use of bone as a raw material has been validated at very few sites, the most famous being the pointed rib implements from Salzgitter–Lebenstedt, Germany (Gaudzinski 1999a, 1999b), although reanalysis of old faunal assemblages is beginning to reveal further examples. Sharpened mammoth ribs might well have serviced the close-encounter, ambush hunting strategies inferred from other Neanderthal hunting sites, as well as being potentially able to produce the kinds of traumas seen on Neanderthal skeletons (Berger and Trinkaus 1995). Nevertheless, Gaudzinski casts doubt on the efficiency of the mammoth rib points for thrusting, given their curvature. Their use as structural supports might therefore be considered. Bone as fuel is also problematic, as it requires another source of fuel to generate sufficient heat for it to ignite (White 2006 and references therein); dried animal dung, grass and shrubs could provide alternative fuels but all carry energetic costs to harvest. These questions could be answered but new examples of hearths, such as those apparently found by Victorian excavators in the Hyaena Den and Robin Hood Cave, will need to be recovered in new excavations to ascertain exactly what fuels were used.

Survival stresses would have been particularly acute in winter, providing an obvious solution to the problems raised above: that Neanderthals mainly used Britain as a summer hunting ground, perhaps following migratory herds, and came equipped with resources from neighbouring parts of Europe. Small, highly mobile, seasonal hunting parties would certainly fit with the technological organisation in the landscape described below (although again, seasonality data from new, well-excavated sites is required to test this). There are differences, however, between the typological character of British and continental handaxes that appear to contradict this easy solution. The radiocarbon evidence can also be interpreted to support the notion that Neanderthals were feasibly only present in Britain during some of the warmer interstadials, which again might help remove some of the obstacles raised by White (2006). However, a recent analysis of Neanderthal energy use during the last interglacial (MIS5e), one of the warmest periods of the last 500,000 years, showed that even then a number of cultural solutions would have been required to solve the problem of survivorship (Sørensen 2009). The British and continental archaeological record contains no physical evidence for these solutions, but the extreme situation in Britain at least reminds us of the skills necessary for survival, and demands that we consider these invisible cultural elements alongside the more traditional concerns with the lithic technologies described below.

THE BRITISH LATE MIDDLE PALAEOLITHIC

The British Late Middle Palaeolithic record comprises a number of lithic findspots usually with single or very few artefacts, without faunal associations and without absolute dating. Superimposed upon this scatter is a handful of larger lithic assemblages, with or without associated fauna and dating, only one or two of which are on a qualitative par with continental sites (Table 6.4). The available absolute chronology reveals that this occupation occurred, probably intermittently and for short periods, broadly between ~60 ka BP and ~41 ka BP (see below), preserving evidence of activity from Lincolnshire in the north to the Isle of Wight in the south, although the apparent northern limit of this occupation is almost certainly an artefact of the extent of the Last Glacial Maximum (LGM) ice advance (see Chapters 7 and 8).

South of the limits of the LGM advance, the basic distribution of findspots ostensibly shows Neanderthal presence throughout Wales, southern England, East Anglia and the English Midlands, but even here the actual distribution is biased by a number of factors. Landscape variability has influenced both the presence of suitable preservational environments and the likelihood of their eventual discovery. The accessibility of useful caves or fissures (both now and in the deep past), fluvial, lacustrine or coastal locations, the accidental and often fleeting character of many exposures and the serendipitous presence of people capable of recognising Palaeolithic implements have all impacted on the distribution and number of Palaeolithic sites. But, as noted above, 200 years of archaeological endeavour amid rapid industrialisation and urban growth as well as enthusiastic interest has failed to produce an embarrassment of riches. It is hardly surprising that the cave sites that are key to understanding the British Late Middle Palaeolithic are concentrated in two main areas – south-west England/south Wales, and the English Midlands – to an extent showing little more than the distribution of presently located caves, although the resources available in these areas may also have made them desirable locations for Neanderthals. Only two open air sites – Lynford and Little Paxton – have to date yielded substantial Late Middle Palaeolithic assemblages, despite extensive quarrying in deposits of relevant age, with all other open-air sites of this period being represented by very small assemblages or isolated handaxes of a particular form (i.e. the classic *bout coupé* as discussed below).

A list of handaxes attributed by others to the Middle Palaeolithic on the basis of typology is provided in Table 6.8 (Roe 1981; Tyldesley 1987); those believed to date firmly to MIS3 are in Table 6.9. Caution is needed, however, as similar forms appear to have been produced simply by chance in a number of demonstrably older assemblages (White and Jacobi 2002), and context is critical. This makes it rather difficult to gauge the true distribution of open-air sites although, taking the entire typological sample, there appear to be several foci of activity centring around major river systems (those of the Thames, Great Ouse, Little Ouse–Wissey and Solent) and the chalk hinterlands of the North and South Downs (Figure 6.2). Taking only the dated examples, the picture is essentially the same – if somewhat more southerly – although the small sample size means that no real clusters can be recognised. Other sites have also yielded very few, or only individual

Table 6.8 A list of claimed bout coupé handaxe findspots, by county. (Data from Tyldesley 1987; Roe 1981; Woodcock 1981; Wymer 1968; 1985; 1999; pers. obs. MJW and PP.) Some find spots have yielded more than one *bout coupé*. Numbers in parenthesis indicate that the piece was accepted by Tyldesley (1987) as a 'true' *bout coupé*.

Bedfordshire	Highbridge, Eastleigh (#53)	Weeting/Grimes Graves
Bedford General (#13)	Southampton General (#54–55)	
Biggleswade (#12)	Warsash, Fleetend	**Northamptonshire**
		Duston
Berkshire	**Isle of Wight**	
Maidenhead, Summerleaze Pit (#20)	Great Pan Farm (#58)	**Oxfordshire**
Sulhamstead Abbots, Abbots Pit		Abingdon (#15)
	Kent	**Radley, Tuckwells Pit (#16)**
Buckinghamshire	Ash, Parsonage Farm	
Bourne End, New Road, Bucks (#19)	Canterbury St Stephens Pit, (#44)	**Somerset**
Fenny Stratford, Brickhill Rd	Canterbury, Wallfield (#45)	Cheddon Fitzpaine (#67)
Iver, Lavender's Pit	Canterbury, Wincheap (#46)	Hazel Farm
Iver, Meads Bridge Pit	Canterbury General	Pitminster (#66)
Marlow Brickyard (#17)	Elham, Dreals & Standardhill Farm (#47 & 48)	Uphill Quarry
Marlow (#18)	Erith, from Thames (#33, 34 & 35)	West Quantoxhead (#68)
Taplow General	Faversham, Brenley Corner (#41)	Wookey Hole, Hyaena Den
	Faversham, Copton in Preston	Wookey Hole, Rhinoceros Hole
Cambridgeshire	Gravesend, Milton (#29)	
Burnt Fen (#7)	Herne Bay (#42)	**Suffolk**
Fenstanton Pits (#10)	Hextable Agricultural College (#28)	Brandon Fields
Fenstanton, close to river	Ightham	Elveden Brickpit (#5)
Hemingford Grey	Maidstone general	Eriswell
Horningsea (#8)	Newington	Icklingham Warren (#6)
Linton (#9)	New Hythe (#40)	Ipswich, Bramford Rd (#14)
St Ives, Meadow Lane	Oldbury 'Rock Shelter' (#39)	Ipswich, Constantine Rd
St Neots, Little Paxton (#11)	Reculver (#43)	Ipswich Hadleigh Road
Fen Drayton	Snodland, Clubbs Ballast Pit (#37–38)	Mildenhall, High Lodge
Willingham/Over		Mildenhall, Hill Farm
	Leicestershire	Santon Downham (#3)
Devonshire	Aylestone	
Broom		**Surrey**
Brixham Cave	**Lincolnshire**	Balham (#27)
Kent's Cavern (#69, 70, 71 & 72)	Fillingham	Richmond (#36)
	Harlaxton	Farnham, Firgrove Pit
Dorset	Risby Warren	Godalming, Hanaway Rd
Bere Regis		Limpsfield
Bournemouth, Boscombe (#62)	**London**	Wrecclesham, Farnham
Bournemouth, Castle Lane (#63)	Acton, Creffield Rd	
Bournemouth, Talbot Woods (#64)	Acton General (#25)	

Table 6.8 Continued

		Sussex
Bournemouth, East Common	East Acton, Berrymead Priory (#26)	Alfriston
Bournemouth, Ensbury Park	Hammersmith from Thames	Alfriston Tye
Bournemouth, Green Road, Winton	Hillingdon, Sipson Lane (#23)	Ashdown Forest
Bournemouth, Pokesdown (#61)	Hillingdon, West Drayton, Claytons Pit (#22)	Billingshurst (#49)
Bournemouth, Southbourne, (#60)	Hillingdon, Yiewsley, Eastwood's/Sabery's (#21)	Burlough Castle
Christchurch, St Catherine's Hill, (#59)	Hillingdon various find spots	Bullock Down
Christchurch General	Hoxton General	Eastbourne
Corfe Mullen	Isleworth, from Thames (#24)	East Dean
Dewlish	Newham, Beckton from Thames	Friston
Hengistbury Head	Putney from Thames	Hassocks
Ifford, Sheepwash	Tilbury Docks (#32)	Lancing
Poole, West Howe	Wandsworth from Thames	Litlington
Purwell		Newhaven
Sherborne, Cemetery (#65)	**Norfolk**	West Chiltington (#50)
	Little Cressingham (#1)	Wilmington Hill
Essex	Lynford Hall	
Brundon, Jordan's Pit	Lynford, West Tofts	**Wales**
Stone Point/Walton on Naze	Mousehold Heath	Coygan Cave (#73–74)
Witham, Coleman's Farm	Narford	Levernock, Cardiff
	Pulham Market	
Hampshire	Saham Toney (#2)	**Wiltshire**
Dunbridge (#52)	Saxlingham Nethergate	Salisbury, Fisherton (#51)
Fareham, Blackbrook Park Ave, (#56–7)	South Wootton	
Gutteridge's Wood (#31)	Thetford General (#4)	
Holybourne (#30)		

Middle Palaeolithic artefacts, such as a double scraper from Ravencliffe Cave in the Derbyshire Peak District, identified by the Abbé Breuil from a layer that included reindeer, rhinoceros and bear (Storrs Fox 1930).

Although the sites are widely distributed in space, their relative paucity and small assemblage sizes are still notable and may provide a number of insights into Neanderthal populations in Britain. Various attempts have been made to estimate the relative population density during the Pleistocene based on the density of lithic artefacts (Hosfield 1999; Ashton and Lewis 2002). The most influential of these – the deserted Britain model discussed at length in Chapter 5 – concluded that population density decreased over time with an abrupt population crash seen in MIS7 (Ashton and Lewis 2002). This pattern was explained as the combined result of an increasing adaptation to the continental steppic environments of central and eastern Europe and a late breach of the Strait of Dover restricting access to Britain around this time (Ashton and Lewis 2002). This fails

Table 6.9 List of *bout coupé* **handaxes that can be attributed to MIS3 or a broader Devensian context.**

MIS3	Undifferentiated Devensian
Coygan Cave, Wales	Berrymead Priory, London
Fisherton, Wiltshire	Castle Lane, Dorset
Kent's Cavern, Devonshire	Fenstanton, Cambridgeshire
Lynford, Norfolk	Little Cressingham, Norfolk
Little Paxton, Cambridgeshire	Marlow, Buckinghamshire
Snodland, Kent	Saham Toney, Norfolk
	Sipson, London
	Southbourne, Dorset
	Summerleaze Pit,
	Tuckwell's Pit, Oxfordshire
	? Eastwoods Pit, London
	? Bramford Road, Suffolk

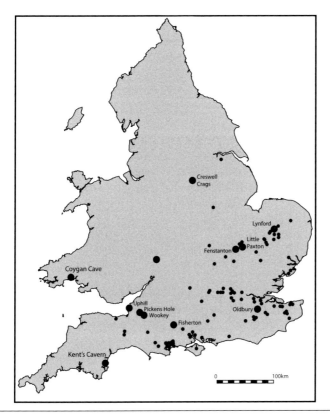

FIGURE 6.2
Major British Late Middle Palaeolithic sites and *bout coupé* findspots. (Modified after Roe 1981.)

Table 6.10 Population estimates for Middle Palaeolithic hominins in Britain based on ethnographically observed densities.

Ethnographic densities	Persons per km²	England 130,000 km²	Wales 20,000 km²	Scotland 78,000 km²	Total Population
High	0.09	11,700	1,800	7,020	20,520
Low	0.05	6,500	1,000	3,900	11,400
Sparse	0.02	2,600	400	1,560	4,560

to explain the patterns seen in MIS3, however, when Britain was part of a wider North European Plain and, according to the faunal evidence discussed above, also had a continental climate. Leaving aside the many problems of using artefact numbers to measure population size, it is unlikely that an area the size of Britain was ever host to particularly large hominin populations. Based on observed data for ethnographic hunter-gatherer population density, Gamble (2002) estimated that Pleistocene populations in England and Wales (the known distribution of Neanderthal settlement) probably varied between ~13,500 and ~3,000 people (greater if Scotland is assumed to have been inhabited; see Table 6.10). Given that estimates for the entire effective population size of Neanderthals amounted to just 3,500 females (a total of 14,000 men, women and children) and that at the maximum extent of their range Neanderthals may have numbered between 38,600 and 147,000 individuals at the very most (Roebroeks et al. 2011), we suspect that even the lower of these figures overestimates the Neanderthal population of Britain: it is entirely possible that only a few hundred individuals were present and then only for very brief periods of time.

CHRONOLOGY AND SETTLEMENT HISTORY

As discussed in Chapter 5, no convincing evidence of Neanderthal presence in Britain in the last interglacial *sensu lato* (MIS5) is known, despite decades of excavation. Early observations that evidence for human activity in Britain was not associated with evidence for *Hippopotamus* (despite mis-identifications, for example at Rhinoceros Hole, Tratman et al. 1971) ruled out occupation during the last interglacial (MIS5e) (Currant and Jacobi 2002, 2011; Ashton 2002). There are also no convincing indications of Middle Palaeolithic activity in the early glacial period (MIS5d–b), nor any archaeological associations with fauna of the Bacon Hole, Banwell or Brean Down MAZs, which appears reasonably well correlated with MIS5a to MIS4 (Currant and Jacobi 2001, 2011; Ashton 2002; Gilmour et al. 2007; Lewis et al. 2011). Judgement on claims of human occupation during MIS5d–5b from Dartford in Kent (Wenban-Smith et al. 2010) – based on OSL dates from mass-movement slope deposits that yielded just two fresh flakes and a number of clearly derived older artefacts – must be reserved until more convincingly contextualised dates and materials are forthcoming. Overall, therefore, it seems that the Neanderthals abandoned Britain around or before the onset of MIS6, ~180 ka BP (Ashton and Lewis 2002; Ashton 2002; Currant and Jacobi 2001) and were absent for at least 120,000 years. Thus a critical issue facing British Late Middle Palaeolithic archaeology is to demonstrate accurately and precisely when the initial reoccupation of Britain by late Neanderthals occurred.

This will be achieved convincingly only by new fieldwork at existing archaeological locales or, better still, the discovery of new sites. There has been too much emphasis on the redating of artefacts from old excavations and too little on new excavation projects. Dating programmes for British sites excavated long ago have to accept that 'associations made between the materials selected for dating and evidence for Middle Palaeolithic activity are the best that can at present be achieved' (Jacobi et al. 2006, 565). There are, however, several problems with this approach. First, one has to reconstruct the original stratigraphic position of the diagnostic Middle Palaeolithic artefacts and of the bones selected for dating, which is imprecise at best, leading to unverifiable assumptions that the two are meaningfully associated. Secondly, one has to possess enough understanding of the sedimentary history of the cave of concern; our own experiences excavating in Kent's Cavern, for example, show that material of widely different ages can be stratified very closely, with little but micromorphological indications that separate sedimentational events have left a uniform-looking cave earth. With the nature of early excavations and the limited documentation that preserves these for posterity, one simply cannot eliminate the possibility that dated bones say nothing about the age of material in close proximity to which they were found. Thirdly, given the almost absolute lack of cut-marked or otherwise modified bones from MIS3, virtually none of the bones and teeth selected for dating demonstrably pertain to Neanderthal activity; instead they often relate to hyaena activity and, although this may have occurred closely in time (as noted above) on the basis of the individual site, such samples do not convincingly serve as archaeological proxies. Finally, the chronometric inaccuracy and imprecision associated with dates of this period further confuses the picture. Published radiocarbon dates represent a mixture of conventional and AMS dates from various periods in the development of the technique, samples for which were prepared using a variety of different pretreatment methods, some of which have been proven to yield very different results. For example, OxA4428 and OxA13880 are the laboratory codes for two dates on the same woolly rhinoceros tibia from Pin Hole Cave, pre-treated using ion-exchanged gelatin and ultrafiltrated gelatin pretreatments respectively: the mean measurements differ by 9,800 radiocarbon years – over one half life of radiocarbon. In some cases measurements are of considerable vintage and almost certainly should be regarded as minimum ages. One also has to make an assumption that radiocarbon dates on hyaena denning material or other naturally accumulated faunal remains do genuinely reflect the age of Neanderthal activity with which they are in broad stratigraphic association which, given the existing precision of the radiocarbon measurements, could in fact amount to a difference of 2–3 ka at 2σ. Uranium-series measurements present different issues, as most are based on speleothem clasts contained in archaeological deposits, and at best provide only a *terminus ante quem* for the age of deposits and their archaeology. Yet another cautionary tale comes from the site of Ilseworth, argued to be Middle Devensian on the basis of stratigraphical correlation with Kempton Park, a conventional radiocarbon measurement of 43,140 ± −1,520 (Birm-319) and a floral and faunal signature entirely consistent with other supposed Devensian sites. The site was recently dated by AAR to MIS5a, ~81 ka (Kirsty Penkman, pers. comm. June 2008), although this date is somewhat at odds with the environmental picture from the site which is totally different to MIS5a sites in Belgium (cf. Hopkinson 2007).

Thus, it can hardly be said that the major British Late Middle Palaeolithic sites are well dated in any sense of the term. As shown in Table 6.4 dates exist for only two open air sites, of which one is a minimum age of dubious relevance. Of the cave sites, non-radio-carbon dates are of little use given their relatively large errors, and many existing radio-carbon measurements are on pre-ultrafiltrated samples that might change if redated today. Only seven sites provide reliable radiocarbon measurements pertinent to British Late Middle Palaeolithic chronology, and three to the chronology of succeeding LRJ (Lincombian–Ranisian–Jerzomanowician leafpoint) assemblages, which are discussed in Chapter 7 (Figure 6.1). OSL dates of 64 ± 5 ka and 67 ± 5 ka BP place Neanderthals at Lynford between ~54 ka BP and ~77 ka BP at 2σ (Boismier et al. 2003). On palaeoen-vironmental grounds one might assume that the activity relates to MIS3 and not MIS4 (see above), thus constraining the age to ~60–54 ka BP. This is consistent with uncali-brated radiocarbon age ranges (again at 2σ) of Late Middle Palaeolithic assemblages at Coygan Cave, Pin Hole Cave, Robin Hood Cave, Kent's Cavern, Ash Tree Cave, Picken's Hole and Hyaena Den, all spanning a period between ~54 ka and ~44 ka BP an age range that, parsimoniously, may be said to represent the bulk of Neanderthal activity in the country. As will be seen in Chapter 7 LRJ leafpoints from Kent's Cavern, Bench Quarry and Badger Hole – the only sites at which they may be regarded as at all reliably dated – span the period between ~41 ka BP and ~42 ka BP. There appears to be no Brit-ish Late Middle Palaeolithic occupation younger than ~44 ka BP. The relevance of LRJ material to this issue is discussed in Chapter 7. Thus, for the formal Late Middle Palaeo-lithic of Britain comparing the reliable radiocarbon measurements with the CalPal curve of Weninger and Jöris (2004) suggests that, very broadly, the calendrical age range of the existing British Middle Palaeolithic is ~44 ka BP to ~54 ka BP. A glance at Figure 6.1 shows that this broadly corresponds to the relatively stable interstadial conditions of GI14, GI13 and GI12. Similarly 'corrected' dates for the three LRJ measurements indicate a broad age range of ~42 ka BP to ~43 ka BP, corresponding perhaps to GI11. We emphasise once again our caution that these are few dates for few assemblages, and such 'corrections' to 'calendrical' dates are at present very approximate, although we hope that the hypothesis of Late Middle Palaeolithic occupation in Britain restricted perhaps to GI14, GI13, GI12 and GI11 may be tested as new sites are discovered and techniques improved. It will be seen in Chapter 7 that the earliest demonstrable age for the Aurignacian presence of *Homo sapiens* in Britain is ~35 ka BP, that is, at least 7,000 years after the LRJ. We suggest, then, that *Homo sapiens* arrived in Britain after a considerable occupation gap following regional Neanderthal extinction and did not play a part in the extinction process. This arrival could have occurred in the interstadial conditions of GI6 or GI7. All one can conclude from the currently available chronometric data is that late Neanderthal activity in Britain need not have amounted to anything more than brief pulses of activity in the period ~44–54 ka BP or possibly to ~42 ka BP if the LRJ represents Neanderthals and that the reasons for the final abandonment of the country by Neanderthals – whatever they were – were similar to those which brought previous dispersals to an end and did not involve competition from a human predator who would not arrive until Neanderthals had long abandoned the rains and snows.

TECHNOLOGY, ORGANISATION AND BEHAVIOUR IN THE BRITISH LATE MIDDLE PALAEOLITHIC

The British Late Middle Palaeolithic is dominated by handaxes, supplemented by typical Mousterian tool forms, notably scrapers, occurring in some of the larger assemblages. In addition to these, a distinct tradition of simple chopper/chopping tool technology on non-flint raw materials is found in several caves at Creswell Crags. At some sites (e.g. Creswell and Oldbury) discoidal technology is evident. Overall, then, it corresponds to the continental Mousterian of Acheulian Tradition (MTA), a comparison that has often been made (e.g. Mellars 1974; Roe 1981). This is not surprising, given that the chrono-logical range of the British material overlaps with that of the French MTA (Mellars 1996). Similarly, continental parallels for simple chopper/chopping tool technologies do occur, for instance at the bovid hunting localities of Mauran (Farizy and David 1992), where this technology seems to have been useful as a rapid and renewable response to the demands of heavy duty butchery of mass/multiple kills. Although the latter are as yet unknown for Britain – and may in any case be inappropriate analogies given the low frequency and low number of Neanderthal sites in Britain – it is consistent with the exploitation of bovids and similarly large-sized animal resources.

British cave assemblages

Many cave sites in Europe have rich, deeply stratified Middle Palaeolithic sequences containing thousands of lithics representing all phases of the technological *chaîne opératoire*. It is often assumed that such caves formed relatively long-term residential foci for Neanderthal groups from which they organised their daily hunting and foraging routines and where a range of economic and social activities took place, sometimes including burial or detachment rituals (Gamble 1999; Pettitt 2011). British assemblages, on the other hand, tend not to correspond to this picture. They tend to be numerically small, dominated by tools, and to show very limited evidence of on-site lithic manufac-ture. Of the sites listed in Table 6.4 only four (Lynford, Robin Hood Cave, Oldbury and Little Paxton, in descending numerical order) have yielded >100 artefacts (see Text Box 6.5). The rest comprise only a few pieces, often handaxes, scrapers, choppers and knives, sometimes accompanied by handaxe trimming flakes. Even the largest cave assemblage – Robin Hood Cave – contained no more than 500 artefacts, probably less. Examples from the clusters in the south-west and South Wales serve to illustrate 'typi-cal' British cave assemblages; those from the English Midlands at Creswell Crags will be discussed in detail below.

THE LATE MIDDLE PALAEOLITHIC OPEN-AIR SITE OF LITTLE PAXTON, CAMBRIDGESHIRE

Until the discovery of Lynford in 2001, the richest open-air Late Middle Palaeo-lithic site in Britain was that at Paxton Park, St Neots (Tebbutt et al. 1927; Paterson and Tebbutt 1947). It comprised a series of gravel pits situated on the low terrace (Terrace 1–2) of the left bank of the Great Ouse River. Tebbutt monitored the site for many years, finding most of his artefacts in the spoil heaps, although he did obtain some better provenanced artefacts and all of the fauna from the quarry workers who provide some contextual details. Of the three pits observed by Tebbutt up to 1927, Pit I –the 'Riverside Pit' – was the most prolific, yielding four handaxes and 18 flakes; only two artefacts in Pit II and a single implement and some fauna from Pit III are reported. Many more finds were subsequently made, the total apparently exceeding 210 artefacts (Paterson and Tebbutt 1947).

The geology of the site was briefly described by Marr (Tebbutt et al. 1927) and more fully by Paterson and Tebbutt (1947) who provided a section through ~3.6 m of fluvial deposits resting on Oxford Clay. It is unclear in which pit this section was recorded, although Tebbutt et al. (1927) had previously noted that Pit 1 could only be excavated to 7–8 ft (~2.1–2.4 m) due to flooding, while Pit II, being further away from the river, could be dug to 8–10 ft (~2.4–3 m). Pit III, however, was noted as being 12 ft (3.6 m) deep, the basal layer being rich in mammalian remains, a description that would appear to show the closest similarity to the published section, including the specific reference to fauna.

The quantity of fauna originally recovered is unknown. Fauna from Bed 1 and Bed 2 consisted of mammoth, woolly rhinoceros, reindeer and horse; while limited this is consistent with the MIS3 Pin Hole MAZ (see main text). The provenance of the archaeology from Little Paxton is, sadly, vague, although it can be fairly confidently assumed that most, if not all, came from the fluvial gravels of Bed 2. The total assemblage included 200 flakes and flake tools, 8 handaxes and 2 cores which Paterson divided into two groups, divisible on the basis of condition and patina. Group A consisted of at least two handaxes, a multiple platform core, and six flakes, all in a rolled and patinated state. Group B comprised the remainder. This group was fresh to slightly rolled, with some edge damage and slight battering, clear evidence of a degree of fluvial disturbance and abrasion. Two flint sources were noted, a grey, and a black flint with worn cortex; both probably obtained from local river gravels (Paterson and Tebbutt 1947). The assemblage included seven small handaxes, one a classic *bout coupé* showing evidence of possible use-wear at the butt produced by heavy-duty battering. Despite the edge damage on the flakes some genuine scrapers including an offset (déjeté) scraper, a 'Quina'-type sidescraper and a convergent scraper with bifacial retouch are present, both similar to forms found at Lynford.

Despite not being an *in situ* assemblage, the absence of cores suggests that handaxe manufacture was the key technological activity at Little Paxton. The range of flakes present appear to reflect complete handaxe reduction sequences:

30% were described as coming from prelimininary preparation, many with fully cortical dorsal surfaces, 45% from shaping or thinning flakes, and 5% from finishing or retouching (Paterson and Tebbutt 1947, 43). Paterson also identified a number of Levallois flakes from both groups, although later researchers have dismissed these as handaxe-thinning flakes (Wymer 1985). The assemblage is today best described as Mousterian of Acheulean Tradition.

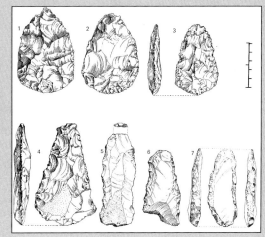

FIGURE 1
Late Middle Palaeolithic lithics from Little Paxton. (After Patterson and Tebbutt 1947.)

The assemblage from Uphill Quarry Cave 8 (Figure 6.3) comprises at least two small triangular handaxes, handaxe fragments, a convergent side scraper/Mousterian point, notched and denticulated flakes, small thinning flakes and a naturally backed knife, as well as some evidence for discoidal core technology (Harrison 1977; Jacobi and Pettitt 2000). While the presence of cores and thinning flakes led Jacobi and Pettitt to suggest that the site was the locus of on-site knapping, Harrison saw the dominant technological activity at the site as the resharpening of broken and damaged tools, probably as a result of limited access to high quality raw materials in the region. This would suggest that the site was only a temporary stopover where a transported and curated tool-kit was being maintained, those tools left behind presumably discarded as not worth taking any further; the triangular handaxe is 6 cm long and was clearly at the end of its use-life. At Coygan, the extant Middle Palaeolithic assemblage comprises three handaxes and two flakes (see Text Box 6.6), one of which is large enough to have served as a handaxe blank. A case for prolonged use of at least one of the handaxes has been made by Jacobi (quoted in Aldhouse-Green et al. 1995, 69) who has noted a polish consistent with a long period of rubbing, in the hand or in a pouch, in association with apparent edge resharpening.

In summary, in most British caves where a Neanderthal presence can be demonstrated, only the most ephemeral of visits are noticeable, perhaps nothing more than a number of overnight forays by well-equipped hunters, who whiled away the hours by repairing items in their tool-kits, some of which they abandoned or otherwise left at the site, and who used local raw materials to produce expedient choppers and other tools to supplement their few curated items. The apparent abundance of hyaenas in MIS3 Britain, and the dominance of their bones and bones of their prey in faunal assemblages, suggests that while potentially desirable residences, most British caves often had very unwelcoming sitting tenants.

NEANDERTHALS AND HYAENAS IN COYGAN CAVE, LAUGHARNE, SOUTH WALES

Coygan Cave, a 34 m long and 35 m wide cave located on an outcrop of carboniferous limestone, was completely destroyed by quarrying in the 1960s (Aldhouse-Green et al. 1995). It was situated at 60 m OD, under the brow of a limestone cliff behind a small, level platform, beyond which the ground sloped steeply downwards to the alluvial flats below (Grimes and Cowley 1935). Our understanding of it results from five excavations from the 1860s to 1960s (Hicks 1867, 1884; Wardle 1919; Clegg 1970; Aldhouse-Green et al. 1995). Excavations varied in standards and recording and some material is now missing (Grimes and Cowley 1935, 103). The most informative were those of McBurney and Clegg (Clegg 1970; Aldhouse-Green et al. 1995).

Remains were excavated from several cave earths which were interspersed with stalagmite development. The fauna comprised the classic MIS3 Pin Hole MAZ (see main text) and the site originally served as the type site for this MAZ (Currant and Jacobi 1997) and was later substituted for Pin Hole as deposits in the former still exist and would therefore allow future reinvestigation (Currant and Jacobi 2002). Material from the cave's Upper Layers (4 and 5) is heavily gnawed and some bones and teeth are acid worn from passage through a carnivores digestive system (Aldhouse-Green et al. 1995). Based on the patterns of destruction and species exploited, the primary agent of accumulation was clearly hyaena, whose coprolites were abundant in the cave. No gnawing was observed on the sparse bone assemblage from underlying Layers 1 and 2, however, suggesting that hyaenas only took up residence in the cave after these had accumulated.

Only three Late Middle Palaeolithic handaxes and two flakes attest Neanderthal presence (see Figure 1). Two of the handaxes were found about one metre apart near the base of Layer 4. The third handaxe and two flakes – one clearly a handaxe-thinning flake – were found towards the base of the cave earth near the third of four entrances (Grimes and Cowley 1935). These are made of fine-grained diorite and rhyolite, probably derived from outcrops ~20–40 km away in Pembrokeshire. Two handaxes are made on flakes, with clear thinning at the butt designed to create a third robust working edge. While their edges are sharp and the general mint condition eliminates the possibility of fluvial abrasion or solutional weathering, the arêtes between the flakes are rounded. Aldhouse-Green et al. (1995) suggested that this might be due to rubbing over a long period, perhaps in the hand or a pouch. The third handaxe also seems to have had an interesting biography: an ancient 'break' running along one margin appears to have been a failed resharpening attempt which formed a burin-like edge rather than a sharp one, in precisely the same manner as the handaxe from Lynford described below. The location within the cave of two of the handaxes, tucked against the north wall, may suggest that they had been cached for future recovery.

Text Box 6.6

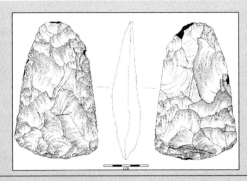

FIGURE 1
Classic *bout coupé* handaxe from Coygan Cave. (From White and Jacobi 2002. Drawings by Julian Cross.)

McBurney (cited in Aldhouse-Green et al. 1995, 47) noted a 'very fine hearth' from a sandy layer below the cave earth. It is unfortunate that this – however fine – was not better recorded; it is unclear whether this was deeply buried within the sand or lay on its surface, whether the sand is the same as the waterlain sand of Bed 2 or whether it was associated with the Middle Palaeolithic use of the cave. Aldhouse-Green et al. (1995, 48) suggested that the most parsimonious hypothesis was to regard the hearth as a feature of the Middle Palaeolithic occupation based on their reconstruction of the stratigraphy.

Neanderthal presence at Coygan Cave appears remarkably fleeting, probably only a single visit, although the proposed caching would suggest at least an intention to return. Neanderthals seem not to have engaged in knapping at the site and the few artefacts left behind were clearly brought from elsewhere, apparently after an extended use-life. Aldhouse-Green et al. (1995, 67) attribute this ephemeral presence to the cave itself for, while it provided spectacular views over the Bristol Channel plain, it was of modest size, had small and limited entrances and did not provide much scope for sitting in the daylight while carrying out daily routines. It was more suitable for use as a hyaena den, at least after Neanderthals had come and gone.

Precisely when Neanderthals used the cave is unclear. A radiocarbon measurement on a red deer bone from Layer 4 produced a date of 38,684 +2,713/−2,024 BP (BM-499), although this is certainly an underestimate. Uranium-series determinations on flow stone samples are also problematic, as they were conducted on derived fragments rather than *in situ* stalagmite. The youngest measurement – 64 ± 2 ka BP obtained on clasts from within or beneath the archaeological horizons – provides a *terminus post quem*, suggesting that the Neanderthal presence in the cave took place ~60–44 ka BP, before which the cave was probably closed to sediment, animals and humans explaining the absence of Joint Mitnor (MIS5e), Bacon Hole (MIS5d–b) and Banwell (MIS5a–4).

Text Box 6.6

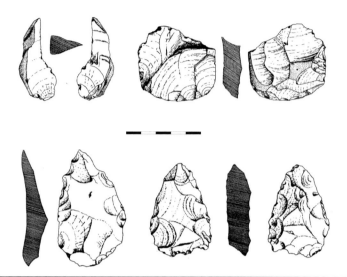

FIGURE 6.3
Middle Palaeolithic artefacts from Uphill Quarry. Top: Naturally backed knife and broken handaxe. Bottom: Mousterian Point and diminutive handaxe. (Scale in cm. After Harrison 1977.)

Open air assemblages

The situation found in British caves is mirrored in the open air sites, only two of which have produced large assemblages, and only one of these – Lynford Quarry, Mundford, Norfolk – having been excavated using modern techniques. The main Lynford assemblage comprises some 565 artefacts in mint condition of ≥20 mm maximum dimension, consisting of 45 handaxes and 489 flakes alongside a small flake-tool element including scrapers, notches and bifacial pieces (Figure 6.4). The assemblage was recovered from slow-moving or still waterlain organic deposits (Facies Association B-ii), infilling an abandoned channel of the River Wissey (Figure 6.5), although it seems likely that much of the lithic assemblage was introduced into the channel through the collapse of the adjacent channel edges where primary activities took place (White in press; Lewis in press). A rich palaeoenvironmental sample including pollen, plant macrofossils, insects, and molluscs was also recovered (Boismier et al. 2003; see Text Box 6.7), alongside an important Pin Hole MAZ faunal assemblage that included horse, reindeer, bison and mammoth.

The Lynford lithic assemblage reveals much about Neanderthal activities and organisation of technology in the landscape. The flakes are dominated by soft hammer pieces from handaxe trimming, with the prevalence of handaxes and low frequency of cores (n=3) indicating that almost the whole sample, including hard-hammer and indeterminate examples, derives from handaxe manufacture. Furthermore, the pattern and number of dorsal scars, butt type and cortex percentage suggest that most come from the later stages of handaxe trimming, with minimal primary working or shaping taking place on site (White in press). In this sense the Lynford assemblage is a numerically larger open air expression of the assemblages found in caves.

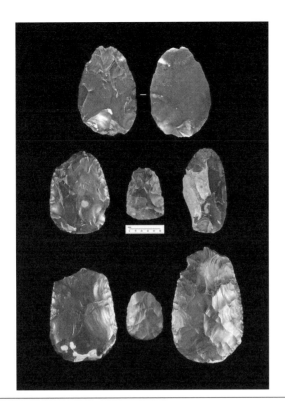

FIGURE 6.4
Handaxes and scrapers from Lynford. Top: two sides of a large unifacial handaxe. Middle, L to R: cordiform handaxe with deliberate notch to right lateral, a *bout coupé* handaxe, a convergent scraper. Bottom, left to right: large handaxe with twin breaks to tip, small ovate handaxe, large ovate handaxe.

FIGURE 6.5
The organic sediments of Facies Association B at Lynford Quarry, Mundford, Norfolk. Artefacts were found throughout the main laminated sequence, with refitting pieces separated by up to 51 cm vertically. (Photograph Mark White.)

AN MIS3 WARM INTERVAL AT LYNFORD

The organic deposits at Lynford, Norfolk, occupy an abandoned palaeochannel on the floodplain of the River Wissey. It was around – and probably sometimes within – this channel that Neanderthals were active, thus the inferred condition of the water reveals much about the conditions Neanderthals were prepared to tolerate. The sedimentology and biota of the organic sediments indicate that they filled pools of still or slow-moving water separate from the main river, with a maximum depth of c.1 m (Green in press, Coope in press, Keen in press). These pools were well vegetated with true aquatics such as water milfoil, bogbean, watercrowfoot and emergent aquatics including bulrush (Green in press). The invertebrate fauna reinforces this picture, with several species of planorbids (ramshorn snails) that feed on various pondweed (Keen, in press) and a number of hydraenid and hydrophilid beetles that in their adult stages feed on decomposing plant matter, indicating that the margins of the pond were choked with aquatic vegetation (Coope in press).

Algae characteristic of shallow pools was also present, as were a number of iron pyrites framboids that develop in stagnant, anaerobic water. This suggests that the water at Lynford was at times rather unpleasant, with poor water and rotting mats of organic matter (Green in press). The ground beetles *Loricela pilicornis*, which is often found beside foul-smelling water with much decomposing organic debris (Coope in press) and *Bembidion obliquum*, which is often found beside stagnant ponds where the earth is damp and sedges and rushes are found, supports this assertion. Similarly, the presence of 'slum' molluscan taxa (i.e. those tolerant of poor water conditions) such as *Pisidium casertanum* and dwarf pond snail *Lymnaea truncatula* (Keen, in press) supports this. The majority of the molluscs avoid such conditions, though, indicating that these periods of stagnation may have been ephemeral. Evidence of oxidation in the organic beds also suggests periodic exposure, although there was no evidence of dessication, suggesting the water body was more or less permanent (Boismier et al. 2003). Fish inhabited these waters, with stickleback, pike and perch found in the organic silts.

Bank erosion was frequent and sometimes dramatic, probably caused by summer melts mobilising sediments, combined with active trampling by the large mammals evident at the site (Boismier et al. 2003). The microstructure of the sediments gave no indication that the ground was ever frozen, although this may be concealed by bioturbation (ibid.); large clasts within the fine organic silts were interpreted as being introduced from the surface of winter ice during the summer thaw (Lewis pers. comm.). The water at Lynford would therefore have only been seasonally accessible; if Neanderthals were present, then the flint nodules may have been deliberately thrown in an attempt to break through it.

The pollen sequence was divided by Green (in press) into several vegetation zones. The character of the terrestrial plants changed little throughout the accumulation of the organic silts and did not indicate major climatic changes.

Text Box 6.7

The zonation is predominantly based on a reduction in the frequency of aquatic plants, probably signalling the transition from virtually still water to faster-moving water. Periods of faster flowing water were also shown by the abundance of *Valvata piscinalis* and *Pisidium subtrucatum*, while high frequencies of land snails probably represent the sweepings of the floodplain while the river was in spate (Keen in press). Few of the beetles suggest running water but *Oreodytes rivilis* lives in streams and rivers where the bottom is firm and the predatory diving-beetle *Potamonectes depressus* lives in larger bodies of running water with little or no vegetation (Coope in press). This clearly shows that the water was only periodically foul.

Around the margins of the water a sedge and reed swamp played host to various beetles, molluscs and frogs, and onto which the herbivores ventured to access the waterbody and rich vegetation. The close proximity of dry, grassy areas with calcareous soils is shown by a number of flowering herbaceous plants including bellflowers, rock roses and gentian, as well as the moss snail *Pupilla muscorum* (Green in press; Keen in press). Relatively bare or short turf vegetation is indicated by dandelion and plantain, alongside the heliophytic ground beetle *Poecilus lepidus* and hairy snail *Trichia hispida* (Coope in press; Keen in press).

Dung beetles are particularly well represented, with many species of *Aphodius* that feed on the dung of large mammals proving that many were feeding on and around the channel. The condition of the insect remains further suggests that they were damaged *in situ*, probably through trampling. Carcass beetles were also present, the carrion beetle *Thanatophilus dispar* particularly abundant (Coope in press), which indicates that animals were also dying at Lynford. Coope (in press) notes, however, that very few Lynford coleoptera are associated with dried carcasses, either those that feed directly off dry meat and skin or indirectly off fly larvae. There are also no fly puparia that would be expected if maggots had quickly infested fresh carcasses and no species that feed on dry bones. Coope considers this an enigmatic record and is of considerable importance in how we interpret the human activity at the site (White 2006).

Green (in press) notes the possibility of some small stands of trees or isolated trees, possibly on the valley sides or farther afield, although the inverbrate faunas contain no obligate woodland species. Willow and birch have been interpreted as dwarf forms and species of beetle that are known to feed on willow (*Melasoma collaris, Phytodecta* sp., *Phylodecta* sp.) are accounted for by these forms.

The relatively small catchment area of the Lynford palaochannel contains evidence of a range of aquatic, marshy and dry grassland environments with a muted and disputed signal for isolated trees. These environments were littered with rotting vegetation, carcasses and dung and at times the smell of stagnant water must have been pervasive. These variations would have impacted on human access to the channel edge and affected the location of hominin action.

Text Box 6.7

Like Robin Hood Cave, Lynford also contains limited evidence for much shorter chains of manufacture–use–discard on site using local fluvial raw materials, including a minimally worked handaxe on a cobble with conjoinable primary removals. Other on-site manufacture is indicated by three flake-based roughouts and two flake 'preforms', most of which were abandoned when flaws became evident in the flint (White in press). However, given the paucity of cores from Lynford, none big enough to produce the preforms, it is assumed that these were introduced to the site from elsewhere, possibly in a dressed state, and thus may again point to logistical lithic movements similar to the apparent cache of quartzite cobbles from Yew Tree Shelter.

The Lynford handaxes form a tight group in terms of shape and technology, tending to be intensively worked, broad and highly refined, with a number of flat-butted cordiforms and one 'true' *bout coupé* (White in press). They also show a number of informative techno-functional features. Twenty-three complete and broken handaxes show varying levels of macroscopic tip damage, generally snaps rather than crushing. In several cases, snaps in opposite directions occur, suggesting that they were produced through a twisting or 'to and fro' prising motion. This recurrent pattern of breakage suggests that one of the major tasks to which the handaxes were being put involved using the tip as a lever, possibly to disarticulate the joints of large animals. In two cases the break surface shows evidence of fine regular 'retouch' and some possibly break-related spalling but others show deliberate modification to thicken and strengthen the broken edge.

Other evidence for repair, recycling and edge modification is widespread (White in press). In two cases fragments of once larger handaxes have been refashioned into new tools by judicious retouch along the break and reorientation of the tools' long axis. Another example of extreme reworking is shown and described in Figure 6.6. Ten handaxes show tranchet removals (twelve tranchet flakes were also found). Given the other indicators of breakage and reworking, these possibly represent the resharpening of broken or blunted tips. Five handaxes also show evidence of notching to the edges and twenty show 'scraper-like' lateral retouch (White in press; cf. Depaepe 2001; Soressi and Hays 2003). The handaxes with retouch are significantly larger than those without, conforming to Dibble's (e.g. 1995) assertion that the larger and better pieces were preferentially selected for extended usage. A number of handaxes also show what appears to be deliberate 'backing', in at least one case on the opposite margin to an area of scraper retouch.

Twenty flake tools were also recovered from the palaeochannel deposits. These show a high frequency of working to both faces with twelve of the scrapers plus a hachoir showing some bifacial working. In eight cases this has been directed towards thinning or removing the butt, with further working occasionally found elsewhere on the ventral surface to regularise edges. In shape and general morphology the distinction between handaxes and scrapers is rather fuzzy, with an arbitrary separation of a technological continuum based on intensity of bifacial working and edge modification. Some of the handaxes, although extensively worked on one face, retain enough evidence of an original ventral flake surface to qualify as partial handaxes under Bordes's (1961) typology.

FIGURE 6.6

Extreme recycling at Lynford. This piece originated as a well-made ovate or pointed ovate handaxe >127 mm in length. At some point in its history it lost its tip and the resulting break surface was used as a platform for two blade-like removals along the lateral margins. These removed the sharp bifacial edges and left two squared edges in their place. Although not recovered, these pieces would have resembled crested blades. A third blade-like removal (found and conjoined) hinged and failed to travel the length of the piece. Finally, a squat hard-hammer flake was removed from one of the flat edges, forming a notch. The conjoinable flake shows that at least part of this sequence of events happened within the palaeochannel. It is difficult to assess its significance. It may represent a failed attempt to resharpen the handaxe following the loss of the tip, or the reuse of a broken handaxe as a core. More emotively, it may just be wanton destruction, the result of an over-heated Neanderthal temper and quite possibly a case of 'flint-rage'.

Recent studies of Middle Palaeolithic handaxe assemblages in Northern France have similarly begun to emphasise a number of blending categories: true handaxes, partial handaxes and bifacial scrapers (papers in Cliquet 2001), with the artefacts from each class serving as either tools in themselves or as supports for other tools (that is, the scraper edges and notches to handaxes described above).

Lynford thus appears to have been a place in the landscape to which handaxes in various states of reduction were brought from manufacturing sites farther afield. Several were broken, repaired and finessed on site, where they were finally lost or discarded. Some of the partial handaxes/bifacial scrapers may represent similar tools at the beginning of an intended longer use-life and only a small number were made on-site from local materials to fulfil an unanticipated need or to replace items irretrievably broken or lost. The Lynford handaxes also conform to recent suggestions that Middle Palaeolithic handaxes possessed prehensive and active edges, the role and location of which may have changed during the life of the tool (Boëda 2001; Soressi and Hays 2003). Middle Palaeolithic handaxes were highly flexible implements with vari-functional edges which formed tools, and supports for other 'tools' such as scrapers and notches, and which were subject to extensive resharpening throughout an extended and mobile use-life (e.g. Boëda et al. 1990; Turq 2000; Soressi and Hays 2003). The partly decorticated preforms and roughouts taken to the channel edge in various stages of advancement would have provided a range of options when it came time to use them. This pattern of artefact curation, rejuvenation and discard is entirely consistent with what we see occurring in the caves.

The conclusions drawn from the Lynford assemblage can be extended to the corpus of British Middle Palaeolithic handaxes. Many of these occur as isolated discards, some (such as Fisherton) apparently in direct association with the remains of large herbivores (Stevens 1870). None are found in situations that imply large social gatherings at domestic foci and nor are they associated with the debris from their manufacture. Nearly all, then, appear to be objects that have been widely transported and modified until finally abandoned in the context of use – highly mobile and morphologically fluid objects. The limited occurrences in precise cave contexts may represent small caches of personal gear stashed by Neanderthal hunters for later use.

This technological behaviour must be viewed in relation to the mammalian assemblage from the site which suggests that mammoths were an important attraction whether or not they were actively hunted or scavenged (see Text Box 6.8). In the broader behavioural and environmental context, the technological organisation suggests a degree of planning, a versatile butchery kit being transported around the open landscape to counter the difficulties of predicting the distribution of mobile (animal) resources, and the possible spatial differentiation between (known) flint sources and the locations in which tools would be needed (Torrence 1989; Nelson 1991; Ashton 1998c). Even if they were simply scavenging dead animals or actively seeking out sick ones on the mammoth steppe, this tool-kit would have helped Neanderthals respond quickly to visual cues like carrion birds and gain early access; thoughtful and prepared Neanderthals reading the signs. The absence of hind limb bones and the flexion breaks on handaxe tips may show that, despite the absence of cut-marks, Neanderthals were dismembering fairly complete mammoth carcasses at Lynford. We also know from isotopic evidence that Neanderthals consumed considerable quantities of mammoth in adjacent areas of Belgium (Bocherens et al. 1999, 2001). An important question is whether the quantity of animals in the small area excavated at Lynford might require a more proactive Neanderthal, perhaps 'shepherding' animals, many of whom were previously wounded, into the marshy palaeochannel, or whether one random encounter every year for twelve years explains it all.

This pattern of transport and curation is not evident at Riverside Pits, Little Paxton, Cambridgeshire, where artefacts were recovered in the basal gravels of the low terrace (Terrace 1–2) of the Great Ouse, alongside a Pin Hole MAZ (Tebbutt et al. 1927; Paterson and Tebbutt 1947; Tebbutt pers. comm. to Jacobi 1982). Some 210 artefacts were recovered, including 200 flakes and flake tools, eight handaxes and two cores, which Paterson divided into two groups based on condition and patina. Paterson's Group B comprised 201 artefacts in fresh to slightly rolled condition, with some edge damage and slight battering, clear evidence of some fluvial disturbance. Two flint sources were noted, a grey 'Lincolnshire' flint and local black flint with a worn cortex; both were probably obtained from local river gravels (Paterson and Tebbutt 1947). The assemblage included seven

NEANDERTHALS AMONG MAMMOTHS AT LYNFORD QUARRY, NORFOLK

In addition to its large Late Middle Palaeolithic lithic assemblage Lynford is important for the mammalian remains found at the site, key species including mammoth, horse, rhinoceros, bison and reindeer. Schreve (2006) reported 1,245 pieces of mammoth bone (91% of the total assemblage), representing a minimum of eleven individuals. The mammoth remains were dominated by fragments of tusk, crania and ribs and had been heavily trampled. Weathering patterns on the surfaces of the bones led Schreve (ibid.) to conclude that the mammalian assemblage was a palimpsest that had entered the channel by various means over a period of tens of years. Neanderthals had played some role in its accumulation, however. Green bone fractures and broken teeth indicative of marrow extraction were found on the remains of horse, reindeer and rhinoceros. The mammoth remains lacked cut-marks or other direct features associated with human butchery, perhaps not surprisingly given their size and condition (cf. Schreve 2006; Haynes 2002; Gaudzinski 1999b).

The mortality profile of the mammoths (mostly young to middle-aged males), the high number of pathologies observable in the prime target area around the ribs (possibly non-fatal humanly inflicted wounds) and the virtual absence of meaty

FIGURE 1
Montage of Lynford during excavation. Main picture: mammoth tusks under excavation from the organic channel deposits. Top right: mammoth mandible. Top left: beetle elytra (wing cases) from the organic channel fill, demonstrating the exceptional preservation at Lynford. (Photos courtesy Nigel Larkin.)

Text Box 6.8

long bones suggested that Neanderthals had interacted with the mammoths, probably removing meatier parts from the site for processing elsewhere (Schreve 2006, 555). Evidence for carnivore gnawing was negligible but where present hyaena was identified as the prime suspect.

The level and nature of human–elephant interaction during the earlier Palaeolithic is still hotly contested (Gaudzinski 1999b) and, as at Lynford, it is seldom possible to demonstrate unequivocally an active link between humans and elephants (cf. Torralba/Ambrona, Spain (Santonja and Villa 1990; Villa 1990) and Bollschweil, Germany (Conard and Niven 2001)). In only a few open-air sites is the claim for direct human interaction with elephant carcasses compelling (e.g. at Aridos, Villa 1990). Even at these places, and in spite of the evidence that Neanderthals were not only highly successful hunters of medium to large game but actually top carnivores (e.g. Gaudzinski 1996; 1999a; Gaudzinski and Roebroeks 2000; Bratlund 1999; Conard and Prindiville 2000; Adler et al. 2006; Stiner et al. 2009), who probably did eat mammoth meat (Bocherens et al. 1999, 2001, 2005), it is often unclear whether Neanderthals were hunting or scavenging mammoths and other elephants. These questions cannot easily be answered by the Lynford data. What it does show, however, is the repeated use of a known area of the landscape in which these giants could be disadvantaged to the benefit of their human predators. The La Cotte de St Brelade mammoth–rhino bone heaps are another obvious example of a disadvantaging site (Scott 1980) but sadly decent lithic associations are lacking from the key contexts (Callow and Cornford 1986).

One should not rule out hunting. White (in press) suggests that the nature of the lithic assemblage, in conjunction with the character of the faunal assemblage, suggested that Neanderthals had repeatedly gone to Lynford 'tooled-up' and ready for action. He suggested that they had anticipated encountering mammoths and had played a primary role in dispatching them, possibly harrying sick and injured animals into the water. Two European examples provide evidence that this practice may have been more widespread. At the MIS5e site of Lehringen, Germany, the carcass of a straight-tusked elephant was found in fully interglacial lakeside deposits, overlying a wooden spear and associated with a small lithic assemblage. The spear suggests that Neanderthals had some role in the final despatching of the elephant. A practically identical situation (albeit without a spear) was found at Neumark-Gröbern, another German MIS5e site (Mania et al. 1990), where an almost complete elephant carcass was found in lake sediments, associated with 27 flint artefacts structurally very similar to those at Lehringen and some of which bore use-traces. A third, strikingly similar site, was described at Pagnano d'Asolo, Italy, but sadly this was excavated in the nineteenth century and poorly documented (Mussi 1999).

Text Box 6.8

small handaxes, one being a classic *bout coupé* showing evidence of possible use-wear at the butt produced by heavy-duty battering, and a number of scrapers including a déjeté scraper, a 'Quina'-type sidescraper and a convergent scraper with bifacial retouch, both similar to forms found at Lynford. Although this is a palimpsest assemblage, the absence of cores suggests that handaxe manufacture was the key technological activity at Little Paxton. The range of flakes present appears to reflect complete handaxe reduction sequences: 30% were from roughing out with fully cortical dorsal surfaces,

45% from shaping or thinning flakes, and 5% from finishing or retouching (Paterson and Tebbutt 1947, 43). Paterson also identified a number of Levallois flakes from both groups although later workers have dismissed these as handaxe-thinning flakes (Wymer 1985). Overall it would appear that, in contrast to Lynford, Little Paxton represents a more complete manufacturing sequence, perhaps one of the places where a rich source of raw material was used to gear-up for activities elsewhere in the landscape.

Levallois technology in Late Middle Palaeolithic Britain

There are remarkably few unambiguous Levallois products in the British Late Middle Palaeolithic, a fact that clearly distinguishes it from the Early Middle Palaeolithic (White and Jacobi 2002; White et al. 2006). This is perhaps not surprising; Levallois points are almost entirely absent in northern France in MIS3, suggesting that the specific technology used to produce them, which was present during MIS5, became regionally extinct when the region was abandoned in MIS4 (Roebroeks et al. 2011). The few British examples that do exist are all flakes and we know of no Levallois core from a firm MIS3 context. A small number of Levallois flakes are known from Kent's Cavern (~5) and Robin Hood Cave (2). A number of flakes hitherto identified as Levallois (Patterson and Tebbutt 1947) have subsequently been reclassified as handaxe thinning flakes (e.g. Little Paxton – Wymer 1985). Evidence from Oldbury and other sites suggests that discoidal core technology was a dominant feature of the British MTA, and it is therefore possible that some of the more ambiguous flakes identified by some as Levallois are actually products of this technology (cf. Cook and Jacobi 1998). At all sites where unambiguous Levallois products have been found it is noticeable that they are in no more than single figures. The extreme rarity of Levallois material among sites and findspots overall, their low number on sites where they do exist and the total absence of cores cannot be an artefact of recovery and one might confidently conclude that Levallois technology was rarely practised in MIS3 Britain.

Interestingly, at the two sites where unambiguous Levallois products occur, leafpoints have also been found. It seems plausible that these Levallois products were generated during the use of laminar technologies aimed at the production of blade blanks for the manufacture of leafpoints. Given the nature of the relevant sites, however, we recognise that this remains speculative. If correct, however, it would again suggest that Levallois technology was not a feature of the British Late Middle Palaeolithic, but of the Early Upper Palaeolithic.

In recent years, a number of studies have suggested that Levallois technology was preferentially selected for long-distance curation in the landscape (Geneste 1985; 1989). White and Pettitt (1995) suggested that this flexible technology would be suited to wide-ranging movements in relatively unfamiliar territory, making its absence in a sparsely and ephemerally occupied Britain puzzling. However, Geneste (1985, 511) also observed that MTA assemblages tend to have a high frequency of exotic raw materials, suggesting that this too is a mobile technology. In France the larger MTA assemblages occur most frequently in open air sites and in regions of good quality raw material; in areas of poor quality raw materials, assemblages tend to be small, often isolated pieces (Turq

2000). The British sites do not appear to conform to these patterns, southern Britain at least being an area of rich primary and secondary chalk flint sources, yet dominated by isolated finds and small assemblages. In summary, we suggest that the reason for the virtual absence of Levallois technology in the British Late Middle Palaeolithic is due to the fact that, when here, Neanderthals were reliant upon a highly curated handaxe-centred tool-kit, superimposed upon which, when necessity demanded, was the simple use of heavy-duty tool-kits made of local resources. A relative unfamiliarity with the landscape due to ephemeral and irregular visits may explain the differences between Britain and Europe in terms of assemblage size and transport practices.

BRITISH LATE MIDDLE PALAEOLITHIC SETTLEMENT SYSTEMS

The procurement and mobility of raw materials in the Neanderthal landscape is now well established, at least for France (Geneste 1985, 1989). The three main procurement distance clusters concerned are local (<5 km), regional (<30 km), and distant (80–100 km). The shortest of these probably reflects the local foraging range immediately surrounding a site – materials found within an hour's walk – while the regional distances presumably reflect longer term foraging patterns over days or weeks. The more distant raw materials are presumed to represent annual ranging behaviour – according to Gamble (2002) an individual's 'landscape of habit' – the maximum 80–100 km transport distances suggesting home ranges with a radius of 40–50 km (encompassing an area of ~5,000 km^2). These data are of heuristic importance for understanding the British material, to which we return below.

Raw material use: local and exotic

A striking contrast between south-west England and south-west France is that, in the latter, raw materials from a variety of sources – usually six or more – are ubiquitous in most Mousterian assemblages, even if these sources were within 5–10 km (Mellars 1996). In Britain, in contrast, most assemblages are produced on only one or two raw material types, most of which were available from sources at the local scale – again possibly reflecting something of an unfamiliarity with the landscape.

British flint is widely distributed in the north and south, although better in quality in the south; igneous rocks are most common in the west, and other fine-quality stones such as cherts are found in the south-west and east. All of these rocks occur as primary outcrops, as components of fluvial terrace gravels, and as glacial erratics. Most British Late Middle Palaeolithic artefacts are made on flint that was available at the local scale, typically <5 km from their findspot, and never more than ~30–40 km (one day's walk). This includes single artefact findspots and larger sites in all of the major river valleys. Non-flint materials were widely employed in regions where these were more abundant than flint, notably quartzite and ironstone in the Creswell region (both available in the immediate vicinity of the caves), and cherts in the south-west. Deposits of Cretaceous greensand chert occur in eastern Devon and Somerset (Roberts 1996), where flint deposits are rare. Late Middle Palaeolithic lithics are most commonly found on this locally available material (ibid., 220). Carboniferous chert, for example, was used for artefacts at Picken's Hole (ApSimon 1986). Greensand chert was used at Kent's Cavern and at Limekiln Quarry (Wells, Somerset; Vranch 1981). At Coygan, handaxes were made of igneous rock obtainable locally (Aldhouse-Green et al. 1995, 67). A small number of Middle Palaeolithic flakes from Creswell are on a grey flint, similar to flint from the Lincolnshire Wolds. The very small amount of material involved could possibly have been obtained locally as glacial erratics; but if it is of the type found in the Wolds and collected at source this still need not represent a transport distance greater than ~30 km.

In contrast, there is little evidence of long-distance raw material movements. The dominance of apparently short transport distances does not, however, imply that this technology was in any way expedient or unplanned but relates to the local landscapes through which Neanderthals operated. The technological signatures at most sites, both cave and open air, the existence of diminutive handaxes consistent with their having been heavily resharpened (e.g. Robin Hood Cave and Uphill) and polish possibly indicative of curation in a pouch (Coygan) indicate that some elements of the tool-kit may have circulated for relatively long periods of time. In flint-poor regions of the north, flint from the south appears to have been preferentially transported as valued personal gear such as handaxes and scrapers but there is no evidence that quartzites or ironstone were moved southwards, perhaps suggesting that this material was not valued outside its local availability, possibly due to difficulties of working (quartzite) or relatively soft and indurable edge (ironstone). This would support the notion that local operational areas were relatively small and knowledge of good quality raw materials was at a premium within these. These observations are not inconsistent with the notion that Britain was occupied by Neanderthals only seasonally.

Bout coupé *handaxes*

The apparent temporal and spatial distribution of *bout coupé* handaxes raises other intriguing issues regarding Neanderthal settlement in Doggerland. A number of MIS3 Middle Palaeolithic facies across Europe have yielded geographically specific handaxe forms, clear evidence of the emergence of cultural geographies at this time: for example the Vasconian Mousterian of the Pyrenees and Northern Cantabria (Bordes 1953; Cabrera-Valdés 1988), the Micoquian of central Europe (Bosinski 1967); the Micoquo–Prondnikian of Southern Poland (Allsworth-Jones 1986) and the MTA of France. As noted above, the British assemblages appear to have undoubted cultural links with the broadly contemporary continental MTA but there are some significant differences in handaxe shape. In Britain the *bout coupé* forms a unique regional variant (Roe 1981; Tyldesley 1987; White and Jacobi 2002: Figures 6.7 and 6.8) while types such as the exaggerated triangulates of northern France and the various 'Micoquian' forms are absent except as very occasional and probably fortuitous specimens. While chronology may explain such typological absences, certain forms being used in Europe during periods when Britain was not visited, this cannot account for the absence of *bout coupés* in Europe.

FIGURE 6.7
Bout coupé handaxes. From left to right: Southbourne, Dorset; Coygan Cave; Castle Lane, Bournemouth, Dorset. (Scale in cm.)

FIGURE 6.8
Bout coupé handaxe from Castle Lane, Bournemouth. (Photo © Trustees of the British Museum.)

This is unlikely to be an artefact of classification (cf. Coulson 1990), as comprehensive surveys (Tyldesley 1987; Soressi 2002) have shown that, while a few examples of *bout coupés* do exist in the Paris Basin, their frequency is extremely low compared to the British situation. Given the tensions between the environmental data and Neanderthal survivorship, we suggested above that Neanderthals were only summer visitors to western Doggerland, perhaps then only during the warmer oscillations. This, though, raises new issues because the clear contrasts in handaxe morphology appear to preclude the notion of movement from contiguous Neanderthal territories in France, Belgium and the Netherlands. It is entirely possible that the main focus of Neanderthal presence in north-west Europe was restricted in the main to the now submerged landscapes of Doggerland and Britain formed merely the temporary western periphery. It is still uncertain whether a sufficient ecological gradient existed between 'upland' Britain and the adjacent lowland plains to make winter survival there any easier (see Barron et al. 2003) but it would certainly fit a number of known distance parameters, including the 300 km seasonal movements inferred from raw material transfers in central Europe, and the total area traversed by modern cold-adapted hunter-gatherers over the course of several decades (Gamble 1993;

Binford 1983). Both further match onto the distribution of Middle Palaeolithic sites in mainland Britain. To resolve these issues we need far more sites like Lynford and new anthropogenic cave assemblages from which we can begin to judge the seasonality of Neanderthal activity in Britain. Future offshore finds of Middle Palaeolithic materials (similar to those mentioned in Glimmerveen et al. 2004; Verhart 2004; and Hublin et al. 2009) may also help resolve the interaction between different Neanderthal groups within these basins.

In terms of Neanderthal behaviour, these seasonal movements would probably have required a high degree of long-term logistical planning and provisioning with resources not apparently available in Doggerland (e.g. wooden shafts and spears), enhanced levels of cooperation, possible task divisions, finely tuned knowledge of the landscape and prey behaviour – a list of traits that includes much often deemed missing from the Neanderthal repertoire (White 2006; cf. Roebroeks 2001; Speth 2004).

Neanderthal local operational areas (LOAs)

Given the relatively high energy requirements and locomotor costs of the Neanderthals (Churchill 2006) one might expect Neanderthals to have foraged over shorter distances than *Homo sapiens*, occupying sites for very short periods and concomitantly investing little effort into the organisation of camps (Verpoorte 2006). Ranges, or local operational areas (LOAs) as we will call them, were probably fairly localised, with relatively high levels of residential mobility within them. We use the concept of LOAs to describe local clusters of Middle Palaeolithic materials, which, we believe, may be linked into an operational whole; and to avoid more behaviourally loaded terms such as 'territories' or 'group ranges'. Local operational areas (LOAs) may be recognised in the previously mentioned 'clusters' of Middle Palaeolithic handaxes, particularly the relative hotspots in the Bournemouth area, in the Great Ouse around Fenstanton, in the Middle Thames around Hillingdon (see Text Box 6.9), the South Downs of Sussex and, of course, the Creswell Heritage Area. It is also worth noting the two *bout coupé* handaxes recovered some five miles north-east of Lynford, in a buried channel beneath the floodplain of the Norfolk Blackwater (a tributary of the Wissey), one on the south-east bank near Little Cressingham (TF888004) and one on the north-east bank in the parish of Saham Toney (TF888005). The gravel from which these were recovered was tentatively correlated with the low-lying, terrace-like gravel deposits of the Wissey at Wretton (Lawson 1978), where a complex sequence of Devensian braided river deposits has been recorded overlying Ipswichian fluvial sediments (Sparks and West 1970; West et al. 1974). The proximity of these two sites to Lynford, their proposed MIS3 age, and the similarity in the handaxes might suggest that they too formed part of the *local operational area* of a single Neanderthal group. The river at Little Cressingham enters a constriction between two spurs, forming low hills to both the north and the south, perhaps vantage points for hunters who subsequently lost their transported handaxes in the context of animal encounters in the landscape (Lawson 1978).

We discuss here two case studies: the Creswell Crags region in the north Midlands, and the Axe valley in Somerset, and speculate that other key site clusters, such as Tor Bay, formed similar foci in other LOAs.

LATE MIDDLE PALAEOLITHIC FINDSPOTS IN THE THAMES VALLEY

Several supposedly Middle Palaeolithic handaxes have been reported from the Thames Valley, a number of which can be assigned to the Late Middle Palaeolithic on the basis of their stratigraphical position in the low-lying or floodplain gravels of the Thames. In the Upper Thames, a *bout coupé* handaxe has been reported from Tuckwell's Pit, Radley, Oxfordshire, lying below a coarse basal gravel (Tyldesley 1983) which probably equates with the Northmoor Gravel, the oldest and lowest units of which are usually attributed to cold-climate phases within the Middle Devensian (cf. Bridgland 1994, 35–41).

A small group of Middle Palaeolithic artefacts was found at Marlow in the Middle Thames between 1928 and 1932, surviving examples of which comprise two *bout coupé* handaxes, a sub-cordiform handaxe and a flake with a facetted butt that may have been removed from a discoidal core (Wymer 1968, 213; cf. Cook and Jacobi 1998; see Figure 1). Treacher (1934, 107–8) noted that the finds derived from 'the brickearth itself or sometimes at its base' overlying a terrace gravel regarded as being the Kempton Park Gravel (Wymer 1996a, 63) and thus of MIS4–2 age. Another *bout coupé* was found 3.5–4 m down *within* the Kempton Park Gravel at Berrymead Priory, Acton, at 15 m (50 ft) OD (Wymer 1968, 268, 1988, 1999, Figure 11). Based on its stratigraphical position, Ashton (2002) inferred that the find derived from an MIS4 deposit, but the Kempton Park Gravel Formation actually spans MIS4–2 (Bridgland 1994) and an MIS3 date is more probable. The same is true for the abraded *bout coupé* from Summerleaze Pit, Maidenhead, recovered with mammoth bones on a reject heap of gravel extracted a few feet above the modern floodplain of the Thames.

Late Middle Palaeolithic artefacts have also been claimed from the various brickearth deposits in north-west London, most found in the nineteenth century by J. Allen Brown (Brown 1887a and b, 1895; Collins 1978; Cotton 1984). Collins (1978) discerned a small series of *bout coupés* (which he termed 'Paxton Type') from this area, united by form, patina and colour. Tyldesley (1987, 46–9) accepted three as 'true' *bout coupé* forms: two from brickearth overlying Lynch Hill Terrace Gravel (MIS 10–9–8, Bridgland 1994) at Clayton's Pit, Yiewsley and Eastwood Pit, West Drayton and one

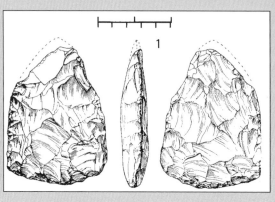

FIGURE 1
Bout coupé handaxe from Marlow. (After Wymer 1968.)

Text Box 6.9

Text Box 6.9

from brickearth overlying Taplow Terrace Gravel (MIS 8–7–6, ibid.) at Sipson, Hillingdon. The latter was found at the base of a banded brickearth overlying the Taplow Formation on the east side of Sipson Village (Cotton 1984). The handaxe lay horizontally 1.1 m into the brickearth, apparently an isolated discard (ibid.). The two faces of the handaxe show different preservational states – the downward face being fresh and mottled blue-white but the upper face showing evidence of pock-marking and weathering and having a lustrous white patina – suggesting that it had lain exposed on the surface for a period prior to burial. Micromorphological anaysis of a lens of pale greenish brickearth associated with the find suggested deposition under very cold conditions (Macphail, cited in Wymer 1988), explaining the thermal damage on the upper surface of the handaxe.

Sadly, the context of the Clayton's Pit specimen is unknown but its condition is clearly different from the Levallois material and Lower Palaeolithic handaxes from the Lynch Hill Gravel at this locality. The other (Allen Brown's #2193) came from Eastwood's Brick Pit. It is labelled as coming from 'loam above gravel' and from a depth of 7 ft (2.1 m), a unique context amongst the finds from this pit. Preservation is also distinctive: both faces have a bluish-white dendritic patina and are polished and pitted in a manner consistent with prolonged surface exposure. Unfortunately, the term 'loam above gravel' does not really allow these deposits to be accurately placed within the complex sequence at Eastwood's Pit, although this must describe brickearth. The find depth, at 7 ft (2.1 m), is close to the maximum depth of the brickearth, which might prompt an earlier age attribution, although the condition suggests that it was at some point exposed on a landsurface, perhaps during the Middle Devensian before being eventually covered by Late Devensian sediments.

The Creswell Crags LOA

By far the densest concentration of Middle Palaeolithic occupation in Britain is found at Creswell Crags (Figure 6.9 and 6.10). This is but one gorge among a number that cut a band of Permian limestone in the wider Creswell Heritage Region of Derbyshire and Nottinghamshire (Figure 6.10). Outside Creswell Crags, at least 30 Late Middle Palaeolithic artefacts are known from Ash Tree Cave, 2 km to the north (Table 6.4 and Text Box 6.10). The recovery of hyaena remains from Ash Tree Cave, and from Langwith Cave in the Poulter Valley (4 km south of Creswell), suggests that the wider region also served as the territory of hyaena clans. Although widespread evidence for Late Middle Palaeolithic activity is rather limited, it seems reasonable to assume that the wider landscape, rather than Creswell *sensu stricto,* formed a Neanderthal local operational area, which possibly extended as far as the aforemen-tioned site of Ravencliffe Cave in the Peak District, some 40 km to the west. This may give an indication of the scale of Neanderthal mobility in the region. The gently undulat-

FIGURE 6.9
Aerial view of Creswell Crags (Nottinghamshire/Derbyshire), looking east. The lake was formed in the 1860s by damming the stream that runs through the gorge. (Photograph courtesy Creswell Heritage Trust.)

ing landscape of the Creswell area, with plentiful rivers draining the plateaux in easterly directions (Mills 2001, 57), provided a rich ecotonal resource during MIS3 and pollen from Robin Hood Cave indicates a grassland with stands of juniper and various herbaceous vegetation at the time that the cave was occupied by Neanderthals (Jenkinson et al. 1986).

All of the major caves in the Creswell gorge have yielded Late Middle Palaeolithic assemblages. In order of size: at least 13 Late Middle Palaeolithic artefacts are known from Mother Grundy's Parlour, 58 from Pin Hole, 93 from Church Hole and 479 (possibly a little over 500 originally) from Robin Hood Cave (Dawkins 1876, 250–251, 1877, 591; Jenkinson 1984; Jacobi 2004; 2007b). Furthermore, the recovery of a number of unworked quartzite pebbles from the Yew Tree Shelter at the eastern end of the Creswell gorge suggests that the shelter was used to cache material in anticipation of future needs (R. Jacobi pers. comm.). It is likely that all of these counts are underestimates: Middle Palaeolithic quartzite flakes were recovered from the spoil heap of the 1875 excavation of Robin Hood Cave (Campbell 1969–1970), and by one of us (PP) from the spoil heap of the 1876 Church Hole excavation (Figure 6.11 and 6.12), which demonstrates that less impressive elements of débitage (at least) were often overlooked. As the majority of pieces have now been lost it is unlikely that the picture will improve. It is unlikely, however, that significant numbers of artefacts were discarded or lost and even assuming under-estimation these are, by continental standards, small assemblages that, as with the rest of British sites, suggest low population numbers and brief periods of occupation.

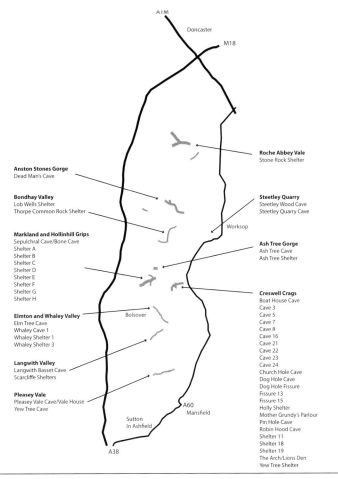

FIGURE 6.10

The Creswell Heritage Area, showing caves with Late Middle Palaeolithic materials. (Modified from Creswell Heritage Trust.)

ASH TREE CAVE, WHITWELL, DERBYSHIRE

Text Box 6.10

Ash Tree Cave, on the north-west side of the Burntfield Grips dry valley, was excavated by Leslie Armstrong from 1949–1956, who described a sequence of deposits some 4.4 m thick (Armstrong 1956). Further excavations by the Hunter Archaeological Society in 1959 and by Charles McBurney in 1960 remain unpublished. The cave's upper deposits yielded evidence of modern, Roman, Iron Age, Neolithic and Mesolithic activity, with Late Magdalenian/Creswellian occupation found throughout a thin Red Cave Earth (Armstrong 1956). In the Yellow Cave Earth beneath, Armstrong reported fauna belonging to the Pin Hole MAZ as well as three distinct areas ('zones') of Mousterian material, the latter 'less well-defined stratigraphically' than in Pin Hole (ibid., 62). AMS radiocarbon measurements on samples collected by McBurney range from 40,900 ± 1,800 BP (OxA-4103) to 30,250 ± 550 (Hedges et al. 1994, 1996). Currant and Jacobi

Text Box 6.10

(2002) suggest that the fauna from the basal clay belongs to the early Devensian Banwell MAZ. However, two radiocarbon measurements of 40,500 ± 1,600 BP (OxA-4580) and 25,660 ± 380 BP (OxA 5798) on bison and hyaena remains from this level do not reflect this (Hedges et al. 1994, 1996) although, as these were conducted prior to ultrafiltration, they are likely to be underestimates.

Armstrong described the evidence for Mousterian occupation as 'scanty and only indicative of occasional use either by man or animals' (ibid., 63) and, although no indication of actual numbers was provided, little material is extant in museum collections. Quartzite tools dominated the small collection which, as Armstrong noted, were similar to those from Pin Hole some 5 km away at Creswell although the Ash Tree Cave examples were of 'inferior quality workmanship' (ibid., 63). A small quantity of chert and flint artefacts including a point and a scraper attest activity in the wider landscape. In addition to these split bones and large quartzite 'pounders' (probably hammerstones, as with Creswell) were found in all three horizons.

At the base of the yellow loam, Armstrong found a concentration of wood ash and charcoal 2 ft in diameter and 3 ft thick lying on bedrock, which he reasonably interpreted as a hearth. Numerous fragments of animal bones, two 'heavy quartzite pounders' and the humerus of an immature rhinoceros were also found at this level. One must reserve judgement on the 'several bone awls' from this palimpsest of material; certainly no readily identifiable examples are extant and it is possible that this was over-interpretation of splintered bone. Similarly doubtful are the bird tibiae from the yellow cave earth which Armstrong saw as 'perforated at the distal ends for suspension' (ibid., 63). He interpreted these as personal ornaments, today a rather contentious claim in any Neanderthal context other than the Châtelperronian (Chase and Dibble 1987; Lindly and Clark 1990; D'Errico et al. 1998; Mellars 1999). In the light of recent demonstration that Neanderthals procured feathers for use (Peresani et al. 2011) it is possible that the modifications Armstrong saw relate to this. Alternatively the modifications – if genuine – may relate to Upper Palaeolithic activity: Jacobi (in Hedges et al. 1994) notes that at least one blade derives from Armstrong's excavations; thus, if the perforated bird bones are genuinely anthropogenic rather than being forms created naturally or by carnivores, then they might more reasonably be associated with this material. Given that in places the Mousterian material merged with the Late Upper Palaeolithic (Armstrong 1956, 62) such a mixture is not inconceivable. Whatever the case one must regard this as currently undemonstrable.

In all of the Creswell caves, quartzite is the dominant raw material (~96–99%), deriving from Triassic deposits commonly referred to as the 'bunter' pebble beds and available in the stream that ran through the gorge itself. Small numbers of artefacts on clay ironstone and flint suggest wider raw material procurement, the latter perhaps 40–60 km distant. Jacobi (2004) has noted a clear link between clay ironstone and handaxe manufacture at Creswell which suggests deliberate selection. The dominant technology, however, is either simple chopper/chopping tool reduction or the discoidal method, both well suited to the small cobbles, although given the presence of handaxes or handaxe-thinning flakes in

FIGURE 6.11
Excavation outside Church Hole Cave, 2006. (Photograph Paul Pettitt.)

Robin Hood Cave, Pin Hole and Mother Grundy's Parlour the collections fall broadly within the definition of the MTA, as with all British Late Middle Palaeolithic material.

Armstrong excavated at least 13 quartzite artefacts from Mother Grundy's Parlour, including 4 sidescrapers, 6 flakes and a handaxe of clay ironstone that is now either lost or represented only by a fragment in Manchester Museum (R. Jacobi, pers. comm). Armstrong noted the similarity of these artefacts 'to those figured from the Robin Hood and Church Hole caves' (1925, 152). Although it is unclear whether Late Middle Palaeolithic artefacts were excavated from the cave by the Dawkins/Mello team and are now lost, it is fair to assume that the cave was probably the least used in the gorge by Neanderthals. Ninety-three Middle Palaeolithic artefacts have been published from Church Hole, of which the majority are flakes and choppers. Of these, 73 were described as 'round pebbles' – apparently unmodified – and 33 pieces were extant, until a further 13 recently emerged out of storage at the University of Cork (P. Woodman, pers. comm. to PP). Among these, chopping tools are most abundant, several of which were also used as hammerstones (PP pers. obs.). In addition to these, three discoidal cores, five sidescrapers (one of flint), two naturally backed knives and various flakes reveal that, as with the other caves in the gorge, a small number of tool forms complemented the otherwise simple chopper/chopping tool assemblage (Figure 6.12 and 6.13).

At least 58 Late Middle Palaeolithic artefacts are known from Pin Hole, a figure probably close to the number originally recovered from the cave (Jacobi 2004; Jacobi et al. 1998).

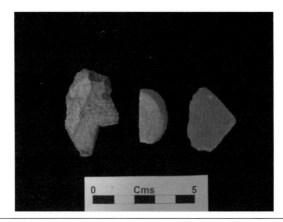

FIGURE 6.12
Church Hole, Creswell Crags (Nottinghamshire). Quartzite flakes from discoidal technology recovered from the 1876 spoil heap during excavations in 2006. (Photograph Paul Pettitt.)

FIGURE 6.13
Middle Palaeolithic quartzite flakes from Creswell Crags (Derbyshire/Nottinghamshire). (Photograph Paul Pettitt and courtesy of Museums Sheffield.)

Armstrong (1931–1932, 179) felt that there were at least three separate Late Middle Palaeolithic assemblages in Pin Hole, each separated by thick layers of cryoclastic slabs, although as Jacobi et al. (1998) noted, there is no reason to separate these stratigraphically, even if they may have derived from a number of brief occupations. The assemblage size and character suggests that *in situ* knapping was limited and, while flakes dominate the quartzite and flint assemblages, the cave is noteworthy for having a large proportion of tools, sidescrapers being the most common tool type on both materials (around 45% of the tool count). Two handaxes are present, although a large quartzite thinning flake (larger than any extant handaxe) and a thinning flake of clay–ironstone (for which there is no matching handaxe) suggest that others were moved in and out of the cave. Quartzite cores, whose colour does not match any known flake, suggest a similar pattern of import and export. Late Middle Palaeolithic artefacts from Pin Hole were re-plotted using

Armstrong's excavation notes which showed a main cluster in the rear of the cave (Jenkinson 1984, 74). Stratigraphically, the artefacts form a relatively discrete 'horizon' clearly distinct from the overlying Early Upper Palaeolithic artefacts, and a large series of Uranium-series and AMS ^{14}C dates on faunal remains associated with the lithics – including mammoth, woolly rhinoceros, horse, reindeer and a bovid – indicate an age for Neanderthal use of the cave between ~44 and ~50 ka BP (Jacobi et al. 1998; 2006 and Figure 6.14).

On the basis of known archaeology it is Robin Hood Cave that clearly received the greatest amount of Neanderthal attention. This is not surprising, given that it has the largest and airiest mouth of all of the Creswell caves. Choppers and flakes dominate the extant quartzite artefacts from Robin Hood Cave, although at least four cordiform handaxes of flint, ironstone and quartzite, several scrapers, and two Levallois flakes are also known. Spatially, their distribution was concentrated in the rear of the cave's western chamber. Radiocarbon measurements on unmodified fauna suggest a broad chronological range for Late Middle Palaeolithic activity in the cave of ~45–43 ka BP.

Dawkins (1877) reported a total of 479 artefacts from the Cave Earth and Red Sand in the Western Chamber (possibly out of a total a little higher than 500), 445 being quartzite chips (flakes); as no stratigraphical details are recorded on the artefacts these can no longer be substantiated. In the 1980s, Coulson (1990) assessed the surviving material (most of which is housed in the British Museum, having been donated by Franks who obtained it directly from Mello in 1883; the remaining objects are distributed around nine museums: Coulson 1990, 292), and was able to reassign 83 pieces to the Middle Palaeolithic (Table 6.11), including a flint handaxe and Tayac point recovered by Campbell (1969) from the Victorian spoil. The material recovered by Robert Laing from the rear of the cave, which reportedly included 'rude' choppers and scrapers, is now completely lost (Jenkinson 1984). This is extremely regrettable, as his short published account describes an area on or within the Red Sand that may represent Mousterian activity around a hearth, with scrapers, charred material and processed bone (Laing 1889, 582).

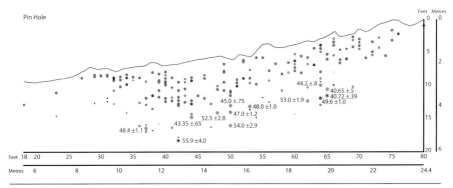

FIGURE 6.14

Section through the archaeological deposits in Pin Hole cave, Creswell, reconstructed by Roger Jacobi, showing Pin Hole MAZ dated fauna. Dots above relate to Late Upper Palaeolithic materials (see Chapter 8). (From Pettitt and Jacobi 2009.)

Table 6.11 Artefacts originally reported by Dawkins vs. Coulson's assessment of the extant assemblage from Robin Hood Cave.

Types after Dawkins 1877	Robin Hood Cave Earth
Oval ironstone implements	2
Ironstone fragments	2
Choppers	8
Hammer stones	19
Scrapers	3
Chips	442 (+3 from Red Sand)
Total	476
Quartzite round stones	48 (+5 from the Red Sand**)**
Types after Coulson 1990	
Levallois flake (Bordes 1)	2 (1 flint)
Single convex side scraper (Bordes 10)	
	2 (1 flint)
Convergent straight/convex side scraper (Bordes 19)	1
Side scraper on ventral surface (Bordes 25)	3 (1 basalt)
Side scraper with a thinned back (Bordes 27)	2
Atypical backed knives (Bordes 37)	1
Naturally backed knives (Bordes 38)	4 (1 basalt)
Raclette (Bordes 39)	1
Denticulate (Bordes 43)	1
Tayac point (Bordes 51)	1
Chopping tools (Bordes 61)	9
Misc. (Bordes 62) (2 utilised flakes, one uniface, one thick flake with slight distal retouch, and one fragment of a retouched flake on flint)	5
Handaxes	5 (2 ironstone, 1 flint)
Flakes	35
Misc. cores	1
Discoidal cores	2
Hammerstones	1
Split pebbles and knapping fragments	7
Total	83

Coulson (1990, 299) observed that seven chopping tools showed signs of having been used as hammerstones and as cores, and in each case the sinuous 'chopping edge' showed use-related damage, suggesting that these objects had ultimately served as tools. The presence of hammerstones, choppers at the end of a varied use-life, flakes and cores – some abandoned due to faults and knapping errors (Coulson 1990) – suggests that a relatively large amount of knapping actually took place in and around this cave. However, there is nothing to suggest that this site served as a longer-term residence and it is equally possible that, simply because of its large size, Robin Hood Cave saw more frequent visits by hunting parties, some of which came equipped with exotic flint objects. Indeed, the assemblage from Pin Hole Cave shows an even greater proportion of flint artefacts, including an elongated Mousterian point, five scrapers and thinning /resharpening flakes from scrapers or handaxes, again showing the introduction of curated items brought into the region from elsewhere. In both sites, though, there is an element of *in situ* knapping of local quartzites to produce heavy-duty tools to service immediate needs, possibly including breaking bone, as at the Pyrenean hunting site at Mauran (Farizy and David 1992; White in press). The absence of any clear human modification on the extant faunal assemblage, however, precludes further speculation.

Jacobi (2004) compared the Middle Palaeolithic lithics from Pin Hole and Robin Hood Cave. Of the 58 artefacts from Pin Hole, over half are formal tools, mostly scrapers. By contrast, although the extant material from Robin Hood Cave is a sample of the original 479 claimed pieces, the greater majority (~80%) comprise cores and débitage. Jacobi has interpreted these differences in functional terms related to the structure of the caves, although the exceptionally high ratio of tools to unretouched forms suggests that the Victorian excavators were selectively retaining tools and discarding débitage, so one must be careful of such interpretations. This being said, Pin Hole is generally very narrow and confined, Robin Hood Cave far more spacious and amenable to housing larger groups. Charcoal is also present in the latter but not the former. Noting that tool manufacture occurred in Robin Hood Cave but not in Pin Hole (to which tools were taken), Jacobi considered that Robin Hood Cave was used as a local operational base (a general purpose camp site), whereas Pin Hole was used for the specific task of hide working, a suggestion previously made by Jenkinson (1984, 75).

Jacobi does, however, caution that the use of caves by hyaenas may well have been another factor that determined which of the Creswell caves were suitable for habitation. Hyaena remains are known from Robin Hood Cave, Pin Hole, Mother Grundy's Parlour and Church Hole, as well as smaller caves and fissures such as C8 (the 'Ossiferous Fissure') and C9 ('The Arch' collapsed cave). Although one should be suspicious of the accuracy of pre-ultrafiltrated radiocarbon measurements, as discussed above, the broad range of measurements for hyaena at Creswell shows that it was a regular visitor to the area in MIS3. Directly dated, shed reindeer antlers at Creswell Crags and at the nearby Whaley 2 rockshelter reveal that the region functioned as a calving ground by ~46 ka BP and, assuming this is a minimum age, may therefore have proven attractive to Neanderthals and hyaenas during the calving season, even if cut-marked reindeer material is lacking from this time period (Pin Hole: OxA-3790 shed male reindeer antler 33,600 ± 670 BP; OxA-3791 shed female reindeer antler 30,940 ± 490 BP, Hedges et al. 1994. Whaley 2: OxA-4433 reindeer antler 42,700 ± 2,300 BP; OxA-4434 reindeer antler 39,600 ± 1,500 BP, Hedges et al. 1996). It is interesting that radiocarbon determinations for hyaena denning at the gorge generally overlap those for reindeer in the area, presumably because this carnivore was exploiting the presence of calving and young reindeer. The presence of hyaena-gnawed reindeer antler at Creswell supports this observation, while a hyaena neonate in the MIS3 deposits of Pin Hole shows that, at least on occasion, the Creswell caves were used as maternity dens. Neanderthals may have been attracted to the reindeer herds for other reasons – their furs. Reindeer furs have very high insulation values and may therefore have been as valuable as their meat in energetic and thermal terms (Stenton 1991; White 2006).

The Axe valley LOA, Somerset

The two richest areas of Late Middle Palaeolithic archaeology in south-west England are the open landscapes of the Solent river and its environs and the Somerset caves area (Hosfield et al. 2007). Within the latter region, it has been observed on the basis of archaeological materials from enclosed sites (Jacobi pers. comm. to PP) that a signifi-cant Neanderthal occupation can be attributed to the valley of the River Axe, despite the fact that with only one exception no palaeoliths have been found in the gravels of its tributaries (Wymer 1996). This apparent lack of Late Middle Palaeolithic archaeology in the gravels of the Axe itself, however, is very likely due to the lack of relevant exposures or commercial exploitation of MIS3 deposits outside the area between Chard and Hawk-church (Wymer 1993, 18). The River Axe rises at Wookey, flowing northwestwards, until today it meets the Severn in the vicinity of Uphill, a little to the south of Weston-super-Mare (Figure 6.15). At source (the caves of Wookey Hole), the Hyaena Den contained what was apparently a rich Late Middle Palaeolithic assemblage in association with fauna of the Pin Hole MAZ, including combustion zones and, with the possible exception of Robin Hood Cave, the largest amount of charred bone recovered from any English or Welsh Lower or Middle Palaeolithic site. Neanderthal occupation is also in evidence at the immediately adjacent Rhinoceros Hole (Proctor et al. 1996). At the other end of the river, some 20 km downstream, Uphill Quarry Cave 8 lay at the point at which the Axe poured onto the great plain that is now the Severn River, and contained small amounts of Late Middle Palaeolithic material in addition to a fragment of an LRJ leafpoint and an Aurignacian lozangic point (Jacobi and Pettitt 2000 (Text Box 6.11)). Between the two, the small cave of Picken's Hole (Tratman 1964), situated in a small box valley suitable perhaps for trapping herbivores, contained a small number of Late Middle Palaeolithic artefacts (see Text Box 6.12). Outside the Axe valley, a number of Middle Palaeolithic handaxes reveal Neanderthal activity in the wider region, notably triangular/sub-trian-gular forms from St Audries, West Quantoxhead (30 km to the west of the Axe valley), *bout coupé* forms from North Petherton, Somerset (20 km south-west) and Chepstow, Gwent (40 km to the north; Jacobi 2000 and pers. comm.).

The Hyaena Den (Figure 6.16) is the most comprehensively documented of the Axe val-ley sites although, as it was excavated by Boyd Dawkins between 1859 and 1863 (and subsequently by several other specialists), its archaeology and palaeontology is relatively poorly understood. Later excavations, of better quality, were conducted by Tratman between 1966 and 1970 (Tratman et al.1971) and by Roger Jacobi and Christopher Hawkes in 1991/1992 (Jacobi and Hawkes 1993), although little of the original contents remained. The site was discovered in 1852 during the removal of Pleistocene deposits that had entirely covered its entrance, for the purpose of constructing a mill leat. It is situated at the base of the Wookey Ravine near to the resurgence of the River Axe. It is a low-arched cave, 10 m wide and 13 m deep, with a rear opening now blocked by spoil

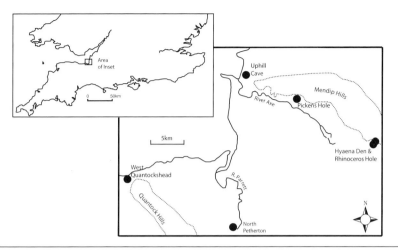

FIGURE 6.15
Map of the Axe Valley and adjacent countryside, showing location of sites mentioned in the text.

Text Box 6.11

THE CAVES OF UPHILL QUARRY, WESTON-SUPER-MARE, SOMERSET

Uphill is located at the western end of the Mendips, only ~10 km west of Picken's Hole and ~25 km from Wookey along the Axe Valley. Since the early nineteenth century, a number of caves and fissures in the carboniferous limestone have been discovered during the course of quarrying here and excavated at different times (Rutter 1829). Harrison (1977) notes up to 13 caves, most now quarried away. Of these, Cave 8, originally probably part of a system joining to Cave 7, yielded Palaeolithic implements and a Pleistocene fauna. These two caves were discovered in 1898 and examined by Edward Wilson on behalf of Bristol Museum (Harrison 1977; Wilson and Reynolds 1901). By 1901 both caves had been destroyed by quarrying. Uphill Cave 8 was described as larger and at a lower level than Cave 7, containing a mass of rubble or cave earth up to 2–2.5m thick and (generally) fragmentary bone and teeth. The artefacts all derive from this cave earth and were apparently recovered in association with the Pleistocene fauna. Wilson thought the rubble and its fauna had been displaced but his views were not shared by Balch (1937).

The original fauna from Caves 7 and 8 has been grouped into a single collection, dominated by elements characteristic of the Pin Hole MAZ (see main text). The artefacts from the site have been described by Davies (1926), Garrod (1926), Harrison (1977) and Campbell 1977. Of the (unknown) original number recovered very few survive but there is no reason to believe that the cave/s ever contained rich assemblages. The extant collection is dominated by Middle Palaeolithic artefacts of chert and flint including a small triangular handaxe, handaxe fragments, a convergent sidescraper, notched and denticulated flakes, small thinning flakes and a naturally backed knife (Harrison 1977; Jacobi and Pettitt 2000).

Text Box 6.11

Evidence of discoidal core technology has also been observed (Jacobi and Pettitt 2000). The association of cordiform handaxes and a naturally backed knife led the latter authors to classify the Uphill assemblage as Mousterian of Acheulean tradition.

The presence of cores and thinning flakes led Jacobi and Pettitt to suggest that the site was the locus of on-site knapping although Harrison saw it as one dominated by the resharpening of broken and damaged artefacts, probably a result of limited high quality raw materials. This would suggest that the site was only a temporary stopover where a transported and curated tool-kit was being maintained, those left behind presumably discarded as not worth taking any further; the triangular handaxe at only 6 cm long was clearly reaching the end of its life. A number of authors have noted technological and typological similarities between the Uphill artefacts and those from the Hyaena Den, Wookey Hole, Harrison going so far as suggesting they were made by the same cultural group, and it has been suggested that the site was one of a number in a Neanderthal local operational area (see main text).

Text Box 6.12

A SMALL NEANDERTHAL SHELTER AT PICKEN'S HOLE, SOMERSET

Located at Compton Bishop on the southern side of the Mendips, 6 km west of Cheddar Gorge, Picken's Hole is one of a series of small caves in a ridge of Carboniferous Limestone ~50 m OD. Extending southeastwards from Crook Peak, these overlook the buried valleys of the Somerset Levels to the south (Apsimon 1986). Their position in a small box-valley suggest that Neanderthals may have been using this to trap prey. The cave was excavated between 1961 and 1967 but has as yet been published only in brief reports (Tratman 1964; ApSimon 1986).

The cave is part of a phreatic system and consists of a short passage ~1–1.5 m wide, opening at the foot of a low cliff onto a platform formed by a former roof collapse (ApSimon 1986). Waterlain sands at the base of the cave represent a final phase of stream activity prior to the downcutting of the Somerset Levels in the Middle Pleistocene; a stalagmite floor above these has been dated by Uranium-series to ~183 ka BP (ibid, 55). ApSimon suggested that the cave was probably closed until the roof collapsed to form a limestone breccia (Unit 6), probably during a cold period.

The most significant archaeological deposit at Picken's Hole is Unit 3, which yielded Late Middle Palaeolithic lithics, a Pin Hole MAZ fauna and two human teeth. An AMS measurement of $4,800 \pm 55$ BP clearly shows that the teeth are intrusive Neolithic specimens (Hedges et al. 1997). The excavations recovered a total of 53 stone items, mostly of Carboniferous chert but with some flint and two sandstone pebbles, which were interpreted as hammerstones (ApSimon 1986).

Text Box 6.12

Such raw materials were locally available in debris fans and river gravels although their absence from other units might suggest that they were humanly introduced (Apsimon 1986). Some of the finds came from the basal clayey subdivision of Unit 3 but most came from a banded silty loam some 20 cm above this. Two conventional radiocarbon dates on associated faunal remains indicate an age of ~32–40 ka BP for these deposits (BM-654, 34,265 + 2,600/–1,950 and BM-2117, 27,540 +/– 2,440: Burleigh et al. 1979, 1984) which clearly places the accumulation, if imprecisely, in MIS3.

The small lithic assemblage included flakes and core fragments plus some naturally shattered pieces. One bipolar core, a small fragment of a discoidal core and a possible handaxe-thinning flake were reported and appear similar to Late Middle Palaeolithic material from Wookey Hole and another core fragment was suggested to have derived from a handaxe. All artefacts are small – none larger than 50 mm in maximum dimension – and the nature of the assemblage again suggests only limited use of this very small cave, probably as a temporary bolt-hole where lithics were dropped and local pebbles idly worked in the context of hunting.

from the adjacent Rhinoceros Hole. Its deposits approached two metres in thickness and contained an abundant Upper Pleistocene fauna ('the 243 bones, the 64 jaws, and 240 teeth obtained from it are to be looked upon as merely a small fraction of the whole': Dawkins 1863, 264). Many of the faunal remains bear traces of gnawing ('the marks of those [hyaena] teeth upon every one of the 800 to 1000 bones': Dawkins 1863, 267) and clearly derive in the main from the eponymous hyaena denning; Middle Palaeolithic artefacts were stratified between layers of hyaena coprolites, suggesting a broad coexistence between Neanderthals and hyaenas in the region. Such interstratification, as Aldhouse-Green (1998, 137) has noted, could suggest that Neanderthals were 'happy to reoccupy carnivore dens littered with faeces and food refuse'.

Dawkins found around 35 Middle Palaeolithic artefacts of flint and chert, including 11 handaxes (Figure 6.17), a handaxe-trimming flake, and an LRJ bladepoint. Most of the finds seem to have been concentrated in the cave's mouth (the current entrance – what Dawkins referred to as the antrum): 'all the ashes and implements were found in positions, near the mouth of the cave, where man himself may have placed them' (Dawkins 1863, 273), and the discovery of lithic micro-débitage in this area by Jacobi and Hawkes (1993) further supports the notion than Neanderthals carried out some knapping in the cave mouth. The fauna from the cave's occupations – probably largely deriving from the hyaena denning – is of a Pin Hole MAZ type and includes hyaena, lion, wolf, bear, horse, bison, woolly rhinoceros, giant deer, red deer, reindeer and mammoth and in part seems to have been recovered from a breccia or within stalagmite (Dawkins 1862, 117). The deposits of burnt bones possibly indicative of a hearth and apparently associated with artefact scatters seem to have clustered in three zones, all within the daylight area of the cave.

FIGURE 6.16
The Hyaena Den, Wookey. Middle Palaeolithic occupation was most intensive just inside the overhang. The mill leat (stream) – the cutting of which exposed the cave – is visible in the foreground. (Photograph Paul Pettitt.)

Dawkins described artefacts as coming from four discreet 'clusters': the first within the bone bed, comprising several chert artefacts including one handaxe; the second in the northern part of the modern entrance, close to where the roof met the floor. This area contained the greatest number of artefacts, alongside charcoal and the bones of horse, rhinoceros and hyaena, many burnt and calcined (Dawkins 1874, 303). This is almost certainly the area where Jacobi and Hawkes (1993) discovered further fragments of charred bone, micro-débitage of flint and chert from knapping or tool-maintenance and faunal remains, among them a cut-marked incisor of red deer. A third cluster was found directly resting on the bedrock floor, beneath the bone bed, from which Dawkins (1874, 303) records both flint and chert artefacts, although no extant tool can be allocated to this group. Finally a single implement was recovered lying on a rock shelf in association with a

FIGURE 6.17
Handaxes from the Hyaena Den. After Tratman et al. 1971. Scale in cm.

hyaena tooth and ashes. It is not clear whether this implement was Middle Palaeolithic or not but, if so, it is tempting to infer that it had been cached on the ledge for later use.

Balch (1914, 168) also recorded hearths 'as low as the present floor of the Den' in the tunnelled section of the south passage and two of his artefacts in Wells Museum, both typologically ambiguous, were considered to be contemporary with these (Tratman et al. 1971, 248). However, as Tratman et al. (1971, 255) pointed out, it would not have been possible to have fires on this spot unless the roof was open to allow the smoke to escape.

Given the stratigraphical location of the artefacts and hyaena denning accumulations, it seems clear that humans were the first occupants of the cave ~50 ka BP and returned for very brief visits a few times thereafter. It is perhaps not surprising that, chronologically, this is similar to Neanderthal activity in neighbouring Rhinoceros Hole (see below) and almost certainly indicates that the artefacts found in that cave were produced by the same Neanderthal group. The sub-divisions of the bone bed also indicate that hyaena denning was brief and episodic (Tratman et al. 1971, 268). Although sparsely used, the cave would appear to have been a desirable location: today, the area under the roof opening receives much daylight and the entrance would have also received a lot of sunshine during the afternoons, although this would not have penetrated far in. The mouth of the cave is also dry although in cold weather ice forms on the roof.

Rhinoceros Hole, only 10 m from Hyaena Den, takes the form of an alcove – probably the result of a roof collapse – leading to two short passages, the lower probably connected with a hyaena den (Proctor et al. 1996, 237). As with Hyaena Den and Badger Hole it originally formed part of the Wookey Hole cave system. Like Hyaena Den, it was the object of several early excavations and, more usefully, excavation by Tratman between 1970 and 1976 (Proctor et al. 1996). Layers 1–5 formed a series of wedges and lenses of sub-aerial cave earth derived from the valley side and cave interior by a combination of wash, soil creep and wall/roof breakdown (Collcutt 1986; Proctor et al. 1996). The silts of Layer 6 are clearly waterlain, the sands above were probably laid down by an active stream, their sedimentology and N–S flow-direction consistent with a backchannel of the River Axe flowing past the entrance of Rhinoceros Hole downstream of the main resurgence at Wookey Hole (Collcutt 1986). The silts, though, were formed in still or slow-flowing pools, possibly representing a minor resurgence within the cave of a stream with a very local catchment (ibid., 242). A small lens of cave earth within Bed 6 (Layer 7) suggested at least two flooding events, the cave drying out in the intervening period. A hanging remnant of *in situ* flowstone towards the roof in the Lower Cave indicates an earlier period of infill, the fragments found within the cave earth probably being derived from this or other hanging remnants in the alcove and two passages. This feature supports the idea that the Axe had flowed passed the cave entrance during one or more flood events, cleaning out earlier deposits from the cave. Uranium-series measurements on samples of flowstone from both sources suggested an age for the hanging floor of ~50–45 ka BP. This would suggest that the entire sedimentary sequence within the cave was deposited after 50 ka BP (Proctor et al. 1996, 248–51). While Low U-Th yields and contamination in the flowstone samples demand some caution in uncritically accepting these dates, they are supported by the presence of the MIS3 Pin Hole MAZ dominated by hyaena, bear and woolly rhinoceros which occurs with no major changes throughout the cave earths and water lain sands.

Only four identifiable Middle Palaeolithic artefacts were recovered from Rhinoceros Hole, a small *bout coupé* handaxe and three handaxe-thinning flakes (Figure 6.18). Stratigraphically these came from the lowermost deposits, one from a burrow through Layer 6, one from the junction of 5/6 and two from a reddened horizon at the base of Layer 6, the latter proposed as the original context for all the Late Middle Palaeolithic finds. An Upper Palaeolithic blade was found in the interstratified Layer 7, although a considerable hiatus may be represented in fluvial activity, a supposition supported by Roger Jacobi's observation of mechanical damage on the surface of the artefacts suggestive of a period of exposure prior to burial. If this is the case then the period of Neanderthal activity in the cave may have taken place soon after the cave became dry, perhaps as early as ~50 ka BP, with EUP activity occurring after a second inundation later in MIS3.

Badger Hole, in close proximity to Rhinoceros Hole and Hyaena Den was, like them, excavated by Balch (1938–1953) and subsequently by Charles McBurney in 1958 and John Campbell in 1968, the latter two excavations remaining unpublished. It contained a number of Early Upper Palaeolithic artefacts probably attributable to the LRJ, including four partly bifacially worked bladepoints. Thus, although our understanding of the Late Middle Palaeolithic of the Wookey sites is poor, it seems that Hyaena Den saw most of the activity.

One can say little about the other sites in the Axe Valley: finds from Uphill Quarry Cave 8 (see Text Box 6.10) were largely destroyed when a bomb hit Bristol Museum during the Second World War; at Picken's Hole, excavation has not been extensive, and publication has been cursory. Uphill Quarry Cave 8, which may have been originally linked to Cave 7, contained at least two Middle Palaeolithic handaxes, both small, triangular forms, one on chert and the other on flint, a flint scraper made on a possible handaxe

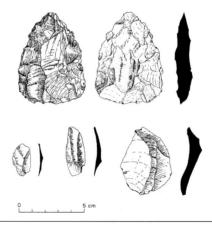

0   5 cm

FIGURE 6.18
Late Middle Palaeolithic artefacts from Rhinoceros Hole, Wookey. (After Proctor et al. 1996 and courtesy Chris Proctor.)

(Harrison 1977), a Mousterian point and blade on chert, a flint naturally backed knife, various chert flakes and fragments of an LRJ leafpoint. The Pin Hole MAZ fauna with which the artefacts were associated is almost identical taxonomically to that from the A2 loamy cave earth at Kent's Cavern. Several chert artefacts from Picken's Hole are compatible with a Late Middle Palaeolithic occupation, notably two hammerstones, a flake, and several handaxe-thinning flakes, again found in association with a Pin Hole MAZ fauna (ApSimon 1986).

The Late Middle Palaeolithic archaeology of the Axe Valley sites shares some common characteristics, enough in our opinion, to link them together as a local operational area. All of the assemblages are very small, utilise a mixture of flint and (mainly) locally available chert for *chaînes opératoires* largely focused on the production of small, irregular ovate/cordiform handaxes which are of similar dimensions and which were heavily retouched; are associated with characteristic Pin Hole MAZ faunas in the context of abundant hyaena denning. Evidence of *in situ* knapping is certain at Hyaena Den and possibly at Picken's Hole, otherwise the degree of economy seen in the use of the handaxes is noticeable – resharpening is attested at Hyaena Den and Uphill, where most handaxes are worked down to a considerable degree, and broken examples are also known from both sites. Roe (1981, 245) saw this as evidence that Neanderthals 'used the same implement for as long as possible'.

Jacobi (2000, 46) has noted that the box-like form of the valley at Wookey would have been tactically suited to trapping game and that the plateau above the valley affords wide panoramic views over the Axe Valley. The plateau above the Hyaena Den and Rhinoceros Hole rises 70 m above the cave and offers an exceptional view of the central part of the Axe Valley (Figure 6.19). The same may be said for Picken's Hole: the valley forms a dead end also presumably of tactical importance and the site is most easily accessed from the valley bottom, although the plateau above is easily reached and affords a long-distance view over at least 25 km (PP pers. obs.). Although the Uphill caves have long been quarried away, the approximate position of Cave 8 and the remaining local topography suggest that it may have been more accessible from the plateau above, from which the view is excellent: at least 30 km eastwards along the Axe valley and a similar distance out to the Severn/Bristol Channel as far as Quantoxhead to the south-west.

Topographic features link the sites. The major river in the region was the Severn, although this would have been considerably reduced in size in the Pleistocene, running through a vast plain ultimately into the Channel River. The Late Middle Palaeolithic occupational traces discussed here, however, relate to a tributary of this major river, a situation that is found also in south-west France (Mellars 1996, 248). Perhaps the Severn acted as a funnel, directing the herds out of the main floodplain of the Severn into the more steeply defined Axe Valley, where the movement of game could be monitored from afar and wherein the small box valleys at its sides could be used to disadvantage and trap game. The viewsheds available from the plateaux above the occupied sites may explain the nature of occupation in the Axe Valley LOA; it is apparent that visibility (assuming a largely treeless landscape) was 20–30 km from these locations (Figure 6.13). Perhaps

FIGURE 6.19
View of the Axe Valley from the plateau above the Hyaena Den, Rhinoceros Hole and Badger Hole, Wookey. (Photograph Paul Pettitt.)

it is no coincidence that distances of this order fall into Geneste's 'regional' scale of raw material movement categories for the Middle Palaeolithic. In the apparent absence of any ability to divide up time and space into arbitrary and exact units and organise hunting behaviour according to these, visual clues to the distribution of resources in the landscape would have been critical. Long-distance viewsheds would have been advantageous in such a 'here-and-now' hunting adaptation; hunting episodes would have begun by scanning the landscape from plateaux and responding to visual clues; hunting opportunities at 20–30 km distances could lead to artefact discard preferentially at these distances. After such resource procurement, in order to return to pivotal sites such as Hyaena Den, one need only find, in this case, the River Axe and walk upstream to source.

It is possible that the Axe valley LOA formed part of a wider system of LOAs, perhaps linked by relocations. The potential LOAs of Tor Bay (Kent's Cavern and Brixham Caves and their environs) and of southern Wales (Coygan and Paviland) could be interpreted in similar ways (see Text Box 6.13). It is of interest that these are respectively ~120 km and ~100–140 km distant from the Axe valley LOA, which corresponds to Geneste's third, 'distant' category of raw material movement. Could it be that the Tor Bay, Axe valley and southern Welsh LOAs represent periodically different activities of the same Neanderthal group? Obviously one cannot hope to test this hypothesis but, we suggest, perspectives of this nature might profitably be used as heuristics for future work.

The last Neanderthals in Britain

As noted above, the youngest reliable radiocarbon measurements for British Late Middle Palaeolithic material indicate a presence ~44 ka BP. The few available for the succeeding LRJ materials, discussed in the next chapter, span a tight period between ~42 and 41 ka BP. Either this period – probably far briefer than the imprecise radiocarbon measurements suggest – saw the last Neanderthal groups in Britain, or the earliest groups of *Homo sapiens,* depending on how one views the authorship of the poorly understood LRJ collections. As will be seen in Chapter 7, most authorities assume that the LRJ represents the last Neanderthals on the Northern European Plain, although the evidence is scanty. Assuming this correlation is correct, however, it indicates that by 41 ka BP Neanderthals had abandoned their brief and tentative grip on this cold, grey steppe. For several thousand years once more, Britain would be a human desert.

Text Box 6.13

THE LATE MIDDLE PALAEOLITHIC OF KENT'S CAVERN

Kent's Cavern is probably the most famous and intensively-worked cave site in Britain. Its fame largely derives from its role in the establishment of human antiquity and development of Palaeolithic archaeology (White and Pettitt 2009), rather than for its Middle Palaeolithic assemblage, which is today difficult to reconstruct. The cave has been subject to numerous excavations since at least the 1820s and William Pengelly alone, who conducted extensive excavations in the cave between 1865 and 1880, recorded over 7,000 finds from his excavations, 1,400 of these being lithics (Pengelly 1884; see Figure 1). Only ~33 of his Late Middle Palaeolithic artefacts are now extant, to which can be added a handful of artefacts

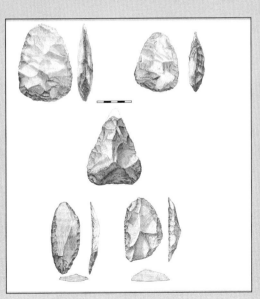

excavated subsequently by Arthur Ogilvie, and several bifaces excavated previously by John MacEnery.

The extant collection of 45 objects (23 of greensand chert, 22 of flint) includes five bifaces, nine scrapers, possible awls/borers, and a variety of débitage including two Levallois flakes. A number of these appear to have been isolated finds, such as those

FIGURE 1
Artefacts from Kent's Cavern.
Scale in cm. (After Evans 1897.)

from the Clinnick's Gallery and Smerdon's Passage parts of the cave system, but accounts suggest that a concentration of Middle Palaeolithic finds occurred near to the cave's south entrance within the Great Chamber, at depths of 1–4 ft (0.3–1.2 m) (Pengelly 1884; Rogers 1955; Campbell and Sampson 1971). From what survives, there is little evidence of on-site manufacture and the whole appears to be a collection of artefacts transported to the cave during a number of relatively brief visits. Technologically, the very small amount of extant débitage includes discoidal or Levallois methods of managed flake production, the latter unusual or unique from other British MIS3 sites. This lead White and Pettitt to wonder whether these pieces related to the LRJ occurrences within the cave, rather than the Mousterian. The known and illustrated handaxes from Kent's Cavern are all small, typical Late Middle Palaeolithic cordiform examples, four of which conform to the *bout coupé* type (Tyldesley 1987). This grouping actually constitutes the largest concentration of *bout coupés* in Britain and, although some show apparent reworking, there is no evidence that once introduced to the cavern they were modified or further worked.

White and Jacobi (2002) suggested that the *bout coupé* form had a social resonance for those who made and carried it (see main text) and that some were deliberately cached in caves, the well-used piece from Coygan being one example (see separate Text Box 6.6), while that from the Wolf's Cave area of Kent's Cavern was certainly found in a relatively inaccessible part of the cave which appears to have functioned as a hyaena den during MIS3, as our recent excavations have shown (see Figure 2). Caching implies not only the deliberate postponement of action – members of task groups storing objects for an anticipated return visit – but also the provisioning of sites, transforming them from spaces into places (Kuhn 1995). In conjunction with the open air discard of transported objects, this suggests that both people and places were provisioned (Kuhn 1995), perhaps another reflection of extreme mobility through the unfamiliar landscapes of Doggerland. If this is the case, then the geographical distribution of *bout coupés* might indicate that the social networks through which these meanings flowed were extensive and complex, stretching amongst the various local groups that, we suggest, moved seasonally into Britain from the surrounding basins.

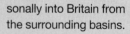

FIGURE 2
View of excavations by the authors in the Wolf's Cave area of Kent's Cavern, Devon, 2009, looking west. Part-articulated leg bones of woolly rhinoceros *Coelodonta antiquitatis*, bearing heavy gnawing, surrounded by hyaena teeth attest to hyaena denning in the MIS3 A2 loamy cave earth. (Photo authors.)

Text Box 6.13

CHAPTER 7

Liminal worlds

The British Early Upper Palaeolithic and the earliest populations of *Homo sapiens*

INTRODUCTION

From a northern European point of view, an interrupted archaeological record indicative of successive dispersals and regional extinctions is the rule throughout the Upper Palaeolithic (Verpoorte 2008). As with the preceding Middle and Lower Palaeolithic, hominin groups dispersed into the region infrequently and the relatively precise chronology available for the British Upper Palaeolithic reveals that it was interstadials, some of which approached the Holocene in terms of mean temperatures, which ultimately facilitated the northwestwards dispersal of grassland faunal communities into Britain. Only towards the end of the Pleistocene can one identify a boreal woodland community – in the second half of the last interstadial before the Holocene – an indication of the Early Holocene and Mesolithic communities to come. As will be seen below, the British Upper Palaeolithic record is remarkably sparse and even the Late Magdalenian/Creswellian record of the first half of the Late Glacial Interstadial need represent, in our opinion, no more than the activities of one group resident for a handful of years.

Traditionally, the British Upper Palaeolithic has been divided into two: an Early Upper Palaeolithic preceding the Last Glacial Maximum, and a Late Upper Palaeolithic following recolonisation of the Northern European Plain as the severe conditions of the LGM ameliorated (Campbell 1977). In this chapter we examine the former.

CLIMATES, ENVIRONMENTS AND RESOURCES

The climatic oscillations of MIS3 and their environmental implications have been discussed fully in Chapter 6 and as the time period covered in this chapter essentially forms part of the continuing climatic instability of the period only a brief summary is necessary here. In the NGRIP core at least eight interstadials are recorded for the period ~38–28 ka cal BP – Greenland Interstadials (GI) 8, 7, 6, 5, 4 and 3 (from oldest to youngest; Svensson et al. 2008). In terms of the terrestrial record, of the five interglacials recognised in northern Europe for the period ~58–28 ka cal BP (Zagwijn 1989; Behre 1992) two are relevant to the concerns of this chapter: the Hengelo (~39–36 ka cal BP) and the Denekamp (~32–28 ka cal BP). In Britain, however, only one clear interstadial – Upton Warren – has been indentified at present (Coope et al. 1961) which, at apparently ~42–44 ka cal BP, precedes the arrival of Upper Palaeolithic groups. However likely it is, therefore, that Early Upper Palaeolithic dispersal into Britain was restricted to certain interstadials, the rarity of dated assemblages and chronological imprecision make this difficult to demonstrate convincingly at present. More broadly speaking, in terms of a three-phase model for MIS3 (see Chapter 6) the arrival of *Homo sapiens* coincides with the phase of climatic deterioration with relatively tightly spaced oscillations down to ~37 ka cal BP and the onset of cold stadial conditions thereafter.

From modest origins in the Scottish Highlands the British–Irish ice sheet (BIIS) expanded between ~40 and 33 ka cal BP (Chiverrell and Thomas 2010) although it would not be until MIS2 that the glaciers reached their Last Glacial Maximum limits across the entirety of Ireland and northern Scotland (see Text Box 7.1). As noted in Chapter 7 the pre-LGM Devensian BIIS was probably highly dynamic, fluctuating in nature over the course of the period, although given the coarseness of the terrestrial data, details of the extent of such fluctuation are at present unavailable. Remains of woolly rhinoceros from Dunbartonshire in central Scotland, for example, have been dated to 31,140 ± 170 ^{14}C BP (OxA-19560) and 32,250 ± 700 ^{14}C BP (OxA-X-2288-33) and reveal that the region must have been free of ice ~34.7–35.8 ka cal BP (Jacobi et al. 2009). Whatever the dynamics, organic deposits immediately south of the BIIS margins indicate that the cold, open tundra landscape that characterised MIS3 persisted until the climatic deterioration into the LGM (Chiverrell and Thomas 2010).

Text Box 7.1

THE LAST GLACIAL MAXIMUM IN BRITAIN

During the Last Glacial Maximum (LGM) Britain, northern Germany and northern France were, it seems, completely depopulated (Roebroeks et al. 2011). Glacial ice began to accumulate once more from ~32 ka BP (Telfer et al. 2009) and it is probably significant that the youngest Mid Upper Palaeolithic activity in Britain dates to ~33 ka BP. Most specialists now agree that approaching the LGM, the maximum extent of the British–Irish Ice Sheet (BIIS) was reached ~27 to ~24 ka BP (Scourse et al. 2009a; Clark et al. in press) corresponding to maximum global ice volumes over the same period (Boulton and Hagdorn 2006; Peltier and Fairbanks 2006; Clark et al. 2009). The BIIS was a relatively small and discrete ice sheet (Hubbard et al. 2009), the growth and deglaciation of which seems to have been dynamic, marked by regional differences in deglaciation rates, standstills and readvances, and there is as yet no consensus on the extent and variability of such dynamism (e.g. Fretwell et al. 2008; Clark et al. 2010). Rapid ice advances and retreats have, for example, been suggested for the North Sea, that is, down the the east coast of England; the west coast of Scotland and Ireland and the Scilly Isles (Clark et al. 2011; Bateman et al. 2011) and such fluctuations are known across the world (Clapperton 1995). The precise extent of the LGM BIIS is unclear, as is the question of whether it was confluent with the Scandinavian Ice Sheet (SIS), although recent micromorphological analysis of sediments from North Sea cores suggest that they were joined during at least two periods within the Devensian (Carr et al. 2006). In contrast to modern ice sheets in Greenland and Antarctica the BIIS had a relatively low elevation and extensive, active, elongated lobes at its margins (Boulton and Hagdorn 2006; Bateman et al. 2011). The extent of the BIIS in the North Sea is still known only imprecisely. Diamictons of the Cape Shore Formation extend across much of the North Sea basin from the Norwegian Channel to the northern parts of East Anglia, indicating extensive glaciation that peaked ~27 ka BP. Those of the succeeding Bolders Bank Formation form a large lobe extending up to 50 km off the north-east coast of England and across much of the southern North Sea to Dutch territory, probably reflecting a readvance *after* ~22 ka BP (Carr et al. 2006).

On land, the extent of the glaciers across the British and Irish land mass is better known (e.g. Boulton and Hagdorn 2006; Clark et al. 2004; Greenwood and Clark 2009; Shennan et al. 2006; Chiverrell and Thomas 2010). This has traditionally been mapped on the basis of the distribution of diamicts, end-moraines, eskers, drumlins, weathered/unweathered landforms, meltwater channels including tunnel valleys, weathering limits (trimlines), ice-dammed lakes and erratic dispersal patterns (Clark et al. 2004; Chiverrell and Thomas 2010; see Figure 1). Two large lobes extended down the Vale of York and the eastern English coast, extending respectively as far as Escrick or Doncaster, and down the east Lincolnshire coast and over the Wash (Bateman et al. 2011).

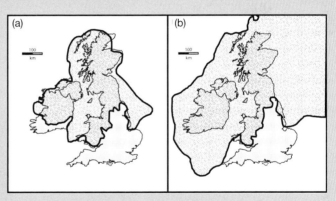

Text Box 7.1

FIGURE 1
Approximate limits of the Last Glacial Maximum ice over Britain; (a) after Boulton et al. 1977; (b) after Scourse et al. 2009a.

A series of moraines mark the southern limits of the LGM BIIS across the Wye Valley in Hertfordshire and in south Wales around Abergavenny and Usk. Periglacial deposits on Gower reveal that most of south Wales was covered by ice (e.g. Hiemstra et al. 2009). Ice streams ran from the southern Irish Sea basin past the coasts of Pembrokeshire and Wexford to west of the Isles of Scilly (Scourse et al. 2009a and references therein). In southern Ireland a subglacial diamicton indicateS its presence over much of the country and an extension well out into the Celtic Sea and moraines off the coast of Connemara indicate probably complete coverage of the west coast. Estimates of the thickness of the ice sheets vary. The highest parts, such as in the Scottish Highlands, could have reached anywhere between ~950 m and over 1,800 m (depending on which physical model one favours) and approached 700 m in Ireland (Ballantyne et al. 1998, 2008). Fretwell et al. (2008) used digital terrain mapping to model the extent and volume of the ice based on three existing ice sheet models. Unlike previous models, this technique takes into account the effects of topography on overlying ice volumes. The results of these models indicate a variable thickness of ice cover with central cores of very thick ice (900-1,600 m) over regions such as the south-east Grampians, the inner Solway Firth and northern and central Ireland. These cores were surrounded by extensive areas of very thin ice (<100 m), and potentially abrupt transitions from ~1,000m to zero in a few kilometres.

Global sea level during MIS2 was ~114–35 m below that of the present day (Shennan et al. 2006) and most of the North Sea basin and eastern parts of the English Channel were dry land (Coles 1998). Coleoptera suggest extensive snowfall during the height of the LGM (Atkinson et al. 1987) and all areas free of ice witnessed severe periglacial conditions during the LGM, as evidenced by significant river incision, solifluction and cryoturbation from the south-west to south-east. The aggrading, braided, gravelly rivers flowed through treeless, polar landscapes barren of mammalian life (Walker 1995; Collins et al. 1996 and references therein). The increased winds of the period distributed coversand and loess across large areas of southern and eastern England throughout the period and even during deglaciation (Bateman 1998; Bateman et al. 2008; Reynolds et al. 1996; Clarke et al. 2007). Apart from the glaciers the large proglacial lakes Humber and Pickering, dammed by North Sea basin ice, were prominent features of Late Devensian Britain, covering ~4,500 km^2 (Bateman et al. 2008).

Biostratigraphy and faunal turnover within later MIS3 and early MIS2

Biostratigraphically, the period is characterised by the taxonomically rich Pin Hole MAZ discussed in Chapter 6 (Currant and Jacobi 1997, 2001, 2011). Dominant taxa were spotted hyaena, mammoth, horse, woolly rhinoceros, bison and reindeer. Fox, lion, arctic hare and humans were also relatively familiar although perhaps unevenly distributed elements. As Turner (2009) has noted, the relatively persistent presence of lion and hyaena throughout MIS3 indicates a relatively rich resource base of herbivores. Following MIS3, the Dimlington Stadial Interzone that opened MIS2 has yielded a comparatively impoverished mammalian fauna, reflecting the severity of the climate as conditions deteriorated towards the Last Glacial Maximum (see Chapter 8). Some faunal changes, however, distinguish the Early Upper Palaeolithic world from the preceding Middle Palaeolithic one. Hyaena and woolly rhinoceros seem to have become extinct in Britain by ~36–37 ka cal BP (Stuart and Lister 2007) and Neanderthals probably followed shortly thereafter depending on whether or not Lincombian–Ranisian–Jerzmanowician (LRJ) assemblages are a proxy indicator of their presence or not (see below). The lesser scimitar-toothed cat, *Homotherium latidens*, may have been active in Britain during MIS3; a dentary of this species from south-east of the Brown Bank has been directly dated to 28,100 ± 220 ^{14}C BP (UtC-11000, tooth) and 27,650 ± 280 BP (UtC-11065, mandibular bone) revealing its presence within 50 km of the current East Anglian coast ~31–32 ka BP (Reumer et al. 2003), and the recovery of a tooth assigned to this species apparently associated with Late Upper Palaeolithic archaeology from Robin Hood Cave at Creswell Crags – although undated – may suggest the Late Pleistocene persistence, or arrival, of this predator on the British Mainland (Jacobi 2006).

It should be remembered that the Pin Hole MAZ is a formal biostratigraphic zone apparently covering ~35,000 years of Upper Pleistocene time, not a reflection of specific faunal communities over this period, which were presumably constantly remodelled in response to the highly unstable climate of the period. One assumes that such fluctuations – probably occurring at the level of centennial- and millennial-scale climate change at the very least – form the context in which successive hominin dispersals and extinctions in Britain occurred although, given the relatively low number of well-understood palaeontological assemblages and the imprecision of chronometric dating for the period, such fluctuations are only very poorly understood. Some indications of MIS3 faunal turnover have been observed in the Goat's Hole at Paviland on the Gower Peninsula, south Wales (often referred to as Paviland Cave) and at Pontnewydd Cave in north Wales, both the result of ambitious radiocarbon dating projects in the context of major new analyses of old archaeological and palaeontological collections (Aldhouse-Green 2000a; Aldhouse-Green et al. in press). At Paviland a relatively impoverished fauna of woolly rhino, reindeer, aurochs and bear, possibly attributable to the MIS4/early MIS3 Banwell MAZ, was replaced by a richer 'mammoth steppe' community ~33 ka BP (Pettitt 2000). This community included humans in the form of Mid Upper Palaeolithic hunter-gatherers, apparently reaching Britain as a small-scale and momentary dispersal prior to the decline of conditions as they began to approach the Last Glacial Maximum (see Text Box 7.2).

Text Box 7.2

DISPERSAL OF THE MAMMOTH STEPPE AND THE ARRIVAL OF THE GRAVETTIANS

Pontnewydd Cave in north Wales and the Goat's Hole, Paviland, in south Wales have yielded large amounts of Pleistocene fauna that have been the subject of major radiocarbon dating projects (Pettitt 2000; Pettitt et al. in press; see Figure 1) in the context of major reassessments of the caves' archaeology and palaeontology (Aldhouse-Green 2000; Aldhouse-Green et al. in press). These have revealed fluctuating faunal communities over the period ~41 to ~28 ka BP and, at Paviland, directly dated human remains and humanly modified artefacts reveal how Gravettian groups were an integral part of this animal community. Despite some taxonomic differences – the presence of hyaenas and humans at Paviland for example – broad similarities exist between the two caves.

With twelve faunal taxa (including humans) Paviland is taxonomically richer than Pontnewydd (nine, lacking humans) (see Table 1). The two caves share seven

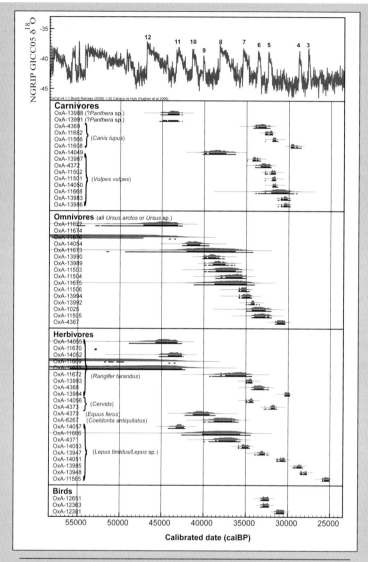

FIGURE 1

Calibrated age ranges of direct AMS radiocarbon measurements on fauna from Pontnewydd Cave, plotted against NGRIP climate curve. (From Pettitt et al. in press.)

taxa (three carnivores – wolf, fox and bear, and four herbivores – reindeer, cervid, horse and woolly rhino). Five of these overlap chronometrically although horse and unspecified cervid appear to have occurred earlier at Pontnewydd. Lion and arctic hare are present at Pontnewydd but are entirely absent from Paviland. With the exception of woolly rhinoceros and reindeer, which may have been present at Paviland before ~41 ka BP, there is an abrupt appearance of several taxa from this time, revealing a quadrupling of taxonomic diversity. Around the same time taxonomic diversity doubled at Pontnewydd, indicating the appearance of the rich mammoth steppe faunal community in the west of Britain at this time.

Text Box 7.2

Table 1 Taxonomic composition at Pontnewydd and Paviland between ~41 and ~28 Ka BP, after Pettitt et al. in press. Shading denotes the presence of a taxon at one site which is unknown from the other.

	Pontnewydd	Paviland
Panthera leo	*	
Canis lupus	*	*
Vulpes vulpes/Alopex lagopus	*	*
Crocuta crocuta		*
Ursus sp.	*	*
Rangifer tarandus	*	*
Cervid	*	*
Equus ferus	*	*
Coelodonta antiquitatis	*	*
Bovid		*
Megaloceros giganteus		*
Mammuthus primigenius		*
Lepus sp.	*	
Homo sapiens		*

Text Box 7.2

At Paviland, bovids and the extinct giant deer *Megaloceros* had appeared by ~36 ka BP, and mammoth by ~33 ka BP. To this one may add the presence of culturally Gravettian humans ~33 ka BP (Jacobi and Higham 2008) and wolves and hyaenas at least from ~32 ka BP. Clearly by this time the faunal community of GI6 was rich enough to support three social carnivores. Similar rises in taxonomic diversity are recorded at Pontnewydd ~41 ka BP and ~33 ka BP, although the absence of humans is notable. By contrast to Paviland, bears (*Ursus arctos* or *Ursus* sp.) were common here between ~41 and ~30 ka BP although, as there is no evidence of Gravettian presence anywhere in north Wales, it seems that this is a genuine regional absence rather than competitive exclusion from the cave by bears. The floruit of fox at Pontnewydd after ~34 ka BP (a rare taxon at Paviland) further reflects a regionally distinct faunal community in the north of Wales from this time.

At both sites very few fauna date to younger than ~30 ka BP. Clearly a significant diminution of populations occurred at each site from this time, presumably reflecting the faunal depopulation of Wales as conditions deteriorated into the Last Glacial Maximum.

A rich fauna from the Upper Breccia at Pontnewydd Cave, Clwyd, spans later MIS3 to the beginning of MIS 2, that is, Currant and Jacobi's Pin Hole MAZ and possibly into the Dimlington Stadial mammalian interzone. Like Paviland, an ambitious programme of radiocarbon dating has clarified a picture of faunal turnover during this period (Pettitt et al. in press). The basic composition of the Pontnewydd fauna shares elements with Currant and Jacobi's biostratigraphy although differences can be observed which may provide important indications of regional differences in the composition of animal communities within the broad mammoth steppe. The radiocarbon dates span the period ~25 ka–~40 ka ^{14}C BP and terminate abruptly at the end of MIS3, presumably reflecting the marked deterioration of climate into the Dimlington Stadial Interzone. It seems that the onset of severe conditions caused the localised extinction of most MIS3 faunal taxa, or at the very least a dramatic impoverishment in taxonomic diversity.

Eight of the dated faunal taxa from Pontnewydd are found in the type locality of Pin Hole cave, Creswell (Currant and Jacobi 2001, Table 5), with Pin Hole lacking only a cervid other than reindeer or *Megaloceros*. Compared with Pin Hole, Pontnewydd lacks mammoth, the giant deer *Megaloceros,* two mustelids and possibly *Bison*. Importantly, taxonomic diversity is relatively low in the Pontnewydd fauna compared with Pin Hole (9 taxa as opposed to 15) and is in fact similar to that for the 'impoverished' fauna of the preceding Bacon Hole MAZ with which it shares five taxa (*Canis lupus, Vulpes vulpes, Ursus* sp., *Rangifer tarandus* and *Lepus* sp.). So, taxonomically, the sampled and dated MIS3 faunal community from Pontnewydd is intermediate between the MIS4 Bacon Hole MAZ and the Pin Hole MAZ with which it is biostratigraphically equated.

Assuming the results are broadly indicative of real faunal turnover and not hopelessly distorted due to the vagaries of preservation, recovery and sampling for dating, a degree of diachronic change can be observed. A major restructuring of the faunal community seems to have occurred ~44 ka BP. Prior to this lion, bear, and possibly red fox seem to have been the only carnivores at the site, and reindeer the only dated herbivore. Taxonomic diversity increased ~42 ka BP with a concentration of dates on bear, the possible persistence of red fox, and the appearance of wild horse, woolly rhino and *Lepus* (hare). Later still, ~34 ka BP, wolves appear, possibly in the context of the diminution or disappearance of bear. The two dated cervids fall into this phase but the only herbivorous taxon that persists through the sequence is *Lepus.* With the exception of one date on *Lepus* at ~27 ka BP, no dates are younger than ~30 ka BP, by which time local conditions may have been too severe to support a mammoth-steppe community.

A small series of radiocarbon dates on fauna from other Welsh caves – Ffynnon Beuno, Coygan Cave, Little Hoyle and Ogof-yr-Ychen – support the broad picture provided by Paviland and Pontnewydd (Aldhouse-Green et al. 1995), in the sense that their dated faunas begin ~44 ka BP and show some evidence of biostratigraphic turnover shortly thereafter. Radiocarbon dates from sites in western England or on a broad latitudinal parallel with Pontnewydd – Bench Tunnel Cavern and Kent's Cavern, Devon; Soldier's Hole, Hyaena Den, Uphill Quarry, Somerset; and Pin Hole, Robin Hood Cave, The Arch, Church Hole and Ash Tree Cave, Derbyshire and Nottinghamshire – although relatively few, are also consistent with the broad picture. Seven taxa dated from Pontnewydd are variably found among these sites and in the case of fox, reindeer, bear, wolf and cervid their broad age ranges overlap; in fact the only taxon conspicuously lacking among the dated examples from western English sites is *Lepus.* The main contrast of other Welsh and English sites with Pontnewydd is, of course, the conspicuous lack of human presence at the latter (see Text Box 7.2).

THE BRITISH EARLY UPPER PALAEOLITHIC RECORD

In this and the following chapter we follow the division of British Upper Palaeolithic into two phases, an earlier (EUP/MUP) and later (LUP) as initially proposed by Campbell (1977), separated by the LGM. One can identify both qualitative and quantitative differences between the EUP/MUP and LUP; the British EUP is represented by very few sites and, as Jacobi and Higham (2011, 181) have noted, is comprised almost entirely of lithic finds, unlike the far larger and better contextualised LUP. On the continent, the Upper Palaeolithic spans the period from ~45 ka BP to the end of the Pleistocene ~11.6 ka BP, a period over 30,000 years in duration. This includes 'leafpoint' assemblages which, although formally defined on technological grounds as Upper Palaeolithic are, by general consensus (although not clear demonstration), thought to have been made by Neanderthals. Britain seems to have been devoid of human occupants for much of this period. Even radiocarbon dates for MIS3 – the few that exist – are relatively imprecise, with errors typically spanning at least 1,000 radiocarbon years at 2σ. Even taking these large degrees of chronological uncertainty into account, the period they cover amounts to no more than ~5,000 total years of radiocarbon time spread over five or so occupational phases. This is of course a small number of measurements, sampling human occupation that may have been more frequent in time, although there are no reasons to believe on the basis of the remarkably poor archaeological record of the British Early Upper Palaeolithic (EUP) and Mid Upper Palaeolithic (MUP) that occupation was anything other than brief. Despite intensive excavations in the country's major known caves, and intensive prospecting of both major and minor river valleys, the EUP and LRJ record amounts to no more than a few hundred finds from around 60 sites, and of these the majority represent single findspots rather than assemblages. The latter, where they exist, are small, usually less than 50 artefacts. Thus, EUP and MUP humans may well have been active in the British landscape for far less than 5,000 radiocarbon years, probably for a total period countable in years or tens of years rather than in centuries. A stringent reading of the existing radiocarbon dates relevant to human activity, taking into account the potentially vast exaggeration of age ranges caused by chronometric imprecision, supports such a parsimonious interpretation. Given Britain's geographical location this is perhaps not surprising; a similar pattern of human settlement can be observed for neighbouring regions of the continent, such as northern France, Belgium and The Netherlands (Housley et al. 1997) and over the entire period one has to look as far south as the Loire or Mittelgebirge to find essentially continuous human presence. From this point of view, animals such as bison, aurochs and horse seem to have been far more successful in their exploitation of the western periphery of Doggerland. Far from lamenting the poor state of the British LRJ and EUP record we should be grateful that these brief dispersals, occurring in such a remote period, have left any archaeology at all.

With regard to the biological species of humans associated with the British Early Upper Palaeolithic the record is effectively non-existent and one is forced to make assumptions about which species the archaeological record acts as a proxy for. The only anatomical remains apparently belonging to the period is the KC4 partial human maxilla from Kent's Cavern (Oakley et al. 1971). This takes the form of a partial right maxilla with associated C, P4 and M1 (Oakley et al. 1971: see Figure 7.1). The taxonomic status of the maxilla has been debated for some time (Stringer 2006; E. Trinkaus pers. comm.) although on morphometric grounds now seems to be *Homo Sapiens* (Higham et al. 2011). The maxilla is small, the teeth are heavily worn and the shapes of the tooth crowns do not display the extreme pattern visible on some Neanderthals but given the range of variation observed in its features there is nothing clearly diagnostic in its anatomy (E. Trinkaus pers. comm.). Attempts to date the maxilla directly also failed and it is assumed to date to ~41.5–44.1 ka BP on the basis of radiocarbon measurements on faunal remains found in close proximity to the maxilla (Higham et al. 2006; Jacobi et al. 2006; Jacobi and Higham 2011; Higham et al. 2011). It is of course an assumption that these measurements broadly relate to the age of the maxilla and that dated and undated artefacts from the Vestibule – an area of intense activity – are relatively undisturbed. It is highly unlikely that such an assumption is justified. Uncalibrated radiocarbon measurements on fauna stratified 50 cm above and below the level of the mandible vary between ~41 and 46 ka BP (OxA-13921, 36,040 ± 330 to OxA-14285, 43,600 ± 3,600: Jacobi and Higham 2011 Table 11.5) but most importantly they are not stratigraphically consistent; several measurements on samples stratified above the maxilla have older mean ages than those on samples stratified below it. This clearly reveals a degree of disturbance, and as this affects dated samples up to one metre above and one metre below it is probable that mixing of material of widely different ages was considerable. Thus, while Bayesian modelling appears to resolve the age of the maxilla, individual radiocarbon measurements pertain only to the samples they date and do not have stratigraphic relevance. Even assuming that the dated samples immediately above and below it provide a reasonable estimate of its age this could still be as young as ~41 ka BP and as old as ~46 ka BP at 2σ (uncalibrated measurements: OxA-13965 37,200 ± 550 BP and OxA-13888 40,000 ± 700 BP). These are but two samples and this is assumption; we suggest that it is sensible to regard the maxilla as dated no more precisely than to MIS3.

Chronometric dating for the British Early Upper Palaeolithic and Mid Upper Palaeolithic is very poor. A handful of radiocarbon dates from a few sites reveals three main periods of activity, which may be taxonomically equated with the leafpoints of the continental LRJ, a phase of the Aurignacian and a phase of the Gravettian. There are no chronometric or typological grounds to indicate the presence of any other technocomplex, or indeed sustained or substantial settlement during these periods. As with the preceding Middle Palaeolithic and succeeding Late Upper Palaeolithic, it seems that humans were more often absent than present.

In a broad sense, British Early Upper Palaeolithic findspots are widely distributed south of the limits of the LGM glaciers (see below). This broad distribution belies other

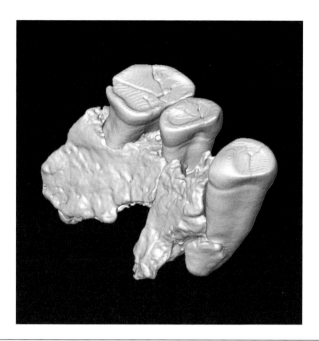

FIGURE 7.1
CT scan of the KC4 human maxilla. (Courtesy Barry Chandler, Torquay Museum.)

patterning, however. By far the majority of finds derive from caves, no doubt because of the intense levels of excavation activity in the nineteenth and early twentieth centuries, which almost always focused on these sites. Where materials have derived from open-air sites these are almost always remarkably small collections and often single finds. A clear contrast with the preceding Middle Palaeolithic is the relative lack of importance of the major rivers in the distribution of EUP materials which, given that this dominates in the distribution of the Middle Palaeolithic, cannot be entirely due to sampling. As Bridgland (2010) has noted, the terrace systems of the major British rivers, so important for pre-MIS5 archaeology, reveal very little for MIS3 in general. Some patterning may, by contrast, relate to real differences in human distribution. The small number of EUP assemblages that can be classified as Aurignacian are all in the west, which may relate to contrasting dispersal and settlement patterns to the preceding LRJ and succeeding Gravettian (Jacobi and Pettitt 2000; Pettitt 2008 and see below).

LEAFPOINTS AND BLADE-POINTS ~42–43 KA BP

Leafpoints *sensu lato* are known from at least 38 findspots in England and Wales (Table 7.1). Although reliable radiocarbon dates exist only for three British leafpoint sites, those noted in the table can be accepted as reliably of Early Upper Palaeolithic age on the basis of:

- their context and/or preservational state (Jacobi 2007, 273);

- the fact that they are distinguishable from later prehistoric 'knives';

- the fact that Britain seems never to have played host to visits from other users of bifacial leaf-shaped points, that is, the Solutreans.

Of the known findspots, 25 have yielded either isolated solitary leafpoints or solitary leafpoints within assemblages where an association with other material is not demonstrable on the basis of available stratigraphic information. Only at three caves – Robin Hood Cave (Figure 7.2), the Goat's Hole at Paviland and Kent's Cavern – and two open sites – Beedings and Warren Livingston Pit in Ipswich – have more than eight examples been found and these are probably all palimpsests. Only at Beedings and Glaston is it possible to associate with any degree of confidence leafpoints with other lithic artefacts. As many of these finds were made long ago, and reported cursorily if at all, it is impossible today to establish precisely whether leafpoints contextually represent chance losses of armatures during hunting or whether they originally formed

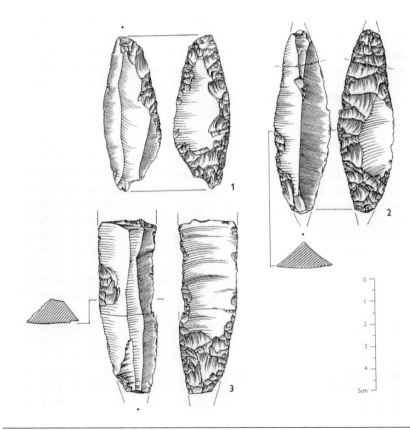

FIGURE 7.2
Bladepoints from Robin Hood Cave, Creswell Crags. (From Pettitt and Jacobi 2009; drawings by Hazel Martingell.)

Table 7.1 Major British Late Middle Palaeolithic sites

Site	Leafpoints	Bladepoints	Chronology	Context	References
Creswell Crags, Derbyshire, Nottinghamshire (no specific cave attribution)		3		Unclear	Jacobi 1990, 2007a
Pin Hole, Creswell Crags, Derbyshire		1	OxA-4754 *Crocuta crocuta* right pre-maxilla 37,800 ± 1600 BP	Unclear: possible associations with Middle Palaeolithic, no Aurignacian	Jacobi 1990, 2007, Jacobi and Higham 2011
Robin Hood Cave, Creswell Crags, Derbyshire	1	10 plus up to 3 possible examples		Unclear: possible associations with Middle Palaeolithic, no Aurignacian	Jacobi 1990, 2007, Jacobi and Higham 2011a
Wallow Camp, Salmonby, Lincolnshire		1		Isolated find	Jacobi 1990, 2007, Jacobi and Higham 2011a
Grange Farm, Glaston, Leicestershire		2		Hunting of wild horse	Jacobi 2007, Jacobi and Higham 2011a
Ffynonn Beuno Cave, Denbighshire		1		Unclear: no Middle Palaeolithic, Aurignacian present	Jacobi 1990, 2007, Green and Walker 1991, Jacobi and Higham 2011a
Goat's Hole, Paviland, Gower	1, possibly 2	7		Unclear: Middle Palaeolithic and Aurignacian present	Campbell 1977, Jacobi 1990, 2007, Jacobi and Higham 2011a
Goldcliff, Monmouthshire		1		Isolated find	Jacobi 1990, Jacobi and Higham 2011a
King Arthur's Cave, Gloucestershire		1		Unclear	Jacobi 1990, 2007, Jacobi and Higham 2011a
Beckford, Gloucestershire	1			Isolated find	Jacobi 2007
Osney Lock, Oxford, Oxfordshire	1			Isolated find	Jacobi 1990, 2007, Jacobi and Higham 2011a
Sutton Courtenay, Oxfordshire	1	1		Isolated find	Jacobi 2007, Jacobi and Higham 2011a

Hyaena Den, Wookey, Somerset	2			Unclear: Middle Palaeolithic and probable Aurignacian present	Jacobi 1990, 2007, Jacobi and Higham 2011a
Badger Hole, Wookey, Somerset	4		OxA-11963 *Equus ferus* right dentary 36,000 ± 450 BP	Unclear: Middle Palaeolithic present	Jacobi 1990, 2007, Jacobi and Higham 2011a
Uphill Quarry Cave 8, Somerset	5			Unclear: Middle Palaeolithic and Aurignacian present	Jacobi 1990, 2007, Jacobi and Higham 2011a
Soldier's Hole, Cheddar, Somerset		3	Radiocarbon measurements available from spits containing leafpoints but unreliable	Unclear: no Middle Palaeolithic or Aurignacian present	Jacobi 1990, Jacobi and Higham 2011a
Kent's Cavern, Devon	9	1	General association with spread of radiocarbon measurements on unmodified fauna ~35–40 uncal BP	Unclear: Middle Palaeolithic and Aurignacian present	Jacobi 1990, 2007, Jacobi and Higham 2011a,
Windmill Hill Cave, Brixham, Devon	1			Unclear: Middle Palaeolithic present	Jacobi 1990, 2007, Jacobi and Higham 2011a
Bench Quarry, Brixham, Devon	1		OxA-13512 *Crocuta crocuta* right dentary 36,800 ± 450 BP; OxA-13324 same sample as above 37,500 ± 900 BP	Isolated find	Jacobi 1990, 2007, Jacobi and Higham 2011a
Moordown, Bournemouth, Hampshire	1			Isolated find	Jacobi 1990, 2007, Jacobi and Higham 2011a
Brighstone, Isle of Wight		1		Isolated find	Poole 1929, Jacobi 2007, Jacobi and Higham 2011a
Cross Bank, Cambridgeshire		1		Isolated find	Jacobi 1990, Jacobi and Higham 2011a
Hainey Hill, Barway, Cambridgeshire	1			Isolated find	Jacobi 2007, Jacobi and Higham 2011a
Drayton, Norfolk	1			Isolated find	Jacobi 2007, Jacobi and Higham 2011a

Location	Number	Date	Status	References
Balding's Hill, Brandon, Suffolk	1		Isolated find	Jacobi 1990, 2007, Jacobi and Higham 2011a
Warren Hill, Suffolk	1		Isolated find	Jacobi 1990, 2007, Jacobi and Higham 2011a
Town Pit, Icklingham, Suffolk	1		Isolated find	Jacobi 1990, 2007, Jacobi and Higham 2011a
Eastall's Pit, Barham, Suffolk	1		Isolated find	Jacobi 1990, Jacobi and Higham 2011a
Warren Livingstone Pit, Bramford Road, Ipswich, Suffolk	5–9	2, plus 2 possible examples	Isolated find	Jacobi 1990, 2007, Jacobi and Higham 2011a
Pit I, White (Earl's) Colne, Suffolk	1		Isolated find	Jacobi 1990, 2007, Jacobi and Higham 2011a
Creffield Road, Acton, London	1			Jacobi 1990, 2007, Jacobi and Higham 2011a
Temple Mills, London	1		Isolated find	Jacobi 2007, Jacobi and Higham 2011a
Earl of Dysart's Gravel Pit, Ham, Surrey	1		Isolated find	Jacobi 1990, 2007, Jacobi and Higham 2011a
Bapchild, Kent	1		Isolated find	Jacobi 1990, 2007, Jacobi and Higham 2011a
Ightham, Kent	1		Unclear	Jacobi 2007, Jacobi and Higham 2011a
Golden Cross, East Sussex	1		Isolated find	Jacobi 2007, Jacobi and Higham 2011a
Conningbrook Manor Pit, Kennington, Kent	1		Isolated find	Jacobi 1990, 2007, Jacobi and Higham 2011a
Beedings, Pulborough, Sussex	43	$31,100 \pm 5,700$ BP (TL on burnt flint)	Technologically EUP material present (see text) although no diagnostically Aurignacian forms	Jacobi 1990, 2007, Jacobi and Higham 2011a
Total number of locations	**28**			
	15			

part of wider assemblages which have not been sampled. The isolation of most finds perhaps supports the former interpretation. Most of the caves which have yielded leafpoints have also yielded Middle Palaeolithic assemblages and it may be that tools and débitage classified as such were originally associated with leafpoints, although the amounts of such material are small, as seen in Chapter 6, and do not suggest intensive occupation.

Leafpoint sites (the LRJ; see below) are found in all major British regions south of the LGM ice limits and there is no discernible geographical patterning to their occurrence. They are found in most counties up to Lincolnshire and Derbyshire in the north (Jacobi 2007; Figures 7.3 and 7.4). Four regions each contain a site with multiple leafpoints: Paviland in south Wales, Kent's Cavern in the south-west, Beedings in the south-east and Robin Hood Cave in the north and the greatest number of sites with multiple examples is in the south west (Hyaena Den and Badger Hole at Wookey (Figure 7.5), Uphill, Kent's Cavern and Paviland) although, given the small numbers of finds nationally, it is unclear as to whether there is any meaning to this. Indeed, the overall distribution of finds – isolated or not – shows that leafpoint users were active, at least at times,

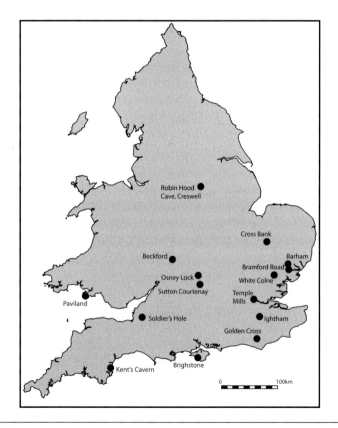

FIGURE 7.3
Distribution of Early Upper Palaeolithic bifacially worked leafpoints in Britain

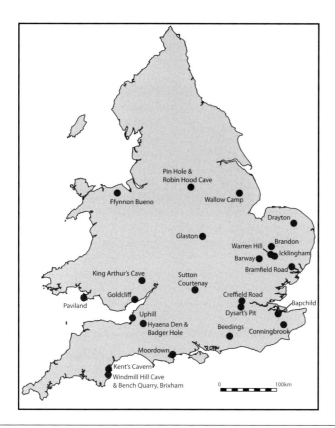

FIGURE 7.4
Distribution of Early Upper Palaeolithic bladepoints in Britain

over the entire landscape that had been exploited by preceding Neanderthals. Both bifacially worked leafpoints and relatively lightly-worked blade-points (see below) can be found at the same sites, suggesting, if they do represent different populations, that their ranges overlapped in space, if not in time. Jacobi (1999, 36), for example, noted that both fully bifacial leafpoints were present at Soldier's Hole, Cheddar, whereas partly bifacial blade-points were found at nearby Hyaena Den, Wookey. It must be said, however, that no leafpoint sites are precisely dated and individual artefacts in most palimpsest assemblages *could* be separated by several centuries. The general imprecision of dates in this period may therefore mask a degree of diachronic change in leafpoint assemblages.

LRJ sites: technological and typological definitions

Among leafpoints in general, Jacobi (1990; 2000; 2007a) has identified two technological categories. Leafpoints *sensu stricto* are bifacially worked pieces showing relatively intensive manufacture through principles of *façonnage* similar to that used to produce

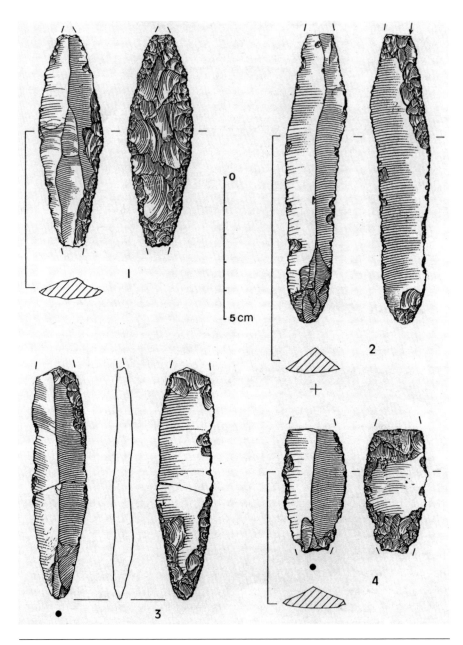

FIGURE 7.5
Bifacially worked 'bladepoints' (leafpoints) from Badger Hole, Wookey, Somerset. (Drawn by Joanna Richards and courtesy Roger Jacobi.)

handaxes. Indeed, the relatively wide form of some of these, such as that shown by the example from Kent's Cavern (Figure 7.6) may indicate that these forms arose straight out of Late Middle Palaeolithic bifacial traditions. By contrast, blade-points (or blade leafpoints to use the term preferred by Jacobi and Higham 2011, 185) are, as the name implies, produced on the products of Middle Palaeolithic opposed-platform blade technology and usually show evidence of minimal working. On these, retouch is restricted to the ventral surface and usually only to the proximal and distal ends, functioning simply to reduce the natural curvature of the blank. Formally speaking the term 'blade-point' also covers partially bifacial leafpoints, Jerzmanowician points, *Pointes du Spy* and unifacial leafpoints. We shall use the terms leafpoint and blade-point to refer to these categories.

Raw material probably accounts for some variability in the intensity and form of leafpoint modification. More intensive, bifacial techniques were appropriate when raw material came in the form of flattened nodules or in tabular form, whereas the relatively minimally or partially worked blade-point production was appropriate for high-quality but irregularly formed materials where the sole requirements were to straighten the longitudinal profile of the blank and point its ends. Variability can be observed in the same collections, however, although it is impossible to establish whether this was due to changes in the availability or quality of raw materials in palimpsest assemblages, or whether it relates to deliberate choice of modification methods, perhaps for different functions. As Jacobi (1990) noted, blade-points represent the manifestation of a desire to produce a straight implement in situations where raw material takes the form of irregular nodules and where thin tabular flint was rare. In such cases the retouch served to reduce the

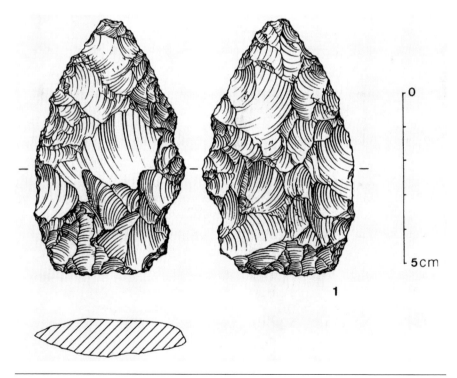

FIGURE 7.6
Bifacially worked leafpoint from Kent's Cavern, Devon. (Courtesy Roger Jacobi.)

natural curvature of the object and bring about a convergence of the proximal and distal ends and thus an elongated leaf shape.

To our knowledge no microwear evidence of function has been established for EUP leafpoints. It is usually assumed that they functioned as weapon heads although there is no reason to suppose why their use may have been restricted to spearpoints and why some may not have been used as knives. Known British examples typically vary from ~6 cm to ~12 cm in length although the example from Cross Bank in Suffolk is ~20 cm long. In view of this one might expect some variation in function although it is of course possible that these tipped variable weapon systems. If this were the case, it may indicate that by this time different weapon systems, such as light and heavy spears, were being deployed on different prey. It is interesting in this light that, very broadly speaking, the LRJ occurs alongside other technocomplexes in which characteristic point forms were becoming more standardised, such as the Châtelperronian and Ulluzian, almost certainly reflecting developments in weaponry, and one cannot rule out the possibility that the LRJ forms part of continent-wide behavioural developments in weapon systems at this time. Several other lines of evidence support the notion that leafpoints were, in the main, weapon heads. Most findspots have yielded only singular finds, suggesting that they were hunting losses rather than tools discarded in occupational contexts; breakage patterns at Beedings are consistent with impact damage and retooling (Jacobi 2007a), and possible impact fractures have also been observed on a broken example from Buhlen, Germany (O. Jöris pers. comm. to PP). It may also be of significance that the locations of the two largest British assemblages – Beedings and Glaston (Cooper 2004; Cooper et al. in press) – are at tactically important points in the landscape suggestive of hunting stands.

Sixty-five per cent of British leafpoint sites and findspots have yielded blade-points. The figure is even greater if one accounts for the total of individual pieces; of a minimum of 125 artefacts classed as leafpoints 104 (83%) are blade-points. Clearly then, blade-points were by far the most common diagnostic element of the British LRJ. As can be seen in Table 7.1, leafpoints and blade-points are found together at only five sites (13% of the total findspots); leafpoints are found without blade-points at 10 sites (66%) and blade-points are found without leafpoints at 23 sites (82%). Clearly, in the main, leafpoints and blade-points have a relatively exclusive occurrence and on four of the five sites on which they co-occur they occur in raised number, suggesting that these sites were probably palimpsests. Although the data are poor, this patterning may suggest that leafpoints and blade-points were taxonomically separate entities during the British LRJ.

Campbell (1977) classified British leafpoint assemblages as Lincombian, after Lincomb Hill in Wellswood on the outskirts of Torquay, Devon, within which Kent's Cavern formed. There is nothing wrong with this term, although in order to stress continental parallels we use here the term Lincombian–Ranisian–Jerzmanowican (LRJ). Jacobi's (1990; 2007a) surveys of leafpoint assemblages included examples from both cave and open contexts. They clearly display technological and typological parallels with broadly contemporary assemblages to the east of Britain, such as Ilsenhöhle (Ranis), Mauern in Germany and Nietoperzowa Cave near Jerzmanovice in Poland (Desbrosse and Kozlowski 1988;

Flas 2008) and can thus be considered to be part of a relatively continuous tradition on the Northern European Plain.

When British leafpoints are found in association with other tool forms (particularly at Beedings, Sussex) these are clearly Upper Palaeolithic in nature (if culturally undiagnostic), including endscrapers on blades and burins, although it must be said that examples of such associations are few. By contrast, there is little evidence to associate them with typologically Mousterian forms (Jacobi 1999), although undiagnostic flakes often found with them are consistent with Middle Palaeolithic technology. Campbell (1977) suggested that leafpoints formed part of a wider technology of which the few known British Aurignacian assemblages were part but, as Jacobi (1990) has noted, there are no known associations between the minimal Aurignacian presence in Britain and leafpoints. Only three sites (Kent's Cavern, Paviland and Ffynnon Beuno) have yielded both assemblage types but this can probably be explained by the strategic position and repeated use of these caves rather than any meaningful connection between the assemblages (Jacobi 1980, 17; Figure 7.7). At Kent's Cavern, the spatial distribution of the two artefact types was mutually exclusive. Furthermore, south of the LGM ice-limit leafpoints are geographically widespread, with many recovered from central and eastern England, a dramatic contrast to the restricted distribution of the few known Aurignacian sites exclusively in the west (Jacobi and Pettitt 2000). Thus if the two were related in a technological whole deployed by the same groups of *Homo sapiens*, one would

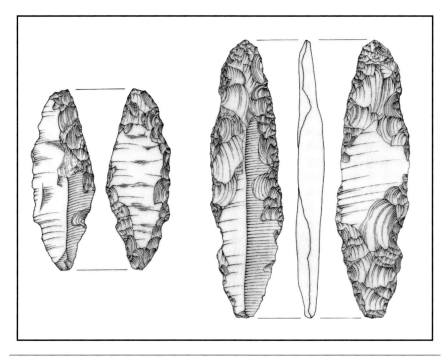

FIGURE 7.7
Welsh Early Upper Palaeolithic bladepoints. Left: Paviland; right: Ffynnon Beuno. (Illustration by Andrew David.)

have to conclude that these groups used weapons tipped with leafpoints across much of England, and then changed their toolkits radically for operating in Wales. Clearly the most parsimonious interpretation is that these two assemblage types represented distinct human populations although the issue of whether these were biologically distinct, that is, *Homo neanderthalensis* and *Homo sapiens*, does remain to be resolved (see below).

Stapert (2007) observed that the frequencies of unifacial leafpoints (i.e. blade points) increases from east to west on the Northern European Plain and at their westernmost distribution – in Britain – dominate over bifacial forms. As stratigraphic observations on central European sites reveal that bifacial points (often referred to as 'Mauern type') apparently pre-date the unifacial forms ('Jerzmanowician type'), he suggested that the east–west patterning may represent an actual westwards movement of Neanderthals, a 'great trek', which may have occurred as a response to expanding populations of *Homo sapiens*. Other interpretations of this patterning are possible; if the leafpoint tradition arose in the west one might expect larger numbers there, especially if the tradition were short-lived as was noted above. It is impossible to say.

At Glaston in Leicestershire, blade-points have been recovered from an assemblage of 83 pieces (see Text Box 7.3). As noted above, however, the only British leafpoint collection that can truly be said to be part of a *large* assemblage is that from Beedings, near Pulborough in Sussex (Jacobi 2007a). The site has yielded by far the largest number of leafpoints in the country, amounting to ~34% of the known sample, and in fact on a continental scale only the assemblage from Nietoperzowa is larger (Flas 2008). Here, material was derived from 'gulls' (erosional fissures) that provided sedimentary traps in which artefacts also accumulated. The site commands extensive views across the landscape of the Sussex Weald, and is therefore suggestive of a hunting camp, although the lack of faunal preservation precludes testing this hypothesis. Originally excavated in the early twentieth century and comprising some 2,300 pieces, the collection has been considerably reduced and now only around 180 can be identified with certainty. In addition, the lack of fauna and thus dating, and the mixing within the gulls of archaeological materials of significantly different ages, severely limits the utility of the Beedings collection for understanding the behaviour of LRJ makers. As Jacobi (2007a, 271) noted, 'there is an inevitable element of subjectivity when it comes to identifying the Early Upper Palaeolithic component of what is very clearly a multi-period collection among which there are few clues, such as condition, as to the relative ages of individual artefacts'. Despite this, his comprehensive analysis of the surviving artefacts provides a rare technological and typological context for leafpoints. The source of the flint used for the Beedings assemblage is unknown, although was probably local in the Sussex Downs. The 36 examples of leafpoint from Beedings are exclusively blade-points *sensu stricto*. Microstructural fabric analysis of the artefacts showed that variable raw materials were used for non-leafpoint artefacts at the site, suggesting an ad hoc use of locally available stone, whereas far less variability was observed for the leafpoints, suggesting greater selectivity of material from a source of finer quality flint.

LEAFPOINTS, HYAENAS AND HORSE HUNTING AT GLASTON, LEICESTERSHIRE

The remains of an open-air LRJ activity site and hyaena den was excavated at Glaston, Leicestershire in 2000 (Cooper 2004; Cooper et al. in press). The site is situated on the top of a ridge flanked by rivers to the north and south and was preserved when the apex subsided into a fault basin. Free standing remnants or 'rafts' of local sandstone presented opportunities for shelter in this otherwise exposed landscape and probably explain, in addition to the views the locale commands over the surrounding landscape, the activity of LRJ makers and hyaenas. The latter had created burrows beneath the rafts and humans exploited the shelter provided in their lee. AMS radiocarbon dates on fauna indicate that the activity occurred between ~42 and 44 ka BP, the age range of the few continental LRJ sites which have reliable dates (see main text).

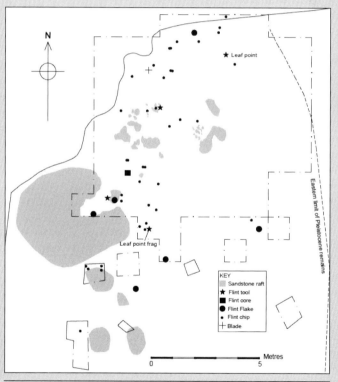

FIGURE 1
The location of Glaston. (Courtesy of Lynden Cooper.)

The site yielded a lithic assemblage of 83 pieces, dominated by flakes (including trimming flakes from leafpoint manufacture or maintenance) alongside two notched flakes, and a laminar core rejuvenation flake (Cooper et al. in press). In addition to these a complete blade-point and a blade-point fragment were

Text Box 7.3

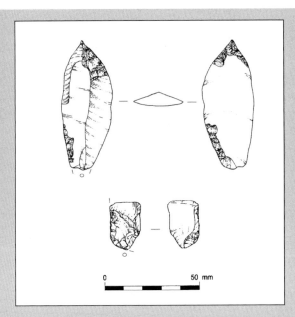

FIGURE 2
Leafpoint and fragmentary leafpoint from Glaston. (Courtesy of Lynden Cooper.)

recovered. No local source for the flint can be identified although it is unclear how far it may have been imported onto the site. The blade-point was produced on a bipolar core in keeping with typical blank production for the LRJ (see main text). The blade-point fragment bears a bending fracture consistent with impact damage supporting the notion that leafpoints *sensu lato* were armatures rather than general purpose knives. Knapping clearly took place on-site, although one need invoke no activities other than the repair of weapon systems – and perhaps a degree of butchery – to account for the lithic assemblage. In this sense Glaston need represent nothing more than a hunting stop at which animals killed in the locale were eaten and weapons repaired.

Faunal remains – which probably relate predominantly to the hyaena denning – indicate the presence of woolly rhinoceros, mammoth, wild horse, reindeer, wolverine and arctic hare, certainly indicative of a Pin Hole MAZ. Anthropogenic modifications have only been found on the remains of horse, which bear spiral fractures suggestive of marrow extraction, and which were found in close proximity to the complete blade-point (see Figure 3).

Text Box 7.3

FIGURE 3
Horse limb bones from Glaston showing fractures. (Courtesy of Lynden Cooper.)

Fifty-five of the Beedings artefacts (30.5%) are formally débitage although a number of these may be of post-Palaeolithic age. Of the retouched tools, two appear to be Late Middle Palaeolithic in age: (1) a piece which can be identified either as a unifacial handaxe on a proximally thinned flake or a partially bifacial double sidescraper (2) and the proximal end of a sidescraper. A number of Late Middle Palaeolithic handaxes have been found at nearby locations in the Sussex Weald and in Kent, so an identification of a small Mousterian element at Beedings is not surprising. Between 30 and 40 retouched tools are identifiably Early Upper Palaeolithic. These include 11 burins of dihedral, break, truncation and Corbiac forms, two of which appear to have been made on fragmentary leafpoints. No single type dominates. Four or five Kostenki knives from the site have been taken by some as an indication that it is of younger (i.e. Mid Upper Palaeolithic) age, although as Jacobi points out these forms are found in Middle Palaeolithic and leafpoint assemblages on the continent. Seven composite tools, three of which are burin/Kostenki knife combinations, one a burin/endscraper, and two Kostenki knives, one with a truncation and the other lateral retouch, form the last group of tool forms. One denticulate and one piercer may also belong to the leafpoint assemblage and ten utilised pieces are indicative of a variety of tasks. Otherwise, the Beedings assemblage is overwhelmingly dominated by leafpoints, all of which, as mentioned above, are of the blade-point form (Figure 7.8). They typically have a triangular cross-section and several

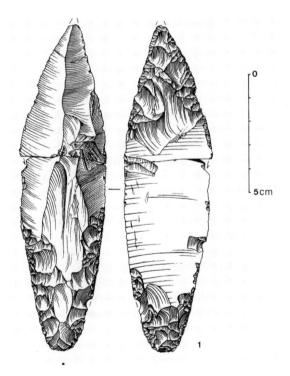

FIGURE 7.8
Bifacially worked bladepoint (leafpoint) from Beedings, Sussex. (Drawn by Joanna Richards and courtesy Roger Jacobi.)

have been fluted, perhaps to assist hafting. All examples are broken and the symmetry displayed on fragmentary points suggests that they were finished pieces. Thus, in the main, the Beedings site represents a place where weapons/knives were being discarded, although at least two examples of leafpoint manufacture survive, suggesting that retooling was practised at least on occasion at the site; the two activities may, of course, have been linked.

LRJ chronology

On the continent, radiocarbon dates place the LRJ between ~42 and 44 ka BP (Jöris and Street 2008, 790; Flas 2008) although it can hardly be said that the number of dated assemblages is comprehensive. The existing chronology for British LRJ assemblages is poor, although enough stratigraphical and chronometric data exist for cave sites such as Kent's Cavern, Pin Hole and Robin Hood Cave to demonstrate at least that they post-date the Late Middle Palaeolithic as they do on the continent. The few existing ^{14}C dates on fauna found in stratigraphic association with leafpoints suggest ages in excess of ~40 ka BP (Jacobi 1999, contra Aldhouse-Green and Pettitt 1998). As Jacobi (1999) has noted, however, there are problems with almost all radiocarbon dates on fauna apparently associated with leafpoints. We critically need new examples of leafpoints, excavated and recorded with modern methods, and ultrafiltrated radiocarbon dates on clearly associated fauna. Only at three sites – Kent's Cavern, Bench Quarry and Badger Hole – are radiocarbon dates at all reliably associated with LRJ materials (see Table 6.1) and, assuming these are broadly representative of LRJ occupation of Britain, indicate a time span between ~42 and 44 ka BP. We are, however, sceptical about the relationship between the two at Kent's Cavern, as discussed below. Broadly speaking then, British LRJ material is contemporary with continental LRJ assemblages in radiocarbon terms. Non-^{14}C dates for British material, such as a TL date of 31,100 ± 5,700 BP on a burnt flint from Beedings (Jacobi 2007a), are so imprecise that they play no role in the chronological definition of Middle and Early Upper Palaeolithic technocomplexes.

Wider issues: faunal context and authorship of the LRJ

On the continental scale, evidence for the LRJ is poor. Actual *assemblages* exist only at Nietoperzowa Cave at Jerzmanowice in Poland (~277 artefacts), the Ilsenhöhle at Ranis, Germany (~63 artefacts) and Beedings and Glaston in Britain (Flas 2008). Its representation, therefore, is largely one of isolated finds and in terms of these the greater majority are in Britain. In view of this, the LRJ may well have been a very brief phenomenon indeed. Furthermore, the lack of LRJ assemblages excavated with modern methods, and lack of clear association with fauna, renders the broader contextualisation of this technocomplex impossible at present. Breakage fractures on wild horse bones at Glaston show that leafpoint users were exploiting this species (Thomas and Jacobi 2001; Cooper et al. in press), otherwise there are no further data, other than a broad chronological overlap between the LRJ and faunas of the Pin Hole MAZ noted above. Their pertinence to Neanderthal extinction is also severely limited; assuming the LRJ does represent the latest Neanderthals in Britain, all one can say is that they became extinct in the region some time before 40 ka BP, although this is questionable.

It is usually assumed that continental LRJ assemblages were produced by late Neanderthals. As noted above the KC4 human maxilla from Kent's Cavern may date to ~40–42 ka BP and for this reason is usually assumed to have an LRJ cultural association (e.g. Jacobi 2007a, 307). The maxilla, however, was excavated in 1927, its location is relatively poorly recorded, one cannot trust apparent stratigraphic relationships between objects in British caves that were the subject of early excavations and, in any case, the maxilla was found in a separate area of the cave (the Vestibule) to the cluster of leafpoints. As such a lack of spatial correlation has been used to argue that leafpoints and Aurignacian materials are not meaningfully connected (Jacobi 1990, 281–5) one must follow the same logic and argue that there is no clear correlation between the maxilla and the LRJ. This situation will not improve and it is futile to continue discussing the maxilla in the context of considering the LRJ.

On the continent the picture is no better. It is usually assumed that Neanderthals were the authors of LRJ assemblages given that they are technologically rooted in the Middle Palaeolithic (e.g. Desbrosse and Kozlowski 1988, 37; Otte 1990b, 248–9; Jacobi 2007a, 305–7; Jöris and Street 2008, 388). There are, however, absolutely no associations between the LRJ and human fossils. Because of this, LRJ assemblages are usually assumed to represent a northern and central European equivalent of the Châtelperronian, which is associated with Neanderthal fossils at two sites, the Grotte du Renne at Arcy-sur-Cure and Saint-Césaire (Bailey and Hublin 2006; Lévêque and Vandermeersch 1980). At neither site are direct causal associations between the human fossils and archaeological industries particularly convincing, however. A major series of radiocarbon measurements on fauna from the Grotte du Renne has indicated considerable stratigraphic mixing (Higham et al. 2010) leaving no reliable cultural context for the Neanderthal teeth from the site; and the apparent Neanderthal burial at Saint-Césaire was devoid of artefactual associations. In any case there is no a priori reason why the curved-backed point tradition Châtelperronian of the south should be at all relevant to LRJ assemblages on the Northern European Plain; the only link between the two is the repeated tendency of specialists to group them under the increasingly meaningless term 'transitional industry'. Human fossil associations are desperately needed and, until new excavations provide these, as Roebroeks (2008, 923) notes, 'exercises in lithic phylogeny are not going to solve the debate over the character of transitional industries or their authorship'.

AURIGNACIAN DISPERSALS AND THE COMING OF *HOMO SAPIENS*

From a north-west European point of view the Aurignacian technocomplex provides the first unambiguous indication of the arrival of *Homo sapiens* (e.g. Davies 2001; Conard and Bolus 2003; Mellars 2005; Jöris and Street 2008). Although associations with fossils classed as *Homo sapiens* are few (Churchill and Smith 2000) a respectable and growing number of diagnostic fossils date to the period ~41 ka BP and thereafter (Pettitt 2011 and references therein). The most parsimonious reading of the continental archaeological record sees the gradual dispersal of culturally Aurignacian *Homo sapiens* from west to east, presumably from the Near East, with 'Protoaurignacian' populations established in the south of Europe by ~42 ka BP, central Europe and the Russian plain by ~40–41 ka BP and across much of Europe from ~36 ka BP (Jöris and Street 2008 and references therein). By ~40 ka BP Neanderthals seem to have disappeared from all of their previous territories whether or not one regards the LRJ and 'transitional' technocomplexes as proxies for their presence.

The British Aurignacian is defined on the basis of the presence of carinated/nosed/shouldered endscrapers, *burins busqués* and related variants and bone/antler *sagaies* (Campbell 1977, Jacobi 1999, 2007a; David 2007; Dinnis 2005; 2008, 2009; Pettitt 2008; Jacobi and Higham 2011). It seems that artefacts formally defined as carinated endscrapers and scrapers functioned primarily as cores for the production of small bladelets which were often subsequently retouched into tool forms such as the dufour bladelet (Chiotti 2003; Le Brun-Ricalens 2005). The production of these bladelet forms was clearly complex, aimed at highly specific forms which presumably formed parts of well-designed, multi-component tool and weapon systems. As Dinnis (2008, 19) has noted, the specific morphology of nosed endscrapers (*grattoirs à museau*), on which the 'nose' is a protrusion of the ventral surface and served as a platform for bladelet removal in a similar manner to larger blade cores, reveals a concern with standardisation of bladelet removals. One of the most diagnostic lithic forms of the Aurignacian is the *burin busqué*.[1] These bear a flat burin scar which functioned as the platform for the removal of a series of regular bladelets, the length of which has been determined by a terminal 'stop-notch' which served to terminate the removal. It is this latter character that distinguishes *burins busqués* from other nosed endscrapers, although their reduction is otherwise broadly similar (Dinnis 2008). *Burins busqués* are known from Paviland (see Text Box 7.4), Ffynnon Beuno and Hoyle's Mouth in Wales, revealing that although bladelets have understandably not survived from these early excavations they were produced as part of the quotidian activities of Aurignacians in Britain.

The earliest Aurignacian in northern Europe is poorly dated. The oldest reliable radiocarbon measurements for a handful of sites indicate that it had arrived in northern Germany somewhere between ~40 and 38 ka BP and in Poland and Belgium by ~41 ka BP, persisting until ~32 ka BP in these regions (Flas 2008). It is no surprise that the few reliable radiocarbon measurements for British Aurignacian sites fall at the younger end of this range, parsimoniously reflecting a gradual north-west dispersal of Aurignacian groups (see below). Assemblages in Northern France possess blade and bladelet production including dufour bladelets, carinated endscrapers and Aurignacian blades, dihedral and truncation burins.

Aurignacian chronology and relationship with the LRJ

At least six British cave sites have yielded demonstrably Aurignacian material and a further six may include a very small number of Aurignacian artefacts although some are ambiguous (Table 7.2). Assuming these represent the earliest arrivals of *Homo sapiens* in Britain (see Jacobi and Pettitt 2000; Jacobi et al. 2006; Jacobi 2007a; Pettitt 2008; Dinnis 2009) there seems to be no chronometric overlap between these and the makers of the LRJ. It now seems fairly clear that Aurignacian implements were not part of LRJ

Table 7.2 British sites with Aurignacian material (possible Aurignacian material in italics). Data from Jacobi 1980, 1999; Swainston 1999, 2000; Jacobi and Pettitt 2000; Dinnis 2005, 2008, 2009. Where details are discrepant we follow the figures of Dinnis 2009.

Site	Nosed/shouldered scrapers	Carinated endscrapers	*Burins Busqués*	Pavil and burins	Aurignacian blades	Organic items	References
Ffynonn Beuno Cave, Denbighshire, Wales			1				Green and Walker 1991, Jacobi and Pettitt 2000, David 2007, Dinnis 2009
Hoyle's Mouth Cave, Pembrokeshire, Wales			1				Green and Walker 1991, Jacobi and Pettitt 2000, David 2007, Dinnis 2009
Goat's Hole, Paviland, Gower, Wales	15		3	23		2 basal fragments of chopped base points (although possibly Gravettian)	Green and Walker 1991, Jacobi and Pettitt 2000, David 2007, Dinnis 2009
Uphill Quarry Cave 8, Somerset						Lozangic bone/antler point	Jacobi and Pettitt 2000, Higham et al. 2006
Hyaena Den, Wookey, Somerset						Square-sectioned bone/antler point	Higham et al. 2006, Jacobi 2007
Kent's Cavern, Devon	2			1			Jacobi and Pettitt 2000, Jacobi 2007a, Dinnis 2009
Aston Mills, Worcestershire	*1 possible*						Jacobi and Pettitt 2000, Dinnis 2009
Windmill Hill Cave, Brixham, Devon							Jacobi 2007a
Tor Court Cave, Devon							Jacobi 2007a
Tornewton Cave, Devon							Jacobi 2007a
Nottle (Northill) Tor, W. Glamorganshire, Wales	*1 possible*						Green and Walker 1991, Jacobi and Pettitt 2000, David 2007, Dinnis 2009
Cae Gronw Denbighshire, Wales	*1 possible*				*1 possible*		Green and Walker 1991, Jacobi and Pettitt 2000, David 2007, Dinnis 2009

assemblages as was suggested for example by McBurney (1965, 26–9); they are usually found fairly exclusively (Jacobi 1999, 38) and, even at sites where LRJ leafpoints and diagnostic Aurignacian artefacts are both present, the two are usually distinguishable on the basis of condition if not stratigraphy (Jacobi 2007a, 299; Swainston 2000, 100) and, at Kent's Cavern at least, on the basis of exclusive distribution (Garrod 1926, 44–5; Jacobi 2007a). Furthermore, the restriction of the Aurignacian to the south-west and the wider distribution of LRJ assemblages is best interpreted as distinct chrono-cultural territories rather than activity facies (Pettitt 2008).

The presence of *burins busqués* and nosed carinated endscrapers in British Aurignacian sites has been seen by several specialists as indicating a recent *Aurignacien Evolué* rather than earlier *Aurignacien Ancien* attribution (e.g. Jacobi 1980; Jacobi and Pettitt 2000; Swainston 2000; Dinnis 2009). Such a late attribution is in keeping with the known chronology for the spread of the Aurignacian in Europe generally (e.g. papers in Zilhão and d'Errico 2003) and for the two absolute dates for British Aurignacian material. A direct AMS radiocarbon date on a lozangic bone/antler point from Uphill Quarry Cave 8 (Somerset) indicates an age of ~35–36 ka BP (OxA-13716, 31,730 ± 250 BP, Jacobi et al. 2006). This is typologically similar to points from continental Aurignacian II (or *Aurignacien Evolué*) assemblages with similar ages and the age is further supported by a direct date on a typologically undiagnostic bone/antler point from the Hyaena Den of 31,550 ± 340 BP (OxA-13803, Jacobi et al. 2006), that is, statistically the same calibrated age range. While these are the only two dates currently existing for the British Aurignacian they are at least consistent and suggest an age of ~34–35 ka BP for the appearance of modern humans in the country. Thus, even assuming the LRJ dates to be as young as ~42 ka BP, and the Aurignacian to as early as ~34 ka BP, there seems on current evidence to have been a gap of perhaps 8,000 years between the two. Although the database is far too poor to allow statements of any confidence we hypothesise, therefore, that contemporaneity, contact and interaction between Neanderthals and modern humans did not occur in Britain; when modern humans dispersed into the country they did so into a landscape devoid of other human predators. With a small and poorly dated set of Aurignacian sites in Britain it is, however, impossible to establish the duration of this pioneer dispersal. Jacobi and Pettitt (2000) drew attention to the geographically restricted range of known assemblages and the similarity of their inventories, suggesting that in all probability they represent a very brief time range, and Dinnis (2008) suggested that this may have been restricted to Greenland Interstadial 7. It is possible that Aurignacian activity in Britain was, in reality, restricted to a single group, perhaps even during only one seasonal visit, although of course this is impossible to establish. There is, however, certainly no reason to assume long-term or even year-round occupation.

AURIGNACIAN SITES AND ASSEMBLAGES

The most stringent identifications of British Aurignacian material are those of Jacobi and Pettitt (2000) and particularly Dinnis (2009), both of which employ strict criteria to identify only typologically diagnostic artefacts. As such they may underestimate the actual amount of known Aurignacian material, although probably only to a very minor extent, as much British Upper Palaeolithic material is typologically LUP as will be seen in Chapter 8. It cannot be ruled out, for example, that some débitage from discoidal reduction from Paviland is of Aurignacian age; although it is generally assumed to be of Middle Palaeolithic age, it can be found in well-stratified Aurignacian assemblages on the continent such as at Abri Pataud and Lommersum (Dinnis 2009, 169). In Britain, however, contextualised examples of discoidal technology are Middle Palaeolithic, as seen in Chapter 6 and, given the very low numbers of EUP artefacts in Britain in general, however, a parsimonious approach seems sensible. Of the six to twelve sites which have yielded Aurignacian material it is noticeable that these belong to a tight geographical area in the south-west, with groups in Devon, Somerset and south Wales (Table 7.2 and Figure 7.9). Those clearly attributable to the Aurignacian include carinated endscrapers, often of nosed or shouldered form, and *burins busqués* as noted above. Formally diagnostic Aurignacian artefacts are remarkably limited in number; the stringent analysis by Dinnis (2009) identified only 49 artefacts as clearly diagnostic markers of the Aurignacian.

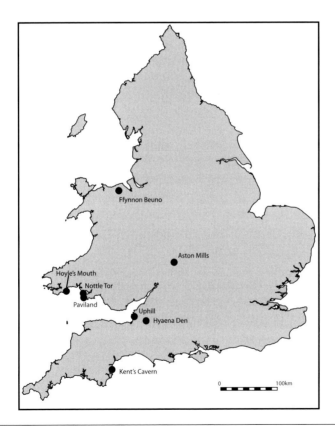

FIGURE 7.9
Distribution of British sites/findspots classified as Aurignacian.

Rather than finished tools, it seems that a number of Aurignacian 'endscraper' and 'burin' forms are actually cores from which small bladelets have been removed, their differing morphologies relating to how the size and shape of resulting bladelets has been determined. On the continent these generally belong to the *Aurignacien Evolué*. They are summarised in Table 7.3.

Only the Goat's Hole at Paviland contained what may be referred to as an Aurignacian assemblage, although even this is remarkably small. Campbell (1977, 144–5) implied that several dozen artefacts from the cave are Aurignacian, although Dinnis (2009, 172) has noted that his overly broad typological classification resulted in this 'entirely erroneous' number; Swainston (2000, 100–101) identified only 55, and Dinnis (2009, 173) arrived at a similar count of 49. The raw materials represented by the diagnostic artefacts suggest procurement to the west (Pembrokeshire), locally, and possibly to the south-east (Somerset; see below). The diagnostic artefacts are dominated by 'Paviland

Table 7.3 Diagnostic Aurignacian endscraper and burin forms (bladelet cores) represented in Britain and on the continent.

English name	Other name/s	Definition	Removals	References
Carinated endscrapers	Grattoirs caréné	Distally retouched convex scraper edge usually produced on laminar blank.	Small bladelets, shape and size of which are controlled by the thickness of blank and angle of scraper edge.	Demars and Laurent 1992, 46.
Nosed endscrapers/ thick-nosed endscrapers	Grattoirs à Museau/ Grattoirs à Museau épais	Distally retouched convex scraper edge usually produced on thick laminar blank and with a protruding carinated 'nose' on the scraper edge.	Small bladelets, shape and size of which is controlled by maintenance of the lateral concavities of the 'nose' and its isolation.	Demars and Laurent 1992, 46, Dinnis 2009.
Shouldered endscraper	Grattoirs à épaulement	Similar to nosed endscraper (a nose is always present) but with only one retouched lateral concavity and thus an asymmetrical 'shoulder' in planform. Usually subsumed in the nosed endscraper category.	Small bladelets, usually curved in section, shape and size controlled as with nosed endscrapers.	Demars and Laurent 1992, 46, Dinnis 2009.
Burins busqués/ hook-nosed burins/hawk-nosed burins/ busked burins	Burins busqués	Burin with flat burin scar opposed by a carinated area of multiple overlapping scars with a retouched 'stop notch' at the termination point of these removals.	Small bladelets, usually curved in section, the size of which is determined by the position of the stop notch. On the continent this technique was used to produce Dufour bladelets and Caminade bladelets.	Demars and Laurent 1992, 54, Dinnis 2009.
Paviland Burins	Paviland burins	Burins made usually on linear flakes and blades with carinations and similar to Burins busqués.	Small bladelets with anti-clockwise twisted aspect in section, struck. obliquely from the dorsal surface across the width/thickness of the blank, sometimes prepared with a dorsally oriented burin scar.	Dinnis 2008, 2009.

Burins' (23; see below) and followed by carinated burins (8), thick-nosed endscrapers (8) and flat-nosed endscrapers (7) with three *burins busqués.*

Swainston (1999, 50; 2000, 109–11) drew attention to the idiosyncratic retouch used to create 'shouldered (nosed) endscrapers' at the site. Breuil had first identified these and defined them as a 'rostrate [beak-like] grattoir [endscraper] with inverse terminal retouches' (Sollas 1913, 344). These are fairly standardised in form and bear four to six diagonal retouch facets (bladelet removals) on the ventral surface (Figure 7.10). Swainston noted that this idiosyncratic type of retouch occurred additionally on an endscraper on a blade and acted as the platform for burin spall removal in at least two cases, the similarity suggesting that the assemblage derived from only a single occupation. Dinnis (2008, 26–8) noted the general similarity of these forms with *burins busqués* although he has demonstrated that they are distinct technological forms due to consistent technological differences. He classified them as 'Paviland Burins', noting that they may represent the final stages of more standardised *burins busqué* reduction or a completely independent reduction sequence.

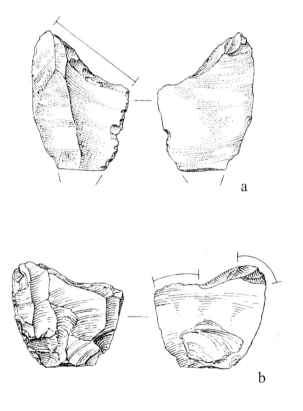

a

b

FIGURE 7.10
Aurignacian shouldered endscrapers from Paviland. (From Swainston 1999, 2000 and courtesy Steph Swainston.)

To the west of Paviland, the small cave of Hoyle's Mouth near Tenby in south-west Wales has yielded a single *burin busqué* in a lithic assemblage otherwise Late Glacial in character (David 2007, 12; Figure 7.11). As Dinnis (2009, 183) has noted, the presence of hyaena and woolly rhinoceros indicate the presence of Mid Devensian deposits in the cave and thus this identification is not surprising, although clearly one is dealing with a very brief occupation, possibly the result of a westward search for raw materials from the Gower area. The *burin busqué* is made on high-quality flint possibly from a source in the now-submerged Bristol Channel (David 1991, 148); if correct this supports the notion of a link to the east.

In north Wales, two caves with Upper Palaeolithic archaeology are found next to each other in the Vale of Clwyd; Ffynnon Beuno and Cae Gwyn. Ffynnon Beuno contained the larger assemblage of the two and its small amount of Early Upper Palaeolithic archaeology includes a leafpoint and a *burin busqué* (David 2007, 8; Figure 7.11), the latter on high-quality flint from a relatively large nodule (Dinnis 2009, 185). At Cae Gwyn the number of artefacts is much smaller. Two objects from the cave have been seen by some as Early Upper Palaeolithic – a blade and endscraper on blade with 'Aurignacian-like' retouch (Green and Walker 1991, 51) – although these are not particularly diagnostic and could be Late Glacial in age.

Kent's Cavern contained a small number of Aurignacian artefacts and, although their actual number is open to question, there is no reason to believe that they represent anything other than a brief occupation. Campbell (1977, 142) grouped these with LRJ

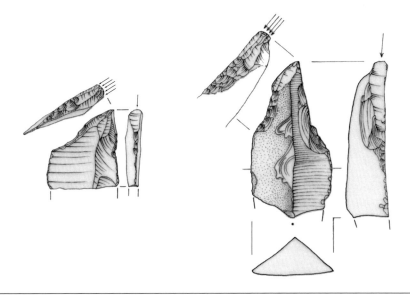

FIGURE 7.11
Burins busqué from the Welsh Aurignacian. Left: Hoyle's Mouth; right: Ffynnon Beuno. (Illustration courtesy Andrew David.)

material, suggesting that the overall count for EUP artefacts from the cave was 112, although this is certainly an over-estimation. Jacobi (2007a, Figure 60) plotted 10 artefacts as Aurignacian on the cave's plan, yet Dinnis (2009, 188) recognised only three apparently diagnostic artefacts – a Paviland Burin and two flat-nosed endscrapers and has subsequently noted the presence of a carinated burin (pers. comm. to PP). At present the source of the flint used for these is unknown. The distribution of diagnostic Aurignacian artefacts in Kent's Cavern is apparently restricted to the eastern (downslope) end of the Vestibule and to the adjacent areas of the Passage of Urns and the northern end of The Great Chamber (Jacobi 2007a).

As noted above, two organic armatures are referrable to the British Aurignacian (Figure 7.12). Although no diagnostic lithics were recovered from Uphill Quarry Cave 8 just

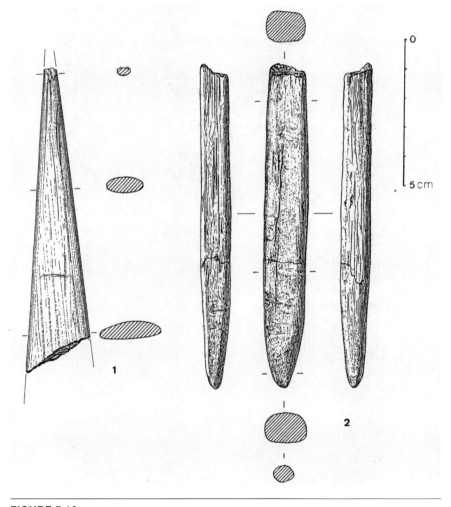

FIGURE 7.12
Organic points from Aurignacian contexts in Somerset. Left: Uphill Quarry; right: Hyaena Den. (From Pettitt 2008 and courtesy Roger and Jacobi.)

outside of Weston-super-Mare (Somerset), a broken lozangic bone/antler point of simi-lar typological form to those from Aurignacian II/*Aurignacien Evolué* assemblages on the continent has a direct AMS radiocarbon measurement of 31,730 ± 250 BP (OxA-13716, Higham et al. 2006). A bone/antler point recovered from the South Passage of the Hyaena Den at Wookey (Somerset) – like Uphill associated with the Axe river – also bears similarities to those from continental Aurignacian sites and has been dated to 31,550 ± 340 (OxA-13803, Higham et al. 2006) but otherwise the cave contained no identifiable Aurignacian artefacts. Both of these indicate calendrical ages of ~35–36 ka BP. Two basal fragments of chopped-base bone points from Paviland may also be Aurignacian but could equally be Gravettian or late glacial in derivation.

In addition to the sites with demonstrable Aurignacian material, several caves have yielded artefacts which may be Aurignacian but which are ambiguous. The number of potential Aurignacian artefacts from such sites is so low that, whether or not they are accepted as Aurignacian, does not change the overall picture of very brief settlement in the south-west. The small fissure (now destroyed) of Nottle Tor on the north part of the Gower peninsula yielded a possible shouldered endscraper which was accepted as Aurignacian by Jacobi and Pettitt (2000, 316) but, as Dinnis (2009, 186) has rightly pointed out, this remains open to question. Similar doubt surrounds the possible flat-nosed endscraper from the terrace deposits of the Carrant Brook in Worcestershire at Aston Mill. The site has yielded a number of MIS3 fauna although, as Dinnis (2009, 185–6) notes, the issue is open. Jacobi (2007a, 298) has suggested that the shared pres-ence of flint available in the vicinity of Kent's Cavern in Tornewton Cave, Tor Court Cave and Windmill Hill Cave in Devon suggests that this material is also attributable to the Aurignacian. No diagnostic artefacts from these additional sites have yet been reported, however, and in view of this such an attribution seems provisional (Dinnis 2009, 85). It is worth noting that Late Upper Palaeolithic artefacts are known from Tornewton and Windmill Hill caves at least and that one cannot therefore rule out a shared Late Upper Palaeolithic raw material source.

Aurignacian settlement

The British Aurignacian record could not contrast more with the larger assemblages of the continental *Aurignacien Evolué,* with their large and varied lithic and organic inven-tories, deep stratigraphies and regional traditions of rock art and *art mobilier*. Typo-logically and chronologically, however, it is understandable as a brief northwestwards dispersal of an *Aurignacien Evolué* group, carrying with it the technological *connaisance* and *savoire-faire* of the lithic and organic technologies of the time. The remarkably low number of British artefacts attributable to the Aurignacian is striking and must reflect at best ephemeral occupation of the northwestern edge of the Aurignacian range. Even assuming that undiagnostic débitage belonging to the Aurignacian has not been rec-ognised and that in the early history of cave investigation in Britain such artefacts have gone unnoticed, the extremely small size of British Aurignacian assemblages is of note. Aurignacian assemblages from the closest regions of continental Europe vary in size, from those which more closely approximate the Paviland assemblage (~30–50 pieces, such as Des Agneux, Côtes-d'Armor, France), to those containing ~100–200 artefacts (e.g. Wildscheuer cave in Hesse and Ilsenhöhle at Ranis), more typical assemblages containing ~400–500 artefacts (e.g. La Pièce de Coinville in the valley of the Orne, northern France), those with up to ≥1,500 artefacts (e.g. Épouville-la-Briquetterie Dupray in Normandy and Herbeville, Yvelines) and even those with ≥5,000 (at Breitenbach in Thuringia) (Gouédo 1996; Flas 2008). The other striking pattern is the total lack of open air findspots in Britain (with the possible exception of one artefact at Aston Mills). Given the predominance of diagnostically Aurignacian artefacts in the caves from which one can identify material, and given that open air findspots are known for the Gravettian (see below) and Late Upper Palaeolithic (see Chapter 8) this cannot, we suggest, be explained by recovery bias. One imagines a chronologically discrete and geographically restricted dispersal to south-west Britain perhaps by one small Aurignacian group. The specific reason for such a modest and probably very brief Aurignacian presence in Britain is unknown. On the basis of the mammoth ivory artefacts from the Goat's Hole, Paviland, Dennell (1983, 132–3) suggested that it may reflect deliberate sourcing of mammoth ivory, although it is now fairly clear that the worked ivory from this site is of Gravettian context, and thus does not pertain to the Aurignacian, and no artefacts of this material are known for the period.

The similarities of the British material to the continental Aurignacian II/*Aurignacien Evolué*, lack of evidence of any typological subdivisions within the British material, and the clustering of the known sites in the western uplands of Britain (Jacobi 1999; Jacobi and Pettitt 2000), adds support to the notion that Britain was visited only by one or a small number of groups. Broad typological similarities suggest potential sources for such a dispersal to the south (e.g. south-west France) and east (e.g. Belgium; see discussion in Dinnis 2009). 'Paviland Burins' (*sensu* Dinnis 2008) for example are known at Spy and Trou Magrite in Belgium and Le Piage in south-west France (ibid.). Aldhouse-Green (2004, 16) suggested that the source of the British Aurignacian was the 'classic' region of south-west France and Pettitt (2008) argued that the distribution of sites in Britain may reflect the importance of the Atlantic coast in the northwards dispersal of an Aurignacian group into Britain, arguing that a parsimonious dispersal would be to follow the Atlantic coastline of the time, along the rugged landscapes of northwestern France into similar landscapes from the west of Cornwall onto the plains of what is now the Bristol Channel and the Severn Valley. This remains plausible and would explain the lack of Aurignacian findspots further east in lowland England. It should be remembered, however, that a major part of Aurignacian territory in north-west Europe could now be submerged, that is, the vast valleys of the Channel River (R. Dinnis pers. comm.). If a westward dispersal occurred along this route there is no reason why finds should be recovered from lowland England.

Whatever the specific direction of dispersal into Britain Aurignacian settlement clearly focussed on the south-west, and if numbers of sites with known archaeology of the period and numbers of artefacts are at all indicators then possibly south Wales was the main focus, the plains of the Severn River/Bristol Channel and its tributaries such as the Axe channelling the movement of herbivorous prey. Upland plateaux on south Gower such as above the Goat's Hole at Paviland and at Uphill could have provided excellent vantages for monitoring prey, as would the plateau above the Hyaena Den at Wookey for observing movements along the Axe Valley.

Lithic raw materials support the notion of connectedness between the known British Aurignacian sites. Swainston (2000, 104–5) noted that imported flint dominates the small Aurignacian assemblage from the Goat's Hole, Paviland (Figure 7.13). It is certain that the Goat's Hole contains the most varied raw material types of all known British Aurignacian sites (Dinnis 2009, 181). To an extent this may be a factor of the remarkably low number of artefacts from all other sites although this supports the notion that if there was any 'centre' of settlement for the brief Aurignacian occupation of Britain it was the Gower region. The Aurignacian blades identified from the site are on flint, as are the *burins busqués,* suggesting, perhaps, that deliberate lithic gearing-up occurred

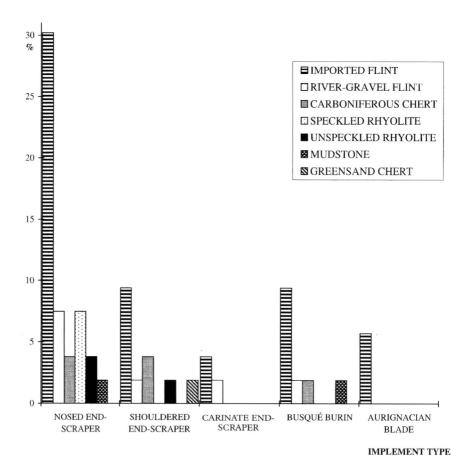

FIGURE 7.13
Representation of raw material types among the Aurignacian lithics from Paviland. (From Swainston 2000 and courtesy Steph Swainston.)

in Pembrokeshire. By contrast the presence of artefacts of Greensand chert – used for example for a shouldered endscraper – suggests a source in Somerset.

It could be said that all known Aurignacian material in Britain relates to armature use and manufacture, that is, the two known *sagaies* from the Axe River and the various 'burins' and 'endscrapers' that were presumably the source for armature-mounted bladelets which early excavations failed to recover. In this sense the whole Aurignacian record of Britain looks like a relatively brief hunting episode in which an Aurignacian group dispersed along the Channel River system or Atlantic coast, inserted themselves tactically into a readily understandable landscape in which rivers channelled herbivores in predictable ways, plateaus were available for monitoring such prey, caves presented shelter and gearing-up was practised at flint and chert sources within and on the periphery of the temporary range. The small nature of the artefact collections at all sites within the range suggest small-scale but highly mobile residential mobility, as noted above, probably during a very brief stay.

THE BRITISH MID UPPER PALAEOLITHIC: GRAVETTIAN LIFE AND DEATH

As with the preceding Aurignacian dispersal into Britain, which may have been restricted to the relatively mild conditions of Greenland Interstadial 7, the subsequent Gravettian dispersal into Britain – probably just as brief and ephemeral – must be seen in the context of the climatic deterioration and build-up of the British–Irish Ice Sheet (BIIS) which had begun by ~40 ka BP and developed to its maximum extent by ~30 ka BP, from which time it may have coalesced with the Fennoscandian ice sheet (Chiverrell and Thomas 2010: see Text Box 7.1). The poor radiocarbon data base suggests that the next human visits to Britain occurred ~33–34 ka BP, that is, after a gap of ~1,000–3,000 years and well into the period of growth of the BIIS. Once again the archaeological record is remarkably sparse and of eight known findspots only the Goat's Hole at Paviland has yielded anything like an assemblage, although much of the Paviland material can be accounted for by the burial of a young adult male (see Text Box 7.4). At Paviland, a direct AMS radiocarbon measurement on the 'Red Lady' suggest internment ~33–34 ka BP and, while a measurement on one of three bone 'spatulae' may suggest occupation somewhat later ~31–32 ka BP (see below), it should be regarded as a minimum age and is thus consistent with only a single phase of Gravettian activity at the site (see Text Box7.4). The existing radiocarbon measurements show that this occurred within either Greenland Interstadial GI5 or 6, probably the latter (Jacobi and Higham 2008, 904). On the other seven sites Gravettian presence is attested solely on the basis of tanged Font Robert points made on blades (Figure 7.14), which is consistent with the notion of a temporally restricted dispersal within GI6, although direct AMS radiocarbon date on a human humerus from Eel Point Cave on Caldey Island, south Wales suggests an age of ~28 ka BP (Schulting et al. 2005) although the provenance of this bone has been disputed and one must regard it questionable (Jacobi et al. 2010; Jacobi and Higham 2011).

PAVILAND AND THE 'RED LADY': A GRAVETTIAN BURIAL ON GOWER

Numerous excavations were undertaken in the small cave of Goat's Hole at Paviland on the Gower Peninsula from the 1820s to 1980s, with major campaigns in 1823 and 1912 removing much of the cave's archaeology and palaeontology (Buckland 1823; Sollas 1913; Aldhouse-Green 1997; Swainston and Brookes 2000; Pettitt and White 2011). In addition to ~12 Mousterian lithics, 6 leafpoints and a small Aurignacian assemblage (see main text) the cave yielded a burial attributable to the Mid Upper Palaeolithic and a small number of artefacts attributable to the Gravettian on either typological or chronometric grounds (Aldhouse-Green and Pettitt 1998; Aldhouse-Green 2000a). A major reassessment of the cave's material in association with a major AMS radiocarbon dating programme has placed the human occupation of the cave in wider perspective, the Gravettians apparently dispersing as part of a taxonomically rich mammoth steppe community.

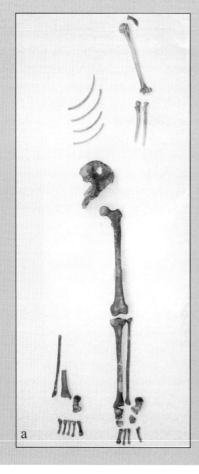

FIGURE 1
The bones of the 'Red Lady' of Paviland in frontal view. (Courtesy of Oxford University Museum of Natural History.)

FIGURE 2
Paviland. The Goat's Hole is the triangular opening to the right. (Courtesy of National Museums and Galleries Wales.)

Text Box 7.4

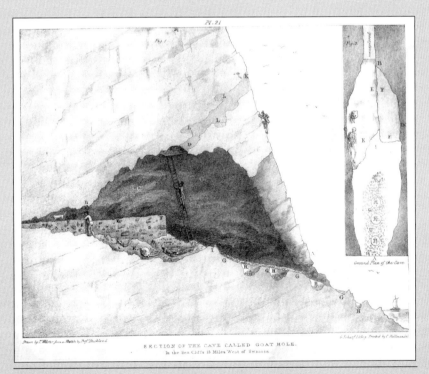

FIGURE 3
Section drawing of excavations in the Goat's Hole, Paviland Cave, from Buckland 1823. The position of the 'Red Lady' is clear, although the missing half of the skeleton has been filled in for artistic licence. The drawing does not do the position of the burial justice: it was tucked into a small alcove.

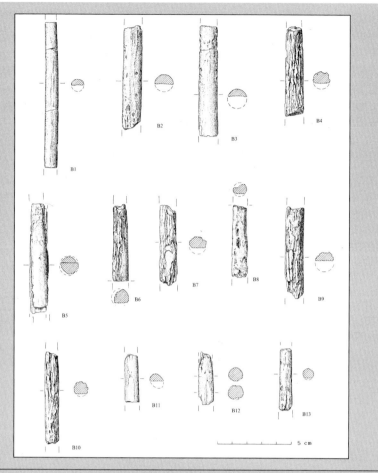

FIGURE 4
Fragments of mammoth ivory rods polished with ochre and apparently associated with the Red Lady burial. (Courtesy of National Museums and Galleries Wales.)

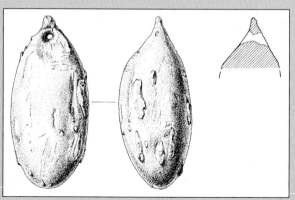

FIGURE 5
The 'Sollas Egg', a pathological fragment of mammoth tusk pierced for suspension. (Courtesy of National Museums and Galleries Wales.)

Text Box 7.4

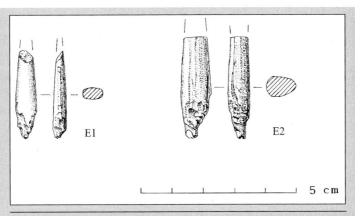

FIGURE 6
Two basal fragments of chopped-base points. (Courtesy of National
Museums and Galleries Wales.)

The 'Red Lady of Paviland' – so named because the bones are stained with
ochre and it was initially thought to be female (of Holocene age) – is actually the
burial of a young adult male in Mid Upper Palaeolithic tradition and has recently
been dated directly by AMS radiocarbon to ~33.3–34 ka BP (Jacobi and Higham
2008).[1] Because of this date Jacobi et al. (2010, 37) have suggested that it 'is
much earlier' than the bulk of Mid Upper Palaeolithic burials and that this tradition 'had its origin in the time before the earliest Gravettian', although they take
no account of equally old measurements for other Gravettian burials and ignore
the fact that a number of apparently younger Gravettian burials were measured
before ultrafiltration pretreatment which, in many cases, has demonstrated that
similar measurements are underestimates (Higham 2011).[2] There is no reason,
therefore, to assume that the Red
Lady is anything other than Gravettian and, although it was excavated
in the infancy of archaeology (Buckland 1823), enough information
survives to reveal striking similarities with ~55 continental burials of
the Gravettian period (Pettitt 2006,
2011). The Red Lady was tucked
into a small alcove to the left side
of the cave, apparently in association with the cranium and partial
tusks of a mammoth, which are
clearly visible in Buckland's
section and plan of the 1823

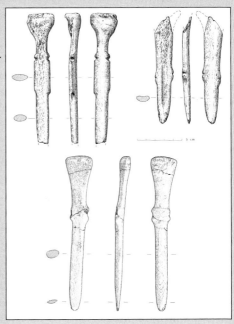

FIGURE 7
Horse bone 'spatulae' from the Goat's
Hole, Paviland. (Courtesy of National
Museums and Galleries Wales.)

Text Box 7.4

FIGURE 8
Basal fragment of Font Robert Point from Paviland. (Courtesy of National Museums and Galleries Wales.)

excavations. The skeleton is now partial: much of the post-cranial bones of the left side and some of the lower right leg survive but the cranium and much of the right side are missing (Trinkaus and Holliday 2000).

All surviving bones are stained with ochre, probably obtained locally (Young 2000). Ochre staining is far stronger on the bones of the lower body than the upper, suggesting that the young male was buried in a two-piece set of clothing, perhaps in the form of a parka and leggings. A number of pierced shells of common periwinkle (*Littorina littorea*) were recovered, according to Buckland (1823, 88), in its 'waist or pubic area', and these were probably sewn onto the male's clothing (Aldhouse-Green 2000b, 115), perhaps a loincloth (Pettitt 2006, 296). Accompanying the shells Buckland also found fragments of rings of mammoth ivory (1823, 88–9). The curvature of surviving ring fragments suggests that these were only ~70 mm in diameter (PP pers. obs.), suggesting that they had either been worn continuously from youth, derived from another, smaller, individual, or were worn suspended about the person rather than on the wrists. Around 40–50 fragments of mammoth ivory rods broken in antiquity and polished with ochre were recovered 'in contact with the ribs' (Buckland 1823, 88) suggesting that tapering elongated rods with bulbous ends were deliberately

FIGURE 9
Recent excavations in the Goat's Hole, Paviland, directed by Stephen Aldhouse-Green. The site of the Red Lady burial is to the left. (Courtesy of National Museums and Galleries Wales.)

Text Box 7.4

broken before being laid over the burial (Aldhouse-Green 2000b, 117). In view of the age and sex of the burial, ochre colouring, personal ornamentation and apparent association with mammoth remains the burial falls into the canon of European Mid Upper Palaeolithic burials, from Lagar Velho, Portugal, in the west, to Sungir', Russia, in the east (Pettitt 2006, 2011). Such an association suggests that the few Gravettians who dispersed into Britain at this time were connected to wider cultural and perhaps cosmological movements.

Several other modified items of organic material were recovered in general proximity to the burial although it is impossible today to ascertain whether they formed part of it or were left at the time or during subsequent visits to the cave. These include the 'Sollas egg' pendant made from an egg-shaped pathology of mammoth ivory (Sollas 1913) which refits to a pathological tusk fragment excavated by Buckland some 90 years beforehand, a small oval bead of mammoth ivory, two perforated reindeer canines (now lost) and two heavily modified teeth of cervid or bear similar to continental examples of perforated *croches de cerf*. Two basal fragments of chopped base points may be of Gravettian or Aurignacian attribution. Several fragments of worked mammoth ivory attest a degree of maintenance or manufacturing activity, possibly a specialised task for which Gravettians were in the region (Dennell 1983, 132–3). More enigmatically, three 'knives/spatulae' of cervid and horse bone were recovered from the cave by collectors in the 1830s, one of which has been directly dated by AMS radiocarbon to ~31–32 ka BP, although this could be an underestimate (Jacobi and Higham 2008, 2011 and see main text). Pettitt (2008) suggested that they may have originally been part of the burial or occupation at the time of its interment. Jacobi and Higham (2011, 212) questioned this as they are not ochre stained, although a number of artefacts clearly interred with continental ochre burials are not stained and this is not grounds to rule this out. The use of these items is unclear; they may have had a physical function (daggers, butchery tools, tent pegs, snow knives or weaving knives for example) although a decorative or symbolic function cannot be ruled out, especially as 'waists' on two of them could have taken line, perhaps for suspension.

With regard to more prosaic occupation of the Goat's Hole little can be said. Only one diagnostic lithic artifact – the broken tang of a Font Robert point (Swainston 2000) – can be attributed to the period. Certainly the lack of any other diagnostically Gravettian material rules out any kind of intensive use of the cave and, in view of the radiocarbon chronology of the burial and 'spatulae', one need account for no more than two separate uses of the cave overnight to account for its Gravettian archaeology, whether or not it had sacred significance (Aldhouse-Green 2000c; Aldhouse-Green and Aldhouse-Green 2005).

NOTES

1 There have been several previous direct AMS radiocarbon measurements on the bones of the 'Red Lady', all of which should be regarded as underestimates. See discussion in Jacobi and Higham 2008.

2 Dolní Věstonice I is at least 26 ka (^{14}C) years old and could be as much as 30 ka; the Kostenki 12 burial could be as old as 29 ka (^{14}C) BP and Kostenki 14 at least 28 ka (^{14}C) BP (see Pettitt 2011, Table 6.2).

Text Box 7.4

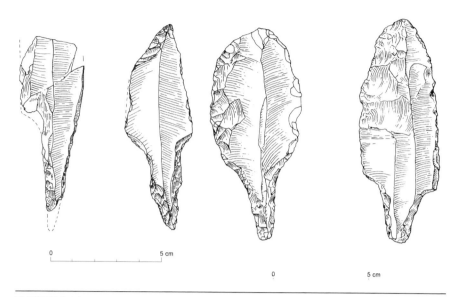

FIGURE 7.14
Tanged points of Font Robert type, left to right: Kent's Cavern, Devon; Mildenhall, Suffolk; Warren Livingstone Pit, Bramford Road, Ipswich, Suffolk; Peper Harrow Park, Godalming, Surrey. (Redrawn by Jerneja Willmott from Jacobi and Higham 2011a.)

Faunal evidence from Paviland and Pontnewydd caves provides a degree of context for the brief Gravettian dispersal in Britain (see Text Box 7.2). As noted above, taxonomic diversity increases at Paviland ~33 ka BP, and at Pontnewydd around the same time wolf appears in an already taxonomically diverse community. In each case it is clear that this represents a rich mammoth steppe community. At Paviland, Gravettians were clearly an element of such a community, although there is no evidence for their presence at Pontnewydd. Given the extremely low number of Mid Upper Palaeolithic finds in Britain this may well represent a genuine human distribution, that is, a brief presence in south Wales but not further to the north of the country, although with so few sites one should of course be cautious about inferring the distribution of British Gravettian groups. Although the amount of material – actually less than the Aurignacian in terms of the number of diagnostic artefacts – the overall distribution of Gravettian sites is wider suggesting that, however temporary Gravettian settlement in Britain was, it was more widely dispersed and it is probable that Gravettians spread as an integral part of a dispersing mammoth steppe community. Findspots are confirmed in Derbyshire, Gloucestershire, Suffolk, Surrey, Devon and, of course, Gower (Table 7.4 and Figure 7.15).

The relatively wide distribution indicates either that they had wider and more mobile foraging patterns than the Aurignacians, although this would be surprising in the absence of any further diagnostic assemblages, or that they were here for a relatively longer period of time than the Aurignacians, although again this would be surprising given the remarkably low amounts of material. A parsimonious interpretation would be that Britain was visited briefly by one Gravettian group, no more; relatively little time would be necessary for a small hunter-gatherer group to cover the distances between the

Table 7.4 British sites and findspots with material attributable to the early Gravettian.

Site	Lithics	Organics and context	Chronology	References
Pin Hole, Creswell Crags, Derbyshire	2 Font Robert points	No organics, from main passage of the cave, otherwise context unknown	Not directly dated.	Jacobi 1990, Jacobi et al. 1998, Pettitt and Jacobi 2009.
Mildenhall, Suffolk	1 Font Robert point	Single find, open air	/	Jacobi 1990
Warren Livingstone Pit, Bramford Road, Ipswich, Suffolk	1 Font Robert point	No known associations, open air	/	Jacobi 1990
Goat's Hole, Paviland, Gower	1 broken Font Robert point	'Red Lady' burial (see Text Box 7.4)	Direct AMS radiocarbon measurement on 'Red Lady; burial of ~33–34 ka BP and minimum age of ~31–32 ka BP on one bone 'spatula'	Jacobi 1990, Swainston 2000, Jacobi and Higham 2008.
Cat Hole (Cat's Hole) Cave, Gower	2 or 3 fragmentary tanged points (2 basal tangs, one virtually complete point), possibly Font Robert points	Context unknown.	/	Jacobi 1990, David 2007.
Forty Acre Field Pit, Barnwood, Gloucester, Gloucestershire	1 Font Robert point	Context unknown.	/	Jacobi 1990
Kent's Cavern, Devon	1 Font Robert point	One bone pin/*poinçon*. Context unknown.	Direct AMS radiocarbon measurement on bone pin of 26,950 ± 500 BP (OxA-21895) is probably an underestimate.	Jacobi 1990, Jacobi and Higham 2011a
Peper Harow Park, Godalming, Surrey	1 Font Robert point	Secondary context: found in gravels used to build a bank, probably from Gravel pit nearby.	/	Winbolt 1929. Jacobi 1990

known find regions. The spread of ^{14}C dates from Paviland have been taken to support this notion (Pettitt 2000) and recent redating of these using ultrafiltration pretreatment at Oxford has revealed diagnostic Gravettian archaeology clusters ~33–34 ka BP. As noted above all British Gravettian sites are characterised by the presence of Font Robert points which, on the continent, are the type fossil of the early Gravettian (Perigordian Va or Fontirobertian). In France this is securely dated to 32–33 ka BP, which is in accord with the available dating evidence from Paviland. Thus, a parsimonious interpretation of the Gravettian material of Britain would be a chronologically tight pulse of activity. If this were the case, the distribution of material – effectively English unlike the Aurignacian – might suggest a derivation of these groups from the east and the parallels between the British lithic material and those from the Gravettian sites of Masières Canal, Belgium, and Cirque de la Patrie in the Paris Basin, noted by Jacobi (1980, 25; see also Jacobi

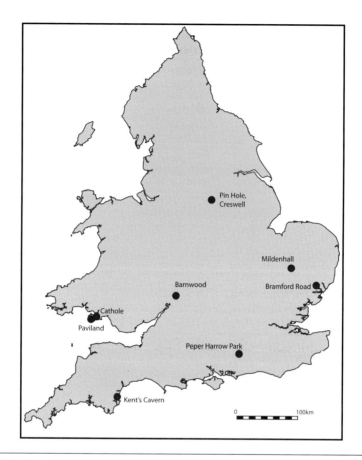

FIGURE 7.15
Distribution of British sites/findspots classified as Gravettian.

et al. 2010), would support this notion. Campbell (1980) coined the term Maisierian to reflect this material and while no examples of Maisières points are known from Britain the similarities of chronology and Font Robert points demonstrate a meaningful link.

With the exception of Paviland, British Gravettian sites reveal nothing about their behaviour except that they were discarding or losing lithic armatures and knives and in one case a bone pin.[2] Two fragmentary tangs from Cat Hole, Gower, suggest that they were discarded after spears had broken, although one cannot say the same for the virtually complete example from Pin Hole, Creswell (see Text Box 7.5). The conically headed pin (Figure 7.16) was found in the Vestibule area of Kent's Cavern apparently stratified above artefacts of Aurignacian attribution and the KC4 human maxilla discussed above. An AMS radiocarbon measurement on this in 1990 indicated that collagen-based contamination may have caused significant age underestimation and the small sample-size of material dated in 2008 suggests the new measurement of 26,950 ± 500 BP is an underestimate. There is therefore no reason to believe why the pin should represent a Gravettian dispersal into Britain later than GI6, although of course this cannot be ruled out.

GRAVETTIAN LITHICS FROM PIN HOLE, CRESWELL CRAGS

As with all of the caves of Creswell Crags, Pin Hole was excavated on several occasions in the infancy of archaeology, notably by John Magens Mello (1875) and Albert Leslie Armstrong (1924–36). Today, it is the type site of the MIS3 Pin Hole MAZ, yielding a rich mammoth steppe fauna (See Table 6.5). Thankfully, Armstrong recorded the location of finds in two dimensions, along and above/below a line strung from the cave's mouth to his rear section, and kept excavation diaries which allow one to reconstruct in some detail the original location of the cave's palaeontology and Mousterian, LRJ, Gravettian, Magdalenian, Federmessergruppen and Mesolithic finds (Pettitt and Jacobi 2009; see Chapters 6 and 8).

Only two diagnostic Gravettian artefacts are known from Pin Hole, both Font Robert points found in the cave's narrow main passage (see Figure 1). One had broken into two in antiquity, the refitting pieces occurring some 10 m apart, having been displaced downslope. The other is virtually complete, a large example some 10 cm in length. Jacobi et al. (1998) were able to plot the context of Armstrong's finds including the three pieces of Font Robert points and place these in the context of directly dated faunal remains from the cave. These were stratified below finds of Late Upper Palaeolithic age (discussed in Chapter 8). No direct radiocarbon measurements are available for this brief Gravettian occupation of the gorge, although measurements on faunal remains from the cave fall into the expected time range and reveal the local presence of at least mammoth and lion at the presumed time of Gravettian activity (Jacobi et al. 1998, 34). The paucity of Gravettian artefacts in the cave and lack of them from any of the other Creswell caves is noticeable and presumably reflects a very brief sojourn at the site. Pin Hole is the narrowest and certainly least accommodating of the four Creswell caves for which Middle and Upper Palaeolithic archaeology is recorded and would not be a sensible choice for a campsite of prolonged duration. Perhaps it sufficed for a very brief shelter in an unfamiliar territory.

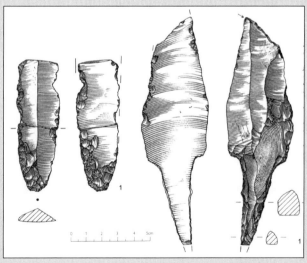

FIGURE 1
Fragmentary leafpoint (left) and complete Font Robert point (right) from Pin Hole. (From Pettitt and Jacobi 2009.)

Text Box 7.5

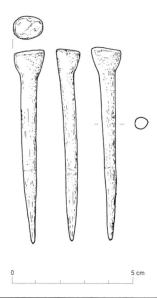

FIGURE 7.16
Conical bone pin from Kent's Cavern, Devon. (Redrawn by Jerneja Willmott from Jacobi and Higham 2001a and courtesy Tom Higham.)

There are no convincing examples of human presence in Britain after ~33 ka BP. An AMS radiocarbon measurements on several artefacts of bone and ivory from Paviland yielded underestimates and the remeasurement of one of the spatulae could still be an underestimation (See Text Box 7.1) and it has been noted above that the provenance of a human humerus from Eel Point, the age of which might suggest a dispersal ~28 ka BP, is of questionable provenance and there are no late Gravettian artefacts known from Britain, at least based on continental parallels. Glacial ice had begun to build up once more over the British Isles shortly after this (see Text Box 7.1). Presumably, after the brief but favourable conditions of Greenland Interstadial GI6, the climatic downturn ensured that no subsequent opportunities were available for humans to return until well after the Last Glacial Maximum, a period of absence of up to 18,000 years, assuming there was no Solutrean dispersal (see Chapter 8).

CHAPTER 8

Settling the north-west frontier

The Late Upper Palaeolithic, ~14.6–11.6 ka BP

INTRODUCTION

This chapter describes in detail the Late Upper Palaeolithic archaeology of Britain. For much of the late Upper Pleistocene Britain was either under ice or experiencing severe periglacial activity with concomitantly little evidence of life. The palaeontological and archaeological record from caves, rockshelters and open air sites from Scotland, Wales and England as far south-west as Devon is patchy, taphonomically sorted, has suffered from the damage caused by early excavation and loss and, in almost all cases, amounts to single findspots or very small assemblages representing little more than brief, ephemeral camp stops. That said, much finer resolution is possible for this period than for any previous era, due to its relative recentness and to the application of major radiocarbon dating projects. It can be seen that it contains a number of temporally discreet assemblage types that are technologically and typologically comparable to contemporary examples on the continent and seems broadly synchronous with continental assemblage change. The British record is, nevertheless, impoverished compared to continental Europe and, despite a relatively high temporal resolution, one is still afforded only partial glimpses of the various behavioural and social themes that run through this book. For much of the period, Britain seems to have been a human desert. The known archaeology could amount to little more than a few years or tens of years of occupation in total.

MIS2: PALAEOCLIMATE FROM THE LAST GLACIAL MAXIMUM TO THE END OF THE PLEISTOCENE

Greenland ice cores typically preserve bi-decadal isotopic information on climate change over the Upper Pleistocene and six of these cores – Camp Century, Dye-3,

GRIP, GISP2, Renland and NorthGRIP (e.g. Stuiver et al. 1995; Johnsen et al. 2001; NGRIP Members 2004) – are in good agreement back to the Last Interglacial (MIS5e, the Eemian/Ipswichian). Sub-orbital millennial-scale and centennial-scale climate variability is particularly noticeable in these cores during MIS3 and 2 (and in more muted fashion in Antarctic cores such as Vostok; Petit et al. 1999), the most clear indication of which is the abrupt Dansgaard–Oeschger cycles of ~2,000–3,000 year periodicity (Bond et al. 1993; Wolff et al. 2010; see Chapter 6). A good degree of correlation is possible between cores at both poles, indicating that the isotopic excursions they record are global in scale. The GICC05 chronology combines closely fitting data from the GRIP, NGRIP and Dye-3 cores and is the basis on which a number of Greenland interstadials (GI) and stadials (GS) are recognised, which are numbered in sequential order back from the Pleistocene–Holocene transition (Lowe et al. 2008). At least 18 D–O oscillations are recorded for MIS4–2, 15 of which fall into MIS3 as discussed in Chapter 6. These were variable in length although all seem to be characterised by rapid and pronounced warming (8–16° C) followed by gradual cooling. Terrestrial pollen records show that European climate change corresponded with such cycles (e.g. Sánchez-Goñi et al. 2000).

Following the Last Glacial Maximum (LGM), the ice and marine cores record five major climatic excursions for the late glacial period which are reflected in terrestrial proxies dated by radiocarbon (Walker 1995). At the Hawes Water lake in Lancashire, for example, pollen, chironomids (nematoceran flies) and mineral magnetic analyses revealed four sub-millennial events prior to the onset of the Younger Dryas: the severe Oldest Dryas within the Dimlington Stadial, and the two relatively temperate stages of the Late Glacial Interstadial (which on the continent have been termed Bølling and Allerød, although see below), separated by the brief cold oscillation of the Older Dryas (Walker 1995; Jones et al. 2002). Although one must be cautious about using chronozones defined in Scandinavia for more widespread climatic and environmental change (Lowe et al. 2008), these do seem to be reflected globally, although regional variations occur as to expression and timing. It is generally acknowledged that this picture is an oversimplification; within these main stadials and interstadials marine and ice core records reveal a number of fluctuations in sea surface temperatures at the centennial scale (Walker 1995 and references therein) and a number of British terrestrial records reveal phases of climate amelioration and deterioration within the classic chronozones. Here, we follow the nomenclature and chronology of the Greenland ice core record (e.g. Lowe et al. 2008) while retaining the traditional chronozones.

Absent for at least 10,000 years: Britain during the Last Glacial Maximum

Between ~31 ka and ~16 ka BP the LGM saw the maximum expansion of the British–Irish ice sheet (BIIS) since MIS4 (see Chapter 7). As glacial activity is in scant evidence at the type locality of the Devensian (Four Ashes, Staffordshire; Morgan 1973), Rose (1985) proposed the term Dimlington Stadial for the period, after the eponymous site at Dimlington (East Yorkshire) where fossiliferous organic materials overlain by glacigenic sediments provide a well-controlled glimpse of the deterioration in conditions (see also Bateman et al. 2011). Similar deposits elsewhere in Eastern England preserve organic deposits above the glacigenic sediments, the entire regional sequence constrained to ~31 ka BP (decline) to ~16 ka BP (amelioration).

During the LGM the polar front was considerably to the south of the British Isles (Jones and Keen 1993). Arctic structure soils developed on the floodplains of braided rivers and other aggrading sequences (Catt 1996). Periglacial activity can be found as far south as Kent and Cornwall (Watson and Morgan 1977) and was, for example, intense in the east and south-east, where braided rivers deposited sands and gravels in the Nar Valley (Jones and Keen 1993, 181) and on the Isle of Thanet, Kent (Murton et al. 2003). The south-west of England remained free of glacial ice although floating ice shelves may have filled most of the Celtic Sea between Ireland, Wales and Cornwall (Jones and Keen 1993, 193) and glacial ice may have reached the northern Scilly Isles (Scourse 1986). Periglacial activity was widespread in the south-west, with widespread development of head deposits from Cornwall to the Bristol area, and thick mantles of loess were deposited on the Lizard peninsula in Cornwall, Britain's most southwesterly extension into the English Channel (Ealey and James 2010). Periglacial features were also widespread in the south-east, with solifluction, cryoturbation and river incision in the Sussex and Kent Weald and Loess deposition in Kent (Jones and Keen 1993, 194). Understandably, few sites exist which provide environmental information about the polar conditions of the period (Lowe and Walker 2008). Coleoptera from several sites including Dimlington reveal an arctic climate (Coope 1977). At Colney Heath in the valley of the River Lea, Hertfordshire, pollen indicated northern and montane plants such as arctic willow (Godwin 1964) and a Late Glacial lake at Hawks Tor on Bodmin Moor, Cornwall, revealed an open grass heath with snow beds immediately prior to the Late Glacial Interstadial (Brown 1977).

The latest convincing radiocarbon dated faunal remains for the Dimlington Stadial occur no later than ~31 ka BP in Britain and Ireland (Currant and Jacobi 2011; Woodman et al. 1997) and dates younger than this are probably underestimates due to contamination (e.g. Lowe and Walker 1984; Currant and Jacobi 2001, 2011). As noted in Chapter 7, the latest pre-LGM human activity in the country seems to have occurred ~33 ka BP. It is not surprising, then, that there is no evidence of human settlement for the entire Dimlington Stadial; one is, in fact, hard pushed to find a single collared lemming, let alone an intrepid hunter-gatherer. If claims that some bifacially worked leafpoints are Solutrean are correct (e.g. Pryor 2003) this would place humans in Britain ~22–24 ka BP based on French chronology for this technocomplex. French Solutrean assemblages are known from the southern parts of the Paris Basin where it meets the Massif Central but none are known further to the north (Schmider 1990a, 1990b; papers in Pautrat and Thévenin 1996) and Solutrean assemblages are unknown in Belgium and the Netherlands (Otte 1990a). In view of this it seems unlikely that British examples are genuinely Solutrean. Furthermore, they all fall within the techno-typological range of Early Upper Palaeolithic leafpoints observed on the continent, as discussed in Chapter 7. On these grounds one can reject the suggestion that some British leafpoints are Solutrean in age. It therefore seems that humans were not present in the country from ~33 ka BP, the youngest reliable date for Gravettian occupation, until conditions had ameliorated significantly after ~16 ka BP.

DEGLACIATION

In northern Europe a series of low-amplitude and short-lived climatic ameliorations can be recognised after ~21 ka BP, the most prominent occurring ~16 ka BP (Walker 1995). In the Paris Basin, culturally Badegoulian hunter-gatherers were hunting horse and reindeer around this time (Schmider 1990a and b; Bignon 2009). Reindeer was re-established in the south-west of Britain – probably briefly – ~17.2–17.8 ka BP, although without human predators (see below). Deglaciation began ~19 ka BP, with a more rapid and sustained melting beginning with the amelioration ~16 ka BP (Lambeck et al. 2002). By this time large areas of Britain – even those close to the centre of the BIIS – were free of ice (Shennan et al. 2006). OSL dates on loess from Morecambe Bay and from the Yorkshire Dales show that these areas of north-west England had deglaciated between ~19 ka and 17 ka BP (Telfer et al. 2009) and Dimlington was deglaciated by ~16 ka BP (Bateman et al. 2011). By contrast, ^{10}Be surface exposure ages indicate that substantial glaciers survived in northern Scotland for the entirety of the following interstadial (Bradwell et al. 2008). Deglaciation seems to have been relatively unstable. In western Scotland it was interrupted by readvances in many regions, probably caused by climatic oscillations and regional glaciodynamic changes, and only by the Late Glacial Interstadial had they largely disappeared (Benn 1997). A similar picture prevailed for eastern Scotland and the North Sea basin (Graham et al. 2009). In the North Irish Sea basin a significant glacial readvance has been observed between ~14.7 and 14 ka BP, probably correlated with Heinrich Event H1 (McCabe et al. 1998).

The most pronounced period of post-glacial climatic amelioration is known in Britain as the Windermere Interstadial or Late Glacial Interstadial ~14.7–12.9 ka BP (Walker 1995) although short episodes of warming occurred over a few centuries prior to this. The Late Glacial Interstadial has often been seen as a 'false start' to the Holocene as conditions deteriorated once more into the Younger Dryas/Loch Lomond Stadial ~12.9–11.6 ka BP before finally entering the Holocene warming trend. Furthermore, at several British localities another cold period *within* the Late Glacial Interstadial can be recognised, (the Older Dryas ~14–13.9 ka BP), which divides the Late Glacial Interstadial into two warmer periods: an earlier phase referred to on the continent previously as the Bølling (now Meiendorf – see below) and a later phase referred to as the Allerød. In northern Europe a number of radiocarbon-dated sites attest to this sequence of Oldest Dryas–Meiendorf–Older Dryas–Allerød–Younger Dryas chronozones which broadly correspond to recognised biozones (Walker 1995). This picture is certainly an oversimplification: δ^{13}C sequences accompanied by pollen profiles reveal three warm oscillations within the Allerød (e.g. Whittington et al. 1996), whereas the entire Late Glacial Interstadial (comprising the Meiendorf–Older Dryas–Allerød sequence) is encompassed in the ice cores by five phases of Greenland Interstadial (GI) 1 (GI1e–a: Wolff et al. 2010).

The early warm peak of GI1e is increasingly referred to as the Meiendorf interstadial, rather than Bølling. This results from complications over the character and age of the apparent pre-Older Dryas warm period recognised at the type site of Bøllingsø in Denmark (de Klerk 2004). We therefore follow here the recommendation of Terberger et al. (2009) and refer to GI1e as the Meiendorf Interstadial. Subsequent to this, Greenland GI1d is equated with the Older Dryas and the three Allerød warm periods GI1c3 (Allerød 1), GI1c1 (Allerød 2) and GI1a (Allerød 3) separated by brief and low-amplitude cold periods (GI1c2 and GI1b) (e.g. Terberger et al. 2009; Reide et al. 2010). Dates vary for the onset of each of these periods; Table 8.1 presents chronological data insofar as it exists. For consistency we refer here to the combined GICC05 chronology of Lowe et al. (2008).

Despite the climatic amelioration, environmental conditions could remain severe. Vegetation did not respond immediately to the interstadial amelioration, with the spread of woodland delayed by up to 800 years (Walker et al. 1993). At Lundin Tower, Fife, the Oldest Dryas cold phase is represented by a cold steppe dominated by sedges and grasses and with evergreen *Juniperus* shrub and *Salix* (willow) in probable dwarf form (Whittington et al. 1996). Sporadic pollen from the Hawes Water Lake in Lancashire reveals exclusively herbaceous vegetation typical of the polar desert conditions that prevailed across end-Devensian Europe (Walker et al. 1994; Jones et al. 2002). Glaciers retreated from the Pennines, leaving behind them moraines, drumlins and sediments infilling kettle holes (Rose 1980). At one such kettle hole, Bingley Bog in Airedale,

Table 8.1 Chronology of the main climatic oscillations of the Late Glacial in calendar (ice core, varve and INTCAL calibrated) years.

Site and method	Oldest Dryas	Meiendorf	Older Dryas	Allerød	Younger Dryas	Reference
Greenland stadials and interstadials	GS2	GS1e	GI1d	GI1c3, c2, c1, 1b, 1a	GS1	Terberger et al. 2009.
Greenland: GISP2	15.07 ice core ka v	14.67 ka v	14.09 ka BP	14.01 ka BP	12.89 ka BP	Stuiver et al. 1995
Greenland: GICC05*	Unclear	14,692 b2k (before 2000 AD)	(GI1d 14,075 b2k?)**	(GI1c 13,954 b2k?)**	12,896 b2k	Lowe et al. 2008
Meerfelder Maar, Germany (varves)	13.8 varve ka BP (duration 130 years)	14.45 varve ka BP	13.54 varve ka BP (duration 190 years)	13.35 varve ka BP (implied from duration of Older Dryas)	12.68 varve ka BP (duration 1090 years)	Brauer et al. 1999
Lough Inchiquin, Ireland dated lake sediments)	15.1 ka BP	14.6 ka BP	14.1 ka – 13.9 ka BP	13.7 ka BP	12.64 ka BP	Diefendorf et al. 2006

Key:

* The GICC05 chronology combines the NGRIP, GRIP and Dye-3 ice core records (Lowe et al. 2008).

** The GICC05 chronology recognises 5 phases of Greenland Interstadial 1 (in sequence GI1e–a). These suggestions assumes that the climatic downturn of GI1d marks the onset of the Older Dryas and the succeeding amelioration of GI1c3; the onset of the Allerød of the traditional scheme. If this is correct, GI1c2, CI1c1, GI1b and GI1a mark oscillations within the Allerød.

Yorkshire, molluscs and ostracods reveal a rapid climatic amelioration followed by a short, colder episode (Keen et al. 1988). Silts indicative of meltwater lakes have been found at the Dimlington Stadial type locality at Holderness, East Yorkshire (Catt 1987). Found within these were thin lenses of loess, probably derived from proglacial outwash in the North Sea basin. Moss remains in the silts have been dated to ~21–22 ka BP. In the Midlands, tundra with scattered birch (again probably the dwarf *Betula nana*) was established at Stafford in an otherwise arctic climate (Morgan 1973), while at Abingdon, Oxfordshire, deposits dating to immediately prior to the onset of the Late Glacial Interstadial include the buttercup *Ranunculus platanifolius,* indicative of alpine meadows (Briggs et al. 1985).

Overall, it appears that a steppic tundra characterised by shrubby-herbaceous vegetation with dwarf birch, willow and juniper had spread in places prior to the pronounced warming of the Late Glacial Interstadial. In this sense the apparent arrival of horses and Late Magdalenian recolonists in the south of England prior to the interstadial warming (Jacobi and Higham 2009) is not surprising, as is discussed below.

THE LATE GLACIAL INTERSTADIAL ~14,670 TO 12,890 BP

The Late Glacial Interstadial marks not the *first* climatic amelioration after the LGM but the first *pronounced* warming, which may well be important in understanding the sequence of recolonisation by flora and fauna. The interstadial warming was rapid. Coleoptera indicate that mean July temperatures probably rose by more than 7° C per century, and winter temperature rose ~20° C overall (Coope and Brophy 1972; Walker et al. 1993). Chironomids reveal that the thermal maximum occurred early in the interglacial (within the Meiendorf) with temperatures reaching ~12° C (Brooks and Birks 2000). At the beginning of the Interstadial the rivers of northern Europe changed their regimes, often downcutting as the water table lowered, and taking on more sinuous, meandering courses (Collins et al. 1996). Lake cores reveal the establishment of scattered dwarf shrub communities around the Atlantic margins, with dwarf willow and birch further inland, and fossil coleoptera and pollen of aquatic plants such as the blue-green algae *Gleotrichia* indicate abrupt and intense warming (Walker 1995).

Lake Windermere has been defined as the type locality for the Windermere/Late Glacial Interstadial in Britain as it provides continuous deposits for the period and reflects both local terrestrial and lacustrine environments (Coope and Pennington 1977). Here, a gradual replacement of proglacial clays by organic sediments occurred, and an alpine herbaceous vegetation and coleopteran assemblage was replaced by woody plants including tree birch and more temperate coleoptera. At nearby Blelham Bog, *Betula* frequencies attained their maximum during the earlier part of the interstadial. At another Windermere site, Low Wray Bay, a periglacial environment dominated by sedges, dwarf willow and fir clubmoss (*Lycopodium selago*) ~14–13.6 ka BP was replaced by a significant expansion of woody plants immediately prior to the Late Glacial Interstadial.

This was marked by the expansion of juniper thickets until a deterioration is noticeable in which plant cover disintegrated, probably caused by increased snowfall of the Older Dryas (Pennington 1977).

The most widespread Pleistocene palaeosols from Britain formed during the Late Glacial Interstadial (Catt 1996). At Pitstone, Buckinghamshire, glacigenic coombe rock formed the foundation for the formation of two phases of soil development during the Late Glacial Interstadial, probably representing Meiendorf and Allerød phases (Rose et al. 1985), a situation also found at Folkestone, Kent (Preece 1994). At Lundin Tower, Fife, birch and willow increase in importance with an associated decrease in herbs (Whittington et al. 1996). At Hawes Water a sharp increase of thermophilous chironomids occurred at the end-Devensian–Late Glacial Interstadial transition alongside the appearance of dwarf birch and willow (Jones et al. 2002). Later in the early interstadial a phase dominated by the thermophile common juniper *Juniperus communis* occurred between ~14,100 and 13,750 GRIP years BP revealing a marked increase of summer and winter temperatures. Pollen from the fill of a kettle hole at Glanlynnaue on the Lleyn Peninsula in north-west Wales indicates the establishment of juniper, *Rumex* (docks and sorrels) and birch early in the Late Glacial Interstadial, the beetles revealing a cold environment with mean July temperatures ~10° C replaced suddenly by relatively temperate conditions with temperatures ~17° C (Coope and Brophy 1972).

The primary environmental change characteristic of the Late Glacial Interstadial was the establishment of woody plants such as birch across Britain. Sediment accumulation began shortly before ~15 ka BP in the Vale of Pickering, at sites such as Star Carr and Roos Carr (Day 1995). Here, the early interstadial landscape was open, with *Artemisia,* scatterings of willow and birch, the latter two again probably dwarf species. These were replaced by low juniper scrub although the landscape remained largely open. This declined in turn ~14 ka BP in response to cooling prior to the Older Dryas and was replaced by open birch woodland. At the other end of the country, open environments of the late LGM were succeeded by juniper scrub and finally tree birch and *Empetrum* (crowberry) heath on the hillsides at Hawkes Tor in Cornwall (Brown 1977). It is often assumed that trees were not established during the Meiendorf and that if birch pollen is present then it represents *Betula nana* rather than tree birch. Evidence for tree birch does exist for the period, however. At Lake Windermere, the type site for the interstadial, 'tree birches were present but did not spread into woodland' (Coope and Pennington 1977, 338). Tree birch and catkin bud scales have been recovered from a ^{14}C dated mid- Meiendorf deposit at Church Moss, Cheshire, in which pollen indicates the presence of *Betula nana* (Hughes et al. 2000). At Hockham Mere near Thetford, Norfolk, open birch woodland was established at the start of the interstadial (Bennett 1983) and at Church Moor, Hampshire, plant macrofossils and pollen from a Meiendorf peat deposit contained high frequencies of both dwarf and tree *Betula* (Scaife 1987). It does seem that the spread of birch forest was a slow process, however. Tree birch reached as far north as the English Midlands during the Meiendorf but only reached more northerly and westerly regions during the Allerød, a process temporarily arrested by the cold conditions of the intervening Older Dryas which seems to have killed off woody plants

(Catt 1996). It is therefore sensible to assume that small, isolated stands of birch trees were established in southern parts of Britain during the Meiendorf, presumably a critical source of wood for fuel and tools such as javelin hafts. In this light it is interesting that a depletion in $\delta^{13}C$ ratios in British wild horses, usually taken to reflect the rise of a degree of woodland canopy, began ~15 ka BP and not later in the interstadial, alongside a rise in $\delta^{15}N$ usually taken to indicate elevated levels of plant cover (Stevens and Hedges 2004). We shall return to this below.

Several animal taxa recolonised Britain as conditions improved, probably shortly before the pronounced interstadial warming, and these constitute the Dimlington Stadial Mammalian Assemblage Zone (Currant and Jacobi 2011; Table 8.2). Radiocarbon evidence of the recolonisation of north-west Europe by grassland herbivores is abundant, if relatively imprecise when calibrated. By ~15 ka BP wild horse was re-established in the Rhineland, the Belgian Ardennes and the Paris Basin; by ~14.8 ka BP it had recolonised the south of England and as far north as Kendrick's Cave, north Wales, Creswell Crags, South Yorkshire and Victoria Cave, North Yorkshire, shortly after (Stevens and Hedges 2004; Lord et al. 2007; Jacobi and Higham 2009, 2011). In all of these regions its reappearance is associated with human predation in the form of Late Magdalenian hunter-gatherers. The earliest dates for recolonising mammals in Britain are for reindeer, dated directly to ~17.2–17.8 ka BP at Kent's Cavern and ~17.3–18 ka BP at Cattedown, Plymouth (Currant and Jacobi 2011). It is interesting that both examples are from the southwest where conditions presumably had ameliorated enough to allow at least a temporary presence. Otherwise, reindeer are recorded in a natural accumulation at Aveline's Hole, Somerset ~14.6–14.8 ka BP (Hedges et al. 1987), at Pin Hole, Creswell early in the interstadial (Hedges et al. 1989) and in modified form as a dated antler *bâton percé* at Gough's Cave, Cheddar Gorge, and four sagaies from Fox Hole in the Peak District and Church Hole, Creswell, in the same calibrated time range (Bramwell 1971; Jacobi 2007b). This is some 3,000 years later than the Devon examples and there is no reason to assume that the animal was present continuously over the Oldest Dryas. One should not be surprised at the relatively early arrival of reindeer in Britain; they form part of an early recolonisation of Scandinavia ~15 ka BP as part of a relatively rich faunal community also including humans (Fischer 1991; Aaris-Sørensen et al. 2007).

Table 8.2 The Dimlington Stadial mammalian assemblage zone, after Currant and Jacobi 2011.

Taxon	Common name
Homo sapiens	(Anatomically) modern humans
Lepus timidus	Arctic (mountain, variegated) hare
Vulpes vulpes	Fox
Ursus arctos	Brown bear
Mammuthus primigenius	Woolly mammoth
Rangifer tarandus	Reindeer
Ovibos moschatus	Musk ox
Indeterminate Large cervid	

Red Deer appear at Gough's Cave in the same Late Magdalenian assemblage and with similar direct dates as the reindeer; a cut-mark on one dated specimen indicates that this was a hunted species. Red deer has also been recorded in smashed form at King Arthur's Cave in the Wye Valley with direct dates of ~13.8–14.2 ka BP (Hedges et al. 1989; Bronk Ramsey et al. 2002). A dated, cut-marked dentary of aurochs from Kent's Cavern attests its exploitation ~14–15 ka BP and further cut-marked bovid remains from Bob's Cave near Plymouth and Kendrick's Cave in North Wales have similar direct dates (Jacobi and Higham 2011). Bovid is also recorded at Pin Hole, Creswell, ~14.2–15 ka BP (Hedges et al. 1989). Arctic hare from King Arthur's Cave has been dated to ~13.8–14.9 ka BP (Bronk Ramsey et al. 2002) and to ~13.8–14.9 ka BP from a hearth deposit at Three Holes Cave, Devon (Hedges et al.1996). At Creswell Crags, it is well attested from this time period in several of its caves and the ubiquity of this animal and widespread appearance of cut-marks reveal that it was an important resource for fur and food (Charles and Jacobi 1994; Jacobi and Higham in press). The rare saiga antelope *Saiga tatarica* is known from Soldier's Hole, Cheddar, directly dated to ~13.8–14.1 ka BP (Currant 1987).

At Gough's Cave, mammoth ivory was used as raw material for a bevel-based rod dated also to the same time range (Jacobi and Higham 2009) and other British sites such as Creswell Crags and Condover attest its presence between ~15 and 14 ka BP (Stuart et al. 2004; Lister 2009, Table 16). At Condover, Shropshire, where several mammoths came to die in kettle hole ponds (see Text Box 8.1), pollen, plant macrofossils and insects provide complex evidence of environmental change between ~14.8 ka and ~10.2 ka BP (Allen et al. 2009). During the Meiendorf a fairly barren open grassland and dwarf birch scrubland provided the context for the death of the mammoths.

Text Box 8.1

CONDOVER: THE DEATH OF SOME OF EUROPE'S LAST WOOLLY MAMMOTHS

The remains of several woolly mammoths were recovered in the 1980s from clayey sandy silts infilling a kettle hole at Norton Farm, Condover (Shropshire). These included the partial skeletons of at least three juveniles and an adult male. A suite of radiocarbon measurements on the mammoth remains themselves, as well as plant macrofossils from the surrounding sediments, showed that the kettle hole infilled from prior to the Late Glacial Interstadial to the Early Holocene but that the mammoths died during the early warming conditions (GI–1e) of the first half of the Late Glacial interstadial (ultrafiltrated measurements: juvenile cranium, OxA-19903, 12,375 ±50 BP (~14.7–14.1 ka BP); adult tooth, OxA-20129, 12,230 ± 50 BP (~14.2–13.9 ka BP).

The sedimentology of the site indicated the presence of a slow-flowing fluvial network comprised of channels, lakes, and pools (such as those that contained the mammoth remains). Beetle remains and pollen preservation allowed the environment of the Condover mammoths to be reconstructed in some detail (Allen et al. 2009). The coleopteran remains found with the skeletons are

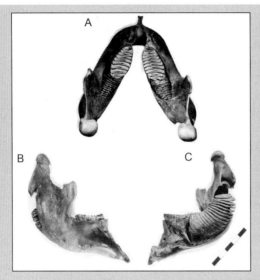

FIGURE 1
The mandible of the adult mammoth from Condover. (A) Occlusal view. (B) Right lateral view. (C) Right ramus in medial view. (From Lister 2009 and courtesy Adrian Lister.)

dominated by cold climate indicators; several taxa revealed the presence of cold-water ponds and a degree of brackishness, among which *Macroplea appendiculata* indicates the presence of pondweeds, milfoils and waterlillies. Terrestrial species showed that these ponds were fringed with sedges, club-rushes and marsh cinquefoil and revealed a largely treeless environment with a mosaic of gravels, heathland, clayey and peaty soils and grassy vegetation. Pollen found in contact with the bones of one juvenile mammoth was dominated by Cyperaceae (sedges, 38–44%) and Poacea (grasses, 19–30%), with low frequencies of pine and willow; while that recovered from the wider C1 unit from which the mammoths derived also indicated the presence of birch in low frequencies. It is probable that both willow and birch were dwarf varieties. The low frequency of dung beetle might suggest that the mammoths were not abundant at the locality.

Most of the mammoth remains from Condover derive from a single adult male, a skeleton that is complete except for the bony cranium, the caudal vertebrae, and about half of the foot bones (Lister 2009). Remains of several juveniles are also present – at least three (MNI based on mandibles) and probably a total of around six. Dental wear, plate

FIGURE 2
Russell Coope holding a bone from the Condover site. (Photo courtesy Adrian Lister.)

Text Box 8.1

counts, and the presence of the M_3 indicate an age at death of ~28 for the adult male and wear stages on the teeth of the juveniles indicate ages at death of ~3, 4 and 6 (Lister 2009). Sexing of the juveniles is more complicated but dimensions of two pelvic girdles suggest the presence of at least one male and one female. As male elephant society is matriarchal, and males wander alone, it is unlikely that the remains comprise a single family group and the radiocarbon measurements noted above indicate that the two dated individuals were deposited at statistically distinct periods.

Several pathologies on the adult male skeleton are of particular interest. Most of these are explainable as by-products of a trauma in the form of a rehealed fracture of the left scapula which is consistent with either a heavy blow behind the forelimb or a fall onto the shoulder. As the latter would almost certainly have resulted in injury or fracture of other limb bones – for which there is no evidence – Lister (2009, 465) favours the former, perhaps a tusking injury. The individual would have been disabled for some time, and was perhaps still weak at the time of death despite the perfect healing of the injury. The lack of steep slopes around the kettle hole suggest that miring, rather than entrapment, were responsible for the mammoths' deaths and the presence of empty fly puparia with the heads of three of the mammoths reveal that they were subaerially exposed for at least two weeks before submergence. As the bones of the right feet of the adult are missing it is probable that it lay on its left side, its left limbs mired and thus protected from erosion. Observations on the carcasses of modern elephants suggest that the cranium is missing because it floated away, its sinuses filled with air (ibid., 469).

It is interesting that the remains date to the end of the first half of the Late Glacial Interstadial (the Meiendorf) during which time Late Magdalenian groups were operating across Britain. The Condover finds place woolly mammoths in the country at the same time as the human groups although direct evidence of the exploitation of this animal is rare. A *sagaie* of mammoth ivory belonging to the Late Magdalenian of Pin Hole, Creswell Crags, and two dated pieces of worked tusk also from Creswell and several engraved fragments from Gough's Cave (see text) do indicate the processing of tusk during this period. But it is during this time that the latest mammoths disappear in Europe; they were probably already a diminishing and disappearing resource.

Reindeer, arctic hare and the giant deer *Megaloceros* had returned to Ireland by the later Meiendorf although most dated records for recolonising faunas of the island belong to the Allerød (Woodman et al. 1997). No evidence of any other taxon is known for the Meiendorf and mammoth, for example, seem not to have recolonised Ireland after the LGM (Stuart et al. 2002). This is a taxonomically impoverished, cold-adapted fauna that perhaps explains – with the absence of horse in particular – why human groups apparently did not recolonise Ireland at this time.

Evidence for the arrival of non-human carnivores is far rarer. Hyaena and lion do not appear to have returned after their local extinction at the start of the LGM (Stuart and

Lister 2007) although rare examples of the latter are known from Paris Basin Magdalenian sites (Bodu 1998, 138). A single dated specimen of lynx from Gough's Cave shows that it had reappeared although probably in low numbers as it remains a remarkably rare species in the British fossil record. Directly dated specimens of brown bear from Three Holes Cave, Devon, attest its presence ~14–15 ka BP (Hedges et al. 1996; Jacobi 2004, 51). Currant and Jacobi (2001) list brown bear, wolf, red fox and arctic fox as Late Glacial Interstadial taxa from Gough's Cave although, as they have not been dated directly, it is unclear whether they returned during the Meiendorf or later in the interstadial. Domesticated wolf is known from Kent's Cavern, where it has been directly dated to ~14–15 ka BP, and from Gough's Cave (Jacobi 2004, 77; Jacobi and Higham 2009).[1]

On the basis of ultrafiltrated radiocarbon measurements reported by Jacobi and Higham (ibid. and see Stevens and Hedges 2004) one cannot distinguish chronologically between the arrival of horse, reindeer, red deer, mammoth, aurochs, arctic hare, brown bear and wolf. Along with humans and domesticated wolves they may have been co-arrivals as a 'mammoth-steppe' community, or the imprecision of dating in the period may mask a more patchy pattern of arrival. These examples of Meiendorf arrivals fall into the Gough's Cave Mammalian Assemblage Zone (MAZ) of Currant and Jacobi (2001). They have noted a degree of regionality of mammals in Britain in the Late Glacial although, as this MAZ covers the entire Late Glacial Interstadial and Younger Dryas, it may, like chronological imprecision, be masking more complex fluctuations of taxa in space and time. On Paris Basin Magdalenian sites, where stratigraphic control at least is better, remains of bears, wolves and mustelids do appear although are rare in the context of faunal processing of reindeer and horse (Bignon 2007). Whatever the case, shortly before or after the start of interglacial warming these species were being exploited by newly arrived humans.

GI1E, THE MEIENDORF, >14,670 – 14,090 BP: HUMAN RECOLONISATION AND THE LATE MAGDALENIAN IN BRITAIN[2]

In recent years our understanding of the Late Upper Palaeolithic recolonisation of the Northern European Plain as the conditions of the Last Glacial Maximum ameliorated has improved considerably. An initial expansion of culturally Badegoulian groups from a Franco-Cantabrian LGM refugium saw the repopulation of areas as far north as the Paris Basin ~16 ka BP (Schmider 1990a and b; Bignon 2009; Gamble et al. 2004). This seems to have been a brief phenomenon, however, and it was only by Gl1e, that is, the start of the pronounced Late Glacial Interstadial warming, that significant recolonisation occurred. Gamble et al. (2004, 2005) identified this with a culturally Magdalenian expansion out of the Franco-Iberian refugium, for which there is much genetic evidence (Richards et al. in press). Direct AMS radiocarbon dates reveal Magdalenian hunting of horse and reindeer in the Belgian Ardennes by ~15–16 ka BP (Otte 1989; Gilot 1994; Charles 1998), in the Rhineland around the same time (Street 2000; Street et al. 1994; Riede et al. 2010), and in the Paris Basin by at least ~14.8 ka BP and probably before (Schmider 1992; Schmider et al. 1996; Bodu 2004). It is probable on typological grounds that Creswellian sites in the northern Netherlands (Stapert and Johansen 2001) and Magdalenian sites such as Orp (Brabant, Belgium; Vermeersch et al. 1987), Eyser- heide and Mesch (Dutch Limbourg; Rensink 1991, 1992) and Kanne (Belgian Limbourg; Vermeersch et al. 1985) were established around this time although they are undated. Using uncalibrated radiocarbon measurements, Housley et al. (1997) suggested that the recolonisation process occurred in two phases: a 'pioneer' phase in which colonists operated seasonally in regions for two or three centuries before establishing year-round cycles during a subsequent 'residential' phase, although the robusticity of this argument has been contested given the imprecision of dates when calibrated (Blockley et al. 2000, 2006; cf. Housley et al. 2000). Whatever the case it is clear that human groups were re- established in southern Britain probably slightly before the interstadial warming ~14.7 ka BP, that is, after the recolonisation of the Ardennes and Paris Basin (Barton 1999; Jacobi and Higham 2009).

It seems that humans spread back into north-west Europe as an integral part of a recolo- nising mammoth-steppe community, as noted above. One should not ignore the possible importance of tree birch in this process. As with stone, this would have been a critical raw material to a hunter-gatherer dependent upon wooden-shafted weapons for survival. As discussed above, tree birch seems to have spread through southern England at least in the earliest phases of the interstadial and, as one cannot rule out its partial establishment immediately prior to the pronounced interstadial warming, the apparently early recoloni- sation of southern England prior to the main warming is perhaps not surprising.

The importance of Doggerland during and after the period of recolonisation should not be forgotten. The extent of this vast landmass – much larger than the British Isles – has been reconstructed by Lambeck (1995) using glacial rebound models and its viability as a place to live has been noted by Coles (1998) in her seminal consideration of Dog- gerland, a term she indeed coined. Recently, seismic reflection data taken by the gas and oil industry has been used to map an area of ~23,000 km^2, revealing deeply incised tunnel valleys relating to major, sinuous rivers (Fitch et al. 2005; Gaffney et al. 2009). To the south the Channel River system continued to flow normally, and eroded sediments from even the Channel Deeps until the Channel was finally flooded by marine transgres- sion in the early Holocene (Antoine et al. 2003). One must therefore regard the Channel as a significant barrier during the Late Glacial.

EARLIER MEIENDORF PERIOD ASSEMBLAGES AND THEIR CONTINENTAL COUNTERPARTS: MAGDALENIAN OR CRESWELLIAN?

Garrod (1926) coined the term 'Creswellian' – after the sites where it is most abundant and variable – to distinguish between British assemblages belonging to the Meiendorf and those of the related, but typologically distinct, Late Magdalenian of the continent. She saw the British material in the sense of regional assemblage variation and believed that enough difference existed to warrant taxonomic distinction, coining the name 'to differentiate it . . . from the classical Magdalenian of France' (ibid., 194). Since Garrod, the nature of the connection between British and continental Late Glacial assemblages has been debated (e.g. Jacobi 1980, 1991, 2007b; Campbell 1977; Barton and Roberts 1996; Charles 1999; Pettitt 2007). Charles (1999) examined Belgian assemblages that have been ascribed by some to the Creswellian, concluding that only two of the caves of Presle (Trou du Docteur and Trou de L'Ossuaire) contain clear Creswellian elements (Cheddar points) among mixed assemblages including Magdalenian elements. She also noted that terms occasionally used in the literature such as 'Creswello–Tjongerian' and 'Creswello–Hamburgian' are meaningless as they have never been defined and make little typological or chronological sense. We couldn't agree more. Similarities do, however, exist.

Technologically, British assemblages belonging to the Meiendorf and defined as Creswellian are characterised by blade production on uni- and bipolar blade cores opened using the cresting technique, a degree of platform preparation, and the use of the *en éperon* technique for isolating a spur on the striking platform to take direct percussion (Barton 1990). Typologically, they are dominated by angle-backed points with one single oblique truncation (Creswell points) and trapezoidal-backed points with two opposed oblique truncations (Cheddar points), endscrapers on blades, burins (often dihedral but also on truncations) and *Zinken,* long-pointed borers made on a thick blank. Curved-backed points, penknife points (*Federmesser*) and shouldered points have been recovered in apparent association with these typological forms but it is unclear whether these belong to these assemblages, whether they are restricted to their later phases, or whether they belong to a later, Allerød phase of occupation (see below). Typical lithic artefacts from the period are shown in Figures 8.1 and 8.2. Microwear analysis of both Cheddar and Creswell points from Dutch 'Creswellian' sites confirms the view that most of these functioned as weapon tips rather than knives, although some were hafted as barbs and others used as borers (Rots et al. 2001, 2002–3). In Paris Basin sites, where such points are absent, microwear analysis suggests that backed bladelets performed the same main role (Audouze et al. 1981, 138–41). Burins seem to have mainly been used to work antler, and endscrapers hide (ibid.).

Continental Magdalenian assemblages are characterised by high frequencies of blade production from unipolar and bipolar cores and blade tools dominated by burins (dihedral and truncation) and straight-backed blades, with becs, perçoirs and truncated blades occurring at lower frequencies (Leroi-Gourhan and Brezillon 1966; Audouze et al. 1981; Vermeersch et al. 1985, 1987; Rensink 1991; Schmider 1992; Otte 1994). In some Magdalenian assemblages burins (particularly dihedral) dominate and backed bladelets are low in frequency, whereas in others it is the latter which dominate (Bosselin and Djindjian 1988). In Hamburgian assemblages shouldered points appear within assemblages in which blacked bladelets are rare or unknown, whereas in Creswellian assemblages obliquely truncated points occur in assemblages with or without blacked bladelets and occasionally with curved-backed points (Kramer et al. 1985; Dewez 1986; Bosselin and Djindjian 1988, 313; Stapert and Johansen 2001).

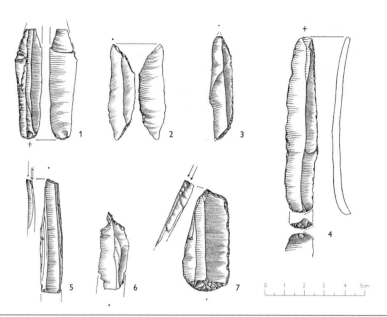

FIGURE 8.1
Late Magdalenian ('Creswellian') lithics from Robin Hood Cave, Creswell Crags. (1) Blade with single oblique truncation ('Creswell Point'); (2–3) blades with two opposed oblique truncations ('Cheddar Points'); (4) endscraper on blade; (5) burin on retouched truncation; (6) piercer; (7) combined endscraper and burin on retouched truncation. (From Pettitt and Jacobi 2009.)

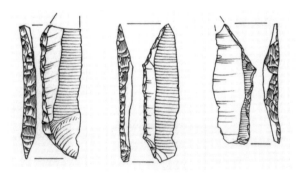

FIGURE 8.2
Cheddar Points from The Hoyle's Mouth, Dyfed, Wales. (Illustrations by Andrew David.)

British assemblages differ from contemporary assemblages on the continent in terms of the *absence* in Britain of elements common on the continent, as well as the *rarity* of British elements on the continent. Straight-backed blades appear to be entirely lacking in Britain before the later Meiendorf culturally Hamburgian assemblages (see below), as are *burins de lacan,* although both are ubiquitous on continental Late Magdalenian sites (Vermeersch et al. 1987; Jacobi 1991; Barton and Roberts 1996). The *en éperon* technique is not known from Dutch sites otherwise classed as 'Creswellian' (Stapert and

Johansen 2001) but it is known from Paris Basin sites such as Pincevent (Karlin 1972) and might therefore be said to have a sporadic continental distribution. Some tools with heavily worn or 'rubbed' ends, such as those from Bradgate Park, Newtown Linford (Cooper 2002), and Wey Manor Farm, Surrey (L. Cooper pers. comm. to PP), are similar to examples known from the continent and probably served as fire starters (Stapert and Johansen 1999).

The concept of oblique truncation of blades is observable in Europe, for example from:

- the Paris Basin, for example at Verberie (Audouze et al. 1981, Figure 12, nos 1 and 2), Marsangy (Schmider 1992, Figure 106, nos 9 and 10) and Pincevent Habitation 1 (Leroi-Gourhan and Brezillon 1966, Figure 45, nos 4 and 5; Figure 46, nos 1, 6 and 7);

- Limbourg, for example at Kanne (Vermeersch et al. 1985, Figure 20, nos 8 and 13, Figure 21, nos 6, 7, 8,12 and 13, Figure 22, no. 2);

- The Ardennes, for example at Trou du Chaleux (Otte 1994, Plate 3, no. 3; Plate 22, nos 4, 9 and 12; Plate 29, nos 10 and 11).

These are, however, infrequent; they are not Cheddar or Creswell Points, and instead often form the platform for burin removals or part of the point of becs or perçoirs. Clearer parallels with Cheddar and Creswell points occur at Marsangy, however, where single-obliquely truncated forms similar to Creswell Points occur, as do shouldered forms approaching Hamburgian Points and bi-truncated forms similar to Cheddar Points (Schmider 1992, Figures 108 and 109). Schmider (ibid., 188), however, has noted a dis-similarity in that the oblique truncation in the Marsangy points occurs over both medial and distal thirds of the pieces rather than solely on their distal third.

It should be noted that, technologically, British assemblages are similar to those on the continent, that is the production of blades typically from bipolar cores, a degree of (spo-radic) usage of en éperon platforms and the use of such blades for most tools. Retouched bladelets seem to form the most common armature on the continent, whereas this role in Britain fell to obliquely truncated points, which nevertheless are found at least in several Dutch sites. Further similarities – notably the appearance of shouldered and curve-backed points – are observable a little later in time and we return to these below. This similarity, in our opinion, is enough to warrant the inclusion of the British material of this age into a wide-spread and regionally variable Late Magdalenian technocomplex, and thus the rejection of 'Creswellian' as a formal term. Hereafter we refer to the British material as Late Magdale-nian. On the basis of structuration analysis of Late Upper Palaeolithic northern European assemblages Bosselin and Djindjian (1988) suggested that the Hamburgian and Creswell-ian arose from Late Magdalenian assemblages in which shouldered and truncated points were dominant; one might therefore see the British material as an evolved (and probably chronologically later) variant of the more 'typical' Late Magdalenian of the Paris Basin.

A degree of similarity is therefore not surprising given the proximity of British sites to those of the continent, as Shackley (1981) noted. A mere 200 km separates the British findspot of Oare in North Kent with the Presle sites in Belgium, about the same distance between the sites of Cheddar Gorge and those of Creswell Crags (Figure 8.3). A degree of regionality is observable in the Late Magdalenian of northern Europe, such as sites in south-east Poland which fall into a regional group (Połtowicz 2006) and differences do exist between the Paris Basin, the Belgian Ardennes, Limbourg, the Middle Rhine and the Thuringian Basin. To a certain extent differences can relate also to functional differences between sites, notably open air and enclosed sites. Otte and Noiret (2009), for example, have observed that Belgian Magdalenian sites fall into two categories; open sites on the plateaux are dominated by burins and endscrapers, whereas those from cave sites are dominated by weapon heads of stone and organic materials. At a smaller

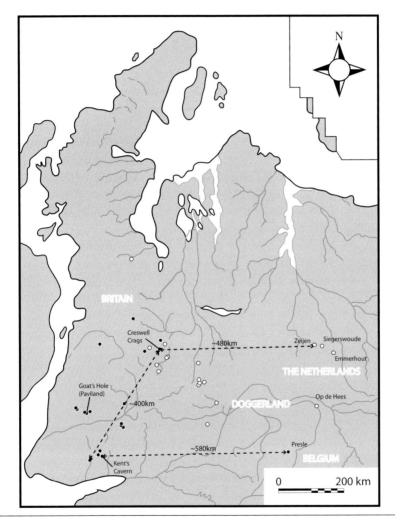

FIGURE 8.3
Proximity of British, Belgian and Dutch Late Magdalenian/Creswellian sites. (Map based on –50m sea level drop and corresponding connnection of Britain, Doggerland and the continent, based on a template courtesy of Roger Jacobi.)

scale most British assemblages could be said to correspond to the latter and thus comparisons with large continental open sites may be misleading.

BRITISH LATE MAGDALENIAN SETTLEMENT, BEHAVIOUR AND SOCIETY

The distribution of British Late Magdalenian sites and findspots relative to the physical geography of the Late Glacial Interstadial can be seen on Figure 8.4. These include at least one findspot in Scotland (Saville 2004, Figure 10.23). There are about 35 in total, of which some of the larger and more useful assemblages are noted in Table 8.3. There is no reason to see the Late Magdalenian occupation of Britain as anything other than small-scale, sporadic and probably very brief. Our understanding of the British Late Magdalenian has been dominated by cave finds, Garrod's regional term itself taking its name from Creswell Crags, the four main archaeological caves of which all contained Late Magdalenian archaeology (see Text Box 8.2). Most caves, however, were excavated in the infancy of archaeology and have been badly sorted by poor excavation and loss; even in the few cases where cave assemblages are relatively well-understood these are small, with one exception. Gough's Cave – by far the largest – amounts to ~2,100 lithic items of which 550 are retouched tools (Jacobi 2004), possibly a considerable underestimate, whereas the Creswell sites (the next largest) amount to no more than 200–400 items each (Jacobi 2007b). No convincing evidence exists in Britain for multiple occupation on any great scale within cave sites, even Gough's (Jacobi 2004, 10). Many of the findspots shown on Figure 8.4. simply record single finds of diagnostic lithics. Patterns of such findspots, such as in Nottinghamshire (Garton 1993; Jacobi et al. 2001), reveal a human presence in areas of the landscape away from caves although densities remain remarkably low despite intensive fieldwalking. An assemblage of ~450 Late Magdalenian lithics recovered from eroding deposits at Bradgate Park, Newtown Linford, Leicestershire, derive from a scatter around 5 m in extent, which suggests at least a small open-air camp (Cooper 2002). A potentially sizable open-air camp is suggested by the partly excavated and partly fieldwalked site of Farndon Fields near Newark, Nottinghamshire, which has yielded <400 lithic artefacts including blades, endscrapers on blades (which dominate the assemblage), obliquely truncated points and a shouldered point (Garton 1993; Garton and Jacobi 2009). Recent fieldwalking on the plateau above Creswell Crags has revealed Late Magdalenian material, although again in low number.

Continental sites are variable in size but typically larger. The size and composition of most British assemblages is similar to those of brief camps on the continent, such as Verberie Loci 1 and 2 in the Oise Valley (248 lithic items; Audouze et al. 1981). By contrast, some continental open air and enclosed site assemblages are very large (Table 8.4). However, as Charles (1998, 212) noted 'there is little to suggest any long-term continuity of human occupation' for the Late Magdalenian occupation of the Belgian Ardennes. All of this suggests that Late Magdalenian occupation of Britain was small-scale and probably relatively brief, possibly similar to that of the Ardennes.

Table 8.3 Selected British Late Magdalenian (Creswellian) sites.

Site	Lithics	Organics and other items	Chronology	Major references
Gough's Cave, Cheddar, Somerset	At least 2,100, including 550 retouched tools	Three antler *batons percés*, one mammoth ivory *sagaie*, incised bones, arctic hare tibiae awls, engraved fragments of mammoth ivory, disarticulated remains of at least 5 humans. Red deer and horse among the hunted fauna.	Large number of radiocarbon measurements cluster ~14.7 ka BP	Jacobi 2004; Jacobi and Higham 2009, 2011; Bello et al. 2011.
Sun Hole, Cheddar, Somerset	Small assemblage includes blades with *talons en éperon*, endscrapers on blades, burins, Cheddar Points	Fauna includes humanly modified horse. Human left ulna.	Ultrafiltrated direct radiocarbon measurement on human ulna, OxA-19557, 12,620 ± 50 BP. Ultrafiltrated measurements from 12,490 ± 45 BP (OxA-18705) to 12,610 ± 90 BP (OxA-14476)	Jacobi 1991, 2004; Jacobi and Higham 2011 (dates).
Soldier's Hole, Cheddar, Somerset	Very small assemblage includes Cheddar Points	Fauna includes arctic hare, reindeer, saiga antelope, although none are humanly modified. Cut-marked bird bones.	Direct radiocarbon dates on unmodified fauna indicate ages of ~13.8–14.8 ka BP.	Jacobi 2004.
Kent's Cavern, Torquay, Devon	Probably rich; blades and bladelets survive in several museums; Cheddar Points, piercers and endscrapers seem common	Three harpoons; one eyed-needle, mammoth ivory rod/*sagaie*, one (probably two) worked horse hyoids. Horse probably the dominant exploited species	Direct radiocarbon measurements on modified fauna from the Black Band range from 12,265 ± 50 BP (OxA-19508 on awl) to 12,500 ± 60 BP (OxA-17545 on horse) and includes measurement of 12,470 ± 50 BP on domesticated wolf (OxA-13588).	Jacobi and Higham 2011.
Three Holes Cave, Devon	Small assemblage	Lithics associated with lower of two hearths. Fauna includes horse, arctic hare and brown bear	Radiocarbon dates on humanly modified fauna: OxA-3890, 12,150 ± 110 BP; OxA-3209, 12,180 ± 130 BP; OxA-3208, 12,260 ± 140 BP.	Barton and Roberts 1996; Hedges et al. 1996 (dating).

Table 8.3 *Continued.*

King Arthur's Cave, Wye Valley, Herefordshire	Very small assemblage	Faunal includes humanly modified red deer.	Radiocarbon measurements on humanly modified fauna range from 12,055 ± 55 BP (OxA-19160 on red deer) to 12,610 ± 55 BP (OxA-17725 on horse).	Jacobi and Higham 2011.
Creswell Crags: Robin Hood Cave	Probably the largest of the Creswell assemblages. Probably 200–400 items originally; extant collections include >40 backed pieces, Cheddar Points, endscrapers on blades, burins, piercers	Horse head engraving on horse rib, arctic hare tibiae awls, parietal engraving ('vulva'). Fauna includes humanly modified arctic hare.	Numerous direct AMS radiocarbon dates on modified fauna range from 12,175 ± 50 BP (OxA-18348 on arctic hare) to 12,465 ± 60 BP (OxA-17525 on arctic hare).	Jacobi 2004, 2007; Pettitt and Jacobi 2009; Jacobi and Higham 2011.
Creswell Crags: Mother Grundy's Parlour	Probably the second-largest of the Creswell assemblages, perhaps with 200–400 items including >57 backed pieces.	Fauna includes humanly modified horse. Possible parietal engravings.	Numerous direct radiocarbon measurements on humanly modified horse range from 12,180 ± 50 BP (OxA-19507) to 12,470 ± 55 BP (OxA-20192)	Jacobi 2004, 2007; Pettitt and Jacobi 2009. Jacobi and Higham 2011.
Creswell Crags: Pin Hole	Probably relatively small; extant collections include 17–23 backed pieces	Engraved humanoid on large rib. Fauna includes humanly modified arctic hare.	Several direct radiocarbon measurements on humanly modified arctic hare range from 12,175 ± 50 BP (OxA-18348) to 12,430 ± 55 BP (OxA-19163).	Jacobi 2004, 2007; Pettitt and Jacobi 2009; Jacobi and Higham 2011.
Creswell Crags: Church Hole and The Crypt	Probably the smallest of the Creswell assemblages: 62 known artefacts from Church Hole including 13	Arctic hare tibiae awls, three eyed needles, horse bone 'spindle', two antler foreshafts, parietal engravings. Fauna includes humanly modified arctic hare.	Direct radiocarbon measurements on humanly modified fauna e.g. 12,395 ± 45 BP (OxA-18704 on arctic hare) and 12,355 ± 50 BP (OxA-18706 on arctic hare).	Jacobi 2004, 2007; Pettitt and Jacobi 2009; Pettitt et al. 2009; Jacobi and Higham 2011.

Site	Assemblage	Preservation	Chronology	References
	retouched tools and ~12 from The Crypt, include endscrapers, burins, Cheddar Points, blades and bladelets		No direct chronology.	Garton 1993; Garton and Jacobi 2009.
Farndon Fields, Nottinghamshire	<400 items dominated by endscrapers on blades	No organic preservation in excavated areas.		
Bradgate Park, Newtown Lynford, Leicestershire	~450 items from small scatter	No organic preservation in excavated areas.	No direct chronology.	Cooper 2002.

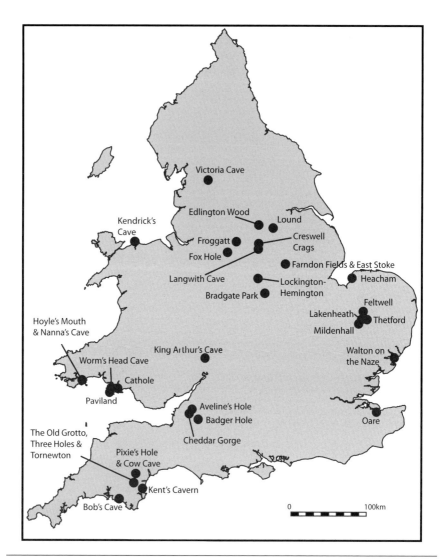

FIGURE 8.4
Distribution of major Late Magdalenian sites and findspots in Britain.

Seasonal hunting grounds and mobility

British Late Magdalenians, like those of the continent, were drawn to the parts of the landscape where uplands meet lowlands, which presumably offered both ecotonal resources as well as landscapes that could be used tactically in the procurement of herbivores (Barton et al. 2003). Findspots cluster in four main areas; south-west Wales, south-west England, the southern Peak District and its periphery, and East Anglia. The latter has yielded only single findspots, whereas the south-west and Peak regions have larger collections and assemblages. This may be due in part to the lack of caves in

Text Box 8.2

LATE MAGDALENIAN ARCHAEOLOGY OF CRESWELL CRAGS

Creswell Crags, a one kilometre long west–east trending limestone gorge straddling Nottinghamshire and Derbyshire was an important focus of Late Magdalenian activity (Figures 1 and 2). Archaeology of the period has been found in four of its caves; Pin Hole, Robin Hood Cave and Mother Grundy's Parlour on the northern (Derbyshire) side of the gorge and Church Hole on the opposite (Nottinghamshire) side and probably existed in other caves with poorly recorded excavation histories (Pettitt and Jacobi 2009). In addition a number of engravings almost certainly of Late Magdalenian age have been found in Church Hole and Robin Hood Cave (see main text). New excavations in The Crypt – a recently discovered rockshelter or small cave just below Church Hole – have revealed that activities were continuous on the platform and slope outside Church Hole and the context of the art in the latter is probably domestic rather than of a more ritual nature as suggested by Pettitt (2007; Pettitt et al. 2009). If the number of backed points – the most dominant Late Magdalenian tool form in the crags – can be taken as a coarse estimate of occupation intensity, Mother Grundy's Parlour was the most used site (n = 57) followed by Robin Hood Cave (n = 40). Pin Hole cave yielded significantly less (n = 17) and Church Hole hardly any (n = 4; Jacobi 2007, Table 7.9) although material from The Crypt has raised this number modestly. Although Gough's cave has yielded the largest single Late Magdalenian assemblage in Britain the caves of the Creswell gorge contain far more, thus the eponym 'Creswellian' for British assemblages of Meiendorf age with broad affiliations to the continental Late Magdalenian (discussed in main text). Despite this, the gorge seems to have attracted only brief, seasonal human visits (Pettitt 2007, 2008). Lithic technology at Creswell was geared towards the production of blades and bladelets, on which were produced points with one or two oblique

FIGURE 1
The Creswell Crags gorge, looking east. The length of the gorge is about 700m. (Courtesy Creswell Heritage Trust.)

FIGURE 2
Creswell Crags in the winter, looking west. (Courtesy Creswell Heritage Trust.)

truncations (the former rare Creswell Points, the latter – far more common – Cheddar Points), endscrapers, dihedral burins, piercers and zinken (see Figure 8.1).

Several organic artefacts are known from the Late Magdalenian at Creswell, including eyed needles, four awls (on the tibiae of arctic hare) and a serially notched horse vertebra erroneously described as a pendant in earlier publications but which may have been used as a line spindle, perhaps for storing line for hare traps or for sewing (Jacobi pers. comm.). All of these derive from Church Hole and may represent a cached or lost sewing kit (see Text Box 8.4). In addition to these are two reindeer antler javelin foreshafts, a curved *sagaie* of the same material (see Figure 2 in Text Box 8.4), an engraved motif on a mammoth ivory *sagaie* and two figurative engravings on ribs (see main text).

Sites in the wider region also possess small Late Magdalenian assemblages and were possibly left during activities in the region by the same group, such as the Whaley rockshelters 3 km south (Radley 1967), Langwith Cave 5 km south (Garrod 1926, Figure 39), Dead Man's Cave in Anston Stones Gorge 8 km north (Mellars 1969), Froggatt 30 km west (Henderson 1973) and possibly Elder Bush Cave in the Manifold Valley of the southern Peak District some 40 km south-west (Bramwell 1964b). The lithic assemblage of the open-air site at Farndon Fields a day's walk (35 km) to the south-east (Garton and Jacobi 2009; see main text) is dominated by endscrapers, suggesting that hide processing was an important activity at that site.

Text Box 8.2

Table 8.4 Quantities of worked lithics from selected European Late Magdalenian sites.

Site	Quantity of lithics	Reference
Pincevent, France, Habitation 1	>31 kg	Leroi-Gourhan and Brézillon 1966
Pincevent, France, Section 36	>11,000	Leroi-Gourhan and Brézillon 1972
Marsangy, France, Ensemble 1	>10,000	Schmider 1992
Marsangy, France Ensemble II	>11,000	Schmider 1992
Tour de Chaleux, Belgium	>4,000	Otte 1994
Eyserheide, The Netherlands	~3,414	Rensink 1991
Zeijen, The Netherlands	~4,275	Rensink 1992
Mesch, The Netherlands	>6,000	Stapert and Johansen 2001

East Anglia, although as Pettitt (2008) noted, the sites cluster broadly along the Trent and Severn rivers, which may have formed a communication axis at the time. A small amount of information of lithic raw material movement is available. In a number of cases visual inspection of flint suggests non-local procurement, although parsimoniously sources could be located within 20–40 km of most sites, for example from Kent's Cavern. Greater distances are suggested at some sites, however. At Gough's Cave, LA-ICP MS trace element analysis of selected artefacts suggested that a high-quality flint was imported from sources at the northern edge of Salisbury Plain, Wiltshire, a distance of ~70 km (Jacobi 1997, 2004; Barton and Dumont 2000; Rockman 2003). A pilot study of lithics from Robin Hood Cave, Creswell, also suggested procurement from this source, in this case a distance of over 200 km. Currently, Late Magdalenian material from at least four sites can be linked to this source, which is specifically identified with the Vale of Pewsey.

Two pebbles of worked Baltic amber were recovered from Gough's Cave (Currant et al. 1989; Charles 1989) and one from Creswell (Probably Robin Hood Cave; Pettitt and Jacobi 2009). In subsequent periods when Britain became an island the source for such Baltic amber was the east coast, although given the lack of such a coast during the Late Pleistocene the most obvious source must have been the northern coast of the North Sea, over 200 km from the Creswell sites, perhaps procured alongside other coastal resources. Beyond this little is known.

Pettitt (2007) has suggested a hypothetical annual round based on several sites. Gough's Cave (and thus the Cheddar region) was used in summer and winter (see Text Box 8.3), particularly for the hunting of horse and red deer, and stable isotope analysis of human remains suggests a more complex diet including aurochs and reindeer, the latter at least perhaps suggesting procurement further to the north. Seasonality indicators are lacking for Creswell, although principle use in autumn may be indicated by the concentration on arctic hare, which is at its best as a source of fur and fatty meat at this time (Owen 2005). The inferred importance of clothing manufacture at Creswell (see Text Box 8.4) supports the notion that gearing-up for winter was an important reason to be amidst the hares of Creswell in autumn. The procurement of reindeer hide, meat and antler at this time – or in spring – may have been another seasonal focus in the region. If correct, these observations suggest that Creswell and Cheddar – both steep-sided gorges with several caves – formed complimentary roles in Late Magdalenian society and perhaps formed critical nodes within an annual round. The two are, in fact, closely linked on a number of grounds. Radiocarbon measurements on humanly modified artefacts from these sites are statistically identical and, given the imprecision of calibrated age ranges, these could in fact be very close in time or date to within the same few years. The lithic inventories are very similar and the two seem to share the same source of high-quality lithic material as noted above. Awls made on arctic hare tibiae from both regions bear the same, highly specific modifications which are unknown elsewhere suggesting, in our opinion, an intimate connection between the two (see Text Box 8.4).

SKULL CUPS FROM THE LATE MAGDALENIAN OF GOUGH'S CAVE, SOMERSET

The partial and disarticulated remains of at least five humans were recovered from Gough's Cave, many of which display cut-marks indicative of defleshing and disarticulation of the cranium and mandible (Currant et al. 1989; Cook 1986, 1991; Andrews and Fernández-Jalvo 2003). Direct AMS radiocarbon measurements indicate an age of ~14.7 ka BP, confirming their association with the Late Magdalenian archaeology found mixed with the human remains close to the cave's wall, where traces of activity seemed greatest (Currant et al. 1989; Jacobi and Higham 2009).

A new analysis of the remains has clarified exactly what practices they represent (Bello et al. 2011). The remains are dominated by cranial fragments including those of the calotte, facial skeleton, basicranium and mandible, and a high degree of refitting of the fragments was possible. They derive from a minimum of five individuals, a ~3-year-old child, two adolescents, an adult and an old adult. Many of the remains – from all of the five recognised individuals – bear cut-marks indicative of slicing, with a few chop and scrape marks. Percussion pits and lunate striations characteristic of breakage indicate that the crania were fractured while green (fresh). Overall, numerous modifications attest the careful and skilled severing of the head, its complete defleshing, and the shaping of the resulting cranial vaults into skull cups. The location of cut-marks on frontal bones reveal scalping, the severing of the *temporalis* muscle, and careful separation of the frontal bones from those of the cranial vault by carefully-aimed blows (see Figure 1). Cut-marked parietal bones also reveal scalping, as well as the severing of the head from the body, and percussion marks on these bones reveal the careful shaping of the edge of the isolated cranial vault. Cut-marks on temporal bones indicate the severing of the ears; on the sphenoid the severing of the mandible from the cranium; on occipital bones the severing of the neck muscles; on the facial the removal of the eyes; and on the mandibles the removal of the *masseter* and *temporalis* muscles, cheeks, tongue and hyoid (see Figure 2). The high-frequency of cut-marks in particular suggests that the skulls were 'scrupulously prepared or "cleaned" using flint tools as an initial stage in the manufacture of skull cups' (Bello et al. 2011).

This is not an isolated phenomenon. Skull cups have been recovered among the remains of

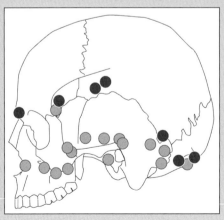

FIGURE 1
Distribution of percussion marks on cranial bones from Gough's Cave: black dots = marks on the vault, grey dots = marks on smaller cranial fragments. (Courtesy Chris Stringer and Silvia Bello and © The Natural History Museum.)

Text Box 8.3

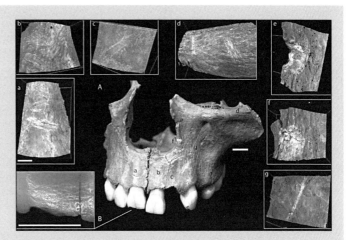

FIGURE 2
Cut-marks and percussion marks on human facial bones from Gough's Cave. (Courtesy Chris Stringer and Silvia Bello and © The Natural History Museum.)

Text Box 8.3

at least twenty-four individuals from the Late Magdalenian site at Le Placard in the Charente (Le Mort and Gambier 1992) and the remains of at least two adults and a child from the Late Magdalenian layers at Brillenhöhle, Germany, were also carefully 'cleaned' and a calotte may have functioned as a container (Orschiedt 2002). Fragmentary remains of at least sixteen individuals were scattered over the abandoned camp at Maszycka Cave in Poland, bearing numerous traces of scalping, severing and scraping (Kosłowski and Sachse-Kosłowska 1993). Clearly, the Gough's Cave remains form part of wider behaviours in Late Magdalenian Europe which may reflect deeply engrained concepts of the fragmentation of the human body (Pettitt 2011).

Text Box 8.4

LATE MAGDALENIAN CLOTHING MANUFACTURE AND MAINTENANCE

One might assume that the seasonal round established in the British Late Magdalenian brought groups into contact with several useful materials for clothing and display. Birds such as partridge, grouse and ptarmigan would have provided black, brown and white feathers for clothing, decoration and fletching of javelins. Reindeer, red deer and aurochs would provide versatile hide and supple calfskin would have been available in spring at the reindeer calving grounds. Sinew, horse hair and plant fibres such as nettle would provide tough materials for plaiting. Arctic hare was clearly procured at Robin Hood Cave, Creswell, and cut-marks on wolf phalanges and a lynx femur from Gough's Cave provide further evidence of the variety of furs available (Charles 1997; Jacobi 2004, 50). Clothing could of course be coloured with ochre; a considerable number of ochre fragments were scattered throughout the occupation area of Hengistbury Head, Dorset (Barton 1992, 136–7) and at Creswell a small crayon of ochre is known from The Crypt under Church Hole (excavated by the authors in 2010), while other single examples came from Robin Hood Cave (Dawkins 1877, 593) and Church Hole (Dawkins 1876). The specific use of these crayons is of course unknown; the examples from Church Hole and The Crypt were found close to the parietal engravings, although no parietal paintings are known and it is perhaps more plausible that they relate to clothing manufacture and maintenance.

Abundant cut-marked bones of arctic hare were recovered from the Late Magdalenian of Robin Hood Cave. Cut and smash marks indicate that their meat and fat were important but also that their fur had been carefully removed (Charles and Jacobi 1994). Four awls made on their tibiae, at least three eyed needles (two now lost) and a possible line spindle from Church Hole (see Figure 1) suggest that a sewing kit was cached or lost in the cave (Jacobi 2007b). Arctic hare tibiae awls are also known from Robin Hood Cave and Pin Hole at Creswell Gough's Cave in Somerset (ibid.) and one is known on a hyoid bone from Kent's Cavern directly dated to ~13.9–15 ka BP (Jacobi 2004, 53). Their relative abundance suggests that they were common items in the Late Magdalenian tool-kit, a testimony to the ubiquity and importance of working soft materials. Individual eyed needles are known from Cat Hole, Gough's Cave and Kent's Cavern. End-scrapers, a common item in British Late Magdalenian tool-kits, seem also to have been used mainly for the working of soft hides and furs (e.g. Audouze et al. 1981, 138).

No shell, teeth or bone items of personal ornamentation have been recovered from clear British Late Magdalenian contexts although some are known from the Early Gravettian of Paviland (see Chapter 7) and from the Allerød at Kendrick's Cave, possibly in association with human remains (see Text Box 8.12).

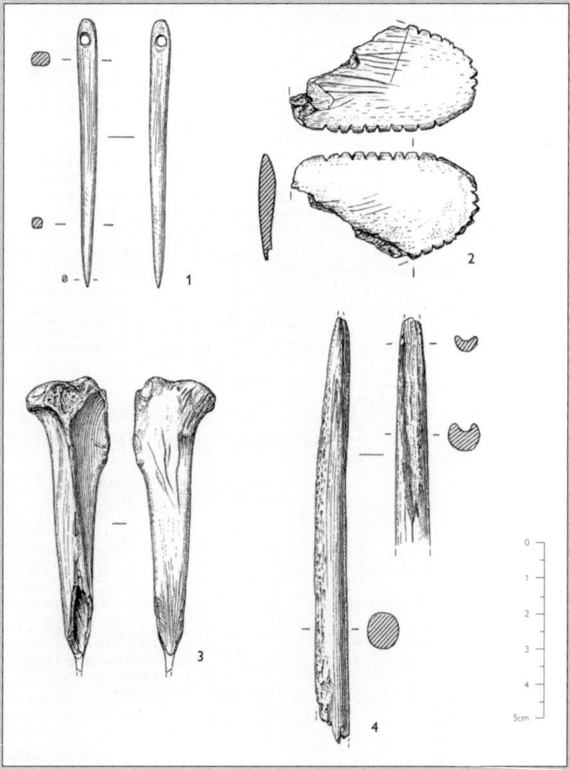

Text Box 8.4

FIGURE 1
(1) eyed bone needle; (2) thread-winder made on vertebral process of horse; (3) Arctic hare tibia awl; (4) Reindeer antler javelin foreshaft. (From Pettitt and Jacobi 2009, drawings by Julian Cross.)

Principal prey species

Horse seems to have been a particularly important prey, perhaps the most critical hunted resource as it dominates the modified faunas of Mother Grundy's Parlour at Creswell, Gough's Cave and Sun Hole in Somerset and Kent's Cavern and Pixie's Hole in Devon. At all of these sites fractured lower molars indicate the removal of marrow (Jacobi 2004, 75–6). Some evidence exists for the tactical use of the landscape for horse procurement, particularly the steep-sided, narrow-mouthed Cheddar Gorge which seems to have been of particular importance for disadvantaging the animal during hunting (Figure 8.5). The gorge narrows immediately above Gough's Cave, an obvious point to trap horse, possibly in association with the use of domesticated wolves (Jacobi 2004, 75). Creswell Crags, another steep-walled gorge but without a narrow mouth, may have been important as it also channelled migrating animals such as horse and reindeer, the latter possibly between winter grazing areas in the lowlands of Lincolnshire/Doggerland and spring calving grounds in the uplands of the Peak District, which were certainly in place by the Younger Dryas and probably before (Pettitt 2007; see below). Cooper (2002, 79) has suggested that the location of the Bradgate Park, Newtown Lynford, camp at the narrow mouth of a pronounced gorge is probably another example of such a natural disadvantaging site. The location of a small lithic assemblage on the slopes overlooking the River Derwent at Froggatt, Derbyshire (Henderson 1973), could conceivably represent a hunting stand, and Garton and Jacobi (2009, 32–6) have speculated

FIGURE 8.5
Cheddar Gorge from above Gough's Cave. (Photograph Paul Pettitt.)

that the position of the large, open air site at Farndon Fields – on the floodplain of the Trent where it is joined by the River Devon – may indicate that it was used to intercept reindeer trying to ford the river.[3]

At Creswell, arctic hare seems to have been a particularly favoured prey of the Late Magdalenians, abundant in the faunal inventories of Church Hole, Pin Hole, Mother Grundy's Parlour and particularly Robin Hood Cave (Charles and Jacobi 1994; Jacobi 2007b; Pettitt 2008; Pettit and Jacobi 2009). In addition to providing fur and sinew for clothing (see Text Box 8.4) smashing on the bones show that the hares also provided an important source of fat and meat (Charles and Jacobi 1994).

Modified bones of red deer (e.g. Gough's Cave, Three Holes Cave, Devon, King Arthur's Cave, Wye Valley), mammoth (e.g. Gough's Cave), aurochs (e.g. Bob's Cave, Devon), badger (Gough's Cave), brown bear (Three Holes Cave) and reindeer indicate that these species were also exploited, in the latter case at least for antler, as at Fox Hole in the southern Peak District and Church Hole, Creswell (Barton and Roberts 1996; Barton and Dumont 2000; Charles 1997; Jacobi 2004, 2007b; Lister 1991; Pettitt 2007; Roberts 1996). Stable isotope analysis of human remains from Gough's Cave (see Text Box 8.5) indicates that aurochs and probably reindeer were important dietary resources – perhaps more so than horse – although the cave furnished no evidence of the processing of these on site (Richards et al. 2000).

LATE MAGDALENIAN ARCHAEOLOGY OF GOUGH'S CAVE, CHEDDAR GORGE

Cheddar Gorge, a one kilometre long, steep-sided gorge in the Mendip Hills, Somerset, contains three caves that have yielded Late Magdalenian archaeology – Gough's Cave, Sun Hole and Soldier's Hole (Figure 8.5). Gough's Cave has yielded Britain's largest Late Magdalenian lithic assemblage as well as tools and other items on organic materials, fauna and disarticulated human remains. The main importance of the gorge at the time seems to have been for the hunting of horse which were processed at Gough's, probably on the platform in front of the cave and within its wide mouth.

Gough's Cave has yielded at least ~2,115 Late Magdalenian lithics, probably only a sample of a much higher original amount (Jacobi 2004). The apparently discrete distribution of the lithics within the cave, the similarity in patination and condition and a degree of refitting, suggest that the assemblage is not mixed. Over 99% are made on black upper Cretaceous chalk flint, the source of which was probably the northern part of Salisbury Plain, particularly around the Vale of Pewsey ~75 km to the east (Rockman 2003). Flakes are numerous although the assemblage is dominated by blades. Cores are low in number, probably because finished blades were transported to the site, although the cores that do exist, as well as a number of complete and partial crested blades, core tablets and platform preparation flakes, indicate that blade production was largely unipolar, as

Text Box 8.5

Text Box 8.5

with other British Late Magdalenian assemblages (see main text). Tools represent 552 pieces of the surviving assemblage (26%) – a high percentage by continental standards that probably indicates only that much débitage has been discarded or lost – and are dominated by points with single and double oblique truncations. Around 79% of these are broken, suggesting that weapons were being repaired at the site. Burins are the next numerous (n = 61), almost always made on blades and dominated by forms on retouched truncations. Forty-seven endscrapers survive, of which thirty are on blades; burins are therefore somewhat more numerous than endscrapers, the reverse of Hengistbury Head (see Text Box 8.10). A number of piercers, becs and truncated pieces form the least numerous categories of tools. The lack of Late Magdalenian/Hamburgian shouldered points is in keeping with radiocarbon dates on humanly modified material from the site, the majority of which cluster ~14.7 ka BP, that is, a little too early (Jacobi and Higham 2009), although the presence of at least 14 curved backed points may hint at a brief occupation during the Allerød or may be an integral part of the Magdalenian assemblage. In addition to these a *sagaie* of mammoth ivory and three antler *batons percés* were also recovered (see main text). The disarticulated remains of at least five humans apparently mixed in with the Late Magdalenian archaeology attests to the production of skull cups (see Text Box 8.3).

Seasonality data indicates that Gough's Cave was used during both summer and winter (Beasley 1987; Parkin et al. 1986). The dominant herbivore among the fauna is horse (Currant 1986b, 1991) which seems to have been hunted without regard for age and from which cut-marks and smashes indicate that both meat and marrow was used. Red deer seems also to have been an important resource, although as Currant (ibid.) has noted there is a marked absence of reindeer (excepting the three antler *bâtons*). The presence of domesticated wolf ('dog') may indicate that this was used in horse hunting. A direct date (OxA-1122; Hedges et al. 1987) of ~15 ka BP on a reindeer antler base from nearby Aveline's Hole (where red deer dominates the fauna) indicates that the species was present in the region during the period, however, and thus its absence at Gough's presumably indicates that it was not a desired resource during these seasons or during activity in the gorge.

Stable isotope analyses of the Gough's Cave and Sun Hole human bones indicates that dietary protein was mainly derived from meat as one would perhaps expect, mainly from red deer, reindeer and aurochs, providing useful contextual data for the horse hunting in the Cheddar region (Richards et al. 2000). Gough's cave forms an important part in an apparent seasonal round in Late Magdalenian Britain (see main text).

The importance of reindeer in the British Magdalenian remains to be elucidated in detail. Although *sagaies* and *bâtons* of reindeer antler are known (see below), little evidence exists of the processing of this animal as a dietary resource. Natural accumulations are known from several sites in southern and northern England, as noted above, although these do not furnish evidence of human exploitation. In the Creswell region Late Glacial unmodified reindeer remains are known from Dead Man's Cave in Anston Stones Gorge (Mellars 1969), Ash Tree Cave near Whitwell (Armstrong 1956), Langwith Cave (Mullins 1913) and at least Robin Hood Cave, Church Hole and Pin Hole at Creswell itself (Jenkinson 1984), all of these caves having yielded Late Magdalenian assemblages. Recent excavations in The Crypt, a small rockshelter under the entrance to Church Hole at Creswell, have uncovered reindeer remains in association with arctic hare and a small Late Magdalenian assemblage (Pettitt et al. 2009) but evidence of processing is lacking and one cannot eliminate the possibility that they were accumulated naturally or by non-human carnivores. Calving grounds had been established in the Peak District by the Younger Dryas although it is unclear whether these existed in the Late Glacial Interstadial. Reindeer bones have been found in Dowel, Elder Bush, Ossom's and Fox Hole caves, all in the southern Peak District and the first three in the valley of the river Manifold (Bramwell 1963, 1964a, 1964b). Fox Hole has yielded two reindeer antler foreshafts (Bramwell 1977, 8; Figure 8.6), alongside an atypical shouldered point (Bramwell 1971). It is therefore likely that the small collection of artefacts from this site belongs to the subsequent Hamburgian-type occupation and it is therefore discussed below. Two antler foreshafts are also known from Church Hole (Jacobi 2007), direct AMS ^{14}C dates

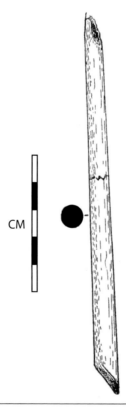

FIGURE 8.6
Reindeer antler javelin foreshaft from Fox Hole, Peak District. (After Bramwell 1977.)

for which are statistically identical to those on the Fox Hole examples (See Text Box on Magdalenian clothing).

Some direct evidence exists for the use of small animals other than hare. At Soldier's Hole, Cheddar, bones of common partridge (*Perdix perdix*) and black grouse (*Lyrurus tetrix*) have been dated directly to ~13.8–14.8 ka BP, along with cut-marked remains of ptarmigan (*Lagopus mutus*) (Jacobi 2004, 75). Together, these indicate the local presence of a mosaic of environments, from tree covered valleys, grassland on the abutting lowlands and barren ground on the plateaux, although only ptarmigan can be directly linked to the human occupation. In addition to their meat birds presumably provided feathers for clothing, fletching and display (see Text Box 8.4).

The organic tool-kit

Four reindeer antler *bâtons percés* are known from the British Late Magdalenian: three from Gough's Cave and one without archaeological associations from the Thames at Syon Reach near Richmond (Figure 8.7). All of the Gough's Cave examples bear helical grooves inside the diagnostic hole and two also bear traces of red ochre within the holes, suggesting that material stained with ochre passed through them, probably as part of their function (PP pers. obs.). Two bear a series of clustered engraved lines which 'wind' diagonally around the *bâtons* and through their holes in a manner reminiscent of line, similar to an example from the Magdalenian of Le Placard in Charente (Marshack 1972, 86ff.). The third example bears no such engraved lines but marks suggestive of chopping appear on its shaft. The helical grooving inside the hole of this example is particularly pronounced. The Syon Reach example is plain, with no traces of scoring, although a degree of asymmetrical wear is observable each side of the hole which is consistent with line

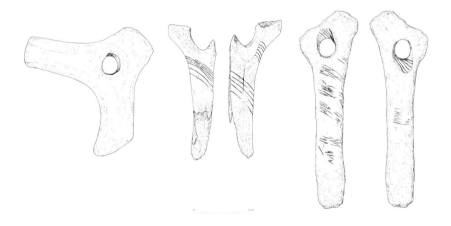

FIGURE 8.7
British Late Magdalenian *bâtons percés*. Left to right: River Thames at Syon Reach, Near Richmond, Greater London; Gough's Cave, Cheddar, Somerset. (Drawn (Left) and redrawn from Garrod 1926 and Campbell 1977 (centre and right) by Jerneja Willmott.)

(PP pers. obs.). All four of the *bâtons* are broken and can be assumed to have been discarded when no longer functional, as with many continental examples (Jacobi 1986, 77). Examples are known from the broadly contemporary Late Magdalenian of the Paris Basin where they are interpreted as relating to textile manufacture (Averbouh 2010).

In addition to the *bâtons* several organic armatures have secure Late Magdalenian attributions. *Sagaies* of mammoth ivory are known from Gough's Cave, Pin Hole and Kent's Cavern (Figure 8.8) and it is probable that three barbed points ('harpoons') of antler – two uniserial and one biserial – from Kent's Cavern are also Late Magdalenian in age as they were stratified within and slightly below the 'Black Band', a thin occupation horizon named for the abundance of charcoal (see Text Box 8.6). That said, the uniserial fragments are similar to those associated with the Poulton Elk of Allerød age (Armstrong 1925; Garrod 1926, 40; Currant et al. 1989; Jacobi 2007a; Pettitt 2007; Text Box 8.7). An undated biserially barbed antler harpoon from Aveline's Hole in Cheddar Gorge may belong to the cave's small Late Magdalenian assemblage and is similar in form to examples from the Late Magdalenian of Goyet Cave, Belgium, as Garrod (1926, 87) noted.

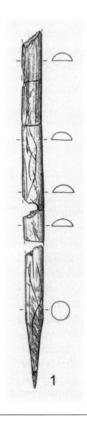

FIGURE 8.8
Mammoth ivory *sagaie* from Pin Hole, Creswell, bearing engraved 'fish/line' decoration. (From Pettitt 2009 and courtesy Roger Jacobi.)

THE LATE MAGDALENIAN OF THE 'BLACK BAND' AT KENT'S CAVERN

Nineteenth- and twentieth century excavations in Kent's Cavern yielded Late Magdalenian artefacts from the Vestibule, the Sloping Chamber immediately beyond this, and the North-East Gallery. They derive from the upper part of the cave earth, immediately below the granular stalagmite that ubiquitously sealed the Pleistocene cave earth in several parts of the cave's outer system. The finds seem to have been most abundant in the cavernous Vestibule, which is not surprising as the cave's north entrance leads directly into this area. The greater number of Late Magdalenian artefacts seem to be associated with a dense area of charcoal and burnt bones – a combustion zone – against the Vestibule's west wall (see Figure 1). The excavator, William Pengelly (1884, 218) noted that the Black Band 'consisted largely of charred wood . . . of irregular outline, covered an area of about 100 square feet, and varied in thickness from 2 to 6 inches'. Of particular interest is his observation that within the Vestibule blocks of old stalagmitic floor 'were so numerous and piled on one another, especially on the western verge of the area occupied by the Black Band, as to assume the aspect of a rudely formed wall' (ibid., 224–5). The Black Band was 'extremely rich in objects, many of them of great interest, and including bones of *Rhinoceros tichorhinus* [*Coeledonta antiquitatis* – woolly rhinoceros], horse, *Hyaena spelaea* [*Crocuta crocuta* – spotted hyaena], fox, bear and badger, as well as human tools of various kinds . . . implements, flakes, and cores of flint; bone tools, and burnt bones . . . the flint specimens formed a total of 366 . . . though many of them were mere chips, and the majority of them simple flakes, no inconsiderable number were more or less perfect lanceolate implements. By far the greater number were white and had an almost chalky texture . . . the bone tools included an awl . . . a portion of a [unbarbed] harpoon' (ibid., 221). Pengelly also noted the discovery of the biserially barbed harpoon discussed in the text 'in the Cave Earth below the black band . . . found 18th March 1887, in the Vestibule, in the second foot level, above which was the Black Band about 3 inches thick; over this again was the Granular Stalagmite 18 inches thick . . .' (see Figure 2). Surviving lithics

FIGURE 1
View of the Vestibule from the Passage of Urns, with approximate location of the original position of the Black Band. Note that no specific size or shape is implied. (Photo Paul Pettitt.)

Text Box 8.6

Text Box 8.6

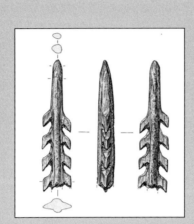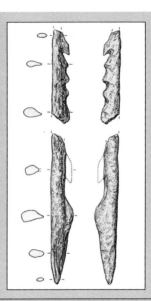

FIGURE 2
Antler uniserial and biserial harpoons from Kent's Cavern. (Drawings by Julian Cross and courtesy Roger Jacobi.)

from the Black Band are typical of the British Late Magdalenian and include, for example, blade and bladelet manufacture and cheddar points. Surviving fauna indicate the presence of horse and a bovid and direct radiocarbon measurements on these taxa indicate an age of ~14–-15 ka BP (Jacobi 2004).

Text Box 8.7

THE POULTON ELK: A WINTER KILL IN THE BOREAL FORESTS

The partial skeleton of a mature male elk (*Alces alces*) was recovered from deposits dating to the second half of the Late Glacial Interstadial at High Furlong, Poulton-le-Fylde, Lancashire (Hallam et al. 1973; see Figure 1). Two incomplete bone harpoons were found in association with the skeleton, at least one of which was originally embedded in the elk's body. This is clearly the remains of a kill by Late Upper Palaeolithic hunters. The skeleton was virtually complete and, although the bones had largely become moderately disassociated and displaced, those of the hind limbs were partly articulated. The size of the animal and the presence of antlers show that it was an adult male. The condition of the antler indicates that it was about to be shed, which suggests that it was hunted in winter, when elk shed their antlers (ibid., 115). Impact lesions consistent with the use of flint-tipped weaponry were found on the animal's left ribs and right scapula, humerus and tibia, most of which occurred at the time of the animal's death. Two bone harpoons were recovered with the skeleton, one in the vicinity of the animal's ribs (point 1), and the second resting against its left metatarsal, having broken in half later due to sediment compaction (point 2). A shallow lesion

Text Box 8.7

was found on the left metatarsal immediately adjacent to point 2, a clear indication that the point had entered the animal's leg, probably from below. Initial radiocarbon dates for the detrital muds in which the elk came to rest indicated a minimum age of 11,665 ± 140 BP (St-3836) and a maximum age of 12,200 ± 160 BP (St-3832), that is, ~13.6–14 ka BP, which were subsequently confirmed by ultrafiltrated radiocarbon dates on the bones of the elk skeleton itself of 11,660 ± 60 BP (OxA-11151) and 11,715 ± 50 BP (OxA-13075: Jacobi et al, 2009), that is, the early part of the Allerød ~13.8–14 ka BP.

The two partial bone harpoons are oval-sectioned, of slender form and uniserially barbed, with barbs cut obliquely to the long axis of the stem (see Figure 2). Hallam et al. (1973, 120–1) suggested a typological association with Early Mesolithic forms of Pre-Boreal and Boreal date, although typologically they are similar to Late Glacial forms from Dinslaken, Germany,

FIGURE 1
The Poulton Elk. (Photo courtesy The Harris Museum and Art Gallery, Preston and with thanks to Emma Heslewood.)

300 km to the east (Jacobi 1980, 60) and more generally to contemporary *Federmessergruppen* forms, clearly falling into the range of variation for harpoons broadly of Late Magdalenian/Azilian attribution (see text).

The context of the skeleton gives some indication of how it may have been hunted. The remains came to rest within a coarse, detrital mud formed within a freshwater lake. The alternating muds and clays in the sequence suggested to the excava-

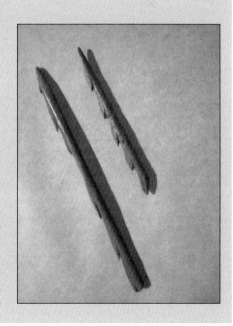

FIGURE 2
Uniserially barbed bone harpoons associated with the Poulton Elk. (Photo PP and courtesy Emma Heslewood and The Harris Museum and Art Gallery, Preston.)

tors a similarity with similar alternating Late Glacial sediments elsewhere. The coarse muds suggest that the skeleton came to rest in shallow water, the plant macrofossils revealing relatively temperate conditions with a shrub and birch-rich forest at the lake edge. Such a watery, boreal woodland context is in keeping with the modern ecology of elk and with the Allerød environment in general. The numerous lesions on the animal's bones suggest that weapons tipped with flint as well as the bone harpoons were used against it, only the harpoons remaining, for some reason, at the death site. The location of the lesions caused by flint-tipped weaponry – on left and right – show that the animal took fire from both sides; shots were aimed at its thoracic region and were probably the main cause of death due to the collapse of its lungs (Hallam et al. 1973, 125). In addition to these, a shot was made from the weapon tipped with point 2. If the proposal that the lesion on the part of the metatarsal in contact with the harpoon took one to two weeks to form is correct, this implies that the animal survived a previous attack in seriously wounded form. It is impossible to say whether the multiple lesions indicate multiple hunters or serial shots at the animal from a solitary hunter. Hallam et al. (ibid., 125) suggested that the entry of point 2 into the elk's foot would have disabled the animal, implying that it was hunted on land. In this case one might envisage a scenario in which it was disabled by harpoon, tracked, and finally killed by flint-tipped javelins. Vang Petersen (2005) has, however, suggested that harpoons were designed to hunt elk and large deer in water, where the animal could be driven and where it would be naturally impeded, a similar situation to that which obtained during reindeer hunting at Stellmoor (Bratlund 1996b). The animals' natural fear of wolves could be exploited; their natural instincts if faced with dogs would be to escape into water. In such a scenario the animal could easily be hunted from boats, the harpoon allowing the recovery of the floating carcass and its transport by lashing behind a canoe. In this case, however, it seems that the carcass was not recovered; perhaps it sank before it could be lashed to the canoe or brought to the lake edge for butchery. Ironically, this important site represents a fatal but nevertheless failed procurement episode.

Art and the social landscape

A number of incised artefacts are known from the British Magdalenian, some of which may have functioned as artificial memory systems, and others are clearly examples of figurative art. These have been summarised by Pettitt and Bahn (2007). Seven small fragments of mammoth ivory from Gough's Cave bear traces of incisions clustered in small groups (Charles 1989). Similar clusters of incisions are known on a length of horse or bovid-sized rib, on one of the arctic hare tibia awls from Gough's Cave and on a worked horse hyoid from Kent's Cavern.[4] The Gough's Cave rib fragment bears clustered incisions along its two long sides and on one truncated end of one side, with a series of diagonal criss-crossed lines originating from a central 'register' on the other. There are similar to incisions seen on the *bâtons* from this site (Hawkes et al. 1970) and the piece also bears traces of ochre colouring (PP pers. obs.). Both the Gough's Cave rib fragment and the engraved rib from Robin Hood (see below) are well polished, suggesting perhaps a degree of curation. Another rib fragment from Gough's Cave bears scrape marks indicative of the removal of the periosteum (Charles 1989), possibly a 'blank' that was never incised. The hare tibia awl from Gough's Cave bears three 'registers' of short incisions on its shaft, each apparently adding up to 28 lines (PP pers. obs.). A mesial fragment of an arctic hare tibia awl recovered from the spoil heap of Church Hole cave (Pettitt et al. 2009) bears more widely spaced incisions although these may relate more to prehension than to notation.

Creswell Crags has yielded three clear examples of *art mobilier* and several examples of engravings on the walls of two caves. Several bones from Mother Grundy's Parlour bear markings that Armstrong (1925) interpreted as 'incised figures of bison and reindeer' although these are very unclear and almost certainly natural, bearing the dull-sectioned character and irregularity of root incisions (PP pers. obs.). A further possible example of Late Upper Palaeolithic incised decoration from Pin Hole, although undated and conceivably post-Palaeolithic in age, is a rib fragment engraved with a series of chevrons. This originated from a trial excavation at the cave's entrance, the contents of which were mixed (Armstrong 1925, 169) and the issue remains open (see discussion in Pettitt and Bahn 2007, 20). A fragment of mammoth ivory excavated by Armstrong from Pin Hole and published as a pendant (Kitching 1963, 48) has, in fact, gone through the stomach of a hyaena, the 'pierced' hole of which has been etched by stomach acids.

A mammoth ivory *sagaie* from Pin Hole is today broken into four fragments, its double-bevelled form common from the continental Middle Magdalenian onwards (Delporte and Mons 1988). This bears incised decoration, truncated at each end by breaks (Figure 8.8), and is clearly an example of the 'fish' design well-known in the French Magdalenian (Campbell 1977, 148; Pettitt and Bahn 2007, 20). Magdalenian examples from the continent contemporary in radiocarbon terms have been found at Trou de Chaleux, Belgium (Otte 1994, Plate 32, no. 6) and La Madeleine (Armstrong 1925, 168). On the second incised fragment, however, the design more closely resembles that of twisted line as found, for example, at Laugerie Basse, France (Breuil 1937). Such continental comparisons are not surprising given those for the horse head engraving from Robin Hood Cave, the engraving of a 'humanoid' on a rib from Pin Hole (see Text Box 8.8) and the parietal art of Church Hole (see below).

At present, Creswell contains the only convincing examples of British Palaeolithic cave art (see papers in Pettitt et al. 2007; Bahn and Pettitt 2009). An engraving of a mammoth has been claimed at Gough's Cave (Mullan et al. 2006) although is clearly formed by natural cracks and spalling in the rock (PP and MJW pers. obs.). By contrast, the Creswell engravings are clearly distinguishable from natural cracks in the permian limestone in which the caves formed (Mawson 2009) and in three cases their Palaeolithic age is verified by Uranium-series dates on stalactites which formed over them (Pike et al. 2005a and b, 2009). With the exception of one 'vulva' comprised of three converging lines in Robin Hood Cave (Figure 8.9), Church Hole cave on the south side of the gorge

LATE UPPER PALAEOLITHIC *ART MOBILIER* FROM CRESWELL CRAGS

Examples of Upper Palaeolithic art are remarkably rare in Britain and it is perhaps an indication of the importance of Creswell Crags, at least during the Late Magdalenian, that most examples of *art mobilier* and all currently known examples of cave art come from this small gorge. Excavations in Robin Hood Cave in the 1870s and in Pin Hole in the 1920s yielded the only two British examples of *art mobilier* which may be regarded as figurative. These take the form of an engraving of a 'humanoid' on the rib of a large mammal (possibly woolly rhinoceros, *Coelodonta antiquitatis*; Figure 1) from Pin Hole and an engraved horse head on the fragmentary rib of a horse (Figure 2), which bears traces of ochre, from Robin Hood Cave.

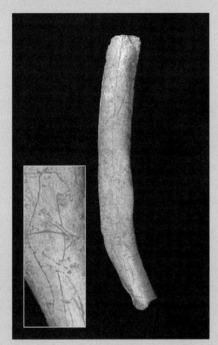

FIGURE 1
The engraved humanoid from Pin Hole.
(© Trustees of the British Museum.)

The humanoid was excavated by A. L. Armstrong (1928, 28) who interpreted it as a 'masked human figure in the act of dancing a ceremonial dance'. Armstrong drew around the outline that he perceived, although recent removal of the graphite from his pencil in an analysis lead by Jill Cook has shown that his interpretation was somewhat exaggerated, as had been his interpretations of artefacts elsewhere (see discussion in Pettitt and Jacobi 2009). The engraving, cleaned of interpretation, is certainly humanoid, but we do not believe that it can be confidently identified as human *sensu stricto.* Given the snout-like face, we wonder whether this depicts a rearing bear.

The horse head engraving from Robin Hood Cave was created on a fragment of horse rib, highly smoothed and polished through wear. In terms of the care taken to draw the head, neck and mane of the animal, the aggressive lines of the mane, and the angular nature of its mouth and jaw, the image has been likened to continental Late Magdalenian depictions of horses (Pettitt 2007). Controversy surrounded the discovery of the engraving, although the excavators – Dawkins and Mello – stressed that it derived from the cave's 'dark cave earth' and there is no reason to disbelieve this (see discussion in Pettitt and Jacobi 2007, 9–11). Several

Text Box 8.8

lines have been engraved over the horse; some have suggested that this represents a 'corral' although these may not be meaningfully associated with the horse or may represent a 'cancelling' of the image rather than a physical object. The reverse of the rib bears a number of engraved lines at oblique angles to the piece. As a polished fragment of horse rib bearing the engravings the piece is similar to examples from Gough's Cave (see main text) and was conceivably one example of a regional tradition of small, portable artificial memory systems.

FIGURE 2
Engraved horse's head from Robin Hood Cave.
(© Trustees of the British Museum.)

contains all of the engravings. These comprise a cervid (probably a young red deer with first year spikes), a bovid (usually identified as bison although in our opinion more likely an aurochs), the dorsal line and front leg of a horse, three (possibly four) 'vulvae', the head of an ibis, a group of images depicting either long-necked birds or stylised Magdalenian females and an enigmatic image that may be a variant on the latter (Figures 8.10, 8.11 and 8.12). With the exception of the birds/women these all cluster in the daylight zone of the cave, the latter marking what was probably the rear of the cave in the Late Pleistocene. Some incorporate natural features in the rock in a manner common in continental cave art, such as an erosional hole ('vug') used to represent an eye and a burrow fragment a mouth in the cervid; a curved section of a remnant burrow as the beak of the ibis, brought into sharper perspective by the *champlevé* technique, and possibly the use of a small erosional depression as a head in one of the 'birds', assuming it actually represents a Gönnersdorf style female (see Text Box 8.9).

A number of continental Magdalenian parallels exist for the Creswell art, such as similar engraved motifs on *sagaies* from south-west France and Belgium, horse engravings on plaquettes and in cave art in France and Germany, bovid images in France and 'vulvae' as far north as Gouy Cave in Normandy (Pettitt 2007). A number of engravings in the latter bear striking similarities with the Creswell art, notably vulvae, incomplete horses, elongated 'birds' and a female of Gönnersdorf type (Martin 2007).

It is of interest that Church Hole, as noted above, seems to have contained less Late Magdalenian archaeology than the three caves of the north side of the gorge (Jacobi 2007b). This could simply reflect the greater desirability of south-facing caves but one

FIGURE 8.9
Engraved 'vulva' of three converging lines on the east wall of the main chamber of Robin Hood Cave, Creswell Crags. (Photo © English Heritage.)

FIGURE 8.10
Engraved cervid (probably red deer) on the east wall of Church Hole, Creswell Crags. Note the difference in condition between the lines that comprise the cervid and the modern graffiti. (Photo © English Heritage.)

FIGURE 8.11
Engraved bovid on the east wall of Church Hole, Creswell Crags. (Photo © English Heritage.)

FIGURE 8.12
Engraved 'vulva' on the west wall of Church Hole, Creswell Crags. (Photo © English Heritage.)

THE CHURCH HOLE REAR ENGRAVINGS: BIRDS OR GÖNNERSDORF-STYLE FEMALES?

Beyond the cave mouth area of Church Hole, where all of the engravings bar one group cluster, the cave narrows into a small phreatic tube with a ceiling only 1 to 1.5 metres high. Although its deposits, like those in the cave mouth, were excavated away in the nineteenth century, the remnants of a Late Pleistocene stalagmite floor which capped the deposits allow the original floor level to be reconstructed. Some 20 m into the cave the ceiling rises, forming a small chamber, beyond which it drops close to the stalagmite floor, probably sealing the rear-most part of the cave at this time. It is probably no coincidence that the only engravings in the dark zone of the cave occur here and possibly significant that they are opposite a small erosional chimney on the eastern wall of the cave in this small chamber.

A small group of interconnected, elongated images was engraved with bold lines onto the western wall in this small chamber. A Uranium-series date on a thin stalactite covering the images provides a *terminus ante quem* of 13,000 BP, clearly supporting the stylistically – and archaeologically – derived notion that they are Late Upper Palaeolithic in age (Pike et al. 2005b, 2009). Although today they are at head height due to the clear fact that the original floor has been excavated away, in antiquity they would have been engraved around 50 cm off the cave's floor. These take the form of four (possibly five) separate images, two of which

share part of a line and one of which is partially superimposed on another (see Figure 1). It is possible that these represent the incomplete (i.e. necks and heads) of long-necked birds, although each image differs from the others and thus do not clearly form a group of the same species of bird. Bird depictions are relatively rare in Upper Palaeolithic art and while one cannot of course rule out this interpretation on those grounds, a group of incomplete and differing long-necked birds would be unique in the currently known Upper Palaeolithic artistic record.

FIGURE 1
Engraved birds or stylised human females from the west wall of the rear chamber in Church Hole, Creswell Crags. (© English Heritage.)

Text Box 8.9

Text Box 8.9

By contrast, highly stylised partial depictions of naked human females are a common character of Late Magdalenian art, occurring on cave walls in Spain and France and as *art mobilier* in Spain, France, Belgium, Germany, the Czech Republic and, arguably, in broadly contemporary Molodovan contexts in Ukraine (see Pettitt 2007 for a fuller discussion). The recovery of over 200 of these engravings on stone plaquettes at Gönnersdorf and carvings on stone and mammoth ivory from Gönnersdorf and Andernach has enabled a strong understanding of this image and its increasingly stylised variants; it appears to depict a naked woman, arms raised (usually missing), with or without breasts, with buttocks thrust out to the rear and legs bent and almost always attenuated below the knee (Höck 1993; Bosinski et al. 2001).

The similarity of the Church Hole examples to Gönnersdorf-style females is clear only if one assumes that they are upside-down to the modern viewer. Elsewhere, Pettitt (2007) has argued that the easiest way to engrave these is to lean against the cave's wall rather than to sit or lie (from which positions engraving hard stone would be very difficult). If the engraver leaned against the rock it would take his/her weight and engraving would be much easier. Assuming a right-handed person (an 80% chance that he/she was so) then the resulting orientation would produce forms remarkably similar to these common continental motifs. It seems to us a more parsimonious interpretation that the Church Hole images form part of this widespread Late Magdalenian tradition rather than unique depictions of birds. Given the similarity of Britain's few examples of Late Magdalenian *art mobilier* to those of the continent (see text) this does not surprise us.

wonders why, in this case, Church Hole contains almost all of the parietal art. This may indicate one way in which the landscape was imbued with meaning, as it is reminiscent of the Magdalenian caves of La Vache and Niaux, which face each other across the Vicdessos Valley of Ariège. In the former, parietal art is non-existent but a rich inventory of archaeology (including *art mobilier*) is known and in the latter no archaeology to speak of has been found, although its parietal art is some of the most spectacular known. Although it would be incorrect to draw too black and white a distinction this does suggest that some caves had more spiritual functions, others more 'prosaic'. Jacobi (2007) has noted that the use of Church Hole came to an end with the Late Magdalenian, whereas later Upper Palaeolithic groups seem to have made use of the other caves, and he has suggested that the creation of the art may have marked it out as special from that point onwards, that is, a place perhaps to be avoided or revered.

Beyond the few examples of art, evidence for ritual activity or cosmological belief is virtually absent from Britain. Given its importance as a resource one might expect horse in particular to have held some ritual significance and it is interesting that the faunal taxa identified in the Creswell art include horse, bovid and cervid, the three most commonly depicted taxa in Palaeolithic art. It has been suggested above that birch trees may have held considerable importance given their use as a raw material and cosmological importance to many small-scale groups in the ethnographic present but this is pure speculation. A degree of 'enculturation' of the landscape may be evident at Creswell; it has been noted that most of the Creswell parietal art occurs in Church Hole, which seems to have received less prosaic attention than the caves of the north side of the gorge, possibly indicating a conceptual difference between the north and south sides of the gorge *sensu* La Vache and Niaux in France (Pettitt 2007). The recovery of knapping waste from new excavations outside Church Hole has, however, revealed that occupational activity in and around Church Hole may have been greater than previously thought and the art may therefore form part of an occupational use of the cave after all (Pettitt et al. 2009). Green and Walker (1991, 59) speculated that given a 40 metre crawl to the back of Hoyle's Mouth cave in southwest Wales it must have served a ritual functon, although the few lithics that indicate humans ventured there could simply represent chance losses while checking the back of the cave for denning or hibernating carnivores before sleeping within it. Cranial and postcranial remains of at least five human individuals (four adults and one juvenile) were recovered from the Late Magdalenian levels of Gough's Cave (Currant et al. 1989). These have been dated directly to ~14.3–15.2 ka BP, confirming a Late Magdalenian attribution (Jacobi and Higham 2009). These bear cut-marks on the cranial vault, mandible and ribs, indicative of careful defleshing and dismembering (Cook 1986, 1991). Although Andrews and Fernández-Jalvo (2003) thought these indicative of cannibalism, the high cut-mark frequency relating to careful removal of the same body parts, remarkably similar to Late Magdalenian processed human remains from Brillenhöhle, southwestern Germany, suggests that they relate to defleshing (Orschiedt 2002) and to the production of skull cups (Bello et al. 2011 and see Text Box 8.3). In this case it is likely that they reflect mortuary rituals relating to a far wider Magdalenian world (Pettitt 2011). Aspects of the Creswell parietal art are interesting in this light. Several images relate either to the fragmented body ('vulvae') or to the highly stylised body (females; see Text Box 8.9) possibly indicating a concern with bodily fragmentation in artistic and mortuary ritual (Pettitt 2011).

The last of the Magdalenians

There is no reason to believe that the Late Magdalenian occupation of Britain was a persistent phenomenon; it may have lasted only for a matter of years. A number of British sites seem on typological grounds to belong to a later period within the Meiendorf Interstadial, however, which may either represent an *in situ* evolution of technology in Britain as part of wider events in Europe or – in our opinion more likely – a later pulse of occupation some time after the Late Magdalenian occupation came to an end. Why this came to an end is, of course, unclear, although one may sensibly assume it related to resources. As this seems to have occurred within the relatively mild conditions of the Meiendorf rather than with the onset of the Older Dryas, it seems that this was not directly related to climate. Perhaps a critical resource disappeared from a vital node in the annual subsistence round, assuming that the hypothetical round noted above is correct. Hares are known to experience profound population crashes on cycles of 5–7 years (Owen 2005); if they disappeared from Creswell such a void would remove this critical node in the year's round and perhaps result in the crash of the annual system overall.

LATER MEIENDORF ADAPTATIONS: SITES OF HENGISTBURY TYPE AND THE HAMBURGIAN

On the continent there is evidence of much change in lithic assemblages during the later part of the Meiendorf, when concave-shouldered 'Hamburgian' points appear in Poland, Denmark, Germany, the Netherlands, Belgium and the Paris Basin alongside a rise in *Zinken* (Stapert 1985; Holm and Rieck 1987; Fischer 1991; Beuker and Niekus 1996; Otte and Noiret 2009). Otte and Noiret (2009) proposed on the basis of calibrated radiocarbon measurements that a Magdalenian–Hamburgian transition occurred on the Northern European Plain within the Meiendorf, a suggestion that has been borne out by recent dating projects. Within much of the continental range of the Hamburgian two phases are apparent; an earlier 'classic' Hamburgian phase in which shouldered points are dominant from south-east Germany to the Netherlands and a later 'Havelte' phase in which tanged Havelte points appeared between Denmark and the Netherlands (Street et al. 2001; Crombé and Verbruggen 2002; Eriksen 2002; Kabaciński et al. 2002; Kabaciński and Kobusiewicz 2007; Terberger and Lübke 2007; Grimm and Weber 2008; Weber and Grimm 2009; Brinch Petersen 2009; Kabaciński and Sobkowiak-Tabaka 2009). The 'classic' Hamburgian appears to have begun around or immediately prior to GI1e, probably as a northern development of the Late Magdalenian, and the 'transition' from Hamburgian to Havelte assemblages occurred within the second half of GI1e, that is, after ~14.6 ka BP or at the start of GI1d, ~14.1 ka BP, when denser forests developed (Grimm and Weber 2008).

In search of the British Hamburgian

In terms of the broad typological composition of its Meiendorf assemblages, Britain groups most clearly with Belgium and The Netherlands. It does not possess strictly Magdalenian sites which dominate in northern France, nor classic Hamburgian and Havelte sites characteristic of the continent from northern Germany eastwards. A degree of blurring is evident, however. On the continent, shouldered points with oblique distal truncations are found in a number of Late Magdalenian lithic assemblages (Jacobi 1980, 44); for example shouldered and obliquely truncated points appear in an otherwise Late Magdalenian assemblage at Le Tureau des Gardes 7 in the Paris Basin in which characteristic Magdalenian backed bladelets are rare (Weber 2006, Figure 4). Chronologically these cannot form a point of origin for the Hamburgian (Burdukiewicz 1989) but may rather presumably reflect a westwards diffusion of Hamburgian ideas, elements or people. In southern Germany sites with angle-backed and/or shouldered points appear by ~14.5 ka BP and seem related to both classic Hamburgian sites and to the English/Dutch 'Creswellian' (e.g. Street et al 2001; Baales and Street 1998). Atypical shouldered points appear in some continental assemblages otherwise classified as 'Creswellian' which contain obliquely truncated points, for example Siegerswoude II in The Netherlands (Kramer et al. 1985, Figure 9.5 and 9.15) and the Presle sites in Belgium (Dewez 1986, Figures 61.41 and 61.42).

With the exception of a possible Havelte point from Cathole, Wales (Figure 8.13: this was classed as a Font Robert Point by David 2007, Figure 2.4.1), British shouldered points and large tanged points are of Hamburgian form. They are rare overall in British assemblages but have been recovered in number and singularly from at least 20 open sites and from at least 5 caves (Gough's Cave, Jacobi 2004, Figure 23.25; Lynx Cave, Blore 1966; Robin Hood Cave, Campbell 1969, Figure 7.4; Mother Grundy's Parlour, Armstrong 1925, Figure 6.3 and 6.5; and Bob's Cave, Kitley, Devon, PP pers. obs.) and several more isolated finds and collections may belong to this group on technological grounds (Figure 8.14). Most are undated, as faunal associations are virtually unknown, and this has lead to a degree of ambiguity as to their specific chrono-cultural affiliation, although it is generally agreed that they relate in some way to the continental Hamburgian (e.g. Barton 1992; Conneller and Ellis 2007). The main distribution is in the south-east, although isolated examples of a large tanged point at Brumby Wood in Humberside and of a shouldered point at Salmonby, Lincolnshire, reveal a presence further north and provide a context for the recent discovery of the Howburn site in Scotland which may belong to this group (see below). The remarkably small size of most assemblages – far smaller than even those of the Late Magdalenian – is probably the result of a very brief presence

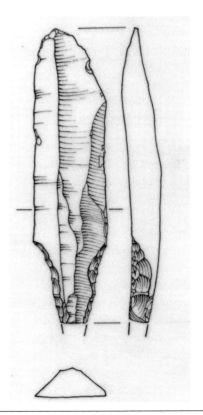

FIGURE 8.13
Possible Havelte Point from Cat Hole, Wales. (Drawing by Andrew David.)

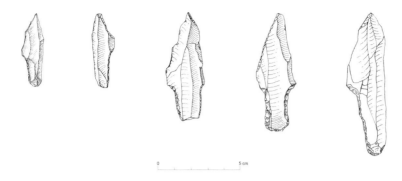

FIGURE 8.14
Shouldered points of Hamburgian affiliation. Left to right: Cranwich, Norfolk; Hengistbury Head, Dorset (three examples); Long Island, Portsmouth, Hampshire (right). (Redrawn by Jerneja Willmott from Jacobi and Martingell 1980, Mace 1959 and Draper 1962.)

in the country by small groups. Only the open-air site of Hengistbury Head could be seen as a repeatedly visited site, although the homogeneity of lithics at the site suggest that even this accumulated over a relatively brief period and there is no reason to see it as anything other than a seasonal aggregation site (Barton 1992; see Text Box 8.10). As it provides the most useful assemblage of this period, similar British sites are usually referred to as being of 'Hengistbury type', although we feel there are enough similarities to warrant use of the term Hamburgian in the sense of a culturally related but geographically peripheral group.

Text Box 8.10

HENGISTBURY HEAD, DORSET, AND SITES OF HENGISTBURY TYPE

Over 13,000 lithic artefacts of Late Upper Palaeolithic age have been recovered from the open-air location of Hengistbury Head near Bournemouth, Dorset, making it, in all probability, the largest British site of the period (Barton 1992). It is not surprising that the site was repeatedly visited, given its position on a promontory commanding a view of the Solent River at the point two south-flowing rivers – the Stour and Avon – converge (see Figure 1). Although fauna was not preserved on site, and TL dates on burnt flint and OSL of sediments from the site are so imprecise that they fail to clarify its chrono-cultural position, the presence of Late Magdalenian/Creswellian lithic elements as well as tanged and shouldered points are certainly consistent with placing the site in the Meiendorf or Older Dryas and in our opinion perhaps most consistent with a position around the transition between the two. The presence of straight-backed blades at Hengistbury (which are absent on continental Hamburgian sites) suggests it may represent Hamburgian influence or contact rather than the Hamburgian *sensu stricto* and, as with the closely preceding Late Magdalenian/Creswellian, it seems one is dealing with a regional variant of the continental norm.

FIGURE 1
Location map of Hengistbury Head. (From Barton 1992, courtesy Nick Barton.)

Text Box 8.10

Technology at Hengistbury was centred on the production of blades and 649 formal tools have been identified from surface collections and three separate excavations. These are dominated by backed blades and bladelets, endscrapers and burins. Of note are 30 refitted knapping sequences, of which 23 allow the refitting of flakes, blades and bladelets to their cores, often opposed-platform blade cores. Core H, for example, comprises 86 refitting artefacts of which 46 are flakes, many from core rejuvenation, and 28 blades including three crested examples (see Figure 2). Blades were typically 13–15 cm in length and bear plain and facetted platforms. A high-degree of refitting allowed the reconstruction of several knapping scatters on site which were consistent in size and shape and only moderately dispersed by post-depositional processes (see Figure 3). Thermally fractured stone slabs and burnt flints suggest the presence of hearths and the spatial distribution of a large amount of lithics suggests the use of one hearth as a focus of activity. The large number of backed blades and bladelets showing signs of burning probably reflect retooling and maintenance activities sitting around the fire. At least two distinct activity areas are recognisable at the site; a high proportion of backed tools, many of which are burnt, occur in the north-west area alongside burnt tools and sandstone fragments indicative of a hearth, whereas a high density of blade cores and débitage – and most refitting sequences – are noticeable in the south-east.

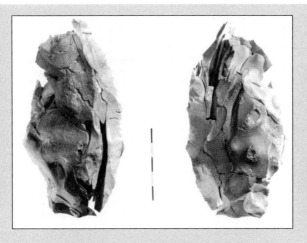

FIGURE 2
Core H refitting group.
(From Barton 1992, courtesy Nick Barton.)

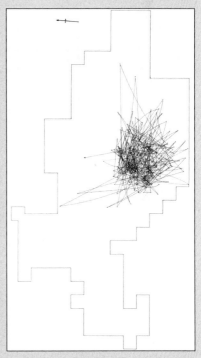

Text Box 8.10

A limited microwear analysis of artefacts revealed that endscrapers were used to scrape hide or softened antler, usually in hafts; backed blades were hafted and used to cut soft materials such as hide or meat; burins functioned as grooving tools, as scrapers and in two cases to scrape a medium or hard material and two bladelets seem to have functioned as projectile points. Fragments of worn ochre and pieces of flint cortex bearing engraved lines suggests other activities consistent with an aggregation site. Barton (1992, 200) has hypothesised that such an aggregation may have occurred during the autumn and/or spring migration of horse and reindeer.

FIGURE 3
Hengistbury knapping scatters. (From Barton 1992, courtesy Nick Barton.)

The location of Hamburgian sites in Britain parallels that of continental sites which are usually clustered around major river valleys (e.g. Bratlund 1996a; Fischer 2004). Certainly the two largest assemblages fit this pattern; the Brockhill open site is located on high ground overlooking a river (Smith 1924) and Hengistbury Head was located high on a promontory commanding excellent views of the Solent River basin where small tributaries flowed into it (Barton 1992, 84). A similar situation might be suggested for the shouldered point and associated blades from Long Island, Portsmouth (Draper 1962: Figure 8.14), a low hill overlooking the Solent River; while Barton (1992, 188–9) has drawn attention to a number of Late Upper Palaeolithic open-air findspots of probable Hengistbury type clustered around the Stour and Avon rivers in the Bournemouth area (including Hengistbury itself). Caves and rockshelters seem to have been used only fleetingly; shouldered points from Lynx Cave, Derbyshire (Blore 1966), Bob's Cave, Devon (PP pers. obs.) and Mother Grundy's Parlour at Creswell (Armstrong 1925 Figure 6) reveal the geographical extent of human presence at this time, although in each case the number of associated artefacts is minimal and each could reflect a single occupation of no intensity, possibly on the edge of the Hamburgian range. A small number of atypical shouldered points occur in the larger, Late Magdalenian assemblages from Gough's Cave (Jacobi 2004, 40) and Farndon Fields, Nottinghamshire (Garton and Jacobi 2009), as well as smaller Magdalenian sites such as Dead Man's Cave at Anston in South Yorkshire (Mellars 1969)

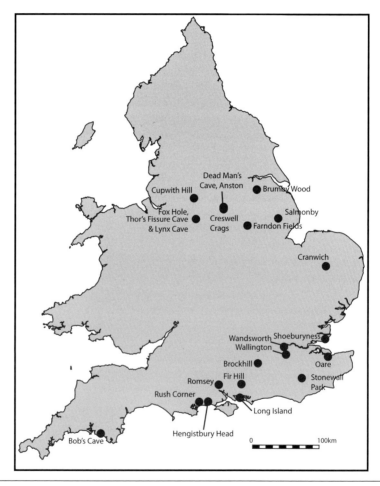

FIGURE 8.15
Distribution of sites and findspots with Hamburgian shouldered points.

although these are probably best seen as an earlier expression of these tool forms in Late Magdalenian assemblages similar, for example, to those at Les Tureau des Gardes 7 discussed above. Fischer (2004) has suggested that the spatial distribution of Hamburgian sites in northern Germany and southern Scandinavia suggests adaptations that were in part coastal, using major rivers such as the Elbe to travel between coastal areas and reindeer migration routes. The distribution of British shouldered points is certainly consistent with a similar activity, clustering in the south-east and perhaps reflecting the importance of the Thames as a route inland from Doggerland (Figure 8.15).

British Hamburgian assemblages are dominated by blade production on unipolar and bipolar cores and the *en éperon* technique is absent (Barton 1990). At La Sagesse Convent, Hampshire, and Hengistbury Head, retouched tools are very low in frequency (~3% and 2% of total assemblage respectively; Barton 1992; Conneller and Ellis 2007).

Other than points, *Zinken* vary in presence, being absent from Hengistbury yet present at Brockhill (Barton 1992, 183). Straight-backed points are present in some assemblages such as Hengistbury Head and La Sagesse Convent, Hampshire (Conneller and Ellis 2007). A certain number of *elements mâchurées* such as 'bruised blades' occur in the larger assemblages, which is of interest as they are thought to be characteristic of terminal Pleistocene/early Holocene Long Blade assemblages; they are present at Hengistbury Head and La Sagesse, both of which appear not to be mixed with later assemblages. Their presence should not be surprising; they occur, for example, in Paris Basin Late Magdalenian sites (P. Bodu pers. comm. to PP). A singular shouldered point was recovered from Fox Hole Cave, Derbyshire, apparently in association with two reindeer antler rods, a penknife point and fragmentary remains of reindeer, horse and a large bovid and in proximity to a hearth (Bramwell 1971). One of the rods can be clearly identified as a javelin foreshaft of a type known at the Hamburgian level at Stellmoor, Germany (Lund 1993) and there is no reason to believe that the second rod, while incomplete, was any different. Two similar rods have been recovered from Church Hole at Creswell, and all have been dated to ~14 ka BP (Hedges et al. 1989, 214; Hedges et al 1994, 339; see Text Box 8.4), which is in keeping with a Hamburgian attribution. Given the lack of any other Late Upper Palaeolithic material in Fox Hole it is tempting to interpret these finds – two lithic and two organic armatures – as weapon losses or discards during a brief hunting excursion. The view from outside the small cave is exceptional (Figure 8.16).

The Scottish Hamburgian

Recently, the geographical spread of the British Late Upper Palaeolithic has been significantly revised by the discovery of Howburn, Lanarkshire, a mixed lithic assemblage but containing elements that belong to the Hamburgian tradition (Ballin et al. 2010). Typologically Upper Palaeolithic products on grey flint and chert cluster in a restricted spatial area amidst a larger, plough-damaged scatter of material of different ages, which includes two tanged points, the probable tang of a third, opposed platform blade technology, three blades with *talons en éperon* (otherwise unknown in British material of this period or younger), several obliquely backed points, *Zinken,* and endscrapers on blades.

FIGURE 8.16
View from just above Fox Hole Cave, Peak District. (Photo courtesy Jon Humble.)

Ballin et al. (ibid.) draw parallels with sites in The Netherlands, northern Germany and southern Scandinavia; one tanged point is similar to classic Hamburgian shouldered points including examples from Hengistbury Head and from Cranwich, Norfolk (Jacobi and Martingell 1980), another is more obviously tanged and is similar to an example from the Hamburgian site at Vledder in The Netherlands ~600 km across Doggerland (Beuker and Niekus 1996, Figure 4). The grey flint on which many of the Hamburgian artefacts are produced is not local and it is interesting that the possible source for this is the Yorkshire Wolds ~300 km to the south and approximately half the distance to Vledder.

Behaviour and society during the British Hamburgian

Little other information is available for the British Hamburgian which is in essence comprised solely of lithics. On the basis of radiocarbon dated faunal remains one might expect a similar suite of mammalian resources to the preceding Late Magdalenian, although imprecision may mask more subtle taxonomic variation. All one can say at present is that the taxa represented in Britain at this time – if not in association with Hamburgian assemblages – is consistent with the notion that reindeer was an important resource, as on the continent (e.g. Bratlund 1996b; Kabaciński and Sobkowiak-Tabaka 2009). Large numbers of ochre fragments of various hues were recovered across the occupation area at Hengistbury Head, a few of which showed traces of utilisation. These include a crayon bearing marks indicative of it having been scraped against a hard material (Barton 1992, 136). Also at Hengistbury two flint artefacts – a small core and a flake – bear engraved marks on their cortical surfaces (ibid., 170). These fine, intersecting incisions extend as much as 35 mm across the surfaces of the pieces in fairly straight lines, resulting in a cross-hatch pattern likely to be deliberate. It is of interest that similar examples are known from the French, Belgian and German Late Magdalenian (ibid., 173).

As noted above, the absolute paucity of assemblages ascribable to the Hamburgian, their small size, and the lack of evidence of multiple occupations, suggests that the Hamburgian incursion into Britain was brief and peripheral. The distribution of sites contrasts with that of the Late Magdalenian; in this case no clustering of sites on the upland/lowland margins along the rivers Trent and Severn occurred. The pattern instead seems more regionalised, sporadic and perhaps focused more on a number of smaller rivers. Why it came to an end is of course unclear although radiocarbon measurements indicate another settlement break rather than a continuous development of the *Feder-messergruppen* in Britain. Presumably this was caused by the deteriorating conditions of the Older Dryas.

The Older Dryas: GI1d, ~14,090–14,010 BP, and the end of the British Hamburgian

Precise dating of the Older Dryas has proven difficult at the continental scale, with ages varying over ~400 radiocarbon years, either reflecting inter-regional time lag or different cold oscillations. All, however, suggest a duration of around two centuries (Walker 1995) and we follow the Greenland chronology here. On the continent, pollen reveals a reduction of trees and shrubs and an increase in plants of open and disturbed soils (ibid.) and in Ireland July temperatures of 11° C or below have been inferred (Walker et al. 1994). In Britain the northern Scottish glaciers were thicker and more extensive than during the succeeding Younger Dryas (Bradwell et al. 2008). In Folkestone, Kent, two phases of soil formation belonging to the Late Glacial Interstadial were separated by a brief period of erosion and deposition of chalky head (Preece 1994), surely evidence of the Older Dryas. At Lundin Tower a marked decline in birch was accompanied by a rise in willow and common sorrel (*Rumex acetosa*, Whittington et al. 1996). No evidence of human presence is known for this period; presumably the severe conditions brought Britain's brief incursions (or incursion) by Hamburgians to an end.

GI 1C–1A: THE ALLERØD, ~14,010 – 12,890 BP, AND THE CURVED-BACKED POINT COMPLEX

Conditions began to ameliorate once more ~14 ka BP, although coleoptera indicate that temperatures appear to have declined by at least 5° C around this time relative to the Meiendorf (Atkinson et al. 1987). Generally, the period is characterised as colder, although with more pronounced woodland. A slight temperature rise in parts of Britain at the close of the interstadial hint at more complex patterns (Walker et al. 1993), however, and in fact several climatic oscillations are reflected in pollen records, notably declines in arboreal pollen and corresponding rises in grasslands, although these short-lived oscillations are difficult to see in most biostratigraphic sequences (Walker 1995).

These may match the three warm peaks represented in the Greenland cores (GI 1c3, 1c1, 1a) separated by two colder oscillations (GI 1c2 and 1b). Evidence for the development of woodland in Britain is fairly compelling from north to south. At Lundin Tower, birch, and later juniper rise in frequency alongside a decline in willow (Whittington et al. 1996). At Low Wray Bay tree birch came to dominate, albeit in an open grass and fern environment with abundant docks and sorrels (*Rumex*, Pennington 1977). At Star Carr birch and juniper shrub-woodland rose once more from the relatively open conditions of the Older Dryas although this recovery was brief (Day 1995). Carpets of fen mosses replaced Allerød trees and sedges at Church Moss, Cheshire, where mean summer temperatures apparently did not fall below 10° C and began to rise in the latter half of the stadial (Hughes et al. 2000). Fossil caddisflies from locations along the River Trent reveal an environment cooler than today, with large river channels running over gravel and sand (Greenwood et al. 2003). Riparian woodland and in-stream vegetation such as aquatic mosses are indicated at Barrow-upon-Trent, whereas cut-off channels or oxbow lakes are revealed at Hemington. At Woolhampton, Berkshire, the levels of the river Kennet began to rise as a response to climatic deterioration (Collins et al. 1996). Pollen indicates damp grasslands on river bars, higher ground and areas of willow scrub and sedge-dominated wetlands and birch trees at the valley margins. At Hawes Water, closed woodland dominated by birch replaced common juniper woodland in the context of isotopic indications of temperature decline (Jones et al. 2002). At Condover, the latter half of the interstadial saw the development of open birch woodland, containing both tree and dwarf forms, juniper, poplar and willow (Allen et al. 2009). At Hawkes Tor, Cornwall, a wetland environment dominated by grasses and sedges in the second half of the interstadial (Brown 1977). Birch forest developed at Folkestone, Kent (Preece 1994).

The faunal record for the Allerød in Britain is relatively poor, although enough securely dated examples exist to demonstrate that it represents a cool, temperate climate. Mammoth are unrecorded, and seem to have become locally extinct within the Meiendorf (Lister 1991; Stuart 2005). Otherwise, mammalian species recorded for the Meiendorf persisted, although the record is so sparse this may conceal temporal or spatial patterning within the period, particularly in response to the intra-Allerød climatic oscilliations or spread of forest cover within it. Direct dates on fauna pertaining to the Allerød are available from Devon to Lancashire, and include arctic hare (Broken Cavern, Devon, Hedges et al. 1996); Reindeer (Torbryan Six cave, Devon, Dowel Cave, southern Peak District and Victoria Cave, North Yorkshire, Hedges et al. 1989); red deer (Hyaena Den, Somerset, Three Hole's Cave, Devon and Lynx Cave, Denbighshire, Hedges et al. 1992, 1996; Currant and Jacobi 2011) and aurochs (Kent's Cavern and Pixie's Hole, Devon; Lynx Cave, Denbighshire, and Kinsey and Victoria Caves in North Yorkshire: Hedges et al. 1988, 1998; Currant and Jacobi 2011). In all cases these accumulations probably reflect human exploitation. Reindeer and horse, for example, were found in association with harpoons at Sproughton, Suffolk (see below). It remains to be established whether horse survived into the Allerød: remains from Three Hole's Cave, Devon, may belong to this period (Hedges et al. 1989) although the record for this species is remarkably sparse (Kaagan 2000) and Currant and Jacobi believe it to be completely absent, at least during the period of maximum development of woodland. New additions to the resource base were the extinct giant deer *Megaloceros giganteus,* which has been recovered on the Isle of Man, and elk (*Alces alces*), which was present ~12.8–13.3 ka BP at Coniston Dib in the Yorkshire Dales (Hedges et al. 1992; Currant and Jacobi 2011). At nearby Poulton-le-Fylde, Lancashire, this species was hunted (see Text Box 8.7). Beyond this, direct evidence of survival strategies is lacking. Stable isotope analyses of human remains (MNI=3) from Kendrick's Cave, Clwyd, indicate a diet high in animal protein although ~30% of dietary protein was obtained from marine sources, probably mammals (Richards et al. 2005), a hint that the mobility of *federmessergruppen* was perhaps not as limited as has been assumed.

Allerød archaeology: continental comparisons

During the Allerød, Britain appears to have been occupied by groups using curved-backed points relating broadly to the 'Azilian' tradition of western and central Europe, including forms with two opposed points (*bipointes*) and those with a single point and a small tang (*monopointes* or *federmesser* – penknife points). The curved-backed point tradition – as with the barbed harpoons that are often associated with it – seems to have originated in southern France during the Meiendorf. They first appear in association with some of the latest-surviving reindeer, although probably spread northwards in the wake of the disappearance of this species as forests spread (Thévenin 1997). North of the Loire, Azilian points (*bipointes*) gave way to *monopointes/federmesser* which may be seen as weapon forms specifically adapted to the Northern European Plain (Schwabedissen 1954). In northern Germany and surrounding areas the Havelte phase Hamburgian was replaced by *Federmessergruppen* assemblages ~13.7–14 ka BP and, in France, curved-backed point assemblages replaced the Late Magdalenian a little before ~14 ka BP, which were then succeeded fairly rapidly by *Federmessergruppen* and less laminar technologies. A degree of chronological change is observable at the multi-stratified site of Le Closeau at Rueil-Malmaison in the Paris Basin, where occupation immediately prior to the Allerød was of a form similar to preceding Late Magdalenian sites and at which horse, red deer and wild boar were exploited and lion was still present (Bodu 1998).

In terms of its lithic scatters, habitation structures and lithic technology (production of large blades and long, elegant endscrapers) the sites reveal close connections between the *Federmessergruppen* and preceding Magdalenian with a rise of *bipointes* in particular through the three subsequent levels ascribed to the *Federmessergruppen.* Interestingly, in the lower *Federmessergruppen* level engraved striations appear on the cortex of several endscrapers, having been produced prior to the removal of the blanks from the core, a practise also found on the *Federmessergruppen* site of Hangest in northern France (Bodu 1995) and, as noted above, Hengistbury Head. If this is a good chronological marker it may suggest that the Hengistbury site, while not formally *Federmessergruppen,* was nevertheless close in time to such sites, although it is unclear whether this implies a close relationship between the two populations. In some areas, such as the Neuwied Basin in the Rhineland, the *Federmessergruppen* seem largely restricted to the later phases of the Allerød, that is, to ~12.9–13.3 ka BP (Baales and Street 1996, 1998, 84; Street et al. 2001). In later *Federmessergruppen* sites straight-backed *Malaurie* points appear, for example at Le Closeau (Bodu 1998) and Bad Breisig in the Rhineland (Baales et al. 2001) and a general decrease in the importance of burins can be seen (Hinout 1997). Generally speaking the use of flint became far more localised than in the preceding Magdalenian/ Hamburgian, although some long-distance transfers are still observable, and long blade cores were replaced by shorter, more tabular forms (e.g. Bodu 1995). Some sites contain tanged point forms, such as Norgervaart in The Netherlands, one tanged point from which is remarkably similar to that from Howburn, as noted above (Paddaya 1973).

Federmessergruppen in Britain: settlement history and settlement patterns

Broadly speaking, British sites are contemporary with the northern French *bipointe* sites, and with *Federmessergruppen* sites in France, Belgium, The Netherlands and Germany.

Directly dated, humanly modified faunal remains are rare and, given their imprecision, range across the entirety of the Allerød at 2σ. Conneller (2007, 218) has suggested that British *Federmessergruppen* occupation may have been restricted to the second half of the interstadial and, while the overall range of direct radiocarbon measurements on organic armatures (see below) may stretch back into the earlier Allerød ~13.8 ka BP, most of these – probably all – cluster between ~12.8 and 13.4 ka BP, reinforcing this suggestion. British sites dating to the Allerød cluster in the south and east and a marked diminution in the use of caves is noticeable, with most material deriving from open sites, possibly indicative of a shift away from horse in hunting strategies (Currant and Jacobi 2011).

At Torbryan Six Cave in the Torbryan Valley, Devon, a cut-marked reindeer dentary dated to ~12.8–13.2 ka BP (OxA-3894; Hedges et al. 1996, 398) was recovered from a remnant hearth. A curved-backed point was among a small and otherwise undiagnostic Late Glacial lithic assemblage in the same stratigraphic horizon as reindeer at Ossum's Cave in the southern Peak District (Jacobi 1987), although the reindeer seem to date to the Younger Dryas and, despite claims that they were exploited (Scott 1986; Bramwell et al. 1987), no cut-marks or other clear modifications exist. A small lithic assemblage including a curved-backed point was recovered from Pixie's Hole, Devon (Barton and Roberts 1996), the archaeological horizon containing a cut-marked aurochs bone and a partially burnt bone of the same species associated with an *in situ* hearth, both dating to ~13.2–14 ka BP (Hedges et al. 1998, 228).

Figure 8.17 shows the distribution of assemblages and single finds of curved-backed points and sites with humanly modified artefacts. Around 22 cave/rockshelter sites and 15 open findspots are known, largely, but not exclusively, south of Yorkshire. It should be noted that some curved-backed points may have been part of Late Magdalenian assemblages, as they are on the continent; they are apparently associated with obliquely truncated points at Nanna's Cave, Dyfed (David 2007, Figure 2.13) and with obliquely truncated points and *en éperon* technology at Hoyle's Mouth, Pembrokeshire, Aveline's Hole, Somerset and Bob's Cave, Devon (Jacobi 2004, 69). At Mother Grundy's Parlour, Creswell, they were recovered mixed with Late Magdalenian and Mesolithic lithics (Armstrong 1925; Figure 8.18) as they were at Gough's cave (Jacobi 2004). In some cases, however, small, exclusively curved-backed point assemblages do occur (e.g. at Priory Farm and Potter's Cave in Wales, David 2007), and in other cases they are demonstrably stratigraphically younger than assemblages containing Cheddar points and do provide reliable indications of Allerød activity. At Three Holes Cave a Late Magdalenian horizon with a hearth was stratified 15 cm below a horizon of burnt bones, a hearth and a small assemblage containing curved-backed points including *federmesser* and no diagnostic Late Magdalenian artefacts (Barton and Roberts 1996). Similar points were recovered

FIGURE 8.17
Distribution of sites with curved backed points/*federmesser*.

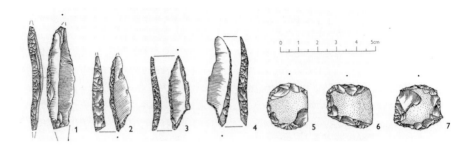

FIGURE 8.18
Federmessergruppen lithics from Mother Grundy's Parlour, Creswell Crags. 1 curved backed point, bi-point; 2–4 *federmesser* (penknife points); 5–7 thumbnail scraper. (From Pettitt and Jacobi 2009. Drawings by Hazel Martingell.)

from Broken Cavern, also in Devon, associated with arctic hare remains directly dated to ~13.1–13.5 ka BP (ibid., 256).

As with the Late Magdalenian there is no reason why the sparse archaeology of the Allerød in Britain need represent anything but the most marginal occupation, presumably deriving from the closest settled regions of the continent – Belgium and The Netherlands – where similar assemblages are known. It is of interest that the number of open-air finds is greater and cave finds fewer than in the preceding Meiendorf, suggesting a more peripheral interest in caves (Jacobi 1980, 45). Jacobi and Higham (2009) have noted that the majority of *federmessergruppen* artefacts derive from southeastern England, with even more fleeting occupation further to the west or north. The recent identification of a curved-backed point assemblage of 743 lithics initially thought to be Mesolithic from Kilmelfort south of Oban, Argyll, however, indicates that *federmessergruppen* activity, however sporadic, reached ~300 km north of the North Yorkshire sites which until recently furnished the most northerly evidence of activity at this time (Saville and Ballin 2009). Amidst a mixture of blade and flake technology the assemblage contains two curved-backed points, a point with two oblique truncations, one of which bears a mild concavity reminiscent of shouldered points, backed blades and bladelets at least two of which can be defined as straight-backed forms, angle- and dihedral burins, and side and endscrapers (Figure 8.19).

Unlike the preceding Late Magdalenian there seems to have been less of a focus on the Trent and Severn rivers and perhaps a more even spread of activities in the landscape. In this sense the British *Federmessergruppen* is more akin to the Hamburgian. Finds are particularly clustered in south-west Wales, the southern Peak District and environs and the Mendip area of Somerset (Jacobi 1980; Green and Walker 1991) although these collections are small and probably represent very brief moments in time. Several dated artefacts, however, attest the presence of humans in the north-west of England, probably the first major presence beyond brief activity in the Meiendorf (Jacobi et al. 2009) and perhaps attracted to the region by the presence of reindeer, on whose antler several of the dated artefacts are made (ibid.). A major assemblage of ~656 pieces has been excavated at Rookery Farm in Cambridgeshire which probably represents a small, specialised camp site positioned to exploit water and a local source of flint (see Text Box 8.11).

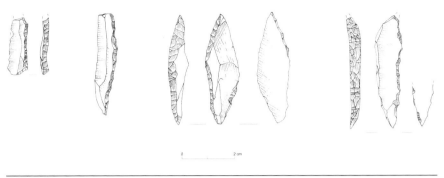

FIGURE 8.19
Backed bladelet and curved backed points from Kilmelfort Cave, Argyll. (Redrawn by Jerneja Willmott from Saville and Ball in 2009.)

ROOKERY FARM, CAMBRIDGESHIRE: AN OPEN-AIR CAMP OF THE *FEDERMESSERGRUPPEN*

The slopes above a pair of springs on the chalklands of South Cambridgeshire attracted brief Upper Palaeolithic settlement and, although collagen preservation in the site's sparse fauna (which included the incisor of a dog) was too poor to facilitate dating, this may be suspected on the basis of the site's lithic assemblage to have occurred during the Allerød (Conneller 2009). The presence of water and high-quality flint presumably made the area attractive.

Some 656 flint artefacts were recovered from an excavated area of some 43 m² and refitting suggests that the majority of the assemblage was recovered from a small, possibly single-episode occupation (see Figure 1). Although almost all of these are heavily patinated, two broken pieces reveal that the flint is black in colour and likely to derive from immediately local sources; the dominance of cortical flakes supports this notion. Much of the assemblage, which includes two cores and several crested blade, relates to the removal of flakes and blades from opposed platform cores. Refitting shows that one platform was preferentially employed, the other serving as a back-up if flaws were encountered or mistakes made. The resulting blades varied in size from 12 cm to 21cm. Seventeen formal tools were recovered, including three utilised blades, a truncation, a microlith and three *federmesser*.

Seventeen per cent of lithic artefacts >10 mm in length could be conjoined, forming three sequences of 9–12 elements each and several smaller refitting groups. One consists of an episode of blade removal, another of a series of platform preparation or maintenance removals, and a third (see Figure 2)

Text Box 8.11

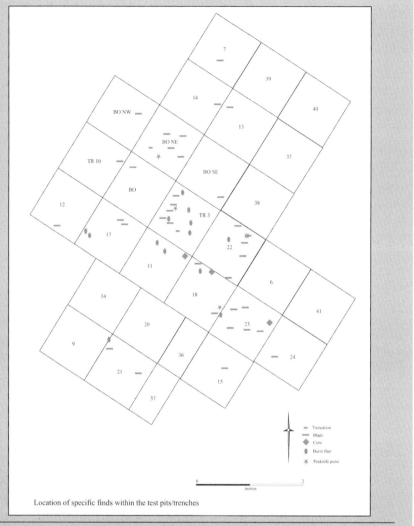

Location of specific finds within the test pits/trenches

FIGURE 1
Distibution of lithics at Rookery Farm. (Courtesy Chantal Conneller.)

FIGURE 2
Conjoined sequence of laminar removals from Rookery Farm. (Courtesy Chantal Conneller.)

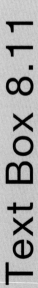

Text Box 8.11

a sequence of blades removed from a missing single-platform core. The sequence began with the removal of a platform maintenance flake across the 'top' of the piece (to the right of figure). Following this several blades were removed, which were not recovered from the site. The platform was rejuvenated once more and another small series of blades were removed, one of which was recovered. A third episode of platform maintenance then occurred, followed by a final series of blades and flakes, one blade among which bears an oblique truncation. Enough is present to show that blades and *federmesser* were manufactured on site and broken tools maintained, and the recovery of a blade 20 m south of its point of manufacture and a backed flake several metres to the east suggest the 'centripetal' distribution of knapped materials from their point of manufacture to specific activity areas on the site. As Conneller (2009, 180) has noted, the Rookery Farm tool-kit is very restricted and lacks the wider range of tools present on other sites of Allerød age, in keeping with a short-term use.

Federmesser and barbed harpoons: weapons of mass destruction

The size of British curved-backed points varies. Small, light forms from Kent's Cavern, King Arthur's Cave and Pin Hole bear impact damage consistent with a use as weapon tips, possibly arrowheads (e.g. Loftus 1982). Larger forms may have served other purposes although continental points thought to form arrowheads vary in size and most of these are likely to have tipped weapons rather than acted as knives. As with continental sites, large, well-made blades are typically lacking in these assemblages and local raw materials – often of poor quality – dominate. This suggests that more localised raw material strategies were employed by the *federmessergruppen* than preceding Late Magdalenian groups, although at Seamer Site C in the Vale of Pickering groups imported blades and finished tools on till flint obtained from Doggerland, implying high levels of transport and mobility even if most raw material use was local (Conneller 2007, 227). It is possible that the availability of high-quality flint in the relatively open conditions of the Meiendorf decreased as forest cover spread, forcing increasing use of poorer-quality, locally available materials.

A small amount of organic tools date to the Allerød, attesting the use of elk and (probably) reindeer antler and bone as raw materials. Barbed harpoons are conspicuously new elements in the armoury and are of uniserial and biserial forms similar to those from continental *Federmessergruppen* sites on the continent (e.g. Schwabedissen 1954, Table 84; Baales and Street 1996, Figure 7.2; Street et al. 2001, Figure 14; Cziesla and Pettitt 2003). An antler uniserially barbed harpoon dredged up from the Leman and Ower Bank in the North Sea attests to Allerød period activity on an area of Doggerland adjacent to 'mainland' Britain ~13.3–13.8 ka BP. A barbed harpoon on antler from Porth-y-Waen, Shropshire, dates to ~13.1–13.5 ka BP and a barbed bone harpoon from Lynx Cave, North Wales, to ~13.4–13.8 ka BP (Blore 1966; Bramwell 1977; Hedges et al. 1990a; Bronk Ramsey et al. 2002, 21). Two incomplete uniserially barbed points were found in association with an elk (*Alces alces*) skeleton in Allerød age deposits at High Furlong, Poulton-le-Fylde, Lancashire (Hallam et al. 1973; see Text Box 8.7). A biserially barbed antler harpoon from Victoria Cave, North Yorkshire, has been dated ~12.8 ka BP (Jacobi et al. 2009: Figure 8.20) and two uniserially barbed harpoons – one of antler and one of bone – found by the River Gipping at Sproughton, Suffolk, date to ~13.2–13.5 ka BP (Wymer et al. 1975; Jacobi et al. 2009). These were associated with the remains of reindeer and wild horse and reveal human activity in the context of a grass and shrub backswamp (Rose et al. 1980). Simple points have also been recovered which indicate the persistence of *sagaies*. A broken base of an antler artefact from Dowel Cave, Earl Sterndale, Derbyshire, dated to ~12.8–3.3 ka BP (Hedges et al. 1989, 214) probably falls into this category. A complete bone point from a fissure at Coniston Dib has been dated to ~12.8–13.3 ka BP (Hedges et al. 1992, 142) and a broken artefact of reindeer antler

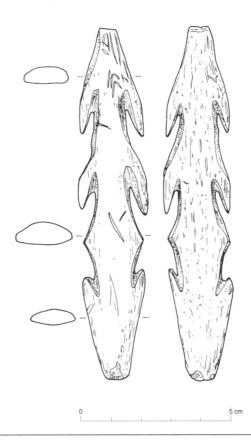

0   5 cm

FIGURE 8.20
Antler harpoon from Victoria Cave, near Settle, North Yorkshire. (Probably culturally *Feder-messergruppen*. Redrawn by Jerneja Willmott from Jacobi et al. 2009.)

from Kinsey Cave, North Yorkshire to the same range (Hedges et al. 1992, 142).

The harpoons from Leman and Ower, Poulton and Sproughton are of similar form, with tightly clustered barbs of either rhomboidal or 'beaked' form cut with criss-cross incisions oblique to the main axis of the pieces, which clearly persisted into the early Holocene on Britain and the continent (Clark 1954; Cziesla and Pettitt 2003). More broadly, the chronological range of British barbed bone/antler harpoons from the mid-Allerød to the early Holocene indicates that these forms, like Late Palaeolithic art forms (see below), had a long chronological currency into the Mesolithic (Cziesla and Pettitt 2003). Vang Petersen (2005) has made a convincing argument that Late Upper Palaeolithic and Mesolithic harpoons were associated with the hunting of reindeer, red deer and, particularly, elk in water. If frightened, these animals tend to run into water to escape, where they may be easily hunted from canoes, the harpoon facilitating the retention of the corpse and its transportation to dry land. The process may have been assisted by (domesticated) wolves, which have a particularly profound effect on elk. As both uniserial and biserial forms arose within the Late Magdalenian it is likely that they were originally associated with reindeer hunting and they are indeed associated with this species at La Madeleine (Thévenin 1997). Clearly these were exapted for the hunting of larger cervids as they spread with the Allerød forests.

Other aspects of British Federmessergruppen settlement

Two sites in the Vale of Pickering, North Yorkshire, have yielded lithic assemblages of *Federmessergruppen* attribution; Seamer C and K (Conneller 2007). Seamer site C is small and reveals little more than the use/discard of backed points and probably small-scale knapping in one area but Seamer site K is more extensive and provides Britain's only evidence of on-site spatial organisation for the period. Although in places mixed with succeeding Mesolithic material, at least three large and three smaller knapping scatters belong to this period (ibid.). Raw material use was predominantly local – as seems often to be the case for the *Federmessergruppen* – in this case of Yorkshire Wolds flints which can be sourced to the south of the Vale. These scatters were probably associated with hearths and include the reduction of a number of blade cores and activities involving the use and resharpening of burins.

Objects of art or functionally ambiguous items are rare on continental sites of the curved-backed points complex and Britain is no exception, the only such items from which are the 'tallies' of Kendrick's Cave (see Text Box 8.12). Small objects similarly engraved are known from continental sites, such as a schist fragment from Niederbeiber and an incised red deer tooth from Andernach-Martinsberg, both in the Neuwied Basin (Baales and Street 1996, Figure 8), although continental sites have also yielded carved animal outlines on Baltic amber. The decline in visible art is noticeable in the period and possibly relates to the growth of art on perishable materials such as wood and bark.

KENDRICK'S CAVE, CONWY, NORTH WALES: BRIEF OCCUPATIONS AND POSSIBLE FUNERARY ACTIVITY IN THE LATE GLACIAL INTERSTADIAL

This small cave on the limestone massif of Great Orme's Head in Conwy, North Wales, takes its name from a lapidary, Mr Kendrick, who occupied the cave in the nineteenth century. Early archaeological discoveries were found when he excavated sediments in order to enlarge the available space (Eskrigge 1880; Dawkins 1880) although the material is mixed and one has little confidence in the early excavations (e.g. David 2007). The Pleistocene material derived from a breccia and an underlying cave earth; bovid bones derived from the latter, but were in a different preservational state to the archaeology and human remains from the breccia. The Late Pleistocene fauna includes horse, bovid, brown bear and human remains, the latter of which may well derive from burials and for which a series of direct AMS radiocarbon dates indicate an Allerød age ~13.4–13.8 ka BP (Richards et al. 2005). The cave's small lithic assemblage, however, contains elements characteristic of Late Magdalenian occupation in the preceding Meiendorf, notably *en éperon* platforms (see main text). Direct AMS radiocarbon measurements on two bovid samples (indeterminate but probably aurochs), one of which bears cut-marks, confirm this attribution, indicating an age of ~14 ka BP (Jacobi and Higham 2011). It is possible that the direct measurements on human remains are understimates given that they were pretreated without the ultrafiltration method (Higham 2011), although one human mandible from the site was pretreated with this method and yielded a result statistically the same age as the others (Jacobi and Higham 2011b). It would seem, therefore, that the cave saw a brief occupation of Late Magdalenian attribution, followed by possible funerary activity in the succeeding Allerød.

The funerary activity is attested by the fragmentary remains of 'portions of the skeletons of four human beings' (Dawkins 1880, 157), although given the lack of information available today it is impossible to establish the exact nature of this activity. Stable isotope analyses of three of the individuals indicate a high animal protein diet as well as the derivation of ~30% of dietary protein from marine sources (Richards et al. 2005).

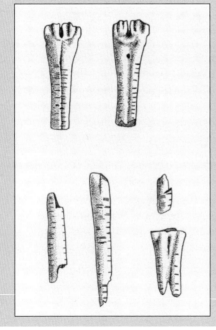

FIGURE 1

Engraved and ochred roe deer metapodia from Kendrick's Cave. (© Trustees of the British Museum.)

Text Box 8.12

Several engraved organic items belong to the Late Glacial inventory of the cave. Two upper canines of bear 'obtained from the same head [i.e. individual] . . . ornamented with transverse lines on the fang . . . [with] the extreme fang perforated for suspension' were apparently found in association with the human remains (Dawkins 1880, 157). Five ochred and incised 'tallies' of roe deer metapodia from the cave seem also to belong to the Allerød on the basis of a direct AMS radiocarbon measurement of ~13 ka BP on one of them (Richards et al. 2005). These may have functioned as personal ornamentation as well as for information storage, again possibly associated with the human remains. Eleven pierced and incised teeth of red deer and bovid and a horse mandible bearing chevron decoration complete the Late Glacial assemblage (Sieveking 1971). One of the teeth yielded a direct AMS measurement of Younger Dryas age and the mandible of terminal Pleistocene age (Richards et al. 2005) although these are likely to be underestimates and it is impossible today to establish their precise chrono-cultural attribution. Thus, although one cannot rule out an Early Holocene age for some of the material (Green and Walker 1991), a parsimonious interpretation would see these as all part of a small but homogeneous assemblage of personal ornamentation and *art mobilier*, possibly associated with the human remains (Pettitt and Bahn 2007). The chevrons engraved on the mandible are of note, as they parallel the appearance of similar motifs on the continent from this time, for example from the Ahrensburgian at Stellmoor (Rust 1943, Figure 21), a series of similar 'registers' of chevrons on an elk antler tine dated to Rusinowo in Pomerania, Poland (Kowalski and Płonka 2009) and herring bone engravings on a small stone plaquette from Zemono in Slovenia (Kavur and Petru 2003: see discussion in Pettitt and Bahn 2007).

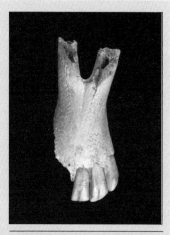

FIGURE 2
Horse maxilla with engraved chevron designs. (© Trustees of the British Museum.)

Text Box 8.12

GS1: THE YOUNGER DRYAS / LOCH LOMOND STADE, ~12,890–11,650 BP, AND EPI-AHRENSBURGIAN GROUPS

An abrupt and rapid climatic deterioration interrupted the Late Glacial amelioration between ~12.9 and 11.6 ka BP, with an initial temperature decline of ~6° C in Britain (Walker 1995). It is no surprise that *Federmessergruppen* appear to have abandoned Britain towards the end of the Allerød. During Greenland Stadial 1 there is much evidence of renewed glaciation in mountainous areas of Britain and associated perigla-cial phenomena more widely, chronologically tied at a number of sites by ^{14}C and [10]Be surface exposure ages (Golledge et al. 2007). A major ice field reoccupied most of the western Scottish Highlands and smaller glaciers developed on the Scottish mainland and islands, the southeast Grampians, Cairngorms, Snowdonia and elsewhere in north Wales, the Lake District, the Pennines and South Wales, as much by snowblow as direct precipitation (Jones and Keen 1993, 190; Mitchell 1996 and references therein; Benn 1997; Ballantyne 1997; 2007; Hughes 2009). The reglaciation of the Loch Lomond region has resulted in the term 'Loch Lomond Readvance' or 'Loch Lomond Stade (LLS)' for the period in Britain. Here, several large Alpine-style plateau glaciers devel-oped, the largest of which was ~55 km^2 (McDougall 2001). At Farmoor in the Upper Thames valley sediments of Younger Dryas age contained the beetle *Helophorus gla-cialis,* indicative of arctic environments (Briggs et al. 1985). Mean summer temperatures have been estimated for the LLS of ~4–5° C based on Scottish chironomid assemblages (Brooks and Birks 2000) but may occasionally have reached 10° C in lowland Britain based on coleoptera (Walker 1995); although these are conservative estimates of mean values, around which the real thermal extremes may have been considerably lower (see Chapter 2). The accumulation of glacially transported debris across the British Isles at this time suggests that the periglacial peaks of the Younger Dryas saw little precipitation but extensive permafrost (Harrison et al. 2008).

Rivers once more adopted aggrading, braided modes, suggesting nival regimes and trees disappeared from the landscape. It is possible that the earlier part of the stadial was drier than the later part with an early increase of steppic taxa such as cold-loving *Artemisia* (Lowe and Walker 1986). At Holderness the landscape was open, character-ised by dwarf birch, juniper and various herbs dominated by *Artemisia* (Jones and Keen 1993, 184). At Stafford, open conditions with some dwarf birch replaced coniferous woodland, although elsewhere in the region patches of willow and tree birch remained in an otherwise grass and sedge environment (Morgan 1973, 174). At Lundin Tower wil-low, sedges*,* and Brassicaceae dominate the pollen with a reduction of juniper and rise of *Artemisia, Rumex* and *Thalicrum* (meadowrue) all indicating a cold, unstable environ-ment (Whittington et al. 1996). At Low Wray Bay, an open, periglacial environment pre-vailed, dominated by grasses, sedges, *Artemisia* and *Rumex* (Pennington 1977). At Star Carr, *Artemisia* gradually increased in abundance, followed by *Rumex*, the sequence ending with a phase of instability and solifluction (Day 1995). At Bingley Bog in York-shire birch woodland was replaced by tundra (Keen et al. 1988) and at Hawes Water a significant decline in arboreal pollen and shift in the chironomid record indicates a thinning of birch woodland and expansion of grassland (Jones et al. 2002). By ~12.5 ka BP open ground taxa such as *Artemisia* dominate the pollen (ibid.). As conditions dete-riorated at Condover – long after the mammoths had disappeared – the frequencies of *Artemisia, Rumex* and *Thalictrum* increased in a generally open landscape (Allen et al. 2009). Church Moor reveals that birch forest was replaced by dwarf shrub and grass vegetation as far south as the Isle of Wight (Scaife 1987) and chalky head was deposited at Folkestone (Preece 1994).

Faunal remains from the Younger Dryas are relatively rare and typically attest to the severe conditions of the period. At Broken Cavern, Devon, cold, steppic conditions are indicated by the presence of steppe pika, *Ochotona pusilla*, and northern vole, *Microtus oeconomus*, the former also at Merlin's Cave in the Wye Valley (Hedges et al. 1996; Bronk Ramsey et al. 2002). Collared lemming *Dicrostonyx torquatus* was present at King Arthur's Cave in the Wye Valley (Bronk Ramsey et al. 2002). Mammals are largely confined to reindeer and horse and the only carnivore on record is wolf, in all an impoverished fauna apparently dominated by reindeer as one finds on the continent in southern Scandinavia, Germany, France, Belgium and Poland although with the presence of *Bos* in Germany (Street et al. 1994, 2001; Baales 1999; Brinch Petersen 2009). At Chelm's Coombe, Somerset, reindeer were accumulating between ~11.6 and 12.6 ka BP (Hedges et al. 1990a; Currant and Jacobi 2011) and have been recorded at nearby Sun Hole in Cheddar Gorge ~11.6–12. ka BP (Jacobi et al. 2009), Dead Man's Cave, South Yorkshire ~11.3–12 ka BP (Hedges et al. 1996) and Victoria Cave and Sewell's Cave in North Yorkshire ~11.6–12.8 ka BP and 12.6–12.8 ka BP respectively in a region where they had probably been calving since at least the Younger Dryas (Hedges et al. 1992; Lord et al. 2007; and see above). A Lyngby 'axe' of reindeer antler places the species at Earl's Barton in Northamptonshire ~11.6 ka BP, that is, at the Pleistocene/Holocene transition. A number of reindeer accumulated in Ossom's Cave in the southern Peak district between ~11.6 and 12.8 ka BP (Gowlett 1986a).[5] Most of these died between 10 and 11 months, suggesting that the region was a calving ground (Scott 1986; Bramwell et al. 1987) and further remains of reindeer from sites in the same valley, notably Elder Bush Cave, may relate to the same period (Bramwell 1964b). Horse are recorded at Chelm's Coombe ~11.8–12.6 ka BP (Hedges et al. 1990a), ~11.6–12.1 ka BP at Kendrick's Cave in north Wales (Gillespie et al. 1985; Jacobi and Higham 2011), Sewell's Cave ~12.6–12.8 ka BP (Lord et al. 2007) and ~11.6–12.4 ka BP at Three Ways Wharf, Uxbridge (Hedges et al. 1990b) where they were hunted (see Text Box 8.13). *Bos* was present at Sewell's Cave ~12.6 – 12.8 ka BP (Lord et al. 2007). Arctic hare are recorded at Merlin's Cave in the Wye Valley ~11.8–12.4 ka BP (Bronk Ramsey et al. 2002). Remains of a red deer from Elderbush Cave in the southern Peak District have been dated to 12.1–12.7 ka BP (Gowlett et al. 1986b), suggesting the presence of this species within the younger Dryas, although this measurement was made in the infancy of the Oxford radiocarbon laboratory and may be incorrect; one other measurement on this species is early Holocene in age and parsimoniously it is sensible to assume that this is the case for all red deer at the site. Wolf is recorded at Broken cavern, Devon (Hedges et al. 1996), and is inferred to be the main accumulating agent of reindeer, horse and *Bos* remains at Sewell's Cave at this time (Lord et al. 2007). Bear dominates the faunal assemblage of nearby Victoria Cave and seems to have been regionally abundant in the Craven area of North Yorkshire at this time (ibid.).

TERMINAL PLEISTOCENE REINDEER HUNTERS AT THREE WAYS WHARF, UXBRIDGE

The Colne River rises in Hertfordshire and flows southwards, joining the Thames at modern Staines in Surrey. It is a major tributary of the Thames and it is no surprise that it attracted Late Glacial groups. Excavations in the 1980s at Uxbridge, north-west Greater London, where it flows southwards, revealed several small scatters of lithics attributable to the Long Blade (Barton 1989) industries of the Late Glacial and Preboreal and Early Holocene Mesolithic industries (Lewis 1991; Lewis and Rackham 2011: see Figure 1). Two scatters – A and C East clearly belong to the former and were associated with reindeer and in the case of Scatter A, possibly horse. A comprehensive dating programme was not possible due to poor collagen preservation; no reindeer remains – the only species clearly associated with the Late Glacial lithics – were datable and results were only produced for horse, which has a questionable relationship to Scatter A. The few measurements on horse bones from Scatter A reveal an age straddling the Pleistocene/Holocene boundary ~12–9.3 ka BP, however imprecise, confirms the chronocultural position of the assemblage.

The Late Glacial material accumulated on a low slope close to the river atop the Late Pleistocene Colney Street Gravels. High ground to the east afforded long-distance views over the floodplain and presumably a nearby fording point facilitated the disadvantaging of reindeer in the hunt. By the Late Glacial a soil had developed on the gravels, supporting a boreal woodland dominated by pine and sedges. Flint and chert was obtained locally from the river's gravels, determining the relatively small size of most cores and blades.

Scatter A, probably not sampled completely, consists of 681 artefacts dominated by flakes and blades, in the form of two distinct low-density lithic scatters, the refitting of elements of which suggest minimal disturbance. These were associated with fauna, and the presence of burnt flints in the northern sub-scatter suggest the position of a hearth. Soft hammer percussion was used for blade production using the cresting technique on opposed platform cores and the main concern seems to have been to produce a relatively small amount of blades while maximising their possible length. Nineteen retouched tools included obliquely truncated microliths and informally retouched blades. The butchered remains of one or two adult reindeer were associated with this scatter and comprise almost entirely only the limbs. Clearly, these meaty elements were brought to the site from a nearby kill.

Over 15,000 lithic artefacts were recovered from Scatter C and, although a sizable proportion of these belong to Early Mesolithic Scatter C West, it was possibly to isolate the Late Glacial Scatter C East on numerous grounds and it seems larger than Scatter A. Technologically, the assemblage seems

Text Box 8.13

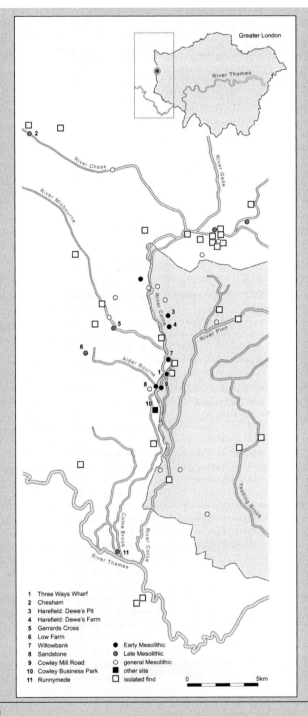

FIGURE 1
Location of the Three Ways Wharf site. (From Lewis and Rackham 2011 and courtesy John Lewis and Museum of London.)

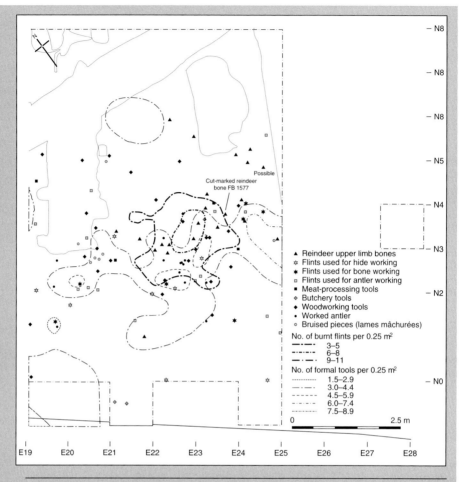

FIGURE 2

Distribution of used lithics, retouched tools and reindeer upper limb bones in Scatter C East. (From Lewis and Rackham 2011 and courtesy John Lewis and Museum of London.)

transitional between the concerns of Scatter A (few blades, maximising length) and Early Mesolithic Scatter C West (larger numbers of blades from smaller nodules, shorter in length). The assemblage includes bruised blades and

FIGURE 3

Refitting group 10. (From Lewis and Rackham 2011 and courtesy John Lewis and Museum of London.)

flakes (*lames et éclats mâchurés*; Barton 1986). As with Scatter A, burnt flints in Scatter C East suggest that activity was organised in proximity to a hearth and the relatively tight clustering of reindeer remains show a clear association with the processing of an adult male, adult female and immature male in this scatter (see Figure 2). Two antler fragments suggest that the site was occupied in winter or early spring. The meatier upper limb bones were clustered close to the presumed hearth and three artefacts with use-wear characteristic of cutting meat support the view that the meat was butchered, and presumably consumed, at the hearth-side and it is possible that the less-dense associations of Scatter A reflect similar activity. Refitted lithics – such as Refitting Group 10 (see Figure 3) reveal extensive decortication, the use of cresting on the backs and sides of cores to facilitate the removal of core tablets and several phases of blade removal often with the continuous adjustment of the platform through faceting. One of the blades from Group 10 is bruised. Use-wear analysis of lithics from Scatters A and C indicate that other activities at the site included cutting fish, whittling wood, boring antler and possibly scraping hide.

The Ahrensburgian and the Long-Blade assemblages: different cultural groups or facies differences?

On the neighbouring parts of the continent the Ahrensburgian clearly corresponds to this period and stretches from the Belgian Ardennes to east of the Oder river (Arts 1988; Kobusiewicz 2002; Brinch Petersen 2009). It is possible that the Ahrensburgian originated in the Bromme (Brommian) of southern Scandinavia; the two are certainly intimately related although this is a debatable point (cf. Kobusiewicz 2002 and Brinch Petersen 2009). Direct dates on humanly modified bone/antler artefacts clearly establish human presence in Britain during the severe conditions of the Younger Dryas although these are remarkably rare.[6] This picture also pertains for the continent; the number of archaeological sites declines in the Younger Dryas in France (e.g. Huchet et al. 1996; Petit and Thévenin 1996; Thévenin 1996; Hinout 1997), Germany (Street et al. 2001, 392; Pasda 2002), Belgium (Dewez 1986; Vermeersch et al. 1996; Crombé and Verbruggen 2003) and The Netherlands (Rensink 2002); southern Scandinavia seems to have been sparsely occupied (Eriksen 2002; Johansson 2002) and Ahrensburgian sites in Poland probably date only to the end of the stadial (Galiński 2007).

The few radiocarbon dates on materials indicative of human presence fall only at the Pleistocene/Holocene transition (Currant and Jacobi 2011) although one may infer a sparse human presence a little earlier on the basis of typological arguments and continental analogy. These are not inconsistent with a human dispersal only towards the end of the stadial. British sites of the Younger Dryas fall into two types; those with diagnostic Ahrensburgian tanged points (which may be referred to the Ahrensburgian) and those defined as Long-Blade assemblages (which may either be a distinct technomplex perhaps chronologically succeeding the Ahrensburgian or simply a facies of this). On the continent, direct radiocarbon dates for the Ahrensburgian show that it originated in the earlier part of the period although they typically cluster in the latter part of the Younger Dryas (Brinch Petersen 2009). Finds of Ahrensburgian points in Britain, although rare, indicate that groups of this cultural affiliation were operating in southeastern Britain in this period. They are lacking in sites further to the north and west despite evidence of contemporary human presence.

At least 28 sites in south-east England possess long blades accompanied by large cores and few retouched tools (Barton 1998; Barton and Dumont 2000). Sites of this type are noticeably absent from Wales (David 2007) although are found as far north as North Yorkshire (Conneller 2007). Where radiocarbon dates exist for English Long-Blade assemblages they straddle the Pleistocene–Holocene transition. Barton (1998) has defined Long-Blade sites on the basis of a dominance of blade production typically from opposed platform cores using direct soft hammer percussion and with the presence of blades >12 cm in length and the presence of a bruised element, particularly *lames mâchuré* (bruised blades: Barton 1986; Figure 8.21). Long-Blade sites on the

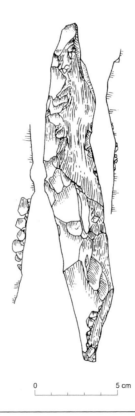

0 _____ 5 cm

FIGURE 8.21
Bruised blade from Avington VI. (Redrawn by Jerneja Willmott from Froom 2005.)

continent are thought to be part of a wider,Epi-Ahrensburgian, adaptation (Jöris and Thissen 1995) but Bodu and Valentin (1991) see examples from the Somme region and the Paris Basin – the Belloisian – as a distinct technocomplex.

Most Younger Dryas archaeology derives from open sites; findspots are few and in every case amount to extremely small numbers of artefacts. One might certainly infer that cave use vanished by the Younger Dryas – and possibly with the Late Magdalenian – and it is conceivable that human presence amounted to anything more than a few months towards the end of the period and possibly around the Pleistocene–Holocene transition as available radiocarbon dates suggest. A survey of directly dated human remains from the British Late Glacial and early Holocene has shown that, while dated examples exist for the Late Magdalenian and for the Early Mesolithic, they are absent for the Younger Dryas (Barton et al. 2003). Given the scarcity of Ahrensburgian archaeology this may simply relate to the infinitely small numbers of humans in the country at the time, although it may relate to changing mortuary practises in the context of more widespread changes in demographic patterns overall. In western Europe the number of open relative to enclosed sites rises for the first time in the Younger Dryas and Gamble et al. (2005) have interpreted this as reflecting a demand for larger camps that can be accommodated in caves in situations where human groups were aggregating in larger numbers that previously known. If this were the case it may explain the rarity of British Younger Dryas archaeology.

A parsimonious interpretation of the limited data than exist would see British Long-Blade assemblages as a *facies* of the Ahrensburian (e.g. Barton 1998). We believe that such a view is justifiable: long blades occur in a number of Ahrensburgian sites which are otherwise technologically consistent with Long-Blade assemblages in which Ahrensburgian points do not occur, such as at Avington VI in the Kennet Valley which also yielded backed bladelets and microliths (Barton and Froom 1986; Froom 2005; Figure 8.22).

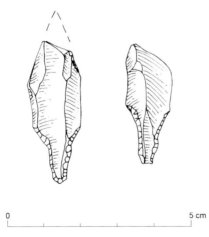

0   5 cm

FIGURE 8.22
Tanged points of Ahrensburgian type, from Avington VI, Berkshire. (Redrawn by Jerneja Willmott from Froom 2005.)

On the continent they also appear on sites otherwise classified as Ahrensburgian, such as at Stellmoor (Rust 1943) and Teltwisch (Barton 1991). A possible functional difference may explain their presence as they seem to have been used to work or 'chop' a hard material; Bodu (pers. comm. to PP) has suggested that they may have mainly been used to maintain hard hammers for direct percussion knapping. Froom (2005) suggested that Long-Blade assemblages accumulate preferentially in situations where good quality flint sources have been worked intensively and the two notions are not inconsistent. If this is the case one might see British examples of Ahrensburg Points – which usually occur alone or as part of very small assemblages – as reflecting hunting activities while long blades reflect lithic manufacture and maintenance.

Organic artefacts of Ahrensburgian attribution

The very small number of organic items dated to the Younger Dryas do not have lithic associations although are consistent with organic armatures found on Ahrensburgian sites on the continent. Two armatures were recovered from Victoria Cave, North Yorkshire (Figure 8.23). One, on reindeer antler dated to ~11.6–12.4 ka BP (Hedges et al.

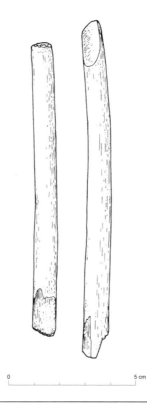

0   5 cm

FIGURE 8.23
Reindeer antler points from Victoria Cave, near Settle, North Yorkshire. (Redrawn by Jerneja Willmott from Garrod 1926.)

1992), although published as a point (Jackson 1945), bears the distal *rainure* (channel) of a javelin foreshaft (PP pers. obs.). It also bears a finely engraved series of chevrons which recall those on the horse mandible from Kendrick's Cave (see Text Box 8.12); they are so fine they resemble stitching (Pettitt and Bahn 2007). The other is a biserially-barbed antler harpoon dated to ~12.6 – 12.9 ka BP (Lord et al. 2007). This is clearly similar to continental Azilian and Ahrensburgian forms in that its barbs are slightly asymmetrical, and remarkably similar to an antler form from an Azilian assemblage at Pont d'Ambon as far south as the Dordogne (Célérier 1996 fig. 13.1). It bears a number of engraved lines on its distal point which bear a 'branching' pattern similar to examples from the continent (Pettitt and Bahn 2007, 35). The 'Lyngby Axe' was discovered at Earl's Barton, Northamptonshire (Figure 8.24). This takes the form of a reindeer antler beam on which the bez tine has been reduced to a bevelled and polished 'stump' reminiscent of the blade of an axe. It is, however, clear that this did not function as an axe or adze and, although the specific use of such forms is unclear, it does correspond to a category of artefacts known from northern Germany and southern Scandinavia (Cook and Jacobi 1994). Wear facets near the bez tine suggest the continuous rubbing of a loop of soft material across the shaft's circumference (ibid., 79) and in this the piece bears similarity to British Late Magdalenian *bâtons percé*. Might the two artefact categories have shared similar functions? If that were the case then Lyngby axes may be the Terminal Pleistocene equivalent of the earlier *bâtons*.

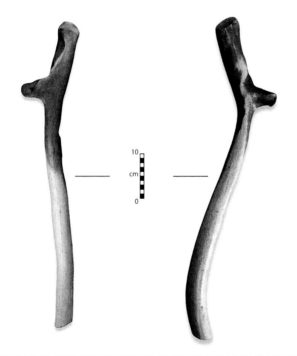

FIGURE 8.24

Reindeer antler 'Lyngby' Axe from Earl's Barton, Northamptonshire. (Photo © Trustees of the British Museum and with thanks to Jill Cook.)

The exploitation of animals during the Younger Dryas

Only the exploitation of reindeer and horse can confidently be identified for British Ahrens-burgian groups. Reindeer may have been exploited while calving in the Peak District as a number of their remains from Ossom's Cave, Staffordshire, show damage possibly indicative of exploitation. However, cut-marks are missing and the few diagnostic lithics from the cave seem to relate to a brief occupation by curved-backed point groups and not Ahrensburgians (Bramwell et al. 1987; Jacobi 1987). Possible cut-marks occur on reindeer and horse remains, also bearing wolf gnaw-marks, from Sewell's Cave in North Yorkshire which have been dated to this time (Lord et al. 2007), and a group of cut-marked horse bones were found in association with a tanged point at Flixton II in the Vale of Pickering (Conneller 2007, 221). By far the most informative site is Three Ways Wharf Site C in the valley of the River Colne at Uxbridge, Greater London (see Text Box 8.13), where both species were exploited by Long-Blade users. Although poor, the British data are consistent with continental evidence. Ahrensburgian groups were hunting reindeer (including calves) in the spring in the upland zone from the river Meuse in the west to the Oder in the east. Baales (1999) has suggested that reindeer spent the winter scattered widely in small groups on the Northern European Plain, aggregating at the beginning of spring to migrate as a large herd southwards to the upland areas of the Eifel, Ardennes and Westphalian highlands for calving. The traditional routes for this migration and, one assumes, the autumn migration back to winter grounds, were probably broad river and stream beds, in which intercept strategies could be employed by Ahrensburgians with a knowledge of the position of valley bottlenecks along these routes. It is possible that similar migrations and intercept strategies occurred in Britain; reindeer seem to have been widely distributed from the south-west to north of England and perhaps major rivers such as the Kennet, Severn and Trent functioned as traditional migration routes. The data are simply too poor to demonstrate this at present.

One can say very little else about human activity in Britain during the Younger Dryas. In the Vale of Pickering groups imported a ready-made set of tools supplemented by a small number of cores and blades derived from a source to the east in Doggerland (Conneller 2007, 227). Three knapping scatters have been identified at Seamer site C, each focused on a hearth, and at one two individuals seem to have been at work (ibid., 229: Figure 8.25). The fact that most lithic material seems to have been imported to the area contrasts strongly to the preceding *Federmessergruppen* occupation which used locally available Wolds flint. Conneller has interpreted the Ahrensburgian pattern as reflecting a concern with provisioning in a flexible mobility strategy in which targeted trips to lithic resources were unnecessary.

A discrete cluster of flakes, blades and bladelets, cores, microlithic points, scrapers, burins and knapping waste at Launde, in east Leicestershire, probably represents hearth-related activities in the open air (Cooper 2006) although, as with most assemblages, faunal associations are lacking here. The assemblage has been assigned to the Long Blade tradition and, as with Three Ways Wharf, projectiles with a concave distal oblique

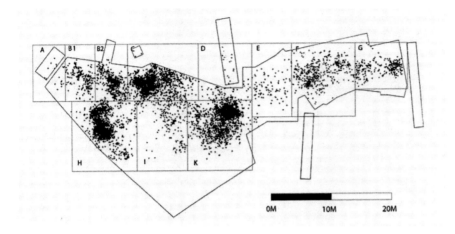

FIGURE 8.25
Knapping scatters at Seamer Site C. (Courtesy Chantal Conneller.)

truncation are notable for their similarities to those on continental Epi-Ahrensburgian sites. The few engraved bones and teeth of the period do have continental parallels (see Text Box 8.12).

It is debatable whether a degree of continuity is observable between the Late Pleistocene/Pre-Boreal Long Blade/Ahrensburgian sites and those of the Early Mesolithic. Barton (1991) has suggested that technological changes over the Pleistocene/Holocene transition lagged behind environmental change and thus adaptation to Postglacial woodlands occurred only gradually. This would certainly fit with an apparent gap of several radiocarbon centuries between the Long Blade sites and the earliest Mesolithic examples, although of course this may be exaggerated by a radiocarbon plateau around 10 ka (uncal) BP (e.g. Barton and Roberts 2004). The close resemblance between Terminal Pleistocene and earliest Holocene lithic assemblages certainly reinforces the view of a continuous cultural tradition across the transition (Barton 1989) although this is not to say that succeeding Mesolithic occupation was itself any more continuous or indeed spatially homogeneous (e.g. Reynier 1998).

Thus came to an end at least 700,000 years of culturally Palaeolithic intermittent hominin dispersals into Britain. If we return to where we began – in Greater London towards the close of the Pleistocene – we are reminded of the vast, untamed world at the edge of humanity's range and the miniscule hominin groups that would from time to time exploit the resources available when climate allowed. How lucky we are that they left an archaeology for us to recover; and what a privilege to unearth it once more. This rarity perhaps explains one of the most exciting characteristics of the Palaeolithic; that it can change overnight.

Notes

2 PIONEERS AT THE EDGE OF THE PLEISTOCENE WORLD: THE EARLIEST HOMININ VISITORS TO BRITAIN, ~1 MA–700 KA BP

1 Claims for occupation as early as 1.6–1.2 ma BP on the Taman Peninsula, Russia, at sites such as Bogatyri/Sinyaya Balka and Rodniki (Shchelinsky et al. 2010) are excluded from this discussion because, in true Short Chronology style, their anthropogenic origin is disputed (Doronichev and Golovanova 2010).

2 The age of the three sites in the Loire Basin are primarily based on ESR. While there is certainly no reason to suggest that humans did not reach this part of France by ~1 ma BP, the ages of the terrace sequences thus produced do not seem to conform to widely accepted models of terrace formation (e.g. Bridgland 1994; Bridgland and Allen 1996; Bridgland and Schreve 2001).

3 Given recent geological work on the Cromerian Complex, and the fact that the key East Anglian deposits originally assigned to it may extend back a further six Marine Isotope Stages comprising at least 200 ka, we wonder about the continued usefulness of this term. It is probably time that Quaternary specialists abandoned this bucket term in favour of a new nomenclature based around appropriate type sites – for example: the Boxgrove Interglacial, the Westbury Interglacial, the Cromerian Interglacial – although we realise that at present dating uncertainties render this difficult in many cases.

4 Although included here for completeness, terrace formations and contained artefacts marked * date to the period of more significant and sustained occupation of the later Middle Pleistocene.

5 Had Reid Moir not been such a confrontational and controversial figure prone to making rash and outlandish claims (White 2004), his findings in the Cromer Forest Bed – some of which represent genuine artefacts – may have been more readily accepted. This would certainly have changed the face of recent debates!

6 For us, it remains somewhat confusing that in other respects Parfitt and colleagues reject the Lee et al. model – see text Box 2.2.

7 It also means that for the late Early Pleistocene and early Middle Pleistocene Europe was probably home to at least two species of archaic human, possibly contemporaneously,

a likelihood that casts a different perspective on our understanding of lithic variability (Chapter 3); one that few modern scholars would have entertained merely a decade ago, but one which caused few conceptual problems for workers of the early twentieth century.

8 These are based on UK Meteorological Office figures for January and July 2010 (http://www.metoffice.gov.uk/). In Britain as a whole, temperatures of −23° C were recorded in Aberdeenshire, and −17° C in Cheshire. Greater variation is evident over longer times-cales. The mean winter temperature for England was 1.6° C, highlighting the problem of using means to determine experiential temperatures.

9 'The lower limit of the thermoneutral zone within which a mammal can regulate its core temperature solely by controlling its thermal conductance…as the temperature falls below this level homeostasis can only be maintained by increasing internal heat production, and incurring additional energetic costs associated with this increase in heat production.' (Aiello and Wheeler 2003, 148).

10 The minimum temperature at which an animal can maintain normal body temperature by raising its basal metabolic rate to its maximum sustainable level, in humans usually about three times normal BMR.

11 Revised estimates for the 'cold-adapted' Neanderthals – a lineage with over a million year pedigree in Eurasia – returned fairly moderate lower critical and minimum sustainable temperatures, of 25.3° C and 1.9° C, respectively (Aiello and Wheeller 2003); we would be surprised if the tolerance limits of the earliest occupants reached these levels.

3   LANDSCAPES OF HABIT: THE HOMININ OCCUPATION OF BRITAIN, ~550–300 KA BP

1 Two conventions exist for dividing the isotopic record. The first uses an alphanumerical record and denotes periods of time (e.g. 13a, 13b and 13c). The second uses a decimal system, each point of which identifies an isotopic event (e.g. 13.3, 13.2, 13.13, 13.11)

2 See Sier et al. (2010) for a discussion on the sometimes considerable time lag between events in the marine isotopic record and their expression in the terrestrial sequences.

3 This realisation has created a rather peculiar situation with regards to nomenclature. That is, the Hoxnian must now be equated only with MIS11c, leaving MIS11a outside its boundaries. To account for this, some workers have begun to refer to MIS11 as the Swanscombe Interglacial (McNabb 2007). We advocate extending the Hoxnian umbrella to include all of MIS11, referring perhaps to MIS11c as the Hoxnian *sensu stricto.*

4   BEHAVIOUR AND SOCIETY IN LOWER PALAEOLITHIC BRITAIN, ~550 KA–300 KA BP

1 See, for example, the number of 'handaxes' for sale on eBay at any given time.

2 Caddington, Biddenham and Kempston, Bedfordshire; Croxley Green, Hertfordshire; Furze Platt and Grovelands Pit; Lent Rise and Baker's Farm, Buckinghamshire; Station Pit, Kennett, Cambridgeshire; Gray's Thurrock and Purfleet Botany Pit, Essex; Cuxton, Sturry and Twydall in Kent; Lower Clapton, Stoke Newington Common and Geldeston Road, East London; and Savernake, Wiltshire. Keswick Norfolk, has 49.

3 It is true that the method can throw up the occasional anomalous classification – for example when a spur on the margin of an obvious pointed handaxe renders it metrically an ovate in Roe's terms (see Roe 1964, 1968a for full details), and beautifully made cordates may span both categories – but generally the method works well.

4   Potentially higher frequencies of humanly struck flake blanks may also account for the differences in cortex retention and refinement levels (but not scar counts), although only large nodules would have been capable of providing flake blanks of a size sufficient to produce these bifaces, again suggesting larger raw materials have been exploited in ovate assemblages.

5   White used Roe's indices for elongation and refinement, and both Roe and Bordes for shape (White 1996; White unpublished data). While for elongation and refinement the methods differ only in terms of where they place the denominator and the numerator in calculating the index (and produce reciprocal figures), there are subtle differences in the methods of calculating shape. Bordes' shape calculation is based on L/L1–4.574 x (midwidth/maxwidth); Roe's simply butt length/length although, when all handaxes used in this study were combined, the correlation between the two methods was r=–0.975. This suggests that by including the midwidth/maxwidth ratio to the calculation, Bordes actually added little to the overall picture of biface shape and that the key to understanding shape lies in the relative position of the maximum width.

6   Perhaps the diminutive size of Middle Palaeolithic handaxes (Chapter 6) therefore explains the demise of the Neanderthals...

7   Both of us have had flirtations with this agenda although, in neither case, thankfully, did the relationship develop fully.

8   McNabb's demonstration that variable frequencies of core working occur in the Acheulean, and that these are indistinguishable from Clactonian ones, means that arbitrarily dividing assemblages into the different cultural elements, especially those from secondary contexts (i.e. most of them) is a high dubious practice. As White (2000) notes, this means that supposed Clactonian elements at sites such as Purfleet Middle Gravel, Essex (Wymer 1985; Schreve et al. 2002); Fordwich, Kent (Smith 1933; Roe 1981); Highlands Farm, Oxfordshire (Wymer 1968); Denton's Pit, Reading (ibid.); Croxley Green, Hertfordshire (ibid.) and Yiewsley, Middlesex (Collins 1978) must be rejected as integral parts of the Acheulean assemblages there. The logical corollary of such a proposition, however, is that many assemblages deemed to be Acheulean may in fact be mixed, making techno-typological comparisons between many 'Acheulean' and 'Clactonian' assemblages fundamentally problematic.

5   NEANDERTHALS OF THE FOREST STEPPE: THE EARLY MIDDLE PALAEOLITHIC, ~325–180 KA BP

1   Bed numbers after Bridgland et al. 1995,; see Text Box 5.2.

2   Scott expresses some concern over the integrity of the surviving collections, which were collected by workmen from the Associated Portland Cement Company and are likely to originate from positions throughout the whole Baker's Hole sequence, although she goes on to propose that much of it really did originate from the Coombe Rock, as reported by Abbott (1911) and Smith (1911).

3   Although Scott (2010) infers that this is simply underrepresented and thus, against the evidence, characterises the technology as predominantly recurrent

4   Scott (2010) divides the Creffield Road material into two assemblages – the St Barnard's Area and the School Site assemblages – and notes a number of preservational and technological contrasts. These are considered together here because the two assemblages are from the same horizon, are only 60 m apart, are both fluvially disturbed and have an imperfect collection history. It is unlikely that the differences have any real behavioural meaning but rather relate to post-depositional channel activity at this terrace level.

5   Although, as shown in Text Box 5.5, the date of the site at Crayford is highly controversial.

6   Although, again, Crayford may belong to MIS65.

6 THE NEANDERTHAL STEPPE: LANDSCAPES AND HUMAN ENVIRONMENTS OF THE LATE MIDDLE PALAEOLITHIC, ~60–35 KA BP

1 This chapter represents an enhanced and edited version of White and Pettitt 2011.
2 Foot loading = the ratio of weight to surface area of the foot (cf. Guthrie 1990).

7 LIMINAL WORLDS: THE BRITISH EARLY UPPER PALAEOLITHIC AND THE EARLIEST POPULATIONS OF HOMO SAPIENS

1 This has in the past been translated by some as 'busked burin' – a meaningless term – or 'beaked burin' (e.g. Jacobi 2007, 298) and although the translation 'hooked (or hawk) nosed burin' is appropriate we follow here the convention of leaving this in the original French.
2 It is generally assumed that Font Robert points were hafted as armatures on spears and javelins. Microwear analysis of 20 Belgian examples suggested, however, a variety of functions amongst which, a use as projectile points was apparently absent (Otte and Caspar 1987). This does not, of course, rule out their use as armatures.

8 SETTLING THE NORTH-WEST FRONTIER: THE LATE UPPER PALAEOLITHIC, ~14.6–11.6 KA BP

1 We use the term 'domesticated wolf' rather than 'dog' to reflect the probability that the wolf was first domesticated as a weapon system (Musil 2000). It is also known from Bonn-Oberkassel at this time (Street 2002) where it is associated with a curved-backed point assemblages and the burial of two adults (Baales and Street 1998) and more widely in Europe at least by the Mid Upper Palaeolithic (Germonpré et al. 2012).
2 We recognise that this is a highly problematic area of research, and Meiendorf itself is not without problems, as De Clerk (2004) has noted. We make no assumptions about climatic, palaeovegetational or inter-regional correlations here, using the term Meiendorf simply to refer to GI1e, the first phase of interstadial warming during the Late Glacial Interstadial, prior to GI1d, the Older Dryas. In the sense we use it, it is simply a replacement for the term Bølling.
3 The site is sometimes referred to as Little Spinney, the name of the house in the garden of which the finds were made. It would certainly be worth further investigation of this locality and there is a very nice pub in the village.
4 Recently, one of us (PP) came across a second horse hyoid bearing regular groups of incised lines in the geological collections in Plymouth City Museum. It is marked 'Kent's Cavern' and seems to derive from the museum's wider collections from the cave, although no further information exists.
5 This site has also been called Ossum's Cave. It is not to be confused with Ossom's Eyrie Cave, which is located just above it and has yielded Holocene fauna (Bramwell et al. 1990).
6 Two uniserially barbed points from Sproughton, Suffolk, were initially dated to the Younger Dryas but recent redating of these using ultrafiltration has demonstrated that they are of Allerød age.

Bibliography

Aaris-Sørensen, K., Mühldorf, R. and Brinch Petersen, E. 2007. The Scandinavian reindeer (*Rangifer tarandus* L) after the last glacial maximum: time, seasonality and human exploitation. *Journal of Archaeological Science* 34: 914–923.

Abbott, W. J. L. 1911. On the classification of British Stone Age industries and some new, little known well marked horizons and cultures. *Journal of the Royal Anthropological Institute of Great Britain and Ireland* 41: 458–481.

Adamenko, O. M. and Gladiline, E. V. 1989. Korolevo, un des plus anciens habitats Acheuléens et Moustériens de Transcarpatie Soviétique. *L'Anthropologie* 93: 689–712.

Adler, D. S., Bar-Oz, G., Belfer-Cohen, A. and Bar-Yosef, O. 2006. Ahead of the game: Middle and Upper Palaeolithic hunting behaviours in the Southern Caucasus. *Current Anthropology* 47: 89–118.

Agustí, J., Blain, H.-A., Cuenca-Bescós, G. and Bailon, S. 2009. Climate forcing of the first hominid dispersal in Western Europe. *Journal of Human Evolution* 57: 815–821.

Agustí, J., Blain, H.-A., Furió, M., De Marfá, R. and Santos-Cubedo, A. 2010. The early Pleistocene small vertebrate succession from the Orce region (Guadix-Baza Basin, SE Spain) and its bearing on the first human occupation of Europe. *Quaternary International* 223/224: 162–169.

Aiello, L. C. and Dunbar, R. 1993. Neocortex size, group size and the evolution of language in the hominids. *Current Anthropology* 34: 184–193.

Aiello, L. C. and Key, C. 2002. The energetic consequences of being a *Homo erectus* female. *American Journal of Human Biology* 14: 551–556.

Aiello, L. C. and Wheeler, P. 1995. The expensive tissue hypothesis: the brain and the digestive system in human and primate evolution. *Current Anthropology* 36: 199–221.

Aiello, L. C. and Wheeler, P. 2003. Neanderthal Thermoregulation and the Glacial Climate. In: Van Andel, T. and Davies, W. (eds), *Neanderthals and Modern Humans in the European Landscape During the Last Glaciation: Archaeological Results of the Stage 3 project.* Cambridge: McDonald Institute, pp. 147–166.

Aldhouse-Green, S. H. R. 1988. Pontnewydd Cave: the selection of raw materials for artefact manufacture and the question of natural damage. In: MacRae, R. J. and Moloney, N. (eds),

Non-flint stone tools and the Palaeolithic Occupation of Britain. Oxford: BAR British Series 189, pp. 223–242.

Aldhouse-Green, M. and Aldhouse-Green, S. H. R. 2005. *The Quest for the Shaman: Shape-Shifters, Sorcerers and Spirit-Healers of Ancient Europe.* London: Thames and Hudson.

Aldhouse-Green, S. H. R. 1995. Pontnewydd Cave, Wales, a later Middle Pleistocene hominid and archaeological site: a review of stratigraphy, dating, taphonomy and interpretation. In: Bermúdez de Castro, J. M., Arsuaga, J.-L. and Carbonell, E. (eds), *Evolución Humana en Europa y los Yacimientos de la Sierra de Atapuerca.* Junta de Castilla y Leon, pp. 37–55.

Aldhouse-Green, S. H. R. 1997. The Paviland Research Project: the field assessment. *Archaeology in Wales* 37: 1–12.

Aldhouse-Green, S. H. R. 1998. The archaeology of distance: Perspectives from the Welsh Palaeolithic. In: Ashton, N., Healey, F. and Pettitt, P. (eds) *Stone Age Archaeology: Essays in Honour of John Wymer.* Oxford: Lithics Studies Society Occasional Papers 6, Oxbow Monograph 102, Oxbow Books, pp. 137–145.

Aldhouse-Green, S. H. R. 2000a. *Paviland Cave and the 'Red Lady': a Definitive Report.* Bristol: Western Academic and Specialist Press.

Aldhouse-Green, S. H. R. 2000b. Artefacts of ivory, bone and shell from Paviland. In: Aldhouse-Green, S. (ed.), *Paviland Cave and the 'Red Lady': a Definitive Report.* Bristol: Western Academic and Specialist Press, pp. 115–132.

Aldhouse-Green, S. H. R. 2000c. Climate, ceremony, pilgrimage and Paviland. The 'Red Lady' in his palaeoecological and technoetic context. In: Aldhouse-Green, S. (ed.), *Paviland Cave and the 'Red Lady': a Definitive Report.* Bristol: Western Academic and Specialist Press, pp. 227–246.

Aldhouse-Green, S. H. R. 2004. The Palaeolithic. In*:* Aldhouse-Green, M. and Howell, R. (eds), *The Gwent County History. Volume 1. Gwent Prehistory and Early History.* Cardiff: University of Wales Press, pp. 1–28.

Aldhouse-Green, S. H. R. and Pettitt, P. B. 1998. Paviland Cave: contextualizing the Red Lady. *Antiquity* 72: 756–772.

Aldhouse-Green, S. H. R., Scott, K., Schwarcz, H., Grün, R., Housley, R., Rae et al. 1995. Coygan Cave, Laugharne, South Wales, a Mousterian site and hyaena den: a report on the University of Cambridge excavations. *Proceedings of the Prehistoric Society* 61: 37–79.

Aldhouse-Green, S., Walker, E. and Peterson, R. in press. *Pontnewydd and the Elwy Valley Caves.* Cardiff: National Museums and Galleries of Wales.

Allen, J. R. M., Scourse, J. D., Hall, A. R. and Coope, G. R. 2009. Palaeoenvironmental context of the Late-Glacial woolly mammoth (*Mammuthus primigenius*) discoveries at Condover, Shropshire, UK. *Geological Journal* 44: 414–446.

Allen, L. G. and Gibbard, P. L. 1993. Pleistocene evolution of the River Solent of southern England. *Quaternary Science Reviews* 12: 503–528.

Allen, P. and White, M. 2004. The geology of Foxhall Road and the surrounding area. In: White, M. J. and Plunkett.S.J. (eds), *Miss Layard Excavates: a Palaeolithic site at Foxhall Road, Ipswich, 1903–1905.* Bristol: Western Academic and Specialist Press, pp. 55–75.

Allen, P., Bridgland, D., Haggart, B. A., Schwenninger, J.-L., White, M. and Wilson, D. 2007. Foxhall Road Ipswich. A Reinvestigation and Reassessment of an Archaeological Site. *Transactions of the Suffolk Naturalists' Society* 43: 26–30.

Allsworth-Jones, P. 1986. *The Szeletian and the Transition from the Middle to Upper Palaeolithic in Central Europe.* Oxford: Oxford University Press.

Andersen, K. K., Svensson, A., Johnsen, S. J., Rasmussen, S. O., Bigler, M., Rothlisberger, R.

et al. 2006. The Greenland ice core chronology 2005, 15–42 ka. Part 1: constructing the time scale. *Quaternary Science Reviews* 25: 3246–3257.

Andrews, P. and Fernández-Jalvo, Y. 2003. Cannibalism in Britain: taphonomy of the Creswellian (Pleistocene) faunal and human remains from Gough's Cave (Somerset, England). *Bulletin of the Natural History Museum, London* 58: 59–81.

Andrews, P., Cook, J., Currant, A. and Stringer, C. 1999. *Westbury Cave: the Natural History Museum Excavations 1976–1984.* Bristol: WASP.

Antoine, P., Coutard, J.-P., Gibbard, P., Hallegouet, B., Lautridou, J.-P. and Ozouf, J.-C. 2003. The Pleistocene rivers of the English Channel region. *Journal of Quaternary Science* 18: 227–243.

Antoine, P., Limondin Lozouet, N., Chaussé, C., Lautridou, J.-P., Pastre, J.-F., Auguste, P. et al. 2007. Pleistocene fluvial terraces from northern France (Seine, Yonne, Somme): synthesis, and new results from interglacial deposits. *Quaternary Science Reviews* 26: 2701–2723.

Antón, M., Galobart, A. and Turner, A. 2005. Co-existence of scimitar-toothed cats, lions and hominins in the European Pleistocene. Implications of the post-cranial anatomy of Homotherium latidens (Owen) for comparative palaeoecology. *Quaternary Science Reviews* 24: 1287–1301.

Antón, S. C. and Leigh, S. R. 2003. Growth and Life History in *Homo erectus*. In: Thompson, J. L., Krovitz, G. E. and Nelson, A. J. (eds), *Patterns of Growth and Development in the Genus Homo.* Cambridge: Cambridge University Press, pp. 219–245.

Antón, S. C. and Swisher, C. 2004. Early dispersals of *Homo* from Africa. *Annual Review of Anthropology* 33: 271–296.

Anzidei, A. P. and Huyzendveld, A. A. 1992. The Lower Palaeolithic site of La Polledrara di Cecanibbio (Rome, Italy). In: Herring, E., Whitehouse, R. and Wilkins, J. (eds), *Papers of the Fourth Conference of Italian Archaeology: New Developments in Italian Archaeology Part 1.* London: Accordia Research Centre.

ApSimon, A. M. 1986. Picken's Hole, Compton Bishop, Somerset: Early Devensian bear and wolf den, and Middle Devensian Hyaena Den and Palaeolithic site. In: Colcutt, S. N. (ed.), *The Palaeolithic of Britain and its Nearest Neighbours: Recent Trends.* Sheffield: University of Sheffield, pp. 55–56.

Armstrong, A. L. 1925. Excavations at Mother Grundy's Parlour, Creswell Crags, Derbyshire. *Journal of the Royal Anthropological Institute of Great Britain and Ireland* 55: 146–178.

Armstrong, A. L. 1928. Pin Hole excavations, Creswell Crags, Derbyshire. Discovery of an engraved drawing of a masked human figure. *Proceedings of the Prehistoric Society of East Anglia* 6: 27–29.

Armstrong, A. L. 1931–2. Excavations at Cresswell Crags, Derbyshire 1928–1934: The Pin Hole Cave. *Transactions of the Hunter Archaeological Society* IV: 178–184.

Armstrong, A. L. 1956. Report on the excavation of Ash Tree Cave, near Whitwell, Derbyshire, 1949 to 1957. *Derbyshire Archaeological Journal* 76: 57–64.

Arnold, N. S., van Andel, T. H. and Valen, V. 2002. Extent and Dynamics of the Scandinavian Ice Sheet during Oxygen Isotope Stage 3 (65,000–25,000 yr B.P.). *Quaternary Research* 57: 38–48.

Arts, N. 1988. A survey of Final Palaeolithic archaeology in the southern Netherlands. In: Otte, M. (ed.), *De la Loire de l'Oder. Les Civilisations du Paléolithique Final dans le Nord-Ouest Européen.* Oxford British Archaeological Reports International Series 444, pp. 287–356.

Arzarello, M., Marcolini, F., Pavia, G., Pavia, M., Petronio, C., Petrucci, M. et al. 2007. Evidence of early human occurrence in Europe: the site of Pirro Nord (Southern Italy). *Naturwissenschaften* 94: 107–112.

Arzarello, M., Marcolini, F., Pavia, G., Pavia, M., Petronio, C., Petrucci, M. et al. 2009. L'industrie lithique du site Pléistocène inférieur de Pirro Nord (Apricena, Italie du sud): une occupation humaine entre 1,3 et 1,7 Ma. *L'Anthropologie* 113: 47–58.

Arzarello, M. and Peretto, C. 2010. Out of Africa: the first evidence of Italian peninsula occupation. *Quaternary International* 223/224: 65–70.

Ashton, N. M. 1992. The High Lodge Flint Industries. In: N. M. Ashton, J. Cook, S. G. Lewis and J. Rose (ed.), *High Lodge; Excavations by G. de G. Sieveking 1962–68 and J. Cook 1988.* London: British Museum Press, pp. 124–163.

Ashton, N. M. 1998a. The technology of the flint assemblages. In: N. M. Ashton, S. G. Lewis and S. Parfitt (eds), *Excavations at the Lower Palaeolithic Site at East Farm, Barnham, Suffolk 1989–94.* London: British Museum Press, pp. 205–236.

Ashton, N. M. 1998b. The spatial distribution of the flint artefacts and human behaviour. In: N. M. Ashton, S. G. Lewis and S. Parfitt (eds), *Excavations at the Lower Palaeolithic site at East Farm, Barnham, Suffolk 1989–94.* London: British Museum Press, pp. 251–258.

Ashton, N. M. 2001. One step beyond. Flint shortage above the Goring Gap: the example of Wolvercote. In: Milliken, S., and Cook, J. (ed.), *A Very Remote Period Indeed: Papers on the Palaeolithic Presented to Derek Roe.* Oxford: Oxbow, pp. 199–206.

Ashton, N. M. 2002. Absence of humans in Britain during the last interglacial (oxygen isotope stage 5e). In: Roebroeks, W. and Tuffreau, A. (eds), *Le Dernier Interglaciaire et les occupations humaines du Palaeolithique moyen.* Lille: Centre d'Etudes et Recherches Préhistoriques, pp. 93–103.

Ashton, N. M. and McNabb, J. 1992. The interpretation and context of the High Lodge industries. In: Ashton, N. M., Cook, J., Lewis, S. G. and Rose, J. (eds), *High Lodge: Excavations by G. de G. Sieveking 1962–68 and J. Cook 1988.* London: British Museum, pp. 164–168.

Ashton, N. M. and McNabb, J. 1994. Bifaces in perspective. In: Ashton, N. M. and David, A. (eds), *Stories in Stones.* London: Lithic Studies Society (Occasional Paper 4), pp. 182–191.

Ashton, N. M. and McNabb, J. 1996. The flint industries from the Waechter excavation. In: Conway, B., McNabb, J. and Ashton, N. (eds), *Excavations at Barnfield Pit, Swanscombe, 1968–72.* British Museum Occasional Paper Number 94. London: British Museum, pp. 201–236.

Ashton, N. M. and Lewis, S. 2002. Deserted Britain: declining populations in the British Late Middle Pleistocene. *Antiquity* 76: 791–798.

Ashton, N. M. and White, M. 2003. Bifaces and raw materials: flexible flaking in the British Lower Palaeolithic. In: Dibble, H. L. and Sorresi, M. (eds), *Multiple Approaches to the Study of Bifacial Technologies.* Pennsylvania: University of Pennsylvania Museum Press, pp. 109–124.

Ashton, N. M. and Hosfield, R. 2009. Mapping the human record in the British early Palaeolithic: evidence from the Solent River system. *Journal of Quaternary Science* 25: 737–753.

Ashton, N., McNabb, J. and Parfitt, S. 1992a. Choppers and the Clactonian: A Reinvestigation. *Proceedings of the Prehistoric Society* 58: 21–28.

Ashton, N., Cook, J., Lewis, S. G. and Rose, J. 1992b. *High Lodge. Excavations by G. de G. Sieveking 1962–68 and J. Cook 1988.* London: British Museum Press.

Ashton, N. M. , McNabb, J., Irving, B., Lewis, S. and Parfitt, S. 1994a. Contemporaneity of Clactonian and Acheulean Flint Industries at Barnham, Suffolk. *Antiquity* 68: 585–589.

Ashton, N. M., Bowen, D. Q., Holman, J. A., Hunt, C. O., Irving, B. G., Kemp, R. A. et al. 1994b. Excavations at the Lower Palaeolithic site at East Farm, Barnham, Suffolk 1989–92. *Journal of the Geological Society of London* 151: 599–605.

Ashton, N. M., Lewis, S. G. and Parfitt, S. 1998. *Excavations at the Lower Palaeolithic Site at East Farm, Barnham, Suffolk 1989–94.* London: British Museum Press.

Ashton, N. M., Jacobi, R. and White, M. J. 2003. The dating of Levallois sites in west London. *Quaternary Newsletter* 99: 25–32.

Ashton, N. M., McNabb, J. and Bridgland, D. R. 2005a. Barnfield Pit, Swanscombe (TQ 598743). In Bridgland, D. R., Allen, P. and Haggart, B. A. (eds), *The Quaternary of the Lower Reaches of the Thames, Field Guide.* Quaternary Research Association: Durham, pp. 129–141.

Ashton, N. M., Lewis, S., Parfitt, S., Candy, I., Keen, D., Kemp, R. et al. 2005b. Excavations at the Lower Palaeolithic site at Elveden, Suffolk, UK. *Proceedings of the Prehistoric Society* 71: 1–61.

Ashton, N. M., Lewis, S., Parfitt, S. and White, M. 2006. Riparian landscapes and human habitat preferences during the Hoxnian (MIS 11) Interglacial. *Journal of Quaternary Science* 21: 497–506.

Ashton, N. M., Lewis, S. G., Parfitt, S., Penkman, K. E. H. and Coope, G. R. 2008a. New evidence for complex climate change in MIS11 from Hoxne, UK. *Quaternary Science Reviews* 27: 652–668.

Ashton, N. M., Parfitt, S. A., Lewis, S. G., Coope, G. R. and N., L. 2008b. Happisburgh Site 1 (TG388307). In: Candy, I., Lee, J. R. and Harrison, A. M. (eds), *The Quaternary of Northern East Anglia, Field Guide.* London: Quaternary Research Association, pp. 151–156.

Ashton, N. M., Lewis, S. and Hosfield, R. 2011. Mapping the human record: population change during the later Middle Pleistocene. In: Ashton, N., Lewis, S. and Stringer, C. (eds), *The Ancient Human Occupation of Britain.* Amsterdam: Elsevier, pp. 39–52.

Atkinson, T. C., Briffa, K. R. and Coope, G. R. 1987. Seasonal temperatures in Britain during the past 22,000 years, reconstructed using beetle remains. *Nature* 325: 587–592.

Audouze, F., Cahen, D., Keeley, L. H. and Schmider, B. 1981. Le site Magdalénien du Buisson Campin à Verberie (Oise). *Gallia Préhistoire* 24: 99–143.

Austin, L. 1994. Life and Death of a Boxgrove Biface. In: Ashton, N. M. and David, A. (ed.), *Stories in Stone.* London: Lithic Studies Society, pp. 119–126.

Austin, L. A., Bergman, C. A., Roberts, M. B. and Wilhelmsen, K. H. 1999. Archaeology of the excavated areas. In: Roberts, M. B. and Parfitt, S. A. (eds), *Boxgrove: A Middle Pleistocene Hominid Site at Eartham Quarry, Boxgrove, West Sussex.* London: English Heritage, pp. 313–378.

Averbouh, A. 2010. Utilisation et transformation des Matieres osseuses au Buisson Campin (Verberie, Oise). In: Zubrow, E., Audouze, F. and Enloe, J. (eds), *The Magdalenian Household: Unravelling Domesticity.* Albany: SUNY Press, pp. 76–90.

Avery, B. W., Bullock, J. A., Catt, J. A., Rayner, J. H. and Weir, A. H. 1982. Composition and origin of some brickearths on the Chiltern Hills, England. *Catena* 9: 153–174.

Baales, M. 1999. Economy and seasonality in the Ahrensburgian. In: Kozłowski, S. K., Gruba, J. and Zaliznyak, L. L. (eds), Tanged points cultures in Europe (Colloquum Lublin 1993). *Lubelskie Materialy Archeologiczne* 13: 64–75.

Baales, M. and Street, M. 1996. Hunter-gatherer behavior in a changing landscape: Allerød archaeology in the Central Rhineland, Germany. *Journal of Anthropological Research* 52: 281–316.

Baales, M. and Street, M. 1998. Late Palaeolithic backed-point assemblages in the Northern Rhineland: current research and changing views. *Notae Praehistoricae* 18: 77–92.

Baales, M., Grimm, S. and Jöris, O. 2001. Hunters of the 'Golden Mile'. The late Allerød Federmessergruppen site at Bad Breisig, Central Rhineland, Germany. *Notae Praehistoricae* 21: 67–72.

Bahn, P. and Pettitt, P. 2009. *Britain's Oldest Art: the Ice Age Cave Art of Creswell Crags.* London: English Heritage.

Bailey, S. E. and Hublin, J.-J. 2006. Dental remains from the Grotte du Renne at Arcy-sur-Cure (Yonne). *Journal of Human Evolution* 50: 485–508.

Baker, A. and Proctor, C. J. 1996. The caves of Berry Head. In: Charman, D. J., Newnham, R. M. and Groot, D. G. (eds), *Devon and East Cornwall, Field Guide.* London: Quaternary Research Association, pp. 147–162.

Baker, A., Smart, P. L. and Edwards, R. L. 2007. Mass spectrometric dating of flowstones from Stump Cross Caverns and Lancaster Hole, Yorkshire: palaeoclimate implications. *Journal of Quaternary Science* 11: 107–114.

Balch, H. E. 1914. *Wookey Hole: Its Caves and Cave Dwellers.* Oxford: Oxford University Press.

Balch, H. E. 1937. *Mendip, its Swallet Caves and Rock Shelters.* Wells: Clare, Son and Co. Ltd.

Balescu, S., Packman, S., Wintle, C. and Grün, R. 1992. Thermoluminescence dating of the Middle Pleistocene Raised Beach of Sangatte (Northern France). *Quaternary Research* 37: 390–396.

Ballantyne, C. K. 1997. Periglacial trimlines in the Scottish Highlands. *Quaternary International* 38/39: 119–136.

Ballantyne, C. K. 2007. The Loch Lomond readvance on north Arran, Scotland: glacier reconstruction and palaeoclimatic implications. *Journal of Quaternary Science* 22: 343–359.

Ballantyne, C. K., McCarroll, D., Nesje, A., Dahl, S. O. and Stone, J. O. 1998. The last ice sheet in north-west Scotland: reconstruction and implications. *Quaternary Science Reviews* 17: 1149–1184.

Ballantyne, C. K., Stone, J. O. and McCarroll, D. 2008. Dimensions and chronology of the last ice sheet in Western Ireland. *Quaternary Science Reviews* 27: 185–200.

Ballentine, C. K. and Harris, C. 1994. *The Periglaciation of Great Britain.* Cambridge: Cambridge University Press.

Ballin, T. B., Saville, A., Tipping, R. and Ward, T. 2010. An Upper Palaeolithic flint and chert assemblage from Howburn Farm, South Lanarkshire, Scotland; first results. *Oxford Journal of Archaeology* 29: 323–360.

Bamforth, D. B. 1988. Investigating microwear polishes with blind tests: the Institute results in context. *Journal of Archaeological Science* 15: 11–23.

Bar-Yosef, O. 1998. Early colonizations and cultural continuities in the Lower Palaeolithic of Western Asia. In: Petraglia, M. D. and Korisettar, R. (eds), *Early Human Behaviour in Global Context: the Rise and Diversity of the Lower Palaeolithic Record.* London: Routledge, pp. 225–279.

Bard, E., Hamelin, B., Arnold, M., Montaggioni, L., Cabioch, G., Faure, G. and Rougerie, F. 1996. Deglacial sea-level record from Tahiti corals and the timing of global meltwater discharge. *Nature* 382: 241–244.

Bard, E., Antonioli, F., Roestek, F., Silenzi, S. and Schrag, D. 2000. The penultimate glaciation as viewed from geochemical data measured in submerged speleothem from Italy. *EOS* 81 (19) Suppl: S79.

Barron, E., Van Andel, T. and Pollard, D. 2003. Glacial Environments II: Reconstructing the Climate of Europe in the Last Glaciation. In: Van Andel, T. and Davies, W. (eds), *Neanderthals and Modern Humans in the European Landscape During the Last Glaciation: Archaeological Results of the Stage 3 project.* Cambridge: McDonald Institute, pp. 57–78.

Barsky, D., Celiberti, V., Cauche, D., Grégoire, S., Lebègue, F., de Lumley, H. et al. 2010. Raw material discernment and technological aspects of the Barranco León and Fuente Nueva 3 stone assemblages (Orce southern Spain). *Quaternary International* 223/224: 201–219.

Barsky, D. and de Lumley, H. 2010. Early European Mode 2 and the stone industry from the Caune de l'Arago's archaeostratigraphical levels 'P'. *Quaternary International* 223/224: 71–86.

Barton, R. N. E. 1986. Experiments with long blades from Sproughton, near Ipswich, Suffolk. In: Roe, D. (ed.) *Studies in the Upper Palaeolithic of Britain and North-West Europe.* Oxford: British Archaeological Reports International Series 296, pp. 129–141.

Barton, R. N. E. 1989. Long Blade technology in southern Britain. In: Bonsall, C. (ed.), *The Mesolithic in Europe.* Edinburgh: John Donald, pp. 264–271.

Barton, R. N. E. 1990. The en éperon technique in the British Late Upper Palaeolithic. *Lithics* 11: 31–33.

Barton, R. N. E. 1991. Technological innovation and continuity at the end of the Pleistocene in Britain. In: Barton, R. N. E., Roberts, A. and Roe, D. A. (eds), *The Late Glacial in North West Europe: Human Adaptation and Environmental Change at the End of the Pleistocene.* London: Council for British Archaeology Research Report 77, pp. 234–245.

Barton, R. N. E. 1992. *Hengistbury Head, Dorset: Volume 2: The Late Upper Palaeolithic and Early Mesolithic Sites.* Oxford: Oxford University Committee for Archaeology Monograph 34.

Barton, R. N. E. 1997. *Stone Age Britain.* London: English Heritage and Batsford.

Barton, R. N. E. 1998. Long Blade technology and the question of British Late Pleistocene/Early Holocene lithic assemblages. In: Ashton, N., Healy, F. and Pettitt, P. (eds), *Stone Age Archaeology: Essays in Honour of John Wymer.* Oxford: Oxbow Monograph 102 and Lithic Studies Society Occasional Papers 6, pp. 158–164.

Barton, R. N. E. 1999. Colonisation and resettlement of Europe in the Late Glacial: a view from the western periphery. *Folia Quaternaria* 70: 71–86.

Barton, R. N. E. and Froom, F. R. 1986. The long blade assemblage from Avington VI, Berkshire. In: Collcutt, S. N. (ed.), *The Palaeolithic of Britain and its Nearest Neighbours: Recent Trends.* Sheffield: University of Sheffield, pp. 80–84.

Barton, R. N. E. and Roberts, A. J. 1996. Reviewing the British Late Upper Palaeolithic: new evidence for chronological patterning in the Lateglacial record. *Oxford Journal of Archaeology* 15: 245–265.

Barton, R. N. E. and Dumont, S. 2000. Recolonisation and resettlement of Britain at the end of the Last Glaciation. *Mémoires de Préhistoire d'ile de France* 7: 151–62.

Barton, R. N. E. and Roberts, A. 2004. The Mesolithic period in England: current perspectives and new research. In: Saville, A. (ed.), *Mesolithic Scotland and its Neighbours. The Early Holocene Prehistory of Scotland, its British and Irish Context, and some Northern European Perspectives.* Edinburgh: Society of Antiquaries of Scotland, pp. 339–358.

Barton, R. N. E., Jacobi, R. M., Stapert, D. and Street, M. J. 2003. The Late-Glacial reoccupation of the British Isles and the Creswellian. *Journal of Quaternary Science* 18: 631–643.

Bassinot, F. C., Labeyrie, L. D., Vincent, V., Quidelleur, X., Shackleton, N. J. and Lancelot, Y. 1994. The astronomical theory of climate and the age of the Brunhes–Matuyama magnetic reversal. *Earth and Planetary Science Letters* 126: 91–108.

Bateman, M. D. 1998. The origin and age of coversand in North Lincolnshire, UK. *Permafrost and Periglacial Processes* 9: 313–325.

Bateman, M. D., Buckland, P. C., Chase, B., Frederick, C. D. and Gaunt, G. D. 2008. The Late-Devensian proglacial Lake Humber: new evidence from littoral deposits at Ferrybridge, Yorkshire, England. *Boreas* 37: 195–210.

Bateman, M. D., Buckland, P. C., Whyte, M. A., Ashurst, R. A., Boulter, C. and Panagiotakopulou, E. 2011. Re-evaluation of the Last Glacial Maximum typesite at Dimlington, UK. *Boreas* 40(4): 573–584.

Bates, M. R. 1993. Quaternary Aminostratigraphy in northwestern France. *Quaternary Science Reviews* 12: 793–809.

Bates, M. R. 1998. Pleistocene sequences at Norton Farm, Chicester, West Sussex (TQ 9257 0655)1. In: Murton, J. B., Whiteman, C. A., Bates, M. B., Bridgland, D. R., Long, A. J., Roberts, M. B. and Waller, M. P. (eds), *The Quaternary of Kent and Sussex: Field Guide.* London: Quaternary Research Association, pp. 168–177.

Bates, M. R., Parfitt, S.A. and Roberts, M.B. 1997. The chronology, palaeogeography and archaeological significance of the marine Quaternary record of the West Sussex Coastal Plain, Southern England, UK. *Quaternary Science Reviews* 16: 1227–1252.

Bates, M. R., Parfitt, S. A. and Roberts, M. B. 1998. Later Middle and Upper Palaeolithic marine sediments of the West Sussex Coastal Plain: a brief review. In: Murton, J. B., Whiteman, C. A., Bates, M. R., Bridgland, D. R., Long, A. J., Roberts, M. B. and Waller, M. P. (eds), *The Quaternary of Kent and Sussex, Field Guide.* London: Quaternary Research Association, pp. 151–165.

Bates, M. R., Bates, C.R, Gibbard, P.L., MacPhail, R.I., Owen, F.J., Parfitt, S.A. et al. 2000. Late Middle Pleistocene deposits at Norton Farm on the West Sussex coastal plain, southern England. *Journal of Quaternary Science* 15: 61–89.

Bates, M. R., Keen, D. H. and Lautridou, J.-P. 2003. Pleistocene marine and periglacial deposits of the English Channel. *Journal of Quaternary Science* 18: 319–337.

Baumann, K.-H., Lackschewitz, K. S., Mangerud, J., Spielhagen, R. F., Wolf-Welling, T. C. W., Heinrich, R. et al. 1995. Reflection on Scandinavian Ice Sheet fluctuations in Norwegian Sea sedminets during the last 150,000 years. *Quaternary Research* 43: 185–197.

Baumann, W. and Mania, D. 1983. *Die Paläolithischen Neufunde von Markkleeberg bei Leibzig.* Berlin: VEB Deutscher Verlag der Wissenschaften.

Baumler, M. F. 1995. Principles and properties of lithic core reduction: implications for Levallois technology. In: Dibble, H. L. and Bar-Yosef, O. (eds), *The Definition and Interpretation of Levallois Technology.* Madison: Prehistory Press, pp. 11–23.

Bayliss, A., Bronk Ramsey, C., Cook, J. and van der Plicht, J. 2007. *Radiocarbon dates from samples funded by English Heritage under the Aggregates Levy Sustainability Fund 2002–4.* Swindon: English Heritage.

Bazely, R., Green, C. and McGregor, D. 1991. Excavation of an early prehistoric site at Creffield Road, Acton. *Transactions of the London and Middlesex Archaeological Society* 42: 17–31.

Beasley, M. J. 1987. A preliminary report on incremental banding as an indicator of seasonality in mammal teeth from Gough's Cave, Cheddar, Somerset. *Proceedings of the University of Bristol Spelaeological Society* 18: 116–128.

Beaumont, P. and Vogel, J. C. 2006. On a timescale for the past million years of human history in central South Africa. *South African Journal of Science* 102: 217–228.

Beck, M., Gaupp, R., Kamradt, I., Liebermann, C. and Pasda, C. 2007. Bilzingsleben site formation processes: geoarchaeological investigations of a Middle Pleistocene deposit: preliminary results of the 2003–2005 excavations. *Archäologisches Korrespondenzblatt* 37: 1–18.

Bee, T. W. 2001. Palaeolithic handaxes from the Lymm Valley, Lincolnshire. *Lithics* 22: 47–52.

Beets, D. J., Meijer, T., Beets, C. J., Cleveringa, P., Laban, C. and van der Spek, A. J. F. 2005. Evidence for a Middle Pleistocene glaciation of MIS 8 age in the southern North Sea. *Quaternary International* 133/134: 7–19.

Behre, K. E. 1992. Biostratigraphy of the Last Glacial Cycle. *Quaternary Science Reviews* 8: 25–44.

Bell, A. M. 1894. Palaeolithic remains at Wolvercote, Oxfordshire, I and II. *Antiquity* 30: 148–152, 192–198.

Bell, A. M. 1904. Implementiferous sections at Wolvercote (Oxfordshire). *Quarterly Journal of the Geological Society of London* 60: 120–132.

Bell, F. G. 1969. The occurrence of southern, steppe and halophyte elements in Weichselian (Last-Glacial) floras from Southern Britain. *New Phytologist* 68: 913–922.

Bell, F. G. 1970. Late Pleistocene floras from Earith, Huntingdonshire. *Philosophical Transactions of the Royal Society of London* B258: 347–378.

Bell, F. G., Coope, G. R., Rice, R. J. and Riley, T. H. 1972. Mid-Weichselian fossil-bearing deposits at Syston, Leicestershire. *Proceedings of the Geologists' Association* 83: 191–211.

Bello, S. M., Parfitt, S. A., Stringer, C. B. 2011. Earliest Directly-Dated Human Skull-Cups. *PLoS ONE* 6(2): e17026. doi:10.1371/journal.pone.0017026

Bellomo, R. V. and Kean, W. F. 1997. Evidence of hominid-controlled fire at the FxJj20 site complex, Karari Escarpment. In: Isaac, G. L. and Isaac, B. (eds), *Koobi Fora Research Project, (Vol. 5): Plio-Pleistocene Archaeology.* Oxford: Clarendon Press, pp. 224–233.

Benn, D. I. 1997. Glacier fluctuation in Western Scotland. *Quaternary International* 38/39: 137–147.

Bennett, K. D. 1983. Devensian Late-Glacial and Flandrian vegetational history at Hockham Mere, Norfolk, England. *New Phytologist* 95: 457–487.

Berger, G. W., Pérez-González, A., Carbonell, E., Arsuaga, J. L., Bermúdez de Castro, J. M. and Ku, T. L. 2008. Luminescence chronology of cave sediments at the Atapuerca paleoanthropological site, Spain. *Journal of Human Evolution* 55: 300–311.

Berger, T. D. and Trinkaus, E. 1995. Patterns of trauma among Neandertals. *Journal of Archaeological Science* 22: 841–852.

Bergman, C. A. and Roberts, M. B. 1988. Flaking Technology at the Acheulean Site of Boxgrove, West Sussex (England). *Revue Archaeologique de Picardie* 1/2: 105–113.

Bergman, C. A., Roberts, M.B., Colcutt, S. and Barlow, P. 1987. Refitting and spatial analysis of artefacts from Quarry 2 at the Middle Pleistocene site of Boxgrove, West Sussex, England. In: Cziesla, E., Eickhoff, S.,Arts, N. and Winter, D. (ed.), *The Big Puzzle; International Symposium on Refitting Stone Artefacts.* Bonn: Holos, pp. 269–279.

Bermúdez de Castro, J. M., Arsuaga, J. L., Carbonell, E., Rosas, A., Martinez, I. and Mosquera, M. 1997. A hominid from the lower pleistocene of Atapuerca, Spain: Possible ancestor to neanderthals and modern humans. *Science* 276: 1392–1395.

Bermúdez de Castro, J. M., Martinón-Torres, M., Robles, A. G. and Carbonell, E. 2010. New human evidence of the Early Pleistocene settlement of Europe, from Sima del Elefante site (Sierra de Atapuerca, Burgos, Spain). *Quaternary International* 223/224: 431–433.

Beuker, J. R. and Niekus, M. J. L. T. 1996. Verder met Vledder; rendierjagers aan de rand een ven. *Niewe Drentse Volksalmanak* 113: 91–129.

Beyries, S. 1987. *Variabilité de l'Industrie Lithique au Moustérien: Approche Fonctionelle sur Quelques Gisements Françaises.* Oxford: British Archaeological Reports International Series 328.

Bietti, A. and Grimaldi, S. 1995. Levallois débitage in Central Italy: technical achievements and raw material procurement. In: Dibble, H. L. and Bar-Yosef, O. (eds), *The Definition and Interpretation of Levallois Technology.* Madison: Prehistory Press, pp. 125–142.

Bignon, O. 2007. La faune du site Magdalénien de Ville-Saint-Jacques 'Le Tilloy' (sondage 'Brezillon'; Seine-et-Marne): perspectives comparatistes dans le Bassin Parisien. *Bulletin de la Société Préhistorique Française* 104: 237–243.

Bignon, O. 2009. Regional populations and exploitation of large herbivores in the Paris Basin during the Late Glacial: in search of an integrated model. In: Street, M., Barton, R. N. E. and

Terberger, T. (eds), *Humans, Environment and Chronology of the Late Glacial of the North European Plain.* Mainz: Verlag des Römisch-Germanischen Zentralmuseums, pp. 27–38.

Binford, L. R. 1979. Organization and formation processes: looking at curated technologies. *Journal of Anthropological Research* 37: 195–208.

Binford, L. R. 1981a. *Bones: Ancient Men and Modern Myths.* New York: Plenum Press.

Binford, L. R. 1981b. Behavioural Archaeology and the 'Pompeii Premise'. *Journal of Anthropological Research* 37: 195–208.

Binford, L. R. 1983. *In Pursuit of the Past: Decoding the Archaeological Record.* London: Thames and Hudson.

Binford, L. R. 1985. Human ancestors: changing views of their behaviour. *Journal of Anthropological Archaeology* 4: 292–327.

Binford, L. R. 1987a. Searching for camps and missing the evidence? In: Soffer, O. (ed.), *The Pleistocene Old World.* London: Plenum Press, pp. 17–31.

Binford, L. R. 1987b. Were there elephant hunters at Torralba? In: Nitecki, M. H. and Nitecki, D. V. (eds), *The Evolution of Human Hunting.* New York: Plenum Press, pp. 47–106.

Binford, L. R. 1989a. Isolating the transition to cultural adaptations: Behaviour. An organisational approach. In: Trinkaus, E. (ed.), *The Emergence of Modern Humans: Biocultural Adaptations in the Later Pleistocene.* Cambridge: Cambridge University Press, pp. 18–41.

Binford, L. R. 1989b. Science to seance, or Processual to 'Post-Processual' archaeology. In: Binford, L. R. (ed.), *Debating Archaeology.* San Diego: Academic Press, pp. 27–40.

Binford, L. R. 2001. *Constructing Frames of Reference. An Analytical Method for Theory Building Using Ethnographic and Environmental Data Sets.* Berkeley: University of California Press.

Binford, L. R. and Stone, N. M. 1986. Zhoukoudian: a closer look. *Current Anthropology* 27: 453–475.

Bischoff, J. L., Williams, R. W., Rosenbauer, R. J., Aramburu, A., Arsuaga, J. L., Garcia, N. et al. 2007. High-resolution U-series dates from the Sima de los Huesos hominids yields 600 + 00/ – 66 kyrs: implications for the evolution of the early Neanderthal lineage. *Journal of Archaeological Science* 34: 763–770.

Blair, K. G. 1923. Some coleopterous remains from the peat-bed at Wolvercote, Oxfordshire. *Transactions of the Royal Entomological Society of London* 71: 558–563.

Bleed, P. 1986. The optimal design for hunting weapons: maintainability or reliability. *American Antiquity* 51: 737–747.

Blezard, R. G. 1966. Field Meeting at Aveley and West Thurrock. *Proceedings of the Geologists' Association* 77: 273–276.

Blockley, S. P. E., Donahue, R. and Pollard, A. M. 2000. Radiocarbon calibration and Late Glacial occupation in northwest Europe. *Antiquity* 74: 112–121.

Blockley, S. P. E., Blockley, S. M., Donahue, R. E., Lane, C. S., Lowe, J. J. and Pollard, A. M. 2006. The chronology of abrupt climate change and Late Upper Palaeolithic human adaptation in Europe. *Journal of Quaternary Science* 21: 575–584.

Blore, J. D. 1966. The excavation of Lynx Cave 1962–1964. *Peakland Archaeological Society Newsletter* 21: 17–19.

Bocherens, H., Billiou, D., Mariotti, A., Patou-Mathis, M., Otte, M., Bonjean, D. et al. 1999. Palaeoenvironmental and palaeodietary implications of isotopic biogeochemistry of last interglacial Neanderthal and mammal bones in Scladina Cave (Belgium). *Journal of Archaeological Science* 26: 599–607.

Bocherens, H., Billiou, D., Mariotti, M., Toussaint, M., Patou-Mathis, M. Bonjean, D. et al. 2001.

New isotopic evidence for dietary habits of Neanderthals from Belgium. *Journal of Human Evolution* 40: 497–505.

Bocherens, H., Drucker, D. G., Billiou, D., Patou-Mathis, M. and Vandermeersch, B. 2005. Isotopic evidence for diet and subsistence pattern of the Saint-Césaire I Neanderthal: review and use of a multi-source mixing model. *Journal of Human Evolution* 49: 71–87.

Bodu, P. 1995. Un gisement à ferdermesser sur les bords de la Seine: Le 'Closeau' à Rueil-Malmaison (Hauts-de-Seine). *Bulletin de la Société Préhistorique Française* 92: 451–455.

Bodu, P. 1998. Magdalenians-Early Azilians in the centre of the Paris Basin: a filiation? The example of Le Closeau (Rueil-Malmaison, France). In: Milliken, S. (ed.), *The Organisation of Lithic Technology in Late Glacial and Early Postglacial Europe.* Oxford: British Archaeological Reports International Series 700, pp. 131–147.

Bodu, P. 2004. Datations absolues sur les sequences archéologiques tardiglaciaires du sud du Bassin Parisien. In: Valentin, B., Bodu, P. and Julien, M. (eds), *Habitats et Peuplements Tardiglaciaires du Bassin Parisien.* Nanterre: Équipe Ethnologie Préhistorique, pp. 175–177.

Bodu, P. and Valentin, B. 1991. L'industrie à pieces mâcherées de Donnemarie-Dontilly (Seine-et-Marne, France): un faciès tardiglaciaire inédit dans le Basin Parisien. *Préhistoire Européenne* 1: 15–34.

Boëda, E. 1986. *Approche technologique du concept Levallois et évaluation de champ d'application.* Unpublished PhD Thesis, Université de Paris.

Boëda, E. 1995. Levallois; A volumetric recontruction, methods, a technique. In: Dibble, H. L. and Bar-Yosef, O. (eds), *The Definition and Interpretation of Levallois Technology.* Madison: Prehistory Press, pp. 41–68.

Boëda, E. 2001. Détermination des unités techno-fonctionnelles de pièces bifaciales provenant de la couche acheuléenne C'3 base du site de Barbas. In: D. Cliquet (ed.), *Les industries á outils bifaciaux du Paléolithique Moyen d'Europe occidentale.* Liège: Études et Recherches Archéologiques de l'Uiversité de Liège, pp. 51–76.

Boëda, E., Geneste, J. M. and Meignen, L. 1990. Identification de chaînes opératoire lithiques du Paléolithique ancien et moyen. *Paléo* 2: 43–80.

Bogin, B. 2003. The Human Pattern of Growth and Development in Paleontological Perspective. In: Thompson, J. L., Krovitz, G. E. and Nelson, A. J. (eds), *Patterns of Growth and Development in the Genus Homo.* Cambridge: Cambridge University Press, pp. 15–44.

Boismier, W., Schreve, D. C., White, M. J., Robertson, D. A., Stuart, A. J., Etienne et al. 2003. A Middle Palaeolithic site at Lynford Quarry, Mundford, Norfolk: Interim statement. *Proceedings of the Prehistoric Society* 69: 315–324.

Bond, G., Broecker, W. D., Johnsen, S., McManus, J., Labeyrie, L., Jouzel, J. et al. 1993. Correlations between climate records from North Atlantic sediments and Greenland ice. *Nature* 365: 143–147.

Bond, G. C. and Lotti, R. 1995. Iceberg discharges into the North Atlantic on millenial timescales during the last glaciation. *Science* 267: 1005.

Bonifay, E. and Vandermeersch, B. (eds) 1991. *Les Premier Européens,* Paris: Editions du C.T.H.S.

Bordes, F. 1950a. L'évolution buissonnante des industries en Europe occidentale. Considérations théoretiques sur le paléolithique ancien et moyen. *L'Anthropologie* 54: 393–420.

Bordes, F. 1950b. Principes d'une méthode d'étude des techniques de débitage et de la typologie du Paléolithique ancien et moyen. *L'Anthropologie* 54: 19–34.

Bordes, F. 1953. Essai de classification des industries Moustériennes. *Bulletin de la Societé Préhistorique Française* 50: 457–466.

Bordes, F. 1961. *Typologie du Paléolithique Ancien et Moyen.* Paris: CNRS.

Bordes, F. 1971. Physical evolution and technological evolution in Man. *World Archaeology* 3: 1–5.

Bordes, F. 1979. Comment on Ohel (1979). *Current Anthropology* 20: 714.

Bordes, F. 1984. *Leçons sur le Paléolithique, Tome II.* Paris: CNRS.

Boreham, S., and Gibbard P.L. 1995. Middle Pleistocene Hoxnian Stage interglacial deposits at Hitchin, Hertfordshire, England. *Proceedings of the Geologists' Association* 106: 259–270.

Bosinski, G. 1967. *Die Mittelpaläolithischen Funde im Westlichen Mitteleuropa.* Köln: Fundamenta Reihe A/4.

Bosinski, G. 1995. Stone Artefacts of the European Lower Palaeolithic: A short note. In: Roebroeks, W. and Kolfschoten, T. V. (eds), *The Earliest Occupation of Europe.* Leiden: University of Leiden, pp. 263–268.

Bosinski, G., d'Errico, F. and Schiller, P. 2001. *Die Gravierten Frauendarstellung von Gönnerdorf (Der Magdalénien Fundplatz Gönnerdorf Vol. 8).* Stuttgart: Franz Steiner.

Bosselin, B. and Djindjian, F. 1988. Un essaie de structuration du Magdalénien français à partir de l'outillage lithique. *Bulletin de la Société Préhistorique Française* 85: 304–331.

Bosselin, B. and Djindjian, F. 1994. La chronologie du Gravettien Française. *Préhistoire Européene* 6: 77–115.

Boswell, P. G. H. and Moir, J. R. 1923. The Pleistocene deposits and their contained Palaeolithic Flint Implements at Foxhall Road, Ipswich. *Journal of the Royal Anthropological Institute* 53: 229–262.

Boulton, G. and Hagdorn, M. 2006. Glaciology of the British Isles ice sheet during the last glacial cycle: form, flow, streams and lobes. *Quaternary Science Reviews* 25: 3359–3390.

Boulton, G. S., Jones, A. S., Clayton, K. M. and Kenning, M. J. 1977. A British ice-sheet model and patterns of glacial erosion and deposition in Britain. In: Shotton, F. W. (ed.), *British Quaternary Studies: Recent Advances.* Oxford: Clarendon Press. 231–246.

Bourillet, J. F., Reynaud, J. Y., Baltzer, A. and Zaragosi, S. 2003. The 'Fleuve Manche': the submarine sedimentary features from the outer shelf to the deep-sea fans. *Journal of Quaternary Science* 18: 261–282.

Bowen, D. Q. (ed.) 1999. *A Revised Correlation of Quaternary Deposits in the British Isles.* London: Geological Society.

Bowen, D. Q., Rose, J., McCabe, A. M. and Sutherland, D. G. 1986. Correlation of Quaternary glaciations in England, Ireland, Scotland and Wales. *Quaternary Science Reviews* 5: 229–340.

Bowen, D. Q., Hughes, S.A., Sykes, G.A.and Miller, G.H. 1989. Land-sea correlations in the Pleistocene based on isoleucine epimerization in non-marine molluscs. *Nature* 340: 49–51.

Bowen, D. Q., Phillips, F. M., McCabe, A. M., Knutz, P. C. and Sykes, G. A. 2002. New data for the last Glacial Maximum in Britain and Ireland. *Quaternary Science Reviews* 21: 89–101.

Bowman, S. G. E. 1993. Thermoluminescence dating of the Lower Industry. In: Singer, R., Gladfelter, B. G. and Wymer, J. J. (eds), *The Lower Paleolithic Site at Hoxne, England.* Chicago: University of Chicago Press, pp. 208–210.

Brain, C. K. and Sillen, A. 1988. Evidence from the Swartkrans cave for the earliest use of fire. *Nature* 336: 464–466.

Bradwell, T., Fabel, D., Stoker, M., Mathers, H., McHargue, L. and Howe, J. 2008. Ice caps existed throughout the Lateglacial Interstadial in northern Scotland. *Journal of Quaternary Science* 23(5): 401–407.

Bramwell, D. 1959. The excavation of Dowel Cave, Earl Sterndale, 1958–9. *Derbyshire Archaeological Journal* 79: 97–109.

Bramwell, D. 1963. The third report on Fox Hole Cave, High Wheeldon. *Peakland Archaeological Society Newsletter* 19: 10–12.

Bramwell, D. 1964a. The fourth report on Fox Hole Cave, High Wheeldon. *Peakland Archaeological Society Newsletter* 20: 8–12.

Bramwell, D. 1964b. The excavations at Elder Bush Cave, Wetton, Staffs. *North Staffordshire Journal of Field Studies* 4: 46–59.

Bramwell, D. 1971. Excavations at Foxhole Cave, High Wheeldon, 1961–1970. *Derbyshire Archaeological Journal* 91: 1–19.

Bramwell, D. 1977. Report on work at Fox Hole for season 1974. *Peak Archaeological Society Bulletin* 30: 4–8.

Bramwell, D., Scott, K., Stuart, A. J. and Cook, J. 1987. Ossom's Cave, Staffordshire: a study of its vertebrate remains and Late Pleistocene environments. *Staffordshire Archaeological Studies* 4: 25–59.

Bramwell, D., Yalden, D. and Yalden, P. E. 1990. Ossom's Eyrie Cave: an archaeological contribution to the recent history of vertebrates in Britain. *Zoological Journal of the Linnean Society* 98: 1–25.

Brandon, A. and Sumbler, M. G. 1991. The Balderton Sand and Gravel: pre-Ipswichian cold stage fluvial deposits near Lincoln, England. *Journal of Quaternary Science* 6: 117–138.

Brantingham, P., Kuhn, S. L. and Kerry, K. (eds) 2004. *The Early Upper Palaeolithic beyond Western Europe*. Berkeley: University of California Press.

Bratlund, B. 1996a. Archaeozoological comments on Final Palaeolithic frontiers in South Scandinavia. In: Larrson, L. (ed.), *The Earliest Settlement of Scandinavia and its Relationship with Neighbouring Areas*. Acta Archaeologica Lundensia 24, pp. 23–33.

Bratlund, B. 1996b. Hunting strategies in the Late Glacial of Northern Europe. A survey of the faunal evidence. *Journal of World Prehistory* 10: 1–48.

Bratlund, B. 1999. Taubach Revisited. *Jahrbuch des Romish-Germanischen Zentralmuseums Mainz* 46: 61–174.

Brauer, A., Endres, C. and Negendank, J. F. W. 1999. Lateglacial calendar year chronology based on annually laminated sediments from Lake Meerfelder Maar, Germany. *Quaternary International* 61: 17–25.

Bray, P. J., Blockley, S., Coope, G. R., Dadswell, L. F., Elias, S. A., Lowe, J. J. et al. 2006. Refining mutual climatic range (MCR) quantitative estimates of palaeotemperature using ubiquity analysis. *Quaternary Science Reviews* 25: 1865–1876.

Breuil, H. 1926. Palaeolithic Industries from the beginning of the Rissian to the beginning of the Würmian glaciation. *Man* 116: 176–179.

Breuil, H. 1932. Les industries a éclats du Paléolithique ancien I: Le Clactonien. *Préhistoire* 1: 148–157.

Breuil, H. 1937. Les subdivisions du Paléolithique Supérieur et leur signification. *Congrès International d'Anthropologie et d'Archéologie Préhistoriques: Compte rendu de la XIVe session, Genève 1912*.

Breuil, H. and Koslowski, L. 1931. Études des stratigraphie paléolithique dans le nord de la France, la Belgique et la Angleterre. *L'Anthropologie* 41: 449–488.

Breuil, H. and Koslowski, L. 1932. Études des stratigraphie paléolithique dans le nord de la France, la Belgique et la Angleterre. *L'Anthropologie* 42: 27–47, 291–314.

Breuil, H. and Koslowski, L. 1934. Études des stratigraphie paléolithique dans le nord de la France, la Belgique et la Angleterre. *L'Anthropologie* 44: 249–290.

Brewer, S., Guiot, J., Sánchez-Goñi, M. F. and Klotz, S. 2008. The climate in Europe during the Eemian: a multi-method approach using pollen data. *Quaternary Science Reviews* 27: 2303–2315.

Briant, R. M., Bates, M. R., Schwenninger, J.-L. and Wenban-Smith, F. F. 2006. An optically stimulated luminescence dated Middle to Late Pleistocene fluvial sequence from the western Solent Basin, southern England. *Journal of Quaternary Science* 21: 507–523.

Bridgland, D. R. 1994. *Quaternary of the Thames.* London: Chapman and Hall.

Bridgland, D. 1996. Quaternary river terrace deposits as a framework for the Lower Palaeolithic record. In: Gamble, C., and A.J. Lawson. (ed.), *The English Palaeolithic Reviewed.* Wessex: Trust for Wessex Archaeology. 24–39.

Bridgland, D. R. 2001. The Pleistocene evolution and Palaeolithic occupation of the Solent River. In: Wenban-Smith, F. F. and Hosfield, R. T. (eds), *Palaeolithic Archaeology of the Solent River.* London: Lithic Studies Society Occasional Paper 7. 15–25.

Bridgland, D. R. 2003. The evolution of the River Medway, S.E. England, in the context of Quaternary palaeoclimate and the Palaeolithic occupation of NW Europe. *Proceedings of the Geologists' Association* 114: 23–48.

Bridgland, D. R. 2006. The Middle and Upper Pleistocene sequence in the Lower Thames: a record of Milankovitch climatic fluctuation and early human occupation of southern Britain. *Proceedings of Geologists' Association* 117: 281–305.

Bridgland, D. R. 2010a. The record from British Quaternary river systems within the context of global fluvial archives. *Journal of Quaternary Science* 25: 433–446.

Bridgland, D. R. 2010b. The record from British Quaternary river systems within the context of global fluvial archives. *Journal of Quaternary Science* 25: 433–446.

Bridgland, D. R. and Harding, P. 1986. An attempt to relocate the 'Wolvercote Channel' in a railway cutting adjacent to Wolvercote brick pit. *Quaternary Newsletter* 48: 12–16.

Bridgland, D. R. and Harding, P. 1989. Investigations at Gaddesden Row Brickpit, Hertfordshire. *Quaternary Newsletter* 59: 2–4.

Bridgland, D. R. and Harding, P. 1993. Middle Pleistocene Thames terrace deposits at Globe Pit, Little Thurrock, and their contained Clactonian industry. *Proceedings of the Geologists' Association* 104: 263–283.

Bridgland, D. R. and Harding, P. 1995. Lion Pit tramway cutting, West Thurrock (TQ 598783). In: Bridgland, D. R., Allen, P. A. and Haggart, B. A. (eds), *The Quaternary of the Lower Reaches of the Thames, Field Guide.* London: Quaternary Research Association, pp. 217–229.

Bridgland, D. R. and Allen, P. 1996. A revised model for terrace formation and its significance for the lower Middle Pleistocene Thames terrace aggradations of north east Essex, U.K. In: Turner, C. (ed.), *The Early Middle Pleistocene in Europe.* Rotterdam: Balkema, pp. 121–134.

Bridgland, D. R. and Schreve, D. C. 2001. River terrace synchrony with long-term climatic fluctuation; supporting mammalian evidence from southern Britain. In: Maddy, D., Macklin, M. and Woodward, J. (ed.), *Proceedings of the Fluvial Archive Group Conference, Cheltenham, September 1998.* Rotterdam: Balkema, pp. 229–248.

Bridgland, D. R. and Westaway, R. 2008. Preservation patterns of Late Cenozoic fluvial deposits and their implications: Results from IGCP 449. *Quaternary International* 189: 5–38.

Bridgland, D. R., Gibbard, P. L. and Harding, P. 1985. New information and results from recent excavations at Barnfield Pit, Swanscombe. *Quaternary Newsletter* 46: 25–39.

Bridgland, D. R., Allen, P., Currant, A. P., Gibbard, P. L., Lister, A. M., Preece, R. C. et al. 1988. Report of Geologists' Association field meeting in north-east Essex, 22—24 May, 1987. *Proceedings of the Geologists' Association* 99: 315–333.

Bridgland, D. R., Allen, P., Blackford, J. J., Parfitt, S. and Preece, R. 1995. New work on the Aveley Silts and Sands – A13 Road Improvement, Purfleet Road, Aveley. In: Bridgland, D. R., Allen,

P. A. and Haggart, B. A. (eds), *The Quaternary of the Lower Reaches of the Thames, Field Guide.* London: Quaternary Research Association, pp. 201–216.

Bridgland, D. R., Keen, D.H., Schreve, D.C. and White, M.J. 1998. Summary dating and correlation of the Stour sequence. In: Murton, J. B., Whiteman, C. A., Bates, M. R., Bridgland, D. R., Long, A. J. et al. (eds), *The Quaternary of Kent and Sussex: Field Guide.* London: QRA, pp. 53–54.

Bridgland, D. R., Field, M. H., Holmes, J. A., McNabb, J., Preece, R. C., Selby, I. et al. 1999. Middle Pleistocene interglacial Thames-Medway deposits at Clacton-on-Sea, England: reconsideration of the biostratigraphical and environmental context of the type Clactonian Palaeolithic industry. *Quaternary Science Reviews* 18: 109–146.

Bridgland, D. R., Preece, R. C., Roe, H. M., Tipping, R. M., Coope, G. R., Field, M. H. et al. 2001. Middle Pleistocene interglacial deposits at Barling, Essex, UK: evidence for a longer chronology for the Thames terrace sequence. *Journal of Quaternary Science* 16: 813–840.

Bridgland, D. R., Maddy, D. and Bates, M. R. 2004. River terrace sequences: templates for Quaternary geochronology and marine terrestrial correlation. *Journal of Quaternary Science* 19: 203–218.

Bridgland, D. R., Howard, A. J., White, M. J. and White, T. S. in press. *Quaternary of the Trent.* Oxford: English Heritage and Oxbow.

Briggs, D. J., Coope, G. R. and Gilbertson, D. D. 1985. *The Chronology and Environmental Framework of Early Man in the Upper Thames Valley: a New Model.* Oxford: British Archaeological Reports British Series 137.

Brinch Petersen, E. 2009. The human settlement of southern Scandinavia 12,500–8,700 cal BC. In: Street, M., Barton, N. and Terberger, T. (eds), *Humans, Environment and Chronology of the Late Glacial of the North European Plain.* Mainz: Verlag des Römisch-Germanischen Zentralmuseums, pp. 89–129.

Bronk Ramsey, C., Higham, T., Owen, D. C., Pike, A. W. G. and Hedges, R. E. M. 2002. Radiocarbon dates from the Oxford AMS system: Archaeometry datelist 31. *Archaeometry* 44 (3) supplement 1: 1–150.

Brooks, S. J. and Birks, H. J. B. 2000. Chironomid-inferred Late-Glacial air temperatures at Whitrig Bog, southeast Scotland. *Journal of Quaternary Science* 15: 759–764.

Brown, A. J. 1887a. *Palaeolithic Man in North-West Middlesex.* London: Macmillan.

Brown, A. J. 1887b. On a Palaeolithic Workshop Floor discovered near Ealing. *Proceedings of the Society of Antiquaries of London* 11: 211–215.

Brown, A. J. 1895. Notes on the high-level river drift between Hanwell and Iver. *Proceedings of the Geologists' Association* 14: 153–173.

Brown, A. P. 1977. Late-Devensian and Flandrian vegetational history of Bodmin Moor, Cornwall. *Philosophical Transactions of the Royal Society of London* B276: 251–320.

Brown, E. J., Rose, J., Coope, G. R. and Lowe, J. J. 2007. An MIS3 age organic deposit from Balglass Burn, central Scotland: significance for the palaeoenvironment of Scotland and the timing of the onset of the LGM in Britain and the adjacent sea. *Quaternary Science Reviews* 22: 295–308.

Brumm, A. and McLaren, A. 2011. Scraper reduction and 'imposed form' at the Lower Palaeolithic site of High Lodge, England. *Journal of Human Evolution* 60: 185–204.

Buckingham, C. M., Roe, D. A. and Scott, K. 1996. A preliminary report on the Stanton Harcourt channel deposits (Oxfordshire, England); geological context, vertebrate remains and Palaeolithic stone artefacts. *Journal of Quaternary Science* 11: 397–415.

Buckland, W. 1823. *Reliquiae Diluvianae: Observations on the Organic Remains Contained in Caves, Fissures and Diluvial Gravel Attesting the Action of an Universal Deluge.* London: John Murray.

Buraczynski, J. and Butrym, J. 1987. Thermoluminescence stratigraphy of the loess in the southern Rhinegraben. In: Pesci, M. (ed.), *Loess and Environment, vol. 9: Catena Supplement*, pp. 81–94.

Burchell, J. P. T. 1935. Evidence of a further glacial episode within the valley of the Lower Thames. *Geological Magazine* 72: 90–91.

Burchell, J. P. T. 1936a. Evidence of a Late Glacial Episode within the Valley of the Lower Thames. *Geological Magazine* 73: 91–92.

Burchell, J. P. T. 1936b. A final note on the Ebbsfleet Channel Series. *Geological Magazine* 73: 550–554.

Burchell, J. P. T. 1957. A Temperate Bed of the last Inter-glacial Period at Northfleet, Kent. *Geological Magazine* 94: 212–214.

Burdukiewicz, J. M. 1989. Le Hambourgien: origine, evolution dans un context stratigraphique, paléoclimatique et paléogeographique. *L'Anthropologie* 93: 189–218.

Burleigh, R., Hewson, A., Meeks, N., Sieveking, G. and Longworth, I. (1979) British Museum natural Radiocarbon measurements X. *Radiocarbon* 21(1): 41–47.

Burleigh, R., Ambers, J. and Matthews, K. (1984) British Museum natural radiocarbon measurements XVII. *Radiocarbon* 26(1): 59–74.

Burriss, R. P. 2009. Symmetry is sexy: a reply to Hidgson's 'Symmetry and humans'. *Antiquity* 83: 1170–1175.

Busschers, F., Van Balen, R., Cohen, K., Kasse, C., Weerts, H., Wallinga, J. et al. 2008. Response of the Rhine-Meuse fluvial system to Saalian ice-sheet dynamics. *Boreas* 37: 377–398.

Cabrera Valdés, V. 1988. Aspects of the Middle Palaeolithic in Cantabrian Spain. In: Otte, M. (ed.), *L'Homme de Néandertal, Vol. 4: La Technique.* Liège: ERAUL, pp. 27–37.

Cahen, D. and Michel, J. 1986. Le site paléolithique moyen ancien de Mesvin IV (Hainault, Belgique). In: Tuffreau, A. and Sommé, J. (eds), *Chronostratigraphie et Facies Culturels du Paléolithique Inferieur et Moyen dans l'Europe du Nord-Ouest.* Paris: Association Française pour l'Etude du Quaternaire, pp. 89–102.

Calkin, J. B. 1934. Implements from the higher raised beaches of Sussex. *Proceedings of the Prehistoric Society of East Anglia* 7: 333–347.

Calkin, J. B.and Green, J. F. N. 1949. Palaeoliths and terraces near Bournemouth. *Proceedings of the Prehistoric Society* 15: 21–37.

Callow, P. 1976. *The Lower and Middle Palaeolithic of Britain and adjacent areas of Europe.* Unpublished Ph.D. Thesis, University of Cambridge.

Callow, P. 1986. A Comparison of British and French Acheulian bifaces. In: Collcutt, S. N. (ed.), *The Palaeolithic of Britain and its Nearest Neighbours: Recent Trends.* Sheffield University of Sheffield, pp. 3–7.

Callow, P. and Cornford, J. M. 1986. *La Cotte de St Brelade: Excavations by C.B.M. McBurney.* Norwich: Geobooks.

Campbell, J. B. 1969. Excavations at Creswell Crags: Preliminary report. *Derbyshire Archaeological Journal* 89/90: 47–58.

Campbell, J. B. 1977. *The Upper Palaeolithic of Britain: a Study of Man and Nature in the Late Ice Age.* Oxford: Clarendon Press.

Campbell, J. B. 1980. Le problèm des subdivisions du Paléolithique Supérieur Britannique dans son cadre Européen. *Bulletin de la Société Royale Belge d'Anthropologie et de Préhistoire* 91: 39–77.

Campbell, J. B. and Sampson, C. G. 1971. *A New Analysis of Kent's Cavern, Devonshire, England.* Oregon: University of Oregon Press.

Campbell, J. B. and Hubbard, R. N. L. 1978. Biological investigation of the Rackley Site. In: Sampson, C. G. (ed.), *Paleoecology and archaeology of an Acheulian site at Caddington, England.* Dallas: Southern Methodist University, pp. 47–60.

Candy, I. and Schreve, D. 2007. Land-sea correlation of Middle Pleistocene temperate sub-stages using high-precision uranium-series dating of tufa deposits from Southern England. *Quaternary Science Reviews* 26: 1223–1235.

Candy, I., Rose, J. and Lee, J. R. 2006. A seasonally 'dry' interglacial climate in eastern England during the early Middle Pleistocene: palaeopedological and stable isotopic evidence from Pakefield, UK. *Boreas* 35: 255–265.

Carbonell, E. and Rodríguez, X. P. 1994. Early Middle Pleistocene deposits and artefacts in the Gran Dolina site (TD4) of the Sierra de Atapuerca, Burgos, Spain). *Journal of Human Evolution* 26: 291–311.

Carbonell, E. and Mosquera, M. 2006. The emergence of symbolic behaviour: the sepulchral pit of Sima de los Huesos, Sierra de Atapuerca, Burgos, Spain. *Comptes Rendus – Palevol* 5: 155–160.

Carbonell, E., Bermúdez de Castro, J. M., Arsuaga, J. L., Allue, E., Bastir, M., Benito et al. 1995. An Early Pleistocene hominin mandible from Atapuerca-TD6, Spain. *Proceedings of the National Academy of Sciences (USA)* 102: 5674–5678.

Carbonell, E., Mosquera, M. Rodriguez, X.P. and Sala, R. 1999a. Out of Africa: the dispersal of the earliest technical systems reconsidered. *Journal of Anthropological Archaeology* 18: 119–136.

Carbonell, E., García-Antón, M. D., Mallol, C., Mosquera, M., Ollé, A., Rodríguez, X. P. et al. 1999b. The TD6 level lithic industry from Gran Dolina, Atapuerca (Burgos, Spain): production and use. *Journal of Human Evolution* 37: 653–693.

Carbonell, E., Bermúdez de Castro, J. M., Parés, J. M., Pérez-González, A., Ollé, A. , Mosquera, M. et al. 2008. The first hominin of Europe. *Nature* 452: 465–469.

Carbonell, E., Ramos, R. S., Rodríguez, X. P., Mosquera, M., Ollé, A., Vergès, J. M. et al. 2010. Early hominid dispersals: A technological hypothesis for 'out of Africa'. *Quaternary International* 223/224: 36–44.

Carr, S. J., Holmes, R., van der Meer, J. J. M. and Rose, J. 2006. The Last Glacial Maximum in the North Sea Basin: micromorphological evidence of extensive glaciation. *Journal of Quaternary Science* 21: 131–153.

Carreck, J. N. 1972. *Chronology of the Quaternary deposits of south-east England, with special reference to their vertebrate faunas.* University of London, Unpublished M.Phil. Thesis.

Cartwright, C. 1992. Charcoal from High Lodge. In: Ashton, N. M., Cook, J., Lewis, S. G. and Rose, J. (eds), *High Lodge: Excavations by G. De G. Sieveking 1962–68 and J. Cook 1988.* London: British Museum Press, p.116.

Cartwright, C. 1998. The wood charcoal from Barnham. In: Ashton, N. M., Lewis, S. G. and Parfitt, S. *Excavations at the Lower Palaeolithic Site at East Farm, Barnham, Suffolk 1989–94.* London: British Museum Press, pp. 165–166.

Caseldine, C. J., McGarry, S. F., Baker, A., Hawkesworth, C. and Smart, P. L. 2008. Late Quaternary speleothem pollen in the British Isles. *Journal of Quaternary Science* 23: 193–200.

Casper, G. and Freund, H. 2001. Vegetation and climate in the Early- and Pleni-Weichselian in northern central Europe. *Journal of Quaternary Science* 16: 31–48.

Catt, J. A. 1978. Sediments from the Rackley Site. In: Sampson, C. G. (ed.), *Paleoecology and archaeology of an Acheulian site at Caddington, England.* Dallas: Southern Methodist University, pp. 39–46.

Catt, J. A. 1987. Dimlington. In: Ellis, S. (ed.), *East Yorkshire. Field Guide.* Cambridge: Quaternary Research Association, pp. 1–14.

Catt, J. A. 1991. The Quaternary history and glacial deposits of East Yorkshire. In: Ehlers, J., Gibbard, P. L. and Rose, J. (eds), *Glacial Deposits on Great Britain and Ireland.* Rotterdam: Balkema, pp. 185–191.

Catt, J. A. 1996. Recent work on Quaternary palaeosols in Britain. *Quaternary International* 34/35: 183–190.

Catt, J. A. and Hagen, R. E. 1978. Geological background. In: Sampson, C. G. (ed.), *Paleoecology and archaeology of an Acheulian site at Caddington, England.* Dallas: Southern Methodist University.

Catt, J. A., Hubbard, R. N. L. B. and Sampson, C. G. 1978. Summary and Conclusions. In: Sampson, C. G. (ed.), *Paleoecology and Archaeology of an Acheulian Site at Caddington, England.* Dallas: Southern Methodist University, pp. 139–150.

Célérier, G. 1996. L'Abri-sous-roche de Pont d'Ambon à Bourdeilles (Dordogne); l'industrie osseuse et la parure. *Gallia Préhistoire* 38: 69–110.

Chandler, R. H. 1914. The Pleistocene deposits of Crayford. *Proceedings of the Geologists' Association* 25: 61–71.

Chandler, R. H. 1916. The implements and cores of Crayford. *Proceedings of the Prehistoric Society of East Anglia* 2: 240–248.

Chandler, R. H. 1930. On the Clactonian Industry at Swanscombe. *Proceedings of the Prehistoric Society of East Anglia* 6: 79–116.

Charles, R. 1989. Incised ivory fragments and other Late Upper Palaeolithic finds from Gough's Cave, Cheddar, Somerset. *Proceedings of the University of Bristol Spelaeological Society* 18: 400–408.

Charles, R. 1997. The exploitation of carnivores and other fur-bearing mammals during the northwestern European Late Upper Palaeolithic and Mesolithic. *Oxford Journal of Archaeology* 16: 253–277.

Charles, R. 1998. *Late Magdalenian Chronology and Faunal Exploitation in the North-Western Ardennes.* Oxford: British Archaeological Reports International Series 737.

Charles, R. 1999. Garrod and the Belgian Creswellian. In: Davies, W. and Charles, R. (eds), *Dorothy Garrod and the Progress of the Palaeolithic.* Oxford: Oxbow, pp. 57–76.

Charles, R. and Jacobi, R. 1994. Lateglacial faunal exploitation at the Robin Hood Cave, Creswell Crags. *Oxford Journal of Archaeology* 13: 1–32.

Chase, P. and Dibble, H. 1987. Middle Palaeolithic symbolism: a review of current evidence and interpretation. *Journal of Anthropological Archaeology* 6: 263–296.

Chazan, M. 1997. Redefining Levallois. *Journal of Human Evolution* 33: 719–735.

Chiotti, L. 2003. Les productions lamellaires dans l'Aurignacien de l'Abri Pataud, Les-Eyzies-de-Tayac. *Gallia Préhistoire* 45: 113–156.

Chiverrell, R. C. and Thomas, G. S. P. 2010. Extent and timing of the Last Glacial Maximum (LGM) in Britain and Ireland: a review. *Journal of Quaternary Science* 25: 535–549.

Chu, W. 2009. A functional approach to Paleolithic open-air habitation structures. *World Archaeology* 41: 348–362.

Churchill, S. E. 2006. Bioenergetic perspectives on Neanderthal thermoregulatory and activity budgets. In: Harvati, H. and Harrison, T. (eds), *Neanderthals Revisited: New Approaches and Perspectives.* Dordrecht: Springer, pp. 113–134.

Churchill, S. E. and Smith, F. H. 2000. Makers of the early Aurignacian of Europe. *Yearbook of Physical Anthropology* 43: 61–115.

Clapperton, C. M. 1995. Fluctuations of local glaciers at the terminations of the Pleistocene 18–8 ka BP. *Quaternary International* 28: 41–50.

Clark, C. D., Evans, D. J. A., Khatwa, A., Bradwell, T., Jordan, C. J., Marsh, S. H. et al. 2004. Map and GIS database of glacial landforms and features related to the last British ice sheet. *Boreas* 33: 359–375.

Clark, C. D., Hughes, A. L. C., Greenwood, S. L., Jordan, C. and Sejrup, H. P. 2011. Pattern at timing of retreat of the last British-Irish Ice Sheet. *Quaternary Science Reviews* doi:10.1016/j.quascirev.2010.07.019.

Clark, J. G. D. 1954. *Excavations at Star Carr.* Cambridge: Cambridge University Press.

Clark, J. G. D. 1969. *World Prehistory: A New Outline.* Cambridge: Cambridge University Press.

Clarke, M. L., Milodowski, A. E., Bouch, J. E., Leng, M. J. and Northmore, K. J. 2007. New OSL dating of UK loess: indications of two phases of Late Glacial dust accretion in SE England and climate implications. *Journal of Quaternary Science* 22: 361–371.

Clark, P. U., Dyke, A. S., Shakun, J. D., Carlson, A. E., Clark, J., Wohlfarth, B. et al. 2009. The Last Glacial Maximum. *Science* 325: 710–714.

Clayton, K. M. 2000. Glacial erosion of the Wash and Fen basin and the deposition of the chalky till of eastern England. *Quaternary Science Reviews* 19: 811–822.

Clegg, J. 1970. Excavations at Coygan Cave, near Laugharne: first draft report. *Carmarthen Antiquary* 5: 13–20.

Cliquet, D., Ladjadj, J., Lautridou, J.-P., Leportier, J., Lorren, P., Michel, D. et al. 2001. Le Paléolithique moyen à outils bifaciaux en Normandie: état des connaissances. In: D. Cliquet (ed.), *Les industries á outils bifaciaux du Paléolithique Moyen d'Europe occidentale.* Liège: ERAUL, pp. 115–127.

Collcutt, S. 1999. *Creswell Crags Nottinghamshire/Derbyshire: Sensitivity Survey.* Oxford: Oxford Archaeological Associates.

Coleman, A. 1952. Some aspects of the development of the Lower Stour, Kent. *Proceedings of the Geologists' Association* 63: 63–86.

Coles, B. J. 1998. Doggerland: a speculative survey. *Proceedings of the Prehistoric Society* 64: 45–82.

Coles, G. M. and Gilbertson, D. D. 1994. The airfall-pollen budget of archaeologically important caves: Creswell Crags, England. *Journal of Archaeological Science* 21: 735–755.

Coles, G. M., Gilbertson, D. D., Hunt, C. O. and Jenkinson, R. D. S. 1989. Taphonomy and the palynology of cave deposits. *Cave Science* 16: 83–89.

Collins, D. 1969. Culture traditions and environment of early man. *Current Anthropology* 10: 267–316.

Collins, D. 1970. Excavations at Oldbury in Kent: The Palaeolithic Occupation. *Archaeologia Cantiana* 85: 211–212.

Collins, D. 1978. *Early Man in West Middlesex: the Yiewsley Palaeolithic Sites.* London: HMSO.

Collins, P. E. F., Fenwick, I. M., Keith-Lucas, M. and Worsley, P. 1996. Late Devensian river and floodplain dynamics and related environmental change in northwest Europe, with particular reference to a site at Woolhampton, Berkshire, England. *Journal of Quaternary Science* 11: 357–375.

Coltorti, M., Feraud, G., Marzoli, A., Peretto, C., Ton-That, T., Voinchet, P. et al. 2005. New 40Ar/39Ar, stratigraphic and palaeoclimatic data on the Isernia La Pineta Lower Palaeolithic site, Molise, Italy. *Quaternary International* 131: 11–22.

Commont, V. 1908. Les industries de l'ancien Saint-Achuel. *L'Anthropologie* 19: 527–572.

Commont, V. 1909. L'industrie moustérienne dans la region de nord de la France. *Congrès préhistorique de France, Compte rendu la 5 session, Beauvais, 1909.*

Commont, V. 1912. Chronologie et stratigraphie des industries protohistorique, néolithiques et paléolithiques dans le depots holocènes et pleistocènes du nord de la France en particulier de la vallée de la Somme. Remarques et comparisons relative aux loess et aux glaciations. *Congrès International d'Anthropologie et d'Archéologie Préhistoriques: Compte rendu de la XIVe session, Genève 1912.* Geneva: Albert Kündig.

Conard, N. J. and Adler, D. 1997. Lithic reduction and hominid behaviour in the Middle Palaeolithic of the Rhineland. *Journal of Anthropological Research* 53: 147–175.

Conard, N. J. and Prindiville, T. J. 2000. Middle Palaeolithic hunting economies in the Rhineland. *International Journal of Osteoarchaeology* 10: 286–309.

Conard, N. J. and Niven, L. 2001. The Paleolithic finds from Bollschweil and the question of Neanderthal mammoth hunting in the Black Forest. In: Cavaretta, G., Gioia, P., Mussi, M. and Polambo, M. R. (eds), *The World of Elephants, Proceedings of the 1st International Congress, Rome, October 2001.* Rome, pp. 194–200.

Conard, N. J. and Bolus, M. 2003. Radiocarbon dating the appearance of modern humans and timing of cultural innovations in Europe: new results and new challenges. *Journal of Human Evolution* 44: 331–371.

Conneller, C. 2007. Inhabiting new landscapes: settlement and mobility in Britain after the Last Glacial Maximum. *Oxford Journal of Archaeology* 26: 215–237.

Conneller, C. 2009. Investigation of a Final Palaeolithic site at Rookery Farm, Great Wilbraham, Cambridgeshire. *Proceedings of the Prehistoric Society* 75: 167–187.

Conneller, C. and Ellis, C. 2007. A Final Upper Palaeolithic site at La Sagesse Convent, Romsey, Hampshire. *Proceedings of the Prehistoric Society* 73: 191–227.

Conway, B. W. 1996. Bifaces in a Clactonian context at Little Thurrock, Grays, Essex. *Lithics* 16: 41–46.

Conway, B. W., McNabb, J. and Ashton, N. (eds) 1996. *Excavations at Barnfield Pit, Swanscombe, 1968–1972,* London: British Museum.

Cook, J. 1986a. Marked human bones from Gough's Cave, Somerset. *Proceedings of the University of Bristol Spelaeological Society* 17: 275–285.

Cook, J. 1986b. A blade industry from Stoneham's Pit, Crayford. In: S. N. Collcutt (ed.), *The Palaeolithic of Britain and its Nearest Neighbours: Recent Trends.* Sheffield: University of Sheffield, pp. 16–19.

Cook, J. 1991. Comment on Stiner, White and Toth. *Current Anthropology* 32: 126–127.

Cook, J. and Jacobi, R. 1994. A reindeer antler or 'Lyngby' axe from Northamptonshire and its context in the British Late Glacial. *Proceedings of the Prehistoric Society* 60: 75–84.

Cook, J. and Jacobi, R.J. 1998. Discoidal core technology in the Palaeolithic at Oldbury, Kent. In: Ashton, N., Healy, F. and Pettitt, P. (ed.), *Stone Age Archaeology: Essays in Honour of John Wymer.* Oxford: Oxbow Books, pp. 124–136.

Cook, J., Ashton, N. M., Coope, G. R., Hunt, C. O., Lewis, S. G. and Rose, J. 1981. High Lodge, Mildenhall, Suffolk (TL 739754). In: Lewis, S. G., Whiteman, C. A. and Bridgland, D. R. (eds), *Central East Anglia and the Fen Basin: Field Guide.* London: Quaternary Research Association, pp. 127–130.

Cook, W. H. and Killick, J. R. 1924. On the discovery of a flint working site of Palaeolithic date in the Medway valley at Rochester, Kent, with notes on the drift stages of the Medway. *Proceedings of the Prehistoric Society of East Anglia* 4: 133–149.

Coope, G. R. 1959. A late Pleistocene insect fauna from Chelford, Cheshire. *Philosophical Transactions of the Royal Society of London* B: 70–86.

Coope, G. R. 1968. An insect fauna from Mid-Weichselian deposits at Brandon, Warwickshire. *Philosophical Transactions of the Royal Society of London* B254: 425–456.

Coope, G. R. 1977. Fossil coleopteran assemblages as sensitive indicators of climatic changes during the Devensian (last) cold stage. *Philosophical Transactions of the Royal Society of London* B280: 313–340.

Coope, G. R. 2000a. The climatic significance of coleopteran assemblages from the Eemian deposits in southern England. *Geologie en Mijnbouw/Netherlands Journal of Geosciences* 79: 257–267.

Coope, G. R. 2000b. Middle Devensian (Weichselian) coleopteran assemblages from Earith, Cambridgeshire (UK) and their bearing on the interpretation of full glacial floras and faunas. *Journal of Quaternary Science* 15: 779–788.

Coope, G. R. 2001. Biostratigraphical distinction of interglacial coleopteran assemblages from southern Britain attributed to Oxygen Isotope Stages 5e and 7. *Quaternary Science Reviews* 20: 1717–1722.

Coope, G. R. 2002. Changes in the thermal climate in Northwestern Europe during Marine Oxygen Isotope Stage 3, estimated from fossil insect assemblages. *Quaternary Research* 57: 401–408.

Coope, G. R. 2006. Insect faunas associated with palaeolithic industries from five sites of pre-Anglian age in central England. *Quaternary Science Reviews* 25: 1738–1754.

Coope, G. R. and Brophy, J. A. 1972. Late Glacial environmental changes indicated by a coleopteran succession succession from North Wales. *Boreas* 1: 97–142.

Coope, G. R. and Pennington, W. 1977. The Windermere Interstadial of the Late Devensian. *Philosophical Transactions of the Royal Society of London* B280: 337–339.

Coope, G. R., Shotton, F. W. and Stachan, I. 1961. A Late Pleistocene Fauna and Flora from Upton Warren, Worcestershire. *Philosophical Transactions of the Royal Society of London* B244: 379–421.

Coope, G. R., Gibbard, P. L., Hall, A. R., Preece, R. C., Robinson, J. E. and Sutcliffe, A. J. 1997. Climatic and environmental reconstructions based on fossil assemblages from Middle Devensian (Weichselian) deposits of the river Thames at South Kensington, Central London, UK. *Quaternary Science Reviews* 16: 1163–1195.

Cooper, J. 1972. Last Interglacial (Ipswichian) non-marine Mollusca from Aveley, Essex. *Essex Naturalist* 33: 9–14.

Cooper, L. 2002. A Creswellian campsite, Newtown Linford. *Transactions of the Leicestershire Archaeology and History Society* 76: 78–80.

Cooper, L. 2004. The hunter-gatherers of Leicestershire and Rutland. In: Bowman, P. and Liddle, P. (eds), *Leicestershire Landscapes.* Leicester: Leicestershire County Council, pp. 12–29.

Cooper, L. 2006. Launde: a Terminal Palaeolithic camp site in the English Midlands and its North European context. *Proceedings of the Prehistoric Society* 72: 53–94.

Cooper, L. and Jacobi, R. M. 2001. Two Late Glacial finds from north-west Leicestershire. *Transactions of the Leicestershire Archaeology and History Society* 75: 118–120.

Cooper, L., Thomas, J. S., Beamish, M. G., Gouldwell, A., Collcutt, S. N., Williams, J. et al. in press. An Early Upper Palaeolithic open-air station and mid-Devensian hyaena den at Grange Farm, Glaston, Rutland, UK. *Proceedings of the Prehistoric Society.*

Copeland, L. and Hours, F. 1993. The Middle Orontes: Palaeolithic flint industries. In: Sanlaville, P., Besançon, J., Copeland, L. and Muhesen, S. (eds), *Le Paléolithique de la Vallée Moyenne de l'Oronte (Syrie): Peulement et Environment.* Oxford: BAR International Series 587, pp. 63–144.

Cotton, J. 1984. A Mousterian handaxe from West London. *Lithics* 5: 40–43.

Coulson, S. D. 1990. *Middle Palaeolithic Industries of Great Britain.* Bonn: Holos.

Cranshaw, S. 1983. *Handaxes and Cleavers: Selected English Acheulean Industries.* Oxford: British Archaeological Reports British Series 113.

Crochet, J.-Y., Welcomme, J.-L., Ivorra, J., Ruffet, G., Boulbes, N., Capdevila, R. et al. 2009. Une nouvelle faune de vertébrés continentaux, associée à des artifacts dans le Pléistocène inférieur de l'Hérault (Sud de la France), ver 1,57 Ma. *Comptes Rendus Palevol* 8: 725–736.

Crombé, P. and Verbruggen, C. 2002. The Lateglacial and early Postglacial occupation of Northern Belgium: the evidence from Sandy Flanders. In: Eriksen, B. V. and Bratlund, B. (eds), *Recent Studies in the Final Palaeolithic of the European Plain. Proceedings of a U.I.S.P.P. Symposium, Stockholm, 14–17 October 1999.* Aarhus: Aarhus University Press, pp. 165–180.

Cruse, J. 1987. Further investigations of the Acheulian Site at Cuxton. *Archaeologia Cantiana* 104: 39–81.

Cunliffe, B. 2001. *Facing the Ocean: the Atlantic and its Peoples.* Oxford: Oxford University Press.

Currant, A. 1986a. Man and the Quaternary interglacial faunas of Britain. In: Colcutt, S. N. (ed.), *The Palaeolithic Of Britain and its Nearest Neighbours: Recent Trends.* Sheffield: University of Sheffield, pp. 50–52.

Currant, A. 1986b. The Lateglacial mammal fauna of Gough's Cave, Cheddar, Somerset. . *Proceedings of the University of Bristol Spelaeological Society* 17: 286–304.

Currant, A. 1987. Late Pleistocene saiga antelope *Saiga tatarica* on Mendip. *Proceedings of the University of Bristol Spelaeological Society* 18: 74–80.

Currant, A. 1991. A Late Glacial Interstadial mammal fauna from Gough's Cave, Somerset, England. In: Barton, R. N. E., Roberts, A. and Roe, D. A. (eds), *The Late Glacial in North West Europe: Human Adaptation and Environmental Change at the End of the Pleistocene.* London: Council for British Archaeology Research Report 77, pp. 48–50.

Currant, A. P. and Jacobi, R. M. 1997. Vertebrate faunas of the British Late Pleistocene and the chronology of human settlement. *Quaternary Newsletter* 82: 1–8.

Currant, A. and Jacobi, R. 2001. A formal mammalian biostratigraphy for the Late Pleistocene of Britain. *Quaternary Science Reviews* 20: 1707–1716.

Currant, A. and Jacobi, R. 2002. Human presence and absence in Britain during the early part of the Late Pleistocene. In: Roebroeks, W. and Tuffreau, A. (eds), *Le Dernier Interglaciaire et les occupations humaines du Palaeolithique moyen.* Lille: Centre d'Etudes et Recherches Préhistoriques, pp. 105–113.

Currant, A. and Jacobi, R. 2011. The Mammal Faunas of the British Late Pleistocene. In: Ashton, N., Lewis, S. and Stringer, C. (eds), *The Ancient Human Occupation of Britain.* Amsterdam: Elsevier, pp. 165–180.

Currant, A. P., Jacobi, R. M. and Stringer, C. B. 1989. Excavations at Gough's Cave, Somerset 1986–7. *Antiquity* 63: 131–136.

Curwen, E. 1925. Palaeolith from raised beach in Sussex. *Antiquaries Journal* 5: 72–73.

Cutler, K. B., Edwards, R. L., Taylor, F. W., Cheng, H., Adkins, J., Gallup, C. D. et al. 2003. Rapid seal evel fall and deep-ocean temperature change since the last interglacial period. *Earth and Planetary Science Letters* 206: 253–271.

Cziesla, E. and Pettitt, P. B. 2003. AMS ^{14}C datierungen von Spätpaläolithischen und Mesolithischen funden aus dem Bützee (Brandenburg). *Archäologisches Korrespondenzblatt* 33: 21–38.

D'Errico, F. and Nowell, A. 2000. A new look at the Berekhat Ram figurine: implications for the origins of symbolism. *Cambridge Archaeological Journal* 10: 123–167.

D'Errico, F., Zilhao, J., Julien, M., Baffier, D. and Pelegrin, J. 1998. Neanderthal acculturation in western Europe? A critical review of the evidence and its interpretation. *Current Anthropology* 39: 1–44.

D'Errico, F., Henshilwood, C., Lawson, G., Vanhaeren, M., Tillier, A.-M., Soressi, M., Bresson, F., Maureille, B., Nowell, A., Lakarra, J., Backwell, L. and Julien, M. 2003. Archaeological Evidence for the Emergence of Language, Symbolism, and Music – An Alternative Multidisciplinary Perspective. *Journal of World Prehistory* 17: 1–70.

Dansgaard, W., Johnsen, S. J., Clausen, H. B., Dahl-Jensen, D., Gundestrup, N. S., Hammer, C. U. et al. 1993. Evidence for general instability of past climate from a 250–kyr ice-core. *Nature* 364: 218–220.

Dapaepe, P. 2001. Pour une poignée de bifaces: les industries en bifaces du Paléolithique moyen de la vallée de la Vanne. In: Cliquet, D. (ed.), *Les industries à outils bifaciaux du Paléolithique Moyen d'Europe occidentale.* Liège: ERAUL, pp. 135–140.

Darvill, T. 2010. *Prehistoric Britain.* London: Routledge.

David, A. 1991. Late Glacial archaeological residues from Wales: a selection. In: Barton, N., Roberts, A. and Roe, D. (eds), *The Late Glacial of Northwest Europe: Human Adaptation and Environmental Change at the End of the Pleistocene.* London: Council for British Archaeology Research Report 77, pp. 141–159.

David, A. 2007. *Palaeolithic and Mesolithic Settlement in Wales, with Special Reference to Dyfed.* Oxford: British Archaeological Reports British Series 448.

Davies, J.A. 1926. Notes on Upper Palaeolithic Implements from Mendip Caves. *Proceedings of the University of Bristol Spelaeological Society* 2: 261–273

Davies, K. H. 1984. *Aminostratigraphy of British Pleistocene beach deposits.* Unpublished Ph.D. Thesis, University of Wales.

Davies, K. H. and Keen, D. H. 1985. The age of the Pleistocene marine deposits at Portland, Dorset. *Proceedings of the Geologists' Association* 96: 217–225.

Davies, P. and Walker, A. 1996. The footprint surfaces at Barnfield Pit, Swanscombe, and the results of analysis of a potential footprint. In: Conway, B., McNabb, J. and Ashton, N. (eds), *Excavations at Barnfield Pit, 1968–1972.* British Museum: London, pp. 169–185.

Davies, W. 2001. A Very Model of a Modern Human Industry: New Perspectives on the Origins and Spread of the Aurignacian in Europe. *Proceedings of the Prehistoric Society* 67: 195–217.

Davies, W. and Gallop, P. 2003. The human presence in Europe during the Last Glacial period II: climatic tolerance and climatic preference of Mid- and Late Glacial hominids. In: Van Andel, T. and Davies, W. (eds), *Neanderthals and Modern Humans in the European Landscape During the Last Glaciation: Archaeological Results of the Stage 3 project.* Cambridge: McDonald Institute, pp. 131–146.

Dawkins, W. B. 1862. On a hyaena-den at Wookey Hole, near Wells. *Quarterly Journal of the Geological Society of London* 18: 115–126.

Dawkins, W. B. 1863. On a hyaena-den at Wookey Hole, near Wells. No. II. *Quarterly Journal of the Geological Society of London* 19: 260–274.

Dawkins, W. B. 1874. *Cave Hunting: Researches on the Evidence Respecting the Early Inhabitants of Europe.* London: Macmillan and Co.

Dawkins, W. B. 1876. On the mammalia and traces of man found in the Robin Hood Cave. *Quarterly Journal of the Geological Society* 32: 245–58.

Dawkins, W. B. 1877. On the mammal fauna of the caves of Creswell Crags. *Quarterly Journal of the Geological Society of London* 33: 389–612.

Dawkins, W. B. 1880a. *Early Man in Britain and his place in the Tertiary Period.* London: Macmillan.

Dawkins, W. B. 1880b. Memorandum on the remains from the cave at Great Orme's Head. *Proceedings of the Liverpool Geological Society* 4 (2): 156–159.

Dawkins, W. B. 1876. *Notes of Caves &c*. Unpublished handwritten notes.

Dawkins, W. B. and Mello, J. M. 1879. Further discoveries at Creswell Crags. *Quarterly Journal of the Geological Society of London* 35: 724–734.

Day, P. 1995. Devensian Late-Glacial and early Flandrian environmental history of the Vale of Pickering, Yorkshire, England. *Journal of Quaternary Science* 11: 9–24.

Dean, C., M. G. Leakey, D. Reid, F. Schrenk, G. T. Schwartz, C. Stringer, and A. Walker. 2001. Growth Processes in Teeth Distinguish Modern Humans from *Homo erectus* and Earlier Hominins. *Nature* 414: 628–631.

De Clerk, P. 2004. Confusing concepts in Lateglacial stratigraphy and geochronology: origin, consequences, conclusions (with special emphasis on the type locality Bøllingsø). *Review of Palaeobotany and Palynology* 129: 265–298.

De Jong, J. 1988. Climatic variability during the past three million years, as indicated by vegetational evolution in Northwest Europe and with emphasis on data from the Netherlands. *Philosophical Transactions of the Royal Society of London B* 318: 601–617.

De Lumley, H. 1969. A Palaeolithic camp site near Nice. *Scientific American* 220: 42–50.

De Lumley, M.-A., Gabunia, L., Vekua, A., Lordkipanidze, D. 2006. Les restes de Pliocene final et du debut du Pleistocene inferieur de Dmanisi, Georgie (1991–2000). I – Les cranes, D 2280, D 2282, D 2700. *L'Anthropologie* 110: 1–110.

De Mortillet, G. 1869. Essai d'une classification des cavernes et des stations sous abri, fondée sur les produits de l'industrie humaine. *Matériaux pour Servir à l'Histoire Primitive de l'Homme* 5: 172–179.

De Mortillet, G. 1873. Classification des diverse période d'Âge de la Pierre. *Compte Rendu du Congrès Internationale d'Anthropologie et d'Archéologie Préhistoriques, 6me Session, Bruxelles, 1872.* Bruxelles: Weissenbruch, pp. 432–444.

Delair, J. B. and Shackley, M. L. 1978. The Fisherton Brickpits: their stratigraphy and fossil contents. *Wiltshire Natural History Society Magazine* 73: 3–19.

Delporte, H. and Mons, L. 1988. Sagaies: fiche sagaie a biseau double. In: Delporte, H., Hahn, J., Mons, L., Pinçon, G. and de Sonneville-Bordes, D. (eds), *Sagaies*. Provence: Publications de l'Universitée Provence. Fiche 4.

Demars, P.-Y. and Laurent, P. 1992. *Types d'Outils Lithiques du Paléolithique Supérieur en Europe.* Paris: Cahiers du Quaternaire 14.

DeMenocal, P. B. 2004. African climate change and faunal evolution during the Pliocene-Pleistocene. *Earth and Planetary Science Letters* 220: 3–24.

Dennell, R. 1983. *European Economic Prehistory: A New Approach.* London and New York: Academic Press.

Dennell, R. 2003. Dispersal and colonisation, long and short chronologies: how continuous is the Early Pleistocene record for hominids outside East Africa? *Journal of Human Evolution* 45: 421–440.

Dennell, R. 2004. *Early Hominin Landscapes in Northern Pakistan.* Oxford: Archaeopress. British Archaeological Reports International Series 1265.

Dennell, R. and Roebroeks, W. 1996. The earliest colonization of Europe: the short chronology revisited. *Antiquity* 70: 535–542.

Dennell, R. and Roebroeks, W. 2005. An Asian perspective on early human dispersal from Africa. *Nature* 438: 1099–1104.

Dennell, R. and Pettitt, P. B. 2007. Review of Brantingham, P., Kuhn, S. and Kerry, K. (eds), *The Early Upper Paleolithic Beyond Western Europe. American Journal of Archaeology* 110: 169–172.

Dennell, R., Rendell, H. M. and Hailwood, E. 1988. Early tool-making in Asia: two-million year-old artefacts in Pakistan. *Antiquity* 62: 98–106.

Dennell, R., Martinón-Torres, M. and Bermúdez de Castro, J. M. 2010. Out of Asia: The initial colonisation of Europe in the Early and Middle Pleistocene. *Quaternary International* 223/224: 439.

Dennell, R., Martinón-Torres, M. and Bermúdez de Castro, J. M. 2011. Hominin variability, climatic instability and population demography in Middle Pleistocene Europe. *Quaternary Science Reviews* 30: 1511–1524.

Desbrosse, R. and Kozlowski, J. 1988. *Hommes et Climats à l'â du Mammouth: le Paléolithique Supérieur d'Eurasie Central.* Paris: Masson.

Desprat, S., Sánchez Goñi, M. F., Turon, J. L., Duprat, J., Malaizé, B. and Peypouquet, J. P. 2005. Climatic variability of Marine Isotope Stage 7: direct land–sea–ice correlation from a multiproxy analysis of a north-western Iberian margin deep-sea core. *Quaternary Science Reviews* 25: 1010–1026.

Despriée, J., Gageonnet, R., Voinchet, P., Bahain, J. J., Falguères, C., Varache, F. et al. 2006. Une occupation humaine au Pléistocène inférieur sur la bordure nord du Massif Central. *Comptes Rendus Palevol* 5: 821–828.

Despriée, J., Voinchet, P., Tissoux, H., Moncel, M.-H., Arzarello, M., Bahain, J.-J. et al. 2010. Lower and Middle Pleistocene human settlements in the Middle Loire River Basin, Centre Region, France *Quaternary International* 223/224: 345–359.

Dewey, H. 1919. On some Palaeolithic Flake-implements from the High Level Terraces of the Thames Valley. *The Geological Magazine* 6: 48–57.

Dewey, H. 1930. Palaeolithic Thames Deposits. *Proceedings of the Prehistoric Society of East Anglia* 6: 146–155.

Dewey, H. 1932. The Palaeolithic deposits of the Lower Thames Valley. *The Quarterly Journal of the Geological Society of London* 88: 35–56.

Dewey, H. and Smith, R. A. 1925. Flints from the Sturry Gravels, Kent. *Archaeologia* 74: 117–136.

Dewez, M. 1986. Research and reflections on the human occupation of Wallonia (Belgium) during the Late Last Glacial. In: Roe, D. A. (ed.), *Studies in the Upper Palaeolithic of Britain and North-west Europe.* Oxford: British Archaeological Reports International Series 296, pp. 227–234.

Dibble, H. 1987. The interpretation of Middle Palaeolithic scraper morphology. *American Antiquity* 52: 109–117.

Dibble, H. 1989. The implications of stone tool types for the presence of language during the Lower and Middle Palaeolithic. In: Mellars, P. and Stringer, C. (eds), *The Human Revolution: Behavioural and Biological Perspectives on the Origins of Modern Humans.* Edinburgh: Edinburgh University Press, pp. 415–433.

Dibble, H. 1995a. Biache-Saint-Vaast, Level IIa: a comparison of approaches. In: Dibble, H. L. and Bar-Yosef, O. (eds), *The Definition and Interpretation of Levallois Technology.* Madison: Prehistory Press, pp. 93–116.

Dibble, H. 1995b. Middle Palaeolithic scraper reduction: background, clarification and review of evidence to date. *Journal of Archaeological Method and Theory* 2: 299–368.

Dibble, H. and Rolland, N. 1992. On assemblage variability in the Middle Palaeolithic of Western Europe: history, perspectives, and a new synthesis. In: Dibble, T. and Mellars, P. (eds), *The Middle Paleolithic: Adaptation, Behavior, and Variability.* Philadelphia: University of Pennsylvania University Museum Monograph 72, pp. 1–28.

Dibley, G. E. and Kennard, A. S. 1916. Excursion to Grays. *Proceedings of the Geologists' Association* 27: 103–105.

Diefendorf, A. F., Patterson, W. P., Mullins, H. T., Tibert, N. and Martini, A. 2006. Evidence for high-frequency late glacial to mid-Holocene (16,800 to 550 cal yr BP) climate variability from oxygen isotope values of Lough Inchiquin, Ireland. *Quaternary Research* 65: 78–86.

Dines, H. G. 1929. The flint industries of Bapchild. *Proceedings of the Prehistoric Society of East Anglia* VI: 12–26.

Dines, H. G. 1964. General account of the 100ft terrace gravels of the Barnfield Pit. *The Swanscombe Skull: a survey of research on a Pleistocene Site.* London: Royal Anthropological Institute, Occasional Paper No. 20, pp. 5–10.

Dines, H. G., Holmes, S. C. A. and Robbie, J. A. 1954. *Geology of the Country Around Chatham. Memoirs of the Geological Survey of Great Britain.* London: HMSO.

Dinnis, R. 2005. A Comprehensive Study of British Aurignacian Artefacts. *Unpublished M.Sc. dissertation, University of Sheffield.*

Dinnis, R. 2008. On the technology of Late Aurignacian burin and scraper production, and the importance of the Paviland lithic assemblage and the Paviland burin. *Lithics* 29: 18–35.

Dinnis, R. 2009. *Understanding the British Aurignacian, Unpublished PhD Thesis.* University of Sheffield.

Dobres, M. A. 2000. *Technology and Social Agency.* Oxford: Blackwell.

Doran, J. E. and Hodson, F. R. 1975. *Mathematics and Computers in Archaeology.* Cambridge: Cambridge University Press.

Doronichev, V. and Golovanova, L. 2010. Beyond the Acheulean: a view on the Lower Paleolithic occupation of Western Eurasia. *Quaternary International* 223/224: 327–344.

Draper, J. C. 1962. Upper Palaeolithic type flints from Long Island, Langstone Harbour, Portsmouth. *Proceedings of the Hampshire Field Club and Archaeological Society* XXII(II): 105–106.

Dudley, T. 1993. Ash Tree Cave, Whitewell, Derbyshire: an examination and analysis of the excavations between 1939 and 1960. Unpublished B.A. Dissertation, Department of Classical and Archaeological Studies, University of Nottingham.

Duigan, S. L. 1956. Interglacial plant remains from the Wolvercote Channel, Oxford. *Quarterly Journal of the Geological Society of London* 112: 363–372.

Dunbar, R. 1996. *Grooming, Gossip and the Evolution of Language.* London: Faber & Faber.

Dunbar, R. 1998. The social brain hypothesis. *Evolutionary Antrhopology* 6: 178–190.

Dunbar, R. 2004. *The Human Story*. London: Faber & Faber.

Dutton, A., Antonioli, F. and Bard, E. 2009a. A new chronoogy of sea level highstand for the penultimate interglacial. *Pages* 17: 66–68.

Dutton, A., Bard, E., Antonioli, F., Esat, T. M., Lambeck, K. and McCulloch, M. T. 2009b. The phasing and amplitude of climate and sea level during the penultimate interglacia. *Nature Geoscience* doi:10.1038/NGEO470.

Ealey, P. J. and James, H. C. L. 2010. Loess of the Lizard Peninsula, Cornwall, SW Britain. *Quaternary International* 231: 55–61.

Ehlers, J. and Gibbard, P. L. 2004a. The extent and chronology of Cenozoic global glaciation. *Quaternary International* 164/165: 6–20.

Ehlers, J. and Gibbard, P. L. 2004b. *Quaternary Glaciations – Extent and Chronology. Part 1; Europe.* Amsterdam: Elsevier.

Elias, S. 1994. *Quaternary Insects and their Environments.* Washington, D.C.: Smithsonian Institution Press.

Eriksen, B. V. 2002. Reconsidering the geochronological framework of Lateglacial hunter-gatherer colonisation of southern Scandinavia. In: Eriksen, B. V. and Bratlund, B. (eds), *Recent Studies in the Final Palaeolithic of the European Plain. Proceedings of a U.I.S.P.P. Symposium, Stock-holm, 14–17 October 1999.* Aarhus: Aarhus University Press, pp. 25–42.

Eskrigge, R. A. 1880. Notes on the human skeletons and traces of human workmanship found in a cave at Great Orme's Head. *Proceedings of the Liverpool Geological Society* IV(ii): 153–155.

Evans, J. 1862. Account of some further discoveries of flint implements in the Drift on the Continent and in England. *Archaeologia* 39: 57–84.

Evans, J. 1872. *Ancient Stone Implements, Weapons and Ornaments of Great Britain, 1st Edition.* London: Longmans and Co.

Evans, J. 1897. *Ancient Stone Implements, Weapons and Ornaments of Great Britain, 2nd Edition.* London: Longmans and Co.

Evans, J., Morse, E., Reid, C., Ridley, E. P. and Ridley, H. N. 1896. The relation of Palaeolithic man to the glacial epoch. *Report of the British Association, Liverpool*, pp. 400–416.

Faegri, K. and Iverson, J. 1989. *Textbook of Pollen Analysis (4th Edition).* Chichester: Wiley.

Falguères, C., Bahain, J.-J., Yokoyama, Y., Arsuaga, J. L., Bermúde Castro, J. M., Carbonell, E. et al. 2001. Datation par RPE et U-Th des sites pléistocenes d'Atapuerca: Sima de los Huesos, Trinchera Dolina et Trinchera Galeriá. Bilan géochronologique. *L'Anthropologie* 105: 71–81.

Farizy, C. and David, F. 1992. Subsistence and behavioural patterns of some middle Paleolithic local groups. In: Dibble, H. and Mellars, P. A. (eds), *The Middle Paleolithic: Adaptation, Behavior and Variability.* Philadelphia: University of Pennsylvania University Museum Monograph 72, pp. 87–96.

Féblot-Augustins, J. 1997. *La circulation des matières premières au Paléolithique.* Liège: Études et Recherches Archéologiques de l'Université de Liège.

Féblot-Augustins, J. 1999. Raw material transport patterns and settlement systems in the European Lower and Middle Palaeolithic: continuity, change and variability. In: Roebroeks, W. and Gamble, C. (eds), *The Middle Palaeolithic Occupation of Europe.* Leiden: University of Leiden, pp. 193–214.

Fernández-Jalvo, Y., Díez, J. C., Rosell, J. and Cáceres, I. 1999. Human cannibalism in the Early Pleistocene of Europe (Gran Dolina, Sierra de Atapuerca, Spain). *Journal of Human Evolution* 37: 591–622.

Field, M. H., Huntley, B. and Müller, H. 1994. Eemian climate fluctuations observed in a European pollen record. *Nature* 371: 779–783.

Fischer, A. 1991. Pioneers in deglaciated landscapes: the expansion and adaptation of Late Palaeolithic societies in southern Scandinavia. In: Barton, R. N. E., Roberts, A. and Roe, D. A. (eds), *The Late Glacial in North West Europe: Human Adaptation and Environmental Change at the End of the Pleistocene.* London: Council for British Archaeology Research Report 77, pp. 100–121.

Fischer, A. 2004. Submerged Stone Age – Danish examples and North Sea potential. In: Flemming, N. C. (ed.), *Submarine Prehistoric Archaeology of the North Sea.* London: Council for British Archaeology Research Report 141, pp. 23–36.

Fitch, S., Thomson, K. and Gaffney, V. 2005. Late Pleistocene and Holocene depositional systems and palaeogeography of the Dogger Bank, North Sea. *Quaternary Research* 64: 185–196.

Flas, D. 2008. *La Transition du Paléolithique Moyen au Supérieur dans la Plaine Septentrionale de l'Europe.* Brussels: Anthropologica et Praehistorica 119.

Fletcher, W., Sanchez-Goñi, M., Allen, J., Cheddadi, R., Combourieu-Nebout, N., Huntley, B. et al. 2010. Millennial-scale variability during the last glacial in vegetation records from Europe. *Quaternary Science Reviews* 29: 2839–2864.

Foley, R. and Lahr, M. M. 1997. Mode 3 technologies and the evolution of modern humans. *Cambridge Archaeological Journal* 7: 3–36.

Fowler, J. 1929. Palaeoliths found at Slindon. *Sussex Archaeology Collections* 70: 197–200.

Francis, E. A. 1974. Quaternary. In: Johnson, G. A. L. and Hickling, G. (eds), *The Geology of Durham County. Transactions of the Natural History of Northumberland, Durham and Newcastle upon Tyne 41*, pp. 134–153.

Frere, J. 1800. Account of flint weapons discovered at Hoxne in Suffolk. *Archaeologia* 13: 204–205.

Fretwell, P. T., Smith, D. E. and Harrison, S. 2008. The Last Glacial maximum British-Irish ice sheet: a reconstruction using digital terrain mapping. *Journal of Quaternary Science* 23: 241–248.

Frison, G. C. 1968. A functional analysis of certain chipped stone tools. *American Antiquity* 33: 149–155.

Froom, F. R. 2005. *Late Glacial Long Blade Sites in the Kennet Valley.* London: British Museum.

Funnell, B. M. 1995. Global sea-level and the (pen-)insularity of late Cenozoic Britain. In: Preece, R. C. (ed.), *Island Britain: a Quaternary Perspective.* London: Geological Society Special Publication No. 96, pp. 3–13.

Funnell, B. M. 1996. Plio-Pleistocene palaeogeography of the southern North Sea Basin (3.75–0.60 Ma). *Quaternary Science Reviews* 15: 391–405.

Gabunia, L., Vekua, A., Lordkipanidze, D., Swisher, C. C. I., Ferring, R., Justus, A. et al. 2000. Earliest Pleistocene hominid cranial remains from Dmanisi, Republic of Georgia: taxonomy, geological setting, and age. *Science* 288: 1019–1025.

Gaffney, V., Fitch, S. and Smith, D. 2009. *Europe's Lost World: the Rediscovery of Doggerland.* York: Council for British Archaeology Research Report 160.

Gagnepain, J., Hedley, I., Bahain, J.-J. and Wagner, J.-J. 1992. Étude magnétostratigraphique du site de Ca' Belvedere di Monte Poggiolo (Forlì, Italie) et de son contexte stratigraphique. Premiers résultats. In: Peretto, C. (ed.), *I primi abitanti della Valle Padana, Monte Poggiolo nel quadro delle conoscenze europee.* Milan: Jaca Book, pp. 319–336.

Gagnepain, J., Laurent, M., Bahain, J.-J., Falguères, C., Hedley, I., Peretto, C., Wagner, J. J. and Yokoyama, Y. 1998. Synthèse des données paléomagnétiques et radiochronologiques du site de Ca' Belvedere di Monte Poggiolo (Romagna, Italie) et de son environnement géologique. *XIII Congresso delle Scienze Preistoriche et Protostoriche, Workshop 13, Forli 1999.* Abacus Editore, pp. 877–888.

Galiski, T. 2007. My own excavations and discoveries of Final Palaeolithic assemblages on the European Plain. In: Kobusiewicz, M. and Kabaciski, J. (eds), *Studies in the Final Palaeolithic Settlement of the Great European Plain.* Poznan: Institute of Archaeology and Ethnology, Polish Academy of Sciences, pp. 129–137.

Gallup, C. D., Edwards, R. L. and Johnson, R. G. 1994. The timing of high-sea levels over the past 200,000 years. *Science* 263: 796–800.

Gamble, C. S. 1986. *The Palaeolithic Settlement of Europe.* Cambridge: Cambridge University Press.

Gamble, C. S. 1987. Man the Shoveller. In: Soffer, O. (ed.), *The Pleistocene Old World.* London: Plenum Press, pp. 82–96.

Gamble, C. S. 1992. Comment on Roebroeks, Conard and van Kolfschoten. *Current Anthropology* 33: 569–571.

Gamble, C. S. 1993. *Timewalkers. The Prehistory of Global Colonisation.* London: Alan Sutton.

Gamble, C. S. 1995a. The earliest occupation of Europe: the environmental background. In: Roebroeks, W. and Kolfschoten, T. V. (eds), *The Earliest Occupation of Europe.* Leiden: University of Leiden, pp. 279–295.

Gamble, C. S. 1995b. Raw materials, technology and variability in Middle Pleistocene Europe. In:

Bermudez de Castro, J. M., Arsuaga, J.-L. and Carbonell, E. (eds), *Evolución Humana en Europa y los Yacimientos de la Sierra de Atapuerca.* Junta de Castilla y Leon, pp. 387–402.

Gamble, C. 1996. Hominid Behaviour in the Middle Pleistocene: An English Perspective. In: Gamble, C. S. and Lawson, A. J. (eds), *The English Palaeolithic Reviewed.* Salisbury: Trust for Wessex Archaeology, pp. 66–71.

Gamble, C. S. 1998. Handaxes and Palaeolithic Individuals. In: Ashton, N., Healy, F. and Pettitt, P. (eds), *Stone Age Archaeology; Essays in Honour of John Wymer.* Oxford: Oxbow Books, pp. 105–109.

Gamble, C. S. 1999. *The Palaeolithic Societies of Europe.* Cambridge: Cambridge University Press.

Gamble, C. 2001. *Archaeology: the Basics.* London: Routledge.

Gamble, C. S. 2002. Early beginnings 500–35,000 years ago. In: Slack, P. and Ward, R. (eds), *The Peopling of Britain: the Shaping of a Human Landscape. The Linacre Lectures 1999.* Oxford: Oxford University Press, pp. 11–37.

Gamble, C. S. 2007. *Origins and Revolutions: Human Identity in Earliest Prehistory.* Cambridge: Cambridge University Press.

Gamble, C. S. 2009. Human display and dispersal: a case study from biotidal Britain in the Middle and Upper Pleistocene. *Evolutionary Anthropology* 18: 144–156.

Gamble, C. S. and ApSimon, A. 1986. Red Barns, Porchester. In: Collcutt, S. N. (ed.), *The Palaeolithic of Britain and its Nearest neighbours: Recent Trends.* Sheffield: University of Sheffield, pp. 8–13.

Gamble, C. S. and Roebroeks, W. 1999. The Middle Palaeolithic: a point of inflection. In: Gamble, C. and Roebroeks, W. (eds), *The Middle Palaeolithic Occupation of Europe.* Leiden: University of Leiden Press, pp. 3–21.

Gamble, C. S. and Steele, J. 1999. Hominid ranging patterns and dietary strategies. In: H. Ullrich (ed.), *Hominid Evolution; Lifestyles and Survival Strategies.* Edition Archaea, pp. 346–409.

Gamble, C. S. and Kruszynski, R. 2009. John Evans, Joseph Prestwich and the stone that shattered the time barrier. *Antiquity* 83: 461–475.

Gamble, C. S. and Moutsiou, T. 2011. The time revolution of 1859 and the stratification of the primeval mind. *Notes and Records of the Royal Society* 65: 43–63.

Gamble, C. S., Davies, W., Pettitt, P. and Richards, M. 2004. Climate change and evolving human diversity in Europe during the last glacial. *Philosophical Transactions of the Royal Society of London* B359: 243–254.

Gamble, C. S., Davies, W., Pettitt, P., Richards, M. and Hazelwood, L. 2005. The archaeological and genetic foundations of the European population during the Lateglacial: implications for 'agricultural thinking'. *Cambridge Archaeological Journal* 15: 193–223.

Ganopolski, A. and Rahmstorf, S. 2001. Simulation of rapid glacial climate changes in a coupled climate model. *Nature* 409: 153–158.

Gao, C., Coope, G. R., Keen, D. H. and Pettitt, M. E. 1998. Middle Devensian deposits of the Ivel Valley at Sandy, Bedfordshire, England. *Proceedings of the Geologists' Association* 109: 127–137.

Gao, C., Keen, D. H., Boreham, S., Coope, G. R., Pettitt, M. E., Stuart, A. J. et al. 2000. Last Interglacial and Devensian deposits of the River Great Ouse at Woolpack Farm, Fenstanton, Cambridgeshire, UK. *Quaternary Science Reviews* 19: 787–810.

Garrod, D. A. 1926. *The Upper Palaeolithic Age in Britain.* Oxford: Clarendon Press.

Garton, D. 1993. A Late Upper Palaeolithic site near Newark, Nottinghamshire. *Transactions of the Thoroton Society of Nottinghamshire* XCVIII: 145.

Garton, D. and Jacobi, R. M. 2009. An extensive Later Upper Palaeolithic flint scatter at Farndon Fields, near Newark, Nottinghamshire. *The Archaeological Journal* 166: 1–37.

Gaudzinski, S. 1995. Wallertheim revisited: a re-analysis of the fauna from the Middle Palaeolithic site of Wallertheim (Rheinhessen/Germany). *Journal of Archaeological Science* 22: 51–66.

Gaudzinski, S. 1996. On bovid assemblages and their consequences for the knowledge of subsistence patterns in the Middle Palaeolithic. *Proceedings of the Prehistoric Society* 62: 19–39.

Gaudzinski, S. 1999a. The faunal record of the Lower and Middle Palaeolithic of Europe: Remarks on human interference. In: Roebroeks, W. and Gamble, C. (eds), *The Middle Palaeolithic Occupation of Europe.* Leiden: University of Leiden, pp. 215–233.

Gaudzinski, S. 1999b. Middle Palaeolithic bone tools from the open-air site Salzgitter-Lebenstedt (Germany). *Journal of Archaeological Science* 26: 125–41.

Gaudzinski, S. and Roebroeks, W. 2000. Adults only. Reindeer hunting at the Middle Palaeolithic site of Salzgitter-Lebenstedt, Northern Germany. *Journal of Human Evolution* 38: 497–521.

Gaudzinski, S., Turner, E., Anzidei, A. P., Alvarez-Fernandez, E., Arroyo-Cabrales, J., Cinq-Mars, J. et al. 2005. The use of Proboscidean remains in everyday Palaeolithic life. *Quaternary International* 126/128: 179–194.

Gaunt, G. D. 1970. A temporary section across the Escrick moraine at Wheldrake, East Yorkshire. *Journal of Earth Sciences* 8: 163–170.

Gaunt, G. D., Coope, G. R. and Franks, J. W. 1970. Quaternary Deposits at Oxbow opencast coal site in the Aire Valley, Yorkshire. *Proceedings of the Yorkshire Geological Society* 38: 175–200.

Geneste, J.-M. 1985. *Analyse lithique des industries Moustériennes du Périgord: une approche technologique du comportement des groups au Paléolithique moyen.* Thesis, Université de Bordeaux.

Geneste, J.-M. 1989. Economie des resources lithiques dans le Moustérien du sud-ouest de la France. In: Otte, M. (ed.), *L'Homme de Neanderthal Vol 6 La Subsistence.* Liège: Etudes et Recherches Archéologique de l'Université de Liège, pp. 75–97.

Germonpré, M. Lázničková-Galetová, M. and Sablin, M. V. 2012. Palaeolithic dog skulls at the Gravettian Předmostí site, the Czech Republic. *Journal of Archaeological Science* 39(1): 184–202.

Gibbard, P. L. 1982. Terrace stratigraphy and drainage history of the Plateau Gravels of north Surrey, South Berkshire and north Hampshire, England. *Proceedings of the Geologists' Association* 93: 369–384.

Gibbard, P. L. 1985. *The Pleistocene History of the Middle Thames.* Cambridge: Cambridge University Press.

Gibbard, P. L. 1988. The history of the great northwestern European rivers during the past three million years. *Philosophical Transactions of the Royal Society of London* B318: 559–602.

Gibbard, P. L. 1994. *The Pleistocene History of the Lower Thames Valley.* Cambridge: Cambridge University Press.

Gibbard, P. L. 1995. Formation of the Strait of Dover. In: Preece, R. C. (ed.), *Island Britain: a Quaternary Perspective.* London: Geological Society Special Publication. No. 96, pp. 15–26.

Gibbard, P. L. 2007. Palaeogeography: Europe cut adrift. *Nature* 448: 259–260.

Gibbard, P. L. and Aalto, M. M. 1977. A Hoxnian interglacial site at Fisher's Green, Stevenage, Hertfordshire. *New Phytologist* 78: 505–523.

Gibbard, P. L. and Lautridou, J. P. 2003. The Quaternary history of the English Channel: an introduction. *Journal of Quaternary Science* 18: 195–199.

Gibbard, P. L., Coope, G. R., Hall, A. R., Preece, R. C. and Robinson, J. E. 1982. Middle Devensian deposits beneath the 'Upper Floodplain' terrace of the River Thames at Kempton Park, Sunbury, England. *Proceedings of the Geologist's Association* 93: 275–289.

Gibbard, P. L., Bryant, I. D. and Hall, A. R. 1986. A Hoxnian interglacial doline infilling at Slade Oak Lane, Denham, Buckinghamshire, England. *Geological Magazine* 123: 27–43.

Gibbard, P. L., Wintle, A.G and Catt, J.A. 1987. Age and origin of clayey silt 'brickearth' in west London, England. *Journal of Quaternary Science* 2: 3–9.

Gilead, D. 1973. Cleavers in Early Palaeolithic industries in Israel. *Paléorient* 1: 73–86.

Gillespie, R., Gowlett, J. A. J., Hall, E. T., Hedges, R. E. M. and Perry, C. 1985. Radiocarbon dates from the Oxford AMS system: Archaeometry datelist 2. *Archaeometry* 27: 237–246.

Gilmour, M., Currant, A., Jacobi, R. and Stringer, C. 2007. Recent TIMS dating results from British Late Pleistocene vertebrate localities: Context and interpretation. *Journal of Quaternary Science* 22: 793–800.

Gilot, E. 1994. Datations C14. In: Otte, M. (ed.), *Le Magdalenien du Trou de Chaleux (Hulsonniaux-Belgique).* Liège: Études et Recherches Archéologiques de l'Université de Liège 60, p. 169.

Gladfelter, B. G. 1972. Cold-climate features in the vicinity of Clacton-on-Sea, Essex (England). *Quaternaria* 16: 121–135.

Gladfelter, B. G. 1993. The geostratigraphic context of the archaeology. In: Singer, R., Gladfelter, B. G. and Wymer, J. J. (eds), *The Lower Paleolithic Site at Hoxne, England.* Chicago: University of Chicago Press, pp. 23–66.

Gleed-Owen, C. 1999. The palaeoclimatic and biostratigraphic significance of herpetofaunal remains from the British Quaternary. In: Andrews, P. and Banham, P. H. (eds), *Late Cenozoic Environments and Hominid Evolution: a Tribute to Bill Bishop.* Bath: Geologial Society.

Glimmerveen, J., Mol, D., Post, K., Reumer, J. W. F., van der Plicht, H., de Vos, J. et al. 2004. The North Sea Project: the first palaeontological, palynological and archaeological results. In: Flemming, N. C. (ed.), *Submarine Prehistoric Archaeology of the North Sea. CBA Research Report 141.* York: CBA, pp. 43–52.

Godwin, H. 1964. Late-Weichselian conditions in southeastern Britain: organic deposits at Colney Heath, Herts. *Philosophical Transactions of the Royal Society of London* B150: 199–215.

Golledge, N. R., Fabel, D., Everest, J. D., Freeman, S. and Binnie, S. 2007. First cosmogenic ^{10}Be age constraint on the timing of Younger Dryas glaciations and ice cap thickness, western Scottish Highlands. *Journal of Quaternary Science* 22: 785–91.

Goren-Inbar, N. 1992. The Acheulian site of Gesher Benot Ya'aqov: an African or Asian Entity. In: Akawaza, T., Aoki, K. and Kimura, T. (eds), *The Evolution and Dispersal of Modern Humans in Asia.* Japan: Hokunsen-Sha, pp. 67–82.

Goren-Inbar, N. and Belfer-Cohen, A. 1998. The technological abilities of the Levantine Mousterians: cultural and mental capacities. In: Akazawa, T., Aoki, K. and Bar-Yosef, O. (eds), *Neanderthals and modern humans in Western Asia.* New York: Plenum Press, pp. 205–221.

Goren-Inbar, N. and Sharon, G. 2006. Invisible handaxes and visible Acheulian biface technology at Gesher Benot Ya'aqov, Israel. In: Goren-Inbar, N. and Sharon, G. (eds), *Axe Age: Acheulian Toolmaking from Quarry to Discard.* London: Equinox, pp. 111–135.

Goren-Inbar, N., Feibel, C. S., Verosub, K. L., Melamed, Y., Kislev, M. E., Tchernov, E. et al. 2000. Pleistocene milestones on the Out-of-Africa corridor at Gesher Benot Ya'aqov, Israel. *Science* 289: 944–947.

Goren-Inbar, N., Alperson, N., Kislev, M. E., Simchoni, O., Melamed, Y., Ben-Nun, A. et al. 2004. Evidence of hominin control of fire at Gesher Benot Ya'aqov, Israel. *Science* 304: 725–727.

Gosden, C. 1994. *Social Being and Time*. Oxford: Blackwell.

Gouédo, J.-M. 1996. Proposition de calage chronologiques de l'industrie Aurignacienne d'Herbeville (Yvelines). In: Pautrat, Y. and Thévenin, A. (eds), *Paléolothique Supérieur et Epipaléolithique dans le Nord-Est de la France.* Dijon: Service Régionale de l'Archéologie de Borgogne, pp. 11–16.

Gowlett, J. A. J. 1984. Mental abilities of early man: a look at some hard evidence. In: Foley, R. A. (ed.), *Hominid Evolution and Community Ecology.* London: Academic Press, pp. 167–193.

Gowlett, J. A. J. 2006. The early settlement of northern Europe: fire history in the context of climate change and the social brain. *Comptes Rendus Palevol* 5: 299–310.

Gowlett, J. A. J., Harris, J. W. K., Walton, D. and B.A., W. 1981. Early archaeological sites, hominid remains and traces of fire from Chesowanja, Kenya. *Nature* 294: 125–129.

Gowlett, J. A. J., Hall, E. T., Hedges, R. E. M. and Perry, C. 1986a. Radiocarbon dates from the Oxford AMS system: Archaeometry datelist 3. *Archaeometry* 28: 116–25.

Gowlett, J. A. J., Hedges, R. E. M., Law, I. A. and Perry, C. 1986b. Radiocarbon dates from the Oxford AMS system: Archaeometry datelist 4. *Archaeometry* 28: 206–221.

Gowlett, J. A. J., Chambers, J. C., Hallos, J. and Pumphrey, T. R. J. 1998. Beeches Pit: first views of the archaeology of a Middle Pleistocene site in Suffolk, UK, in European context. *Anthropologie* 36: 91–97.

Gowlett, J. A. J., Hallos, J., Hounsell, S., Brant, V. and N.C., D. 2005. Beeches Pit — archaeology, assemblage dynamics and early fire history of a Middle Pleistocene site in East Anglia, UK. *Journal of Eurasian Prehistory* 3: 3–40.

Graham, A. G. C., Lonergan, L. and Stoker, M. S. 2009. Seafloor glacial features reveal the extent and decay of the last British ice sheet, east of Scotland. *Journal of Quaternary Science* 24: 117–138.

Graham, J. M. and Roe, D. A. 1970. Discrimination of British Lower and Middle Palaeolithic handaxe groups using canonical variates. *World Archaeology* 1: 321–342.

Grayson, D. K. 1983. *The Establishment of Human Antiquity*. New York: Academic Press.

Green, C. P. 1984. *Pontnewydd Cave; A Lower Palaeolithic Hominid Site in Wales.* Cardiff: National Museum of Wales.

Green, C. P., Keen, D. H., McGregor, D. F., Robinson, J. E. and Williams, R. B. W. 1983. Stratigraphy and environmental significance of Pleistocene deposits at Fisherton, near Salisbury, Wiltshire. *Proceedings of the Geologist's Association* 94: 17–22.

Green, C. P., Coope, G. R., Currant, A., Holyoak, D., Ivanovich, M., Jones, R. et al. 1984. Evidence for two temperate episodes in the late Pleistocene deposits at Marsworth, Buckinghamshire. *Nature* 309: 778–781.

Green, C. P., Coope, G. R., Jones, R. L., Keen, D. H., Bowen, D. Q., Currant, A. P. et al. 1996. Pleistocene deposits at Stoke Goldington in the valley of the Great Ouse, UK. *Journal of Quaternary Science* 11: 59–87.

Green, C. P., Gibbard, P. L. and Bishop, B. J. 2004. Stoke Newington: geoarchaeology of the Palaeolithic 'floor'. *Proceedings of the Geologists' Association* 115: 193–208.

Green, C. P., Branch, N. P., Coope, G. R., Field, M. H., Keen, D. H., Wells, J. M. et al. 2006. Marine Isotope Stage 9 environments of fluvial deposits at Hackney, north London, UK. *Quaternary Science Reviews* 25: 89–113.

Green, H. S. and Walker, E. 1991. *Ice Age Hunters: Neanderthal and Early Modern Humans in Wales.* Cardiff: National Museum of Wales.

Green, R. E., Krause, J., Briggs, A. W. et al. 2010. A draft sequence of the Neandertal genome *Science* 328: 710–722.

Greenhill, J. E. 1884. The Implementiferous Gravels of North-East London. *Proceedings of Geologists' Association* 8: 336–343.

Greenland Ice Core Project Members. 1993. Climate instability during the last interglacial period recorded in the GRIP ice core. *Nature* 364: 203–207.

Greenwood, M. T., Agnew, M. D. and Wood, P. J. 2003. The use of caddisfly fauna (Insecta: Trichoptera) to characterise the Late-Glacial River Trent, England. *Journal of Quaternary Science* 18: 645–661.

Greenwood, S. L. and Clark, C. D. 2009. Reconstructing the last Irish ice sheet 2: a geomorphologically-driven model of ice-sheet growth, retreat and dynamics. *Quaternary Science Reviews* 28: 3101–3123.

Grimes, W. F. and Cowley, L. F. 1935. Coygan Cave, Llansadyrnin, Carmarthenshire. *Archaeologia Cambrensis* 90: 95–111.

Grimm, S. B. and Weber, M.-J. 2008. The chronological framework of the Hamburgian in the light of old and new ^{14}C dates. *Quartär* 55: 17–40.

Grootes, P. M., Stuiver, M., White, J. W. C., Johnsen, S. J. and Jouzel, J. 1993. Comparison of oxygen isotope records from the GISP2 and GRIP Greenland ice cores. *Nature* 366: 552–554.

Grün, R. and Schwarcz, H. P. 2000. Revised open system U-series/ESR age calculations for teeth from Stratum C at the Hoxnian Interglacial type locality, England. *Quaternary Science Reviews* 19: 1151–1154.

Gupta, S., Collier, J. S., Palmer-Felgate, A. and Potter, G. 2007. Catastrophic flooding origin of the shelf valley systems of the English Channel. *Nature* 448: 342–345.

Guthrie, R. D. 1982. Mammals of the mammoth steppe as paleoenvironmental indicators. In: Hopkins, D. M., Matthews, J. V., Schweger, C. E. and Young, S. B. (eds), *Paleoecology of Beringia.* New York: Academic Press, pp. 307–376.

Guthrie, R. D. 1984. Mosaics, allelochemics and nutrients: an ecological theory of late Pleistocene megafaunal extinctions. In: P. S. Martin and R. G. Klein (eds), *Quaternary Extinctions: a Prehistoric Revolution.* Tuscon: University of Arizona Press, pp. 259–298.

Guthrie, R. D. 1990. *Frozen Fauna of the Mammoth Steppe.* Chicago: Chicago University Press.

Haidle, M. N. and Pawlik, A. F. 2010. The earliest settlement of Germany: is there anything out there? *Quaternary International* 223/224: 143–153.

Hallam, J. S., Edwards, B. J. N., Barnes, B. and Stuart, A. J. 1973. The remains of a Late Glacial elk associated with barbed points from High Furlong, Near Blackpool, Lancashire. *Proceedings of the Prehistoric Society* 29: 100–128.

Hallos, J. 2005. '15 minutes of fame': Exploring the temporal dimension of Middle Pleistocene lithic technology. *Journal of Human Evolution* 49: 155–179.

Hamblin, R., Moorlock, B. S. P., Booth, S. J., Jeffery, D. H. and Morigi, A. N. 1997. The Red Crag and Norwich Crag formations in eastern Suffolk. *Proceedings of the Geologists' Association* 108: 11–23.

Hamblin, R., Moorlock, B. and Rose, J. 2000. A new glacial stratigraphy for eastern England. *Quaternary Newsletter* 92: 35–43.

Hamblin, R. J. O., Moorlock, B. S. P., Rose, J., Lee, J. R., Riding, J. B., Booth, S. J. et al. 2005. Revised pre-Devensian glacial stratigraphy in Norfolk, England, based on mapping and till provenance. *Geologie en Mijnbouw/Netherlands Journal of Geosciences* 84: 77–85.

Hardaker, T. 2001. New Lower Palaeolithic finds from the Upper Thames. In: Milliken, S. and Cook, J. (eds), *A Very Remote Period Indeed: Papers on the Palaeolithic Presented to Derek Roe.* Oxford: Oxbow Books, pp. 180–198.

Harding, P. and Gibbard, P. L. 1984. Excavations at Northwold Road, Stoke Newington, north-east London. *Transactions of the London and Middlesex Archaeological Society,* 34: 1–18.

Harding, P., Bridgland, D. R., Keen, D. H. and Rogerson, R. J. 1992. A Palaeolithic site rediscovered at Biddenham, Bedfordshire. *Bedfordshire Archaeology* 19: 87–90.

Hardy, B. L. 2010. Climatic variability and plant food distribution in Pleistocene Europe: Implications for Neanderthal diet and subsistence. *Quaternary Science Reviews* 29: 662–679.

Harrison, B. 1892. Report of the Committee appointed to carry on excavations at Oldbury Hill near Ightham. *Report of the Sixty-First Meeting of the British Association for the Advancement of Science, Cardiff* 1891: 353–354.

Harrison, K. 1938. A note on High Lodge, Mildenhall. *Proceedings of the Prehistoric Society* 4: 326–328.

Harrison, R. A. 1977. The Uphill Quarry Caves, Weston-Super-Mare, A Reappraisal. *Proceedings of the University of Bristol Spelaeological Society* 14: 233–254.

Harrison, S., Whalley, B. and Anderson, E. 2008. Relict rock glaciers and protalus lobes in the British Isles: implications for Late Pleistocene mountain geomorphology and palaeoclimate. *Journal of Quaternary Science* 23: 287–304.

Hawkes, C. J., Tratman, E. K. and Powers, R. 1970. Decorated piece of rib bone from the Palaeolithic levels at Gough's Cave, Cheddar, Somerset. *Proceedings of the University of Bristol Spelaeological Society* 12: 137–142.

Hawkes, K., O'Connell, J. F. and Blurton-Jones, N. G. 1997. Hadza women's time allocation, offspring provisioning and the evolution of long post-menopausal lifespans. *Current Anthropology* 38: 551–577.

Hawkes, K., O'Connell, J. and Blurton-Jones, N. 2003. Human life histories: primate trade-offs, grandmothering socioecology, and the fossil recor. In: Kappeler, P. M. and Pereira, M. E. (eds), *Primate Life Histories and Socioecology.* Chicago: University of Chicago Press, pp. 204–231.

Hawkins, A. B. and Tratman, E. K. 1977. The Quaternary deposits of the Mendip, Bath and Bristol Areas; including a reprinting of Donovan's 1954 and 1964 Bibliographies. *Proceedings of the University of Bristol Spelaeological Society* 14: 197–232.

Hayden, B. and Villeneuve, S. 2009. Sex, symmetry and silliness in the bifacial world. *Antiquity* 83: 1163–1170.

Haynes, G. 1991. *Mammoths, Mastodonts, and Elephants: Biology, Behavior and the Fossil Record.* Cambridge: Cambridge University Press.

Haynes, G. 2002. *The Early Settlement of North America: The Clovis Era.* Cambridge: Cambridge University Press.

Head, M. J. and Gibbard, P. 2005. Early-Middle Pleistocene transitions: an overview and recommendation for the defining boundary. In: Head, M. J. and Gibbard, P. L. (eds), *Early-Middle Pleistocene Transitions: The Land-Ocean Evidence.* London: Geological Society Special Publications 247, pp. 1–18.

Hedges, R. E. M., Housley, R. A., Law, I. A., Perry, C. and Gowlett, J. A. J. 1987. Radiocarbon dates from the Oxford AMS system: Archaeometry datelist 6. *Archaeometry* 29: 289–306.

Hedges, R. E. M., Housley, R. A., Law, I. A. and Perry, C. 1988. Radiocarbon dates from the Oxford AMS system: Archaeometry datelist 7. *Archaeometry* 30: 155–164.

Hedges, R. E. M., Housley, R. A., Law, I. A. and Bronk, C. R. 1989. Radiocarbon dates from the Oxford AMS system: Archaeometry datelist 9. *Archaeometry* 31: 207–234.

Hedges, R. E. M., Housley, R. A., Law, I. A. and Bronk, C. R. 1990a. Radiocarbon dates from the Oxford AMS system: Archaeometry datelist 10. *Archaeometry* 32: 101–108.

Hedges, R. E. M., Housley, R. A., Bronk, C. R. and van Kinken, G. J. 1990b. Radiocarbon dates from the Oxford AMS system: Archaeometry datelist 11. *Archaeometry* 32: 211–237.

Hedges, R. E. M., Housley, R. A., Bronk, C. R. and van Klinken, G. J. 1991. Radiocarbon dates from the Oxford AMS system: Archaeometry datelist 13. *Archaeometry* 33: 279–296.

Hedges, R. E. M., Housley, R. A., Bronk, C. R. and van Klinken, G. J. 1992. Radiocarbon dates from the Oxford AMS system: Archaeometry datelist 14. *Archaeometry* 34: 141–159.

Hedges, R. E. M., Housley, R., Bronk Ramsey, C. and van Kinken, G. J. 1993. Radiocarbon dates from the Oxford AMS system: Archaeometry datelist 17. *Archaeometry* 35: 305–326.

Hedges, R. E. M., Housley, R. A., Bronk Ramsey, C. and van Klinken, G. J. 1994. Radiocarbon dates from the Oxford AMS system: Archaeometry datelist 18. *Archaeometry* 36: 337–374.

Hedges, R. E. M., Pettitt, P. B., Bronk Ramsey, C. and van Klinken, G. J. 1996. Radiocarbon dates from the Oxford AMS system: Archaeometry datelist 22. *Archaeometry* 38: 391–415.

Hedges, R. E. M., Pettitt, P. B., Bronk Ramsey, C. and van Klinken, G. J. 1997. Radiocarbon dates from the Oxford AMS system: Archaeometry datelist 23. *Archaeometry* 39: 247–262.

Hedges, R. E. M., Pettitt, P. B., Bronk Ramsey, C. and van Klinken, G. J. 1998. Radiocarbon dates from the Oxford AMS system: Archaeometry datelist 25. *Archaeometry* 40: 227–239.

Heinrich, H. 1988. Origin and consequences of cyclic ice-rafting events in Northeast Atlantic Ocean during the past 130,000 years. *Quaternary Research* 29: 142–152.

Hemmer, H. 2000. Out of Asia: a paleoecological scenario of man and his carnivorous competitors in the European Lower Pleistocene. *Études et Recherches Archéologiques de l'Université de Liège* 92: 99–106.

Hemming, S. R. 2004. Heinrich events: Massive late Pleistocene detritus layers of the North Atlantic and their global climate imprint. *Reviews of Geophysics* 42: doi: 10.1029/2003RG000128.

Henderson, A. H. 1973. Flint and chert implements from Froggatt, Derbyshire. *Transactions of the Hunter Archaeological Society* 10: 138–144.

Henrich, J. 2004. Demography and cultural evolution: how adaptive cultural processes can produce maladaptive losses – the Tasmanian case. *American Antiquity* 69: 197–214.

Hicks, H. 1867. Discovery of a hyaena-den near Laugharne, Carmarthenshire. *Geological Magazine* 4: 307–309.

Hicks, H. 1884. On some recent researches in bone caves in Wales. *Proceedings of Geologists Association* 9: 1–42.

Hicks, S. 2006. When no pollen does not mean no trees. *Vegetation History and Archaeobotany* 15: 253–261.

Hiemstra, J. F., Rijsdijk, K. F., Shakesby, R. A. and McCarroll, D. 2009. Reinterpreting Rotherslade, Gower Peninsula: implications for the Last Glacial ice limits and Quaternary stratigraphy of the British Isles. *Journal of Quaternary Science* 24: 399–410.

Higham, T. F. G. 2011. European Middle and Upper Palaeolithic radiocarbon dates are often older than they look: problems with previous dates and some remedies. *Antiquity* 55: 235–249.

Higham, T. F. G., Jacobi, R. M. and Bronk Ramsey, C. 2006. AMS radiocarbon dating of bone from the European Palaeolithic using ultrafiltration. *Radiocarbon* 48: 179–195.

Higham, T. F. G., Jacobi, R., Julien, M., David, F., Basell, L., Wood, R. et al. 2010. Chronology of the Grotte du Renne (France) and implications for the context of ornaments and human remains within the Châtelperronian. *Proceedings of the National Academy of Sciences (USA)* 107: 20234–20239.

Higham, T. F. G., Compten, T., Stringer, C., Jacobi, R., Shapiro, B. Trinkhaus, E. et al. (2011). The earliest evidence for anatomically modern humans in northwest Europe. *Nature* (doi: 10.1038/nature 10484).

Hillson, S. W., Parfitt, S. A., Bello, S. M., Roberts, M. B. and Stringer, C. B. 2010. Two hominin incisor teeth from the Middle Pleistocene site of Boxgrove, West Sussex, England. *Journal of Human Evolution* 59: 493–503.

Hinout, J. 1997. Quelques aspects de l'épipaléolithique dans le Nord du Bassin Parisien. *Bulletin de la Societé Préhistorique Française* 94: 337–340.

Hinton, M. A. C. and Kennard, A. S. 1905. The relative ages of the stone implements of the Lower Thames valley. *Proceedings of Geologists Association* 19: 76–100.

Höck, C. 1993. Die frauenstatuetten des Magdalénien von Gönnerdorf und Andernach. *Jahrbuch des Römisch-Germanischen Zentralmuseums Mainz* 40: 253–316.

Hollin, J. T. 1977. Thames interglacial sites, Ipswichian sea-levels and Antarctic ice surges. *Boreas* 6: 33–52.

Holm, J. and Rieck, F. 1987. Die Hamburger Kultur in Dänemark. *Archälogisches Korrespondenzblatt* 17: 151–165.

Holman, J. A. 1998. The herpetofauna. In: Ashton, N. M., Lewis, S. G. and Parfitt, S. A. (eds), *Excavations at the Lower Palaeolithic site at East Farm, Barnham, Suffolk 1989–94.* London: British Museum Press, pp. 101–106.

Holman, J. A., Stuart, A. J. and Clayden, J. D. 1990. A Middle Pleistocene herpetofauna from Cudmore Grove, Essex, England, and its paleogeographic and paleoclimatic implications. *Journal of Vertebrate Paleontology* 10: 86–94.

Holmes, J. A., Atkinson, T. C., Darbyshire, D. P. F., Horne, D. J., Joordens, J., Roberts, M. B. et al. 2010. Middle Pleistocene climate and hydrological environment at Boxgrove hominin sites (West Sussex, UK) from ostracod records. *Quaternary Science Reviews* 29: 1515–1527.

Holyoak, D. T. 1983. A Late Pleistocene interglacial flora and molluscan fauna from Thatcham, Berkshire, with notes on Mollusca from interglacial deposits at Aveley, Essex. *Geological Magazine* 120: 823–829.

Hopkinson, T. 2007. The transition from the Lower to Middle Palaeolithic in Europe and the incorporation of difference. *Antiquity* 81: 294–307.

Hopkinson, T. and White, M. J. 2005. The Acheulean and the handaxe: structure and agency in the Palaeolithic. In: Gamble, C. and Porr, M. (eds), *The Hominid Individual in Context: Archaeological Investigations of Lower and Middle Palaeolithic landscapes, locales and artefacts.* London: Routledge, pp. 13–28.

Horton, A., Worsaam, B. C. and Whittow, J. B. 1981. The Wallingford Fan Gravel. *Philosophical Transactions of the Royal Society of London* B293: 215–255.

Hosfield, R. 1999. *The Palaeolithic of the Hampshire Basin: A Regional Model of Hominid Behaviour during the Middle Pleistocene.* Oxford: British Archaeological Reports British Series 286.

Hosfield, R. 2005. Individuals among palimpsest data: fluvial landscapes in Southern England. In: Gamble, C. and Porr, M. (eds), *The Hominid Individual in Context: Archaeological Investigations of Lower and Middle Palaeolithic landscapes, locales and artefacts.* London: Routledge, pp. 220–243.

Hosfield, R. 2011. The British Lower Palaeolithic of the early Middle Pleistocene. *Quaternary Science Reviews* 30: 1486–1510.

Hosfield, R., and Chambers, J. C. 2002. The Lower Palaeolithic site of Broom: geoarchaeological implications of optical dating. *Lithics* 23: 33–42.

Hosfield, R., Straker, V., Gardiner, P., Brown, A., Davies, P., Fyfe, R. et al. 2007. Palaeolithic and Mesolithic. In: Webster, C. J. (ed.) *The Archaeology of South-West England: South West Archaeological Framework.* Taunton: Somerset County Council, pp. 23–62.

Housley, R. 1991. AMS dates from the Lateglacial and early Postglacial in north-west Europe: a review. In: Barton, N., Roberts, A. J. and Roe, D. A. (eds), *The Late-Glacial in North-West Europe: Human Adaptation and Environmental Change at the End of the Pleistocene.* London: Council for British Archaeology, pp. 25–39.

Housley, R., Gamble, C., Street, M. and Pettitt, P. B. 1997. Radiocarbon evidence for the Lateglacial human recolonisation of Northern Europe. *Proceedings of the Prehistoric Society* 63: 25–54.

Housley, R., Gamble, C. and Pettitt, P. 2000. Reply to Blockley, Donahue and Pollard. *Antiquity* 74: 117–119.

Howard, A. J., Bridgland, D., Knight, D., McNabb, J., Rose, J., Schreve, D. et al. 2007. The British Pleistocene fluvial archive: East Midlands drainage evolution and human occupation in the context of the British and NW European record. *Quaternary Science Reviews* 26: 2724–2737.

Hubbard, A., Bradwell, T., Golledge, N., Hall, A., Patton, H., Sugden, D. et al. 2009. Dynamic cycles, ice systems and their impact on the extent, chronology and deglaciation of the British-Irish ice sheet. *Quaternary Science Reviews* 28: 758–776.

Hubbard, R. 1978. Pollen analysis of the Pleistocene deposits at Yiewsley. In: Collins, D. (ed.) *Early Man in West Middlesex: the Yiewsley Palaeolithic Sites.* London: HMSO, pp. 15–22.

Hubbard, R. 1982. The environmental evidence from Swanscombe and its implications for Palaeolithic Archaeology. In: Leach, P. E. (ed.), *Archaeology in Kent to AD 1500.* London: Council for British Archaeology Research Report 48, pp. 3–7.

Hubbard, R. 1996. The palynological studies from the Waechter excavations. In: Conway, B., McNabb, J. and Ashton, N. M. (eds), *Excavations at Barnfield Pit, Swanscombe, 1968–72, British Museum Occasional Paper Number 94.* London: British Museum Press, pp. 191–199.

Hublin, J.-J. and Roebroeks, W. 2009. Ebb and flow or regional extinctions? On the character of Neandertal occupation of northern environments. *Comptes Rendus Palevol* 8: 503–509.

Hublin, J.-J., Weston, D., Gunz, P., Richards, M., Roebroeks, W., Glimmerveen, J. et al. 2009. Out of the North Sea: the Zeeland Ridges Neandertal. *Journal of Human Evolution* 57: 777–785.

Huchet, A., Pautrat, Y. and Thévenin, A. 1996. Présences Ahrensburgiennes et Mésolithiques en Puisaye. In: Pautrat, Y. and Thévenin, A. (eds), *Paléolithique Supérieur et Epipaléolithique dans le Nord-Est de la France*. Dijon: Service Régional de l'Archéologie de Bourgogne, pp. 106–118.

Hughes, P. D. 2009. Loch Lomond Stadial (Younger Dryas) glaciers and climate in Wales. *Geological Journal* 44: 375–391.

Hughes, P. D. M., Kenward, H. K., Hall, A. R. and Large, F. D. 2000. A high-resolution record of mire development and climatic change spanning the Late-Glacial-Holocene boundary at Church Moss, Davenham (Cheshire, England). *Journal of Quaternary Science* 15: 697–724.

Hughes, T. M. and Thomas, D. R. 1874. On the occurrence of felstone implements of Le Moustier type in Pontnewydd cave, near Cefn, St. Asaph. *Journal of the Anthropological Institute of Great Britain and Ireland* 3: 387–392.

Hunt, C. 1992. Pollen and algal microfossils from the High Lodge clayey-silts. In: Ashton, N. M., Lewis, S. G. and Rose, J. (eds), *High Lodge; Excavations by G. de G. Sieveking 1962–68 and J. Cook 1988.* London: British Museum Press, pp. 109–115.

Huntley, B. and Allen, P. 2003. Glacial Climates III: Palaeo-vegetation patterns in Late Glacial Europe. In: Van Andel, T. and Davies, W. (eds), *Neanderthals and Modern Humans in the European Landscape During the Last Glaciation: Archaeological Results of the Stage 3 project.* Cambridge: McDonald Institute, pp. 79–102.

Imbrie, J., Hays, J.D., Martinson, D.G., McIntyre, A., Mix, A.C., Morley, J.J. et al. 1984. The orbital theory of Pleistocene climate: support from a revised chronology of the marine $\delta^{18}O$ record. In: Berger, A., Imbrie, J., Hays, J., Kukla, G., Saltzman, B. (eds), *Milankovitch and Climate, Part 1.* Dordrecht: Plenum Reidel, pp. 269–305.

Ingold, T. 1993. Tool-use, sociality and intelligence. In: Gibson, K. R. and Ingold, T. (eds), *Tools, Language and Cognition in Human Evolution.* Cambridge: Cambridge University Press, pp. 429–445.

Irving, B. G. 1996. The ichthyofauna from the Waechter excavations, Barnfield Pit, Swanscombe. In: Conway, B., McNabb, J. and Ashton, N. (eds), *Excavations at Barnfield Pit, Swanscombe, 1968–72, British Museum Occasional Paper Number 94.* London: British Museum, pp. 145–147.

Isaac, G. 1972. Chronology and tempo of cultural change during the Pleistocene. In: Bishop, W. W. and Miller, J. (eds), *Calibration in Hominid Evolution.* Edinburgh: Scottish Academic Press, pp. 381–430.

Isaac, G. 1977. *Olorgesailie: Archaeological Studies of a Middle Pleistocene Lake Basin in Kenya.* Chicago: University of Chicago Press.

Isaac, G. 1978. Food sharing and human evolution: archaeological evidence from the Plio-Pleistocene of East Africa. *Journal of Anthropological Research* 34: 311–325.

Iverson, J. 1954. The late interglacial flora of Denmark and its relation to climate and soil. *Danmarks Geologiske Undersögelse II* 80: 87–119.

Jackson, J. W. 1945. A lance-point of Upper Palaeolithic type from Victoria Cave, Settle, Yorkshire. *The Antiquaries Journal* 22: 147–148.

Jacobi, R. M. 1980. The Upper Palaeolithic of Britain with special reference to Wales. In: Taylor, J. A. (ed.), *Culture and Environment in Prehistoric Wales.* Oxford: British Archaeological Reports (British Series) 76, pp. 15–100.

Jacobi, R. M. 1986. The Lateglacial archaeology of Gough's Cave at Cheddar. In: Collcutt, S. N. (ed.), *The Palaeolithic of Britain and its Nearest Neighbours: Recent Trends.* Sheffield: University of Sheffield, pp. 75–79.

Jacobi, R. M. 1987. On some flint and chert artefacts from Ossom's Cave, Staffordshire. *Staffordshire Archaeological Studies* 4: 93.

Jacobi, R. M. 1990. Leaf-points and the British Early Upper Palaeolithic. In: Kozlowski, J. (ed.), *Feuille de Pierre. Les Industries à pointes foliacées du Paléolithique supérieur européen.* Liège, pp. 271–289.

Jacobi, R. M. 1991. The Creswellian, Creswell and Cheddar. In: Barton, R. N. E., Roberts, A. J. and Roe, D. A. (eds), *The Late Glacial in north-west Europe: human adaptation and environmental change at the end of the Pleistocene.* London: Council for British Archaeology, pp. 128–140.

Jacobi, R. M. 1997. The 'Creswellian' in Britain. In: Fagnart, J. P. and Thévenin, A. (eds), *Le Tardiglaciaire en Europe du Nord Ouest.* Paris: Éditions du Comité des Travaux Historiques et Scientifiques, pp. 497–505.

Jacobi, R. M. 1999. Some observations on the British Earlier Upper Palaeolithic. In: Davies, W. and Charles, R. (eds), *Dorothy Garrod and the Progress of the Palaeolithic: Studies in the Prehistoric Archaeology of the Near East and Europe.* Oxford: Oxbow Books, pp. 35–40.

Jacobi, R. M. 2000. The Late Pleistocene archaeology of Somerset. In: Webster, C. J. (ed.) *Somerset Archaeology; Papers to mark 150 years of the Somerset Archaeological and Natural History Society.* Somerset County Council, pp. 45–52.

Jacobi, R. M. 2004. The Late Upper Palaeolithic lithic collection from Gough's Cave, Cheddar, Somerset and human use of the cave. *Proceedings of the Prehistoric Society* 70: 1–92.

Jacobi, R. M. 2005. Some observations on the lithic artefacts from Aveline's Hole, Burrington Coombe, North Somerset. *Proceedings of the University of Bristol Spelaeological Society* 23: 267–295.

Jacobi, R. M. 2006a. Creswell Crags and the sabre-toothed cat. *Studies in Spelaeology* 14: 33–38.

Jacobi, R. M. 2006b. Some observations on the non-flint lithics from Creswell Crags. *Lithics* 25 (for 2004): 39–64.

Jacobi, R. M. 2007a. A collection of Early Upper Palaeolithic artefacts from Beedings, near Pulborough, West Sussex and the context of similar finds from the British Isles. *Proceedings of the Prehistoric Society* 73: 229–325.

Jacobi, R. M. 2007b. The Stone Age archaeology of Church Hole, Creswell Crags, Nottinghamshire. In: Pettitt, P., Bahn, P. and Ripoll, S. (eds), *Palaeolithic Cave Art at Creswell Crags in European Context*. Oxford: Oxford University Press, pp. 71–111.

Jacobi, R. M. and Martingell, H. E. 1980. A Late-Glacial shouldered point from Cranwich, Norfolk. *Norfolk Archaeology* XXXVII: 312–314.

Jacobi, R. M. and Hawkes, C. J. 1993. Work at the Hyaena Den, Wookey Hole. *Proceedings of the University of Bristol Spelaeological Society* 19: 369–71.

Jacobi, R. M. and Pettitt, P. B. 2000. An Aurignacian point from Uphill Quarry, Somerset, and the colonization of Britain by *Homo sapiens*. *Antiquity* 74: 513–518.

Jacobi, R. M. and Grun, R. 2003. ESR dates from Robin Hood Cave, Creswell Crags, Derbyshire and the age of its early human occupation. *Quaternary Newsletter* 100: 1–12.

Jacobi, R. M. and Higham, T. F. G. 2008. The 'Red Lady' ages gracefully: new ultrafiltration AMS determinations from Paviland. *Journal of Human Evolution* 55: 898–907.

Jacobi, R. M. and Higham, T. F. G. 2009. The early Lateglacial re-colonisation of Britain: new radiocarbon evidence from Gough's Cave, southwest England. *Quaternary Science Reviews* 28: 1895–1913.

Jacobi, R. M. and Higham, T. F. G. 2011a. The British Earlier Upper Palaeolithic: settlement and chronology. In: Ashton, N., Lewis, S. and Stringer, C. (eds), *The Ancient Human Occupation of Britain*. Amsterdam: Elsevier, pp. 181–222.

Jacobi, R. M. and Higham, T. F. G. 2011b. The Late Upper Palaeolithic recolonisation of Britain: new results from AMS radiocarbon dating. In: Ashton, N., Lewis, S. and Stringer, C. (eds), *The Ancient Human Occupation of Britain*. Amsterdam: Elsevier, pp. 223–247.

Jacobi, R. M., Garton, D. and Brown, J. 2001. Field-walking and the Late Upper Palaeolithic of Nottinghamshire. *Transactions of the Thoroton Society of Nottinghamshire* 105: 17–22.

Jacobi, R. M., Rowe, P. J., Gilmour, M. A., Grün, R. and Atkinson, R. C. 1998. Radiometric dating of the Middle Palaeolithic tool industry and associated fauna of Pin Hole Cave, Creswell Crags, England. *Journal of Quaternary Science* 13: 29–42.

Jacobi, R. M., Higham, T. F. G. and Bronk Ramsey, C. 2006. AMS radiocarbon dating of Middle and Upper Palaeolithic bone in the British Isles: improved reliability using ultrafiltration. *Journal of Quaternary Science* 21: 557–573.

Jacobi, R. M., Higham, T. F. G. and Lord, T. C. 2009a. Improving the chronology of the human occupation of Britain during the Late Glacial. In: Street, M., Barton, N. and Terberger, T. (eds), *Humans, Environment and Chronology of the Late Glacial of the North European Plain. Proceedings of Workshop 14 (Commission XXXII 'The Final Palaeolithic of the Great European Plain' of the 15th U.I.S.P.P. Congress, Lisbon, September 2006*. Mainz: Römisch-Germanischen Zentralmuseums, pp. 7–25.

Jacobi, R. M., Rose, J., MacLeod, A. and Higham, T. F. G. 2009b. Revised radiocarbon ages on woolly rhinoceros (*Coelodonta antiquitatis*) from western central Scotland: significance for timing the extinction of woolly rhinoceros in Britain and the onset of the LGM in central Scotland. *Quaternary Science Reviews* 28: 2551–2556.

Jacobi, R. M., Higham, T. F. G., Haesaerts, P., Jadin, I. and Basell, L. S. 2010. Radiocarbon chronology for the Early Gravettian of northern Europe: new AMS determinations for Maisières-Canal, Belgium. *Antiquity* 84: 26–40.

James, S. R. 1989. Hominid use of fire in the Lower and Middle Palaeolithic. *Current Anthropology* 30: 1–26.

Jaubert, J. and Farizy, C. 1995. Levallois Débitage: exclusivity, absence or coexistence with other operative schemes in the Garonne, Basin, Southwestern France. In: Dibble, H. L. and Bar-Yosef, O. (eds), *The Definition and Interpretation of Levallois Technology.* Madison: Prehistory Press, pp. 227–248.

Jaubert, J., Lorblanchet, M., Laville, H., Slott-Moller, R., Truro, A. and J.P, B. 1990. *Les Chasseurs d'Auroches de La Borde.* Paris: Editions de la Maison des Sciences de l'Homme.

Jenkinson, R. D. S. 1984. *Creswell Crags: Late Pleistocene Sites in the East Midlands.* Oxford: British Archaeological Reports International Series 122.

Jenkinson, R. D. S., Gilbertson, D. D., Griffin, C. M., Hunt, C. O., Rowe, P. J. and Coles, G. M. 1986. New Upper Palaeolithic human remains from Robin Hood Cave, Creswell Crags SSSI, UK. In: Roe, D. (ed.), *Studies in the Upper Palaeolithic of Britain and Northwest Europe.* Oxford: British Archaeological Reports British Series 296, pp. 89–98.

Johansson, A. D. 2002. Late Palaeolithic settlement in South Zealand, eastern Denmark. In: Eriksen, B. V. and Bratlund, B. (eds), *Recent Studies in the Final Palaeolithic of the European Plain. Proceedings of a U.I.S.P.P. Symposium, Stockholm, 14–17 October 1999.* Aarhus: Aarhus University Press, pp. 75–83.

Johnsen, S., Dahl-Jensen, D., Gundestrup, N., Steffensen, J., Clausen, H., Miller, H., Masson-Demotte, V., Sveinbjornsdottir, A. and White, J. 2001. Oxygen isotope and palaeotemperature records from six Greenland ice core stations: Camp Century, Dye-3, GRIP, GISP2, Reinland and NorthGRIP. *Journal of Quaternary Science* 16: 299–307.

Jones, R. L. and Keen, D. H. 1993. *Pleistocene Environments in the British Isles.* London: Chapman and Hall.

Jones, R. T., Marshall, J. D., Crowley, S. F., Bedford, A., Richardson, N., Bloemendal, J. et al. 2002. A high resolution, multiproxy Late-Glacial record of climate change and intrasystem responses in northwest England. *Journal of Quaternary Science* 17: 329–340.

Jöris, O. and Adler, D. 2008. Setting the record straight: toward a systematic chronological understanding of the Middle to Upper Palaeolithic boundary in Eurasia. *Journal of Human Evolution* 55: 761–763.

Jöris, O. and Street, M. 2008. At the end of the ^{14}C timescale – the Middle to Upper Palaeolithic record of western Eurasia. *Journal of Human Evolution* 55: 782–802.

Jöris, O. and Thissen, J. 1995. Übach-Palenberg. In: Schirmer, W. (ed.), *INQUA 1995: Quaternary Field Trips in Central Europe 2.* Munich: INQUA, pp. 957–961.

Junkmanns, J. 1991. Die Steinartefakte aus Achenheim in der Sammlung Paul Wernet. *Archäologisches Korrespondenzblatt* 17: 409–417.

Junkmanns, J. 1995. Les ensembles lithiques d'Achenheim d'apres la collection de Paul Wernet. *Bulletin de la Société Préhistorique Française* 92: 26–36.

Kaagan, L. 2000. *The Horse in Late Pleistocene and Holocene Britain.* Unpublished Ph.D. Thesis, University of London.

Kabacinški, J. and Kobusiewicz, M. 2007. Kragola near Koło (Central Poland) – the easternmost settlement of Hamburgian culture. In: Kobusiewicz, M. and Kabacinški, J. (eds), *Studies in the Final Palaeolithic Settlement of the Great European Plain.* Poznaš: Institute of Archaeology and Ethnology, Polish Academy of Sciences, pp. 21–52.

Kabacinški, J. and Sobkowiak-Tabaka, I. 2009. Big game versus small game hunting – subsistence strategies of the Hamburgian culture. In: Street, M., Barton, N. and Terberger, T. (eds), *Humans, Environment and Chronology of the Late Glacial of the North European Plain. Proceedings of Workshop 14 (Commission XXXII 'The Final Palaeolithic of the Great European Plain' of the 15th U.I.S.P.P. Congress, Lisbon, September 2006.* Mainz: Römisch-Germanischen Zentralmuseums, pp. 67–76.

Kabacinški, J., Schild, R., Bratlund, B., Kubiak-Martens, L., Tobolski, K., van der Borg, K. et al. 2002. The Lateglacial sequence at the Hamburgian site at Mirkowice: stratigraphy and geochronology. In: Eriksen, B. V. and Bratlund, B. (eds), *Recent Studies in the Final Palaeolithic of the European Plain. Proceedings of a U.I.S.P.P. Symposium, Stockhold, 14–17 October 1999.* Aarhus: Aarhus University Press, pp. 109–116.

Kahlke, R.-D. 2002. The Quaternary large mammal faunas of Thuringia (central Germany). In: Meyrick, R. A. and Schreve, D. C. (eds), *The Quaternary of Central Germany (Thuringia and surroundings): field guide.* London: The Quaternary Research Association, pp. 59–78.

Kahlke, R.-D., Maul, L. C., Meyrick, R. A., Stebich, M. and Grasselt, T. 2002. The Quaternary sequence from the late Middle to Upper Pleistocene site of Weimar-Ehringsdorf. In: Meyrick, R. A. and Schreve, D. C. (eds), *The Quaternary of Central Germany (Thuringia and Surroundings): Field Guide.* London: Quaternary Research Association, pp. 163–177.

Kahlke, R.-D., García, N., Kostopoulos, D. S., Lacombat, F., Lister, A. M., Mazza, P. P. A. et al. 2011. Western Palaearctic palaeoenvironmental conditions during the Early and Early Middle Pleistocene inferred from large mammal communities, and implications for hominin dispersal in Europe. *Quaternary Science Reviews* 30: 1368–1395.

Kaplan, H. S. 2002. Human Life Histories. In: Pagel, M. (ed.), *Encyclopedia of Evolution.* Oxford: Oxford University Press, pp. 627–631.

Karlin, C. 1972. In: Leroi-Gourhan, A. and Brézillon, M, 1972. Fouilles de Pincevent: essai d'analyse ethnographique d'un habitat Magdalénien (La Section 36). *VIIe Supplément à Gallia Préhistoire*: 263–78.

Kavur, B. and Petru, S. 2003. Poznopaleolitski tabor lovcev in nabiralcev. In: Djuriš, B. and Prešeren, D. (eds), *Zemla pod Vasšimi Nogami: Arheologija na Autoccestah Slovenije: Vodnik po Najdiš ih.* Ljubljana: Narodna in Univerzitetna Knjižnica, pp. 27–31.

Keeley, L. H. 1980. *Experimental Determination of Stone Tool Uses.* Chicago: University of Chicago Press.

Keeley, L. H. 1993. The Utilization of Lithic Artefacts. In: Singer, R., Gladfelter, B. G. and Wymer, J. J. (eds), *The Lower Palaeolithic Site at Hoxne, England.* Chicago and London: University of Chicago Press, pp. 129–138.

Keen, D. H. 1990. Significance of the record provided by Pleistocene fluvial deposits and their included molluscan faunas for palaeo-environmental reconstruction and stratigraphy: a case study from the English Midlands. *Palaeogeography, Palaeoclimatology, Palaeoeology* 80: 25–34.

Keen, D. H. 1995. Raised beaches and sea-levels in the English Channel in the Middle and Late Pleistocene: problems of interpretation and implications for the isolation of the British Isles. In: Preece, R. C. (ed.), *Island Britain: a Quaternary Perspective.* London: Geological Society Special Publication 96, pp. 63–74.

Keen, D. H. 1999. The chronology of Middle Pleistocene ('Wolstonian') events in the English Midlands. In: Andrews, P. and Banham, P. H. (eds), *Late Cenozoic Environments and Hominid Evolution: A Tribute to Bill Bishop.* London: The Geological Society, pp. 159–168.

Keen, D. H. 2001. Towards a late Middle Pleistocene non-marine molluscan biostratigraphy for the British Isles. *Quaternary Science Reviews* 20: 1657–1665.

Keen, D. H., Hardaker, T. and Lang, A. T. O. 2006. A Lower Palaeolithic industry from the Cromerian (MIS 13) Baginton Formation of Waverley Wood and Wood Farm Pits, Bubbenhall, Warwickshire, UK. *Journal of Quaternary Science* 21: 457–470.

Keen, D. H., Jones, R. L., Evans, R. A. and Robinson, J. E. 1988. Faunal and floral assemblages from Bingley Bog, West Yorkshire, and their significance for Late Devensian and early Flandrian environmental changes. *Proceedings of the Yorkshire Geological Society* 47: 125–138.

Kelley, H. 1937. Acheulian flake tools. *Proceedings of the Prehistoric Society* 3: 15–28

Kelly, M. R. 1968. Floras of the Middle and Upper Pleistocene Age from Brandon, Warwickshire. *Philosophical Transactions of the Royal Society of London* B254: 401–416.

Kelly, R. 1995. *The Foraging Spectrum: Diversity in Hunter-gatherer Lifeways.* Washington and London: Smithsonian Institution Press.

Kemp, R. A. 1985. The decalcified Lower Loam at Swanscombe, Kent: a buried Quaternary soil. *Proceedings of the Geologists' Association* 96: 343–355.

Kemp, R. A. 1995. The Middle and Upper Loam at Northfleet. In: Bridgland, D. R., Allen, P. and Haggert, B. A. (eds), *The Quaternary of the Lower Reaches of the Thames. Field Guide.* Durham: Quaternary Research Association, pp. 165–166.

Kennard, A. S. 1904. Notes on a Palaeolith from Grays, Essex. *Essex Naturalist* 13: 112–113.

Kennard, A. S. 1916. The Pleistocene succession in England. *Proceedings of the Prehistoric Society of East Anglia* 2: 249–267.

Kennard, A. S. 1942a. Discussion on Pleistocene Chronology. *Proceedings of the Geologists' Association* 53: 24–25.

Kennard, A. S. 1942b. Faunas of the High Terrace at Swanscombe. *Proceedings of the Geologists' Association* 53: 105.

Kennard, A. S. 1944. The Crayford Brickearths. *Proceedings of the Geologists' Association* 55: 121–169.

Kennedy, G. E. 2003. Paleolithic Grandmothers? Life History Theory and Early *Homo. Journal of the Royal Anthropological Institute* 9: 549–572.

Kenward, H. 2006. The visibility of past trees and woodland: testing the value of insect remains. *Journal of Archaeological Science* 33: 1368–1380.

Kenward, H., Engleman, C., Robertson, A. and Large, F. 1985. Rapid Scanning of Urban Archaeological Deposits for Insect Remains. *Circaea* 3: 163–172.

Kenworthy, J. W. 1898. Palaeolithic flakes from Clacton. *Essex Naturalist* 17: 15.

Kerney, M. P. 1971. Interglacial deposits at Barnfield Pit, Swanscombe, and their molluscan fauna. *Journal of the Geological Society of London* 127: 69–86.

Kerney, M. P. and Sieveking, G. de. G. 1977. Northfleet. In: Shepherd-Thorne, E. R. and Wymer, J. J. (eds), *South East England and the Thames Valley. Guide Book for Excursion A5, X INQUA Congress, Birmingham.* Norwich: Geoabstracts, pp. 44–46.

King, W. B. R. and Oakley, K. P. 1936. The Pleistocene Succession in the Lower Parts of the Thames Valley. *Proceedings of the Prehistoric Society* 2: 52–76.

Kitching, J. W. 1963. *Bone, Tooth and Horns of Palaeolithic Man: an Account of the Osteodontokeratic Discoveries in Pin Hole Cave, Derbyshire.* Manchester: Manchester University Press.

Klein, R. 1999. *The Human Career: Human Biological and Cultural Origins.* Chicago: Chicago University Press.

Kleindienst, M. R. 1962. Components of the East African Acheulean assemblage: an analytical approach. In: Nenquin, G. M. A. J. (ed.) *Actes du IVe Congrès et du l'étude du Quaternaire.* Tervuren: Musée Royal d'Afrique Centrale, pp. 81–112.

Klotz, S., Müller, U., Mosbrugger, V., de Beaulieu, J.-L. and Reille, M. 2004. Eemian to early Würmian climate dynamics: history and patterns of changes in Central Europe. *Palaeogeography, Palaeoclimatology, Palaeoecology* 11: 107–126.

Kobusiewicz, M. 2002. Ahrensburgian and Swiderian: two different modes of adaptation? In: Eriksen, B. and Bratlund, B. (eds), *Recent Studies in the Final Palaeolithic of the European Plain. Proceedings of a U.I.S.P.P. Symposium, Stockholm, 14–17 October 1999.* Aarhus: Aarhus University Press, pp. 117–122.

Kohn, M. and Mithen, S. 1999. Handaxes: products of sexual selection? *Antiquity* 73: 518–526.

Kolen, J., De Loecker, D., Groenendijk, A. J. and de Warrimont, J. P. 1999. Middle Palaeolithic surface scatters: how informative? A case study from southern Limburg (the Netherlands). In: Roebroeks, W. and Gamble, C. (eds), *The Middle Palaeolithic Occupation of Europe.* Leiden: University of Leiden Press, pp. 177–192.

Kooi, H., Johnston, P., Lambeck, K., Smither, C. and Molendijk, R. 1998. Geological causes of recent (~100 yr) vertical land movement in the Netherlands. *Tectonophysics* 299: 297–316.

Koop, H. 1987. Vegetative reproduction of trees in some European natural forests. *Plant Ecology* 72: 103–110.

Kosłowski, S. K. and Sachse-Kosłowska, E. 1993. Maszycka Cave: a Magdalenian site in Southern Poland. *Jahrbuch der Römisch-Germanischen Zentralmuseums Mainz* 40: 115–205.

Kowalski, K. and Płonka, T. 2009. New ornamented artefacts from the Polish lowland and Final Palaeolithic symbolism. In: Street, M., Barton, N. and Terberger, T. (eds), *Humans, Environment and Chronology of the Late Glacial of the North European Plain. Proceedings of Workshop 14 (Commission XXXII 'The Final Palaeolithic of the Great European Plain' of the 15th U.I.S.P.P. Congress, Lisbon, September 2006).* Mainz: Römisch-Germanischen Zentralmuseums, pp. 179–187.

Kramer, E., Houtsma, P. and Schilstra, J. 1985. The Creswellian site at Siegerswoude II (gemeente Opsterland, province of Friesland, the Netherlands). *Palaeohistoria* 27: 67–88.

Krovitz, G. E., Thompson, J. L. and Nelson, A. J. 2003. Hominid Growth and Development from Australopithecines to Middle Pleistocene *Homo*. In: Thompson, J. L., Krovitz, G. E. and Nelson, A. J. (eds), *Patterns of Growth and Development in the Genus Homo.* Cambridge: Cambridge University Press, pp. 271–294.

Kruuk, H. 1972. *The Spotted Hyena.* Chicago: University of Chicago Press.

Kuhn, S. L. 1995. *Mousterian Lithic Technology: An Ecological Perspective.* Princeton: Princeton University Press.

Kuhn, S. L. 2002. Paleolithic Archaeology in Turkey. *Evolutionary Anthropology* 11: 198–210.

Kuhn, S.L., 2006. Trajectories of change in the Middle Paleolithic of Italy. In: Hovers, E., Kuhn, S.L. (eds), *Transitions Before the Transition: Evolution and Stability in the Middle Paleolithic and Middle Stone Age*. Springer, New York, 109–120.

Kuhn, S. L. and M. C. Stiner. 2006. What's a mother to do? A hypothesis about the division of labor and modern human origins. *Current Anthropology* 47: 953–980

Kukla, G. 2005. Saalian supercycle, Mindel/Riss interglacial and Milankovitch's dating. *Quaternary Science Reviews* 24: 1573–1583.

Kukla, G. and Cílek, V. 1996. Plio-Pleistocene megacycles: record of climate and tectonics. *Palaeogeography, Palaeoclimatology, Palaeoecology* 120: 171–194.

Lacaille, A. D. 1938. A Levallois side-scraper from the Brickearth at Yiewsley, Middlesex. *The Antiquaries Journal* 18: 55–57.

Lacaille, A. D. and Oakley, K. P. 1936. The Palaeolithic sequence at Iver, Bucks, with an appendix on the geology. *The Antiquaries Journal* 16: 421–443.

Lagarde, J., Amorese, D., Font, M., Laville, E. and Dugu, O. 2003. The structural evolution of the English Channel area. *Journal of Quaternary Science* 18: 201–213.

Laing, R. 1889. On the bone caves of Creswell and the discovery of an extinct Pleistocene feline (*Felis brevirostris*) new to Great Britain. *Report to the British Association for the Advancement of Science*. Newcastle, pp. 582–584.

Lambeck, K. 1995. Late Devensian and Holocene shorelines of the British Isle and North Sea from models of glacio-hydro-isostatic rebound. *Journal of the Geological Society of London* 152: 437–448.

Lambeck, K., Yokoyama, Y. and Purcell, T. 2002. Into and out of the Last Glacial Maximum: sea-level change during Oxygen Isotope Stages 3 and 2. *Quaternary Science Reviews* 21: 343–360.

Lang, A. T. O. and Keen, D. 2005. 'At the edge of the world ...' Hominid colonisation and the Lower and Middle Palaeolithic of the West Midlands. *Proceedings of the Prehistoric Society* 71: 63–84.

Larsson, L. 1991. The Late Palaeolithic in southern Sweden: investigations in a marginal region. In: Barton, R. N. E., Roberts, A. and Roe, D. A. (eds), *The Late Glacial in North West Europe: Human Adaptation and Environmental Change at the End of the Pleistocene.* London: Council for British Archaeology Research Report 77, pp. 122–127.

Lawson, A. J. 1978. A hand-axe from Little Cressingham. *East Anglian Archaeology* 8: 1–8.

Layard, N. F. 1903. A recent discovery of Palaeolithic implements in Ipswich. *Journal of the Anthropological Institute of Great Britain and Ireland* 33: 41–43.

Layard, N. F. 1904. Further excavations on a Palaeolithic site in Ipswich. *Journal of the Anthropological Institute of Great Britain and Ireland* 34: 306–310.

Layard, N. F. 1906a. A winter's work on the Ipswich Palaeolithic site. *Journal of the Anthropological Institute of Great Britain and Ireland* 36: 233–236.

Layard, N. F. 1906b. Account of a Palaeolithic site in Ipswich. *Proceedings and Communications of the Cambridge Antiquarian Society* 11: 493–502.

Layard, N. F. 1912. Animal remains from the railway cutting at Ipswich. *Proceedings of the Suffolk Institute of Archaeology and Natural History* 14: 59–68.

Layard, N. F. 1920. The Stoke Bone-Bed, Ipswich. *Proceedings of the Prehistoric Society of East Anglia* 3: 210–219.

Le Brun-Ricalens, F. 2005. Chronique d'une reconnaissance attendee. Outils 'carénés', outils 'nucléiformes': nucléus à lamelles. Bilan aprés un siécle de recherché typologiques, technologiques et traceologiques. In: Le Brun-Ricalens, F., Bordes, J.-G. and Bon, F. (eds), *Productions Lamellaires attribuées à l'Aurignacien: Chaînes Opératoires et Perspectives Techno-Culturelles. Actes de la Table-ronde organisée dans le cadre du XVe Congrès de l'UISPP, Liège, 2001.* Luxembourg: Archéologiques 1, pp. 23–72.

Le Mort, F. and Gambier, D. 1992. Diversité du traitement des os humains au Magdalénien un exemple particulier, le cas du gisement du Placard (Charente). In: Rigaud, J.-P., Laville, H. and Vandermeersch, B. (eds), *Le Peuplement Magdalénien. Paléographie, Physique et Humaine.* Paris: Editions du C. T. H. S. , pp. 29–40.

Lea, D. W., Martin, P. A., Pak, D. K. and Spero, H. J. 2002. Reconstructing a 350 ky history of sealevel using planktonic Mg/Ca and oxygen isotope records from a Cocos Ridge core. *Quaternary Science Reviews* 21: 283–293.

Leakey, M. D. 1971. *Olduvai Gorge Vol. 3, Excavations in Beds I and II, 1960–63.* Cambridge: Cambridge University Press.

Lee, H. W. 2001. *A study of Lower Palaeolithic stone artefacts from selected sites in the upper and middle Thames Valley, with particular reference to the R. J. MacRae Collection.* Oxford: British Archaeological Reports British Series 319.

Lee, J. 2009. Patterns of preglacial sedimentation and glaciotectonic deformation within early Middle Pleistocene sediments at Sidestrand, north Norfolk, UK. *Proceedings of Geologists' Association* 120: 34–48.

Lee, J., Rose, J., Hamblin, R. J. O. and Moorlock, B. S. P. 2004. Dating the earliest lowland glaciation of eastern England: a pre-MIS 12 early Middle Pleistocene glaciation. *Quaternary Science Reviews* 23: 1551–1566.

Lee, J., Rose, J., Candy, I. and Barendregt, R. 2006. Sea-level changes, river activity, soil development and glaciation around the western margins of the southern North Sea Basin during the Early and early Middle Pleistocene: evidence from Pakefield, Suffolk, UK. *Journal of Quaternary Science* 21: 155–179.

Leroi-Gourhan, A. and Brézillon, M. 1966. L'habitation Magdalénienne No. 1 de Pincevent près Montereau (Seine-et-Maritime). *Gallia Préhistoire* 9: 263–371.

Leroi-Gourhan, A. and Brézillon, M. 1972. Fouilles de Pincevent: essai d'analyse ethnographique d'un habitat Magdalénien (La Section 36). *VIIe Supplément à Gallia Préhistoire.*

Leroy, S. A. G., Arpe, K. and Mikolajewicz, U. 2011. Vegetation context and climatic limits of Early Pleistocene hominin dispersal in Europe. *Quaternary Science Reviews* 30: 1448–1463.

Lev, M. 1973. *British Lower and Middle Palaeolithic Industries.* Unpublished Ph.D. Thesis. University of London.

Lévêque, F. and Vandermeersch, B. 1980. Découverte de restes humains dans un niveau castelperronien à Saint-Césaire (Charente-Maritime). *Comptes Rendus de l'Académie des Sciences* 291: 187–189.

Lewin, R. and Foley, R. 2004. *Principles of Human Evolution.* Oxford: Blackwell.

Lewis, J. 1991. A Late Glacial and early Postglacial site at Three Ways Wharf, Uxbridge, England: interim report. In: Barton, R. N. E., Roberts, A. and Roe, D. A. (eds), *The Late Glacial in North West Europe: Human Adaptation and Environmental Change at the End of the Pleistocene.* London: Council for British Archaeology Research Report pp. 77, 246–255.

Lewis, J. and Rackham, J. 2011. *Three Ways Wharf, Uxbridge. A Lateglacial and Early Holocene Hunter-Gatherer Site in the Colne Valley.* London: Museum of London Archaeology Monograph 51.

Lewis, S. G. 1992. High Lodge – Stratigraphy and depositional environments. In: Ashton, N. M., Cook, J., Lewis, S. G. and Rose, J. (eds), *High Lodge: Excavations by G. de G. Sieveking 1962–68 and J. Cook 1988.* London: British Museum Press, pp. 51–85.

Lewis, S. G. 1998. Quaternary stratigraphy and Lower Palaeolithic archaeology of the Lark Valley, Suffolk. In: Ashton, N. M., Healy, F. and Pettitt, P. (eds), *Stone Age Archaeology: Essays in Honour of John Wymer.* Oxford: Oxbow, pp. 43–51.

Lewis, S. G., Maddy, D., Buckingham, C., Coope, G. R., Field, M. H., Keen, D. H. et al. 2006. Pleistocene fluvial sediments, palaeontology and archaeology of the upper River Thames at Latton, Wiltshire, England. *Journal of Quaternary Science* 21: 181–205.

Lewis, S. G., Ashton, N. and Jacobi, R. 2011. Testing human presence during the Last Interglacial (MIS5e): a review of the British evidence. In: Ashton, N., Lewis, S. and Stringer, C. (eds), *The Ancient Human Occupation of Britain.* Amsterdam: Elsevier, pp. 125–164.

Lindly, J. M. and Clark, G. A. 1990. Symbolism and modern human origins. *Current Anthropology* 31: 233–261.

Lister, A. 1991. Late Glacial mammoths in Britain. In: Barton, R. N. E., Roberts, A. and Roe, D. A. (eds), *The Late Glacial in North West Europe: Human Adaptation and Environmental Change at the End of the Pleistocene.* London: Council for British Archaeology Research Report 77, pp. 53–59.

Lister, A. 2004. The impact of Quaternary ice ages on mammalian evolution *Philosophical Transactions of the Royal Society of London* B359: 221–241.

Lister, A. 2009. Late-Glacial mammoth skeletons (*Mammuthus primigenius*) from Condover (Shropshire, UK): anatomy, pathology, taphonomy and chronological significance. *Geological Journal* 44: 447–479.

Lister, A. and Bahn, P. 1995. *Mammoths.* London: Boxtree.

Lister, A. and Sher, A. V. 2001. The origin and evolution of the woolly mammoth. *Science* 294: 1094–1097.

Lister, A., Sher, A. V., van Essen, H. and Wei, G. 2005. The pattern and process of mammoth evolution in Eurasia. *Quaternary International* 126/128: 49–64.

Locht, J.-L. and Antoine, P. 2001. Caractérisation techno-typologique et position chronostratigraphique de plusieurs industries á rares bifaces ou amnicissements bifaciaux du nord de la France. In: Cliquet, D., Ladjadj, J., Lautridou, J.-P., Leportier, J., Lorren, P., Michel, D. et al. (eds) *Les industries á outils bifaciaux du Paléolithique Moyen d'Europe occidentale.* Liège: Études et Recherches Archéologiques de l'Université de Liège, pp. 129–134.

Loftus, J. 1982. Ein verzierter pfeilschaftglätter von fläsch 64/74–73/78 des Spätpaläolithischen fundplatzes Niederbeiber, Neuweider Becken. *Archäologisches Korrespondenzblatt* 12: 312–316.

Lord, T. C., O'Connor, T. P., Siebrandt, D. C. and Jacobi, R. M. 2007. People and large carnivores as biostratinomic agents in Lateglacial cave assemblages. *Journal of Quaternary Science* 22: 681–694.

Lordkipanidze, D., Vekua, A., Ferring, R., Rightmire, G. P., Zollikofer, C., Ponce de Leon, M. et al. 2006. A fourth hominin skull from Dmanisi. *The Anatomical Record Part A: Discoveries in Molecular, Cellular, and Evolutionary Biology* 288: 1146–1157.

Loveday, J. 1962. Plateau deposits of the southern Chiltern Hills. *Proceedings of Geologists' Association* 73: 83–102.

Lovejoy, O. 1981. The origin of man. *Science* 211: 341–350.

Lowe, J. J. and Walker, M. J. C. 1984. *Reconstructing Quaternary Environments.* Harlow: Longman and Co.

Lowe, J. J. and Walker, M. 1997. *Reconstructing Quaternary Environments (2nd Edition).* Harlow: Longman.

Lowe, J. J. and Walker, M. J. C. 1986. Lateglacial and early Flandrian environmental history of the Isle of Mull, Inner Hebrides, Scotland. *Transactions of the Royal Society of Edinburgh: Earth Sciences* 77: 1–20.

Lowe, J. J., Rasmussen, S. O., Björk, S., Hoek, W. Z., Steffensen, J. P., Walker, M. J. C. et al. 2008. Synchronisation of palaeoenvironmental events in the North Atlantic region during the last termination: a revised protocol recommended by the INTIMATE group. *Quaternary Science Reviews* 27: 6–17.

Lund, M. 1993. Vorshäft für Kerbspitzen der Hamburger Kultur. *Archäologisches Korrespondezblatt* 23: 405–411.

Lundberg, J. and McFarlane, D. A. 2007. Pleistocene depositional history in a periglacial terrane: A 500ka record from Kents Cavern, Devon, United Kingdom. *Geosphere* 3: 199–219.

McCabe, M., Knight, J. and McCarron, S. 1998. Evidence for Heinrich Event 1 in the British Isles. *Journal of Quaternary Science* 13(6): 549–568.

McBurney, C. B. M. 1950. The geographical study of the older Palaeolithic stages in Europe. *Proceedings of the Prehistoric Society* 16: 163–183.

McBurney, C. B. M. 1965. The Old Stone Age in Wales. In: Foster, I. L. and Daniel, G. (eds), *Prehistoric and Early Wales.* London: Routledge and Kegan Paul, pp. 17–34.

McDougall, D. A. 2001. The geomorphological impact of Loch Lomond (Younger Dryas) stadial plateau icefields in the central Lake District, northwest England. *Journal of Quaternary Science* 16: 531–543.

MacEnery, J. and Vivian, E. 1859. *Cavern Researches: Or Discoveries of Organic Remains, and of*

British and Roman Reliques, in the Caves of Kent's Hole, Anstis Cove, Chudleigh, and Berry Head. London: Simpkin, Marshall and Co.

Mace, A. 1959. An Upper Palaeolithic open-site at Hengistbury Head, Christchurch, Hants. *Proceedings of the Prehistoric Society* 25: 233–59.

McManus, J. F., Oppo, D. W. and Cullen, J. L. 1999. A 0.5–million-year record of millennial-scale climate variability in the North Atlantic. *Science* 283: 971–974.

McNabb, J. 1992. *The Clactonian: British Lower Palaeolithic flint technology in biface and non-biface assemblages.* Unpublished Ph.D. Thesis, University of London.

McNabb, J. 1996a. More from the cutting edge: Further discoveries of Clactonian bifaces. *Antiquity* 70: 428–436.

McNabb, J. 1996b. Through the looking glass: an historical perspective on archaeological research at Barnfield Pit, Swanscombe, ca.1900–1964. In: Conway, B., McNabb, J. and Ashton, N. (eds), *Excavations at Barnfield Pit, Swanscombe, 1968–72, British Museum Occasional Paper Number 94.* London: British Museum Press, pp. 31–51.

McNabb, J. 2007. *The British Lower Palaeolithic: Stones in Contention.* London: Routledge.

McNabb, J. and Ashton, N. 1992. The Cutting Edge, Bifaces in the Clactonian. *Lithics* 13: 4–10.

McNabb, J. and Ashton, N. M. 1995. Thoughtful flakers: a reply to Mithen. *Cambridge Archaeological Journal* 5: 289–298.

MacPhail, R. I. 1999. Sediment micromorphology. In: Roberts, M. B. and Parfitt, S. (eds), *Boxgrove. A Middle Pleistocene Hominid Site at Eartham Quarry, Boxgrove, West Sussex.* London: English Heritage, pp. 118–149.

McPherron, S. 1994. *A Reduction Model for Variability in Acheulian Biface Morphology.* Unpublished Ph.D. Dissertation, University of Pennsylvania.

McPherron, S. 1996. A Reexamination of British Biface Data. *Lithics* 16: 47–63.

McPherron, S. 2006. What typology can tell us about Acheulian handaxe production. In: Goren-Inbar, N. and Sharon, G. (eds), *Axe Age: Acheulian Toolmaking from Quarry to Discard.* London: Equinox, pp. 267–285.

Machin, A. J. 2008. Why handaxes just aren't that sexy: a response to Kohn and Mithen. *Antiquity* 82: 761–766.

Machin, A. J., Hosfield, R. T. and Mithen, S. J. 2007. Why are some handaxes symmetrical? testing the influence of handaxe morphology on butchery effectiveness. *Journal of Archaeological Science* 34: 883–893.

Macrae, R. J. 1982. Palaeolithic artefacts from Berinsfield, Oxfordshire. *Oxoniensa* 47: 1–11.

Macrae, R. J. 1988. Belt, shoulder-bag or basket: an enquiry into handaxe transport and flint sources. *Lithics* 9: 2–8.

Macrae, R. J. 1991. New Lower Palaeolithic finds from gravel pits in central southern England. *Lithics* 12: 12–20.

Maddy, D., Green, C. P., Lewis, S. G. and Bowen, D. Q. 1995. Pleistocene geology of the Lower Severn Valley, UK. *Quaternary Science Reviews* 14: 209–222.

Maddy, D., Lewis, S. G., Scaife, R. G., Bowen, D. Q., Coope, G. R., Green, C. P. et al. 1998. The Upper Pleistocene deposits at Cassington, near Oxford, England. *Journal of Quaternary Science* 13: 205–231.

Maddy, D., Bridgland, D. R. and Green, C. P. 2000. Crustal uplift in southern England: evidence from the river terrace records. *Geomorphology* 33: 167–181.

Madsen, B. and Goren-Inbar, N. 2004. Acheulian giant core technology and beyond: an archaeological and experimental case study. *Eurasian Prehistory* 2: 3–52.

Mania, D. 1991. The zonal division of the Lower Palaeolithic open-air site at Bilzingsleben. *Anthropologie* 29: 17–24.

Mania, D. 1995. The earliest occupation of Europe: the Elbe-Saale region. In: Roebroeks, W. and Van Kolfshoten, T. (eds), *The Earliest Occupation of Europe.* Leiden: University of Leiden, pp. 85–102.

Mania, D., Thomae, M., Litt, T. and Weber, T. 1990. *Neumark-Gröbern. Beiträge zur Jagd des mittelpaläolithischen Menhen. Publication of the Landesmuseum für Halle 42.* Berlin: Deutscher Verlag der Wissenschaft.

Mania, D. and Mania, U. 2005. The natural and socio-cultural environment of *Homo erectus* at Bilsingsleben, Germany. In: Gamble, C. and Porr, M. (eds), *The Hominid Individual in Context: Archaeological Investigations of Lower and Middle Palaeolithic landscapes, locales and artefacts.* London: Routledge, pp. 98–114.

Marean, C. W. and Assefa, Z. 2005. The Middle and Upper Pleistocene African Record for the biolgical and behavioural origins of modern humans. In: Stahl, A. (ed.), *African Archaeology: A Critical Introduction.* Oxford: Blackwell, pp. 93–129.

Marr, J., Moir, J. R. and Smith, R. A. 1921. Excavations at High Lodge, Mildenhall in 1920 A.D. I. Report on the Geology. II. A description of the humanly fashioned flints found during the excavations at High Lodge, Mildenhall. III. Summary of previous finds. *Proceedings of the Prehistoric Society of East Anglia* 3: 353–379.

Marshack, A. 1972. *The Roots of Civilisation.* London: Weidenfeld and Nicholson.

Marston, A. T. 1937. The Swanscombe Skull. *Journal of the Royal Anthropological Institute of Great Britain and Ireland* 67: 339–406.

Martin, Y. 2007. The engravings of Gouy: France's northernmost decorated cave. In: Pettitt, P. B., Bahn, P. and Ripoll, S. (eds), *Palaeolithic Cave Art at Creswell Crags in European Context.* Oxford: Oxford University Press, pp. 142–193.

Martínez-Navarro, B. and Palmqvist, P. 1995. Presence of the African Machairodont *Megantereon whitei* (Broom, 1937) (Felidae, Carnivora, Mammalia) in the Lower Pleistocene Site of Venta Micena (Orce, Granada, Spain), with some Considerations on the Origin, Evolution and Dispersal of the Genus. *Journal of Archaeological Science* 22: 569–582.

Martínez-Navarro, B. and Palmqvist, P. 1996. Presence of the African sabre-toothed felid *Megantereon whitei* (Broom. 1937) (Mammalia, Carnivora, Machairodontinae) in Apollonia-1 (Mygdonia Basin, Macedonia, Greece). *Journal of Archaeological Science* 23: 869–872.

Martínez-Navarro, B., Pérez-Claros, J. A., Palombo, M. R., Rook, L. and Palmqvist, P. 2007a. The Olduvai buffalo *Pelorovis* and the origin of *Bos. Quaternary Research* 68: 220–226.

Martinón-Torres, M., Bermúdez de Castro, J. M., Gómez-Robles, A., Arsuaga, J. L., Carbonell, E., Lordkipanidze, D., Manzi, G. et al. 2007b. Dental evidence on the hominin dispersals during the Pleistocene. *Proceedings of the National Academy of Sciences (USA)* 104: 13279–13282.

Martinón-Torres, M., Bermúdez de Castro, J. M., Gómez-Robles, A., Margvelashvili, A., Prado, L., Lordkipanidze, D. and Vekua, A. 2008. Dental remains from Dmanisi (Republic of Georgia): Morphological analysis and comparative study. *Journal of Human Evolution* 55: 249–273.

Martinez, K., Garcia, J., Carbonell, E., Agusti, J., Bahain, J.-J., Blain, H.-A. et al. 2010. A new Lower Pleistocene archaeological site in Europe (Vallparadis, Barcelona, Spain). *Proceedings of the National Academy of Sciences (USA)* 107: 5762–5767.

Maul, L. C. and Markova, A. K. 2007. Similarity and regional differences in Quaternary arvicolid evolution in Central and Eastern Europe. *Quaternary International* 160: 81–99.

Mawson, M. 2009. The bedrock geology of Creswell Crags. In: Bahn, P. and Pettitt, P. (eds), *Britain's Oldest Art: the Ice Age Cave Art of Creswell Crags.* London English Heritage, pp. 96–103.

Meijer, T. and Preece, R. 1995. Malacological evidence relating to the insularity of the British Isles during the Quaternary. In: Preece, R. C. (ed.) *Island Britain: a Quaternary Perspective.* London: Geological Society Special Publication 96, pp. 89–110.

Meijer, T. and Preece, R. 1996. Malacological evidence relating to the stratigraphical position of the Cromerian. In: Turner, C. (ed.), *The Early Middle Pleistocene in Europe.* Rotterdam: Balkema, pp. 53–82.

Mellars, P. 1969. Radiocarbon dates for a new Creswellian site. *Antiquity* 43: 308–311.

Mellars, P. 1974. The Palaeolithic and Mesolithic. In: Renfrew, A. C. (ed.) *British Prehistory: a New Outline.* London: Duckworth, pp. 41–99.

Mellars, P. 1996. *The Neanderthal Legacy.* Princeton: Princeton University Press.

Mellars, P. 1999. The Neanderthal Problem continued. *Current Anthropology* 40: 341–363.

Mellars, P. 2005. Neanderthals and the modern human colonization of Europe. *Nature* 432: 461–465.

Mello, J. M. 1875. On some Bone-Caves in Creswell Crags. *Quarterly Journal of the Geological Society of London* 31: 679–691.

Mello, J. M. 1877. The bone caves of Creswell Crags. *Quarterly Journal of the Geological Society of London* 33: 579–588.

Messager, E., Lordkipanidze, D., Kvavadze, E., Ferring, C. R. and Voinchet, P. 2010. Palaeoenvironmental reconstruction of Dmanisi site (Georgia) based on palaeobotanical data. *Quaternary International* 223/224: 20–27.

Messager, E., Lebreton, V., Marquer, L., Russo-Ermolli, E., Orain, R., Renault-Miskovsky, J. et al. 2011. Palaeoenvironments of early hominins in temperate and Mediterranean Eurasia: new palaeobotanical data from key-sites and synchronous natural sequences. *Quaternary Science Reviews* 30: 1439–1447.

Mgeladze, A., Lordkipanidze, D., Moncel, M.-H., Despriée, J., Chagelishvili, R., Nioradze, M. et al. 2010. First human settlement of the Caucasus: Technical behavior and raw material acquisition at Dmanisi, Georgia (1.77 Ma). *Quaternary International* 223/224: 422–425.

Mills, M. G. L. 1990. *Kalahari Hyenas: The Comparative Behavioural Ecology of Two Species.* London: Chapman and Hall.

Mills, N. 2001. *Creswell Crags Conservation Plan.* Creswell: Creswell Heritage Trust.

Mishra, S., Gaillard, C., Deo, S., Singh, M., Abbas, R. and Agrawal, N. 2010a. Large Flake Acheulian in India: Implications for understanding lower Pleistocene human dispersals. *Quaternary International* 223/224: 271–272.

Mishra, S., Gaillard, C., Hertler, C., Moigne, A.-M. and Simanjuntak, T. 2010b. India and Java: Contrasting records, intimate connections. *Quaternary International* 223/224: 265–270.

Mitchell, G. F., Penny, L. F., Shotton, F. W. and West, R. G. 1973. *A Correlation of Quaternary Deposits in the British Isles.* Special Report of the Geological Society of London 4.

Mitchell, J. C. 1996. Studying biface utilisation at Boxgrove: Roe deer butchery with replica handaxes. *Lithics* 16: 64–69.

Mitchell, J. C. 1997. Quantitative image analysis of lithic microwear on flint handaxes. *Microscopy and analysis* 61: 15–17.

Mitchell, J. C. 1998. *A use-wear analysis of selected British lower palaeolithic handaxes with special reference to the site of Boxgrove (West Sussex): a study incorporating optical microscopy, computer aided image analysis and experimental archaeology.* Unpublished D.Phil. Thesis, University of Oxford.

Mitchell, W. A. 1996. Significance of snowblow in the generation of Loch Lomond Stadial (Younger Dryas) glaciers in the western Pennines, northern England. *Journal of Quaternary Science* 11: 233–248.

Mithen, S. 1994. Technology and Society during the Middle Pleistocene: Hominid group size, social learning and industrial variability. *Cambridge Archaeological Journal* 4: 3–32.

Mithen, S. 1996. *The Prehistory of the Mind.* London: Thames and Hudson.

Mithen, S. 2008. 'Whatever turns you on': a response to Anna Machin, 'Why handaxes just aren't that sexy'. *Antiquity* 82: 766–769.

Moir, J. R. 1917. A Piece of Humanly-Shaped Wood from the Cromer Forest Bed. *Man* 17: 172–173.

Moir, J. R. 1921a. Flint Implements from the Cromer Forest Bed. *Nature* 106: 756–757.

Moir, J. R. 1921b. On an Early Chellian-Palaeolithic Workshop-Site in the Pliocene 'Forest Bed' of Cromer, Norfolk. *Journal of the Royal Anthropological Institute of Great Britain and Ireland* 51: 385–418.

Moir, J. R. 1922. An Early Palaeolithic Flint Implement from West Runton, Norfolk. *Man* 22: 34–36.

Moir, J. R. 1926. The silted-up lake of Hoxne and its contained implements. *Proceedings of the Prehistoric Society of East Anglia* 5: 137–165.

Moir, J. R. 1931. Ancient man in the Gipping-Orwell Valley, Suffolk. *Proceedings of the Prehistoric Society of East Anglia* 6: 182–221.

Moir, J. R. 1935. Lower Palaeolithic man at Hoxne, England. *Bulletin of the American School for Prehistoric Research* II: 43–53.

Moir, J. R. 1939. The Cromer Forest Bed Implements. *Nature* 144: 205–206.

Moir, J. R. and Hopwood, A. T. 1939. Excavations at Brundon, Suffolk (1935–7). *Proceedings of the Prehistoric Society* 5: 1–32.

Moncel, M.-H. 2010. Oldest human expansions in Eurasia: favouring and limiting factors. *Quaternary International* 223/224: 1–9.

Moncel, M.-H., and Combier, J. 1992. L'outillage sur éclat dan l'industrie lithique du site Pléistocène moyen D'Orgnac 3 (Ardèche, France). *L'Anthropologie* 96: 5–48.

Moncel, M.-H., Moigne, A.-M. and Combier, J. 2005. Pre-Neanderthal behaviour during isotopic stage 9 and the beginning of stage 8. New data concerning fauna and lithics in the different occupation levels of Orgnac 3 (Ardèche, South-East France): occupation types. *Journal of Archaeological Science* 32: 1283–1301.

Monnier, G. 2006. The Lower/Middle Paleolithic Periodization in Western Europe. *Current Anthropology* 47: 709–744.

Montagu, M. F. A. 1949. A report of archaeological work at Swanscombe and Galley Hill, Kent, England: June to September 1948. *Bulletin of the Philadelphia Anthropological Society* 2: 2–3.

Morgan, A. 1973. Late Pleistocene environmental changes indicated by fossil insect faunas of the English Midlands. *Boreas* 2: 173–212.

Morigi, A., Schreve, D. and White, M. 2011. Introduction and the Pre-Anglian geological, palaeoenvironmental and archaeological records. In: Morigi, A., Schreve, D. and White, M. (eds), *The Thames through Time. The Archaeology of the Gravel Terraces of the Upper and Middle Thames. Early Prehistory to 1500 BC. PART 1: The Ice Ages.* Oxford: Oxford Archaeology Thames Landscape Monograph No. 32, pp. 1–40.

Mottershead, D. M., Gilbertson, D.D. and Keen, D. H. 1987. The raised beaches and shore platform of Torbay: a re-appraisal. *Proceedings of the Geologists' Association* 98: 241–257.

Mullan, G. J., Wilson, L. J., Farrant, A. R. and Devlin, K. 2006. A possible engraving of a mammoth in Gough's Cave, Cheddar, Somerset. *Proceedings of the University of Bristol Spelaeological Society* 24: 37–47.

Mullenders, W. W. 1993. New palynological studies at Hoxne. In: Singer, R., Gladfelter, B. G. and Wymer, J. J. (eds), *The Lower Paleolithic Site at Hoxne, England.* Chicago: University of Chicago Press, pp. 150–55.

Mullins, E. H. 1913. The ossiferous cave at Langwith. *Derbyshire Archaeological Journal* 35: 137–158.

Murton, J. B., Baker, A., Bowen, D. Q., Caseldine, C. J., Coope, G. R., Currant, A. P. et al. 2001. A Middle Pleistocene temperate-periglacial-temperate sequence (Oxygen Isotope Stages 7–5e) near Marsworth, Buckinghamshire, UK. *Quaternary Science Reviews* 20: 1787–1825.

Murton, J. B., Bateman, M. D., Baker, C. A., Know, R. and Whiteman, C. A. 2003. The Devensian periglacial record on Thanet, Kent, UK. *Permafrost and Periglacial Processes* 14: 217–246.

Musil, R. 2000. Evidence for the domestication of wolves in Central European Magdalenian sites. In: Crockford, S. J. (ed.), *Dogs Through Time: an Archaeological Perspective.* Oxford: British Archaeological Reports International Series 889, pp. 21–28.

Mussi, M. 1995. The Earliest Occupation of Europe: Italy. In: Roebroeks, W. and Kolfschoten, T. v. (eds), *The Earliest Occupation of Europe.* Leiden: University of Leiden, pp. 27–41.

Mussi, M. 1999. The Neanderthals in Italy: a tale of many caves. In: Roebroeks, W. and Gamble, C. (eds), *The Middle Palaeolithic Occupation of Europe.* Leiden: Leiden University Press, pp. 49–80.

Muttoni, G., Scardia, G. and Kent, D. V. 2010. Human migration into Europe during the late Early Pleistocene climate transition. *Palaeogeography, Palaeoclimatology, Palaeoeology* 296: 79–93.

Narr, K. 1979. Comment on Ohel (1979). *Current Anthropology* 20: 717.

Nelson, M. 1991. The study of technological organisation. *Archaeological Method and Theory* 3: 57–100.

Newcomer, M. 1971. Some quantitative experiments in handaxe manufacture. *World Archaeology* 3: 83–94.

Newcomer, M. 1979. Comment on Ohel (1979). *Current Anthropology* 20: 717.

Newcomer, M. 1984. Flaking experiments with Pontnewydd raw materials. In: Green, H. S. (ed.) *Pontnewydd Cave: a Lower Palaeolithic Hominid Site in Wales: the First Report.* Cardiff: National Museum of Wales, pp. 153–158.

Newcomer, M., Grace, R. and Unger-Hamilton, R. 1986. Evaluating microwear analysis with blind tests. *Journal of Archaeological Science* 13: 203–208.

Nicholls, G., Cripps, J. A., Collinson, M. E. and Scott, A. C. 2000. Experiments in waterlogging and sedimentology of charcoal: results and implications. *Palaeogeography, Palaeoclimatology, Palaeoecology* 164: 43–56.

North Greenland Ice Core Project Members. 2004. High-resolution record of Northern Hemisphere climate extending into the Last Interglacial Period. *Nature* 431: 147–151.

Nowell, A. and Chang, M. L. 2009. The case against sexual selection as an explanation of handaxe morphology. *Paleoanthropology* 2009: 77–88.

Nowell, A. and White, M. J. 2010. Growing Up in the Middle Pleistocene: Life History Strategies and Their Relationship to Acheulian Industries. In: Nowell, A. and Davidson, I. (eds), *Stone Tools and the Evolution of Human Cognition.* Colorado: University of Colorado Press, pp. 67–82.

O'Connell, J. F., Hawkes, K. and Blurton Jones, N.G. 1999. Grandmothering and the evolution of *Homo erectus. Journal of Human Evolution* 36: 461–485.

O'Connor, A. 2007. *Finding Time for the Old Stone Age: A History of Palaeolithic Archaeology and Quaternary Geology in Britain, 1860–1960.* Oxford: Oxford University Press.

O'Regan, H., Turner, A. and Wilkinson, D. M. 2002. European Quaternary refugia: a factor in large carnivore extinction? *Journal of Quaternary Science* 17: 789–795.

O'Regan, H. J., Turner, A., Bishop, L. C., Elton, S. and Lamb, A. L. 2009. Hominins without fellow travellers? First appearances and inferred dispersals of Afro-Eurasian large-mammals in the Plio-Pleistocene. *Quaternary Science Reviews* 11/12: 1343–1352.

Oakley, K. 1949. *Man the Tool-Maker (1st edition).* London: British Museum (NH).

Oakley, K. 1981. Emergence of Higher Thought 3.0–0.2 Ma B.P. *Philosophical Transactions of the Royal Society of London* B292: 205–211.

Oakley, K., Andrews, P., Keeley, L. H. and Clark, J. D. 1977. A reappraisal of the Clacton spear-point. *Proceedings of the Prehistoric Society* 43: 13–30.

Oakley, K. P. 1939. Geology and Palaeolithic Studies. In: Oakley, K. P., Rankine, W. F. and Lowther, A. W. G. (eds) *A Survey of the Prehistory of the Farnham District (Surrey).* Guildford: Surrey Archaeological Society, pp. 3–58.

Oakley, K. P. 1948. Survey of the Present Position in British Prehistoric and Early Historic Archae-ology 1: The Palaeolithic Age. *A Survey and Policy of Field Research in the Archaeology of Great Britain. I. The Prehistoric Ages to the Seventh Century A.D.* London: Council For British Archaeology, pp. 13–25.

Oakley, K. P. 1964a. *Frameworks for Dating Fossil Man.* London: Weidenfeld and Nicholson.

Oakley, K. P. 1964b. The evidence of fire at Swanscombe. In: Ovey, C. D. (ed.) *The Swanscombe Skull: a Survey of Research on a Pleistocene Site.* London: Royal Anthropological Institute Occasional Paper No. 20, pp. 63–66.

Oakley, K. P. and Leakey, M. D. 1937. Report on Excavations at Jaywick Sands, Essex (1934), with some Observations on the Clactonian Industry, and on the Fauna and Geological Significance of the Clacton Channel. *Proceedings of the Prehistoric Society* 3: 217–260.

Oakley, K. P. and King, W. B. R. 1945. Age of Baker's Hole, Coombe Rock, Northfleet, Kent. *Nature* 155: 51–52.

Oakley, K. P., Campbell, B. G. and Molleson, T. L. 1971. *Catalogue of Fossil Hominids, Part II, Europe.* London: British Museum (Natural History).

Obermaier, H. 1924. *Fossil Man in Spain.* New Haven, CT: Yale University Press.

Ohel, M. Y. 1987. The Acheulean Handaxe: A Maintainable Multifunctional Tool. *Lithic Technology* 16: 54–55.

Ohel, M. Y. 1979. The Clactonian: an independent complex or an integral part of the Acheulean? *Current Anthropology* 20: 685–726.

Ohel, M., Y. and Lechevalier, C. 1979. The 'Clactonian' of Le Havre and its bearing on the English Clactonian. *Quartär* 29/30: 85–103.

Oms, O., Parés, J. M., Martínez-Navarro, B., Agustí, J., Toro, I., Martínez-Fernández, G. et al. 2000. Early human occupation of Western Europe: paleomagnetic dates for two paleolithic sites in Spain. *Proceedings of the National Academy of Sciences (USA)* 97: 10666–10670.

Oppo, D. W., McManus, J. and Cullen, J. L. 1998. Abrupt climate events 500,000 to 340,000 years ago: evidence from subpolar North Atlantic sediments. *Science* 279: 1335–1338.

Orschiedt, J. 2002. Secondary burial in the Magdalenian: the Brillenhöhle (Blauberen, Southwest Germany). *Paleo* 14: 241–256.

Otte, M. 1989. Le Magdalénien de Belgique: un apercu. In: Rigaud, J.-P. (ed.) *Le Magdalénien en Europe: La Structuration du Magdalénien.* Liège: Études et Recherches Archéologiques de l'Université de Liège 38, pp. 63–80.

Otte, M. 1990a. The northwestern European plain around 18000 BP. In: Soffer, O. and Gam-ble, C. (eds), *The World at 18000 BP: Volume One, High Latitudes.* London: Unwin Hyman, pp. 54–68.

Otte, M. 1990b. Les industries aux pointes foliacées du Nord-Ouest Européen. In: Kozlowski, J.

(ed.) *Les Industries a Pointes Foliacées du Paléolithique Supérieur Européen.* Liège: Études et Recherches Archéologiques de l'Université de Liège, pp. 247–269.

Otte, M. (ed.) 1994. *Le Magdalénien du Trou du Chaleux (Hulsonniaux-Belgique),* Liège: Études et Recherches Archéologiques de l'Université de Liège 60.

Otte, M. and Caspar, J.-P. 1987. Les 'pointes' de la Font-Robert: outils emmanchés? In: Stordeur, D. (ed.) *Le Main et l'Outil: Manches et Emmanchements Préhistoriques.* Lyon: Travaux de la Maison de l'Orient 15, pp. 75–88.

Otte, M. and Noiret, P. 2009. Le territoire de la Basse Vallée du Rhin, de la Meuse et de leurs affluents à la fin du Paléolithique Supérieur (Belgique, Hollande, Allemagne du Nord-Ouest). In: Djindjian, F., Kozlowski, J. and Bicho, N. (eds), *Le Concept de Territoires dans le Paléolithique Supérieur Européen.* Oxford: British Archaeological Reports International Series 1938, pp. 143–155.

Owen, L. 2005. *Distorting the Past: Gender and the Division of Labor in the European Upper Palaeolithic.* Tübingen: Kerns Verlag.

Owen-Smith, N. 1988. *Megaherbivores: the influence of very large body size on ecology.* Cambrigde: Cambridge University Press.

Paddaya, K. 1973. A federmesser site with tanged points at Norgervaart, Province of Drenthe (Netherlands). *Paleohistoria* 15: 167–205.

Palmer, S. 1975. A Palaeolithic site at North Road, Purfleet, Essex. *Transactions of the Essex Archaeological Society* 7: 1–13.

Palmqvist, P., Martínez-Navarro, B., Toro, I., Patrocinio Espigares, M., Ros-Montoya, S., Torregrosa, V. et al. 2005. Réévaluation de la présence humaine au Pléistocène inférieur dans le Sud de l'Espagne. *L'Anthropologie* 109: 411–450.

Palombo, M. R. 2010. A scenario of human dispersal in the northwestern Mediterranean throughout the Early to Middle Pleistocene. *Quaternary International* 223/224: 179–194.

Parfitt, S. A. 1998a. The interglacial mammalian fauna from Barnham. In: Ashton, N. M., Lewis., S.G., and Parfitt, S. (ed.) *Excavations at the Lower Palaeolithic Site at East Farm, Barnham, Suffolk 1989–94.* London: British Museum Press, pp. 111–147.

Parfitt, S. A. 1998b. Pleistocene vertebrates faunas of the West Sussex Coastal Plain: their environment and palaeoenvironmental significance. In: Murton, J. B., Whiteman, C. A., Bates, M. R., Bridgland, D., Long, A. J., Roberts, M. B. and Waller, M. P. (eds), *The Quaternary of Kent and Sussex: Field Guide.* London: Quaternary Research Association, pp. 121–135.

Parfitt, S. A. 1999. Mammalia. In: Roberts, M. B. and Parfitt, S. A. (eds), *Boxgrove. A Middle Pleistocene Hominid Site at Eartham Quarry, Boxgrove, West Sussex.* London: English Heritage, pp. 197–290.

Parfitt, S. A. 2008. Pakefield cliffs: archaeology and palaeoenvironment of the Cromer Forest-bed formation. In: Candy, I., Lee, J. R. and Harrison, A. M. (eds), *The Quaternary of Northern East Anglia: Field Guide.* London: Quaternary Research Association, pp. 130–136.

Parfitt, S. A., Barendregt, R. W., Breda, M., Candy, I., Collins, M. J., Coope, G. R. et al. 2005. The earliest record of human activity in northern Europe. *Nature* 438: 1008–1011.

Parfitt, S. A., Ashton, N. M., Lewis, S. G., Abel, R. L., Coope, G. R., Field, M. H. et al. 2010. Early Pleistocene human occupation at the edge of the boreal zone in northwest Europe. *Nature* 466: 229–233.

Parkin, R. A., Rowley-Conwy, P. and Sergeantson, D. 1986. Late Palaeolithic exploitation of horse and red deer at Gough's Cave, Cheddar, Somerset. *Proceedings of the University of Bristol Spelaeological Society* 17: 311–330.

Pasda, C. 2002. A short note on man in the Allerød/Younger Dryas environment of Lower Lusatia (Brandenburg, Germany). In: Eriksen, B. and Bratlund, B. (eds), *Recent Studies in the Final Palaeolithic of the European Plain. Proceedings of a U.I.S.P.P. Symposium, Stockholm, 14–17 October 1999.* Aarhus: Aarhus University Press, pp. 123–128.

Paterson, T. T. 1937. Studies on the Palaeolithic succession in England No. 1. The Barnham Sequence. *Proceedings of the Prehistoric Society* 3: 87–135.

Paterson, T. T. 1942. *Lower Palaeolithic Man in the Cambridge District.* Unpublished Ph.D. Thesis, University of Cambridge.

Paterson, T. T. and Fagg, B. E. B. 1940. Studies in the Palaeolithic succession in England II: the Upper Brecklandian Acheul (Elveden). *Proceedings of the Prehistoric Society* 6: 1–29.

Paterson, T. T. and Tebbutt, C. F. 1947. Studies in the Palaeolithic succession in England No. III. Palaeoliths from St. Neots, Huntingdonshire. *Proceedings of the Prehistoric Society* 13: 37–46.

Pautrat, Y. and Thévenin, A. (eds) 1996. *Paléolithique Supérieur et Epipaléolithique dans le Nord-Est de la France.* Dijon: Cahiers Archéologiques de Bourgogne.

Pawley, S. M., Bailey, R. M., Rose, J., Moorlock, B. S. P., Hamblin, R. J. O., Booth, S. J. et al.. 2008. Age limits on Middle Pleistocene glacial sediments from OSL dating, north Norfolk, UK. *Quaternary Science Reviews* 27: 1363–1377.

Peltier, W. R. and Fairbanks, R. G. 2006. Global ice volume and Last Glacial Maximum duration from an extended Barbados sea level record. *Quaternary Science Reviews* 25: 3322–3337.

Pengelly, W. 1873. The cavern discovered in 1858 at Windmill Hill, Brixham, South Devon. *Transactions of the Devonshire Association for the Advancement of Science, Literature and Art* 6: 775–856.

Pengelly, W. 1884. The Literature of Kent's Cavern, Part V. *Transactions of the Devonshire Association for the Advancement of Science, Literature and Art* 14: 189–334.

Penkman, K. E. H. 2005. *Amino acid geochronology: a closed system approach to test and refine the UK model.* Unpublished Ph.D. Thesis, University of Newcastle.

Penkman, K. E. H., Preece, R., Keen, D. H. and Collins, D. 2010. Amino acid geochronology of the type Cromerian of West Runton, Norfolk, UK. *Quaternary International* doi:10.1016/j.quaint.2010.06.020.

Pennington, W. 1977. The Late Devensian flora and vegetation of Britain. *Philosophical Transactions of the Royal Society of London* B280: 247–271.

Peresani, M., Fiore, I., Gala, M., Romandini, M. and Tagliacozzo, A. 2011. Late Neandertals and the intentional removal of feathers as evidenced from bird bone taphonomy at Fumane Cave 44 ky B.P., Italy. *Proceedings of the National Academy of Sciences (USA)* 108: 3888–3893.

Peretto, C., Amore, O., Antoniazzi, A., Bahain, J. J., Cattani, L., Cavallini, E. et al. 1998. L'industrie lithique de Ca` Belvedere i Monte Poggiolo: stratigraphie, matière première, typologie, remontage et traces d'utilisation. *L'Anthropologie* 102: 343–466.

Pérez-González, A., Santonja, M. and Benito, A. 2001. Geomorphology and stratigraphy of the Ambrona site (central Spain). In: Caverretta, G., Gioia, P., Mussi, M. and Palomba, M. R. (eds), *The World of Elephants.* Rome: Consiglio Nazionale delle Ricerche, pp. 587–591.

Perpére, M. 1986. Apport de la typométrie à la définition des éclats Levallois. *Bulletin de la Société Préhistorique Française* 83: 115–118.

Perrin , R. M. S., Rose, J. and Davies, H. 1979. The distribution, variation and origins of pre-Devensian tills in Eastern England. *Philosophical Transactions of the Royal Society of London* 287: 535–570.

Pesesse, D. and Michel, A. 2006. Le burin des Vachons: approts d'une relecture technologique à la comprehension de l'Aurignacien recent du Nord d'Aquitaine et des Charentes. *Paléo* 18: 143–160.

Petit, C. and Thévenin, A. 1996. Paléolithique Supérieur et Epipaléolithique dans le Nord-Est de la France. In: Pautrat, Y. and Thévenin, A. (eds), *Réflexions sur quelques armatures épipaléolithiques du Pays de Langres (Haute-Marne)*. Dijon: Service Régional de l'Archéologie de Bourgogne, pp. 88–96.

Petit, J. R., Jouzel, J., Raynaud, D., Barkov, N. I., Barnola, J.-M., Basile, I. et al. 1999. Climate and atmospheric history of the past 420,000 years from the Vostok ice core, Antarctica. *Nature* 399: 429–436.

Petraglia, M. D. 1998. The Lower Palaeolithic of India and its bearing on the Asian record. In: Petraglia, M. D., and Korisettar, R. (ed.) *Early Human Behaviour in Global Context: the Rise and Diversity of the Lower Palaeolithic Record.* London: Routledge.

Pettitt, P. B. 1992. High Lodge and Human Behaviour. Unpublished MA Dissertation, Institute of Archaeology, University College London

Pettitt, P. B. 2000. Radiocarbon chronology, faunal turnover and human occupation at the Goat's Hole, Paviland. In: Aldhouse-Green, S. (ed.) *Paviland Cave and the 'Red Lady': a Definitive Report.* Bristol: Western Academic and Specialist Press, pp. 63–71.

Pettitt, P. B. 2006. The living dead and the dead living: burials, figurines and social performance in the European Mid Upper Palaeolithic. In: Knüsel, C. and Gowland, R. (eds), *The Social Archaeology of Funerary Remains.* Oxford: Oxbow, pp. 292–308.

Pettitt, P. B. 2007. Cultural form and context of the Creswell images: an interpretative model. In: Pettitt, P. B., Bahn, P. and Ripoll, S. (eds), *Palaeolithic Cave Art at Creswell Crags in European Context.* Oxford: Oxford University Press.

Pettitt, P. B. 2008. The British Upper Palaeolithic. In: Pollard, J. (ed.) *Prehistoric Britain.* London: Blackwell Studies in Global Archaeology, pp. 18–57.

Pettitt, P. B. 2009. François Bordes. *Lithics 30: Great Prehistorians: 150 years of Palaeolithic Research, 1859–2009*: 201–212.

Pettitt, P. B. 2011. *The Palaeolithic Origins of Human Burial.* London: Routledge.

Pettitt, P. B. and Bahn, P. 2007. Rock art and art mobilier of the British Upper Palaeolithic. In: Mazel, A., Nash, G. H. and Waddington, C. (eds), *Art as Metaphor: The Prehistoric Rock-art of Britain.* Oxford: Archaeopress, pp. 9–38.

Pettitt, P. B., Bahn, P. and Ripoll, S. (eds) 2007. *Palaeolithic Cave Art at Creswell Crags in European Context,* Oxford: Oxford University Press.

Pettitt, P. B. and Jacobi, R. M. 2009. The Palaeolithic archaeology of Creswell Crags. In: Bahn, P. and Pettitt, P. (eds), *Britain's Oldest Art: the Ice Age Cave Art of Creswell Crags.* London: English Heritage, pp. 16–35.

Pettitt, P. B. and White, M. J. 2011. Cave Men: stone tools, Victorian science and the 'primitive mind' of deep time. *Notes and Records of the Royal Society* 24(1): 25–42.

Pettitt, P. B., Housley, R. A. and Higham, T. F. G. in press. Radiocarbon chronology and faunal turnover in the Upper Pleistocene at Pontnewydd cave. In: Aldhouse-Green, S., Walker, E. and Peterson, R. (eds), *Pontnewydd and the Elwy Valley Caves.* Cardiff: National Museums and Galleries of Wales.

Pettitt, P. B., Jacobi, R. M., Chamberlain, A., Pike, A. W. G., Schreve, D., Wall, I. et al. 2009. Excavations outside Church Hole, Creswell Crags: the first three seasons (2006–8). *Transactions of the Thoroton Society of Nottinghamshire* 113: 35–53.

Pevzner, M., Vangengeim, E. and Tesakov, A. 2001. Quaternary subdivisions of Eastern

Europe based on vole evolution. *Bollettino della Societa Palaeontologica Italiana* 40: 269–274.

Pike, A., Eggins, S., Grun, R., Hedges, R. E. M. and Jacobi, R. 2005a. U-series dating of the Late Pleistocene mammalian fauna from Wood Quarry (Steetley), Nottinghamshire, UK. *Journal of Quaternary Science* 20: 59–65.

Pike, A. W. G., Gilmore, M., Pettitt, P. B., Jacobi, R., Ripoll, S., Bahn, P. et al. 2005b. Independent U-Series verification of the Pleistocene antiquity of the Palaeolithic cave art at Creswell Crags, UK. *Journal of Archaeological Science* 32: 1649–1655.

Pike, A. W. G., Gilmour, M. and Pettitt, P. B. 2009. Verification of the age of the Palaeolithic cave art at Creswell Crags using uranium-series disequilibrium dating. In: Bahn, P. and Pettitt, P. B. (eds), *Britain's Oldest Art: The Ice Age Cave Art of Creswell Crags.* London: English Heritage, pp. 87–95.

Pike, K. and Godwin, H. 1953. The interglacial at Clacton-on-Sea, Essex. *Quarterly Journal of the Geological Society of London* 108: 261–270.

Piperno, M., Lefèvre, D., Raynal, J. P. and Tagliacozzo, A. 1998. Notarchirico. An Early Middle Pleistocene site in the Venosa Basin. *Anthropologie* 36: 85–90.

Pitts, M. and Roberts, M. B. 1997. *Fairweather Eden: Life in Britain Half a Million Years Ago as revealed by the Excavations at Boxgrove.* London: Century.

Plisson, H. and Beyries, S. 1998. Pointes ou outils triangulaire? Donneés fonctionelles dans le Moustérian levantin. *Paléorient* 24: 5–24.

Połtowicz, M. 2006. The eastern borders of the Magdalenian culture range. *Analecta Archaeologica Ressoviensia* 1.

Poole, H. W. 1929. A laurel-leaf point from Brighstone. *Proceedings of the Isle of Wight Natural History and Archaeology Society* 1: 690–693.

Pope, M. 2002. *The significance of biface-rich assemblages: an examination of behavioural controls on lithic assemblage formation in the Lower Palaeolithic.* Unpublished Ph.D. Thesis, Department of Archaeology, University of Southampton.

Pope, M. 2004. Behavioural implications of biface discard: assemblage variability and land-use at the Middle Pleistocene site of Boxgrove. In: Walker, E., Wenban-Smith, F. and Healy, F. (eds), *Lithics in Action.* Oxford: Oxbow Books, Lithics Studies Society Occasional Paper No. 8, pp. 38–47.

Pope, M. and Roberts, M. B. 2005. Observations between the relationship between Palaeolithic individuals and artefact scatters at the Middle Pleistocene site of Boxgrove, UK. In: Gamble, W. and Porr, M. (eds), *The Hominid Individual in Context: Archaeological Investigations of Lower and Middle Palaeolithic landscapes, locales and artefacts.* London: Routledge, pp. 81–97.

Pope, M., Roberts, M. B., Maxted, A. and Jones, P. 2009. The Valdoe: archaeology of a locality within the Boxgrove palaeolandscape. *Proceedings of the Prehistoric Society* 75: 239–304.

Potts, R. 1988. *Early Hominid Activities at Olduvai.* New York: Aldine de Gruyter.

Preece, R. C. 1994. Radiocarbon dates from the 'Allerød' soil in Kent. *Proceedings of the Geologists' Association* 105: 111–123.

Preece, R. C. (ed.) 1995. *Island Britain: a Quaternary perspective,* London: Geological Society Special Publication 96.

Preece, R. C. 2001. Molluscan evidence for differentiation of interglacials within the 'Cromerian Complex. *Quaternary Science Reviews* 20: 1643–1656.

Preece, R. C. and Bates, M. R. 1999. Mollusca. In: Roberts, M. B. and Parfitt, S. A. (eds), *Boxgrove.*

A Middle Pleistocene Hominid Site at Eartham Quarry, Boxgrove, West Sussex. London: English Heritage, pp. 170–175.

Preece, R. C. and Parfitt, S. A. 2000. The Cromer Forest-bed Formation: new thoughts on an old problem. In: Lewis, S. G., Whiteman, C. A. and Preece, R. C. (eds), *The Quaternary of Norfolk and Suffolk: Field Guide.* London: Quaternary Research Association, pp. 1–27.

Preece, R. C. and Penkman, K. E. H. 2005. New faunal analyses and amino acid dating of the Lower Palaeolithic site at East Farm, Barnham, Suffolk. *Proceedings of the Geologists' Association* 116: 363–377.

Preece, R. C. and Parfitt, S. 2008. The Cromer Forest-bed Formation: some recent developments relating to early human occupation and lowland glaciation. In: Candy, I., Lee, J. R. and Harrison, A. M. (eds), *The Quaternary of Northern East Anglia: Field Guide.* London: Quaternary Research Association, pp. 60–83.

Preece, R. C., Scourse, J. D., Houghton, S. D., Knudson, K. L. and Penney, D. N. 1990. The Pleistocene sea-level and neotectonic history of the eastern Solent, southern England. *Philosophical Transactions of the Royal Society of London* B328: 425–477.

Preece, R. C., Lewis, S. G., Wymer, J.J., Bridgland, D. R. and Parfitt, S. A. 1991. Beeches Pit, West Stow, Suffolk (TL 798719). In: Lewis, S. G., Whiteman, C. A. and Bridgland, D. R. (eds), *Central East Anglia and the Fen Basin: Field Guide.* London: Quaternary Research Association, pp. 94–104.

Preece, R. C., Bridgland, D. R., Lewis, S. G., Parfitt, S. A. and Griffiths, H. I. 2000. Beeches Pit, West Stow, Suffolk (TL 798719). In: Lewis, S. G., Whiteman, C. A. and Preece, R. C. (eds), *The Quaternary of Norfolk and Suffolk: Field Guide.* London: Quaternary Research Association, pp. 185–195.

Preece, R. C., Gowlett, J. A. J., Parfitt, S. A., Bridgland, D. R. and Lewis, S. G. 2006. Humans in the Hoxnian: habitat, context, and fire use at beeches Pit, West Stow, Suffolk, UK. *Journal of Quaternary Science* 21: 485–496.

Preece, R. C., Parfitt, S., Coope, G. R., Penkman, K. E. H., Ponel, P. and Whittaker, J. E. 2009. Biostratigraphic and aminostratigraphic constraints on the age of the Middle Pleistocene glacial succession in north Norfolk, UK. *Journal of Quaternary Science* 24: 557–580.

Proctor, C. J. 1994. *A British Pleistocene chronology based on uranium series and electron spin resonance dating of speleothems.* Unpublished Ph.D. Thesis, University of Bristol.

Proctor, C. J. and Smart, P. L. 1991. A dated cave sediment record of Pleistocene transgressions on Berry Head, Southwest England. *Journal of Quaternary Science* 6: 233–244.

Proctor, C. J., Collcutt, S. N., Currant, A. P., Hawkes, C. J., Roe, D. A. and Smart, P. L. 1996. A report on the excavations at Rhinoceros Hole, Wookey. *Proceedings of the University of Bristol Spelaeological Society* 20: 237–262.

Prokopenko, A. A., Karabanov, E. B., Williams, D. F., Kuzmin, M. I., Shackleton, N. J., Crowhurst, S. J. et al. 2001. Biogenic silica record of the Lake Baikal response to climatic forcing during the Bruhnes. *Quaternary Research* 44: 205–15.

Pryor, F. 2004. *Britain BC.* London: Harper Collins.

Radley, J. 1967. Excavations at a rock shelter at Whaley, Derbyshire. *Derbyshire Archaeological Journal* LXXXVII: 1–17.

Radmilli, A. M. 1984. Scavi nel giacimento del Paleolitico inferiore a Castel di Guido presso Roma. In: Bietti Sestieri, A. M. (ed.), *Preistoria e Protostoria nel territorio di Roma.* Rome: Lavori e Studi di Archaeologia pubblicati dalla Soprintendenza Archeologica di Roma, pp. 75–85.

Ranov, V. A. 2001. Cleavers: their distribution, chronology and typology. In: Milliken, S. and Cook,

J. (eds), *A Very Remote Period Indeed: Papers on the Palaeolithic Presented to Derek Roe.* Oxford: Oxbow, pp. 105–113.

Raynal, J.-P., Magoga, L., Sbihi-Alaoui, F.-Z. and Geraads, D. 1995. The earliest occupation of Atlantic Morocco: the Casablanca evidence. In: Roebroeks, W. and Van Kolfshoten, T. (eds), *The Earliest Occupation of Europe.* Leiden: University of Leiden, pp. 255–262.

Raynal, J.-P., Sbihi-Alaoui, F.-Z., Geraads, D., Magoga, L. and Mohi, A. 2001. The earliest occupation of North Africa: the Moroccan perspective. *Quaternary International* 75: 65–75.

Raynal, J.-P., Sbihi-Alaoui, F.-Z., Magoga, L., Mohib, A. and Zouak, M. 2002. The Lower Palaeolithic sequence of Atlantic Morocco revisited after recent excavations at Casablanca. *Bulletin d'Archeologie Marocaine* 20: 1–18.

Read, A., Godwin, M., Mills, C. A., Juby, C., Lee, J. R., Palmer, A. P. et al. 2007. Evidence for Middle Pleistocene temperate-climate high sea-level and lowland-scale glaciation, Chapel Hill, Norwich, UK. *Proceedings of Geologists' Association* 118: 143–156.

Reich, D., Green, R. E., Kircher, M., Krause, J., Patterson, N., Durand, E. Y. et al. 2010. Genetic history of an archaic hominin group from Denisova Cave in Siberia. *Nature* 468: 1053–1060.

Reid, C. 1899. *The Origin of the British Flora.* London: Dalau.

Reimer, P. J., Baillie, M. G. L., Bard, E., Bayliss, A., Beck, J. W., Blackwell, P. G. et al. 2009. INTCAL09 and MARINE09 radiocarbon age calibration curves, 0–50,000 years cal BP. *Radiocarbon* 51: 1111–1150.

Rensink, E. 1991. L'observation du gibier et le débitage des nucleus: un poste de guet du Magdalénien à Mesch (Limbourg, Pays-Bas). *Helinium* XXXI: 5–59.

Rensink, E. 1992. Eyserheide: a Late Magdalenian site on the fringe of the northern loessbelt (Limburg, The Netherlands). *Archäologisches Korrespondenzblatt* 22: 315–327.

Rensink, E. 2002. Late Palaeolithic sites in the Maas Valley of the southern Netherlands: prospects, surveys and results. In: Eriksen, B. and Bratlund, B. (eds), *Recent Studies in the Final Palaeolithic of the European Plain. Proceedings of a U.I.S.P.P. Symposium, Stockholm, 14–17 October 1999.* Aarhus: Aarhus University Press, pp. 181–188.

Reumer, J., Rook, L., van der Borg, K., Post, K., Mol, D. and de Vos, J. 2003. Late Pleistocene survival of the saber-toothed cat *Homotherium* in northwestern Europe. *Journal of Vertebrate Palaeontology* 23: 260–262.

Reumer, J., Mol, D. and Borst, W. 2010. The first Late Pleistocene coprolite of *Crocuta crocuta spelaea* from the North Sea. *Deinsea* 14: 15–18.

Révillion, S. 1995. Laminar flaking in the European Middle Palaeolithic of Northern Europe. *Bulletin de la Société Préhistorique Française* 92: 425–441.

Reynier, M. J. 1998. Early Mesolithic settlement in England and Wales: some preliminary observations. In: Ashton, N., Healy, F. and Pettitt, P. (eds), *Stone Age Archaeology: Essays in Honour of John Wymer.* Oxford: Oxbow Monograph 102 and Lithic Studies Society Occasional Papers 6, pp. 174–184.

Reynolds, P. J., Catt, J. A., Weir, A. H. and Fisher, G. C. 1996. Stratigraphy and origin of New Forest brickearths, England. *Journal of Quaternary Science* 11: 203–216.

Richards, M. P. 2007. Diet shift at the Middle/Upper Palaeolithic transition in Europe? The stable isotope evidence. In: Roebroeks, W. (ed.), *Guts and Brains: an Integrative Approach to the Hominin Record.* Leiden: Leiden University Press, pp. 223–234.

Richards, M. P., Hedges, R. E. M., Jacobi, R. M., Currant, A. P. and Stringer, C. B. 2000. Gough's Cave and Sun Hole Cave human stable isotope values indicate a high animal protein diet in the British Upper Palaeolithic. *Journal of Archaeological Science* 27: 1–3.

Richards, M. P., Jacobi, R., Cook, J., Pettitt, P. B. and Stringer, C. B. 2005. Isotope evidence for the intensive use of marine foods by Late Upper Palaeolithic humans. *Journal of Human Evolution* 49: 390–394.

Richards, M. P., Gamble, C., Pettitt, P. B. and Davies, W. in press. Genetic and archaeological perspectives on population contraction and expansion in Lateglacial Europe. In: Gosden, C. and Ward, R. (eds), *Archaeology and Genetics.* London: Routledge.

Riede, F., Grimm, S. B., Weber, M.-J. and Fahlke, J. M. 2010. Neue daten für alte grabungen – ein beitrag zur spätglazialen archäologie und faunengeschichte Norddeutschlands. *Archälogisches Korrespondenzblatt* 40: 297–316.

Rightmire P. 2004. Brain size and encephalization in Early to Mid-Pleistocene *Homo. American Journal of Physical Anthropology* 124:109–123.

Rightmire, G. P., Lordkipanidze, D. and Vekua, A. 2006. Anatomical descriptions, comparative studies and evolutionary significance of the hominin skulls from Dmanisi, Republic of Georgia. *Journal of Human Evolution* 50: 115–141.

Ritchie, J. C. and Lichti-Fedorovich, S. 1967. Pollen dispersal phenomena in arctic-subarctic Canada. *Review of Palaeobotany and Palynology* 3: 255.

Robb, J. 2001. Social agency and anti-social agency: archaeology in the grey zone. *Society for American Archaeology.* New Orleans.

Roberts, A. 1996. Evidence for Late Pleistocene and Early Holocene human activity and environmental change from the Torbryan Valley, south Devon. In: Charman, D. J., Newnham, R. M. and Croot, D. G. (eds), *The Quaternary of Devon and East Cornwall: Field Guide.* London: Quaternary Research Association, pp. 168–204.

Roberts, A. and Barton, R. N. E. 2001. A Lyngby point from Mildenhall, Suffolk, and its implications for the British Late Upper Palaeolithic. In: Milliken, S. and Cook, J. (eds), *A Very Remote Period Indeed: Papers on the Palaeolithic Presented to Derek Roe.* Oxford: Oxbow, pp. 234–241.

Roberts, A. and Grün, R. 2010. Early human northerners. *Nature* 466.

Roberts, M. B. 1986. Excavation of the Lower Palaeolithic Site at Amey's Eartham Pit, Boxgrove, West Sussex: A preliminary report. *Proceedings of the Prehistoric Society* 52: 215–245.

Roberts, M. B. 1990. Amey's Eartham Pit, Boxgrove. In: Turner, C. (ed.) *The Cromer Symposium: SEQS Field Excursion Guidebook.* Norwich: SEQS, pp. 62–67.

Roberts, M. B. 1996a. 'Man the Hunter' Returns at Boxgrove. *British Archaeology* 18: 8–9.

Roberts, M. B. 1996b. And then came speech and clothing. *British Archaeology* 19: 8–9.

Roberts, M. B. 1999. Flintwork from other contexts. In: Roberts, M. B. and Parfitt, S. A. (eds), *Boxgrove. A Middle Pleistocene Hominid Site at Eartham Quarry, Boxgrove, West Sussex.* London: English Heritage, pp. 378–384.

Roberts, M. B. and Parfitt, S. A. (eds) 1999. *Boxgrove: A Middle Palaeolithic Pleistocene Hominid Site at Eartham Quarry, Boxgrove, West Sussex,* London: English Heritage.

Roberts, M. B., Stringer, C. and Parfitt, S. A. 1994. A hominid tibia from Middle Pleistocene sediments at Boxgrove. *Nature* 369: 311–13.

Roberts, M. B., Gamble, C. S. and Bridgland, D. R. 1995. The earliest occupation of Europe: The British Isles. In: Roebroeks, W. and Van Kolfshoten, T. (eds), *The Earliest Occupation of Europe.* Leiden: Leiden University Press, pp. 165–191.

Roberts, M. B., Parfitt, S. A., Pope, M. I., and Wenban-Smith, F. F. 1997. Boxgrove, West Sussex: Rescue excavations of a Lower Palaeolithic Landsurface (Boxgrove Project B, 1989–91). *Proceedings of the Prehistoric Society* 63: 303–358.

Robinson, J. E. 1996. The ostracod fauna from the Waechter excavations. In: Conway, B., McNabb, J. and Ashton, N. M. (eds), *Excavations at Barnfield Pit, Swanscombe 1968–1972. British Museum Occasional Papers 94.* London: British Museum Press, pp. 187–190.

Robinson, P. 1986. An introduction to the Levallois industry at Baker's Hole (Kent), with a description of two flake cleavers. In: Collcutt, S. N. (ed.), *The Palaeolithic of Britain and its Nearest Neighbours: Recent Trends.* Sheffield: University of Sheffield, pp. 20–22.

Rockman, M. 2003. *Landscape Learning in the Late Glacial Recolonisation of Britain.* Unpublished Ph.D. dissertation, University of Arizona.

Roe, D. A. 1964. The British Lower and Middle Palaeolithic: Some Problems, Methods of Study and Preliminary Results. *Proceedings of the Prehistoric Society* 30: 245–267.

Roe, D. A. 1968a. British Lower and Middle Palaeolithic handaxe groups. *Proceedings of the Prehistoric Society* 34: 1–82.

Roe, D. A. 1968b. A Gazetteer of British Lower and Middle Palaeolithic Sites. CBA Research Report No. 8.

Roe, D. A. 1979. Comment on Ohel (1979). *Current Anthropology* 20: 718.

Roe, D. A.1981. *The Lower and Middle Palaeolithic Periods in Britain.* London: Routledge and Kegan Paul.

Roe, D. A. 1986. The Palaeolithic period in the Oxford Region. In: Briggs, G., Cook, J. and Rowley, T. (eds), *The Archaeology of the Oxford Region.* Oxford: Oxford University Department for External Studies, pp. 1–17.

Roe, D. A. 1994a. The Palaeolithic archaeology of the Oxford Region. *Oxoniensia* 59: 1–15.

Roe, D. A. 1994b. A metrical analysis of selected sets of handaxes and cleavers from Olduvai Gorge. In: Leakey, M. D. and Roe, D. A. *Olduvai Gorge Volume 5: Excavations in Beds III, IV and the Masek Beds, 1968–1971.* Cambridge: Cambridge University Press, pp. 146–234.

Roe, H. M. 1994. *Pleistocene Buried Channels in Eastern Essex, Unpublished Ph.D. Thesis.* University of Cambridge.

Roe, H. M. 1999. Late Middle Pleistocene sea-level change in the southern North Sea: the record from eastern Essex. *Quaternary International* 55: 115–128.

Roe, H. M. 2001. The Late Middle Pleistocene biostratigraphy of the Thames Valley, England: new data from eastern Essex. *Quaternary Science Reviews* 20: 1603–1619.

Roe, H. M. and Preece, R. C. 1995. A new discovery of the Middle Pleistocene 'Rhenish' fauna in Essex. *Journal of Conchology* 35: 272–273.

Roe, H. M., Coope, G. R., Devoy, R. J., Harrison, C. J., Penkman, K. E., Preece, R. C. et al. 2009. Differentiation of MIS 9 and MIS 11 in the continental record: vegetational, faunal, aminostratigraphic and sea-level evidence from coastal sites in Essex, UK. *Quaternary Science Reviews* 28: 2342–2373.

Roebroeks, W. 1988. *From find scatters to early hominid behaviour: A study of Middle Palaeolithic riverside settlements at Maastricht-Belvédère (the Netherlands).* Leiden: University of Leiden.

Roebroeks, W. 1996. The English Palaeolithic Record: Absence of Evidence, Evidence of Absence and the First Occupation of Europe In: Gamble, C. S. and Lawson, A. J. (eds), *The English Palaeolithic Reviewed.* Wessex: Trust For Wessex Archaeology.

Roebroeks, W. 2001. Human behaviour and the earliest occupation of Europe: an exploration. *Journal of Human Evolution* 41: 437–461.

Roebroeks, W. 2005. Life on the Costa del Cromer. *Nature* 438: 921–922.

Roebroeks, W. 2006. The human colonisation of Europe: where are we? *Journal of Quaternary Science* 21: 425–435.

Roebroeks, W. 2008. Time for the Middle to Upper Palaeolithic transition in Europe. *Journal of Human Evolution* 55: 918–926.

Roebroeks, W. and Van Kolfshoten, T. 1994. The earliest occupation of Europe: A short chronology. *Antiquity* 68: 489–503.

Roebroeks, W. and Van Kolfshoten, T. (eds) 1995. *The Earliest Occupation of Europe,* Leiden: Leiden University Press.

Roebroeks, W. and Tuffreau, A. 1999. Palaeoenvironment and settlement patterns of the Northwest European Middle Palaeolithic. In: Gamble, C. and Roebroeks, W. (eds), *The Middle Palaeolithic Occupation of Europe.* Leiden: University of Leiden Press, pp. 121–138.

Roebroeks, W. and Speleers, B. 2002. Last interglacial (Eemian) occupation of the North European Plain and adjacent areas. In: Tuffreau, A. and Roebroeks, W. (eds), *Le Dernier Interglaciaire et les occupations humaines du Palaeolithique moyen.* Lille: Centre d'Etudes et Recherches Prehistorique, pp. 31–40.

Roebroeks, W. and Villa, P. 2011. On the earliest evidence for habitual use of fire in Europe. *Proceedings of the National Academy of Sciences (USA)* 108: 5209–5214.

Roebroeks, W., Connard, N.J. and van Kolfschoten, T. 1992. Dense Forests, Cold Steppes, and the Palaeolithic Settlement of Northern Europe. *Current Anthropology* 33: 551–586.

Roebroeks, W., Kolen, J., van Poecke, M. and van Gijn, A. 1997. 'Site J': An early Weichselian (Middle Palaeolithic) flint scatter at Maastricht-Belvedere, The Netherlands. *Paléo* 9: 143–172.

Roebroeks, W., Hublin, J.-J. and MacDonald, K. 2011. Continuities and discontinuities in Neanderthal presence: a closer look at Northwestern Europe. In: Ashton, N., Lewis, S. and Stringer, C. (eds), *The Ancient Human Occupation of Britain.* Amsterdam: Elsevier, pp. 113–123.

Rogers, E. H. 1955. Stratification of the cave earth in Kents Cavern. *Proceedings of the Devonshire Archaeological Exploration Society* 1954/1955: 1–25.

Rohling, E., Bigg, G. R., Jorissen, F. J., Bertrand, P., Ganssan, G. and Caulet, J.-P. 1998. Magnitudes of sea-level low stands of the past 500,000 years. *Nature* 394: 162–165.

Rolland, N. 1981. The Interpretation of Middle Palaeolithic Variability. *Man* 16: 15–42.

Rolland, N. 1992. The palaeolithic colonization of Europe: an archaeological and biogeographic perspective. *Trabajos De Prehistoria* 49: 69–111.

Rolland, N. 1995. Levallois technique emergence: single or multiple? A review of the Euro-African record. In: Dibble, H. L. and Bar-Yosef, O. (eds), *The Definition and Interpretation of Levallois Technology.* Madison: Prehistory Press, pp. 333–359.

Rolland, N. 1998. The Lower Palaeolithic settlement of Eurasia, with special reference to Europe. In: Petraglia, M. D. and Korisettar, R. (eds), *Early Human Behaviour in Global Context: the Rise and Diversity of the Lower Palaeolithic Record.* London: Routledge, pp. 187–220.

Rolland, N. 1999. The Middle Palaeolithic as Development Stage: Evidence from Technology, Subsistence, Settlement Systems, and Hominid-Socio-ecology. In: Ullrich, H. (ed.), *Hominid Evolution; Lifestyles and Survival Strategies.* Bonn: Edition Archaea, pp. 315–334.

Rolland, N. 2010. The early human occupation of high latitudes, boreal, continental and periglacial habitats: Middle Paleolithic milestones in Northern Eurasia. *Acta Universitatis Wratislaviensis* 3207: 15–46.

Rolland, N. and Dibble, H. L. 1990. A new synthesis of Middle Palaeolithic assemblage variability. *American Antiquity* 55: 480–499.

Ronen, A. (ed.) 1982. *The Transition from the Lower to Middle Palaeolithic and the Origins of Modern Man,* Oxford: British Archaeological Reports International Series 151.

Ronen, A., Burdukiewicz, J. M., Laukhin, S. A., Winter, Y., Tsatskin, A., Dayan, T. et al. 1998. The Lower Paleolithic site Bitzat Ruhama in the northern Negev. *Archäologisches Korrespondenzblatt* 28: 163–173.

Rose, J. 1980. Landform development around Kisdon, Upper Swaledale, Yorkshire. *Proceedings of the Yorkshire Geological Society* 43: 201–219.

Rose, J. 1985. The Dimlington Stadial/Dimlington Chronozone: a proposal for naming the main glacial episode of the Late Devensian in Britain. *Boreas* 14: 225–230.

Rose, J. 1987. The status of the Wolstonian glaciation in the British Quaternary. *Quaternary Newsletter* 53: 1–9.

Rose, J. 2009. Early and Middle Pleistocene landscapes of eastern England. *Proceedings of the Geologists' Association* 120: 3–33.

Rose, J. and Allen, P. 1977. Middle Pleistocene stratigraphy in south-east Suffolk. *Journal of the Geological Society of London* 133: 83–102.

Rose, J., Turner, C., Coope, G. R. and Bryan, M. D. 1980. Channel changes in a lowland river catchment over the last 13,000 years. In: Cullingford, R. A., Davidson, D. A. and Lewin, J. (eds), *Timescales in Geomorphology.* London: Allen Unwin, pp. 159–175.

Rose, J., Boardman, J., Kemp, R. A. and Whiteman, C. A. 1985. Palaeosols and the interpretation of the British Quaternary stratigraphy. In: Richards, K. S., Arnett, R. R. and Ellis, S. (eds), *Geomorphology and Soils.* London: Allen Unwin, pp. 348–375.

Rose, J., Lee, J. A., Candy, I. and Lewis, S. G. 1999. Early and Middle Pleistocene river systems in eastern England: evidence from Leet Hill, southern Norfolk. *Journal of Quaternary Science* 14: 347–360.

Rose, J., Moorlock, B. S. P. and Hamblin, R. J. O. 2001. Pre-Anglian fluvial and coastal deposits in Eastern England: lithostratigraphy and palaeoenvironments. *Quaternary International* 79: 5–22.

Rose, J., Candy, I., Moorlock, B. S. P., Wilkins, H., Lee, J. A., Hamblin, R. J. O. et al. 2002. Early and early Middle Pleistocene river, coastal and neotectonic processes, southeast Norfolk, England. *Proceedings of the Geologists' Association* 113: 47–67.

Rots, V., Stapert, D. and Johansen, L. 2001. De Cheddar-en Creswell-Spitzen van Zeijen (Dr.): 'projectilen' of messen? *Paleo-Aktuel* 13: 24–29.

Rots, V., Stapert, D. and Johansen, L. 2002–3. Spitsen van Siegerswoude (Fr.), Emmerhout (Dr.) en Luttenberg (Ov.): gebruikssporenonderzoek. *Paleo-Aktuel* 14: 11–15.

Rouffignac, C. d., Bowen, D. Q., Coope, G. R., Keen, D. H., Lister, A. M., Maddy, D. et al. 1995. Late Middle Pleistocene interglacial deposits at Upper Strensham, Worcestershire, England. *Journal of Quaternary Science* 10: 15–31.

Rowe, P. J., Richards, D. A., Atkinson, T. C., Bottrell, S. H. and Cliff, R. A. 1997. Geochemistry and radiometric dating of a Middle Pleistocene peat. *Geochimica and Cosmochimica Acta* 61: 4201–4211.

Rust, A. 1943. *Die Alt- und Mittelsteinzeitlichen Funde von Stellmoor.* Neumünster: Karl Wachholz.

Rutter, J. 1829. *Delineations of the north western division of the County of Somerset, and of its antediluvian bone caverns, with a geological sketch of the district.* London: Longman, Rees and Co.

Sampson, C. G. 1978. *Palaeoecology and Archaeology of an Acheulian Site at Caddington, England.* Dallas: Southern Methodist University.

Sánchez Goñi, M. F. 1993. The identification of European Upper Palaeolithic interstadials from cave sequences. *Palynology* 17: 1–21.

Sánchez Goñi, M. F., Turon, J.-L., Eynaud, F. and Gendreau, S. 2000. European climatic response to millennial-scale changes in the atmosphere-ocean system during the last glacial period. *Quaternary Research* 54: 394–403.

Sánchez Goñi, M. F., Cacho, I., Turon, J.-L., Guiot, J., Sierro, F. J., Peypouquet, J.-P. et al. 2002. Synchroneity between marine and terrestrial responses to millennial scale climatic variability during the last glacial period in the Mediterranean region. *Climate Dynamics* 19: 95–105.

Sandford, K. S. 1924. The River Gravels of the Oxford District. *Quarterly Journal of the Geological Society of London* 80: 113–179.

Sandford, K. S. 1926. Pleistocene deposits. In: Pringle, J. (ed.) *The Geology of the Country around Oxford. Memoir of the Geological Survey of Great Britain.* London: HMSO.

Santonja, M. and Villa, P. 1990. The Lower Palaeolithic of Spain and Portugal. *Journal of World Prehistory* 4: 45–94.

Saville, A. 2004. The material culture of Mesolithic Scotland. In: Saville, A. (ed.) *Mesolithic Scotland and its Neighbours. The Early Holocene Prehistory of Scotland, its British and Irish Context, and some Northern European Perspectives.* Edinburgh: Society of Antiquaries of Scotland, pp. 185–220.

Saville, A. and Ballin, T. B. 2009. Upper Palaeolithic evidence from Kilmelfort Cave, Argyll: a re-evaluation of the lithic assemblage. *Proceedings of the Society of Antiquaries of Scotland* 139: 1–36

Scaife, R. F. 1987. The Late-Devensian and Flandrian vegetation of the Isle of Wight. In: Barber, K. E. (ed.) *Wessex and the Isle of Wight: Field Guide.* Cambridge: Quaternary Research Association, pp. 156–180.

Schick, K. 1987. Modelling the formation of early stone age artefact concentrations. *Journal of Human Evolution* 16: 789–807.

Schlanger, N. 1996. Understanding Levallois: Lithic technology and cognitive archaeology. *Cambridge Archaeological Journal* 6: 231–254.

Schmider, B. 1990a. The last pleniglacial in the Paris Basin (22,500–17,000 BP). In: Soffer, O. and Gamble, C. (eds), *The World at 18,000 BP: Volume One High Latitudes.* London: Unwin Hyman, pp. 41–53.

Schmider, B. 1990b. Le Solutreen dans de Bassin Parisien. In: Kozlowski, J. (ed.) *Feuilles de Pierre: les Industries à Pointes Foliacées du Paléolithique Supérieur Européen.* Liège: Études et Recherches Archéologiques de l'Université de Liège 42, pp. 321–33.

Schmider, B. 1992. *Marsangy. Un Campement des Derniers Chasseurs Magdaléniens, sur les Bords de l'Yonne.* Liège: Études et Recherches Archéologiques de l'Université de Liège 55.

Schmider, B., Valentin, B., Baffier, D., David, F., Julien, M., Leroi-Gourhan, A. et al. 1996. L'Abri du Lagopède (fouilles Leroi-Gourhan) et le Magdalénien des Grottes de la Cure (Yonne). *Gallia Préhistoire* 37: 55–114.

Schreve, D. C. 1997. *Mammalian biostratigraphy of the later Middle Pleistocene in Britain.* Unpublished Ph.D. Thesis, University of London.

Schreve, D. C. 2001a. Differentiation of the British late Middle Pleistocene interglacials: the evidence from mammalian biostratigraphy. *Quaternary Science Reviews* 20: 1693–1705.

Schreve, D. C. 2001b. Mammalian evidence from Middle Pleistocene fluvial sequences for complex environmental change at the oxygen isotope substage level. *Quaternary International* 79: 65–74.

Schreve, D. C. 2006. The taphonomy of a Middle Devensian (MIS3) vertebrate assemblage from Lynford, Norfolk, UK, and its implications for Middle Palaeolithic subsistence strategies. *Journal of Quaternary Science* 21: 543–557.

Schreve, D. C., Bridgland, D. R., Allen, P., Blackford, J. J., Gleed-Owen, C. P., Griffiths, H. I. et al. 2002. Sedimentology, palaeontology and archaeology of late Middle Pleistocene River Thames terrace deposits at Purfleet, Essex, UK. *Quaternary Science Reviews* 21: 1423–1464.

Schreve, D. C., Harding, P., White, M. J., Bridgland, D. R., Allen, P., Clayton, F. et al. 2006. A Levallois knapping site at West Thurrock, Lower Thames, UK: its Quaternary context, environment and age. *Proceedings of the Prehistoric Society* 72: 21–52.

Schreve, D. C., White, M. and Morigi, A. 2011. Chapter 5 – The Archaeology of Absence in the Late Middle Pleistocene (MIS6–4). *The Thames Through Time: The Archaeology of the Gravel Terraces of the Upper and Middle Thames. Part 1: The Ice Ages*. Oxford: Oxford Archaeology Thames Valley Landscapes Monograph No. 32.

Schreve, D. C., Bridgland, D.R., Allen, P., Blackford, J.J., Russell Coope, G., Cooper, J.H. et al. In prep. Late Middle Pleistocene River Thames terrace deposits at Aveley, Essex, UK: a multi-proxy framework for the penultimate (MIS 7) interglacial.

Schulting, R. J., Trinkaus, E., Higham, T., Hedges, R., Richards, M. and Cardy, B. 2005. A Mid Upper Palaeolithic human humerus from Eel Point, South Wales, UK. *Journal of Human Evolution* 48: 493–505.

Schwabedissen, H. 1954. *Die Federmesser-Gruppen des nordwesterneuropäischen flachlandes*. Neumünster: Karl Wachholtz Verlag.

Schwarcz, H. and Grün, R. 1993. Electron Spin Resonance Dating of the Lower Industry. In: Singer, R., Gladfelter, B. G. and Wymer, J. J. (eds), *The Lower Paleolithic Site at Hoxne, England*. Chicago: University of Chicago Press, pp. 210–211.

Scott, A. C., Cripps, J. A., Collinson, M. E. and Nichols, G. 2000. The taphonomy of charcoal following recent heathland fire and some implications for the interpretation of fossil charcoal deposits. *Palaeogeography, Palaeoclimatology, Palaeoecology* 164: 1–31.

Scott, G. R. and Gibert, L. 2009. The oldest hand-axes in Europe. *Nature* 461: 82–85.

Scott, K. 1980. Two hunting episodes of Middle Palaeolithic age at La Cotte de Saint-Brelade, Jersey (Channel Islands). *World Archaeology* 12: 137–152.

Scott, K. 1986. Man in Britain in the Late Devensian: evidence from Ossom's Cave. In: Roe, D. (ed.) *Studies in the Upper Palaeolithic of Britain and Northwest Europe*. Oxford: British Archaeological Reports International Series 296, pp. 63–87.

Scott, K. 2007. The ecology of late middle Pleistocene mammoths in Britain. *Quaternary International* 169/170: 125–136.

Scott, K. and Buckingham, C. 2001. A river runs through it: a decade of research at Stanton Harcourt. In: Milliken, S. and Cook, J. (eds), *A Very Remote Period Indeed: papers on the Palaeolithic presented to Derek Roe*. Oxford: Oxbow, pp. 207–213.

Scott, R. 2006. *The Early Middle Palaeolithic of Britain*. Durham University.

Scott, R. 2010. *Becoming Neanderthal: The Earlier British Middle Palaeolithic*. Oxford: Oxbow.

Scott, R., Ashton, N., Penkman, K., Preece, R. and White, M. 2010. The position and context of Middle Palaeolithic industries from the Ebbsfleet Valley, Kent, UK. *Journal of Quaternary Science* 25: 931–933.

Scott, R., Ashton, N., Lewis, S. G., Parfitt, S. and White, M. 2011. The Early MIddle Palaeolithic of the Thames Valley. In: Ashton, N., Lewis, S. G. and Stringer, C. (eds), *The Ancient Human Occupation of Britain*. Amsterdam: Elsevier, pp. 67–90.

Scourse, J. D. 1986. Pleistocene Stratigraphy. In: Scourse, J. D. (ed.) *The Isles of Scilly: Field Guide*. Cambridge: Quaternary Research Association, pp. 12–28.

Scourse, J. D. 1999. Late Pleistocene stratigraphy and palaeoenvironments of west Cornwall. In: Scourse, J. D. and Furze, M. F. A. (eds), *The Quaternary of West Cornwall, Field Guide*. London: QRA, pp. 27–45.

Scourse, J. D., Haapaniemi, A. I., Colmenero-Hidalgo, E., Peck, V. L., Hall, I. R., Austin, W. E. N. et al. 2009a. Growth, dynamics and deglaciation of the last British-Irish ice sheet: the deep-sea ice-rafted detritus record. *Quaternary Science Reviews* 28: 3066–3084.

Scourse, J. D., Coope, G. R., Allen, J. R. M., Lister, A. M., Housley, R. A., Hedges, R. E. M. et al. 2009b. Late-Glacial remains of woolly mammoth (*Mammuthus primigenius*) from Shropshire, UK: stratigraphy, sedimentology and geochronology of the Condover site. *Geological Journal* 44: 392–413.

Sejrup, H. P., Nygård, A., Hall, A. M. and Haflidason, H. 2009. Middle and Late Weichselian (Devensian) glaciation history of south-western Norway, North Sea and Eastern UK. *Quaternary Science Reviews* 28: 370–380.

Shackleton, N. J. 1987. Oxygen isotopes, ice volumes and sea-level. *Quaternary Science Reviews* 6: 183–190.

Shackleton, N. J. 2000. The 100,000–year Ice-Age cycle identified to lag temperature, carbon dioxide and orbital eccentricity. *Science* 289: 1897–1902.

Shackley, M. 1981. On the Palaeolithic archaeology of Hampshire. In: Shennan, S. and Shadla-Hall, T. (eds), *The Archaeology of Hampshire from the Palaeolithic to the Industrial Revolution*. Hampshire Field Club and Archaeological Society Monograph 1, pp. 4–9.

Sharon, G. 2007. *Acheulean Large Flake Industries: Technology, Chronology and Significance*. Oxford: British Archaeological Reports International Series 1701.

Shaw, A. D. 2008. *The Earlier Palaeolithic of Syria: Settlement History, Technology and Landscape-Use in the Orontes and Euphrates Valleys*. Unpublished Ph.D. Thesis, Durham.

Shaw, A. D. and White, M. J. 2003. Another look at the Cuxton handaxes. *Proceedings of the Prehistoric Society* 69: 305–314.

Shchelinsky, V.E., Dodonov, A.E., Baigusheva, V.S., Kulakov, S.A., Simakova, A.N., Tesakov, A.S. et al. 2010. Early Palaeolithic sites on the Taman Peninsula. (Southern Azov Sea region, Russia). *Bogatyri/Sinyaya Balka and Rodniki Quaternary International* 223/224: 28–35.

Shea, J. J. 1993. Lithic Use-Wear Evidence for Hunting by Neandertals and Early Modern Humans from the Levantine Mousterian. In: Peterkin, G. L., Bricker, H. and Mellars, P. (eds), *Hunting and Animal Exploitation in the Later Palaeolithic and Mesolithic of Europe*. Washington: American Anthropological Association Archaeological Papers 4, pp. 189–198.

Shea, J. J., Davis, Z. and Brown, K. 2001. Experimental tests of Middle Palaeolithic spear points using a calibrated crossbow. *Journal of Archaeological Science* 28: 807–816.

Shennan, I., Bradley, S., Milne, G., Brooks, A., Bassett, S. and Hamilton, S. 2006. Relative sea-level changes, glacial isostatic modeling and ice-sheet reconstructions from the British Isles since the Last Glacial Maximum. *Journal of Quaternary Science* 21: 585–599.

Shennan, S. 2001. Demography and cultural innovation: a model and its implications for the emergence of modern human culture. *Cambridge Archaeological Journal* 11: 5–16.

Shennan, S. 2002. *Genes, memes, and human history. Darwinian archaeology and cultural evolution*. Thames and Hudson: London.

Shepherd-Thorne, E. R. and Kellaway, G. A. 1977. Amey's Eartham Pit, Boxgrove Common. In: Shepherd-Thorne, E. R. and Wymer, J. J. (eds), *South East England and the Thames Valley: INQUA Excursion Guide*. Norwich: INQUA, pp. 66–68.

Shotton, F. W. 1968. The Pleistocene Succession around Brandon, Warwickshire. *Philosophical Transactions of the Royal Society of London* B254: 387–400.

Shotton, F. W. and Wymer, J. 1989. Hand-axes of andesitic tuff from beneath the standard Wolstonian succession in Warwickshire. *Lithics* 10: 1–7.

Shotton, F. W., Keen, D. H., Coope, G. R., Currant, A. P., Gibbard, P. L., Aalto, M. et al. 1993. The Middle Pleistocene deposits of Waverly Wood pit, Warwickshire, England. *Journal of Quaternary Science* 8: 293–325.

Siddall, M., Rohling, E. J., Almogi-Labin, A., Hemleben, C., Meischner, D., Schmelzer, I. et al. 2003. Sea level fluctuations during the last glacial cycle. *Nature* 423: 853–858.

Sier, M. J., Roebroeks, W., Bakels, C. C., Dekkers, M. J., Brühl, E., De Loecker, D. et al. 2011. Direct terrestrial and marine correlation demonstrates surprisingly late onset of the last interglacial in central Europe. *Quaternary Research* 75: 213–218.

Sieveking, A. 1971. The Kendrick's Cave mandible. *British Museum Quarterly* 35: 230–250.

Sieveking, A. 1987. *A Catalogue of Palaeolithic Art in the British Museum.* London: British Museum.

Singer, R., Wymer, J. J., Gladfelter, B. G. and Wolff, R. 1973. Excavations of the Clactonian industry at the Golf Course, Clacton-on Sea, Essex. *Proceedings of the Prehistoric Society* 39: 6–74.

Singer, R., Gladfelter, B.G. and Wymer, J.J. (ed.) 1993. *The Lower Palaeolithic Site at Hoxne, England,* Chicago: Chicago Press.

Skinner, J. D. and van Aarde, R. J. 1991. Bone collecting by brown hyaenas *Hyaena brunnea* in the Central Namib Desert, Namibia. *Journal of Archaeological Science* 18: 513–523.

Smith, A. J. 1985. A catastrophic origin for the palaeovalley system of the eastern English Channel. *Marine Geology* 64: 65–75.

Smith, A. J. 1989. The English Channel – by geological design or accident? *Proceedings of the Geologists' Association* 100: 325–37.

Smith, R. A. 1911. A palaeolithic industry at Northfleet, Kent. *Archaeologia* 62: 515–532.

Smith, R. A. 1918. On flint implements from the Palaeolithic floor at Whipsnade. *Proceedings of the Society of Antiquaries of London* 31: 39–50.

Smith, R. A. 1921. Implements from plateau brickearths at Ipswich. *Proceedings of the Geologists' Association* 32: 1–16.

Smith, R. A. 1924. Stone Age site near Woking. *The Antiquaries Journal* 4: 415.

Smith, R. A. 1926. *A Guide to the Antiquities of the Stone Age.* London: British Musem.

Smith, R. A. 1931. *The Sturge Collection: an illustrated selection of flints from Britain bequeathed in 1919 by William Allen Sturge, M.V.O., M.D., F.R.C.P.* London: British Museum.

Smith, R. A. 1933. Implements from high-level gravel near Canterbury. *Proceedings of the Prehistoric Society of East Anglia* 165–170.

Smith, R. A. and Dewey, H. 1913. Stratification at Swanscombe: report on excavations made on behalf of the British Museum and H. M. Geological Survey. *Archaeologia* 64: 177–204.

Smith, R. A. and Dewey, H. 1914. The High Terrace of the Thames: Report on Excavations made on behalf of the British Museum and H. M. Geological Survey in 1913. *Archaeologia* 65: 187–212.

Smith, W. G. 1878. On Palaeolithic Implements from the Valley of the Lea. *Journal of the Anthropological Institute of Great Britain and Ireland* 8: 275–279.

Smith, W. G. 1884. On a Palaeolithic Floor at North-East London. *Journal of the Anthropological Institute of Great Britain and Ireland* 13: 357–384.

Smith, W. G. 1894. *Man the Primeval Savage: his haunts and relics from the hill-tops of Bedfordshire to Blackwall.* London: Stanford.

Smith, W. G. 1916. Notes on the Palaeolithic floor near Caddington. *Archaeologia* 67: 49–74.

Snelling, A. 1964. Excavations at the Globe Pit, Little Thurrock, Grays, Essex 1961. *Essex Naturalist* 31: 199–208.

Snelling, A. 1975. A fossil molluscan fauna from Purfleet, Essex. *Essex Naturalist* 33: 104–8.

Snodgrass, J. J. and Leonard, W. R. 2009. Neandertal energetics revisited: Insights into population dynamics and life history evolution. *Palaeoanthropology* 2009: 220–237.

Sollas, W. J. 1913. Paviland cave: an Aurignacian Station in Wales. *Journal of the Royal Anthropological Institute of Great Britain and Ireland* 43: 325–374.

Sommé, J., Paepe, R., Baeteman, C., Beyens, L., Cunat, N., Geeraerts, R.A.F.H., Hus, J., Juvigné, E., Mathieu, L.J.T. and Vanhoorne, R. 1978. La Formation d'Herzeele: un nouveau stratotype du Pléistocène moyen marin de la Mer du Nord *Bulletin de l'Association Française pour l'Etude du Quaternaire* 54–56: 81–149.

Sommé, J., Antoine, P., Cunat-Bogé, N., Lefèvre, D. and Munaut, A. V. 1999. Le Pléistocène moyen marin de la mer du Nord en France: falaise de Sangatte et formation d'Herzeele. *Quaternaire* 10: 151–160.

Sommer, M. 2007. *Bones and Ochre: The Curious Afterlife of the Red Lady of Paviland.* Cambridge, MA: Harvard University Press.

Sørensen, B. 2009. Energy use by Eem Neanderthals. *Journal of Archaeological Science* 36: 2201–2205.

Sorensen, M. V. and Leonard, W. R. 2001. Neanderthal energetic and foraging efficiency. *Journal of Human Evolution* 40: 483–495.

Soressi, M. 2002. Le Moustérien de tradition acheuléene du sud-ouest de la France. Discussion sur la signification du faciès à partir de l'étude comparée de quatre sites: Pech-de-l'Azé, Le Moustier, La Rochette et la Grotte XVI. *Dissertation. Université Bordeaux I.*

Soressi, M. and Hays, M. A. 2003. Manufacture, transport and use of Mousterian bifaces: a case study from the Perigord (France). In: Soressi, M. and Dibble, H. (eds), *Multiple Approaches to the Study of Bifacial Technologies.* Pennsylvania: University of Pennsylvania Museum Press, pp. 125–148.

Sparks, B. W. and West, R. G. 1963. The interglacial deposits at Stutton, Suffolk. *Proceedings of the Geologists' Association* 74: 419–432.

Sparks, B. W. and West, R. G. 1970. Late Pleistocene deposits at Wretton, Norfolk. 1. Ipswichian Interglacial Deposits. *Philosophical Transactions of the Royal Society of London* B258: 1–30.

Speleers. 2000. The relevance of the Eemian for the study of the Palaeolithic occupation of Europe. *Geologie en Mijnbouw/Netherlands Journal of Geosciences* 79: 283–291.

Spencer, F. 1991. *Piltdown: A Scientific Forgery*. Oxford: Oxford University Press

Spencer, H. E. P. 1958. Mammalia of the Stutton Brickearth. *Transactions of the Suffolk Naturalists Society* 10: 242.

Spencer, H. E. P. 1962. Prehistoric animal remains at Harkstead. *Transactions of the Suffolk Naturalists Society* 12: 59–60.

Spencer, H. E. P. 1970. A contribution to the geological history of Suffolk: Part 4: The interglacial epochs. *Transactions of the Suffolk Naturalists Society* 15: 148–196.

Speth, J. D. 1987. Early hominid subsistence strategies in seasonal habitats. *Journal of Archaeological Science* 14: 13–29.

Speth, J. D. 1989. Early hominid hunting and scavenging: The role of meat as an energy resource. *Journal of Human Evolution* 18: 329–343.

Speth, J. D. 2004. News flash: negative evidence convicts Neanderthals of gross mental incompetence. *World Archaeology* 36: 519–526.

Spurrell, F. C. J. 1880a. On the discovery of the place where Palaeolithic implements were made at Crayford. *Quarterly Journal of the Geological Society of London* 36: 544–548.

Spurrell, F. C. J. 1880b. On implements and chips from the floor of a Palaeolithic Workshop. *Archaeological Journal* 38: 294–299.

Spurrell, F. C. J. 1883. Palaeolithic implements found in west Kent. *Archaeologia Cantiana* 15: 89–103.

Spurrell, F. C. J. 1884. On some Palaeolithic knapping tools and modes of using them. *Journal of the Anthropological Institute of Great Britain and Ireland* 13: 109–118.

Spurrell, F. C. J. 1892. Excursion to Grays Thurrock, Essex. *Proceedings of the Geologists' Association* 12: 194.

Stapert, D. 1985. A site of the Hamburg tradition with a constructed hearth near Oldeholtwold (province of Friesland, The Netherlands); first report. *Palaeohistoria* 24: 53–89.

Stapert, D. 2007. Bladspitsen en de 'Grote Trek naar het Westen' van de laatste Neanderthalers in Noordelijk Europa. *Paleo-Aktueel* 18: 10–20.

Stapert, D. and Johansen, L. 1999. Flint and pyrite: making fire in the Stone Age. *Antiquity* 73: 765–767.

Stapert, D. and Johansen, L. 2001. The Creswellian site at Zeijen (Prov. of Drenthe, The Netherlands): an encampment with a probable tent ring. In: Metz, W. H., van Beek, B. L. and Steegstra, H. (eds), *Patina: essays Presented to Jay Jordan Butler on the Occasion of His 80th Birthday.* Groningen/Amsterdam: Metz, van Beek and Steegstra, pp. 503–526.

Steegmann, A. T., Cerny, F. J. and Holliday, T. W. 2002. Neanderthal cold adaptation: physiology and energetic factors. *American Journal of Human Biology* 14: 566–583.

Stenton, D. R. 1991. The adaptive significance of Caribou winter clothing for arctic hunter-gatherers. *Inuit Studies* 15: 3–28.

Stevens, E. T. 1870. *Flint Chips: a guide to prehistoric archaeology, as illustrated by the collection in the Blackmore Museum, Salisbury.* London: Bell and Daldy.

Stevens, R. E. and Hedges, R. E. M. 2004. Carbon and nitrogen stable isotope analysis of northwest European horse bones and tooth collagen, 40,000 BP-present: palaeoclimatic interpretations. *Quaternary Science Reviews* 23: 977–991.

Stewart, J. 2005. The ecology and adaptation of Neanderthals during the non-analogue environment of Oxygen Isotope Stage 3. *Quaternary International* 137: 35–46.

Stewart, J. R. and Lister, A. M. 2001. Cryptic northern refugia and the origins of the modern biota. *Trends in Ecology and Evolution* 16: 608–613.

Stiner, M. 2002. Carnivory, coevolution and the geographic spread of the genus *Homo*. *Journal of Archaeological Research* 10: 1–62.

Stiner, M. C., Barkai, R. and Gopher, A. 2009. Cooperative hunting and meat sharing 400–200 kya at Qesem Cave, Israel. *Proceedings of the National Academy of Science (USA)* 106: 13207–13212.

Stopp, M. P. 1993. Taphonomic analysis of the faunal assemblage. In: Singer, R., Gladfelter, B. G. and Wymer, J. J. (eds), *The Lower Palaeolithic Site at Hoxne, England.* Chicago and London: University of Chicago Press, pp. 138–149.

Storrs Fox, W. 1930. Ravencliffe Cave. *Derbyshire Archaeological Journal* 3: 71–78.

Straw, A. 1996. The Quaternary record of Kent's Cavern: a brief reminder and update. *Quaternary Newsletter* 80: 17–25.

Street, M. 2000. Aspects of Late Upper Palaeolithic settlement and chronology in northern Central Europe. In: Bodu, P. and Christensen, J. A. (eds), *L'Europe Centrale et Septentrionale au Tardiglaciaire: Table-Ronde de Nemours 13–16 Mai 1997.* Mémoires du Musée de Préhistoire d'Ile de France 7, pp. 55–71.

Street, M. 2002. Ein wiedersehen mit dem hund von Bonn-Oberkassel. *Bonner Zoologische Beitrag* 50: 269–290.

Street, M., Baales, M. and Weninger, B. 1994. Absolute chronologie des späten Paläolothikums und des frühmesolithikums im nördlichen Rhineland. *Archäologisches Korrespondenzblatt* 24: 1–28.

Street, M., Baales, M., Cziesla, E., Hartz, S., Heinen, M., Jöris, O. et al. 2001. Final Paleolithic and Mesolithic research in reunified Germany. *Journal of World Prehistory* 15: 365–453.

Stringer, C. 2006. *Homo Britannicus: the Incredible Story of Human Life in Britain.* London: Penguin/Allen Lane.

Stringer, C. and Gamble, C. 1994. *In Search of the Neanderthals: Solving the Puzzle of Human Origins.* London: Thames & Hudson.

Stringer, C. and Hublin, J.-J. 1999. New age estimates for the Swanscombe hominid, and their significance for human evolution. *Journal of Human Evolution* 37: 873–877.

Stringer, C. , Currant, A. P., Schwarcz, H. P. and Collcutt, S. N. 1986. Age of Pleistocene faunas from Bacon Hole, Wales. *Nature* 320: 59–62.

Stuart, A. J. 1976. The history of the mammal fauna during the Ipswichian/last interglacial in England. *Philosophical Transactions of the Royal Society of London* B276: 221–250.

Stuart, A. J. 1991. Mammalian extinctions on the Late Pleistocene of northern Eurasia and North America. *Biological Reviews* 66: 453–562.

Stuart, A. J. 1992. The High Lodge mammalian fauna. In: Ashton, N. M., Cook, J., Lewis, S. G. and Rose, J. (eds), *High Lodge: Excavations by G. de G. Sieveking 1962–68 and J. Cook 1988.* London: British Museum Press, pp. 120–123.

Stuart, A. J. 1995. Insularity and Quaternary vertebrate faunas in Britain and Ireland. In: Preece, R. C. (ed.) *Island Britain: a Quaternary Perspective.* London: Geological Society Special Publication 96, pp. 111–126.

Stuart, A. J. 1996. Vertebrate faunas from the early Middle Pleistocene of East Anglia. In: Turner, C. (ed.) *The Early Middle Pleistocene in Europe.* Rotterdam: Balkema, pp. 9–24.

Stuart, A. J. 2005. The extinction of woolly mammoth (*Mammuthus primigenius*) and straight-tusked elephant (*Palaeoloxodon antiques*) in Europe. *Quaternary International* 126/128: 171–177.

Stuart, A. J. and Lister, A. M. 2001. The mammalian faunas of Pakefield/Kessingland and Corton, Suffolk, UK: evidence for a new temperate episode in the British early Middle Pleistocene. *Quaternary Science Reviews* 20: 1677–1692.

Stuart, A. J. and Lister, A. M. 2007. Patterns of Late Quaternary megafaunal extinctions in Europe and North Asia. *Courier Forschungsinstitut Senckenberg* 259: 287–297.

Stuart, A. J., Wolff, R. G., Lister, A. M., Singer, R. and Egginton, J. M. 1993. Fossil Vertebrates. In: Singer, R., Gladfelter, B. G. and Wymer, J. J. (eds), *The Lower Paleolithic Site at Hoxne, England.* Chicago: University of Chicago Press, pp. 163–206.

Stuart, A. J., Sulerzhitsky, L. D., Orlova, L. A., Kuzmin, Y. V. and Lister, A. M. 2002. The latest woolly mammoths (*Mammuthus primigenius* Blumenbach) in Europe and Asia: a review of the current evidence. *Quaternary Science Reviews* 21: 1559–1569.

Stuart, A. J., Kosintsev, P. A., Higham, T. F. G. and Lister, A. M. 2004. Pleistocene to Holocene extinction dynamics in giant deer and woolly mammoth. *Nature* 431: 684–689.

Stuiver, M., Grootes, P. M. and Braziunas, T. F. 1995. The GISP2 180 climate record of the past 16,500 years and the role of the sun, ocean, and volcanoes. *Quaternary Research* 44: 341–354.

Sturge, W. A. 1911. The chronology of the Stone Age. *Proceedings of the Prehistoric Society of East Anglia* 1: 43–105.

Sutcliffe, A. J. 1964. The mammalian fauna. In: Ovey, C. D. (ed.) *The Swanscombe Skull: a survey of research on a Pleistocene Site.* London: Royal Anthropological Institute, Occasional Paper No. 20, pp. 85–111.

Sutcliffe, A. J. 1970. Spotted hyaena: Crusher, gnawer, digester and collector of bones. *Nature* 227: 1110–1113.

Sutcliffe, A. J. 1975. A hazard in interpretation of glacial-interglacial sequences. *Quaternary Newsletter* 17: 1–3.

Sutcliffe, A. J. 1995. Insularity of the British Isles 250,000–30,000 years ago: the mammalian, including human, evidence. In: Preece, R. C. (ed.), *Island Britain: a Quaternary Perspective.* London: Geological Society Special Publication 96, pp. 127–140.

Svensson, A., Andersen, K. K., Bigler, M., Clausen, H. B., Dahl-Jensen, D., Davies, S. M. et al. 2008. A 60,000 year Greenland stratigraphic ice core chronology. *Climate of the Past* 4: 47–57.

Svoboda, J. 1989. Middle Pleistocene adaptations in Central Europe. *Journal of World Prehistory* 3: 33–70.

Swanscombe Committee 1938. Report on the Swanscombe Skull, prepared by the Swanscombe Commitee of the Royal Anthropological Institute. *Journal of the Royal Anthropological Institute of Great Britain and Ireland* 68: 17–98.

Swainston, S. 1999. Unlocking the inhospitable. In: Davies, W. and Charles, R. (eds), *Dorothy Garrod and the Progress of the Palaeolithic: Studies in the Prehistoric Archaeology of the Near East and Europe.* Oxford: Oxbow, pp. 41–56.

Swainston, S. 2000. The lithic artifacts from Paviland. In: Aldhouse-Green, S. (ed.) *Paviland Cave and the 'Red Lady': a Definitive Report.* Bristol: Western Academic and Specialist Press, pp. 93–113.

Swainston, S. and Brookes, A. 2000. Paviland Cave and the 'Red Lady'. The history of collection and excavation. In: Aldhouse-Green, S. (ed.) *Paviland Cave and the 'Red Lady': a Definitive Report.* Bristol: Western Academic and Specialist Press, pp. 19–46.

Swisher, C. C., Curtis, G. H., Jacob, T., Getty, A. G. and Widiasmoro, S. A. 1994. Age of the earliest known hominids in Java, Indonesia. *Science* 263: 118–121.

Szabo, B. J. and Collins, D. 1975. Ages of fossil bones from British interglacial sites. *Nature* 254: 680–681.

Tardieu, C. 1998. Short Adolescence in Early Hominids: Infantile and Adolescent Growth of the Human Femur. *American Journal of Physical Anthropology* 197: 163–178.

Tebbutt, C. F. 1982. Letter to Roger Jacobi. *Copy Held by Mark White*.

Tebbutt, C. F., Marr, J. E. and Burkitt, M. C. 1927. Palaeolithic industries from the Great Ouse gravels at and near St. Neots. *Proceedings of the Prehistoric Society of East Anglia* 5: 166–73.

Telfer, M. W., Wilson, P., Lord, T. C. and Vincent, P. J. 2009. New constraints on the age of the last ice sheet glaciation in NW England using optically stimulated luminescence dating. *Journal of Quaternary Science* 24: 906–915.

Terberger, T. and Lübke, H. 2007. Between east and west – Hamburgian in northeastern Germany? In: Kobusiewicz, M. and Kabaciski, J. (eds), *Studies in the Final Palaeolithic Settlement of the Great European Plain.* Pozna: Institute of Archaeology and Ethnology, Polish Academy of Sciences, pp. 53–66.

Terberger, T., Barton, N. and Street, M. 2009. The Late Glacial reconsidered – recent progress and interpretations. In: Street, M., Barton, N. and Terberger, T. (eds), *Humans, Environment and Chronology of the Late Glacial of the North European Plain. Proceedings of Workshop 14 (Commission XXXII 'The Final Palaeolithic of the Great European Plain' of the 15th U.I.S.P.P. Congress, Lisbon, September 2006).* Mainz: Römisch-Germanischen Zentralmuseums, pp. 189–207.

Tester, P. J. 1950. Palaeolithic flint implements from the Bowman's Lodge Gravel Pit, Dartford Heath. *Archaeologia Cantiana* 63: 122–134.

Tester, P. J. 1965. An Acheulian Site at Cuxton. *Archaeologia Cantiana* 80: 30–60.

Texier, P.-J. and Francisco-Ortega, I. 1995. Main technological and typological characteristics of the lithic assemblage from Level 1 at Bérigoule (Murs-Vaucluse). In: Dibble, H. L. and Bar-Yosef, O. (eds), *The Definition and Interpretation of Levallois Technology.* Madison: Prehistory Press, pp. 213–226.

Thévenin, A. 1996. Azilien et Ahrensbourgien dans l'est de la France: le point sur le question. In: Pautrat, Y. and Thévenin, A. (eds), *Paléolithique Supérieur et Epipaléolithique dans le Nord-Est de la France.* Dijon: Service Régional de l'Archéologie de Bourgogne, pp. 119–130.

Thévenin, A. 1997. L'Azilien et les cultures a pointes a dos courbe: esquisse géographique et chronologique. *Bulletin de la Société Préhistorique Française* 94: 393–411.

Thieme, H. 1997. Lower Palaeolithic Hunting Spears from Germany. *Nature* 385: 807–810.

Thieme, H. 2005. The Lower Palaeolithic art of hunting: the case of Schöningen 13 II-4, Lower Saxony, Germany. In: Gamble, C. and Porr, M. (eds), *The Hominid Individual in Context: Archaeological Investigations of Lower and Middle Palaeolithic landscapes, locales and artefacts.* London: Routledge, pp. 115–132.

Thomas, G. N. 2001. Late Middle Pleistocene pollen biostratography in Britain: pitsfalls and possibilities in the separation of interglacial sequences. *Quaternary Science Reviews* 20: 1621–1630.

Thomas, J. and Jacobi, R. M. 2001. Glaston. *Current Archaeology* 173: 180–184.

Thompson, W. G. and Goldstein, S. L. 2005. Open-System Coral Ages Reveal Persistent Suborbital Sea-Level Cycles *Science* 308: 401–404.

Torrence, R. 1989. Retooling: Towards a behavioural theory of stone tools. In: Torrence, R. (ed.), *Time, Energy and Stone Tools.* Cambridge: Cambridge University Press, pp. 57–67.

Toth, N. 1985. The Oldowan re-assessed: a close look at early stone artifacts. *Journal of Archaeological Science* 12: 101–120.

Toth, N. and Schick, K. 1993. *Making Silent Stones Speak: Human Evolution and the Dawn of Technology.* London: Weidenfeld and Nicolson.

Toucanne, S., Zaragosi, S., Bourillet, J. F., Cremer, M., Eynaud, F., Van Vliet-Lanoë, B. et al. 2009. Timing of massive 'Fleuve Manche' discharges over the last 350 kyr: insights into the European ice-sheet oscillations and the European drainage network from MIS 10 to 2. *Quaternary Science Reviews* 28: 1238–1256.

Tratman, E. K. 1955. Second report on the excavations at Sun Hole, Cheddar. *Proceedings of the University of Bristol Spelaeological Society* 7: 61–70.

Tratman, E. K. 1964. Picken's Hole, Crook Peak, Somerset: A Pleistocene site, preliminary note. *Proceedings of the University of Bristol Spelaeological Society* 10: 112–115.

Tratman, E. K., Donovan, D. T. and Campbell, J. B. 1971. The Hyaena Den (Wookey Hole), Mendip Hills, Somerset. *Proceedings of the University of Bristol Spelaeological Society* 12: 245–79.

Trauth, M. H., Maslin, M. A., Deino, A. and Strecker, M. R. 2005. Late Cenozoic moisture history of East Africa. *Science* 309: 2051–2053.

Trauth, M. H., Larrasoaña, J. C. and Mudelsee, M. 2009. Trends, rhythms and events in Plio-Pleistocene African climate. *Quaternary Science Reviews* 28: 399–411.

Treacher, L. 1934. Field Meeting in the Marlow District. *Proceedings of the Geologists' Association* 45: 107–8.

Trinkaus, E. and Holliday, T. W. 2000. The human remains from Paviland. In: Aldhouse-Green, S. (ed.) *Paviland Cave and the 'Red Lady': a Definitive Report.* Bristol: Western Academic and Specialist Press, pp. 141–204.

Tryon, C. A. 2006. Early Middle Stone Age Lithic Technology of the Kapthurin Formation (Kenya). *Current Anthropology* 47: 367–375.

Tryon, C. A., McBrearty, S. and Texier, P.-J. 2006. Levallois lithic technology from the Kapthurin Formation, Kenya: Acheulean origin and Middle Stone Age Diversity. *African Archaeology Review* 22: 199–229.

Tuffreau, A. 1982. The transition Lower/Middle Palaeolithic in Northern France. In: Ronen, A. (ed.) *The transition from Lower to Middle Palaeolithic and the Origin of Modern Man.* Oxford: Oxford Archaeological Reports International Series 151, pp. 137–149.

Tuffreau, A. 1995. The variability of Levallois technology in northern France and neighbouring areas. In: Dibble, H. L. and Bar-Yosef, O. (eds), *The Definition and Interpretation of Levallois Technology.* Madison: Prehistory Press, pp. 413–427.

Tuffreau, A. and Antoine, P. 1995. The earliest occupation of Europe: Continental Northwest Europe. In: W. Roebroeks and Kolfshoten, T. V. (eds), *The Earliest Occupation of Europe.* Leiden: Leiden University Press, pp. 147–164.

Tuffreau, A. and Lamotte, A. 2010. Oldest Acheulean settlements in Northern France. *Quaternary International* 223/224: 455.

Turner, A. 1992. Large carnivores and earliest European hominids: changing determinants of resource availability during the Lower and Middle Pleistocene. *Journal of Human Evolution* 22: 109–126.

Turner, A. 2009. The evolution of the guild of large carnivora of the British Isles during the Middle and Late Pleistocene. *Journal of Quaternary Science* 24: 991–1005.

Turner, C. 1968. A Lowestoftian Late-Glacial flora from the Pleistocene deposits at Hoxne, Suffolk. *New Phytologist* 67: 327–332.

Turner, C. 1970. The Middle Pleistocene Deposits at Marks Tey. *Philosophical Transactions of the Royal Society of London* Series B 257: 373–440.

Turner, C. 1985. Problems and pitfalls with the application of palynology to Pleistocene archaeological sites in Western Europe. In: Renault-Miskovsky, J. (ed.) *Palynologie Archaeologie. Centre de Recherches Archaeologiques Notes et Monographies Techniques Vol. 17*, pp. 347–372.

Turner, C. (ed.) 1996. *The early Middle Pleistocene in Europe,* Rotterdam: Balkema.

Turner, C. 1996. A brief survey of the early Middle Pleistocene in Europe. In: Turner, C. (ed.) *The early Middle Pleistocene in Europe.* Rotterdam: Balkema, pp. 295–317.

Turner, C. 2000. The Eemian interglacial in the North European plan and adjacent areas. *Geologie en Mijnbouw/Netherlands Journal of Geosciences* 79: 217–231.

Turner, C. and Kerney, M. P. 1971. A note on the age of the Freshwater Beds of the Clacton Channel. *Journal of the Geological Society of London* 127: 87–93.

Turq, A. 1988. Le Paléolithique inférieur et moyen en Haute-Agenais: état des recherches. *Revue de l'Argenais* 115: 83–112.

Turq, A. 1989. Exploitation des matières premières lithiques et occupation du sol: l'example du Moustérien entre Dordogne et Lot. In: Laville, H. (ed.) *Variation des Paléomilieux et Peuplement Préhistorique.* Paris: CNRS, pp. 179–204.

Turq, A. 2000. Paléolithique Inférieur et Moyen entre Dordogne et Lot. *Paléo* Supplément 2.

Turq, A. 2001. Réflexions sur le biface dans quelques sites du Paléolithique ancien-moyen en en grotte ou abri du Nord-Est du Bassin Aquitaine. In: D. Cliquet (ed.) *Les industries á outils bifaciaux du Paléolithique Moyen d'Europe occidentale.* Liège: Études et Recherches Archéologiques de l'Université de Liège, pp. 141–150.

Turq, A., Brenet, M., Colonge, D., Jarry, M., Lelouvier, L.-A., O'Farrell, M. and Jaubert, J. 2010. The first human occupations in southwestern France: A revised summary twenty years after the Abbeville/Saint Riquier colloquium. *Quaternary International* 223/224: 383–398.

Tyldesley, J. A. 1983. Two bout coupé handaxes from Oxfordshire. *Oxoniensia* 48: 149–152.

Tyldesley, J. A. 1986a. *The Wolvercote Channel handaxe assemblage: a comparative study.* Oxford: British Archaeological Reports British Series 153.

Tyldesley, J. A. 1986b. A reassessment of the handaxe assemblage recovered from the Wolvercote Channel. In: Collcutt, S. N. (ed.) *The Palaeolithic of Britain and its nearest Neighbours: Recent Trends.* Sheffield: University of Sheffield, pp. 23–25.

Tyldesley, J. A. 1987. *The bout coupé handaxe: a typological problem.* Oxford: British Archaeological Reports British Series 170.

Tyráček, J., Westaway, R. and Bridgland, D. 2004. River terraces of the Vltava and Labe (Elbe) system, Czech Republic, and their implications for the uplift history of the Bohemian Massif. *Proceedings of Geologists' Association* 115: 101–124.

Tzedakis, P. C., Andrieu, V., de Beaulieu, J. L., Birks, H. J. B., Crowhurst, S., Follieri, M. 2001. Establishing a terrestrial chronological framework as a basis for biostratigraphical comparisons. *Quaternary Science Reviews* 20: 1583–1592.

Urban, B. 2007. Interglacial pollen records from Schöningen, north Germany. In: Sirocko, F., Litt, T., Claussen, M. and Sánchez Goñi, M. F. (eds), *The Climate of Past Interglacials.* New York: Springer, pp. 417–444.

Van Andel, T. and Davies, S. W. G. 2003. *Neanderthals and Modern Humans in the European Landscape During the Last Glaciation: Archaeological Results of the Stage 3 project.* Cambridge: McDonald Institute.

Van der Made, J. and Mateos, A. 2010. Longstanding biogeographic patterns and the dispersal of early Homo out of Africa and into Europe. *Quaternary International* 223/224: 195–200.

Van Kolfschoten, T. and Turner, E. 1996. Early Middle Pleistocene mammalian faunas from from Kärlich and Miesenheim I and their biostratigraphical implications. In: Turner, C. (ed.) *The early Middle Pleistocene in Europe.* Rotterdam: Balkema, pp. 227–253.

Van Peer, P. 1992. *The Levallois Reduction Strategy.* Madison: Prehistory Press.

Vang Petersen, P. 2005. Stortandede harpooner og jagt på hjortevildt til vands. *Arbøger for Nordisk Oldkyndighed og Historie*, pp. 43–54.

Ventris, P. A. 1996. Hoxnian Interglacial freshwater and marine deposits in northwest Norfolk, England and their implications for sea-level reconstruction. *Quaternary Science Reviews* 15: 437–450.

Vereshchagin, N. K. and Baryshnikov, G. F. 1982. Palaeoecology of the Mammoth fauna in the Eurasian arctic. In: Hopkins, D. M., Matthews, J. V., Schweger, C. E. and Young, S. B. (eds), *Paleoecology of Beringia.* New York: Academic Press, pp. 267–279.

Verhart, L. M. B. 2004. The implications of prehistoric finds on and off the Dutch coast. In: Flemming, N. C. (ed.) *Submarine Prehistoric Archaeology of the North Sea. CBA research report 141.* York: CBA, pp. 57–61.

Vermeersch, P. M., Lauwers, R., Van Peer, P., Munaut, A. V. and Gullentops, F. 1985. Un site Magdalénien à Kanne (Limbourg). *Archaeologica Belgica* I: 17–54.

Vermeersch, P. M., Symens, N., Vynckier, P., Gijselings, G. and Lauwers, R. 1987. Orp, site Magdalénien de plein air (comm. de Orp-Jauche). *Archeologia Belgica* III: 7–56.

Vermeersch, P. M., Peleman, C., Rots, V. and Maes, R. 1996. The Ahrensburgian site at Zonhoven-Molenheide. *Notae Praehistoricae* 16: 117–121.

Verpoorte, A. 2006. Neanderthal energetic and spatial behaviour. *Before Farming* 2006 (3): 1–6.

Verpoorte, A. 2008. Limiting factors on early modern human dispersals: the human biogeography of late pleniglacial Europe. *Quaternary International* 201: 77–85.

Vèrtes, L. and Dobosi, V. T. 1990. Fireplaces of the Settlement. In: Kretzoi, M. and Dobosi, V. T. (eds), *Vèrtesszöllös - Man, Site and Culture.* Budpest: Akadémiai Kiadó, pp. 519–521.

Vidal, L., Schneider, R. R., Marchal, O., Bickert, T., Stocker, T. F. and Wefer, G. 1999. Link between the North and South Atlantic during the Heinrich events of the last glacial period. *Climate Dynamics* 15: 909–919.

Villa, P. 1982. Conjoinable Pieces and Site Formation Processes. *American Antiquity* 47: 276–290.

Villa, P. 1983. *Terra Amata and the Middle Pleistocene Archaeological Record of Southern France.* Berkeley and Los Angeles: University of California Press.

Villa, P. 1990. Torralba and Aridos: elephant exploitation in Middle Pleistocene Spain. *Journal of Human Evolution* 19: 299–309.

Villa, P. 2001. Early Italy and the Colonization of Western Europe. *Quaternary International* 75: 113–130.

Villa, P. and Santonja, M. 2006. The Acheulean in Southwestern Europe. In: Goren-Inbar, N. and Sharon, G. (eds), *Axe Age: Acheulean Toolmaking, from Quarry to Discard.* Jerusalem: Equinox, pp. 429–478.

Villa, P. and Lenoir, M. 2009. Hunting and hunting weapons of the Lower and Middle Paleolithic of Europe. In: Hublin, J. J. and Richards, M. (eds), *The Evolution of Hominin Diets: Integrating Approaches to the Study of Palaeolithic Subsistence.* New York: Springer, pp. 59–85.

Vishnyatsky, L. B. 1999. The Paleolithic of Central Asia. *Journal of World Prehistory* 12: 69–122.

Voelker, A. H. L. and Workshop-Participants. 2002. Global distribution of centennial-scale records for Marine Isotope Stage (MIS) 3: a database. *Quaternary Science Reviews* 21: 1185–1212.

Vollbrecht, J. 1995. Achenheim. In: Bosinski, G., Street, M. and Baales, M. (eds), *The Palaeolithic and Mesolithic of the Rhineland. INQUA 1995, Quaternary Field Trips in Central Europe.* Munich: INQUA, pp. 855–857.

Von Koenigswald, W. 1992. Various Aspects of Migrations in Terrestrial Mammals in Relation to Pleistocene Faunas of Central Europe. In: von Koenigswald, W. and Werdelin, L. (eds), *Mammalian Migration and Dispersal Events in the European Quaternary.* Courier Forschungsinstitut Senckenberg, pp. 39–47.

Voormolen, B. 2008. *Ancient Hunters, Modern Butchers. Schöningen 13II-4, a kill-butchery site dating from the northwest European Lower Palaeolithic.* Unpublished Ph.D. Thesis, University of Leiden.

Vranch, R. D. 1981. A note on Pleistocene material from Lime Kiln Hill Quarry, Mells, Somerset. *Proceedings of the University of Bristol Spelaeological Society* 16: 70.

Vrba, E. S. 1995. The fossil record of African antelopes (Mammalia, Bovidae) in relation to human evolution and paleoclimate. In: Vrba, E. S., Denton, G. H., Partridge, T. C. and Burckle, L. H. (eds), *Paleoclimate and Evolution.* New Haven: Yale University Press, pp. 385–424.

Waechter, J. D. A. 1970. Swanscombe 1969. *Proceedings of the Royal Anthropological Institute*, pp. 83–5.

Waechter, J. D. A. 1971. Swanscombe 1970. *Proceedings of the Royal Anthropological Institute*, pp. 43–49.

Waechter, J. D. A. 1973. The Late Middle Acheulean Industries in the Swanscombe Area. In: Strong, D. E. (ed.) *Archaeological Theory and Practice.* London: Seminar Press, pp. 67–86.

Waelbroeck, C., Labeyrie, L., Michel, E., Duplessy, J. C., McManus, J. F., Lambeck, K. et al. 2002. Sea-level and deep water temperature changes derived from benthic foraminifera isotopic records. *Quaternary Science Reviews* 21: 295–305.

Walker, M. 2005. *Quaternary Dating Methods.* Chichester and New York: Wiley.

Walker, M. J. C. 1995. Climatic changes in Europe during the Last Glacial/Interglacial transition. *Quaternary International* 28: 63–76.

Walker, M. J. C., Bohncke, S. J. P., Coope, G. R., O'Connell, M., Usinge, R. H. and Verbruggen, C. 1994. The Devensian/Weichselian Late-Glacial in northwest Europe (Ireland, Britain, north Belgium, the Netherlands, northwest Germany). *Journal of Quaternary Science* 9: 109–118.

Walker, M. J. C., Coope, G. R. and Lowe, J. J. 1993. The Devensian (Weichselian Lateglacial palaeoenvironmental record from Gransmoor, East Yorkshire, England. *Quaternary Science Reviews* 12: 659–680.

Wardle, F. C. 1919. The Coygan Bone Cave. *Transactions of the Carmarthenshire Antiquarian Society* 13: 50–52.

Warren, S. H. 1911. Palaeolithic wooden spear from Clacton. *Quarterly Journal of the Geological Society of London* 67: 119.

Warren, S. H. 1912. Palaeolithic remains from Clacton-on-Sea, Essex. *Essex Naturalist* 17: 15.

Warren, S. H. 1922. The Mesvinian industry of Clacton-on-Sea, Essex. *Proceedings of the Prehistoric Society of East Anglia* 3: 597–602.

Warren, S. H. 1923a. The sub-soil flint flaking sites at Grays. *Proceedings of the Geologists' Association* 34: 38–42.

Warren, S. H. 1923b. The *Elephas antiquus* bed of Clacton-on-Sea (Essex) and its flora and fauna. *Quarterly Journal of the Geological Society of London* 79: 606–636.

Warren, S. H. 1924. The elephant bed of Clacton-on Sea. *Essex Naturalist* 21: 32–40.

Warren, S. H. 1926. The Classification of the Lower Palaeolithic with especial reference to Essex. *The South-Eastern Naturalist*: 38–51.

Warren, S. H. 1933. The Palaeolithic industries of the Clacton and Dovercourt districts. *Essex Naturalist* 24: 1–29.

Warren, S. H. 1941. The Foundations of Prehistory. *Essex Naturalist* 27: 89–98.

Warren, S. H. 1951. The Clacton flint industry: a new interpretation. *Proceedings of the Geologists' Association* 62: 107–135.

Warren, S. H. 1955. The Clacton (Essex) channel deposits. *The Quarterly Journal of the Geological Society of London* 111: 283–307.

Warren, S. H. 1958. The Clacton flint industry: a supplementary note. *Proceedings of Geologists' Association* 69: 123–129.

Watson, E. and Morgan, A. V. 1977. The periglacial environment of Great Britain (and discussion). *Philosophical Transactions of the Royal Society of London* B280: 183–198.

Weber, M.-J. 2006. Typologische und technologische aspekte des fundplatzes Le Tureau des Gardes 7 (Seine-et-Marne, Frankreich) – ein zur erforschung des Magdalénien im Pariser Becken. *Archäologisches Korrespondenzblatt* 36: 159–178.

Weber, M.-J. and Grimm, S. B. 2009. Chapter One. Dating the Hamburgian in the Context of Lateglacial Chronology. In: Crombé, P., Van Strydonck, M., Sergant, J., Boudin, M. and Bats, M. (eds), *Chronology and Evolution within the Mesolithic of North-West Europe: Proceedings of an International Meeting, Brussels, May 30th-June 1st 2007.* Newcastle upon Tyne: Cambridge Scholars Publishing, pp. 3–21.

Wenban-Smith, F. F. 1995. The Ebbsfleet Valley, Northfleet (Baker's Hole). In: Bridgland, D. R., Allen, P. and Haggart, B.A. (ed.), *The Quaternary of the Lower Reaches of the Thames, Field Guide.* Durham: Quaternary Research Association, pp. 147–164.

Wenban-Smith, F. F. 1996. Another One Bites the Dust. *Lithics* 16: 99–107.

Wenban-Smith, F. F. 1998. Clactonian and Acheulian Industries in Britain: Their chronology and significance reconsidered. In: Ashton, N., Healy, F. and Pettitt, P. (ed.), *Stone Age Archaeology: Essays in Honour of John Wymer.* Oxford: Oxbow, pp. 90–97.

Wenban-Smith, F. 2004. Handaxe typology and the Lower Palaeolithic cultural development: ficrons, cleavers and two giant handaxes from Cuxton. *Lithics* 25: 11–21.

Wenban-Smith, F. F. 2006 Handaxe typology and the Lower Palaeolithic cultural development: ficrons, cleavers and two giant handaxes from Cuxton. *Lithics* 25 (for 2004): 11–21.

Wenban-Smith, F. F. and Ashton, N. 1998. Raw material and lithic technology. In: Ashton, N., Lewis, S. G. and Parfitt, S. (eds), *Excavations at the Lower Palaeolithic Site at East Farm, Barnham, Suffolk, 1989–1994.* London: British Museum, pp. 237–244.

Wenban-Smith, F., Gamble, C. S. and Apsimon, A. 2000. The Lower Palaeolithic site at Red Barns, Porchester, Hampshire: bifacial technology, raw material quality, and the organisation of archaic behaviour. *Proceedings of the Prehistoric Society* 66: 209–255.

Wenban-Smith, F. F., Allen, P., Bates, M. R., Parfitt, S. A., Preece, R. C., Stewart, J., Turner, C. and Whittaker, J. 2006. The Clactonian elephant butchery site at Southfleet Road, Ebbsfleet, UK. *Journal of Quaternary Science* 21: 471–484.

Wenban-Smith, F., Bates, M. and Schwenninger, J.-L. 2010. Early Devensian (MIS 5d–5b) occupation at Dartford, southeast England. *Journal of Quaternary Science* 25: 1193–1199.

Weninger, B. and Jöris, O. 2004. Glacial radiocarbon calibration: The CalPal program. In: Higham, T., Bronk Ramsey, C. and Owen, C. (eds), *Radiocarbon and Archaeology. Fourth International Symposium, St Catherine's College, Oxford (9th–14th April 2002).* Oxford: Oxbow, pp. 9–15.

Weninger, B. and Jöris, O. 2008. A ^{14}C age calibration curve for the last 60 ka: the Greenland-Hulu U/Th timescale and its impact on understanding the Middle to Upper Paleolithic transition in Western Eurasia. *Journal of Human Evolution* 55: 772–781.

West, R. G. 1956. The Quaternary deposits at Hoxne, Suffolk. *Philosophical Transactions of the Royal Society of London* B239: 265–356.

West, R. G. 1969. Pollen analyses from interglacial deposits at Aveley and Grays, Essex. *Proceedings of the Geologists' Association* 80: 271–282.

West, R. G. 1977. East Anglia. *X INQUA Congress Excursion Guide.* Norwich: Geo Abstracts.

West, R. G. 1980. *The Pre-Glacial Pleistocene of the Norfolk and Suffolk Coasts.* Cambridge: Cambridge University Press.

West, R. G. 1987. A note on the March gravels and Fenland sea levels. *Bulletin of the Geological Society of Norfolk* 37: 27–34.

West, R. G. and McBurney, C. M. B. 1954. The Quaternary deposits at Hoxne, Suffolk and their archaeology. *Proceedings of the Prehistoric Society* 20: 131–154.

West, R. G. and Sparks, B. W. 1960. Coastal interglacial deposits of the English Channel. *Philosophical Transactions of the Royal Society of London* B243: 95–133.

West, R. G., Dickson, C. A., Catt, J. A., Weir, A. H. and Sparks, B. W. 1974. Late Pleistocene deposits at Wretton, Norfolk II. Devensian Deposits. *Philosophical Transactions of the Royal Society of London* B267: 337–420.

Westaway, R. 2009a. Quaternary vertical crustal motion and drainage evolution in East Anglia and adjoining parts of southern England: chronology of the Ingham River terrace deposits. *Boreas* 38: 261–284.

Westaway, R. 2009b. Calibration of decomposition of serine to alanine in *Bithynia opercula* as a quantitative dating technique for Middle and Late Pleistocene sites in Britain. *Quaternary Geochronology* 4: 241–259.

Westaway, R. in press. The age of the sediments at Happisburgh, eastern England. *Proceedings of Geologists' Association*.

Westaway, R., Bridgland, D. and White, M. J. 2006. The Quaternary uplift history of central southern England: evidence from the terraces of the Solent River system and nearby raised beaches. *Quaternary Science Reviews* 25: 2212–2250.

Weston, R. 2008. John Traherne, FSA, and William Buckland's 'Red Lady'. *The Antiquaries Journal* 88: 347–364

Whitaker, K., Beasley, M., Bates, M. and Wenban-Smith, F. 2004. The Lost Valley. *British Archaeology* 74: 22–27.

Whitaker, W. 1885. *The Geology of the Country around Ipswich, Hadleigh and Felixstowe.* Memoirs of the Geological Survey.

Whitaker, W., Woodward, H. B., Bennett, F. J., Skertchly, S. B. J. and Jukes-Browne, A. J. 1891. *The Geology of Parts of Cambridgeshire and of Suffolk (Ely, Mildenhall, Thetford). Memoir of the Geological Survey of Great Britain.* London: HMSO.

White, M. J. 1995. Raw materials and biface variability in Southern Britain: a preliminary examination. *Lithics* 15: 1–20.

White, M. J. 1996. *Biface variability and human behaviour: a case study from south-east England.* Unpublised Ph.D. Thesis, University of Cambridge.

White, M. J. 1997. The earlier Palaeolithic occupation of the Chilterns (southern England): re-assessing the sites of Worthington G. Smith. *Antiquity* 71: 912–931.

White, M. J. 1998a. On the significance of Acheulean biface variability in Southern Britain. *Proceedings of the Prehistoric Society* 64: 15–44.

White, M. J. 1998b. Twisted Ovate Bifaces in the British Lower Palaeolithic: Some Observations and Implications. In: Ashton, N., Healy, F. and Pettitt, P. (ed.) *Stone Age Archaeology; Essays in honour of John Wymer.* Oxford: Oxbow Books, pp. 98–104.

White, M. J. 1998c. Palaeolithic Archaeology of the Stour Terraces. In: Murton, J. B., Whiteman, C. A., Bates, M. B., Bridgland, D. R., Long, A. J., Roberts, M. B. et al. (eds), *The Quaternary of Kent and Sussex: Field Guide.* London: Quaternary Research Association, pp. 50–52.

White, M. J. 2000. The Clactonian Question: On the interpretation of core-and-flake assemblages in the British Lower Palaeolithic. *Journal of World Prehistory* 14: 1–63.

White, M. J. 2004. Moir, (James) R. (1879–1944). *Oxford Dictionary of National Biography.* Oxford: Oxford University Press.

White, M. J. 2006. Things to do in Doggerland when you're dead: surviving OIS3 at the north-western-most fringe of Middle Palaeolithic Europe. *World Archaeology* 38: 547–575.

White, M. J. 2008. Review of Clive Gamble's Origins and Revolutions. *American Journal of Archaeology* 112: 355.

White, M. J. in press. The lithic assemblage from Lynford Quarry and its bearing on Neanderthal behaviour in Late Pleistocene Britain. In: Boismier, W., Gamble, C. and Coward, F. (eds), *Neanderthals Among Mammoths: Excavations at Lynford Quarry, Norfolk.* London: English Heritage.

White, M. J. and Pettitt, P. B. 1995. Technology of Early Palaeolithic Western Europe: innovation, variability and a unified framework. *Lithics* 16: 27–40.

White, M. J. and Schreve, D. C. 2000. Island Britain – Peninsula Britain: palaeogeography, colonization, and the Lower Palaeolithic settlement of the British Isles. *Proceedings of the Prehistoric Society* 66: 1–28.

White, M. J. and Jacobi, R. 2002. Two sides to every story: *bout coupé* handaxes revisited. *Oxford Journal of Archaeology* 21: 109–133.

White, M. J. and Ashton, N. M. 2003. Lower Palaeolithic core technology and the origins of the Levallois method in NW Europe. *Current Anthropology* 44: 598–609.

White, M. J. and Plunkett, S. J. 2004. *Miss Layard Excavates: a Palaeolithic site at Foxhall Road, Ipswich, 1903–1905.* Liverpool: Western Academic and Specialist Press.

White, M. J. and Pettitt, P. B. 2009. The demonstration of human antiquity: Three rediscovered illustrations from the 1825 and 1846 excavations in Kent's Cavern (Torquay, England). *Antiquity* 84: 758–768.

White, M. J. and Pettitt, P. 2011. The British Late Middle Palaeolithic: an interpretative synthesis of Neanderthal occupation at the northwestern edge of the Pleistocene World. *Journal of World Prehistory* 24(1): 25–97.

White, M. J., Bridgland, D. R., Ashton, N., McNabb, J. and Berger, M. 1995. Wansunt Pit, Dartford Heath (TQ 513737). In: Bridgland, D. R., Allen, P. and Haggart, B. A. (eds), *The Quaternary of the Lower Reaches of the Thames: Field Guide.* London: Quaternary Research Association, pp. 117–128.

White, M. J., Lewis, S. G. and McNabb, J. 1999a. Excavations at the Lower Palaeolithic site of Whipsnade 1992–4. *Proceedings of Geologists' Association* 110.

White, M. J., Mitchell, J., Bridgland, D. R. and McNabb, J. 1999b. Rescue Excavations at an Acheulean Site at Southend Road, South Woodford, London Borough of Redbridge, E18 (TQ 407905). *Archaeological Journal* 155: 1–21.

White, M. J., Scott, R. and Ashton, N. 2006. The Early Middle Palaeolithic in Britain: archaeology, settlement history and human behaviour. *Journal of Quaternary Science* 21: 525–542.

White, M. J., Scott, B. and Ashton, N. M. 2011. The Emergence, Diversity and Significance of Mode 3 (Prepared Core) Technologies. In: Ashton, N., Lewis, S. and Stringer, C. (eds), *The Ancient Human Occupation of Britain.* Amsterdam: Elsevier, pp. 53–68.

White, T. D. 1995. African omnivores: global climatic change and Plio-Pleistocene hominids and suids. In: Vrba, E. S., Denton, G. H., Partridge, T. C. and Burckle, L. H. (eds), *Paleoclimate and Evolution.* New Haven: Yale University Press, pp. 369–385.

White, T. S., Bridgland, D. R., Westaway, R., Howard, A. J. and White, M. J. 2010. Evidence from the Trent terrace archive, Lincolnshire, UK, for a lowland glaciation of Britain during the Middle and Late Pleistocene. *Proceedings of the Geologists' Association* 121: 141–153.

Whitehead, P. F. 1977. Vertebrate fauna from the Carrant main terrace. In: Shotton, F. W. (ed.), *The English Midlands.* X INQUA Congress Excursion Guide A2, pp. 45–47.

Whiteman, C. A. and Rose, J. 1992. Thames river sediments of the British Early and Middle Pleistocene. *Quaternary Science Reviews* 11: 363–375.

Whittaker, J. 1999. Foraminifera. In: Roberts, M. B. and Parfitt, S. (eds), *Boxgrove: A Middle Pleisticene hominid site at Eartham Quarry, Boxgrove, West Sussex.* London: English Heritage.

Whittington, G., Fallick, A. E. and Edwards, K. J. 1996. Stable oxygen isotope and pollen records from eastern Scotland and a consideration of Late-Glacial and early Holocene climate change for Europe. *Journal of Quaternary Science* 11: 327–340.

Wilson, E. and Reynolds, S. H. 1901. The Uphill Bone Caves. *Proceedings of the Bristol Natural History Society* 9: 152–160.

Wilson, L. 1988. Petrography of the Lower Palaeolithic tool assemblage of the Caune de l'Arago (France). *World Archaeology* 19: 376–387.

Winbolt, S. E. 1929. A Late-Pleistocene flint point. *The Antiquaries Journal* IX: 152–153.

Wolff, E. W., Chappellaz, J., Blunier, T., Rasmussen, S. O. and Svensson, A. 2010. Millennial-scale variability during the last glacial: the ice core record. *Quaternary Science Reviews* 29: 2828–2838.

Woodcock, A. G. 1981. *The Lower and Middle Palaeolithic Periods in Sussex.* Oxford: British Archaeological Reports British Series 94.

Woodman, P., McCarthy, M. and Monaghan, N. 1997. The Irish Quaternary Fauna Project. *Quaternary Science Reviews* 16: 129–159.

Wymer, B. O. 1955. Discovery of the right pariental bone at Swanscombe. *Man* 55: 124.

Wymer, J. J. 1957. A Clactonian industry at Little Thurrock, Grays, Essex. *Proceedings of the Geologists' Association* 68: 159–177.

Wymer, J. J. 1961. The Lower Palaeolithic succession in the Thames Valley and the date of the ancient channel between Caversham and Henley. *Proceedings of the Prehistoric Society* 27: 1–27.

Wymer, J. J. 1964. Excavations at Barnfield Pit, 1955–1960. In: Ovey, C. D. (ed.) *The Swanscombe Skull: a survey of research on a Pleistocene Site.* London: Royal Anthropological Institute, Occasional Paper No. 20, pp. 19–60.

Wymer, J. J. 1968. *Lower Palaeolithic Archaeology in Britain, as Represented by the Thames Valley.* London: John Baker.

Wymer, J. J. 1974. Clactonian and Acheulean industries in Britain: their chronology and significance. *Proceedings of the Geologists' Association* 85: 391–421.

Wymer, J. J. 1979. Comment on Ohel (1979). *Current Anthropology* 20: 719.

Wymer, J. J. 1980. The excavation of the Acheulean site at Gaddesden Row. *Bedfordshire Archaeological Journal* 4: 2–4.

Wymer, J. J. 1983. The Lower Palaeolithic site at Hoxne. *Proceedings of the Suffolk Institute of Archaeology and History* 35: 169–89.

Wymer, J. J. 1985. *Palaeolithic Sites of East Anglia.* Norwich: Geobooks.

Wymer, J. J.1988. Palaeolithic Archaeology and the British Quaternary Sequence. *Quaternary Science Reviews* 7: 79–98.

Wymer, J. J. 1992. Region 3 (The Upper Thames Valley, the Kennet Valley) and Region 5 (The Solent Drainage System). Southern Rivers Palaeolithic Project Report. Salisbury: Wessex Archaeology.

Wymer, J.J. 1993. Region 1 (The South West) and Region 4 (South of the Thames). Southern Rivers Palaeolithic Project Report. Salisbury: Wessex Archaeology.

Wymer, J. J. 1994. Region 6 (Sussex Raised Beaches) and Region 2 (Severn River). Souther Rivers Palaeolithic Project Report. Salisbury: Wessex Archaeology.

Wymer, J. J. 1996a. Regions 7 (Thames) and 10 (Warwickshire Avon). English Rivers Palaeolithic Project Report. Salisbury: Wessex Archaeology.

Wymer, J. J. 1996b. Regions 9 (Great Ouse Drainage) and 12 (Yorkshire and Lincolnshire Wolds). English Rivers Palaeolithic Project Report. Salisbury: Wessex Archaeology.

Wymer, J. J. 1997. Regions 8 (East Anglian Rivers) and 11 (Trent Drainage): English Rivers Project Report. Salisbury: Wessex Archaeology.

Wymer, J. J. 1999. *The Lower Palaeolithic Occupation of Britain.* Salisbury: Trust for Wessex Archaeology.

Wymer, J. J., Jacobi, R. M. and Rose, J. 1975. Late Devensian and early Flandrian barbed points from Sproughton, Suffolk. *Proceedings of the Prehistoric Society* 41: 235–41.

Wymer, J. J., Lewis, S.G., and Bridgland, D.R. 1991. Warren Hill, Mildenhall, Suffolk (TL 744743). In: Lewis, S. G., Whiteman, C.A., and Bridgland, D.R. (ed.), *Central East Anglia and the Fen Basin: Field Guide.* London: QRA, pp. 50–57.

Wynn, T. 1995. Handaxe Enigmas. *World Archaeology* 27: 10–24

Young, T. 2000. The Paviland ochres: characterization and sourcing. In: Aldhouse-Green, S. (ed.) *Paviland Cave and the 'Red Lady': a Definitive Report.* Bristol: Western Academic and Specialist Press, pp. 205–225.

Zagwijn, W. H. 1985. An outline of the Quaternary stratigraphy of the Netherlands. *Geologie en Mijnbouw/Netherlands Journal of Geosciences* 64: 17–24.

Zagwijn, W. H. 1989. Vegetation and climate during warmer intervals in the Late Pleistocene of western and central Europe. *Quaternary International* 3/4: 57–67.

Zagwijn, W. H. 1996. The Cromerian Complex Stage of the Netherlands and correlation with other areas in Europe. In: Turner, C. (ed.), *The early Middle Pleistocene in Europe.* Rotterdam: Balkema, pp. 145–172.

Zazo, C. 1999. Interglacial Sea Levels. *Quaternary International* 55: 101–113.

Zilhão, J. and d'Errico, F. (eds) 2003. *The Chronology of the Aurignacian and of the Transitional Technocomplexes: Dating, Stratigraphies, Cultural Implications,* Lisbon: Português de Arqueologia Trabalhos de Arqueologia 33.

Zimmermann, E. and Radespiel, U. 2007. Primate Life Histories. In: Henke, W. and Tattersall, I. (eds), *The Handbook of Paleoanthropology.* Berlin: Springer-Verlag. 1163–1205.

Index

Acheulean 146–173

Acton: see West London

Africa: hominin dispersals out of 16–17

Ahrensburgian 495–501

Allerød 477–479; archaeology 479–489

Amber 447

Amiens, discovery of human antiquity at 4

Ancaster-Trent River 29

Ancient Human Occupation of Britain (AHOB)
    Project 29, 54

Anglian Glaciation (MIS12) 109

Antediluvianism 4

Art mobilier 461–463, 488–489

Ash Tree Cave (Derbyshire) 300, 321, 353,
    355–356, 454

'Asia, out of' (model) 22, 49

Aston Mills (Hereford and
    Worcestershire) 301, 401, 408

Atapuerca Gran Dolina TD6 (Spain) 11

Aurignacian: definition 400–401;
    dispersals 399–400; relationship with
    LRJ 401–402; settlement 408–411; sites
    and assemblages 402–408

Aveley (Essex) 223–226, 245–246

Aveline's Hole (Somerset) 430, 481

Avington VI (Berkshire) 496–498

Axe River (Dorset) 139

Axe Valley Local Operational Area
    (LOA) 362–370

Azilian 479

Badger Hole, Wookey (Somerset) 368, 388

Baker's Hole (Kent) 259, 263–264

Bapchild (Kent) 261

Barnham (Suffolk): Clactonian at 178, 183;
    geological context 109; sequence and
    archaeology 79–81; environments
    78–83

Barnham Heath (Suffolk) 261

Barnwood, Gloucester (Gloucestershire) 419

Bâtons percés 455–456

Beeches Pit, West Stowe (Suffolk): fire
    at 194–195; sequence, archaeology and
    fire 81–83; environments 84

Beedings (West Sussex) 300, 388, 394–398

Beetles: see Coleoptera

Bench Quarry (Somerset) 322

Berry Head (Devon) 216

Biddenham (Bedfordshire) 140

Bifaces: see handaxes

Biomass, primary production of 52

Biostratigraphy: small mammal 24;
    mammalian 47; MIS7 230–231;
    MIS3-MIS2 376–381

Blade-Points 383–388

Bleadon Cave (Cornwall) 232

Bluelands Pit, Purfleet (Essex) see Purfleet
    (Essex)

Bob's Cave, Kitley, Nr. Plymouth (Devon) 431, 470, 474, 481

Bølling: see Meiendorf

Boucher de Perthes, Jacques 4

Boxgrove (Sussex): Acheulean at 147; antler soft hammer 202; functional analysis of handaxes at 167–168; handaxe variation at 152, 157; hominin incisors 168; knapping scatters 199–200; sequence, environments and archaeology 117–120; hominin presence at 114, 123–124; hominin remains 144; hominin environments 62–65; horse hunting 204; rhinoceros butchery 205

Bowman's Lodge (Essex) 152, 200

Bradgate Park, Newtown Lynford (Leicestershire) 440, 443

Bramford Road, Ipswich (Suffolk) 261, 419

Brandon (Warwickshire) 296

Britain: drainage networks and fluvial archive 108–109; palaeogeography 98–102; sea levels and marine transgressions 102–104

British-Irish Ice Sheet (BIIS) 374–376

Brockhill (Surrey) 473

Broken Cavern (Devon) 482, 491

Broom Pits (Dorset) 139, 260

Brumby Wood (Humberside) 470

Brundon (Suffolk) 246

Buckland, William 4

Butlins Holiday Camp, Clacton-on-Sea (Essex): see Clacton-on-Sea

Bytham River 28–29, 108, 138

Caddington (Bedfordshire) see Chiltern Hills

Cae Gronw/Gwyn (Denbighshire, Wales) 401, 406

Campsites 196–198

Castlepook Cave (Ireland) 322

Cat Hole Cave (Gower, Wales) 419, 420, 470

Cattedown, Plymouth (Devon) 430

Cave art 461–468

Channel River Basin 12, 99–102, 299–300

Cheddar Gorge (Somerset) 451. See also Gough's Cave, Soldier's Hole, Sun Hole

Chelm's Coombe (Somerset) 491

Chiltern Hills (Bedfordshire and Hertfordshire: Caddington, Round Green Gaddesten

Row, Whipsnade): individuals at 161; knapping scatters 200; sequence, environments and archaeology 135–137; handaxe variation at 152

Church Hole, Creswell Crags (Nottinghamshire) 300; cave art 461–468; hyaenas from 322, 354; Magdalenian 442; organic artefacts 449–450

Clacton-on-Sea (Essex): Clacton Spear 160–161; Clactonian at 178, 183; sequence, environments and archaeology at 76–83; in context of history of Palaeolithic archaeology 5;

Clacton Spear: see Clacton-on-Sea

Clactonian: 173–193; chopper cores 165–166; context in history of Palaeolithic archaeology 5; definition of 175–176, 183–184; explanations of 184–193; handaxes within 176–180

Clast lithology: and dating 47

Cleavers 157–159

Climate, British 50

Clothing 52

Coleoptera (beetles): and environmental reconstruction 34–35, 50, 297; Mutual Climatic Range (MCR) 50

Condover (Shropshire) 431–433

Coygan Cave (South wales) 300, 322, 336–337

Cranwich (Norfolk) 471, 476

Crayford Brickearths (Kent: Stoneham's Pit, Norris's Pit, Rutter's Pits, Furner's Pits, Slade Green) 234, 246, 281; refitting assemblage from Stoneham's Pit 244, 270–272

Creffield Road, Acton (London) 245, 254, 261–263, 274

Creswell Crags (Derbyshire/Nottinghamshire) 5; art mobilier 461–463; cave art 461–468; Creswell Heritage Area 355; Local Operational Area (LOA) 353–362; Magdalenian (Creswellian) 440, 445–446; Magdalenian clothing 449–450; raw materials 356–358; and see Church Hole, The Crypt, Mother Grundy's Parlour, Robin Hood Cave, Pin Hole and Yew Tree shelter

Creswellian: see Magdalenian

Creswello-Hamburgian 436

Creswello-Tjongerian 436

Cromer Forest Bed Formation (CF-bF) 23, 29, *30*

Cromerian Complex 22ff.

Crypt, Creswell Crags (Nottinghamshire) 442, 454

Cryptic refugia 314

Cudmore Grove (Essex): environments 85–93

Curation 198–203

Curved-backed Point Complex 479–480, 485

Cuxton (Kent): Clactonian at 183; sequence, environments and archaeology 128–130; handaxe variation at 152, 154; Levallois at 245

Dansgaard-Oeschger events 295

Dartford (Kent) 330

Dead Man's Cave, Anston Stones Gorge (Derbyshire) 454, 474, 491

Deglaciation 424, 426–428

Denekamp Interstadial 296

Deserted Britain model 284

Dimlington Stadial 424–426, 428, 430

Discoidal technology 333

Dix's Pit, Stanton Harcourt: see Stanton Harcourt Channel, Dix's Pit (Oxfordshire)

Doggerland 299, 435

Dover Straight 98–100

Dmanisi (Georgia) 12

Dovercourt (Essex) 152

Dowel Cave (Derbyshire) 454, 486

Earith (Cambridgeshire) 296, 309–310

Earl's Barton (Northamptonshire) 491, 499

Ebbsfleet Valley (North Kent): sequence, environments and archaeology 245, 264–267, 281

Eel Point cave (Caldey Island, Wales) 411

Elder Bush Cave (Staffordshire) 454, 491

Elveden (Suffolk): geological context 109; sequence and archaeology at 79–81; handaxe variation at 152;

English Rivers Project 242–244

Environments: Allerød 477–479; Meiendorf 434–435; MIS13 60–67; MIS11 68–85; MIS9 85–97; MIS7 220–242; MIS3 298–319, 373–381; MIS2 426–434, Older Dryas 477; Younger Dryas 489–491

Eolith debate 5

Evans, John 4

Façonnage 15

Farndon Fields (Nottinghamshire) 440, 443, 474

Federmesser 479–480

Federmessergruppen: chronology 480; settlement 480–485

Fenstanton (Cambridgeshire) 303

Ffynon Beuno Cave (Denbighshire, Wales) 401, 406

Fire, use of 51–52, 193–196, 481; see also Hearths

Fisherton Brick Pits, Salisbury (Wiltshire) 304

Flixton II, Vale of Pickering (North Yorkshire) 500

Fluvial archive 3

Fordwich (Kent) 152

Four Ashes (West Midlands) 296

Foxhall Road, Ipswich (Suffolk): geological context 109; handaxe variation at 152; individuals at 161; raw material and 200; sequence, environments and archaeology 110–111

Fox Hole, Peak District (Staffordshire) 430, 454, 476

Functional analysis: see Microwear analysis

Furner's Pits, Crayford: see Crayford Brickearths

Furze Platt (Berkshire) 152

Gaddesten Row (Hertfordshire) see Chiltern Hills

Gipping Valley (Suffolk) 268–270

Glaston (Leicestershire) 394–396

Glinde Interstadial 296

Globe Pit, Little Thurrock (Essex) see Little Thurrock (Essex)

Goat's Hole, Paviland (Gower, Wales): Aurignacian 401, 404–405; in context of history of Palaeolithic archaeology 4; Gravettian, mammoth steppe and 377–379, 419; LRJ 388; Red Lady' of Paviland burial 412–417

Golf Course, Clacton-on-Sea (Essex): see Clacton-on-Sea

Gough's Cave (Cheddar, Somerset): curved-backed points 481; engraved bone and ivory 460–461; fauna 430–431; in context of history of Palaeolithic archaeology 5; Magdalenian 441, 452–453, 455–456; shouldered points 474; skull cups 448–449

Grandmother hypothesis 171–172

Grasslands 17

Gravettian 377–379, 411–422; chronology 418–419; dispersals 377–379, 418, faunal context 418; 'Red Lady' of Paviland burial 412–417; sites 419–422

Gray's Inn Lane (London): in context of history of Palaeolithic archaeology 4; handaxe from 145

Greenland ice cores 294, 374, 411, 422, 423–424

Greenland interstadials 295, 374, 411, 422, 434–435, 477–479

Greenland stadials 295, 374, 477, 489–491

Greenlands Pit, Purfleet (Essex) see Purfleet (Essex)

Habitat preferences, hominin 133–138

Hamburgian 469–477: definition 469–471

Handaxes: explanations for variation 149–163; *bout coupé* type 327–329, 349–351; individuals and 159–160; nature of variation 147–149; raw materials and 151–155; temporal trends 168–171; reduction (resharpening) and 155–159; retaining fossil inclusions 208; social functions of 191–192

Happisburgh (Norfolk) 12, 36–47; age of 45–47; climate at 50; environments 62

Harnham (Wiltshire) 260

Harpoons 485–487

Harrison, Benjamin 5

Hearths 161, 194–195, 481

Heinrich events 294–295

Hengelo Interstadial 296

Hengistbury Head (Dorset) 471–473

Hengistbury-Type sites: see Hamburgian

High Furlong: see Poulton Elk

High Lodge (Suffolk): sequence, environments and archaeology 121–123; handaxe variation at 152; hominin presence at 114; in context of history of Palaeolithic archaeology 5;

Hillingdon: see West London

Hitchin (Hertfordshire) 152

Holbrook Bay (Suffolk) 246

Holderness (East Yorkshire) 428

Holybourne (Hampshire) 152

Homo antecessor 11; 20–21, 54

Homo erectus 20–21, 48, 171–172

Homo cf. *ergaster* 48

Homo georgicus 20–21

Homo heidelbergensis 20–21, 50, 54, 133, 207, 282

Homo helmei 282

Homo sapiens 382–383, 399, 411

Homotherium 8

Howburn (Lanarkshire, Scotland) 470, 475–476

Hoxne (Suffolk): environments 84; geological context 109; handaxe from 145; sequence and archaeology at 69–72; in context of history of Palaeolithic archaeology 4; raw material and 200

Hoxnian Interglacial (MIS11) 68–86, 134

Hoyle's Mouth Cave (Pembrokeshire, Wales) 401, 406, 437, 481

Hunting 53–54

Hyaenas 319–324, 372

Hyaena Den (Wookey, Somerset): Aurignacian 401, 408; deposits, environments and archaeology 304; in context of history of Palaeolithic archaeology 5; Late Middle Palaeolithic 362–367; LRJ 388; pollen 313

Ipswichian Interglacial (MIS5a) 284–292

Ismaili centre (London) 296

Jaywick Sands, Clacton-on-Sea (Essex): see Clacton-on-Sea

Kempton Park (Surrey) 296

Kendrick's Cave (Conwy, North Wales) 430, 487, 488–489, 499

Kent's Cavern (Torquay, Devon): Aurignacian 401, 406–407; 'Black Band' 457–458; deposits, environments and archaeology 305; in context of

Kent's Cavern (*cont*.):
history of Palaeolithic archaeology 4;
Gravettian 419; hyaenas of 322; KC4
maxilla 382, 399; Levallois technology
in 347; Late Middle Palaeolithic 371–372;
LRJ 388; Magdalenian 441; organic
artefacts 407–408; pollen 313; post-LGM
faunal recolonisation 430

King Arthur's cave (Herefordshire) 431, 442,
485, 491

Kirkdale Cave (North Yorkshire): in context of
history of Palaeolithic archaeology 4

Kilmelfort (Argyllshire, Scotland) 482–483

Kinsey Cave (North Yorkshire) 486

Lancaster Hole (Lancashire) 313–314

Landscapes of habit 198–203

Langwith Cave (Derbyshire) 454

Lankaster, Ray 5

Last Glacial Maximum (LGM) 374–376,
424–426

Lateglacial Interstadial 428–489; Lake
Windermere type site 428–429

Latton (Wiltshire) 296

Launde (Leicestershire) 500–501

Leafpoints 383–388

Leman and Ower Bank 485

Levallois technology: Botany Pit (Purfleet) 257–
258; concept and organisation 253–254;
history and definitions 247–249; in
MIS9 282–284; origins 250–253; Late
Middle Palaeolithic 347–348; temporal
fluctuations 254

Lincomb Hill,Wellswood, Torquay (Devon) 392

Lincombian-Ranisian-Jerzomanowician
(LRJ) assemblages: 383–399;
authorship 398–399; chronology 332,
398; definition 389–398

Lion Point, Clacton-on-Sea (Essex) see
Clacton-on-Sea

Little Cressingham (Norfolk) 306

Little Hoyle cave (Dyfed, Wales) 322

Little Paxton, St. Neots, Riverside Pit
(Cambridgeshire) 306, 334–335,
344–347

Little Thurrock (Essex) Clactonian and 178,
181, 183; sequence, environments and
archaeology 130–131

Local Operational Areas (Neanderthal) 274–
275, 351–370

Loch Lomond Readvance: see Lock Lomond
Stade

Loch Lomond Stade 489–490

Long Blade Assemblages: see Ahrensburgian

Long Island, Portsmouth (Hampshire) 471,
473

Lower Pleistocene: faunas 17–19, 52;
palaeogeography 25–27

Lynford (Norfolk) 296, 307, 332, 338–346

Lyngby Axe 491, 499

Lynx Cave, Clywdd 470, 474, 486

MacEnery, Rev. John 4

Magdalenian (alt. Creswellian): annual
round 447; art 460–468; clothing 449–
450; definition 435–439; organic
artefacts 455–460; prey species 451–
453; settlement, behaviour and
society 440–468

Magnetostratigraphy 46

Mammalian Assemblage Zone (MAZ): Bacon
Hole MAZ 330; Banwell MAZ 330; Brean
Down MAZ 330; Dimlington Stadial
MAZ 430; Gough's Cave MAZ 434; Pin
Hole MAZ 317–318, 377

Mammoth Steppe 283, 291, 317–319,
377–379

Marine Isotope Stages (MIS): explanation 7;
Middle Pleistocene 23, 58–60;
MIS15 114; MIS13 60–67; MIS11 68–86,
139; MIS9 85–97, 139; MIS7 211–212;
MIS6 (absence of hominins during) 278,
285–288; MIS5e (Last Interglacial) 284–
292; MIS5 *sensu lato* 330–332;
MIS4 298–299; MIS3 293–298, 373–381;
MIS2 423–428

Marine transgressions 102–104, 214–217

Marks Tey (Essex): environments 68

Marlow (Buckinghamshire) 296, 352

Marsworth (Buckinghamshire) 221–223

'Mediterranean Type' environments 19

Meindorf Interstadial (alt. Bølling) 434–435

Merlin's Cave (Herefordshire) 491

Microwear analysis 163–165

Middle Pleistocene: climatic cycles 17;
palaeogeography 27–29

Mildenhall (Suffolk) 419
Mode 1 lithic assemblages 14–15
Moershooft Interstadial/Moershooft
    Complex 296
Mortillet, Gabriel de 5
Mother Grundy's Parlour, Creswell Crags
    (Derbyshire) 302, 354; engraved
    bones 461; Federmessergruppen 482;
    Late Middle Palaeolithic 357;
    Magdalenian 442, 451; shouldered
    points 470, 474
Mousterian of Acheulian Tradition (MTA) 333

Nanna's Cave (Dyfed, Wales) 481
Neanderthals: early Neanderthal
    behaviour 279–281; and hyaenas
    319–324; late Neanderthal presence in
    Britain 332, 371; multiple kill sites 282;
    ranges 324; raw material use 348–349;
    survival strategies 324–325
New Hythe (Kent) 261
Nightingale Estate, Hackney (London):
    environments 93
Norris's Pit, Crayford: see Crayford Brickearths
Northfleet (Kent) 245
North Sea 12, 102–104
Nottle Tor (West Glamorganshire, Wales) 401,
    408

Oerel Interstadial 296
Oldbury (Kent) 307, 347
Older Dryas 477
Oreston Cave (Cornwall) 232
Ossom's Cave (Staffordshire) 454, 500
Overwintering, problems of 51
Oxbow open coal mine (West Yorkshire) 296
Oxygen Isotope Stages (OIS): see Marine
    Isotope Stages

Pakefield (Suffolk) 12, 29, *30,* 30–34; age
    of 45; climate at 50
Paviland: see Goat's Hole, Paviland
Peper Harrow Park, Godalming (Surrey) 419
Picken's Hole (Somerset) 307, 362, 364–365
Piltdown (hoax) 5
Pin Hole, Creswell Crags (Derbyshire) 302;
    engraved objects 461–462; hyaenas
    from 321; Gravettian 419, 420–421;

Late Middle Palaeolithic 357–361;
    Magdalenian 442, 456
Pontnewydd Cave (Clwydd): sequence,
    environments and archaeology 232–234,
    245; Gravettian, mammoth steppe
    and 377–380
Population: artefacts as proxy for 275–277;
    estimates 282, 330; history 112–125;
    132–133, 192–193; population sinks 3,
    133
Porth-y-Waen (Shropshire) 486
Poulton Elk 458–460, 486
Poulton-le-Fyld, Lancashire: see Poulton Elk.
Prestwich, Joseph 4
Purfleet (Essex): Botany Pit early Levallois 245,
    257–258, 261; Clactonian at 183;
    sequence and environments 96–97,
    105–108, 254

Quartzites 356–358
Quinton, Birmingham (West Midlands):
    environments 68

Radiocarbon: calibration 8–9
Raised beaches 214–217
Range size, hominin 52–53
Ravencliffe Cave (Derbyshire) 328, 353
Raw material distribution 348–349
Red Barns, Portchester (Hampshire) 154
Reid Moir, James 5
Rhenish (molluscan) faunas 74, 104
Rhine terraces 24
Rhinoceros Hole, Wookey (Somerset) 308,
    362, 367–368
Riwat (Pakistan) 12
Robin Hood Cave, Creswell Crags
    (Derbyshire) 303; engraved
    artefact 461–462; hyaenas from 321;
    Late Middle Palaeolithic 354; 359–360;
    Levallois technology in 347; LRJ 388;
    Magdalenian 437, 442; organic
    artefacts 449–450; pollen 313; shouldered
    points 470
Rookery Farm (Cambridgeshire) 482–485
Round Green (Bedfordshire)
    see Chiltern Hills
Rutter's Pits, Crayford: see Crayford
    Brickearths

Saalian Complex 211–212

Saham Toney (Norfolk) 306

Salmonby (Lincolnshire) 470

Sandford Hill, Mendip (Somerset) 322

Sandy (Bedfordshire) 296, 315–316

Sea level 102–104, 213–214

Seamer Site C, Vale of Pickering (North Yorkshire) 485, 487, 500–501

Seamer Site K, Vale of Pickering (North Yorkshire) 487

Selsey LBS (Life Boat Station) (Sussex) 220–221, 230–231, 245

Settlement history 49

Severn-Avon River system 139

Sewell's Cave (North Yorkshire) 491, 500

Short Chronology (for initial hominin dispersals into Europe) 11–12

Slade Green, Crayford: see Crayford Brickearths

Soldier's Hole, Cheddar (Somerset) 321, 388, 441

Solent River 29

South Woodford 166–167

Sproughton (Suffolk) 486–487

Stage 3 Project 314–317

Stanton Harcourt Channel, Dix's Pit (Oxfordshire) sequence, environments and archaeology 237–238, 246

Stoke Newington, Hackney (London): environments and archaeology 93–95; handaxe variation at 152

Stoke Tunnel, Ipswich (Suffolk) 246

Stoneham's Pit, Crayford: see Crayford Brickearths

Stour Valley (Suffolk) 268–270

Structures (e.g. dwellings) 52

Sun Hole, Cheddar (Somerset) 441, 451, 491

Swanscombe (Kent): archaeology of the Barnfield Pit at 56–58; Clactonian at 178, 183; handaxe variation at 152, 154; hominin remains 144; sequence and environments at 73–76; in context of history of Palaeolithic archaeology 5;

Syon Reach, Richmond (Surrey) 455

Syston Terraces (Leicestershire) 296

Tautavel (France) 11

Terrace formation (rivers) 88–91

Thames-Medway River: ancestral form of 28–29, 86, 108–109; terraces 88–91; archaeology of 138–139

Thames Valley Late Middle Palaeolithic findspots 352–353

Theory of mind 207

Thermoregulation and energetic s 51

Three Hole's Cave (Devon) 431, 441, 481

Three Way's Wharf (Uxbridge, Middlesex) 2, 492–495, 500

Torbryan Six Cave (Devon) 480

Tor Court Cave (Devon) 401, 408

Tornewton Cave (Devon) 401, 408

Uphill Quarry Caves, Weston-super-Mare (Somerset) 308, 335, 362–364, 401, 407–408

Upton Warren (Worcestershire) 296

Victoria Cave (North Yorkshire) 430, 486, 491, 498

Vivian, Edward 4

Wansunt (Essex) 152, 200

Waverley Wood (Warwickshire) 29, 114, 115–117

West Cliff, Clacton-on-Sea (Essex): see Clacton-on-Sea

West London, Hillingdon to Acton: sequence, environments and archaeology 255–257

West Runton (Norfolk) 49

West Thurrock, Lion Pit Tramway Cutting (Kent): sequence, environments and archaeology 217–219, 245, 267–268, 281

Westbury-sub-Mendip (Somerset) 29, 114

Whipsnade (Bedfordshire) see Chiltern Hills

Whitlingham (Norfolk) 152, *158*

Windermere Interstadial 428–429

Windmill Hill Cave, Brixham (Devon) 308, 401

Wolvercote Channel (Oxfordshire): sequence, environments and archaeology 97, 125–127; handaxe variation at 152

Yew Tree Shelter, Creswell Crags (Derbyshire) 353

Younger Dryas 489–501; environments 489–491